Music and Dance as Everyday South Asia

Edited by

SARAH L. MORELLI and ZOE C. SHERINIAN

OXFORD
UNIVERSITY PRESS

OXFORD
UNIVERSITY PRESS

Oxford University Press is a department of the University of Oxford. It furthers
the University's objective of excellence in research, scholarship, and education
by publishing worldwide. Oxford is a registered trade mark of Oxford University
Press in the UK and certain other countries.

Published in the United States of America by Oxford University Press
198 Madison Avenue, New York, NY 10016, United States of America.

© Oxford University Press 2024

Chapter 2 "A Melody of Lucknow: Hearing History in North Indian Music"
has been adapted from a previously published work. From Lineage of Loss:
Counternarratives of North Indian Music © 2017 by Max Katz. Published by
Wesleyan University Press. Used by permission.

All rights reserved. No part of this publication may be reproduced, stored in
a retrieval system, or transmitted, in any form or by any means, without the
prior permission in writing of Oxford University Press, or as expressly permitted
by law, by license, or under terms agreed with the appropriate reproduction
rights organization. Inquiries concerning reproduction outside the scope of the
above should be sent to the Rights Department, Oxford University Press, at the
address above.

You must not circulate this work in any other form
and you must impose this same condition on any acquirer.

Library of Congress Cataloging-in-Publication Data
Names: Morelli, Sarah L., editor. | Sherinian, Zoe C., editor.
Title: Music and dance as everyday South Asia /
Sarah L. Morelli and Zoe C. Sherinian, editors.
Description: New York, NY : Oxford University Press, 2024. |
Includes index.
Identifiers: LCCN 2024030363 (print) | LCCN 2024030364 (ebook) |
ISBN 9780197791974 (paperback) | ISBN 9780197566237 (hardback) |
ISBN 9780197566251 (epub)
Subjects: LCSH: Music—Social aspects—South Asia. |
Music—South Asia—History and criticism. | Dance—Social aspects—
South Asia. | Dance—South Asia—History.
Classification: LCC ML3917.A78 M87 2024 (print) |
LCC ML3917.A78 (ebook) | DDC 306.4/840954—dc23/eng/20240702
LC record available at https://lccn.loc.gov/2024030363
LC ebook record available at https://lccn.loc.gov/2024030364

DOI: 10.1093/oso/9780197566237.001.0001

Paperback printed by Marquis Book Printing, Canada
Hardback printed by Bridgeport National Bindery, Inc., United States of America

Music and Dance as Everyday South Asia

For our mentors, teachers, family members, friends, and colleagues who helped make this project possible.

Contents

Acknowledgments — xi
List of Contributors — xiii
About the Companion Website — xvii
Note on Translation and Transliteration — xix

Introduction: Comprehensive Approaches to South Asian Sound and Movement — 1
   Sarah L. Morelli and Zoe C. Sherinian

SECTION I: IDENTITY IN PLACE AND COMMUNITY
Introduction by Peter Kvetko and Sarah L. Morelli

1. A Sense of the City: Embodied Practice and Popular Music in Mumbai — 17
   Peter Kvetko

2. A Melody of Lucknow: Hearing History in North Indian Music — 29
   Max Katz

3. Sufi Devotional Performances in Multan, Pakistan, a "City of Saints" — 41
   Karim Gillani

4. *Hale da Divan*: Trance, Historical Consciousness, and the Ecstasy of Separation in Namdhari Sikh Services — 56
   Janice Protopapas

5. "Small Voices Sing Big Songs": Music as Development in the Thar Desert — 73
   Shalini R. Ayyagari

SECTION II: PERFORMANCE DYNAMICS: STYLE, GENRE, CODING, AND FUNCTION
Introduction by Zoe C. Sherinian

6. Changing Musical Style and Social Identity in Tamil Christian *Kirttanai* — 97
   Zoe C. Sherinian

7. Professional Weeping: Music, Affect, and Hierarchy in a South Indian Folk Performance Art — 113
   Paul D. Greene

8. Sindhi *Kafi* and Vernacular Islam in Western India — 127
   Brian E. Bond

9. Music, Religious Experience, and Nationalism in Marathi *Rashtriya Kirtan* — 142
   Anna Schultz

10. Prestige, Status, and the History of Instrumental Music in North India — 155
    George E. Ruckert

SECTION III: INTERSECTIONAL DYNAMICS: CASTE, CLASS, AND TRIBE
Introduction by Zoe C. Sherinian

11. Mundari Performance after the Revolution: Did Dance Save the Tribe? — 179
    Carol M. Babiracki

12. Systematic and Embodied Music Theory of Tamil *Parai* Drummers — 193
    Zoe C. Sherinian

13. Caste, Class, Aesthetics, and the Making of Modern Bharatanatyam Dance — 209
    Hari Krishnan and Davesh Soneji, with a contribution by Nrithya Pillai

14. Sacred Song, Food, and the Affective Embodied Experience of Non-Othering in the Sikh Tradition — 229
    Inderjit N. Kaur

15. Following in the Footsteps of Muria Music and Dance — 243
    Roderic Knight

SECTION IV: IDENTITY IN GENDER AND SEXUALITY
Introduction by Zoe C. Sherinian

16. *Bhangra* Brotherhood: Gender, Music, and Nationalism in *Rang De Basanti* — 265
    Pavitra Sundar

17. Disrupted Divas: Conflicting Pathways of India's Socially Marginalized Female Entertainers — 277
    Amelia Maciszewski

18. "All the Parts of Who I Am": Multi-Gendered Performance in Kathak Dance — 291
    Sarah L. Morelli

19. Music and the Trans-*thirunangai* Everyday at Koovagam, Tamil Nadu — 305
    Jeff Roy

20. Performing Youthful Desires: Bihu Festival Music and Dance in Assam, India — 317
    Rehanna Kheshgi

SECTION V: TECHNOLOGY, MEDIA, AND TRANSMISSION
Introduction by Sarah L. Morelli

21. "We Know What Our Folk Culture Is from Commercial Videos": Rethinking the Popular-Folk Dynamic in the Indian Himalayas — 337
    Stefan Fiol

22. The Female Voice in Hindi Cinema: Agency, Representation, and Change — 350
    Natalie Sarrazin

23. Love, Politics, and Life between Village and City in Nepali *Lok Dohori*: One Album, Three Titles — 364
    Anna Marie Stirr

24. Pedagogy and Embodiment in the Transmission of Kerala Temple Drumming — 377
    Rolf Groesbeck

25. Sonic Gift-Giving in Sri Lankan Buddhism — 389
    Jim Sykes

SECTION VI: DIASPORA AND GLOBALIZATION
Introduction by Nilanjana Bhattacharjya and Sarah L. Morelli

26. Contemporizing Kandyan Dance   413
    Susan A. Reed

27. *Desi* Dance Music: A Transnational Phenomenon   427
    Nilanjana Bhattacharjya and DJ Rekha

28. Dance In The Round: Embodying Inclusivity and Interdependence through *Garba*   439
    Parijat Desai

29. Tamil Rap and Social Status in Malaysia   453
    Aaron Paige

30. Beyond the Silver Screen: *Filmi* Aesthetics in Bollywood Fitness Classes   466
    Ameera Nimjee

Index   479

Acknowledgments

Our sincere thanks go, first and foremost, to this volume's authors, whose years of research, scholarship, and artistry, developed within broad networks of friendships, teacher-student relationships, and other associations, are the soul of this book. We gratefully acknowledge our mentors, *guru*s, *asan*s, and *ustad*s, including the Reverend James Theophilus Appavoo (1940–2005), Pandit Chitresh Das (1944–2015), Ustad Ali Akbar Khan (1922–2009), T. Viswanathan (1927–2002), Ramnad Raghavan (1927–2009), Smt. Madhuri Devi Singh the drummers of Kurinji Malar, A. Manimaran, Drs. Mark Slobin, Kay Kaufman Shelemay, Gage Averill, Rod Knight, Carol Babiracki, Beth Bullard, Truman Bullard (1938–2024), and George Ruckert, Gretchen Hayden, Sister Chandra and Sister Felci, and Drs. Ted Adams (1944–2015) R. Venkatraman (1933–2018), Arun Raja Selvan and Rev. Dr. Jeevakani Aruldoss. Early articulations of this book's concept were presented at the Society for Ethnomusicology's 2010 South Asia pre-conference honoring Nazir Ali Jairazbhoy. Select authors' pedagogical materials were workshopped at the virtual SEM meeting in 2020 and presented in classes at the University of Denver and the University of Oklahoma. Our thanks to many DU and OU students, whose questions, insights, and spirited workshopping of these chapters helped make them stronger. We are grateful to colleagues and friends who read and commented on drafts of this work or provided other help, including Nilanjana Bhattacharjya, Brian Bond, Julia Byl, Alice Campbell, Parijat Desai, Stefan Fiol, Inderjit Kaur, Peter Kvetko, Philip Lutgendorf, Carrie McCune, Hannah O'Toole, Aaron Paige, Indira Viswanthan Peterson, Shilpa Sharma, Jack Sheinbaum, Davesh Soneji, Kristin Taavola, Patricia Tang, Jeremy Wallach, Keith Ward, Aleysia Whitmore, Sean Williams, and our anonymous reviewers. For their crucial help in bringing this publication to fruition, we thank Norman Hirschy and Rachel Ruisard at Oxford University Press, and Hemalatha Arumugam at Newgen Knowledge Works. Thanks to Lokesh Ohri for the considerable work of indexing this book and to the Book Publishing Support Fund of the University of Denver's College of Arts, Humanities, and Social Sciences. Finally, thanks to other friends and family members, including Richard and Sylvia Morelli, Stephen Scaringe, David and Hali Morelli, and artists, students, and leaders at the Leela Institute of Kathak, the Sakthi Folk Cultural Centre, Oberlin Shansi, and the Tamil Nadu Theological Seminary for their love and support.

Contributors

Shalini R. Ayyagari is Associate Professor of Music at the University of Pittsburgh. She is the author of *Musical Resilience: Performing Patronage in the Indian Thar Desert* (Wesleyan University Press, 2022).

Carol M. Babiracki retired in 2020 from Syracuse University, where she was Associate Professor of Ethnomusicology in the Department of Art and Music Histories and Director of the South Asia Center in the Moynihan Institute of Global Affairs.

Nilanjana Bhattacharjya is Principal Lecturer and Honors Faculty Fellow at Barrett, the Honors College at Arizona State University. Her work on music, film, and visual culture has been published in multiple journals including *Asian Music* and *South Asian Popular Culture*, and in edited collections such as *Global Bollywood* (2008), *South Asian Transnationalisms* (2012), and *Industrial Networks and Cinemas of India* (2021).

Brian E. Bond is Visiting Lecturer at the University of California at Berkeley with a PhD in ethnomusicology from the CUNY Graduate Center and a student of Sindhi Sufi vocal genres. His published work appears in the journals *Asian Music, Journal of Sindhi Studies*, and *Culture, Theory & Critique,* and the edited volume *Modern Sufis and the State: The Politics of Islam in South Asia and Beyond*.

Parijat Desai is a dance artist/educator living and working in Lenapehoking (New York City). She is Founder and Artistic Director of Parijata Dance Company and Dance in the Round.

Stefan Fiol is Professor of Ethnomusicology at the University of Cincinnati and author of *Recasting Folk in the Himalayas* (University of Illinois Press, 2017). He currently conducts interdisciplinary research on the role of music in stimulating memory, cognitive function, and awe, and investigates central Himalayan drumming as a mode of historiographic inquiry.

Karim Gillani lectured at the University of Alberta from 2010 to 2016. A freelance composer, producer, and performer of Sufi music, he has released five Sufi music albums and is currently writing a book and making a documentary film on the topic.

Paul D. Greene is Professor of Ethnomusicology and Integrative Arts at Penn State Brandywine. He is author and coeditor of several publications including the volumes *Wired for Sound: Engineering and Technologies in Sonic Cultures* and *Metal Rules the Globe: Heavy Metal around the World*.

Rolf Groesbeck is Professor of Music History/Musicology/Ethnomusicology at the University of Arkansas at Little Rock and has performed the *chenda* drum frequently in the United States and India.

Max Katz is Associate Professor in the Department of Music at William & Mary. His book, *Lineage of Loss: Counternarratives of North Indian Music*, was published by Wesleyan University Press in 2017.

Inderjit N. Kaur is Assistant Professor of Ethnomusicology at the University of Michigan and a native scholar and practitioner of Sikh *sabad kīrtan*. Her work on Sikh musical worship appears in journals such as *The Yearbook of Traditional Music* and *MusiCultures* and edited volumes including *The Oxford Handbook of the Phenomenology of Music Cultures*.

Rehanna Kheshgi is Assistant Professor of Music at St. Olaf College. Her research on contemporary performances of gender and sexuality through the springtime Assamese New Year's festival, Bihu, has been published in journals including *Indian Theatre Journal* and *MUSICultures*.

Roderic Knight (MA and PhD, UCLA) is an Emeritus Professor of Ethnomusicology at the Oberlin College Conservatory. He is known for his publications and audio/video documentaries on the Mandinka of West Africa, several Adivasi genres of central India, and organology.

Hari Krishnan is Professor and Chair of the Dance Department at Wesleyan University, and also Professor of Feminist, Gender and Sexuality Studies. A dancer, choreographer, scholar, and educator who has trained extensively with hereditary courtesan teachers in South India, he is Artistic Director of inDANCE and author of *Celluloid Classicism: Early Tamil Cinema and the Making of Modern Bharatanāṭyam* (Wesleyan University Press, 2019).

Peter Kvetko is Professor and Chair of the Music and Dance Department at Salem State University where he teaches courses in ethnomusicology and popular music studies.

Amelia Maciszewski is a sitarist, teaching artist, public ethnomusicologist, and creative culture worker. Her training includes degrees from Santiniketan, the University of Texas at Austin, and the University of Alberta, and intensive training with Pandit Suresh Misra, Ustad Aashish Khan, and Padmavibhushan Girija Devi.

Sarah L. Morelli is Professor of Ethnomusicology at the University of Denver and author of *A Guru's Journey: Pandit Chitresh Das and Indian Classical Dance in Diaspora* (University of Illinois Press, 2019). Also a performing kathak dancer, she is a Founding Artist and Soloist with the Leela Dance Collective and Director of Leela Denver.

Ameera Nimjee is Assistant Professor in the Department of Music at Yale University. She is active in the research, performance, and programming of global South Asian arts.

CONTRIBUTORS

Aaron Paige is an ethnomusicologist, public folklorist, performing mridangam artist, and educator. He is currently Director of Folk & Traditional Arts at ArtsWestchester and oversees public folklife programs in Westchester and Rockland Counties, New York.

Nrithya Pillai is a dancer, singer, writer, speaker, and dance pedagogue, and holds a degree in Journalism from MOP Vaishnav College for Women, Chennai. She runs a series entitled "Re-casteing Culture" for *The News Minute*, and is a regular contributor to *The Economic and Political Weekly*, *The Hindu*, *The Times of India*, *The Telegraph*, *Firstpost*, and a host of other digital news platforms.

Janice Protopapas is an ethnomusicologist and Sikh music specialist affiliated with Punjabi University at Patiala. She is the author of *Sikh Shabad Kirtan: The Musicology of Sacred Memory* (Punjabi University Press, 2013), along with numerous articles on Sikh sacred music.

Susan A. Reed is Associate Professor of Women's & Gender Studies and Anthropology at Bucknell University. She is the author of *Dance and the Nation: Performance, Ritual and Politics in Sri Lanka* (University of Wisconsin Press, 2010).

DJ Rekha (born Rekha Malhotra) is a producer, curator, educator, and founder of Basement Bhangra, one of NYC's longest-running club nights (1997–2017). They have performed in festivals, clubs, and community spaces worldwide and have taught at NYU Tisch School of the Arts and have a MS in Comparative Media at MIT. They have been featured on Broadway, NPR, *Taste the Nation*, Obama's White House, Celebrate Brooklyn, and Central Park SummerStage.

Jeff Roy is a musician, filmmaker, and Associate Professor in Liberal Studies at Cal Poly Pomona whose work centers the politics and performance of queer and trans-*hijra*-gender expansive cultural formations at the intersections of race, class, caste, and religion. Roy has recently published the guest-edited themed issue "Queer Elsewheres ←→ South Asian Imaginaries" in *Feminist Review* (2023) and co-authored the book *Badhai: Hijra-Khwaja Sira-Trans Performance across Borders in South Asia* (2022).

George E. Ruckert retired in 2020 from the Massachusetts Institute of Technology's Department of Music and Theater Arts. A senior disciple of the *sarod* maestro Ali Akbar Khan, he is the author of several books, including *Music in North India: Experiencing Music, Expressing Culture* (Oxford University Press, 2004).

Natalie Sarrazin is Professor of Music at SUNY Brockport, ethnomusicologist, and music educator with primary research in India. She is the author and editor of several books, including *Focus: Popular Music in Contemporary India* (Routledge, 2019) and *Music in Contemporary Indian Film: Memory, Voice and Identity* (with coeditor Jayson Beaster-Jones, Routledge, 2016).

Anna Schultz is Associate Professor of Music and the Humanities at the University of Chicago. Her book *Singing a Hindu Nation: Marathi Devotional Performance and Nationalism* (Oxford University Press) was published in 2013.

Zoe C. Sherinian is Professor of Ethnomusicology at the University of Oklahoma. She has published the monograph *Tamil Folk Music as Dalit Liberation Theology* (Indiana University Press, 2014) and coedited *Making Congregational Music Local: Indigenous Songs and Cosmopolitan Styles in the Music of Global Christianity* (Routledge, 2017).

Davesh Soneji is Associate Professor in the Department of South Asia Studies at the University of Pennsylvania. He is author of *Unfinished Gestures: Devadāsīs, Memory, and Modernity in South India* (University of Chicago Press, 2012), editor of *Bharatanāṭyam: A Reader* (Oxford University Press, 2010; 2012), and coeditor of *Performing Pasts: Reinventing the Arts in Modern South India* (Oxford University Press, 2008).

Anna Marie Stirr is Associate Professor in Asian Studies and the Director of the Center for South Asian Studies at the University of Hawaii at Manoa. Her book *Singing Across Divides: Music and Intimate Politics in Nepal* was published by Oxford University Press in 2017.

Pavitra Sundar is Associate Professor of Literature at Hamilton College, where she teaches courses on film, literature, and sound, with a focus on South Asia. She is the author of *Listening with a Feminist Ear: Soundwork in Hindi Cinema* (University of Michigan Press, 2023) and coeditor of *Thinking with an Accent: Toward a New Object, Method, and Practice* (University of California Press, 2023).

Jim Sykes is Associate Professor of Music at the University of Pennsylvania and the author of *The Musical Gift: Sonic Generosity in Post-War Sri Lanka* (Oxford University Press, 2018).

About the Companion Website

www.oup.com/us/MDESA

Video and Audio examples, glossaries for each chapter, and additional supplemental materials can be found on the companion website. Video and Audio examples are referenced throughout this book with Oxford's symbol: ⏵. These online resources are, in many cases, central elements of the author's chapter, and are particularly valuable in engaging with participatory exercises, which are offset in Boxes throughout.

Note on Translation and Transliteration

This book draws from research involving more than twenty South Asian languages, including Assamese, Bhojpuri, Gondi, Gujarati, Hindi, Kachchhi, Malayalam, Marathi, Marwari, Mundari, Nagpuri, Nepali, Pali, Panjabi, Persian, Tamil, Telegu, Sanskrit, Saraiki, Sindhi, Sinhala, and Urdu, as well as Arabic, Hokkien, and Malay. Due to the considerable number of languages and artistic practices encompassed here, we have chosen to limit the use of diacritic marks, with some exceptions.

Most terms in this volume are spelled most of the time without diacritic marks. In these cases, our spelling choices are meant to balance accuracy with visual clarity. For example, when transliterating from Tamil, *ch* or *s* is used instead of the more common *c*, which can represent either sound. We recognize that certain distinctions, however, are not reflected in our transliteration choices. For example, dental and retroflex/cerebral sounds that are not distinguished in English (such as *t* and *ṭ*, or *l*, *ḷ*, and *ḻ*) are spelled with the same unmodified Roman letter. Similarly, long and short vowels (such as *a* and *ā*) are not differentiated; common *aa*, *ee*, and *oo* spellings are not used except for words (such as *raas*) that have a widely accepted English spelling. Some spellings (e.g., *rag*, *raga*) may vary by author and context. A glossary is available for each chapter among the book's online references.

For terminology central to each chapter and included in the glossary, we include more precise transliterations parenthetically following the terms' first use. These transliterations employ diacritic marks broadly consistent with the Romanization tables available from the Library of Congress.[1] (Nasalizations [*anusvāra*] follow the Urdu Romanization table and are designated with *ṉ*.) In addition to key terms, we employ diacritic marks for all Romanized titles, song lyrics, and direct quotations, with the exception of titles/lyrics (e.g., from Bollywood films) that appear in the public domain using a specific Roman-alphabet spelling. We also forgo the use of diacritic marks in all introductions unless a central term introduced there will not be discussed in subsequent chapters.

Finally, many chapters draw on specialized terminology, including oral/aural systems for representing music and dance practices. When discussing melody, many authors navigate between Western terminology and the *sargam* system of solfège syllables (Sa Re/Ri Ga Ma Pa Dha Ni) that are widely, though not exclusively, utilized across the subcontinent. Rhythm is often communicated and represented with mnemonics/mnemonic systems (such as *bols*, *solkattu*, *son adi*, and *vayttari*) in which specific syllables represent drum strokes, rhythmic structure, and/or dance movements. In general, when rhythm is written in this book, a dash represents a unit of time equal to each surrounding rhythmic syllable. (One notable exception is Berava drumming, which does not generally utilize a standard pulse [Sykes*]). These systems vary rather widely and often have not been subject to written standardization. As such, when representing rhythm, each author utilizes a system of Romanization that is most applicable to the practice/s they discuss.

Note

1. https://www.loc.gov/catdir/cpso/roman.html.

Introduction

Comprehensive Approaches to South Asian Sound and Movement

Sarah L. Morelli and Zoe C. Sherinian

This book offers an inclusive lens through which to study the music, dance, and allied arts of South Asia, its diasporas, and the people who produce and use these as cultural expressions. Based largely on the perspectives of ethnomusicologists, who study cultural meaning as constructed in sound and movement, most of these studies draw from years of ethnographic fieldwork, language study, and hands-on music and dance training. The contributors to this collection understand music and dance as everyday lived experience. By "everyday South Asia," we mean the practices of South Asians living in a multitude of countries and regions, whose identities include numerous castes, classes, tribes, genders, sexualities, language groups, religions, nationalities, and other overlapping affiliations. In taking an inclusive and expansive approach, this collection aims to present a more accurate picture of the many arts practiced, experienced, and appreciated by the broadly diverse people of the subcontinent and its diasporas. Through these chapters, we show how the arts are a meaningful expression of human relationships and interactions among ordinary people as well as by virtuosic performers for elite patrons. The realities, experiences, and artistic practices of the everyday person, however, have not typically been accessible to most students of South Asian music in university settings. Our intent in curating this collection is to make these diverse perspectives more readily available to teachers and students of the arts and cultures of South Asia and the world.

South Asia is a geographic region encompassing approximately 3.5 percent of the world's land and 25 percent of the world's population, within the nations of Afghanistan, Bangladesh, Bhutan, India, the Maldives, Nepal, Pakistan, and Sri Lanka (Map 0.1).[1] Its diasporas include Malaysia, the

---

[1] These eight countries make up the South Asian Association for Regional Cooperation; the United Nations definition of the region also includes Iran.

Sarah L. Morelli and Zoe C. Sherinian, *Introduction* In: *Music and Dance as Everyday South Asia*. Edited by: Sarah L. Morelli and Zoe C. Sherinian, Oxford University Press. © Oxford University Press 2024. DOI: 10.1093/oso/9780197566237.003.0001

2 MUSIC AND DANCE AS EVERYDAY SOUTH ASIA

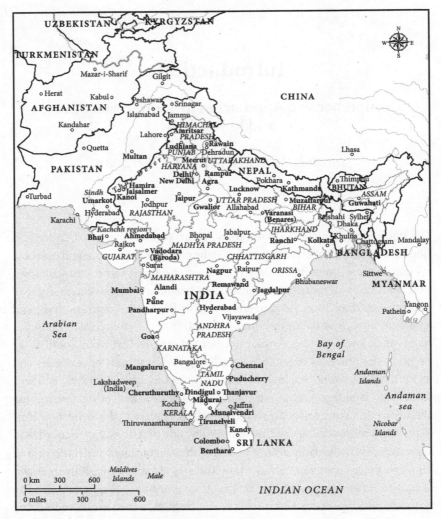

Map 0.1 Map of South Asia highlighting places discussed in this volume.

United Kingdom, the United States, Canada, countries in the Caribbean, and elsewhere. South Asia boasts twenty-five national and regionally recognized languages and hundreds of others in daily use. Its geography ranges from tropical islands and rainforests to arid deserts and some of the world's highest mountains. This diversity also extends, unsurprisingly, to artistic practices. Within the so-called classical realm alone, there are two music systems and eight recognized dance forms in India, the largest country in the region.

Imagine the diversity of folk, devotional, and popular styles. Additionally, many practices exist on a continuum between these fixed canonic categories.

History of South Asian Ethnomusicology Scholarship

Within the field of ethnomusicology, early scholars of South Asia tended to focus on teaching and concert presentation of classical performing arts. There are several possible reasons for this. First, within Eurocentric fine arts departments—home to most North American and European ethnomusicologists from the 1950s to 1980s—the curriculum, scholarship, positions, and research of ethnomusicologists and dance scholars competed for legitimacy and acceptance with the Western music/dance canon's "value-free," positivist ideologies of virtuosity and perfection. In this context, the study of elite court and temple cultures of Asia was more readily validated than folk, popular, or so-called primitive musics might have been.

A two-hundred-year Eurocentric hegemony in South Asian music scholarship that can be traced to nineteenth-century Western colonialism and racism, as well as eighteenth-century Indology and orientalism, supported this tendency toward privileging the classical.[2] In 1784, Sir William Jones wrote Indic ethnomusicology's foundational treatise on Indian classical music, *On the Musical Modes of the Hindus*. Historian Thomas Trautmann labels Jones's work—which also argued that Sanskrit was a civilized European protolanguage—as the result of "Indomania" circulating among British cultural elites (1997). Trautmann contrasts the enthusiasm of Jones and other scholars with the more common "Indophobia" perpetuated by colonialists and British missionaries at the height of imperial colonialism in the mid-nineteenth century.[3]

Among scholars, enthusiasm for elite music and dance continued into the nineteenth and twentieth centuries. Augustus Willard wrote an English treatise on North Indian music in 1834 (*Treatise on the Music of Hindoostan*), followed by A. H. Fox Strangways's early prototype of comparative musicology, *The Music of Hindustan*, in 1914 (which does include transcription of

---

[2] Trautmann (1997) uses the terms "Indomania" and "Indophobia" to distinguish and nuance the qualities of orientalism prevalent in India before and after 1800 (distinct from the Middle East). These terms may or may not be broadly applicable to South Asian performing arts scholarship, especially today.

[3] Indophobia led to the inculcation of some Indians, particularly Christian converts, to Western four-part harmonic practices and the use of well-tempered instruments like the harmonium (see Sherinian* [Section II]). Authors followed by an asterisk reference chapters in the book.

Garhwali folk songs in *raga* [Fox Strangways 1914, 51–72, in Fiol 2015, 1]). Detailed analyses of the classical *raga* systems and some transcriptions of folk and Christian songs were published by two Protestant missionaries: H. A. Popley (*The Music of India*, 1921) and Emmons White (*Appreciating India's Music*, 1957). Some of these works drew from field studies and included detailed transcriptions in Western notation or were based on firsthand study with a teacher/guru who may have limited the scope of their studies to classical music. Nevertheless, many of these works contain subtle traces of ethnocentrism, rationalistic comparison, generalization, paternalism, and the impetus to codify structural procedures and performance practice. Despite these scholars' great personal appreciation for the karnatak and Hindustani systems, their methodological focus on scientifically and practically "knowing" the classical systems, particularly that of "pure *raga*," strongly influenced a focus in later South Asian ethnomusicology on musical structure and theory over cultural meaning and context.

In his analysis of the contemporary Hindu fundamentalist movement, historian Thomas Bloom Hanson argues, "the Brahmanical high scriptural tradition . . . [was] regarded as the classical center of the Aryan-Vedic high civilization" (1999, 65). Early proto-ethnomusicologists like William Jones, supported by the Indomania of scholarly communities such as the Asiatic Society of Bengal (1784) and larger colonial initiatives, produced and structured the concept of a single classical Hinduism organized around a central high culture and extending across the subcontinent as a "great tradition" (Trautmann 1997).[4] With the support of both Indian scholars/practitioners and Western intellectuals, this value hierarchy further extended to knowledge production about elite Indian musics. This resulted in the simplistic and essentialist construction of karnatak and Hindustani musics as "great traditions" with shared "ancient" theoretical foundations in Sanskrit texts like the *Natyashastra* (AD 100) and stretching across the subcontinent as a single musical system that diverged in the thirteenth century through Islamic influence. Hanson argues that "the construction of a great tradition allowed . . . intellectuals to classify and order the vast mélange of cultural differences in the subcontinent into systems of core and periphery, exclusion and inclusion" (1999, 66). Ethnomusicologist Carol Babiracki further contends that this construction led to categorization of both Hindu religious

---

[4] This construction emboldened Hindutva majoritarian ideology and politics in the twentieth century (see Schultz, Krishnan et al., and Sundar*).

and South Asian musical practices as either "great" or "little" traditions (1991). The Orientalist imagination of India as mystical, spiritual, ahistorical, and ancient was reinforced by a focus on the "pure" Indian classical great traditions—those "oceans of knowledge" (Hanson 1999, 67) that evolved from a golden age and that no single person can ever fully comprehend.

As this book demonstrates, scholarly interest in the once-unmarked "little"—non-elite, regional, popular, devotional, and other—practices has grown significantly. Nevertheless, relative indifference continues to perpetuate the hierarchical privileging of classical arts over all others, as well as the "embeddedness of the classical arts in the world of right-wing Hindu nationalism" in India (Krishnan et al.*). This erasure sets up a singular framework for the Indian nation and the region that forgets its oppressed internal minorities (Dalit-Bahujan numerical majorities) and excludes those deemed foreign (particularly Muslims and Christians), further sanctioning Brahminization, sanitization, and elite appropriation (see Krishnan et al.*, Menon 2009). Such homogeneity also disregards other national and culture groups on the subcontinent.

Organization of This Book

Previous world music textbooks have focused primarily, or extensively, on the "classical" music and dance practices of South Asia, emphasizing "Indian" classical music and its positivist analysis of *raga*, *tala*, and form over the relationship of musical elements with South Asian cultural values and people.[5] In order to de-emphasize an approach that fetishizes analysis of classical form and its technical virtuosity, we instead contextualize the understanding of aesthetic meaning within a wider context of social life. Further, we undermine the implied hegemonic hierarchies of value that are encoded by the fixed divisions of "classical," "popular," and "folk," and we seek to blur the often-artificial boundaries between "music" and "dance" studies.

We organize our chapters to show how the performing arts construct and reflect the following themes: (1) Identity in Place and Community; (2) Performance Dynamics: Style, Genre, Coding, and Function; (3)

---

[5] Among these texts, *Music in South India* (Viswanathan and Allen 2004) and *Music in North India* (Ruckert 2003) can serve as valuable supplements to this book for those wishing to delve more deeply into karnatak and Hindustani theoretical systems, respectively.

Intersectional Dynamics: Caste, Class, and Tribe; (4) Identity in Gender and Sexuality; (5) Technology, Media, and Transmission; and (6) Diaspora and Globalization. Additional themes woven throughout include migration, politics, nationalism, religion, modernity, and disciplinary inclusivity. To deconstruct both the epistemological approach of fixed style categories inherited from Western art music as well as South Asian ethnomusicology's emphasis on art/court performance practices, we highlight overlapping fusions, continuums, and complexities of influence in stylistic lineages and performers' repertoire. Chapters highlight processes and dynamics such as folklorization, eclecticism (e.g., Bollywood *masala*), Brahminization, queering, the popular-folk dynamic, community re-creation, activism, and geographic unmooring of style sources.

This collection of essays emphasizes music and dance as intersectional arts. Their aesthetic relationships are expressed in elite practices by the Sanskrit term *sangeet (saṅgīt)*—encompassing vocal music (*gītam*), instrumental music (*vādyam*), and dance (*nṛtyam*)—which, along with drama (*nāṭyam*), are inextricably intertwined elements of South Asian performance. Similarly, in folk (Hindi: *lok* or Tamil: *girāmiya*)[6] practices, tune/melody types, accents, rhythmic mnemonics and timbres, along with rhythmic and dance step patterns typically are subsumed under a single genre term reflecting ritual purpose/function and experienced as a whole.[7] Finally, we highlight the relationships between people from various class/caste levels and locations that are facilitated by the arts. Therefore, some chapters emphasize intersections created and articulated through performance across social identity categories, between performance styles, and across specific geographic spaces, such as homeland and diaspora. With these strategies, we aim to expand simplistic understandings of South Asia, its music/dance, and people.

Pedagogical Uses of This Book

Ethnomusicological pedagogy aims to convey an understanding of cultural values through, and on the terms of, indigenous aesthetic elements. In this book, our pedagogical approach is to associate South Asian aesthetics

---

[6] *Lok* means people and *giramiya* means village.
[7] See, e.g., studies in this book of Tamil *parai-attam* (Sherinian* [Section III]), Gujarati *garba* (Desai*), and Mundari *or jadur* (Babiracki*).

explicitly with social values by providing participatory exercises that draw on various multi-sensory modes of learning. Every chapter includes participatory exercises that connect learners experientially to the author's thesis. With these exercises, we aim to provide a counterpoint to critical textual analysis and empower classroom communications that draw on multiple ways of understanding and engaging with cultural meaning. In this process, we offer embodied experience as a vital mode of inquiry to help cultivate attentive, responsive, and ethical dispositions vis-à-vis the music and dance practices of other human beings and their contextualized life experiences.

Each chapter is a discrete, self-contained study situated within the book's six broad thematic sections. Syllabi can be structured around these themes or by other means. One might consider a regional focus, selecting, for example, chapter sets covering Northwest India and Pakistan (Ayyagari, Bond, Gillani, Kaur, Protopapas), or South India, Sri Lanka, and their Malaysian diaspora (Greene, Groesbeck, Krishnan et al., Paige, Reed, Sherinian, Sykes). The chapters discussing similarities in communal dance genres practiced within North and Northeast rural and tribal communities would make for a rewarding unit of study (Babiracki, Fiol, Kheshgi, Knight). Chapter authors utilize a range of framing strategies, for example, analyzing one song as it appears through history (Katz, Sherinian [Section II]), focusing on one artist (Kvetko, Reed), one collective of artists (Morelli, Sherinian [Section III]), or one city (Kvetko, Gillani). Several chapters focus on the role of music and dance in creating or sustaining community (Ayyagari, Babiracki, Desai, Kaur, Maciszewski, Protopapas, Roy, Schultz, Sherinian [Section II], Sundar). Some chapters work especially well in dialogue with one another; for example, readers might compare approaches to the teacher-student (*guru-śiṣyan*) relationship practiced in Kerala temple drumming pedagogy (Groesbeck) and consciously rejected by the contemporary Kandyan dancer Venuri Perera (Reed), or consider the question of what is "music" through community-specific frameworks (Greene, Sykes, Gillani). While history is not the primary focus of most chapters in this volume (with the exception of Ruckert, Katz, Knight, and Krishnan et al.), historical understandings and meanings infuse the majority. A focus on technologically mediated music and dance (Bhattacharjya and DJ Rekha, Fiol, Nimjee, Paige, Sarrazin, Stirr, and Sundar) additionally generates a useful study of diverse genres created in studios and transmitted through various media. Highlighting the role of religion in artistic practice would lead to another collection of readings (Bond, Gillani, Kaur, Morelli, Protopapas, Ruckert, Schultz, Sherinian [Section

II], and Sykes). A focus specifically on music/scholarship as activism—reframing, rewriting, contesting hegemonic practices or understandings—would productively include a distinct set of chapters (Babiracki, Desai, Krishnan et al., Maciszewski, Paige, Reed, Roy, Schultz, Sherinian [Section III], Stirr). Some authors also speak from the position of heritage scholars, having grown up in a specific artistic practice (Gillani, Kaur, Desai, Nimjee, Krishnan et al.), and most chapters include first-person discussions of fieldwork methodology and experiences.

Conclusion

While South Asian ethnomusicological scholarship has changed significantly, the important work of scholars engaging with a wide diversity of music/dance practices has not permeated "world music" pedagogical texts. As a product of contemporary ethnomusicological scholarly activism, this book embraces a broad spectrum of South Asian artists and their diverse repertoires, aesthetics, and practices as a means of creating shared experiences and of making meaning through human relationships and interactions. While this volume does not include all the countries that make up South Asia and its many diasporas, it is our hope that this approach will fundamentally alter how the arts of South Asia are taught in university classrooms and will lead to similar pedagogically oriented scholarly contributions representing a greater diversity of topics, individuals, and communities. In an era of conscious decolonization of the academy, from a South Asian perspective, in addition to attending to culturally elite and "popular" artists, we must retune our ears to Dalit-Bahujan artists who assertively drum, sing, and dance their subjectivities. They thereby not only challenge Western colonial knowledge constructions, but also decaste and declass what and who have been internally endorsed as worthy of study.

Works Cited

Babiracki, Carol. 1991. "Tribal Music in the Study of Great and Little Traditions of Indian Music." In *Comparative Musicology and the Anthropology of Music*, edited by Bruno Nettl and Philip V. Bohlman, 69–90. Chicago: University of Chicago Press.

Fiol, Stefan. 2015. "One Hundred Years of Indian Folk Music: The Evolution of a Concept." In *This Thing Called Music: Essays in Honor of Bruno Nettl*, edited by Victoria Lindsay Levine and Philip V. Bohlman, 317–329. Lanham, MD: Rowman & Littlefield.

Fox Strangways, A. H. 1914. *The Music of Hindustan*. Oxford: Clarendon Press.

Hanson, Thomas Bloom. 1999. *The Saffron Wave: Democracy and Hindu Nationalism in Modern India*. Princeton, NJ: Princeton University Press.

Jones, Sir William. 1784. *On the Musical Modes of the Hindus*. London: Asiatic Researches.

Menon, Dilip M., 2009. *The Blindness of Insight: Essays on Caste in Modern India*. Pondicherry: Navayana Press.

Popley, H. A. 1921. *The Music of India*. 3rd ed. 1966. New Delhi: YMCA.

Ruckert, George. 2003. *Music in North India: Experiencing Music, Expressing Culture*. Oxford: Oxford University Press.

Trautmann, Thomas. 1997. *Aryans and British India*. Berkeley: University of California Press.

Viswanathan, T., and Matthew Harp Allen. 2004. *Music in South India: The Karṇāṭak Tradition and Beyond*. New York: Oxford University Press.

White, Emmons. 1957. *Appreciating India's Music: An Introduction to the Music of India, with Suggestions for Its Use in the Churches of India*. Madras: Christian Literature Society.

Willard, Augustus. 1834. *Treatise on the Music of Hindoostan: Comprising a Detail of the Ancient Theory and Modern Practice*. Calcutta: Baptist Mission Press.

SECTION I
IDENTITY IN PLACE AND COMMUNITY

Introduction by Peter Kvetko and Sarah L. Morelli

There is an intrinsic relationship between the performing arts, place, community, and identity. Through place, we "organize our experiences and order our memories. . . . Place tells us who we are" (Von Glahn 2021, 2). South Asian music and dance making occurs in locales as varied as those presented in this book's thirty chapters: in Adivasi (indigenous) communities, music and dance may take place in community-owned spaces (*akhaṛas*); music and dance happen in sites of religious worship; and some rural practices associated with community celebrations have been adapted to urban stages in a process known as folklorization. Artists might perform on large proscenium stages with professional sound and lighting; and for many, the site of meaning-making is a recording studio, a movie set, the listeners' headphones, or an online interface. The same artist may be involved in many of these seemingly disparate performance locations.

In South Asia, as elsewhere, the notions of identity and community are equally varied. Any reductive views of identity as fixed and stable face immediate challenges from the volatile nature of modern existence in the context of colonialism and its aftermath, migration and forced displacement, rapid technological change, and the recontextualization of traditional values and customs in an era of globalization. The chapters in this section illustrate that identity in South Asia is a fluid category, sometimes emerging from acts of performance within specific geographic and social contexts and other times constructed through the imagination and mediated via mass media technology. As you read these chapters, consider how concepts of place, community, and identity contribute to meaning-making in music and dance practices. Their intertwined relationships have long interested social theorists and continue to invite critical thought. In order to better understand these case studies, we will briefly step back for a broader view of the legacy of ideas upon which these chapters are built.

The classical period in modern social theory (peaking between 1875 and 1920) emerged in western Europe from an era of rapid social change that destabilized concepts of identity, place, and community. Anxiety about the relationship between self and society pervaded much of this work, by scholars including Marx, Weber, Durkheim, and Freud. As a result of the breakdown of collective norms and values in modernity, foundational ideas in the social sciences centered on community as precarious and shifting rather than predetermined and fixed. In the United States, scholars associated with the "Chicago School" included more ethnographic fieldwork with theorizing specifically about the urban experience. Like their European counterparts, they wavered between optimism and pessimism, citing the creative energy that emerges from urbanization and social mobility as well as the strain on traditional norms and relationships.

By the mid-twentieth century, one prevailing model emphasized not the difference between, but the interplay among, the "great" traditions of elite classes and the "little" traditions of villagers (Redfield and Singer, 1954). In South Asian music studies, these categories became reified for a time due to both the hierarchies that dominated Western music scholarship and the terms' relationship to South Asian indigenous concepts of "classical" (*marga*) and "non-classical" (*desi*) music (Allen 1998). These concepts artificially separated what were considered elite, trans-regional artistic practices from localized, diverse ones, influencing scholarly approaches and methodology (Babiracki 1991).[1] By the 1980s, music scholars (e.g., Henry 1981; Kothari 1981; Neuman 1981; Slawek 1988) focused on the interplay between urban and rural experiences, locating musical interaction among people in place and community. As Neuman notes, "The primary assumption . . . at once both obvious and yet commonly overlooked, is that it is *individuals* who transmit and receive ideas . . . in the context of social relationships" (1981, 604). Performing artists, in particular, tend to "straddle . . . musical world[s]" (Thompson 1995, 428; see also Morcom 2022). They are often more mobile

---

[1] Babiracki observes that scholars of "great traditions" tended to concern themselves with "great individuals, the historical development of the tradition, and aspects of the musical sound" while "those studying the little musical traditions . . . tended to focus on the ethnographic present rather than the past and . . . on the texts and contexts of musical expressions rather than their musical structure" (Babiracki 1991, 69).

than their neighbors, experiencing what Zoe Sherinian calls "indigenous cosmopolitanism" (personal communication, January 4, 2021). For example, Ayyagari* examines the "double lives" of Manganiyar musicians; some perform on international stages, aurally representing the stereotyped romance of Rajasthani deserts where, in reality, they suffer caste discrimination at local and governmental levels.

Despite a century of intense urbanization, the Indian subcontinent retains among the world's largest rural populations (World Bank 2021). Some, including those involved in the 2020–2021 Indian farmers' protest, fight to preserve agrarian livelihoods, though many—especially members of often landless Dalit-Bahujan and tribal communities—must travel to cities for unskilled wage labor. Rural lifeways documented by Knight's* account of 1970s fieldwork among Muria Gonds (Section III) have long been threatened by governmental efforts to displace tribal communities from their ancestral lands (Yadav 2018). As Stirr* demonstrates (Section IV), migrant laborers in Nepal moving between rural and urban spaces use music to give voice to their longing for home, customs they left behind, and dangers of urban life.

The integral relationship of place, community, and artistic practice is clearly demonstrated in the concept of *gharana* within Hindustani music and kathak dance. Place names mark the lineages and stylistic characteristics unique to specific communities of artists. For example, the city of Lucknow boasts at least four "Lucknow gharanas": *tabla* drumming, *kathak* dance, instrumental music, and voice. This richness is due in large part to the patronage of the Nawab (king) Wajid Ali Shah (r. 1847–1856). An arts lover and practitioner, he is credited with composing the song "Bābul Morā," whose history and meanings are traced by Katz.* Compare the nostalgia for colonial Lucknow that Katz examines with what Kvetko* refers to as "phantom nostalgia" crafted by Indipop artist Lucky Ali for the American Southwest—a place never experienced by the majority of listeners to his song "Dekha Hai Aise Bhi."

Language plays a central role in our understanding of self, community, and place. Responding to the foundational ideas of Ferdinand de Saussure and Charles Sanders Peirce, cultural theorists have focused their attention on how meaning is created and conveyed within the specific codes, symbols, and expectations of a given society. Emphasizing the multiplicity of meanings that can emerge from a single act of communication, anthropologist Clifford Geertz advocated for "thick description" of everyday moments and the potentials of interpretation over explanation (1973). Similarly, Victor Turner encouraged scholars to focus on transitory, performative aspects of culture (particularly those with a ritual element) and popularized the concepts of "communitas" and "liminality" (1969).

"Communitas" evokes the powerful feelings of solidarity often experienced through performance. Such feelings can be applied to local social relationships or larger "imagined" communities such as the nation (Anderson 2006), as demonstrated in Schultz's* analysis of performances by two female *rashtriya kirtankar*s constructing different frameworks for who belongs to the Indian nation (Section II). Gillani* examines the roles of music and dance in generating individual and community religious experience at two Sufi shrines in Multan, Pakistan—a "city of saints" where Sufi orders have flourished since the tenth century. For Namdhari Sikhs, a small, marginalized Sikh community discussed by Protopapas*, *hale da divan* services generate communitas and liminality, which Turner describes as the state of being in transition, where the codes and norms that govern a society often reveal themselves. Protopapas posits that the collective, "interdividual" experience of trance-inducing singing and movement additionally serves to assuage intergenerational trauma experienced at the hands of British colonizers. Indeed, music- and dance-facilitated experiences of communitas can be beneficial to individual health, well-being, and sense of connection (Turino 2008). The chapters in this section highlight the varied ways in which our individual and collective identities are interwoven with our sense of place in the world.

Works Cited

Allen, Matthew. 1998. "Tales Tunes Tell: Deepening the Dialogue between 'Classical' and 'Non-Classical' in the Music of India." *Yearbook for Traditional Music* 30: 22–52.

Anderson, Benedict. 2006. *Imagined Communities: Reflections on the Origin and Spread of Nationalism*. 2nd ed. London: Verso.

Babiracki, Carol. 1991. "Tribal Music in the Study of Great and Little Traditions of Indian Music." In *Comparative Musicology and the Anthropology of Music*, edited by Bruno Nettl and Philip V. Bohlman, 69–90. Chicago: University of Chicago Press.

Geertz, Clifford. 1973. *The Interpretation of Cultures*. New York: Basic Books.

Henry, Edward O. 1981. "Changing Channels in Urban/Rural Music: Interchange in India." In *Report of the Twelfth Congress of the International Musicological Society, Berkeley 1977*, edited by Daniel Heartz and Bonnie Wade, 590–595. Kassel: Bärenreiter.

Kothari, Komal. 1981. "Rural-Urban Transitions." In *Report of the Twelfth Congress of the International Musicological Society, Berkeley 1977*, edited by Daniel Heartz and Bonnie Wade, 595–603. Kassel: Bärenreiter.

Morcom, Anna. 2022. "Following the People, Refracting Hindustani Music, and Critiquing Genre-Based Research." *Ethnomusicology* 66(3): 470–496.
Neumann, Daniel M. 1981. "Country Musicians and Their City Cousins: The Social Organization of Music Transmissions in India." In *Report of the Twelfth Congress of the International Musicological Society, Berkeley 1977*, edited by Daniel Heartz and Bonnie Wade, 603–608. Kassel: Bärenreiter.
Redfield, Robert, and Milton B. Singer. 1954. "The Cultural Role of Cities." *Economic Development and Cultural Change* 3(1): 53.
Slawek, Stephen. 1988. "Popular Kīrtan in Benares: Some 'Great' Aspects of a Little Tradition." *Ethnomusicology* 32(2): 77–92.
Thompson, Gordon. 1995. "What's in a *Dhal*? Evidence of *Raga*-like Approaches in a Gujarati Musical Tradition." *Ethnomusicology* 39(3): 417–432.
Turino, Thomas. 2008. *Music as Social Life*. Chicago: University of Chicago Press.
Turner, Victor. 1969. *The Ritual Process*. Piscataway, NJ: Transaction Publishers.
Von Glahn, Denise. 2021. *The Sounds of Place: Music and the American Cultural Landscape*. Champaign: University of Illinois Press.
World Bank. 2021. "Rural Population (% of Total Population)—Afghanistan, Bangladesh, Bhutan, India, Maldives, Nepal, Pakistan, Sri Lanka." The World Bank Group. Accessed December 26, 2021. https://data.worldbank.org/indicator/SP.RUR.TOTL.ZS?end=2020&locations=AF-BD-BT-IN-MV-NP-PK-LK&start=1960&view=chart.
Yadav, Smita. 2018. *Precarious Labor and Informal Economy: Work, Anarchy, and Society in an Indian Village*. London: Palgrave Macmillan.

1
A Sense of the City

Embodied Practice and Popular Music in Mumbai

Peter Kvetko

This chapter examines three music videos by Lucky Ali in order to explore the ways in which place and intimacy were constructed in Indipop, a primarily Hindi-language, non-film pop music movement that peaked between 1995 and 2001. This short but significant window of time, just following the liberalization of India's economy in 1991, deserves close scrutiny. This period in Indian history witnessed the consolidation of global capitalism, as well as the emergence of digital technology as a fixture in the home, workplace, and public sphere. Indipop flourished in this context and, as such, provides a window into the ways that globalization was experienced at the local level. As a televisual (as opposed to cinematic) popular music genre, Indipop was fueled by the collision of local talent with the influx of foreign investment in the Indian market by international music industry giants such as MTV, BMG, Sony, and Virgin Records. It is my contention that the sounds and images of Indipop were symptomatic of a shift from public to private that came to define many aspects of post–Cold War bourgeois life, including the ways that popular music was produced and consumed.

My research on this topic occurred primarily between 1998 and 2001 and was largely based in Mumbai. I approached the topic skeptical of the "cultural gray-out" thesis, which posits that with increased globalization, the world's music cultures will inevitably all begin to sound the same (Lomax 1972), and I wanted to hear the voices of artists and executives themselves as they navigated the rapidly converging worlds of technology, commerce, and style. But as I traveled from recording studios to record company offices to the homes of singers and studio musicians, I realized that not only was I thinking about the rhetorical content of my interviews and conversations, but I was also deeply aware of the physical context of those interactions. The contrast between quiet, air-conditioned interior spaces and public spaces abundant with crowds, noise, and heat was often striking. Looking back, I now see that I was thinking about one of the most basic themes in ethnomusicology and the social sciences: the relationship between culture and environment. Classic studies such as Steven Feld's work on the Kaluli (1982), a people whose melodies and rhythms mimic the birds and waterfalls surrounding them in the Papua New Guinean rainforest, have revealed the importance of one's physical environment in the shaping of identity and experience. If I truly wanted to understand the people who made Indipop music, I needed to pay attention to the space that produced them.

At a population near 20 million and ranked as one of the most densely populated cities in the world, Mumbai is a hub of commerce and entertainment for not only India but the entire Indian Ocean region and beyond. Like that of most major port cities, Mumbai's history is written on its physical landscape: colonial ambition and commerce are still on display in the aging Victorian buildings of the "Fort" district, hopeful immigrants struggle to establish themselves in the sprawling slums of Dharavi, and imported cars pass under billboards promoting the latest soap operas in the western suburbs. In many ways, Mumbai offers a model of the urban experience that was fast becoming a norm across the globe. Thus, the title of this chapter: "a sense of the city." For while I started my research thinking about music, I realized that I was also trying to understand the city as a particular kind of environment.

In theorizing the relationship between culture and environment, between music and city life, I have come to use the term "embodied practice" to conceptualize the everyday ways in which people inhabit (and are inhabited by) their physical space. Drawing on foundational work in the social sciences,[1] I base my research on the idea that culture is not a fixed set of ideas that resides within us, but rather that culture is an assemblage of actions, performances, decisions, and speech that changes depending on one's context. "Practice" is a useful word to encapsulate this dynamic model of culture in action, and "embodied" reminds us that each of us performs culture using our own unique bodies navigating our specific physical environments.

Trying to come to terms with the relationship between individuals and urban spaces is a problem that has occupied the minds of social scientists for quite some time. In the early twentieth century, sociologists of the "Chicago School" examined life in their city using an ecological model, arguing that

---

[1] Particularly relevant studies include Goffman (1959), Bourdieu (1977), Bauman (1984), and de Certeau (1984).

crime and delinquency were products of certain places (the environments of certain neighborhoods) rather than the people (often working-class immigrants) who lived there. A few decades earlier in Europe, the German thinker Ferdinand Tönnies popularized the terms *Gemeinschaft* and *Gesellschaft*[2] to describe two ends of a spectrum of human relationships in the modern era: the former consists of close emotional bonds and face-to-face relationships (within a family, for example), while the latter is based on rational understanding of mutual needs (a business contract, for instance). Tönnies takes a rather pessimistic tone, arguing that life in the city leads to a society built more and more on the cold, self-interested calculations of *Gesellschaft* rather than on the warm bonds of *Gemeinschaft*.[3] Another German scholar and contemporary of Tönnies, Georg Simmel, argues that city dwellers become dull and detached (because of the excessive stimulation of their nervous system, he claims) and that impersonal transactions based on money increasingly displace traditional social relationships. The urban environment, Simmel contends, produces hollow, flat, reserved interactions among people he describes as "blasé."[4]

While unsatisfied by the overriding pessimism and deterministic nature of these arguments, my own lived experience had evoked similar concerns. Just as Tönnies and Simmel's world was transformed by new ideas and technologies, mine had changed dramatically with the emergence of one new technology after another: personal computers, email, mobile phones, the Internet, MP3 music files, digital cameras, and more. The unifying feature of all of these technologies was their tendency to replace public, face-to-face interactions with individualized, face-to-screen activity. If the warmth of *Gemeinschaft* emerges from embodied practice, from the everyday experiences that one *feels* in the body (the smells of a library or place of worship, the sounds of a large crowd or a familiar voice, or even the sensation of other bodies in one's proximity), could the new techno-environment that began to flourish in the 1990s, with its individualist narrative of efficiency and

---

[2] In Tönnies (2001), an English translation of this work, *Gemeinschaft* is translated as "community" and *Gesellschaft* as "civil society."

[3] It's important to note that for women or historically marginalized communities, what is described here as the "cold, self-interested calculations" of *Gesellschaft* might instead imply order, fairness, and equality, in contrast to the "old boys' network"—the face-to-face, intimate interactions of *Gemeinschaft* in which a limited few may enjoy greater advantages.

[4] See Simmel (1998) for a collection of essays on money, fashion, leisure, and the senses. It should be noted that neither Tönnies nor Simmel paints an entirely negative picture of cities. Simmel, for example, recognizes the creative and liberating potential that cities offer over the sometimes stagnant and restrictive environment of the village.

rationality revolving around the computer chip, actually end up producing blasé individuals motivated by the cold calculus of *Gesellschaft*?

With this question in the back of my mind, in Mumbai I discovered that the city's residents were experiencing a profound and rapid transformation of their own lived environments. Alongside the "liberalizing" shift from socialism to capitalism in India, air-conditioned cars and shopping malls were emerging as alternatives to open-air buses and crowded bazaars. Trips to noisy cinema halls (where boisterous audience members might sing and dance along to the film songs) could be avoided by watching movies in the comfort of the middle-class home. In short, I found that *the privatization of the Indian economy seemed to have tangible—even aural—counterparts in the privatization of individual experience in Mumbai.* And for the people most benefiting from the privatization of India's economy—English-speaking, middle- and upper-class, urban cosmopolitans—the difference between public and private physical space was especially pronounced.[5] Thus, if culture is something that we "practice" within and among our environmentally conditioned bodies, would the changing physical environments of everyday life in Mumbai come out in the sounds, words, and images of pop songs from that historical moment? Was there a new "soundscape" accompanying India's neoliberal transformation?[6] To put it even more grandly, is it possible to discover what capitalism *sounds* like?

The next section of this chapter examines several Indipop music videos by Lucky Ali[7] with an eye toward ways in which ideas of public and private space are constructed, how intimacy is evoked through music, lyrics, and images of specific physical environments, and how these examples of mass-mediated pop songs evoke the social bonds of *Gemeinschaft*[8] to "warm up" a cold and impersonal mediascape.

---

[5] Nowhere is the contrast between public and private more palpable than when you leave the noisy, sweaty city streets and enter a silent, chilly recording studio!

[6] The Canadian composer R. Murray Schafer popularized the term "soundscape" in the 1970s and is seen as a founder of what is now called "acoustic ecology," a movement that emphasizes an aural awareness of our environment in opposition to what is understood as an increasingly visual way of being. See Schafer (1977).

[7] Despite extensive interactions with his band and promoters, my encounters with Lucky Ali himself were limited (primarily centered on an interview conducted while observing him work in a recording session in 2001) when compared to my ethnographic experience with other Indipop figures such as Alisha Chinai and The Colonial Cousins. Yet I chose to focus on Lucky Ali in this chapter for several reasons. First, his music has received little attention by scholars despite its enduring quality. And second, his conflicted relationship with cinema (he is the son and nephew of very famous actors yet frequently distances himself from "filmi" culture in interviews) is emblematic of the Indipop movement's entangled relationship with Bollywood.

[8] While most people have some bonds that are more intimate and familiar and other relationships that are more formulaic and impersonal, *Gemeinschaft* and *Gesellschaft* are just ways to categorize

> **Box 1.1 Video Analysis**
>
> For each music video by Lucky Ali discussed in this chapter, consider the following questions:
>
> 1. What sorts of physical environments are represented in the video? Is there a marked difference between public and private spaces?
> 2. How many identifiable characters are there, and how do they interact with each other and with their environment? In what ways does the video evoke warm, intimate relationships (*Gemeinschaft*) or formal, rigid (*Gesellschaft*) ones?
> 3. How is culture represented in the video? Are there identity markers in dress or gesture that seem to evoke tradition, authenticity, nostalgia, or modernity?
> 4. Can you describe the timbre/fidelity of the audio track? How does the sonic texture of the recording correspond to the action depicted on-screen?
> 5. Is there evidence of societal differences represented in the video? Do differences in gender, social class, sexuality, ethnicity, or religion come into play?
> 6. What else caught your eye when watching the video?

Analysis: Three Indipop Videos by Lucky Ali

Let's take a look at three examples of Indipop music videos from the genre's boom years of 1996 to 2001. All of these videos are easy to find on the Internet. The lyrics to these songs are sung in Hindi, and you can find full translations of the lyrics online and on the book's accompanying website. Your task, outlined in Box 1.1, is to analyze these videos in relation to the discussion above about embodied practice, the changing physical environment of "neoliberal" India, and your own home environment. The purpose of this exercise is to generate ideas about the relationship between

our diverse interactions. Other famous examples would fit into this discussion as well, such as Emile Durkheim's model of "organic" versus "mechanical" solidarity (2014) or Karl Marx's claim that modern factory workers are "alienated" from their full human capacity and made to feel disconnected from themselves and from each other (1978).

culture and environment in the digital age and to explore the ways in which music videos (or other products of the entertainment industry) can be analyzed as texts—open to interpretation and filled with the tensions and contradictions that permeate our societies as a whole.

Example 1.1: Lucky Ali's "O Sanam"

Album: *Sunoh* (BMG Crescendo), 1996

This video (▶ Video example 1.1), shot in Egypt, was Lucky Ali's breakthrough hit and was released amid the rush of new, non-film music coming from Mumbai-based record companies in the mid-1990s. The song's lyrics draw on conventions from South Asian poetry (such as the Urdu *ghazal*) that have informed Hindi film songs for generations. Words such as *taḍap* ("agitation"), *majbūr* ("compelled"), and *kasam* ("oath") evoke a tradition of courtly love and duty that aligns with the melodrama of the video's storyline. Indeed, each of the three verses of the song ends with a vow to honor the memory and emotions of the singer's relationship with the beloved.[9] Feelings of separation and nostalgia also feature in several of Lucky Ali's greatest hits, here most notably with the line *mil ke bichharnā to dastūr ho gayā* ("these days it has become a custom to be separated after coming together"), which can be read as a reference to anything from the impermanence of life to friends moving abroad for professional opportunities and the growing trend toward casual dating (issues that carried particular weight for Lucky Ali's middle-class, cosmopolitan fans at that time). In a more recent interview with 93.5 RED FM in Bangalore, Lucky Ali reflected, "There was a sense of desperation in that song. A desperation of search, of not finding, of remembering. Also of contemplating and almost feeling bad for a certain situation that you can't control" (see ▶ Video example 1.2, Red FM Bengaluru 2020).[10]

In many ways, Indipop was still trying to get on its feet in 1996, and "O Sanam" comes across as rather *filmi*. That is, it strategically employs many elements that are characteristic of Bollywood cinema in order to draw on

---

[9] In South Asian poetic traditions, the idea of the "beloved" often carries religious connotations. Thus, one's longing to be close to a lover also implies a longing for closeness with God (see Gillani*).

[10] In the interview, radio jockey Tuhin raises the topic of "O Sanam," stating that it is still "engraved in everybody's mind/heart." Nostalgia for Lucky Ali's music has been steadily on the rise alongside the growing indie music scene in contemporary urban India.

the familiar while introducing audiences to a new form of popular music. For example, the piece has a relatively long instrumental introduction, and Lucky Ali hums and sings vocables before introducing the lyrics, a nod to the free-rhythmic *alap* (*ālāp*) that one finds in many traditions in North India. The juxtaposition of sustained chords from a "synth pad" with acoustic instruments (in this case, hand drums and acoustic guitar) is reminiscent of music director A. R. Rahman's sound from that era as well. Yet Lucky Ali comes to the Bollywood connections naturally, as he is the son of famous film actor Mehmood. And the melodramatic, tortured passion for a forbidden love depicted in the video also has a personal meaning, as the blue-eyed woman who captures his heart in the video is, in fact, played by Lucky Ali's first wife, New Zealander Meaghan McCleary (also the sister of Ali's songwriting and producing partner Mikey McCleary).

Example 1.2: Lucky Ali's "Dekha Hai Aise Bhi"

Album: *Sifar* (Sony Music India), 1998
Recorded for his second studio album, "Dekha Hai Aise Bhi" (▶ Video example 1.3) takes Lucky Ali to the southwestern United States, along the famous Route 66. As we saw in the video for "O Sanam," the narrative for this video explores memory and place with layers of loss, longing, and love—themes with a long history in South Asia. The song's title, loosely translated as "I've seen someone just like that before," could be inferred by South Asian listeners as a reference to love poetry influenced by Islamic mysticism, in which the Beloved only offers us a tantalizing, fleeting glimpse, or as a reference to Hindu folk songs about a deity's many forms or Krishna's mysterious presence just beyond our field of view. While the song's lyrics do not specify a location for Ali's journey, the video also evokes a kind of "phantom nostalgia"[11] for the American southwest, compounding the resonances of Native American history with Lucky Ali's own experience of having briefly lived in Arizona into the already dense layers of memory and history that permeate the song.

---

[11] See Emoff (2002) for an evocative account of nostalgia for unseen people, places, or eras within spirit possession practices in Madagascar.

In his pop persona as well as his real life, Lucky Ali's identity as something of a wandering minstrel has been a constant. Appearing on the well-known talk show *Movers and Shakers* at the time of *Sifar*'s release, Lucky Ali characterized the album as follows: "It's about journey, it's about understanding. It's about hope and aspirations and goals in life" (▶ Video example 1.4, SET India 2020). From having attended boarding school at a young age to living and working abroad as a young man, a keen sensitivity to place is evident in his music and videos. This continues today with Lucky Ali's preference for a somewhat reclusive life and his passion for organic farming and reforestation projects. He says, "For me I find my romance with nature..... I love quiet places. I even like deserts. I like a place that is by nature quiet.... [There are] very few places left that way" (see ▶ Video example 1.5, The Show Time 2017).

Example 1.3: Lucky Ali's "Tere Mere Saath"

Album: *Aks* (Sony Music India), 2001

The final music video example, "Tere Mere Saath" (▶ Video example 1.6), comes from Lucky Ali's third solo album. Here we travel to Cuba, where the narrative again places our singer in between the known and unknown, present and past. As Lucky Ali explores Havana in a vintage convertible, he sings *tere mere sāth jo hotā hai, bāt samajh mein ātī nahīn* ("what happens between you and me is something I can't understand"). The viewer is again transported to an "exotic" and "foreign" yet familiar locale where love, companionship, and community must be discovered. Musically, this song follows a more binary form, with relatively choppy lyrics recited over the verses in a minor key alternating with contrastingly soaring singing in a major key for the song's chorus.

His sense of separation from the city is amplified by lyrics such as *jab sārā jag hī sotā hai, phir nīnd hamein kyūn ātī nahīn* (when the world is asleep, why aren't I/we sleepy). As in the previous videos, contrasting levels of color temperature and saturation produce visual markers of the layered histories being conjured in Lucky Ali's songs. Those paying close attention will also notice the intertextual references in his dress: the untucked blue shirt and white pants he wears here evoke memories of Lucky Ali's breakthrough video "O Sanam" of five years earlier.

Conclusion

As you consider your own interpretations of these videos you may wonder: if this chapter is about the bodily experience of living in a crowded megacity like Mumbai, why did we watch videos of a singer wandering around the world like a lonely tourist? I selected these three videos for a variety of reasons. First of all, they are representative of the "global imagination"[12] that fueled both Indipop and Bollywood beginning in the 1990s. Filming in foreign locations became a common strategy to capture an audience's attention in an increasingly crowded media space. Furthermore, it is not easy to film in Mumbai, especially for those on a smaller budget. Bollywood producers might have the clout to block off city streets or an entire neighborhood, but not so with Indipop video directors. Nevertheless, as stated above, many Indipop videos borrow from *filmi* models and clichés in order to appeal to the established consumer base in India.

Shooting videos abroad was also in line with the marketing strategies of international record companies during the 1990s. Lucky Ali's promoters at BMG and Sony Music emphasized quality when competing not only with Bollywood but also against the glut of locally produced Indipop music clamoring for air time on MTV India and other music television channels. For artists like Lucky Ali, Alisha Chinai, and the Colonial Cousins, recording albums abroad became both an aesthetic decision and a marketing resource to appeal to an aspirational class of consumers. With their ears tuned outward to the rest of the world, it's not a surprise that the visualizations of these songs share a similar international orientation.[13]

Reflecting on the impact of Lucky Ali's debut, singer-songwriter Uday Benegal told me:

> Lucky Ali's first album had sensitive lyrics, beautifully written stuff. Really nice songs, and for me he represented one of the best things about Hindi

---

[12] See Appadurai (1990) and Erlmann (1996).

[13] I should note, however, that I encountered very little concern among industry executives with selling Hindi pop music to an international audience beyond the NRI (non-resident Indian) communities of South Asians settled in North America, Europe, and Australia. They assumed that songs in Hindi would not "cross over" to the international charts. And despite the success of Ricky Martin and Shakira at that time, few Indian record companies were interested in promoting English-language recordings. Perhaps this conundrum helps to explain Indipop's struggles to connect with a broader audience base. The music aspired to an international standard, thus eschewing some of the elements that sounded "too Indian." Yet Indipop was being marketed exclusively to Indians, implying that this was strictly a domestic product and thus undermining its own claim to being international.

pop. . . . [It] was a symbol of hope for me as well. That if this exists in the middle of all the other stuff that Hindi pop world is producing, there is hope. And he did very well—it's an album that did very well, I think, critically and commercially. It made me feel good because it meant that there were people with taste and a good sense of judgment, who were buying these things, and therefore it made marketing sense for a record company. (Personal communication, 2009)

Given the international production aesthetic and the relative luxury of buying recorded music (in the late 1990s, buying a compact disc in India would cost roughly the same as fifteen tickets to a local movie theater), Lucky Ali's record labels targeted a cosmopolitan, upper-middle-class audience. During the same time period, this demographic was experiencing a steady outflow of young professionals who were migrating to the United States, United Kingdom, and Australia in significant numbers. Lucky Ali's songs about being in a strange land looking for love, community, and continuity with the past would have spoken powerfully to this audience.[14]

More symbolically, though, I argue that in pop songs such as those by Lucky Ali, what is for sale is the artists themselves. While the emotional content in Bollywood cinema flows between characters on the big screen, and the audience watches as if a fly on the wall, Indipop songs aim to evoke a depth and intimacy of personal experience. Though this is primarily accomplished through musical textures and lyrics, the physical environment of videos can play a critical role in evoking this intimacy. After all, profound personal thoughts and feelings are better contextualized in a lonely desert or on a mountaintop than amid a busy train station or crowded market.

Thus, while there are no scenes of contemporary urban India in these three videos, Lucky Ali's music resonated with an emerging experience of urban cosmopolitanism in India. Like stepping into an air-conditioned shopping mall, "stepping into" a Lucky Ali video offers a palpable, tangible, embodied experience of being in a quiet bubble of individual consumption. The listener traveling around Mumbai wearing headphones or the NRI (Non-Resident Indian) worker heading to Silicon Valley could identify with Lucky Ali

---

[14] The Bollywood industry also tapped into these themes of immigration, nostalgia, and the quest for identity during the 1990s, with the heroes of blockbuster films such as *Dilwale Dulhaniya Le Jayenge* and *Hum Dil De Chuke Sanam* being NRIs who return to India to find love, happiness, and self-identity.

wandering around the world, observing without being compelled to interact. Like the emerging generation whose social identities were increasingly mediated through computer technology and eventually social media, Lucky Ali's music speaks to an experience shared by many today, of surfing alone through the Internet, feeling that there's always something more out there to be discovered, yet also that there's something from our past that has been lost and deserves to be recovered.

In a song Lucky Ali contributed to a 1997 album commemorating the fiftieth anniversary of India's independence from the British, he sings *anjānī rāho<u>n</u> mei<u>n</u> tū kyā ḍhūṇḍhtā phere / dūr jisko samjhā voh to pās hai tere* (What do you seek on these unknown roads? What you thought to be far away is actually close to you).

Works Cited

Appadurai, Arjun. 1990. "Disjuncture and Difference in the Global Cultural Economy." *Public Culture* 2: 1–24.

Bauman, Richard. 1984. *Verbal Art as Performance*. Long Grove, IL: Waveland Press.

Bourdieu, Pierre. 1977. *Outline of a Theory of Practice*. Cambridge: Cambridge University Press.

de Certeau, Michel. 1984. *The Practice of Everyday Life*. Translated by Steven Rendall. Berkeley: University of California Press.

Durkheim, Emile. 2014. *The Division of Labor in Society*. Edited by Stephen Lukes. New York: Free Press.

Emoff, Ron. 2002. "Phantom Nostalgia and Recollecting (from) the Colonial Past in Tamatave, Madagascar." *Ethnomusicology* 46(2): 265–283.

Erlmann, Veit. 1996. "The Aesthetics of the Global Imagination: Reflections on World Music in the 1990s." *Public Culture* 8: 467–487.

Feld, Steven. 1982. *Sound and Sentiment: Birds, Weeping, Poetics, and Song in Kaluli Expression*. Philadelphia: University of Pennsylvania Press.

Geertz, Clifford. 1973. *The Interpretation of Cultures*. New York: Basic Books.

Goffman, Erving. 1959. *The Presentation of Self in Everyday Life*. New York: Anchor.

Lomax, Alan. 1972. "Appeal for Cultural Equity." *World of Music* 14(2): 3–17.

Marx, Karl, and Friedrich Engels. 1978. *The Marx-Engels Reader*. Edited by Robert C. Tucker. New York: W. W. Norton.

Red FM Bengaluru. 2020. "Conversations over a Jam Session with Lucky Ali FT. RJ Tuhin." YouTube, last modified January 25, 2020. https://www.youtube.com/watch?v=ynMrIvQ2PnY.

Schafer, R. Murray. 1977. *The Soundscape: Our Environment and the Tuning of the World*. Rochester, VT: Destiny Books.

SET India. 2020. "In Conversation with Lucky Ali and Rani Mukherjee—Full Episode 26—Movers and Shakers." YouTube, last modified March 11, 2020. https://www.youtube.com/watch?v=sviyaggXoVI.

Show Time, The. 2017. "The Most Soulful Ru-Ba-Ru Interview of Lucky Ali | Episode 11 | The Show Time." YouTube, last modified August 10, 2017. https://www.youtube.com/watch?v=yoZ1kkW_imc.

Simmel, Georg. 1998. *Simmel on Culture: Selected Writings*. Edited by David Frisby and Mike Featherstone. London: Sage Publications.

Tönnies, Ferdinand. 2001. *Tönnies: Community and Civil Society*. Translated by Margaret Hollis. Cambridge: Cambridge University Press.

2

A Melody of Lucknow

Hearing History in North Indian Music

Max Katz

At the climax of the 1938 Hindi film *Street Singer*, the protagonist, Bhulwa, angrily disrupts opening night at the theater, outraged by the newly composed melody imposed upon his most cherished traditional song. Tossed from the hall, Bhulwa (played by famed actor-singer K. L. Saigal) shuffles off, clutching his harmonium and intoning to himself the piece as he believes it was intended (see Majumdar 2009, 183, and ▶ Video example 2.1). Recorded live on set, this performance by Saigal rocketed the song—a *thumri* (*ṭhumrī*) or light-classical vocal composition titled "Babul Mora" (*bābul morā*)—to commercial success throughout India. A hit from "Kashmir to Kanyakumari," Saigal's recording inspired classical singers of Hindustani (North Indian) and karnatak (South Indian) music alike to adopt "Babul Mora" into their concert repertoire (Misra 1981, 42). Indeed, despite gaining its widest recognition as a film song, "Babul Mora" is embraced by discerning classical musicians and connoisseurs as "one of the most moving pieces in Hindustani music" (Deva 1995, 64).

Undoubtedly the song's renown today derives in large measure from the heart-rending brilliance of Saigal's 1938 recording. In this chapter, however, I argue that "Babul Mora" continues to resonate among both popular and classical audiences due in part to its long history preceding Saigal's famed rendition. I pursue this argument through a genealogical study of the song itself, including a hands-on engagement with its pivotal melodic phrase, revealing that "Babul Mora" carries with it more than a century and a half of accumulated meanings and associations. Specifically, I argue that the song—which uses the form of a wedding lament—presents a compressed, iconic representation of the grievous cultural loss wrought by the imposition of British colonialism, the transition to modernity, and, ultimately, the attainment of democratic self-rule in 1947.

"Babul Mora"

"Babul Mora" has been performed and recorded countless times over the past century with numerous variations in text and melody, yet there remains an identifiable, if flexible, core to the song that presents a union of lyrics and tune. The pivotal lyrical line, which expresses the lament of a bride leaving her parents' home, is this:

Bābul morā naihara chūṭo hī jāe
Oh Father, my maternal home is (verily) being left behind.

The essential melodic movement of the song corresponds with the words *naihara* ("maternal home") *chūṭo* ("left behind") *hī* ("verily") *jāe* ("is being") and is used repeatedly throughout performances of "Babul Mora" as a *mukhra* (*mukhṛā*) or relatively stable, recurring signpost that concludes sections of improvisational elaboration. A transcription of this *mukhra* as sung by eminent vocalist Girija Devi (1929–2017) is presented below (Figure 2.1, see ⏵ Audio example 2.1, cue point 0:26).[1]

The goal of this chapter is to prepare you to recognize "Babul Mora" when you hear it, and further to hear a complex historical narrative within it. But in Indian music (as in musical practices throughout the world), learning to *hear* requires learning to *sing*. Let's begin by singing a simplified version of the basic intervals involved in the *mukhra* of "Babul Mora" (Box 2.1). Both Hindustani and karnatak music are taught aurally through a system of solfège called *sargam* in which each of seven scale degrees carries its own name, abbreviated to a single syllable. For this exercise, we will only need

Figure 2.1 *Mukhra* of "Babul Mora" in Western staff notation and *sargam*. Transcription by the author.

---

[1] Note that the tonic pitch is C, and thus the key signature of four flats indicates not A♭ major, but a mode akin to C Phrygian.

> **Box 2.1 Exercise**
>
> - Sing: *Sa, Re, <u>Ga</u>* (like the first three notes of a minor scale) and hold each note for a second or two.
>
> Next, we expand the phrase by adding a descent, using the lowered 2nd scale degree (<u>Re</u>) instead of the raised 2nd (*Re*).
>
> - Sing: *Sa, Re, <u>Ga</u>* (pause), <u>*Re*</u>, *Sa*.
>
> Next, we will add the raised 7th, or leading tone, preceding a final *Sa*.
>
> - Sing: *Sa, Re, <u>Ga</u>* (pause), <u>*Re*</u>, *Sa* (pause), *Ni, Sa*.

five discrete scale degrees: *Ni* (raised 7th, or leading tone), *Sa* (tonic, C in this case), <u>*Re*</u> (lowered 2nd), *Re* (natural or raised 2nd), and <u>*Ga*</u> (lowered 3rd). The transcription presents the melody in the key of C, but it may be transposed to any tonal center, depending on the range and preferences of the vocalist.

Notice how the lowered 2nd and raised 7th degrees encircle the tonic pitch at the end of the phrase. Now listen to the first few moments of the performance of "Babul Mora" by Girija Devi (▶ Audio example 2.1). Notice how she sings the words *naihara chūṭo hī jāe* beginning at 0:26 in the recording. Do you recognize the melodic shape that you practiced singing? Does it feel like a mournful lament to you? You probably also notice many other melodic turns and subtle gestures rendered with virtuosic vocal control and artistry. What is Girija Devi doing? Is she just singing random, pleasing sounds? Indeed not. The melodic material of "Babul Mora" derives from a specific *raga* (*rāga*) or modal entity called *bhairavi* (*bhairavī*). This *raga* is understood to have as its most basic structure a heptatonic (seven-note) scale with flat 2nd, 3rd, 6th, and 7th degrees. The intervals you practiced singing also included *bhairavi*'s two most common accidentals: the raised 2nd degree and the raised 7th degree. Those notes are technically outside of the *bhairavi* scale and would not be heard in an orthodox treatment, but are regularly employed when the *raga* is performed in the light-classical style, in which case it is also sometimes called *sindhi bhairavi*.

A deep understanding of Hindustani music requires technical language and specialized skills, but the great majority of those who know and love *raga*-based music connect with it not through esoteric theory or disciplined practice, but rather through its emotional appeal. Since the earliest texts in which the term is given a musicological definition, *raga* has referred to a combination of modal structure and emotional affect (Widdess 1995, 40–42). The word *raga* derives from the Sanskrit *ranj*, meaning "to color"—for centuries, *raga*s have been understood to "give color." The best-known contemporary definition of *raga* is "that which colors the mind" (e.g., Shankar 2007 [1968], 28), suggesting that the capacity to evoke emotions, feelings, or colors remains the defining characteristic of *raga* music today. For some two millennia, Indian music scholars have systematized these colors through a theory of *rasa*s, or "aesthetic sentiments" (Widdess 1995, 37). *Bhairavi* has often been associated with the ancient *rasa*s of *shringara* (*śṛṅgāra*, romantic love), *karuna* (*karuṇā*, pathos or compassion), and *bhakti* (religious devotion). Even in the present day, *bhairavi* is widely interpreted to express "the poignancy of separation" (Bor 1999, 34).

*Raga*s are also associated with seasons, times of day, and even, in some cases, geographic locations. Such is the case with *bhairavi*, which is an early-morning *raga*, but also conjures in the minds of contemporary music lovers the legendary city of Lucknow. In Abdul Halim Sharar's classic history, *Lucknow: The Last Phase of an Oriental Culture*, originally published as a series of Urdu essays between 1914 and 1919, the author extensively cites musician and scholar Asadullah "Kaukab" Khan, who notes that "Today Lucknow's *bhairvin* raginis, sung in the early morning, have become as famous throughout India as Lucknow's melons" (2001 [1975], 138).[2] Indeed, from the mid-nineteenth century until today, *raga bhairavi* has aroused nostalgic reverie for the once-great city of Lucknow.

Lucknow: Lost City of the Arts

Lucknow marks the approximate center of the vast region of the Indo-Gangetic Plain that spreads from Pakistan to Bangladesh. In the eighteenth and nineteenth centuries, the city was a pivotal site of royal patronage for

---

[2] Kaukab uses the now-archaic term "ragini" to refer to *bhairavi* (here with the alternate spelling *bhairavi*) as a lighter, female-coded *raga*.

North India's most elite musicians. Delhi, the capital of the Mughal Empire, was the unrivaled cultural center of North India from the sixteenth to the eighteenth centuries, yet as the empire foundered, Delhi's loss was Lucknow's gain. From the time of its establishment as the capital of the state of Awadh in 1775, Lucknow became a magnet for musicians fleeing the embattled imperial capital. By the mid-nineteenth century, and especially during the reign of its last king, Wajid Ali Shah (r. 1847–1856), Lucknow not only was North India's preeminent musical and cultural center, but was the subcontinent's "largest and most prosperous" city outside of the new British colonial centers of Calcutta, Bombay, and Madras (Oldenburg 2001 [1984], 3–4).

Throughout this period, various forms of *raga*-based art music flourished in the royal courts and salons of Lucknow, where performer-composers both conserved and transformed the repertoires of the fading Mughal courts. Still North India's most elite and revered musical heritage, today these arts are known collectively as Hindustani music, or Hindustani classical music. Lucknow remains most intimately associated with Hindustani music's light-classical vocal genre called *thumri*.

The "quintessential" genre of "dance-song" performed by North India's professional female courtesans (Walker 2014, 133), *thumri* was particularly beloved by the king, Wajid Ali Shah. Most significant for our purposes, Wajid Ali Shah, a prolific composer of *thumri*s himself, is universally credited as the author of "Babul Mora." Though this ascription as yet lacks documentary evidence, there remains an intimate connection in the South Asian popular imagination between the *thumri* "Babul Mora" and the composer-king Wajid Ali Shah. To grasp the powerful associations between the king, the city, the *raga*, and the *thumri*, we must return to the royal court of Lucknow and review the circumstances that led to its demise—and to the beginning of official British colonial rule in India—early in 1856.

"A Cherry Which Will Drop into Our Mouths"

The decline of the Mughal Empire throughout the eighteenth century opened the door for new, independent princely states to emerge and prosper. The largest and wealthiest of these was the state of Awadh, ruled from 1722 to 1856 by a dynasty of Shia Muslims of Persian extraction titled Nawabs (*navābs*). However, the collapse of the unified Mughal Empire also empowered the British East India Company, whose appetite for expansion set it on a collision course with the Nawabs of Awadh.

The situation came to a head under the reign of the final King of Awadh, Nawab Wajid Ali Shah. Lord Dalhousie, the British governor-general of India from 1848 to 1856, saw Awadh (spelled "Oude" by the British) as a territory crucial to the expansion of the British Empire, famously describing it as "a cherry which will drop into our mouths some day" (Dalhousie 1910, 169; Mukherjee 2001 [1984], 32). In January 1856, as a finale to his tenure as governor-general, Dalhousie ordered the Lucknow Resident, General James Outram, to present the King of Awadh with an ultimatum: sign a new treaty ceding all administrative responsibilities for the kingdom to the British East India Company or face a military attack.

Captain Fletcher Hayes was among General Outram's small entourage present at the fateful meeting in Lucknow on the morning of February 4, 1856. As Hayes documents in his eyewitness report, at the conclusion of the meeting Wajid Ali Shah removed his turban, handed it to General Outram, and stated that he was now "in the hands of the British Government" which could, "at its pleasure, consign him to obscurity" ("Oude Blue Book" 1856, 288–289; Bhatnagar 1968, 149). While helpless to resist the Company militarily, the king raged against the insult of his ouster, refused to sign a new treaty, and vowed to seek immediate redress at the highest levels of government, first in the Company's administrative center of Calcutta, and then, if necessary, in London before the Queen herself (Bhatnagar 1968, 150). On March 13, 1856, in a quest for justice, the king departed Lucknow, never to return.

According to legend—and some historians—it was at this very moment of crisis, as the king bade farewell to his beloved city, that he penned the *thumri* "Babul Mora" (Oldenburg 2007, 26–27; Metcalf and Metcalf 2002, 122). It is especially significant that Wajid Ali Shah should choose to lament his ouster with a *thumri*. Not only was the king believed by many—though incorrectly—to have invented the genre of *thumri* itself (see Manuel 1989, 34; Du Perron 2007, 52), his very reputation as a lover of music, dance, and poetry provided Lord Dalhousie with his primary justification for the removal of the king. Indeed, the stated rationale for the Company's overthrow of Awadh rested upon the conviction that the king was neglecting the affairs of the state through his fanciful obsession with the arts.

The claim of "misrule" was documented by Dalhousie through reference to the reports of successive British Residents, close witnesses to the Lucknow court. For example, Colonel William Sleeman (Resident from 1849 to 1854) writes in an undated letter to Lord Dalhousie that the "King's ambition seems to be limited to the reputation of being the best drum-beater, dancer, and poet of the day" (quoted in Chatterjee 2004, 4161). In his own statement to the Company's court of directors in London, Lord Dalhousie insists that it is the solemn responsibility of the British Government to protect the people of Awadh from the depredations of their successive rulers, citing "avarice, as in one; intemperance, as in another; or, as in the present King, effeminate sensuality, indulged among singers, musicians, and eunuchs, the sole companions of his confidence, and the sole agents of his power" ("Oude Blue Book" 1856, 180). Even contemporaneous critics of British imperialism understood that such claims against the King of Awadh served as mere pretext for the amassing of colonial power (e.g., Lucas 1857), yet in the popular imagination the notion remains even today that Wajid Ali Shah was deposed due to his "misrule," itself a result of his excessive fascination with dance, poetry, and music. In this regard, "Babul Mora" constitutes an art song written in lament of a fate that was itself a consequence of the love of art song.

Yet the *thumri* carries further historical significance still: as a depiction of the exile of Wajid Ali Shah from his kingdom, "Babul Mora" identifies a pivotal moment of social and cultural rupture in Indian history. While Dalhousie was convinced that the administration of Awadh must be transferred to the East India Company, he was not in favor of outright annexation. As Dalhousie writes in explanation of his position, "We should lower the dignity and authority of the Sovereigns of Oude no further than is absolutely necessary for the accomplishment of our righteous ends" ("Oude Blue Book" 1856, 184). Of course, Dalhousie's concern for the "dignity" of the king was entirely tactical: as noted by Colonel Sleeman, "Were we to take advantage of the occasion to *annex* or *confiscate* Oude, or any part of it, our good name in India would inevitably suffer" (quoted in Chatterjee 2004, 4161). Thus, Dalhousie's plan was to leave the king in place as a figurehead while quietly taking over the administration of Awadh for the Company.

In fact, however, the king successfully thwarted this plan by refusing to sign a new treaty and fleeing his kingdom. He thereby forced Dalhousie to annex the territory, replace the entire government with British officials, and rule it directly in an undisguised colonial coup. The result, far exceeding the stated fears of Sleeman or Dalhousie, was the righteous indignation of the masses of Awadh, who joined a broad rebellion against the British colonizers in a year-long war that permanently tore the fabric of North Indian society.

As numerous historians have argued, the war of 1857–1858, though beginning as a mutiny by soldiers of the Bengal Army in the city of Meerut, quickly spread throughout North India as a popular uprising embraced by all levels of society. Fighting was particularly fierce in Awadh, where peasants and landlords were unified by their shared outrage at the ignominious ouster of their king (e.g., Metcalf and Metcalf 2002, 100; Bhattacharya 2010 [2007], xv; Mukherjee 2001 [1984], 82–134). Because of the radical social and political rupture of the war, the year 1857 has "conventionally been taken as the dividing point that marks the beginning of modern India" (Metcalf and Metcalf 2002, 91). Such modernity entailed the full onslaught of direct colonial rule, the subsequent birth of the anticolonial nationalist movement, the end of feudal states, and, eventually, independence and democracy in 1947.

It is debatable whether the war itself constituted the birth of nationalist consciousness in India, but there is no doubt that it was an unprecedented anticolonial rebellion and continues to live in the collective memory of the subcontinent today: as historians Bose and Jalal write, 1857 is a "date to conjure with" in historical narratives of South Asia (1998, 88). While the leaders of the rebellion did not themselves advocate thoroughgoing changes to the social order (Bhattacharya 2010 [2007], xxv–xxvi), they did observe democratic principles of organization and, during their rule, produced newspapers that spoke to the public at large, presenting the newly imagined community "enticing vistas of what it would gain from an Indian (not necessarily, royal) regime" (Habib 2010 [2007], 61). Moreover, events that culminated along with the war highlight massive shifts in the politics, economy, culture, and communications of India, including the birth of "the railway, the telegraph, the postal service, and improved steam transport" (Metcalf and Metcalf 2002, 95).

The shift to modernity in India did not take place in a momentous epiphany, and scholars still debate the roles of colonialism, capitalism, and precolonial history in shaping India's modernity. However, if one were to posit that a single lyrical tableau might capture the emotional experience of India's transition to modernity, the meeting of Wajid Ali Shah with General Outram on February 4, 1856, would not be an entirely outlandish choice. The king's resignation, his pain and anger, the war that followed, and the resulting transformation of life in India all speak to the radical ruptures of modernity. In this regard, the king's lament—"Babul Mora"—may be understood as an iconic artistic rendering of the agony attending the birth of modern India.

Marriage, Modernity, and Loss

Prior to K. L. Saigal's hit recording of "Babul Mora," the song was already well known in India. In 1925, famed classical singer Faiyaz Khan performed the song at the Fourth All India Music Conference held at the heart of Wajid Ali Shah's ruined palace complex in Lucknow (Report 1925, 40). Faiyaz Khan's rendition of "Babul Mora" was likely influenced by the 1907 recording of the song by Malka Jan of Agra (Kinnear 1994, 237–239), a famed courtesan with whom Faiyaz Khan reportedly enjoyed a "romantic involvement" (Mukherji 2006, 180). According to Mukherji, Faiyaz Khan acknowledged that it was Malka Jan who "inspired" him to perform *thumri*s (2006, 180), a repertoire that fell outside of the orthodox traditions of high-status singers such as himself. As music writer Susheela Misra reports, "Many a time I have witnessed Faiyaz Khan rendering the Bhairavi Thumri 'Babul Mora' and drawing tears out of the listeners' eyes" (Misra 1981, 101). Even into the second half of the twentieth century, as historian Veena Oldenburg writes, "Lucknow's most famous singer, Begum Akhtar, sang ['Babul Mora'] often on request . . . and brought her audiences to tears" (2007, 27).

What was so potent about "Babul Mora" and why does it continue to capture the imaginations of South Asians today, more than a century since it was first recorded, and more than one hundred and fifty years since it was composed? As I have argued, the *thumri* directly references, even memorializes, the traumatic separation of the king from his kingdom and thus evokes the massive political and cultural calamity that befell Lucknow—and likewise the entire subcontinent—in the wake of the ouster of Wajid Ali Shah. But perhaps it resonates on a deeper level yet.

The lyrics of the song's recurring refrain literally reference the pain of separation felt by a young bride as she is carried away from her childhood home to the household of her husband's family. In *Sunlight on a Broken Column* (1992 [1961]), a novel set in mid-twentieth-century Lucknow, author Attia Hosain likewise explores the emotional complexity of South Asian marriage as a metaphor of broader social change. In the novel, Laila, the daughter of a wealthy family of landed gentry, defies centuries of tradition by rejecting an arranged marriage, marrying instead for love, and thereby embracing the very modernity that will ultimately disenfranchise her entire clan. While the story revolves around Laila's own ambivalent freedom struggle, it simultaneously depicts the last days of British rule in India, highlighting the dependence of the Indian feudal aristocracy on the economic and political structures of colonialism. Because of this dependency, the birth of independent India as a democratic republic in 1947 not only toppled the British Empire, but also devastated those elite families—like Laila's—whose refined culture and generous patronage of the arts were premised on a long-standing system of feudal exploitation of peasant workers. In the novel, Laila's family is torn apart not only by the forfeiture of their land holdings to the new democracy, but also by emigration to Pakistan, India's conjoined twin, separated at birth through a bloody and brutal partition whose pain is still felt today.

In South Asia, as in much of the world, marriage is virtually unavoidable. It constitutes one of life's most significant rites of passage, opening a new future even as it marks a wrenching rupture with the past, as encapsulated in the image of the weeping bride torn from her father's embrace only to start a new life as a wife and mother in a strange new home. Likewise, the death of feudalism, the defeat of colonialism, the rise of democracy, and the birth of the nation delivered political freedom but also undermined centuries-old courtly traditions celebrated across lines of class, caste, region, and religion. One might rightly note that the great majority of the Indian masses never embraced elite culture as their own, but the ouster of the King of Awadh in 1856 shocked and enraged his subjects at all levels of society, and even today, everyday Indians continue to identify with the high artistic achievements—especially in the realm of classical music—nurtured by the feudal aristocracy of the anti-democratic past.

Wajid Ali Shah's legendary *thumri* has been interpreted on multiple levels. For instance, beyond the understanding of the song as a wedding lament, scholars note that the second line of the *thumri* evokes an image of the bride being carried away on a palanquin, which may also be read as a reference to the funeral procession that transports the deceased (e.g., Manuel 1989, 20; Du Perron 2007, 57). Thus, separation from the childhood home may also be read as a metaphor illuminating the severance from the material realm awaiting us all. In this chapter, I have argued for an additional interpretation in which the *thumri* may offer a cutting critique of modernity itself, drawing on the metaphor of marriage to highlight a strain of ambivalence within India's struggle for freedom from colonialism and feudalism.

"Babul Mora" reminds us that the progress extolled in the story of India's embrace of Western modernity—its enlightened values, its democratic institutions—demanded the destruction of the very social and economic systems that birthed and sustained the traditions celebrated today as India's enduring musical heritage. Humming along with the plaintive contours of *raga bhairavi*, we may momentarily inhabit the experience of the young bride leaving home, of the aesthete king fleeing Lucknow, and of everyday South Asians who look forward to an unfolding future of technological discovery, global connectivity, and economic expansion while casting longing glances over their shoulder at the rarefied world of courtly dance, poetry, and music left behind.

Works Cited

Bhatnagar, G. D. 1968. *Awadh under Wajid 'Ali Shah*. Varanasi: Bharatiya Vidya Prakashan.
Bhattacharya, Sabyasachi. 2010 [2007]. "Rethinking 1857." In *Rethinking 1857*, edited by Sabyasachi Bhattacharya, ix–xl. Hyderabad: Orient Blackswan.
Bor, Joep, et al., eds. 1999. *The Raga Guide: A Survey of 74 Hindustani Ragas*. Netherlands: Nimbus Records.
Bose, Sugata, and Ayesha Jalal. 1998. *Modern South Asia: History, Culture, Political Economy*. New Delhi: Oxford University Press.
Chatterjee, Partha. 2004. "Empire after Globalization." *Economic and Political Weekly* 39(37): 4155–4164.
Dalhousie, James Andrew Broun Ramsay. 1910. *Private Letters of the Marquess of Dalhousie*. Edited by John George Alexander Baird. London: William Blackwood & Sons.
Deva, B. C. 1995. *Indian Music*. New Delhi: New Age International.
Du Perron, Lalita. 2007. *Hindi Poetry in a Musical Genre: Ṭhumrī Lyrics*. New York: Routledge.
Habib, Irfan. 2010 [2007]. "Understanding 1857." In *Rethinking 1857*, edited by Sabyasachi Bhattacharya, 58–66. Hyderabad: Orient Blackswan.
Hosain, Attia. 1992 [1961]. *Sunlight on a Broken Column*. New Delhi: Penguin Books.
Kinnear, Michael. 1994. *The Gramophone Company's First Indian Recordings, 1899–1908*. Bombay: Popular Prakashan.
Lucas, Samuel. 1857. *Dacoitee in Excelsis: Or, the Spoliation of Oude by the East India Company*. London: J. R. Taylor.
Majumdar, Neepa. 2009. *Wanted Cultured Ladies Only!: Female Stardom and Cinema in India, 1930s–1950s*. Urbana: University of Illinois Press.
Manuel, Peter. 1989. *Ṭhumrī in Historical and Stylistic Perspectives*. Delhi: Motilal Banarasidass.
Metcalf, Barbara, and Thomas Metcalf. 2002. *A Concise History of India*. Cambridge: Cambridge University Press.
Misra, Susheela. 1981. *Great Masters of Hindustani Music*. New Delhi: Hem Publishers.
Mukherjee, Rudrangshu. 2001 [1984]. *Awadh in Revolt: 1857-1858*. Delhi: Permanent Black.
Mukherji, Kumar Prasad. 2006. *The Lost World of Hindustani Music*. New Delhi: Penguin Books.
Oldenburg, Veena Talwar. 2001 [1984]. *The Making of Colonial Lucknow: 1856–1877*. In *The Lucknow Omnibus*. New Delhi: Oxford University Press.

Oldenburg, Veena Talwar, ed. 2007. *Shaam-e-Awadh: Writings on Lucknow*. New Delhi: Penguin Books.
"Oude Blue Book." 1856. *Oude, Papers Relating to*. Presented to both Houses of Parliament by Command of Her Majesty. London: Harrison & Sons.
Report. 1925. *The 4th All-India Music Conference*. Lucknow: Taluqdar Press.
Shankar, Ravi. 2007 [1968]. *My Music, My Life*. San Rafael, CA: Mandala.
Sharar, Abdul Halim. 2001 [1975]. *Lucknow: The Last Phase of an Oriental Culture*. Translated by E. S. Harcourt and Fakhir Hussain. In *The Lucknow Omnibus*. New Delhi: Oxford University Press.
Walker, Margaret. 2014. *India's Kathak Dance in Historical Perspective*. Burlington, VT: Ashgate.
Widdess, Richard. 1995. *The Rāgas of Early Indian Music: Modes, Melodies, and Musical Notations from the Gupta Period to c. 1250*. Oxford: Clarendon Press.

3
Sufi Devotional Performances in Multan, Pakistan, a "City of Saints"

Karim Gillani

Mainstream media often associates the practices of Muslims with inequality and terrorism. Terms such as "Islamophobia" and "Islamic terrorism" are used in discourses that stereotype the great diversity of people—totaling approximately 1.6 billion—practicing different forms of Islam around the world. Another common misconception is that music is outlawed in Islam. Indeed, there are minor segments among extremists who deny the position of music in Islam and threaten those who engage with it (Shiloah 1995). However, other interpretations place music at the heart of Islam's devotion and piety (Qureshi 1995; Waugh 2005). For the majority of Sufi orders, music plays a vital role. Sufism is the mystical dimension of Islam in which music is often a means to connect with the divine. It is practiced by millions around the world, particularly by Muslims in Pakistan, India, Iran, Senegal, and Turkey. Sufis, in general, are peace-loving people who accept pluralist ideas and convey human love through poetry and music. A love of God rather than a fear of God lies at the heart of Sufism. In this chapter, I highlight two important performance contexts in the city of Multan, Pakistan, where *qawwali* (*qavvālī*)—one of the most popular music genres of Muslim devotional performance in South Asia—is central to religious experiences of devotion and ecstasy.

Multan is an ancient capital and crossroads with a significant Muslim presence since the tenth century. As one of the most important trading centers of medieval Islamic India, it attracted a multitude of Sufi mystics and became known as *Madīnat al-Awliyā*, a "city of saints," and a vibrant center for learning and teaching. The famous Persian saying about Multan is "*Chār chīz ast Taufa-e-Multan, gard va garmā, gadā va gorīstān*" ("With four rare things Multan abounds: heat, beggars, dust, and burial grounds") (Gillani, S. 1990). Multan is located in the center of the province of Punjab, in eastern Pakistan.

Karim Gillani, *Sufi Devotional Performances in Multan, Pakistan, a "City of Saints"* In: *Music and Dance as Everyday South Asia*. Edited by: Sarah L. Morelli and Zoe C. Sherinian, Oxford University Press. © Oxford University Press 2024. DOI: 10.1093/oso/9780197566237.003.0004

While the majority of the population are Sunni Muslims, a large number of Shi'a Muslims also live there.[1] The population mostly speaks Punjabi and Saraiki languages.

Multan has been an important place for Sufi practices since the tenth century. Its saints and shrines attract large numbers of devotees throughout the year. Besides various Sufi orders, the city has also attracted many mystics, the most significant among them Bahauddin Zakariya, Pir Shams Sabzwari, and Shah Rukn-e-Alam. These venerable holy men contributed greatly to spreading Islam in the area, especially through peaceful means of religious performance and devotion.

According to oral tradition, Hazrat Amir Khusrau (1253–1325) is widely acknowledged as the creator of the genre that is today called *qawwali* (Qureshi 1995). Today many of his poems are still sung by *qawwals* during the *mehfil-e sama'* (*mehfil-e samā'*, assembly of listening). In this chapter, I argue that within different shrine contexts in Multan, people integrate poetry, ritual, and belief through *qawwali* performance, making Multan dynamic and distinct. The two examples below, drawn from my ethnographic field research in 2002, demonstrate diverse perspectives and shrine contexts through which people of Multan experience and accept a variety of religious beliefs and teachings in their daily lives. In the first, a male emotionally expresses his devotion for a Chishtiyya (*Chishtīyyā*) Sufi saint accompanied by the *qawwals* singing a Chishtiyya poem at Shah Rukn-e-Alam shrine. In the second, an entranced woman conveys her devotion toward the Sufi Saint Lal Shahbaz Qalandar in the male-dominated context of the Bahauddin Zakariya shrine. She uses *dhamal* (*dhamāl*), a popular style of Sufi dance whose increasing rhythmic tempos encourage *wajd* (*vajd*), religious ecstasy. The coexistence of many Sufi orders within Multan has promoted tolerance of a variety of Islam's belief systems and practices, leading to a common "Multani" culture. That is, people associate Multan with pluralistic cultural, social, and religious identities that challenge the narrow understanding of conservative Muslim practices often associated with radicalism.

Qawwali performance serves many musical, cultural, social, economic, and religious functions for members of all sects of Islam in Multan. However, its main objective is to arouse mystical love and remembrance (*dhikr*) of the divine: the core experience of Sufism. In her book *Sufi Music of India and Pakistan*, Regula Qureshi describes *qawwali* as both "a method of worship"

---

[1] Sunni (85%) and Shi'a (15%) are the two mainstream sects of Islam.

and "a means of spiritual advancement"; it is also "a feast for the soul" for both performers and participants (1995). Participants at shrines make up a Sufi *sama'* (*samā'*), an assembly of active "listeners" who respond to devotional music with vocal utterances, gestures, and body movements. In the two case studies below and accompanying video examples, we examine the diversity of spiritual practice facilitated by *qawwali* performance, including (1) devotees' distinct emotional experiences and connections with the Sufi saints; and (2) the experience of trance during *dhamal* performance as facilitated by particular qualities in the music that evoke emotions in its active listeners. Finally, the video examples provide an opportunity to consider the intimate, emotionally expressive connections between poetry, dance, and music.

The *Qawwali* Genre

While *qawwali* is by far the most popular style of devotional music practiced by Sufi musicians from both sides of the India-Pakistan border, there are other Sufi genres, such as *kafi* and *vai*, that are also accompanied with musical instruments (see Bond*). *Qawwali* takes stylistic inspiration from Hindustani music set to mystical poetry in various languages including Farsi, Urdu, Sindhi, Hindi, Punjabi, and Saraiki. The performers of *qawwali*, *qawwals*, are usually professional hereditary musicians attached to a particular Sufi order and shrine (Qureshi 1995, see Figure 3.1). The song structure and performance style are text-dominated; thus performance tends to involve less "classical" music elaboration.[2] During *qawwali* performance, hand clapping and a strong drumbeat increase emotional arousal, while improvisational singing serves the changing needs of individual listeners (Qureshi 1992/93, 111).

The Belief System Underlying *Qawwali*

South Asian Sufism is rooted in the classical tradition of Islamic mysticism as it developed in Arab and Persian cultures between the ninth and

---

[2] There are exceptions, including celebrated singer Nusrat Fateh Ali Khan (1948–1997), who performed very elaborately.

Figure 3.1 Hereditary *qawwal*s of Hazrat Shah Rukn-e-Alam shrine. Multan, Pakistan. August 2002. Photo by the author.

eleventh centuries (Nicholson 1962). From the tenth to fifteenth centuries, Sufis migrated to many parts of South Asia, where they learned local languages and cultural practices, producing rich poetry in vernacular languages to peacefully spread the messages of Islam. Qureshi describes Sufi ideology as "a response to orthodox Islam, at the same time emanating from its very tenets. Thus, while affirming the unity of God (*tauhid*) and the absolute distinction between Creator and Created, Sufism also assumes an inner kinship between God and man and creates a bridge between them through the dynamic force of love (*muhabbat*)" (Qureshi 1995, 79).

The two dimensions of Sufism's central concept of mystical love are (1) to reach the salvation of God through the way (*tarīqah*) under the direction of a spiritual guide in order to achieve "stages" or a "situation" (*maqāmat*) of nearness to God; and (2) ecstatic intuitive fulfillment through God's gift of "states of nearness" or *hal* (*ḥāl*), leading ultimately to union (*viṣāl*) with God (Qureshi 1995, 79–80). These guides, Sufi *pir*s (*pīr*), are fundamental to leading devotees on the path of experiencing nearness to God.

According to the twelfth-century Muslim philosopher and theologian al-Ghazali, "what is most essential to Sufism cannot be learned, but can only be reached by immediate experience, ecstasy and inward transformation" (Nicholson 1962, 211). For mystical love to become the dynamic force of both *maqam* (*maqām*, stages)[3] and *hal*, it must be cultivated spiritually and emotionally (Qureshi 1995, 82). This is achieved through ritual or devotional practice, in particular, the reciting or chanting of God's name (*dhikr*), and active listening to devotional recitation/performance (*sama'*). This is typically practiced collectively in gatherings led by a spiritual leader.[4]

The Sufi approach to Islam is strongly grounded in the philosophical teachings of Ibn al-'Arabi (1165–1240 CE), especially his immensely influential cosmological theory of *wahdat al-wujud* (Arabic: *waḥdat al-wujūd*), "unity of being." According to Ibn al-'Arabi, the ultimate goal of love is to know its reality and that it is identical to God's essence. Love is not an abstract quality superadded to that essence. It is not a relationship between a worldly lover and beloved. This is the true love of the "gnostics" who know no particular object of love. The lyrics below exemplify Ibn al-'Arabi's idea of divine, mystical love.

> When my Beloved appears,
> With what eye do I see Him?
> With his eye, not with mine,
> For none sees Him except Himself.
>
> (in Nicholson 1914, 165–166)

> My heart has become capable of every form;
> it is a pasture for gazelles and a convent for Christian monks,
> And a temple for idols and the pilgrim's Kaaba
> and the tables of the Tora and the book of the Koran.
> I follow the religion of Love:
> whatever way Love's camels take, that is my religion and my faith.
>
> (Ibn al-'Arabi 1911, iii)

The core value of love, regardless of specific school of thought, allows Sufis to inclusively accept everyone as a member of one large family. The practice of acceptance is implemented in people's daily lives through participating in *qawwali* performance. Below, I explore how these ideas of mystical love and oneness with God are variously applied in the shrine contexts in Multan through *qawwali* performance.

---

[3] *Maqām* refers to the stages a Sufi soul must attain in its search for Allah.
[4] When accompanied by musical instruments, *samā'* has sometimes been a controversial practice theologically in Islam.

Case Study 1: An Emotional Devotee at Shah Rukn-e-Alam Shrine

Sufi tombs and shrines have been vital religious places of contemplation, peace, and devotion for centuries. Every day, hundreds of devotees, both male and female, visit shrines to pray to their spiritual masters (see Figure 3.2). In this first example, the *qawwal*s of Shah Rukn-e-Alam, who are from Suhrawardiyya *tariqah* (*tarīqah*, school), performed a *qawwali* in praise of the *pir* (spiritual master) of a different, Chishtiyya *tariqah*. Devotees also gathered around the *qawwal*s to participate in the *samaʿ* (listening) ceremony, paying humble tribute to the *pir* Hazrat Farid Shakar Ganj Baksh of the Chishtiyya school. Two musicians playing harmonium and *tabla* sang *qawwali* in call-and-response manner. The style of playing *tabla* was distinct as compared to other genres such as *bhajan* and *kirtan*. In traditional *qawwali*, the *bayan* (left drum) does not have a black spot in the middle and is held under the arm. It is thus played more like a *dhol* barrel drum, facilitating a highly resonant, powerful sound. The other key instrument, a single reed fixed harmonium, accompanies the singer. This *qawwali samaʿ* performance took place mid-morning, a time when shopkeepers and small business owners leave their homes, typically attend shrines for blessings, and then proceed to their jobs.

Figure 3.2 A Sufi meditating inside the mausoleum of Hazrat Bahauddin Zakariya Multani. Multan, Pakistan. August 2002. Photo by the author.

The example below is a *qawwali* in praise of the Chishtiyya Sufi saint Farid Shakar Ganj sung by hereditary *qawwal*s of Shah Rukn-e-Alam (from the Suhrawardiyya Sufi *tariqah*): *"Manzil terī kaṭhin hai is se zara na ḍar"* ("Your destination is difficult, but don't be afraid"). Its message is one of hope, reminding the listeners not to give up, but to always remember their spiritual master Farid in order to have strength and remain steadfast on their path toward understanding faith. The original anonymous Urdu text and English translation (by the author) is as follows:

Yā Farīd
Kyā Farīd-ud-dīn Bābā lo khabar chaltī merī
Āa paṛā hūn dar pe tere, pār kar naiyā merī
Kāba hai āshiqon kā, kounvārā Farīd kā
Hain Chishtīyyon ko kāfī sahāra Farīd kā

Oh Farid
Oh Farid, what news can I share with you regarding my own life?
I have come to your shrine, please remove all my troubles [literally bring my boat ashore].
The Kaaba [pilgrimage to Mecca] belongs to lovers, I am a devotee of Farid.
We Chishtiyya only rely upon the support from Farid.

Verse 1:
Manzil terī kaṭhin hai is se zara na ḍar (repeat twice)
Tū har qadam pe yā Farīd yā Farīd kar
Tū Chishtīyya malang hai ghabrānā chor de
Aur dar badar hāth ko pehlāna chor de
Ganj-ē-Shakar se māng terī jholī jāye bhar
Tu har qadam pe yā Farīd yā Farīd kar.

Your destination is difficult, but don't be afraid,
In every step, call out, "Oh Farid, oh Farid."
You are a devotee of Chishtiyya so don't be afraid,
And do not seek help from place to place.
Plea only from Ganj-e-Shaker, all your wishes will come true.
At every step, call out, "Oh Farid, oh Farid."

Verse 4:
Sāre jahān men̲ charchā hai Bābā Farīd kā
Khālī nahīn̲ jātā koī māngtā Farīd kā
Sadqa Moīnuddin kā dete hain Ganj Shakar
Ke tū har qadam pe yā Farīd yā Farīd kar

The entire world praises Baba Farid.
No one goes empty-handed seeking help from Farid.
Ganj-e-Shakar gives humble submission to Moinuddin.[5]
At every step, call out, "Oh Farid, oh Farid."

This *qawwali*, unlike others in praise of Sufi saints, is uniquely relevant to the everyday life of devotees. Here, the poet reminds us of how to cope with worldly challenges faced in our daily lives through hope and prayers, especially by chanting the name of the *pir* Farid.

These lyrics focus on the Chishtiyya belief in *pir*s, like Farid, who serve as spiritual guides for devotees. Most other Sunni Muslims do not believe in having a spiritual guide. This distinction between Chishtiyya Sufi and orthodox Muslim understandings of the means to salvation is seen in the line "The Kaaba (pilgrimage to Mecca) belongs to lovers." With the term "lovers," the poet subtly critiques orthodox Muslims who believe that going on pilgrimage to Mecca is enough to bring them closer to God, but reject the equal significance of following a spiritual guide. The next two lines emphasize the importance of devotion to and reliance upon one's *pir*, Farid. Sufis believe in using spiritual masters (referred to as *pir*, *sheikh*, or *murshid*) as intercessors to guide them according to a specific *tariqah* (school of thought). They believe that to achieve oneness or presence with God through denial of self (*fanā*), one needs a spiritual guide to help understand (in one's local language, context, or place, and through cultural idioms like music) the esoteric, inner aspects of faith that can lead one toward their spiritual goals and answers. This oneness with God can be briefly experienced through trance states brought on by devotional music such as *qawwali*.

During the *qawwali* performance of "Oh Farid" (▶ Video example 3.1), I witnessed one devotee eating *langar* (free food distributed among devotees at the shrine as a *naẓrāna* or gift, cf. Kaur*) behind the *qawwal*s (cue point

---

[5] Moinuddin Chishti was the founder of the Chishtiyya Sufi order in South Asia.

> **Box 3.1 Syllables for Basic Drum Strokes of** *keherwa tal*
>
> Dha ge na ti | na ka dhi na
> 1   2 3 4 | 5 6   7   8

Figure 3.3 A devotee cries while listening to *qawwali*, Hazrat Shah Rukn-e-Alam shrine. Multan, Pakistan. August 2002. Photo by the author.

0:10–2:10). In this performance, the *tabla* player acted as an oral prompter. He recalled the lyrics by heart, singing first so the older main singer could remember the lines. From cue point 4:45 onward, a devotee raised both of his hands, gently moved along with the eight-beat *tal* (*tāl*, rhythmic cycle) called *keherwa*, then suddenly started crying in utmost devotion and love for his spiritual master (see Box 3.1, Figure 3.3).

By performing *qawwali*, these artists provide healing, peace, and devotion for their listeners. At cue point 6:10, one can see clearly how emotionally charged this devotee was as he cried out loud in a public place. He also chanted along with the singers "*yā Farīd*," moving his hands upward as he became entranced (see Box 3.2).

> **Box 3.2 Exercise 1**
>
> 1. Watch ▶ Video example 3.1, of a *qawwali* performance at Shah Rukn-e-Alam Shrine.
> 2. Describe some key features of the performance, such as the timbre of the instruments and the musical accompaniment.
> 3. What is the form of the music, and how does it contribute to participation and easy transmission of the lyrics?
> 4. What is the quality of the *keherwa* rhythmic pattern used in this *qawwali*? How does the tempo of the piece change?
> 5. Based on what you can observe in this example, how does this *qawwali* differ from other devotional music you are familiar with (from South Asia and elsewhere)? Besides the musical sound, what other elements do you observe in the video and how do they intersect?
> 6. Discuss the devotee who cried while paying tribute to his spiritual master. Which elements in the music do you think can influence listeners to this degree?

Case Study 2: *Dhamal* at Hazrat Bahauddin Zakariya Shrine

For almost a thousand years in Sufi performances and rituals, listening and chanting have been incorporated into dance and music as catalysts for experiencing *wajd*, or religious ecstasy (Racy 2003, 4). At shrines in Multan, I witnessed both common people and religious mystics experiencing trance while fully immersed in *qawwali* performance. When I asked them, no one was able to use mere words to describe their spiritual encounters. According to Asghar, a hereditary *qawwal* at Hazrat Bahauddin Zakariya's shrine, *dhamal* performance is a spiritual experience gifted to chosen devotees who are beloved by their Sufi master (*pir*).

One day at the Bahauddin Zakariya shrine, I encountered a *mastani* (*mastānī*). *Mastani* literally means someone who fully surrenders themselves to a state of ecstasy. This *mastani* was a mystical woman lost in spiritual devotion who had devoted her life to serve her *murshid* (Sufi saint). She agreed to be interviewed by me and shared the painful life story of how she became a *mastani*. Someone killed her husband and then took her children away from her due to distribution of wealth issues in her family. As a result, she suffered immensely and did not have a place to live. One day while in grief, she visited the shrine of Bahauddin Zakariya Multani and cried and prayed to be cured of this worldly pain. On that day, she met an elderly man whom she called uncle. He was the caretaker of Bahauddin Zakariya's shrine. He offered her shelter, and she had been living at the shrine since. As signs of her devotional transformation, she rarely wore sandals, even in the hottest month of June; she often ate the free food (*langar*) offered at the shrine and served her spiritual master with utmost sincerity and devotion.

Sometime before I witnessed her dance (Video example 3.2, Figure 3.4), I was having difficulty convincing the *darbari qawwals* (shrine *qawwals*) of Shah Rukn-e-Alam to support my research project and was quite upset. When the *mastani* saw me at Bahauddin Zakariya, she approached me with a surprising question, "Why are you upset; do you have any problems?" I told her that the *darbari qawwals* of Shah Rukn-e-Alam would not allow me to conduct my ethnographic research and refused to participate in interviews. After our meeting, she went to the *darbari qawwals* and informed them about my

Figure 3.4 *Mastani* performing *dhammal* at Hazrat Bahauddin Zakariya Multani shrine. Multan, Pakistan. August 2002. Photo by the author.

research. They did not say a word to me, but simply agreed to work with me. I was completely surprised by their response. Did the *qawwal*s agree to cooperate with me because they knew her and trusted the intensity of her spiritual experience? Or was she able to convince them of the importance of this research based on her own experience? The questions remain unanswered.

The *dhamal* form of Sufi music and dance can be witnessed in various Sufi shrines in Pakistan, especially at Hazrat Lal Shahbaz Qalandar (in Sewan, Sindh) and Hazrat Baba Bulleh Shah (in Kasur, Punjab). *Dhamal* music features a fast, increasing tempo. Its poetry is performed with a distinct vocal timbre and range. The names of holy figures are chanted repeatedly, and the accompanying ecstatic dance often includes whirling patterns. In every ʿurs (death anniversary of a saint) at Lal Shahbaz Qalandar and Bulleh Shah, musicians play two-headed barrel drums called *nal* and *dhol* to accompany hours of music and dance at the shrines.[6]

It is also a common practice to play popular Sufi and commercial *filmi* songs at the shrine to attract an audience. For example, the *darbari qawwal*s of Bahauddin Zakariya shrine performed a popular *dhamal* song, "Mere Dil De Sheeshe Wich Sajna," originally sung by the famous Pakistani singer Noor Jahan in 1997. In general, women's participation in religious ceremony and ritual is seen as controversial by orthodox Muslims. However, it is common practice in the provinces of Punjab and Sindh especially, where women participate regularly in Sufi dance and *qawwali samaʿ* performances. According to the (male) *qawwal*s from Bahauddin Zakariya, women are generally more sensitive and pious in their religious duty than men; therefore, they felt it evident that women feel spiritually connected and experience trance during the *dhamal* performances. Because of this connection, no one prevented women's involvement. The lyrics of the *dhamal* performed in ⏵ Video example 3.2 further elaborate on the sense of female spirituality articulated by the *qawwal*s and displayed by the *mastani* I met at Bahauddin Zakariya:

> *Main terīyān mendīyān gāvān Lāl sāīn sonīyān* (3x)
> *Main tere jashn manāwān te raj dhamālān pāvān* (2x)
> *Main tere sadqē jāvān Lāl sāīn sonīyān*
> *Lāl sāīn sonīyān, Lāl sāīn sonīyān*
> *Main terīyān mendīyān gāvān Lāl sāīn sonīyān*

---

[6] See, for example, "Dhamal Nobat at Sehwan Sharif 2019": https://youtu.be/0LLsZBr_MMY.

I sing while ornamenting my hands in *mehndi* (henna) oh Lal, my
master and beloved;
I celebrate and dance in ecstasy in your devotion.
I dedicate my entire life, oh my master, oh my beloved.
Oh Lal, my master and beloved, oh Lal, my master and beloved,
I sing in utmost devotion, oh Lal, my master and beloved.

Is mehndī de ajab nazāre, chup chup vēkhan arshān vāle (4x)
Tarāne gānde havāvān Lāl sāīn sonīyān

The hidden mysteries of this *mehndi*, even angels see it from above
Even winds blow songs in praise of my master and beloved.

Aye mehndī aye karmā vālī koī na jāve aithūn khālī (4x)
Main bhar bhar jholīyān jāvān, Lāl sāīn sonīyān
Main terīyān mendīyān gāvān Lāl sāīn sonīyān

This *mehndi* brings good fortune, and no one goes empty-handed
My wishes are fulfilled, oh my master and beloved
I sing in utmost devotion, oh Lal, my master and beloved.

Mehndī dā din karmavālā murshid dī sab jhap de mālā
Main qadmī sīs na māvān, Lāl sāīn sonīyān

The day of *mehndi* is auspicious, and everyone praises my beloved
I am at the feet of my master for mercy, oh my beloved.

In this song, the poet uses various symbols to emphasize the eternal love between a devotee and her beloved. The symbol of *mehndi* (henna), which women in South Asia apply during wedding events, is metaphorically used. Here, the lover applies henna to her hands as she mystically submits herself to her spiritual master as his devoted wife. The idea of a woman portrayed as "lover" is also seen in *bhakti*, and Sufi and Ismaili *ginan* devotional practices (Gillani, K. 2004). A famous *qawwali* written by Hazrat Amir Khusrau from the fourteenth century says, *chāp tilak sab chīnī re mose nainā milāike*, "You have taken away my existence, my whole self, by glancing into my eyes." This reflects the concept of *didar* or *darshan*, meaning physical union with one's beloved or a deity. Box 3.3 further engages readers

> **Box 3.3 Exercise 2**
>
> 1. Watch ⊙ Video example 3.2 of the *mastani* performing *dhamal* dance.
> 2. Discuss and share your observations engaging the following questions:
>   - What musical differences do you discern between this performance and the first example of *qawwali* discussed above?
>   - What are the key features of the woman's dance at the shrine?
>   - What kind of symbolism might her hand gestures be conveying?
>   - What is the response from the audience while seeing her dance?
>   - What does this suggest about the role of ecstasy in religious music?
>   - What do you think might be the function of the music's relatively fast tempo?
>   - What connections do you observe between poetry, dance, and music in this performance?

with the experiences and meanings of *qawwali* and *dhamal* dance in Sufi shrines in Multan.

Conclusion

This chapter illuminates aspects of Muslim society that differ from stereotypical, conservative practices of Islam in which music has little place in ritual and women have very limited access to religious performance and devotion. This study goes beyond historical focus on manuscripts to engage the lived, inclusive practices of contemporary people in the South Asian city of Multan, Pakistan. Through examples of Sufi shrine devotional practices, we see how *qawwali* music performance emphasizes the values of communal harmony, integration of religious ideas, and appreciation of music that transcends individual beliefs/schools of thought. These examples demonstrate the significance of local towns and cities like Multan in shaping individual religious experience through devotional music.

In the first case study, a *qawwali* song and its poetic lyrics provided the means through which a devotee reflected and contemplated on the hope and belonging available from the *pir* Farid. The devotee's intense pleading and crying likely helped him put aside and heal from the challenges of his worldly concerns. The second case explored the public role of women in *dhamal* shrine dance and demonstrated how *qawwali* music evokes emotions of devotional love and spiritual union, such as those of a bride toward her groom, that assist devotees to experience trance. Both cases emphasize the common value of respect for all the Sufi saints among devotees and listeners in Multan. At any shrine in the city, everyone is welcome to participate and share their community bonds, symbols, myths, and stories through devotional music that expresses the devotee's love toward God, the Prophet Muhammad, and the Sufi saints.

Works Cited

Gillani, Karim. 2004. "The Ismaili 'Ginan' Tradition from the Indian Subcontinent." *Middle East Studies Association Bulletin* 38(2): 175–185.

Gillani, Sabtain. 1990. *Multan-Mazi wa hal ka aienee main*. Galgist Multan: Beacon Books.

Ibn al-'Arabi, Muhyi'ddin. 1911. *The Tarjumān al-Ashwāq: A Collection of Mystical Odes by Muḥyī'ddīn Ibn al-'Arabī*. Translated by Reynold A. Nicholson. London: Theosophical Publishing House.

Nicholson, Reynold A. 1962 [1914]. *The Mystics of Islam*. Chester Springs, PA: Routledge.

Qureshi, Regula. 1992/93. "Muslim Devotional Popular Religious Music and Muslim Identity under British, Indian and Pakistani Hegemony." *Asian Music* 24(1): 111–121.

Qureshi, Regula. 1995 [1986]. *Sufi Music of India and Pakistan, Sound, Context and Meaning in Qawwali*. Chicago: University of Chicago Press.

Racy, A. J. 2003. *Making Music in the Arab World: The Culture and Artistry of Tarab*. Cambridge: Cambridge University Press.

Shiloah, Amnon. 1995. *Music in the World of Islam*. Aldershot: Scolar Press.

Waugh, Earl. 2005. *Memory, Music, and Religion: Morocco's Mystical Chanters*. Columbia: University of South Carolina Press.

4
Hale da Divan
Trance, Historical Consciousness, and the Ecstasy of Separation in Namdhari Sikh Services

Janice Protopapas

The Namdhari (*nāmdhārī*) Sikhs, also known as Kukas (*kukā*s, the "shriekers") hold a time-honored place in India's struggle for freedom. Led by Baba Ram Singh (1816–1885), this puritanical religious community launched a political and social reform campaign against the British based on the principles of non-cooperation and *swadeshi* (boycotting foreign goods and services and supporting the local economy). Considered by some as "a fanatic sect of Sikhs," they developed a mystico-political musical service, *hale da divan (halē dā divān)*, "verses of attack," as a sonic weapon through which to impart persuasive messages for freedom and social change. Drawing from the rhythms and melodies of Punjabi folk culture, these services not only acted as a music forum but also worked to solidify Namdhari Sikh identity and sense of community. In current practice, *hale da divan* is performed to commemorate the struggles and strife this community has endured, thus activating historically inherited memory. The song texts, tunes, and rhythms encode memories of past events, bringing them into the present, reconstructed through performance.

In this chapter, I argue that the musical, textual, and other performance features of *hale da divan* services continue to act as a medium of historical consciousness, arousing emotional memories of resilience and resistance against colonization. Chanting Sikh hymns with the accompaniment of the harmonium and percussion, members are often induced into altered states of *mast* (spiritual intoxication or trance-like ecstasy), as seen in ▶ Video example 4.1 of the song, "Kālī Kamblī Wāliyā Kadon Ku Ferā Pāvengā" (Punjabi: "When will my black-cloaked Lord return home?"). The lyrics are particularly associated with the theme of Namdhari martyrdom and the deportation of their beloved leader, Ram Singh. Through repetition and a

> **Box 4.1 Discussion**
>
> Think of a musical event you have either attended or observed that triggered strong emotions and/or memories. This may be a religious event, political rally, or even a rave. Consider how the specific aspects of music in that context were used to trigger strong emotions or sentiments. What do you think was the association between those particular emotions and memories? Where else has music been used as a political weapon or as a means to help people remember specific events, or unite them under a common cause?

quickening pace of the song's lyrics accompanied by incessant throbbing timbres from the percussion, congregants are emotionally overcome by memories of martyrdom, loss, oppression, and spiritual separation (*bairāg*) and become *mastana* (*mastāna*, one who has entered a state of trance), performing these communal memories through dance, trance, and catharsis. Through the lens of "interdividuality," the interconnectedness of individuals in the community, this chapter examines participants' physical and verbal responses to understand how a *hale da divan* event unfolds through many bodies simultaneously, creating a community-generated tapestry of music and movement (Box 4.1).

The Kuka Movement (1857–1947)

The Kuka movement arose in mid-nineteenth-century India during a period of intense social and political instability as one of several socio-religious groups promoting the rejuvenation of Indian spiritual values and freedom from British occupation. Their leader, Baba Balak Singh (1799–1862), a pious and charismatic Sikh preacher, reacting against the proselytizing activities of both Christian missionaries and Hindu *Arya Samaj* reformers, instructed Sikhs to return to a spiritual life of simplicity and piety by taking only the support of God's name (Namdhari).[1] Baba Balak Singh's disciple, Baba Ram Singh (1816–1885), continued this initiative for national independence, launching a revolt against the British.

---

[1] Namdhari derives from *nām* (name) and *dhārī* (support).

Ram Singh's messianic mission and social reforms attracted thousands of followers, mostly low-caste Hindus and Muslims. His growing popularity became a threat to the British, who responded by banning all public meetings of Namdharis and detaining Ram Singh for seven years at Bhaini Sahib (Singh and Singh 1995).[2] However, when the detainment was lifted in 1870, Namdhari agitation against the British continued to escalate as the British grew increasingly abusive of local customs, inciting religious animosity among Hindus, Sikhs, and Muslims.

The pivotal event that caused the ultimate decline of the Kuka movement occurred in 1871 when a judge ordered an ox to be butchered in front of a protesting Namdhari named Gurmukh Singh.[3] A clash ensued, and 200 Kukas marched on the Muslim-dominated town of Malerkotla to avenge the wrongful death of this innocent creature. Prompt action by the British resulted in their arrest; on January 14, 1872, sixty-six Kukas were cannoned to death; and Baba Ram Singh was arrested and exiled to Burma. For the next fifty years, a permanent police post was established at Bhaini Sahib, halting the activities of Namdhari rebels. Baba Ram Singh's next three successors, Satguru Hari Singh (1819–1906), Satguru Pratap Singh (1890–1959), and Satguru Jagjit Singh (1920–2012), worked diligently on the campaign for India's independence while never again engaging in the fanatic and violent activity of the earlier Kukas. While the aim of gaining independence was achieved in 1947, the legacy of the Kuka identity lives on in the hearts and minds of Namdharis as inherited memories of resistance and resilience. Today, they remain a tightly bound and prosperous community, remembering their turbulent history through the repertoire of emotive songs in *hale da divan*, in which key historical events are revisited, reimagined, and remembered.[4] Carried on by the diasporic spread of over 1.5 million members, throughout India, Thailand, United Kingdom, United States, Canada and various countries in Africa, *hale da divan* continues to act as a powerful performance medium of protest, transformation, and remembering.[5]

---

[2] Bhaini Sahib is located in south-central Punjab in the district of Ludhiana.

[3] As strict vegetarians, Namdharis are staunch animal rights activists, adhering to all aspects of nonviolence.

[4] I use the term "remembering" to signify a special type of recollection, calling attention to the reaggregation of members who have been displaced through political or social oppression.

[5] The current (2023) spiritual head of the Namdharis is Satguru Uday Singh, who is headquartered at Bhaini Sahib.

Hale da Divan as a Sonic Weapon

The origin of the *hale da divan* has its roots in the folklore of Punjab, drawing from folk songs and rhythms using drums and cymbals.[6] Joyce Pettigrew, writing on the Dadhi singers of Punjab (balladeers of Sikh chivalry), remarks, "the tradition of recording history in song is a very popular one in rural Punjab. The principal theme of these particular songs is one of bravery of those who fight the oppression of the Indian state in order to establish justice. The songs describe the heroism in the face of adversity" (1995, 85).

The fearless spirits of Namdhari freedom fighters fueled the pens of many poets that describe the affective power of *hale da divan* services with drum, cymbal, and song as sonic weapons. Sikh scholar Gurdit Singh relates, "During the period of British occupation, the jathedars, leaders of the musical ensemble, would recite such hymns as: 'We will create havoc in India, we will drive out the British.' During these hymns, they would jump about and create a lot of mayhem and cry as if they would take rest only after driving out the British" (Singh 2009, 98, translation by the author). Thus, the songs themselves became both the fuel for nonviolent protest and a medium for emotional release. Another popular poem whose lyrics were set to song reads, "Beating the drum and clanking the cymbals, *hale da divan* causes heart burning. Ladies dance like pigeons, while dancing their feet do not get tired, open hair spreads over their necks" (Singh 1985, 299). These songs refer to the emotionally exhilarating experience of *mast*. In such experiences, the congregant enters a cathartic, trancelike state, which is physically expressed through uncontrollable vocalizations and dance gestures, causing the head coverings of this ultra-conservative community to fly off, exposing their hair.[7]

The Service

Services are conducted by Namdhari *jathedars* (preachers), who play an intrinsic role as oral historians, preachers, and evangelists with a very charismatic appeal to the congregation. Their responsibilities include transmitting

---

[6] *Hala* means "strike" in Punjabi; a *hale da divan* is a "service" (*divān*) involving striking or beating, popularized by Baba Ram Singh.
[7] Compare with case study 2 in Gillani*.

history and heroic ballads, and narrating stories and songs of love and praise of the Gurus. Through their sermons, *jathedar*s weave together and invoke the memories of gurus' lives, of martyrs, and of miracles, eliciting strong emotional expressions, which often result in some congregants experiencing and demonstrating highly charged states of spiritual intoxication. This state of exaltation may result in outbursts of cries, gesticulations, spinning heads, swaying bodies, rocking, and falling to the ground as participants reach a state of total absorption, often producing intermittent cries such as *"Dhan dhan Satguru Jagjit Singh!"* (Blessed, blessed is my Guru Jagjit Singh!), or *"Bakshish de!"* (Give mercy!).

The service, rendered through both preaching and hymn singing, acts as a spiritual exegesis or homily in which the *jathedar* punctuates a point in the sermon with either a hymn from the Guru Granth Sahib (the primary Sikh scripture) or a poem from a saint. The following section examines a service conducted by *jathedar* Baba Chinda during a 2007 celebration of *Hola Mohalla*, an annual spring festival during the month of March–April held at Bhaini Sahib. Baba Chinda, a fourth-generation exponent of *hale da divan*, is well known for his services, which inspire much participation among the congregants. One of the most popular themes related to Namdhari martyrdom is the exile of Ram Singh, presented as a musical narrative in this service.

The Song

This song of lamentation, "Kālī Kamblī Wāliyā Kadon̠ Ku Ferā Pāvengā" ("When will my black-cloaked Lord return home?"), recalls the painful memory of Ram Singh's exile. As Rana explains: "Ram Singh was given a black blanket as a symbol of sadness and separation before his departure. People wear black to lament the departure of their savior [Ram Singh]" (interview with the author, June 16, 2020). Figure 4.1, painted by Musvar Varyam Singh (1980), depicts the heart-wrenching experience of devotees watching their leader being taken away from them.

The melody, transcribed in Figure 4.2, follows the tonal framework of many Punjabi folk melodies, which is based on a seven-note scale (F, G, A, B♭, C, D, E) with the tonic, in this example, centering on F. The song follows a typical three-part ABA format with an opening section (A), a following section (B), and a repetition of the first section (A), concluding with

Figure 4.1 A folk depiction by painter Musvar Varyam Singh of a congregation (black-cloaked) lamenting Ram Singh's deportation to Burma; used with permission.

an instrumental coda. The lyrics of the tune consist of the title phrase: *kālī kamblī wāliyā kado<u>n</u> ku ferā pāvengā* sung in a call-and-response format, followed by the second half of the line: *kado<u>n</u> ku ferā pāvengā* ("When will he return?") also repeated in call-and-response. The song's transcription provides an outline of the sung refrain with four component instrumental parts: harmonium, *chimta* (*chimṭā*, finger cymbals), *kartal* (*kartāl*, a pair of wooden blocks with small metal jingles mounted on them), and *dholak* (*ḍholak*, a double-headed barrel drum). The tune is set to a popular four-beat rhythmic cycle *tal* (*tāl*) and syncopated pattern called *partali*, performed on the *dholak* (Figure 4.2, bottom, includes the rhythm in Western staff notation). In this performance of the song, the *jathedar* and ensemble engage in a musical dialogue that unfolds in a call-and-response form. The harmonium, played by a member of the ensemble, reinforces the melody of the voices, while the percussion section powerfully impacts the overarching sonic experience as it accelerates in tempo and intensity. The incessant sounds of the *chimta* and *kartal* enhance the mesmerizing state of trance. Rana explains the impact of this rhythmical entrainment:

> The dholak plays a big role in *hale da divan*. It starts out slow, but as it gradually speeds up, like the train wheels on a rail going "*choo-choo*" and rapidly speeding up to "*choo-choo-choo-choo-choo*," that aids in the trance

Figure 4.2 "Kālī Kamblī Wāliyā Kadon Ku Ferā Pāvengā." Transcription by Jan Protopapas.

Figure 4.2 Continued

Figure 4.2 Continued

mode that people go into — the *masti birthi*, state of trance. Like the *shabad* [words of the hymn] is fed into someone's mind slowly, and then as it speeds up and as it goes faster, the emotions start building, and eventually they burst. (June 16, 2020)

Analyzing the Song

Although the majority of my interlocutors would likely learn Namdhari musical repertoire aurally, I have transcribed the 2007 performance led by Baba Chinda using Western staff notation (Figure 4.2) to assist in analyzing and understanding the song. The score commences with a brief musical intro on *harmonium*, followed by the lyrics sung in call-and-response format (mm. 4–20). Percussion accompaniment commences at measure 4, continuing to build in intensity and tempo throughout the entire song, continuing on for eight more measures following the completion of the song. As the cry of lamentation builds, the second part of the lyrics *kadon ku ferā pāvengā* are sung and repeated (mm. 21–28), followed by a D.S. al coda, meaning a return to the sign ⊕ found in measure 4, where the main lyrics are sung a third and fourth time with yet greater intensity and engagement. At this point, the music becomes louder, more rhythmically guided, and repetitive, driving a high trajectory of musical and emotional engagement, leading to the coda ⁌, where the voices fall away and instrumentation takes over entirely. The instrumental coda continues at high intensity, propelling *mastana*s (trancers) to more ecstatic behavior, reaching a peak at measure 36 where the harmonium ceases playing with the percussion, leading the trancers into an ultimate climax. Following the instructions in Box 4.2, try to sing and play this song as a group.

Analyzing the Performance from April 19, 2007

This hymn, composed by Baba Chinda himself, captures the emotional intensity felt at this stage of the service, in which he invokes the painful memory of their beloved leader's exile to Burma and the participants' resultant method of coping with such loss: entering into an ecstatic state of *mast* and *bairag*. In ▶ Video example 4.1, Baba Chinda prefaces the song stating that Baba Ram Singh was himself *masti* (in a state of *mast*) from this emotional separation (cue point

> **Box 4.2 Recreating the Song "Kālī Kamblī Wāliyā"**
>
> 1. If you have enough people, divide into six groups, each led by someone who can read and render the music notated in Figure 4.2. Each group will practice one of the song's parts. The percussion lines (*chimta*, *kartal*, and *dholak*) can be performed by clapping, tapping a table, or reciting a syllable of your choosing ("ching," "ta," etc.). The tenor and bass lines can be sung, and the harmonium part can either be sung or be rendered on melodic instruments, perhaps piano.
> 2. After becoming familiar with your individual parts, try to combine them, first in smaller groups of two to three parts at a time, and finally performing all six parts at once.
> 3. Repeat the song several times. As you become more familiar with producing your individual part, listen to how your part relates to the others in the ensemble. Discuss your experience with members of your group and the full ensemble.
> 4. Watch ⊙ Video example 4.1. Then, practice the song again and collectively try to speed up in imitation of the *hale da divan* ensemble. Does varying the tempo impact your emotional involvement? For those who are ambitious, attempt to "play along" with the video recording.

0:12).[8] Even before this song was performed, halfway into the hour-long service, the congregation was already "heated up," as community member Rana Singh put it, meaning the space was charged with an emotionally intoxicated energy through preaching, dancing, and singing. (interview with the author, April 14, 2007). Men and women had been involuntarily and uncontrollably swaying to the music, and I was surrounded by several *mastana*s with many congregants bare-headed, freely dancing around the front of the stage. Rana further explained that: "They [devotees] go into *bairag*, a spiritual state of separation from the Divine, and feel close to Satguruji [Baba Ram Singh]. Baba Chinda's *divan* produces a lot of *bairag* due to the memory of Satguru" (April 14, 2007). As Baba Chinda led the twelve-member musical ensemble, he also inspired many listeners to recall and experience the ecstatic memory. (Notice people

---

[8] The large poster seen behind Baba Chinda in Video example 4.1 features pictures of Baba Ram Singh along with the tenth Sikh Guru, Gobind Singh, and Satguru Pratap Singh, the third leader of the Namdhari Sikhs.

calling out "Satguru Ram Singh!" as Baba Chinda narrates the story, cue point 0:15). Considered a *bairagi*, one who is detached from worldly life and continuously pining for Divine union, Baba Chinda was emotionally overcome by this musical memory and can be seen wiping his tear-ridden face continuously throughout the song's performance (cue point 2:33–2:41).[9]

The repetition of these lyrics, sung repeatedly, reinforces the pain of loss and separation, exciting the swaying and weeping *mastana*s to spin, fall, and roll on the ground with flailing arms (cue point 1:25). As the tempo and high-pitched singing intensifies (cue point 1:45), the listeners become more emotionally overwhelmed and the singing ceases, leaving the harmonium to exclusively carry the melody at the coda (cue point 2:10). Shortly after (cue point 2:30), the harmonium ceases playing, leaving percussion to carry the *mastana*s into a final apotheosis. By cue point 3:02, the music stops; the dozen or so *mastana*s have reached a climactic peak, and many fall down in exhaustion.

Interdividual Participation

Baba Chinda's *hale da divan* service provides a perfect opportunity to explore the interdividuality of a musical event. This term, based on theories of mimesis (imitation) and interconnectedness, was coined by Lebanese neuropsychiatrist/psychologist Jean-Michel Oughourlian to analyze trancing as an experience that happens across many bodies simultaneously (Oughourlian 1991). Watch ▶ Video example 4.1 and take note of the varied ways participants respond to this musical experience. While *hale da divan* appears to be filled with chaotic and uncontrolled activity by those becoming *mastana*, the various congregants involved (Figure 4.3) are navigating the spectacle quite easily.

One can witness many types of engagement and degrees of participation occurring during this performance. Next to Baba Chinda and his ensemble, located on the uppermost platform, are seated elders and active members of the community. The *Gur Gaddi* ("Guru's throne") of the late Satguru Jagjit Singh (which comes into focus at cue point 1:32), was empty because he was ill and unable to be present for the event. There are several trained dancers, including a young boy on stage (visible at cue point 1:04), who facilitate the

---

[9] Thirteen years later, tears again streamed from the then seventy-five-year-old Baba Chinda's eyes as he reminisced about composing this song, explaining: "because of my love for Satguru, I composed this song of separation" (interview with the author, June 12, 2020).

1. Baba Chinda (standing at the mic) and music ensemble (seated on the highest platform)
2. Elders and Respected Members of the Community (also seated on the platform)
3. The *Gur Gaddi*, throne of the Satguru (center of the platform)
4. Trained child dancers
5. Trained senior dancers
6. Congregants engaged in *mast* (standing and seated)
7. Congregation at large (seated)
8. Congregants offering abeyances
9. Spectators

Figure 4.3 Layers of collective engagement and involvement.

state of emotional arousal by dancing around while rhythmically striking *kartal*s. In the foreground, both men and women enter states of *mast*. Seated behind me was a crowd of approximately 500 congregants, some entering spaces of *mast* while seated. What I witnessed was an overwhelming experience of different degrees of trance-like behavior: from the simple "choreographed" dancing of the young boy on stage, to ladies seated in front of and beside me with spinning bodies and freely moving hair (cue point 2:12), to men running wildly across the front of the stage, wailing loudly. As the song intensified in volume and speed, the ensemble accelerated their tempo, most apparent in the high-pitched cymbal sounds of the *kartal* and *chimta*. Participants reached even greater degrees of spiritual arousal, some shrieking out in agonizing cries of *wah, wah!* Their high states of arousal may be synonymous with the state of *hal* (*hāl*), spiritual intoxication, found in Sufi (Islamic mysticism) ceremonies in which devotees lose their sense of individual separateness and merge into a space of undifferentiated "communitas" (Turner 1969; see Qureshi 1986; Sakata 1997). In such a gathering, each member is organically connected to others and does not act as a solitary unit. Judith Becker explains that in community experiences of trancing, "No one person is responsible, no one person is existentially alone. . . . The group acts as a unit. Ritual practitioners . . . trancers, musicians, onlookers, even hecklers in some situations become part of the larger, ongoing, largely predictable event"

> **Box 4.3 Video Analysis**
>
> Watch ▶ Video example 4.1 again and write a descriptive analysis of the musical performance, separating out its several layers. Consider this performance through the lens of "interdividuality," focusing on how the actions of one person influences those of others. Consider these questions:
>
> - What events occur with each section of the song?
> - How are the musicians interacting with the congregants?
> - How do the physical responses of one individual influence those of others?

(2004, 124). The *hale da divan*, similarly, provides an expressive space for the community as a whole to explore, embody, and remember the deep emotional connections and even the wounds that unite them. (See Box 4.3.)

Music, Memory, and Martyrdom: The Ecstasy of Separation

In this *hale da divan* service, we can witness structural coupling—changes that occur within an individual as a result of interaction with others, each adapting and conforming to the immediacy of the moment (Maturana and Varela 1987, 180). From the moment Baba Chinda introduces the theme "mastana" and sings the opening line of the song (cue point 0:30), he triggers a series of psycho-emotional and physical responses from congregants. While in the video we can observe people doing many different things, the whole event unfolds as a unified spectacle, organized and reorganized over time through individual participants' small structural changes. The community is focused on commonly shared events in Namdhari history (martyrdom and exile) and consequent ways of coping (entering into ecstatic trance). As such, participants act and react in ways that reinforce their unity yet allow for fluidity, spontaneity, and individual expression.

These performances create a space in which community is constituted and in which selective memories are reenacted. The performance space becomes a container where intense experiences can be relived, and where music helps induce a trance-state leading to emotional catharsis. The services often produce varying levels of excitation in devotees, from mild feelings of tranquility and joy to deeper arousal, sometimes leading devotees to weep or shout. One Namdhari explained that when some congregants hear songs of their gurus, they are overcome with agonizing feelings of loss and longing for their leader. During a series of interviews about Baba Chinda's service, Rana Singh expressed that such songs "awaken the wounds [of Ram Singh's deportation]. It touches the soul, and when the soul feels sadness, it feels strength and *josh* [exhilaration]" (April 14, 2007).

The relationship between music, memory, and emotion is a popular area of study for ethnomusicologists, and one that is key to understanding *hale da divan*. In this video performance, we witness many types of expression associated with musical experience that can be summed up as a "habitus of listening" (Becker 2004). Such listening involves a set of trained behaviors and ways of acting and responding to a musical experience. It is a "disposition to listen with a particular kind of focus, to expect and experience particular kinds of emotions, to move with certain stylized gestures, and to interpret the meaning of the sounds and one's emotional responses to the musical event in somewhat predictable ways'" (Becker 2004, 71). For those Namdhari Sikhs familiar with experiencing *mast*, a service of *hale da divan* triggers specific responses from the autonomic nervous system (ANS). The ANS controls physiological processes in the body that are in charge of respiration, heart functions, and temperature and may produce levels of arousal that induce "shivering, goosebumps, changes in breathing and heart rate, tears, weeping, changes in skin temperature, all involuntary reactions that precede language and evaluation" (Becker 2004, 24). Rana Singh similarly refers to the psychoemotional states produced when devotees are moved by musical memories, describing *hale da divan* as:

> A vehicle to remember . . . when someone starts crying. Then, somebody else is weeping . . . another is screaming . . . because of happiness or sadness. It's a matter of feeling. The *mastana* are not there . . . physically they are there, or they are not. They are *behosh* (unconscious). The actual purpose of *hale da divan* . . . no one is sure. . . . However, Satguruji knew that he would be exiled, so he prepared his devotees with this music as a way of expression . . . to express injustice. They could protect and protest. (April 14, 2007)

Transmission of this historical consciousness is of key importance in the education of Namdhari youth, and their participation in a habitus of listening is also observable in the accompanying video. Notice how several young boys actively participate in the performance as they hold *kartal*s and dance around the front of the stage. To this day, all Namdhari children (both boys and girls) undergo a rigorous education in the music of *hale da divan* and in classical Hindustani music, and they are encouraged to perform and compete on a regular basis. Accordingly, participating in these musical events plays an integral role in activating collectively held cultural memories and perpetuating Namdhari identity.

Conclusion

I have approached the study of *hale da divan* by considering the effects of this style of service as a powerful stimulus of memories: collective, personal, and transcendental. Music's emotional impact gains power by repeatedly invoking feelings associated with memories—in this case, feelings of pain associated with oppression, loss, and martyrdom. These songs and performances keep alive the collectively held memories and identity of the Namdhari community. Furthermore, singing, playing percussion instruments, dancing, and trancing in these musical events provide a forum to experience interdividuality. The transmission of this musical genre continues to be an instructional source of musical and cultural repertoire for Namdhari youth, welding generations of the community together by revisiting and re-enacting songs and stories that ignite collectively held memories of the past.

Works Cited

Azad, S. S. 2008. "Contributions of the Kuka Movement to the Anti-Colonial Struggle." *Gadar Jari Hai*, April 2008. Accessed October 1, 2017. http://www.ghadar.in/Index_page/index_vol2_issue2.html.
Becker, Judith. 2004. *Deep Listeners: Music, Emotion and Trancing*. Bloomington: University of Indiana Press.
Maturana, Humberto, and Francisco Varela. 1987. *The Tree of Knowledge: The Biological Roots of Human Understanding*. Boston: New Science Library.
Protopapas, Janice. 2012. "Verses of Attack: Nāmdhārī Sikh Services of *Halē dā divān* as Sonic Weapons." *Journal of Popular Music Studies* 24(4): 554–577.
Oughourlian, Jean-Michel. 1991. *The Puppet of Desire: The Psychology of Hysteria, Possession and Hypnosis*. Stanford, CA: Stanford University Press.

Pettigrew, Joyce. 1995. *The Sikhs of the Punjab: Unheard Voices of State and Guerrilla Violence*. London: Zed Books.
Qureshi, Regula. 1986. *Sufi Music of India and Pakistan: Sound, Context and Meaning in Qawwali*. Cambridge: Cambridge University Press.
Sakata, Hiromi Lorraine. 1997. "Spiritual Music and Dance in Pakistan." *Etnofoor* 10(1/2): 165–173.
Singh, Gurdit. 2009. "Sat Guru Jagjit Singhji da Lok Sangeett Ate Sugam Sangeet Nu Yogadaan." *Varyam* 16: 89–106.
Singh, Bhai Nahar, and Bhai Kirpal Singh. 1995. *Rebels Against the British Rule*. New Delhi: Atlantic Publishers.
Singh, Jaswinder. 1985. *Kuka Movement: Freedom Struggle in Punjab*. New Delhi: Atlantic Publishers.
Turner, Victor. 1969. *The Ritual Process: Structure and Anti Structure*. New York: Routledge.

Interviews with the Author

Baba Chinda. Interview, June 12, 2020. Conducted via Zoom.
Rana Singh. Interview, April 14, 2007. Bhaini Sahib, India.
Rana Singh. Interview, June 16 2020. Conducted via telephone.

5

"Small Voices Sing Big Songs"

Music as Development in the Thar Desert

Shalini R. Ayyagari

On the first morning of a fieldwork trip to the Thar Desert of western Rajasthan in 2009, I awoke to the sound of the tuning of a *kamaicha* (*kamaichā*), a bowed lute instrument unique to the Manganiyar community of musicians. Stepping onto the porch of Sakar Khan Manganiyar's home in Hamira Village, I sat down in the winter morning sun. Sakar Khan (1938– 2013) did not acknowledge my presence in words but through music (see Figure 5.1). He began to play *rag* Sorath, a musical mode/melody common in Manganiyar musical repertoire. His voice had a raspy timbre but was soothing; its slow, syrupy deepness complemented the ease with which he pulled the bow across his instrument's strings as an extension of his body, having played the instrument for the past sixty-five years. Sakar Khan's eldest son, Ghewar Khan, also a virtuosic *kamaicha* player, sat down next to me and said in English, with a nod to his father, "Small voices sing big songs."

At that moment listening to Sakar Khan play the *kamaicha*, I was just beginning to realize the vastness of his "small voice" and the resonance of the "big songs" he performed. Sakar Khan was an unassuming and humble musician despite the many national and international awards he received for his music, decades of international touring, and the countless students he trained. He passed away at the age of seventy-five, but his small voice and big songs have lived on in the Manganiyar community, assuming mythic proportions through his influence, archived performance recordings, teaching, and his descendants (all talented musicians in their own right).

I propose that we listen to Manganiyar voices considered to be small through being societally marginalized, discriminated against for religio-caste affiliations (entanglements of religion and caste), and maligned for their hereditary profession as musicians. The Manganiyar community was left out of historical colonial and government records and continues to be

Figure 5.1 Sakar Khan playing the *kamaicha* on his porch. Hamira Village, 2007. Photo by author.

passed over in government initiatives and development schemes in the Thar Desert region. Despite their marginalization, many Manganiyar musicians lead double lives. At one moment, they are low-class musicians ingrained in a caste-based patronage system and pushed down by government regulations and policies. At another, they are jet-setting international and acclaimed superstars performing on renowned concert stages like Sydney Opera House, for national reality television shows like *Indian Idol* and *Coke Studio India*, and on frequent international performance tours abroad— some six months out of the year in Australia, Europe, and North America (Ayyagari 2013).

In this chapter, I argue that Manganiyar musicians who have gained a broader worldview through performing for traditional village patrons and on global stages possess the seemingly contradictory positionality of low-caste and cosmopolitan at the same time. This positionality has enabled some Manganiyar musicians to take on leadership roles to help community members access government services and desired development through what I call "music as development." In what follows, I entreat you, the reader, to listen to "small voices singing big songs." Hear the extraordinary story that emerges in which the seeming lifestyle contradictions of feudal servitude and contemporary stardom do not hinder musicians from success in diverse musical arenas, but instead act as impetus for action and aspiration for cultural, social, and economic uplift.

The Manganiyar in Focus

The Manganiyar are a community of hereditary professional musicians hailing from the Thar Desert borderland that straddles western Rajasthan, India, and eastern Sindh, Pakistan. For at least the past three centuries, they have provided family genealogies, oral histories, and ceremonial music for their Hindu hereditary patrons for remuneration in cash, gold, livestock, land, grain, and informal insurance that can be called on in times of family hardship, drought, and famine. The name most used to describe their community, Manganiyar, literally means "one who begs." Most Manganiyar musicians consider themselves to be Muslim, although their lived religious practices incorporate tenets from both Hinduism and Islam due to their patrons being Hindu and their conversion to Islam from Hinduism over 300 years ago (Neuman et al. 2006). With very few exceptions, public-performing musicians in the community are male.

The settings for their music are traditionally life-cycle ceremonies for their patrons—weddings, births, and religious festivals. A traditional performance usually consists of one or a few musicians from the same family: a singer who provides his own melodic accompaniment on the *kamaicha* or harmonium (a portable reed organ keyboard instrument) accompanied by a drummer playing the *dholak* (*ḍholak*, a double-headed cylindrical drum), and a musician playing the *khartal* (*kartāl*, idiophone made from two pairs of flat pieces of wood) (see Figure 5.2).

Patronage relations between Manganiyar musician families and high-caste village patron families have continued uninterrupted for at least the past 300 years. But by the 1950s, traditional musical patronage had declined steadily due to postcolonial economic and political rearrangements when India gained its independence and was partitioned

Figure 5.2 A typical Manganiyar performing ensemble consisting of an accompanying singer, *khartal* player, lead singer accompanying himself on the harmonium, and a *dholak* player. Kanoi Village, 2016. Photo by author.

into two nations, India and Pakistan, in 1947. It was at this time that the Rajasthani folklorist Komal Kothari became a transformative figure for the Manganiyar community. As a well-educated, high-caste outsider to the Manganiyar community, Kothari founded Rupayan Sansthan, an organization that was granted Indian national NGO (non-governmental organization) status in 1965 with the goals of promoting diverse communities of Rajasthani artists and artisans and publishing a journal on Rajasthani oral textual traditions.

Soon after establishing Rupayan Sansthan, Kothari first met musicians from the Manganiyar community in 1958 (Bharucha and Kothari 2003). From the 1960s until the early 2000s, he served as an impresario for musicians from the Manganiyar community, among other communities. He led rehearsals, crafted appearances, curated repertoire, and promoted musicians. First locally, nationally, and then internationally, Kothari presented troupes of Manganiyar musicians on stages across the world and made Manganiyar a common name on world music concert and festival circuits. In many ways,

Kothari and his NGO took the place of many Manganiyar musicians' waning patrons. Not only did he support the musicians financially, but he also encouraged their musical creativity through performance, just as traditional patrons have done for centuries.

Music as Development in Western Rajasthan

While Kothari and Rupayan Sansthan functioned as makeshift patrons for the Manganiyar as their traditional means of livelihood waned, Rupayan Sansthan's interventions went beyond patronage and into the realm of development. Development is generally thought of in terms of building roads and infrastructure, providing food and public health services, and educating people; however, it can also be conceptualized more broadly, encompassing cultural interventions and institutions that work with the challenges of alleviating poverty, addressing social injustices, and engaging communities (Warren et al. 1995).

Although Rupayan Sansthan did not directly intervene in traditional development initiatives, Kothari addressed the social injustices against the Manganiyar community and worked to help them sustain musical practice as livelihood. Rupayan Sansthan took on the prevailing model of NGO-based development that emphasized external intervention through a top-down approach, with Kothari not as the organization's leader, but as the organization itself. Rupayan Sansthan also reproduced the development organization model of top-down power and the dependence of Manganiyar musicians on the organization (Keare 2001; Panda 2007).

As part of a trend seen throughout the Global South, India became a hub of both international and local development initiatives beginning in the 1970s (Chant and McIlvaine 2009). Later, economic liberalization in India in the 1990s led to increased resources for NGOs from international aid agencies; Rajasthan quickly became an epicenter for NGO development (Bhargava 2007; Government of Rajasthan 2002). After decades of international development implementation in the Global South, it became clear that the ways development was discussed and approached directly impacted how it was received. Postmodern, postcolonial, and feminist shifts in scholarship and policy affected development practice in the 1990s. As scholars and practitioners acknowledged the power of rhetoric in theorizing and implementing development, "development as discourse" described sets of localized ideas that, in addition to being discussed and written about, shape reality and frame human relationships (Escobar 1995).

In a parallel turn toward postmodernism and postcolonialism in the 1990s, scholars began to theorize music in a similar fashion, "music as discourse." Jean-Jacques Nattiez proposed, "Music is not a narrative, but an incitement to make a narrative, to comment, to analyze" (1990, 128). Similarly, Kofi Agawu posited that if music is performed live, it can never be frozen and is therefore always contested and shaped by discourse (2009, 4).

The Manganiyar community became enmeshed in a world of development—from the infrastructural projects developing around them to Kothari's interventions into their music through Rupayan Sansthan. Development quickly became part of musical discourse among the Manganiyar. They began speaking of their music using development rhetoric; words like sustainability, preservation, and empowerment entered the everyday Manganiyar lexicon. If development as discourse refers to the ways discourse shapes development's application, and if music as discourse relates to ways language can powerfully determine how music is made and received, then is it possible for development to be linked to music through Manganiyar lived experience and discourse? I use the phrase "music as development" to analyze and explain the entrenchment of the Manganiyar community in development and entanglements with music. I use the following case study to examine ways Manganiyar musicians harness development as a musical resource and become mediating figures between the arenas of culture and development.

Gazi Barna and Music as Development

By the time Kothari died in 2004, many Manganiyar musicians were left feeling helpless and began wondering where their livelihood would come from if Kothari, their patron, was not there to promote them. It was at this time that a few musicians who had worked closely with Rupayan Sansthan rose up to take on leadership roles in the Manganiyar community. Gazi Barna is one of those musicians and serves as the main case study of this chapter. Born in 1968 in Barna Village near Jaisalmer City, Barna is a prominent *khartal* player and self-recognized conductor/bandleader from the Manganiyar community (see Figure 5.3).

Figure 5.3 Gazi Barna leading a rehearsal for a performance of his "Desert Symphony" at the Jawahar Kala Kendra Outdoor Amphitheatre. Jaipur, 2006. Photo by author.

As the son of the famous Chugga Khan, a musician who enjoyed a close working relationship with Komal Kothari and Rupayan Sansthan, Gazi Barna began his performance career as a child with the guidance of Kothari. Barna maintained close ties with Kothari until his death. In an interview I conducted with Gazi Barna, he expressed the impact that Kothari had on him as a musician and community leader:

> Komalda [as Kothari was affectionately called by the musicians] took me under his wing after my father died. In the last years of Komalda's life, I spent many weeks by his side—watching him, listening to him, and learning from him. I observed how he did his work with musicians and how he was able to teach them new things in an unimposing way, while also allowing them to be themselves and express their music personally. (January 14, 2007)

Inspired by Kothari, Gazi Barna founded his own NGO in 1997 under the guidance of Kothari and named it Pehchan Lok Sangeet Sansthan

("Recognition Folk Music Institute") to grapple with cultural, economic, political, and ecological change that the Manganiyar community was facing.[1] Although Pehchan is currently non-functioning and Gazi Barna spends most of his time touring, performing, and promoting his sons as performers, Pehchan was one of the first organizations of many to come out of the Manganiyar community, influencing how development can shape music and vice versa.

From its beginnings, Pehchan seemed to have a different organizational structure than did other regional development NGOs (Fisher 1997). Founded and headed by an "insider" from the Manganiyar community, Barna aimed to create a local Manganiyar brand of development where concerns for cultural difference and autonomy to change music culture were coupled with those of development and community uplift. Pehchan had three aims, as outlined on the organization's now-defunct website: education for Manganiyar children, preservation of Manganiyar culture, and control of the local cultural tourism market through musical performance.

Preservation through Education

One of the main facets of Pehchan was musical preservation in an attempt to keep traditional Manganiyar musical knowledge in circulation in contemporary musical practice. Until recently, music was not taught in a formal setting; Manganiyar children gained a musical education from watching, listening, and imitating their older male family members, and accompanying them to patronage functions (Kothari 1994). But when elder musicians are on tour many months of the year, how can Manganiyar children learn music by traditional means? To combat this dilemma, in 2007 Gazi Barna established a small schoolhouse in his village as part of Pehchan.

The establishment of a Manganiyar school was, at the time, unique in a community where children did not routinely go to school beyond the age of twelve. Barna's goal with the Pehchan Lok Sangeet Sansthan school was both to provide a traditional education of reading, writing, and math to Manganiyar children and to teach them music. The children who attended

---

[1] While Gazi Barna's organization was the first of its kind to be established to aid in Manganiyar community uplift, an earlier Manganiyar organization, Arba Sangeet Club, was founded by Akbar Khan in the 1970s with the help of the ethnomusicologist Nazir Jairazbhoy.

Pehchan's school were taught by a select group of elders considered master musicians in the community; these elders were, for the most part, the same musicians Komal Kothari chose to perform on his national and international tours in past decades. Due to the similar performance experiences of these elder renowned musicians, they taught a standardized musical curriculum. In this context, children learned not how to perform for traditional patrons but instead how to perform for tourists and foreign audiences. Lessons focused on a small, fixed repertoire that emphasized percussion while de-emphasizing lyrical content and poetry in an effort to appeal to non-specialist audiences. This approach differed greatly from the traditional way that children learned music by watching, listening, and participating, in a region where repertoire and language dialect varied from village to village due to the far distances between villages and the individual nature of traditional patronage.

In this way, Gazi Barna conceptualized music as development (see Box 5.1). On the organization's website, he described Pehchan's educational mission as follows:

> The school grew from the Manganiyar community's desire to preserve their musical legacy. The school brings together arts and literacy education into an empowering curriculum. Through sustainable education of the Manganiyar they will be able to actively preserve their own artistic legacy and participate in the construction of a more just social landscape.

Through the use of development discourse, Gazi Barna was able to harness a brand of music as development in order to attract donors and international

---

Box 5.1 Discussion: Development Rhetoric

Review the passage describing Pehchan's educational mission, which is quoted from Gazi Barna's institutional website. In small groups, engage in the following exercise:

- Highlight and define specific terms Barna uses that connote development.
- What purpose does this kind of language serve? To whom is it directed?

attention, and use Pehchan Lok Sangeet Sansthan to educate Manganiyar children. In this context, musical education serves as a form of music as development.

A Manganiyar Archive

The second aim of Barna's Pehchan Lok Sangeet Sansthan was the collection and transcription of Manganiyar sung poetry. *Doha*s (*dohā*), or rhyming poetic couplets, form an integral part of Manganiyar musical knowledge and provide oral history of the Manganiyar community and their patrons (see Box 5.2). When *doha*s are sung at the beginning of traditional patronage performances, they honor the patron for whom the musicians are performing and are called *shubhraj*s (*shubhrāj*). *Shubhraj*s can take the form of a sung list of names of the patron's ancestors or may recount genealogical stories of bravery and generosity of the patron's ancestors. When *doha*s are sung at the beginning of *kacheri* (*kacherī*), intimate listening sessions of patrons or other Manganiyar musicians, they instead praise a personification of the *rag* (*rāg*, musical mode/melody type) being performed or elucidate the subject of the song.

Manganiyar musicians were traditionally required to recite *doha*s for their patron to pay them. For many younger Manganiyar musicians, *doha*s symbolize servitude to patrons and reinforce their low-caste status. They choose not to sing *doha*s in non-traditional contexts. As younger musicians move away from performing for patrons and toward cultural tourists, much of the knowledge of *doha*s is being lost. Gazi Barna, therefore, hired

---

Box 5.2 Exercise. Compose Your Own *Doha*

Watch ▶ Video example 5.1, a short two-minute video of Thanu Khan singing a *doha* during a recording session I conducted with him and his group of musicians in 2008. While you are watching the video, jot down notes about the rhyming scheme, musical characteristics, and setting. Then compose your own *doha*. Your *doha* may be sung in a similar Manganiyar style or may be recited. When you compose your *doha*, consider drawing on what you have learned from Manganiyar contemporary performance contexts and development.

a literate Manganiyar musician to travel throughout the region to visit elder Manganiyar musicians to collect, transcribe, and archive *doha*s.

Gazi Barna's goal with this project was to preserve musical knowledge he deemed to be dying out in the community. On a visit to Barna Village in 2013, I asked Gazi Barna about the results of the *doha*s preservation project. He proudly showed me several books filled with transcribed *doha* texts and told me he had plans to teach these *doha*s to children at the Pehchan Lok Sangeet Sansthan school in an effort to revitalize them. For Gazi Barna, these transcriptions served as a symbol of the productivity of Pehchan and represented an effort toward collecting and promoting local community knowledge.

Organization founders from within the Manganiyar community like Gazi Barna are using Manganiyar *doha*s as a cultural form of preservation, which stimulates feelings of self-worth in Manganiyar musicians. By inverting *doha*s' value, from a symbol of their low caste status and ingrained servitude to a musical tradition worth preserving, Manganiyar musicians feel a sense of pride. Such preservation and inversion of meaning thus serves as another form of music as development. At the same time, Gazi Barna has taken on the role of cultural arbiter, deciding what to preserve and for whom.

Cultural Tourism

Cultural tourism, which comprises both domestic tourism and Manganiyar musicians touring abroad, served as a third aim of Gazi Barna's NGO. While only a relatively select few were given touring opportunities by Komal Kothari, Pehchan Lok Sangeet Sansthan provided an opening for other musicians in the Manganiyar community to be recognized as talented musicians locally and globally. Since the 1980s, many Manganiyar musicians have supplemented their income from traditional patronage with performances in the seasonal tourism industry in Jaisalmer City and Thar desert camel safaris. For many Manganiyar musicians, cultural tourism has replaced traditional patronage as a means of maintaining music as a livelihood.

Such new forms of patronage have greatly changed the way musicians perform. Gazi Barna and Pehchan were at the forefront of these musical and contextual changes. I have identified four distinct changes in Manganiyar music that were initiated by Barna as a result of performing in cultural tourism settings.

1. Repertoire choices are based on songs that will appeal to non-patron audiences who are not musically educated in Manganiyar traditional music, do not understand *rag* theory, and do not speak the languages in which the songs are sung. Songs that require audience specialist knowledge are thus passed over in non-traditional performance contexts and/or not passed down to the younger generations of musicians.
2. Instrumentation has changed. The *kamaicha*, the bowed lute introduced at the beginning of the chapter and a symbol of the Manganiyar community, is not prevalently played anymore, as the instrument requires years of training and is no longer commonly being made. Instead, musicians more often play the harmonium, a non-specialist instrument considered to be more versatile across musical genres, readily available, easily tuned, and portable. Another instrumental change is a new emphasis placed on percussion. There are often multiple *dholak* drummers and *khartal* players in ensembles. Within the musical form, space is given for percussion solos. Manganiyar musicians believe that audiences less familiar with Manganiyar music can more easily appreciate percussion virtuosity.
3. The Manganiyar now incorporate the Hindustani classical practices of *jugalbandi* ("entwined twins") and *sawal-jawab* ("question-answer") into their performances. These musical, often rhythmically oriented conversations between two soloists were first made popular in Hindustani classical performances outside of traditional contexts (Lavezzoli 2006). Gazi Barna believes that non-specialist audiences enjoy this fast-paced back-and-forth between performers that puts an emphasis on rhythm rather than sung poetry.
4. Gazi Barna has innovated a large ensemble format that incorporated the above three changes through the Pehchan Lok Sangeet Sansthan's "Desert Symphony." With a large group of musicians, he showcased a variety of instruments and featured sections made up of many musicians performing on the same instrument. Barna himself served as the conductor of the ensemble.

These four changes can be read as music as development. Development in the form of cultural tourism has required Manganiyar musicians to change their

> **Box 5.3 Discussion: Tourism and Cultural Change**
>
> In small groups, discuss the above-listed four changes in Manganiyar music as a result of performing in cultural tourism settings. In what ways do Manganiyars and other professional musicians need to regularly change to meet audience demands? When is musical change not beneficial to the artists, traditions, or audiences? In your discussions, engage with the concepts of "Westernization" and "classicization" in musical change.

music accordingly. In the case of cultural tourism, Manganiyar musicians must cater to non-Indian audiences who do not understand the nuances of their traditional music (repertoire, *rag*, and language) and high-class Indian audiences who may only appreciate classical forms of Indian music and dance. Manganiyar musicians, therefore, change the music through these processes of Westernization and classicization (see Box 5.3).

Conclusion

Komal Kothari's Rupayan Sansthan, although innovative in the 1960s for its focus on local Rajasthani music and culture at a time when institutions were mostly concerned with national and classical culture, maintained the same top-down international development model prevalent in other local development initiatives. Kothari, while intimately involved with the Manganiyar community, was not Manganiyar himself and was therefore an outsider. He seemed to be everything Manganiyar musicians were not—he did not perform music, he was from a high caste and class, he had a graduate-level education, and his family was well-respected in society, owning one of the largest and most powerful newspapers in the state.

During my ethnographic fieldwork, Gazi Barna often reminded me that Kothari could do what he did for the Manganiyar community precisely because he was an outsider and had the means to do it. In these reminders, I sensed that Gazi Barna felt an affinity with Kothari as an outsider. Barna communicated to me that his many international traveling experiences gave him a vantage point to see his own community from the perspective of an outsider, allowing him to cultivate an international frame of reference while maintaining connections and an identity as an insider. It is his unique positionality as a powerful, cosmopolitan insider that allowed Gazi Barna to found Pehchan Lok Sangeet Sansthan and envision music as development.

In this chapter, I have told one story of how "small voices sing big songs." These songs and stories tell us of the possibilities of reconceptualizing development as a locally initiated effort to sustain a community's livelihood, and how music can be conceptualized as development. Although I have focused this chapter on Gazi Barna and Pehchan, several other Manganiyar musicians have founded their own organizations in a similar vein throughout the Thar Desert after Komal Kothari's death. They are looking inward to their own local traditions through the cosmopolitan lens of development, viewing their music and traditions as cultural capital. For all these musicians, a local notion of development means acquiring tools of dominant development discourse that might empower them to implement a future for the Manganiyar community that will enable them to continue practicing music as a viable profession.

Contemporary Manganiyar musicians' expanded worldview and utilization of music as development requires adaptations of repertoire, instrumentation, musical form, and ensemble to meet the needs of new patrons and audiences. With their unique cosmopolitan positioning of having one foot in traditional village patronage relationships and the other on international concert stages, Manganiyar musicians have been able to envision development in innovative ways and embed it into their everyday musical lives. This story of music as development is not a story unique to the Manganiyar, as this is where music as development's power resides—in its ability to articulate dynamic struggles commonly found in musical communities around the world.

Works Cited

Agawu, Kofi. 2009. *Music as Discourse: Semiotic Adventures in Romantic Music*. New York: Oxford University Press.

Ayyagari, Shalini. 2013. "At Home in the Studio: The Sound of Manganiyar Music Going Popular." In *More than Bollywood: Studies in Indian Popular Music*, edited by Gregory Booth and Bradley Shope, 256–275. New York: Oxford University Press.

Bhargava, Pradeep. 2007. "Civil Society in Rajasthan: Initiatives and Inhibitions." In *Rajasthan: The Quest for Sustainable Development*, edited by Vijay Vyas, Sarthi Acharya, Surjit Singh, and Vidya Sagar, 257–282. New Delhi: Academic Foundation.

Bharucha, Rustom, and Komal Kothari. 2003. *Rajasthan: An Oral History, Conversations with Komal Kothari*. New Delhi: Penguin Global.

Chant, Sylvia, and Cathy McIlvaine. 2009. *Geographies of Development in the 21st Century: An Introduction to the Global South*. Cheltenham: Edward Elgar Publishing.

Escobar, Arturo 1995. *Encountering Development: The Making and Unmaking of the Third World*. Princeton, NJ: Princeton University Press.

Fisher, William. 1997. "Doing Good? The Politics and Antipolitics of NGO Practices." *Annual Review of Anthropology* 26: 439–64.

Government of Rajasthan. 2002. *Rajasthan Human Development Report: Some Facts*. Jaipur: Office of the Chief Minister.

Keare, Douglas. 2001. "Learning to Clap: Reflections on Top-Down versus Bottom-Up Development." *Human Organization* 60(2): 159–165.

Kothari, Komal. 1994. "Musicians for the People: The Manganiyars of Western Rajasthan." In *The Idea of Rajasthan: Explorations in Regional Identity*, edited by Karine Schomer, Joan Erdman, Derych Lodrick, and Lloyd Rudolph, 205–237. Columbia: South Asia Publications.

Lavezzoli, Peter. 2006. *The Dawn of Indian Music in the West*. New York: Continuum.

Nattiez, Jean-Jacques. 1990. *Music and Discourse: Toward a Semiology of Music*. Princeton, NJ: Princeton University Press.

Neuman, Daniel, and Shubha Chaudhuri, with Komal Kothari. 2006. *Bards, Ballads and Boundaries: An Ethnographic Atlas of Music Traditions in West Rajasthan*. New York: Seagull Books.

Panda, Biswambhar. 2007. "Top Down or Bottom Up? A Study of Grassroots NGOs' Approach." *Journal of Health Management* 9(2): 257–273.

Warren, Dennis, Jan Slikkerveer, and David Brokensha, eds. 1995. *The Cultural Dimension of Development: Indigenous Knowledge Systems*. London: Intermediate Technology Publications Ltd.

SECTION II
PERFORMANCE DYNAMICS
Style, Genre, Coding, and Function

Introduction by Zoe C. Sherinian

This book is intentionally *not* organized around the categories of music/dance style or genre, but instead around social themes. In South Asia, performance categories often imply a value hierarchy. Such an organization further encourages the focus of analysis to privilege aesthetic form and stylistic elements over the cultural meanings that they encode. However, style and genre remain important concepts with which many of our authors engage. Associations between identity and specific sound and movement categories are essential to understanding music and dance as everyday cultural expression.

Style and Genre

Analyses of style, genre, semiotic coding, and function are interrelated ways to understand cultural meaning in the arts. "Style" can be defined as a package of culturally preferred sound elements that constitute a musical identity. Musical elements of style can include rhythmic type, melodic type, instrumental and vocal timbre, associated forms and genres, as well as texture—or the number of sounded parts and their relationship. Styles studied in Section II include the following: Hindustani "classical" (Ruckert*) and styles that are Hindustani-like, but not considered classical (Bond; Schultz*); karnatak "classical" (Sherinian*); "light" or film music (Sherinian*);[1] and folk music (Greene; Sherinian*).

---

[1] Kaur* (Section III) discusses "classical," "light," and "AKJ" styles of Sikh kīrtan. She describes the "light style" as using melodies drawn from popular music, whereas "light" Christian *kirttanai* discussed in Sherinian* (Section II) draws on popular stylistic elements generally, but not specific tunes.

Differences in purpose often distinguish performance categorizations and artistic choices. Presentational devotional music with distinct performers and audience members leans toward classical virtuosity, while participatory styles with little artist-audience distinctions tend to be relatively simple, repetitive, and use call-and-response form in a congregational setting (e.g., Schultz*). Performance genres, while seemingly fixed and immutable, are more often fluid and exist on a continuum of aesthetic choices and practices. For example, the *kafi* song genre, based on Sufi poetry, may be considered an "intermediate" genre of South Asian music, distinct from, though related to, Hindustani music (Manuel 2015, in Bond*). To enhance the emotional impact of poetry, Sindhi *kafi* performers use a variety of melody types known as *sur*, *rāgiṇī*, or *rāg*; some are shared with Hindustani music, and others are particular to *kafi* repertoire. Manganiyar musicians in western Rajasthan, similarly, utilize some *rags* that are common to Hindustani music and others specific to their locale (Ayyagari 2012).

Genre typically signifies a function or purpose. Three chapters in this book introduce the important genre category of devotional music, specifically common song forms called *kirtan* or *kirttanai* used in Hindu, Sikh, and Christian contexts (Schultz; Kaur; and Sherinian*). While the purpose of *kirtan* is typically to generate participatory congregational singing through call-and-response form, it can also have a more solo/presentational style drawing on classical idioms of improvisation and melody (Schultz*). Tamil *kirttanai* in the style of Tamil folk song and *oyilattam* dance has been used to create a celebratory/festival atmosphere (Sherinian*). Other genres discussed in this section include *dhrupad* and *khyal* (Ruckert*)—Hindustani vocal genres that have influenced twentieth-century instrumental performance—and *oppari* funeral lament (Greene*). Distinguishing style, genre, and function is important, while each author approaches aesthetic analysis and meaning in distinct ways.

Semiotic Coding

Style elements and genres of music and dance carry associated semiotic codes or musical signs. As Thomas Turino writes, "music and dance create and communicate emotion and meaning through signs" (2008, 5). Generally, a sign, as understood by the philosopher Charles Peirce, is "anything that is perceived by an observer [listener] which stands for or calls to mind something else [an object] and by doing so creates an effect in the observer" (Turino 2008, 5). These "vehicles" of perception include iconic and indexical codes. An iconic musical code culturally signifies what the musical utterance "sounds like" or represents as the object or idea indicated by the sign. The sound (and its associated meaning) then generates an effect, typically an emotion, physical reaction, or thought (5–6). For example, the complexity of Hindustani improvisation resembles or iconically encodes virtuosity and, thus the social idea of eliteness. The way a handkerchief is twirled in *oyilattam* dance iconically evokes sword fighting, generating a feeling of strength and confidence in the dancers that they might feel in preparation for war (Sherinian* [Section III]).

Indexical codes, more typically present in the arts, mean that sounds *can be associated with* an idea or an event. In music, they are often generated through instrumental timbre. Thus, the buzzing wash of a *tambura* drone encodes karnatak or Hindustani style (the object), evoking for many Westerners, for example, an orientalist feeling of mystery. The harmonium and *tabla* together similarly encode devotional music in South Asia. The *parai* frame drum plays specific rhythmic patterns (*adis*) that communicate function—that a specific ritual/event is occurring—generating associated feelings of excitement in the case of a festival or concern if a funeral (Sherinian* [Section III]). The high range and thin, sweet timbre of Bollywood singers such as Lata Mangeshkar both indexically encode mid-to-late twentieth-century Bollywood style and iconically represent the naïve, virginal character the actress portrays (Sarrazin* [Section V]). Another category of sign is symbol. Notation or mnemonic syllables (*son adi*s, *bol*s, *solkattu*, and *sargam* pitch names) act as symbolic signs. Whether verbalized or written, these music and dance symbols carry specific meanings.

Historical Construction of the "Classical" Arts

In South Asia, the style categories of classical, folk, and popular all carry indexical associations with cultural identities of caste, class, gender, and religion. These categories are relatively recent historical constructions embedded within political discourses that require critical deconstruction. The aesthetic attribute of "classical" began to be applied to Indian performing arts through both an encounter with colonialism and a reaction to its orientalism, becoming a conscious part of the cultural project of nationalism at the turn of the twentieth century. Before this period, the stylistic practices today called karnatak and Hindustani music, as well as bharatanatyam, kathak, and other now-"classical" dance styles, were primarily performed by professional hereditary artists as salaried employees meant to entertain, in courtly contexts patronized by elite landowners and royalty (e.g., Allen 1997; Bakhle 2005).

The process of defining an indigenous "classical" music style was secured by socio-religious elites, primarily Brahmins, and entwined with defining a modern, middle-class, English-speaking, and educated cosmopolitan subject. On the one hand, elites reacted to the colonialist and orientalist discourses of Indian music and dance as exotic and mysterious as well as the judgment of melodic filigree and improvisation as feminine, and thus, degenerate (Katz*). Conversely, this process of securing a "classical tradition" was an attempt to render Indian arts commensurate with the cultural esteem ascribed to Western arts. To do so, it was simultaneously necessary to retain an authentic difference packaged in a discourse of ancientness, especially the derivation of a "spiritual classicalness" in Sanskrit treatises. In music, the voice and its association with oral tradition were privileged as the source of distinction in karnatak (and Hindustani) music. "The voice came to be associated with Indianness and not Westernness, originality and not reproduction, humanity and not mechanization, tradition and not modernity" (Weidman 2006, 5).

In the South Indian city of Madras (Chennai), the designation "classical" was applied to the newly coined "bharatanatyam" dance by the nationalists E. Krishna Iyer and Rukmini Arundale, leaders of the occultist Madras Theosophical Society. In the 1930s, these upper-caste elites tethered the production of "Indian classical dance" with notions of metaphysics, spiritual enlightenment, and nationalism by reinventing and repopulating the dance, previously only performed by courtesans, with Brahmin women to (re)embody the idea of "India's classical heritage" (Krishnan et al.*).

The cultural movement to (re)create the classical arts was further codified through independent India's central arts organization, the Sangeet Natak Akademi (1952), which designated particular forms as "classical" and others as "folk" partly for funding purposes. "Nearly all oppressed caste art forms were classified by the state as 'folk,' and therefore were not accorded the prestige and patronage afforded to the so-called classical forms practiced by the upper castes" (Davesh Soneji, personal communication, December 2023). Further, this false binary reflected class and caste distinctions more than the actual flow of artists across genres and the variety of repertoires used among them (Morcom 2022).

Construction of "the Folk"

The constructed discourse of "the folk" in South Asian arts draws on indigenous terminology. Most such terms reflect a sense of local people (such as *makkal isai*, "people's music," and *lokgeet*, "folk song"); music of the rural-agricultural milieu or country (*nāṭṭupuṟa isai*, "country music"); or village song or music (*girāmiya pāṭṭu* or *grāmiya isai*) (Paige 2010, 34). While the Hindi term *lok* has a common Indo-European etymology with "folk/volk," Stefan Fiol argues that the English word "folk" appears in India in the late nineteenth century only because of "encounters between British and Bengali social elites, 'who deployed the concepts of folk music and folk culture as part of a broader worldview rooted in cultural nationalism and colonial dominance'" (Korom 2006, 39, in Fiol 2015, 3).

As a result of this colonial history, as well as regionalism and caste and class dynamics, folk music and dance continue to indexically convey notions of tradition, heritage, cultural authenticity (a sense of unchanging difference), backwardness, degradedness (low-caste, uncivilized, without theoretical structure or conception), and rootedness in local, rural village practices (isolated and authentic). The designation *folk* thus socially marks the artist as lower-class (typically male) and Dalit-Bahujan or Adivasi, while hereditary female folk artists have been considered prostitutes who display themselves for public consumption (Seizer 2005). Recent urban staging of folk performance, called folklorization, however, has facilitated the possibility of women to perform without this stigma (Fiol* [Section V]; Kheshgi*; Maciszewski* [Section IV]; Sherinian* [Section III]). However, the purpose of folklorization tends to be driven by middle-class values of propriety and excellence, while others would advocate collective self-determination and social justice for folk artists (Fiol 2017, 3).[2]

Dalit folklorist Rev. J. T. Appavoo defines folk music in a contemporary political sense as a form of protest and alternative communication of

---

[2] Several chapters in this book consider urban, folkloric staging and its effect on artists' status, including Babiracki* (Section III); Fiol* (Section V); Maciszewski* (Section IV); Kheshgi* (Section IV); and Sherinian* (Section III).

Dalit-Bahujans, especially for the purpose of social liberation. Appavoo contends that if the message of a song is meaningful to the oppressed—if it is politically and spiritually empowering—it will spread quickly through humanly produced and transmitted communication systems. If it is not meaningful, its message and style will either be changed/recreated to become so, or it will naturally die from lack of use (Appavoo 1993, 75). Further, Appavoo believes folk arts should be economically and socially accessible, participatory, and draw on community skills.

As an amalgamation of aesthetic elements, folk music-dance styles across South Asia have commonalities. Their elements are organized around genres, usually oriented toward local purposes: work, games, lullabies, lament, life-cycle celebrations, and rituals for local deities (Paige 2010). These elements within the genre are intersectional in that one determines the other. These include tune type, syllables for memory and transmission, and a cyclical rhythmic pattern, often in a metrical cycle of three or six with duple accents against it creating a polymetrical feel. Rhythmic patterns also use mnemonics to recognize, communicate, and encode genre purpose. Dance steps and movements are associated with rhythmic patterns and accents. Folk genres have flexible song texts in vernacular languages, adaptable to the expressive and political needs of the moment and context.

The authors in this book, based on their fieldwork, direct study, and interviews with artists, challenge the primitivist, colonialist, and casteist construction of "folk" to recognize a greater fluidity between divergent performance spaces, styles, and genres. They demonstrate that "it is impossible to draw clear boundaries between the folk and classical, the rural and urban, and the modern and traditional" (Paige 2010, 59). Analogously, Peter Manuel describes a circular process of tune borrowing and "parody" between folk and film music (1993). Film music producers commonly borrow tunes/tune types, rhythms, and instrumental timbres from folk musicians, arranging them in a *filmi* style by adding reverb, background string orchestras, and high-pitched female voices. Folk artists (re)localize these mediated songs into their live performance repertoire, often "folkifying" the song through ensemble arrangement and timbre, to successfully use them as a source of entertainment and recreation (Manuel 1993, 143). This process reflects the folk practice of listening to and absorbing from the environment, however broad and mediated those sources are. "Folk" artists continually expand and recreate their forms of expression to meet the needs of the sociopolitical moment (Appavoo 1986, in Sherinian 2014).

Bollywood Film Music

For most of the twentieth century, Bollywood film music has been India's and, by extension, much of South Asia's popular music. Its style is often described as *filmi* or *masala*: a mixture of musical style and genre "spices" from the subcontinent as well as the rest of the world sautéed in a distinctly Indian pot of musical arrangement, vocal quality, form, and performance by studio musicians. "Playback" singers pre-record songs to which actors lip-sync on-screen (Sarrazin* [Section V]). As creators of a national music style, musicians similarly reflect a wide diversity of communities from throughout the country. Goans, Parsis, Sikhs, Christians, Muslims, Bengali Hindus, and others contribute a variety of skills and instruments to the Bollywood sound including Western music theory, choral singing, and performance of European string instruments, all taught in the schools and churches of the Portuguese colony of Goa for the last 500 years. What may sonically appear to the uninitiated Bollywood listener to be Western mimicry has been composed, arranged, and performed by Indian musicians in a distinctly Indian, "Bollywood" style (Booth 2008).

Chapters in Section II analyze how style, genre, and function in South Asian music and dance construct cultural meaning associated with identity, affect, religion, nationalism, and social status. While music and gesture analysis have been foundational in South Asian performing arts scholarship for over 100 years, the approach in this text is to always contextualize sound and movement in cultural meaning to better understand the identities and purposes of the people who produce and use the arts.

Works Cited

Allen, Matthew. 1997. "Rewriting the Script for South Indian Dance." *TDR: The Drama Review* 41(3): 63–100.

Appavoo, J. T. 1986. *Folklore for Change*. Madurai: Tamil Nadu Theological Seminary.

Appavoo, J. T. 1993. "Communication for Dalit Liberation: A Search for an Appropriate Communication Model." Master of Theology thesis, University of Edinburgh.

Ayyagari, Shalini. 2012. "Spaces Betwixt and Between: Musical Borderlands and the Manganiyar Musicians of Rajasthan." *Asian Music* 43(1): 3–33.

Bakhle, Janaki. 2005. *Two Men and Music: Nationalism and the Making of an Indian Classical Tradition*. New York: Oxford University Press.

Booth, Gregory D. 2008. *Behind the Curtain: Making Music in Mumbai's Film Studios*. New York: Oxford University Press.

Fiol, Stefan. 2015. "One Hundred Years of Indian Folk Music: The Evolution of a Concept." In *This Thing Called Music: Essays in Honor of Bruno Nettl*, edited by Victoria Lindsay Levine and Philip V. Bohlman, 317–329. Lanham, MD: Rowman & Littlefield.

Fiol, Stefan. 2017. *Recasting Folk in the Himalayas: Indian Music, Media, and Social Mobility*. Urbana: University of Illinois Press.

Korom, Frank J. 2006. *South Asian Folklore: A Handbook*. Greenwood Folklore Handbooks. New York: Bloomsbury Publishing.

Manuel, Peter. 1993. *Cassette Culture: Popular Music and Technology in North India*. Chicago: University of Chicago Press.

Manuel, Peter. 2015. "The Intermediate Sphere in North Indian Music Culture: Between and Beyond 'Folk' and 'Classical'." *Ethnomusicology* 59(1): 82–115.

Morcom, Anna. 2022. "Following the People, Refracting Hindustani Music, and Critiquing Genre-Based Research." *Ethnomusicology* 66(3): 470–496.

Paige, Aaron. 2010. "Subaltern Sounds: Fashioning Folk Music in Tamil Nadu." MA thesis, Wesleyan University.

Seizer, Susan. 2005. *Stigmas of the Tamil Stage: An Ethnography of Special Drama Artists in South India*. Durham, NC: Duke University Press.

Sherinian, Zoe. 2014. *Tamil Folk Music as Dalit Liberation Theology*. Bloomington: University of Indiana Press.

Turino, Thomas. 2008. *Music as Social Life: The Politics of Participation*. Chicago: University of Chicago Press.

Weidman, Amanda. 2006. *Singing the Classical, Voicing the Modern: Postcolonial Politics of Music in South India*. Durham, NC: Duke University Press.

6
Changing Musical Style and Social Identity in Tamil Christian *Kirttanai*

Zoe C. Sherinian

The history of Christianity in India began with St. Thomas coming to Kerala in AD 52. In the mid-1500s, St. Xavier converted entire fishing communities on the Southern coast. The first Lutheran Protestant missionaries arrived in Tamil Nadu in 1706 and by 1724 had published pamphlets containing Christian *kirttanai* (*kīrttaṉai*), likely used in their congregations and schools. However, upper-caste Hindus, in the process of negotiating their conversion with missionaries, insisted that they retain their caste and practices of separation from lower and outcaste converts. Tamil converts also brought cultural idioms, like musical genres, that carried caste and class values into Christian practice. Borrowing the devotional genre from Hindu congregational and elite court karnatak music contexts of the Tanjore area, upper-caste Vellalar Christians first composed Christian *kirttanai* (also called "lyrics" in English) in the eighteenth century. These used karnatak *raga*s (modes), *tala*s (rhythmic cycles), and a three-part *kriti* form. From the late eighteenth century, *kirttanai* continued to be the most widely performed indigenous Christian music genre among Tamil Protestants. However, lower-caste Christians, particularly Nadars and Paraiyars, consciously made musical style changes to *kirttanai* performance practice to encode shifts of power and identity.

In 1853, the American Congregational missionary Edward Webb collected more than 100 Christian *kirttanai* from the Vellalar Christian poet of Tanjore, Vedanayakam Sastriar (1774–1864). These formed the core of the first Tamil Protestant hymnal, *Christian Lyrics for Public and Social Worship* (1875 [1853]), widely disseminated to villages and towns by missionaries and Tamil lay teachers, soon becoming a canon of karnatak hymnody among the diverse Protestant missions. Thereby, *kirttanai* became the primary liturgical music for poor rural Christian Paraiyar (outcaste[1]) and Nadar (Bahujan or lower-caste) communities. *Kirttanai* also became a useful tool for Christian evangelism to transmit the gospel stories and theology of Tamil Protestant Christianity (Sherinian 2014). This process of musical localization, or creating Christian music to reflect or reclaim local cultural identity, included using both "indigenous" and "foreign" performance idioms. These processes transcended the construction of cohesive, cultural continuity within the community, reflecting instead internal complexity, discontinuity, and "rupture with the past" (Ingalls, Reigersberg, and Sherinian 2018, 11–13). In the case of Dalit, Bahujan, and lower-class people, such ruptures with histories of oppression empower the development of cultural and psychological self-esteem.

Mid-nineteenth-century transmission of *kirttanai* resulted in different caste groups adapting their use to various musical styles. This included changes of tune and rhythm from classicized karnatak to Tamil folk and to Western hymn-like performances with organ accompaniment. *Kirttanai* has been used in multiple contexts: in Tamil folk dances such as *oyilattam*, on devotional cassettes by popular Hindu playback singers in the style of Tamil film or light music, and in urban church services and community events where *kirttanai* are sung in Western major scales. Christians and Hindus with formal karnatak training also perform light-classical, concert-style *kirttanai*. While transmission of *kirttanai* to the lower castes in the nineteenth century symbolized inculcation into upper-caste culture and values (Sherinian 2005), later stylistic changes signified shifting social identities and socio-religious needs of the diversity of Tamil Christians. In this chapter, transformations in performance practice of *kirttanai* by lower-caste Protestants reveal aspirations for upward mobility for some and civil rights for others.

The localization of *kirttanai* to "Indian" and "foreign" styles, I argue, manifests the need to create Christian musical and theological expressions relevant to changing socio-religious identities, particularly to shifting dynamics of caste, class, and location among Tamil Protestants. Musical style indexes the hierarchical distinctions of Tamil Christian caste and class. Specifically, lower-class and lower-caste Christians (re)create liturgical music

---

[1] Today, politicized Tamils who formerly identified with this so-called outcaste, or untouchable group, call themselves by the anti-caste term Dalit, meaning oppressed. Some reject their caste designation of Paraiyar altogether, while others reverse the devaluation of their caste names to reclaim it as positive.

to reflect their indigenous understandings of Christianity, thereby realizing the Christian message of equality and justice in their lives; music becomes liberation theology.

Through musical and performance analysis of three versions of the same *kirttanai*, "Tōttiram Ceyvēṉe" (pronounced "Seyvēṉe"), by Tanjore Sathiyanathan Pillai (born c. 1840), I demonstrate that, while theology and language are significant elements that code the meaning of Christian musical localization, it is musical style[2] that encodes changing arrangements of class, caste, and cultural meaning within ritual contexts. Indeed, by representing the style spectrum (karnatak, folk, Western, and light) of Tamil Christian music within a single genre, I reinforce how musical style determines the reconstruction of socio-religious identity and meaning.

The "Original" Karnatak Style

The *kirttanai* "Tōttiram Ceyvēṉe" is one of several hundred karnatak-style Tamil Christian compositions published in editions of the Tamil Hymnal between 1853 and the 1930s. In the mid-to-late nineteenth century, composer Tanjore Sathiyanathan Pillai infused it with the style markings of an upper-class/caste socio-religious identity. Pillai was a Vellalar, or upper-caste Christian who lived in the city of Tanjore, the seat of classical Brahminical Saivite music culture and a center of Lutheran and Anglican mission societies.

"Tōttiram Ceyvēṉe's" elite cultural sensibility is apparent in its lyrics, which reflect poetic ornamentation and Hindu ritual praise typical of *kriti* and *kirttanai* composers (Figure 6.1). Florid praise of the deity's attributes is illustrated by claims that Jesus is "like pure gold." He is "the heavenly son who is wise and good." He is "the true guru" sought by *tecikarkal* "seekers of truth." Christian *bhakti* (devotion) is expressed in the third *caranam* (verse, pronounced *charanam*) by the devotee who so desires Jesus' love that he intends to shower him with flowers of pure gold, not the ordinary flowers Hindus place on icons. The centrality of *bhakti* devotion is emphasized in the *pallavi*: "I will sing praise to you." Other Brahminical Hindu images in the text include a description of the baby Jesus crying for divine nectar (*amirtam*). Despite Jesus' lower-class status depicted in "Tōttiram Ceyvēṉe"

---

[2] I define musical style as a package of sound-identity elements.

Pallavi

tōttiram ceyvēṉe raḍsakaṉai
tōttiram ceyvēṉe

I will sing praises—Oh savior
I will sing praises

Anupallavi

pāttiramāhha immātram karuṇaivaita
pārttibaṉai yudah kōttiraṇai yeṉṟum

He who has taken me into his trusted fold by
Showering his mercy upon me,
The king of the Jews—forever (I will sing)

Caranam 1

Mother Mary's son—who, lying on the grass of the manger
Cried for divine nectar.
The small boy lying in the manger,
Who came into the world as it was prophesized in the scriptures.

Caranam 2

The one wrapped in tattered cloth,
To whom the angels came and bowed down.
The one who gave joyful revelation of his glory to the shepherds,
The heavenly son who is wise and good.

Caranam 3

The one who is like pure gold.
The true guru sought by seekers of truth.
To receive your love, I will
Shower you with pure golden flowers,
Joining with the heavenly beings
Who came into this world (I will sing)

Figure 6.1 Lyrics to "Tōttiram Ceyvēṉe" by Sathiyanathan Pillai. Translation by Christopher Sherwood.

Figure 6.2 "Tōttiram Ceyvēṉe" composed by Tanjore Sathiyanathan Pillai in Bhairavi *raga*. Transcribed by the Rev. H. A. Popley in 1932.

through the baby being wrapped in tattered cloth, Pillai localized the song within an elite Tamil religious and musical context. Accordingly, he used karnatak idioms, the only acceptable or appropriate indigenous alternative to Western hymns for liturgical use at the time.

"Tōttiram Ceyvēṉe" was originally composed in the *raga bhairavi* and eight-beat *adi tala*. Karnatak *bhairavi* contains a lowered *ga* or third, a lowered *dha* or sixth, and a lowered *ni* or seventh (▶ Video example 6.1).[3] Beyond its setting in *bhairavi raga*, we cannot know exactly how the tune sounded in the late nineteenth century. However, the Rev. H. A. Popley, a British Methodist missionary, includes it in his 1932 set of 400 *kirttanai* transcribed from congregational singing before organ accompaniment was added in the 1940s. Closest to the originals, they provide only a melodic skeleton of pitches without appropriate *gamaka* (ornamentation) (see Figure 6.2[4] and ▶ Audio example 6.1).

Many Tamil Christians today associate karnatak style *kirttanai* with Brahminical upper-caste cultural hegemony, aspirations of upward class mobility, and a non-intelligible Sanskritized Tamil. However, Christians with theological and social identities outside the upper-caste/class milieu have adapted the *kirttanai* to folk and light music styles, to make them personally relevant and meaningful.

---

[3] Compare to Hindustani *raga* Bharavi in Katz*.
[4] This transcription of the skeleton tune of the *pallavi* and *anupallavi* (refrain) are taken from H. A. Popley, *Tune Book to Tamil Christian Lyrics*, vol. 1 (1932).

Folk/Village Style Inculturation of the *Kirttanai*

In the mid-twentieth century, Paraiyar (outcaste) villagers adapted the performance style of the *kirttanai* to rural-style (folk) Christian ritual to bolster their cultural self-esteem and resist the hegemony of upper-caste culture. Considering the style degraded, missionaries and Tamil pastors allowed these to be used only in events held outside formal church services. In the central village gathering place, lower- and outcaste Christians adapted the *kirttanai* to festival-style folk music. In 1912, the American missionary John Chandler noted the process of training villagers, likely without previous access to karnatak music, to sing *kirttanai*.

> The common people were not skilled even in their own music, [implying karnatak] and that caused the objections to be raised, that they [*kirttanai*] were not sung correctly. But in congregational use they were bound to be changed, because many native tunes are adapted to solo singing and yet under the modification of singing in [congregational] unison are sweet and effective. Training and practice under instruction were needed to make these lyrics effective in Christian worship; and these are what Webb secured. (Chandler 1912, 248)

Chandler argues further that congregational singing of these karnatak-style *kirttanai* "disassociated" them from "idolatrous worship" linked with their Hindu origins (Chandler 1912, 393). Yet this "indigenous" hymnody was still stylistically "foreign" to lower-caste villagers. Villagers' deep expressions of faith or identification with liberation theology would unlikely be expressed through karnatak music, Sanskritized Tamil, and theology that reflected upper-caste values. A radical transformation of musical style was necessary for lower-castes to find and express liberation from social bondage.

In 1991, I documented "Tōttiram Ceyvēṉe" used in a folk performance of *oyilattam*, a men's line dance once considered a war dance, in the village of Koppuchittampatti near Aruppukkottai by Paraiyar Christians belonging to the Church of South India denomination (Figure 6.3). They reported that they had performed this version of "Tōttiram Ceyvēṉe" since the 1950s, and had been encouraged to do so by the American Congregational missionaries Emmons and Ruth White, there since the 1920s.

In this performance (transcribed by the author), the song's tune matched neither the original *bhairavi raga* version published by Rev. Popley nor

STYLE AND IDENTITY IN TAMIL CHRISTIAN *KIRTTANAI*   103

Figure 6.3 Village folk style version of "Tōttiram Ceyvēṉe" performed to *oyilattam* line dance by Paraiyar Christians of Koppuchittampatti Village.

the congregational version commonly heard after the 1960s. Instead, it corresponds to the narrow melodic range (of a fifth) and style of other *oyilattam* songs, while its accompaniment by *tavil* drum and cymbals brings to it the twelve-pulse rhythmic feel with the three-against-two polyrhythmic accents characteristic of Tamil folk music. The tune, however, has a flatted third, which may indicate a retention of the pitches of the lower tetrachord in the original Bhairavi *raga* tune.

Several Tamil Christian music scholars believe that remote village versions of *kirttanai* have retained the "original" karnatak-style tunes as well as musical characteristics like *gamaka* (J. T. Appavoo, personal communication, March 1994). Tune retention is likely because many village congregations could not afford an organ or harmonium that, for urban Christians, made equal-tempered tuning and Western harmony available. Rev. J. T. Appavoo (1940–2005), a Dalit theologian composer, believed that villagers learned these karnatak characteristics and retained them, while in the case of *oyillatam* dance, the rhythm has been purposely adapted to the village context (Sherinian 2014).

The Christian *kirttanai-oyilattam* tune, particularly its melodic rhythm and form, has been molded to the dynamic twelve-pulse ostinato pattern with its polyrhythmic accent and call-and-response style of Tamil folk music. In ▶ Video example 6.2, the single older man dressed in *veshti* and white shirt performs as a singing-preacher, leading a group of younger men dancing and singing in a single-line formation. In his responsorial call, he emphasizes the important theological points of the *pallavi* (refrain) by waving his finger above his head and repeating key lyrics on higher melodic notes. The younger men, dressed in shorts and T-shirts with small bells strapped to their ankles, repeat the musical line as a synchronized chorus moving forward and backward with complex foot-crossing patterns while twirling colorful handkerchiefs. *Oyilattam* serves multiple functions: as a means of recreation, of re-identification of Christian worship with the Tamil folk/Dalit music and dance form, of theological identification with Jesus as poor, and the subversive function of developing agility for self-defense. The handkerchief substitutes for the sword originally used in this war dance (Gunasekaran 1988, 65). Dalits, like other oppressed people, have hidden attempts to develop skills of self-defense and empowerment under the guise of music, dance, and religion (Roberts 1972, 27).

Through the dissemination of karnatak *kirttanai* to this rural context, outcaste people were inculcated to a hegemonic elite-modeled Christian theology and hymnody with its associated upper-caste values and musical elements. However, by combining *kirttanai* texts with the empowering folk expression of *oyilattam* dance and tune types, Dalit Christians created a liberation theology in dance and musical sound. The tune, rhythm, agile movements, and responsorial performance style of this folk version of "Tōttiram Ceyvēṉe" direct their message of village-style Christian *bhakti* toward a loving, protecting deity who suffered as they do (Sherinian 2014). Furthermore, because missionaries and middle-class Christians believed that folk music was unfit for use in liturgy, its use became an act of cultural reclamation promoting cultural and psychological self-esteem for Dalits and Bahujans.

The Rev. J. T. Appavoo advocated Christianity as a means for social liberation, using local music and cultural perspectives. In the mid-1980s, he introduced folk songs and liturgies to Tamil churches. He argued that its content and language, its participatory performance style, and its ease of transmission and re-creation in spoken Tamil made it the most viable vehicle for an anti-caste, class-conscious, liberation theology in South India. Appavoo posited that the folk style signifies liberation because its form of transmission inherently allows for continuous re-creation of music and lyrics, making its performance emotionally and socially transformative (Appavoo 1986; Sherinian 2014).

Modern Congregational Style: Westernizing the *Kirttanai*

Many Christian *kirttanai* tunes were originally composed in difficult *raga*s. By the mid-twentieth century, as lower-caste Christians became upwardly mobile and urbanized, they simplified the *kirttanai* melodies and added tonal harmony, thereby expressing a modern, sophisticated identity in congregations throughout Tamil Nadu. This simplification was a result of oral transmission that involved moving lowered and raised notes found in many *raga*s to conform to the Western major scale. Reasons for these changes include the following: oral transmission of tunes; lack of formal training in and access to karnatak music theory by Christians, often because of caste discrimination; the introduction of harmony through organ accompaniment of *kirttanai* in urban areas from the 1940s; the influence of equal-tempered scales from both the organ and harmonium; and the influence of diatonic melodies through the simultaneous use of Western hymnody by Tamil Christians.

Changing social dynamics within the Protestant community, the most significant being the economic and educational development of lower-caste Nadars, spurred these musical changes. Through the conservative Anglican missions (Society for the Propagation of the Gospel and Church Mission Society), Nadars were inculcated into the High-Church practices of British hymnody, four-part harmonic singing, and Victorian sensibilities. Partha Chatterjee calls these practices "bourgeois virtues characteristic of the new social forms of 'disciplining'—of orderliness, thrift, cleanliness, . . . a personal sense of responsibility [and] the practical skills of literacy" (1993, 129). Eliza Kent describes this as a "discourse of respectability" among Tamil Christian communities "articulated in moral statements about space, mobility, self-restraint and sexuality... [that] tended to narrow the already restricted range of behaviors and choices deemed appropriate [particularly] for women" (2004, 4). In the nineteenth century, the Calvinist CMS missionaries discouraged Nadars from using Christian *kirttanai* as they considered celebratory practices unchristian and the *kirttanai* "heathen," as related to Hinduism and Catholicism (Hudson 2000, 141 and 148). Thus, most Nadars supported either the use of English hymnody or no music and celebration at all.

By the early twentieth century, Nadars imbued with Victorian cultural values and education became upwardly mobile. With the creation of the Protestant Church of South India (CSI) in 1947, Anglican liturgical practices and clerical hierarchy dominated the new ecumenical institution. Concurrently, middle-class Nadars migrated to urban areas where they became administrators of Christian institutions, schoolteachers, and organists. The Nadars carried the Anglican preference for English hymnody to formerly Methodist and Congregational CSI parishes, which had encouraged the indigenous *kirttanai* for the previous century.

The result was the dissemination of a congregational *kirttanai* style that, when accompanied by organ, sounded more like a John Wesley hymn than a karnatak *kriti* by Tyagaraja; in Tirunelveli district, they even sang the *kirttanai* in four-part harmony (M. Thomas Thangaraj, interview with the author, March 12, 1997). Although Nadar organists used the correct *raga* scale positions of the *kirttanai*, *raga*-specific melodic movement and *gamaka* were omitted (or never known) by most musicians. Further, they rarely used written music but relied on oral memory, for only the *raga* and *tala* names, not the melodies were published in the hymnals. "Foreign" pitches were introduced through oral transmission or experimenting with harmonic accompaniment, denying the *raga*s their distinctive modal qualities. Musical Westernization occurred when the lowered seconds, sevenths, sixths, and raised fourths characteristic of many *raga*s moved to natural or Western "major scale" positions. Composer and theologian Thomas Thangaraj described this as "Anglicizing," saying, "when you have people who don't know karnatak [music theory] sing karnatak songs, they... make it into light music."[5] This process of melodic simplification through oral

---

[5] Thangaraj believes that "Anglicizing" and the movement toward light music sound was prevalent

Figure 6.4 Congregational light music version of "Tōttiram Ceyvēṉe."

transmission resulted in Christian *kirttanai* becoming more accessible to urban congregations untrained in karnatak music and more sonically compatible with the Western hymns they valued. By the mid-twentieth century, the sound of *kirttanai* no longer represented the indigenized creations of upper-caste Vellalar Christian composers, but had become enculturated songs of middle- and lower-class/caste urban Christians who identified with them as modern and Western.

"Tōttiram Ceyvēṉe" is popularly performed today in church services and at events like house blessings. The melody shown in Figure 6.4 (transcribed by the author) was the most widespread congregational version in the early 1990s. The pitch C—the first and last note of the *pallavi* along with the prominent presence of its fifth, G—defines the tonal center. The harmonically significant first phrase of the *pallavi* begins on C. In measures 6 and 7 the melodic movement outlines a V chord (G major) and returns to the tonic C. Accompanying instruments on several light music recordings of this version also use C-major tonality; however, C is practically absent as the fourth pitch in the scale of the original *bhairavi raga* (Figure 6.2, G-tonic *sruti* version). C is only used as the final (liminal and unresolved) note of the *anupallavi*, a passing tone to return to D (*Pa*), the fifth the first pitch of the *pallavi*.

among the Nadars because "they were quick to jump on the westernization band wagon." By contrast, he believes the Paraiyar villagers, who also had no formal training in karnatak music, have retained the karnatak flavor of the *kirttanai*, particularly the "grace note tradition" or *gamaka* (interview with the author, March 12, 1997).

If the new congregational melody (Figure 6.4) defines C major tonality, the B♭ in measure 3 seems melodically foreign. I argue it is a retention of the flatted third from the original karnatak *bhairavi raga* melody (Figure 6.2) with its G tonic. If one compares the original and congregational melodies considering G as the tonal center, and the B♭ as the lowered third, then the third measures of both examples (with the lyric "Tōttiram Ceyvēṉe") echo the same pitches and melodic contours. The new version's melodic retention reinforces the significant Westernizing influence that organists had on the *kirttanai* through harmonic accompaniment by oral transmission.

Although some elements of Bhairavi *raga* have been retained in the congregational melody, its setting in C major tonality associates the *kirttanai* with sophisticated urban and modern culture through its fusion with Western musical (tonal) values. For upwardly mobile, lower-caste Christians, Westernization symbolizes an escape from, or subversion of, their oppressed status in the caste hierarchy, where karnatak Brahminical cultural expressions are valued above all other indigenous styles. To presume that the Nadar's borrowing of the major scale from the British is simply a mimicry of Western culture denies lower-caste Christian musical agency within the caste economy. Substitution of the major scale for the *kirttanai*'s *raga* subverts the elitism of upper-caste culture—a more locally meaningful act.

Light Music Cassettes and Urban Pentecostals

In 1994, I documented a housewarming for a middle-class (lower-caste) family who had built a new home in the suburbs of Madurai. As is typical in most middle-class urban Christian settings, the spaces in which people listened to and performed music were segregated by sex. The women, wearing silk *saris* with hair neatly placed in a bun (typical of a schoolteacher), sat inside the house on the polished floor. They surrounded a large oil lamp placed in the middle of an elaborate Christian *kolam*, a design drawn on the floor with colored powder, and slowly sang an a cappella congregational version of "Tōttiram Ceyvēṉe" (see ▶ Video example 6.3).

The men sat outside in rows of folding chairs wearing Western-style pants and dress shirts listening to catchy, "filmi" Christian music on cassette. The women, with their more traditional dress and reserved behavior, representing a morally conservative sensibility and newly middle-class status, remained protected in the interior space (Kent 2004). While the soundscapes of the live a cappella female voices and recorded music overlapped, they did not clash because both styles of music performed urban modern expressions. Cassette recordings of light music, particularly by the Ceylon Pentecostals, broadcast from Radio Ceylon (Sri Lanka) since the 1950s, have contributed to codification and standardization of the congregational-style *kirttanai*.[6]

Despite using the same simplified melody, cassette versions differ from congregational ones by their "light," film-style accompaniment, exhibited in two versions of "Tōttiram Ceyvēṉe" by popular playback singers who lip-sync songs for films. One by Jikki, likely recorded in the 1960s, includes a string orchestra accompaniment, mixing Cuban cha-cha-cha rhythms played on the *tabla* with a two-beat country-and-western feel borrowed from American gospel music (⊙ Audio example 6.2, Figure 6.5). The other by Chitra, a Hindu playback singer, produced in 1989, exhibits a disco-style drum machine groove, an electric bass playing throbbing off-beats, and synthesized piano riffs copying the Tamil film music producer Ilaiyaraja's mid-1980s style (⊙ Audio example 6.3).

Light music arrangements and recordings of *kirttanai* by evangelists and Pentecostals have attracted copious middle- and lower-middle-class Christians to join and support their ministries financially. As lower-caste Christians have gained education, upward mobility, and urbanization, they have discarded their village folk styles in favor of allying with the Anglican missionary preference for harmony. Many seek support for expression of emotional religious sentiments and transformation—a form and style of worship practiced in their former village goddess religions. Up-tempo, light-style performance of simplified and westernized *kirttanai* melodies fulfills both those needs, and is indigenous and sophisticated in both an urban Indian and a modern Western sensibility.

Conclusion

Since their publication for a broad Tamil Christian community in 1853, the repertoire of Tamil Protestant *kirttanai* have been re-localized or

---

[6] Many of the earliest congregational singing changes were introduced as light music recordings by the Ceylon Pentecostals in the 1950s and broadcast on Radio Ceylon when All India Radio banned popular music from being aired (Mohan 1994, 55). The Pentecostals were the first to use light music in their churches and conventions. They produced the earliest cassettes in which *kirttanai* tunes were simplified and arranged in a "light" fashion using guitars and drum sets (Thangaraj, March 12, 1997).

Figure 6.5 Cassette cover for Jiki's recording *Thanthannai Thuthippom: Tamil Christian Songs* (GCI, 1988).

enculturated from karnatak to folk, congregational, and light music styles by different subcommunities of Tamil Protestant Christians. The musical styles chosen by Paraiyar villagers, upwardly mobile lower-caste Nadar urbanites, and evangelical Christians both mirror and reveal the process of meaningful renegotiations of Christian class, caste, and cultural identity. Furthermore, musical ritual functions as a primary context in which Tamil Christians have reconstructed themselves. Adaptation of the *kirttanai* to a folk aesthetic expresses cultural self-esteem for Paraiyars (Dalits), who boldly reclaim folk culture as a worthy vehicle for Christian liturgical content. Simplifying and harmonizing the *kirttanai* with Western harmonic organ accompaniment to a congregational style has made *kirttanai* more accessible and modern for upwardly mobile Nadar Christians, who choose to align themselves with a Western cultural model to gain status vis-à-vis local caste and class elites.

Box 6.1 Exercise

The purpose of this exercise is to associate musical style with cultural meaning.

1. Listen to Indira Peterson sing "Tōttiram Ceyvēṉe" in Bhairavi *raga* (▶ Video example 6.1). Try singing with her, feeling the oscillation of the *gamaka*s (ornamentation) of the karnatak style. (The lyrics can be found in Figures 6.1, 6.2, 6.3, and 6.4)
2. Clap and recite the rhythm ("Jen – ja na ka –") in a six-pulse feel, (which happens twice for every measure of the percussion notation in Figure 6.3). Half the group should continue to recite the rhythmic syllables while the other half claps the melodic rhythm of the Koppuchittampatti village folk version. Then clap the *tavil* percussion line (notated) against the melodic rhythm. Notice how the parts interlock (▶ Video example 6.2 and Figure 6.3 notation).
3. Sing the melody of the folk version Figure 6.3 noting the effect of the flatted seventh scale degree.
4. Sing the congregational version of "Tōttiram Ceyvēṉe" (Figure 6.4) noting any familiarity with the tonality of the melody in C major.

Questions for discussion: Which version do you prefer, and why? Consider both musical and cultural factors. Do qualities of each style suggest specific identities or values? Is one version rhythmically or melodically more interesting? If so, what does that reveal about your own musical preferences and their associations with cultural identities in your musical world?

Finally, Evangelists have used contemporary technology to create light music arrangements of congregational style *kirttanai* to attract the financial support of urban Christians. Performance of these songs contributes to middle-class financial and spiritual prosperity (for Indian missions) and serves as a realm in which village ecstatic expression finds an urban Christian idiom.

The spectrum of Western and indigenous styles employed by Tamil Protestants in Christian songs and liturgies is reflected in various arrangements and inculturations of the *kirttanai*. Musical style aligns with social identity codes, as well as with complex interdynamics of colonial, mission, and local agency that shaped the historical development of Christianity in India. Moreover, musical style becomes the determinant and primary symbol for changing socio-religious identity and meaning.

Works Cited

Appavoo, J. T. 1986. *Folklore for Change*. Madurai: Tamil Nadu Theological Seminary.
Chandler, John S. 1912. *Seventy-Five Years in the Madura Mission*. Madurai: American Madurai Mission.
Chatterjee, Partha. 1993. *The Nation and Its Fragments: Colonial and Postcolonial Histories*. Princeton, NJ: Princeton University Press.
Gunasekaran, K. A. 1988. *Nattuppura Mannum Makkalum*. Chennai: New Century Book House.
Hudson, D. Dennis. 2000. *Protestant Origins in India: Tamil Evangelical Christians, 1706–1835*. Grand Rapids, MI: William B. Erdsman.
Ingalls, Monique M., Muriel Swijghuisen Reigersberg, and Zoe C. Sherinian, eds. 2018. *Making Congregational Music Local in Christian Communities Worldwide*. New York: Routledge.
Kent, Eliza. 2004. *Converting Women: Gender and Protestant Christianity in Colonial South India*. New York: Oxford University Press.
Mohan, Anuradha. 1994. *Ilaiyaraja; Composer as Phenomenon in Tamil Film Culture*. MA thesis, Wesleyan University.
Popley, H. A. 1932. *Tune Book to Tamil Christian Lyrics* (revised), Vol. 1 (kirttanai 1–100). Madras: Christian Literature Society.
Roberts, John Storm. 1972. *Black Music in Two Worlds*. New York: Praeger.
Sherinian, Zoe. 2005. "The Indigenization of Tamil Christian Music: Transculturation and Transformation." *The World of Music* 47(1): 125–165.
Sherinian, Zoe. 2014. *Tamil Folk Music as Dalit Liberation Theology*. Bloomington: University of Indiana Press.
Webb, Rev. Edward. 1875 [1853]. *Christian Lyrics for Public and Social Worship*. 5th ed., revised by G. T. Washburn. Nagercoil, Madras Tract and Book Society.

Archival Sources

Edward Webb to Rufus Anderson, secretary of the ABCFM in Boston. 1854. From Letters and Papers of ABCFM, Vol. 226. Madura Mission, vol. II.

Interviews

M. Thomas Thangaraj. Interview, March 12, 1997. Atlanta, Georgia.

7
Professional Weeping

Music, Affect, and Hierarchy in a South Indian Folk Performance Art

Paul D. Greene

This chapter examines *oppari* (*oppāri*), a lament genre in South Indian folk culture, as performed by professional men from Dalit communities.[1] *Oppari* involves expressive song texts as well as wails, shrieks, sobs, and breathy intakes, sound elements that professionals craft, deploy, and develop deliberately and strategically in performance. The professional performer uses these sounds as music—as performance art—to distance himself from reputation-damaging associations with death, widowhood, and spontaneous emotion. I therefore argue that to define *oppari* as music or non-music is to take sides in ongoing struggles of Dalit musicians over their status within Tamil society.

Although the chapter focuses on professional male performers, *oppari* is primarily understood as a woman's expression. *Oppari* typically takes the form of the grieving lament of a widow at the funeral of her husband. Other *oppari* themes include a woman grieving her husband's unfaithfulness, or a decline in her wealth or standing (Saraswathi 1982). *Oppari* are also used as songs of repentance in a Tamil Christian liturgy composed by Rev. J. T. Appavoo (see Sherinian 2014). Women sometimes perform *oppari* at home, grieving a range of problems and injustices, and their laments carry beyond the home's open-air structures to be overheard by others. Thus, *oppari* constitutes an undercurrent, or secondary code of emotional and substantive expressions.

Although Dalit women appear in public and voice social concerns in work songs (Greene 1995, 240–246), Tamil women of other caste communities,

---

[1] The term Dalit (Marathi: "broken, crushed") is used by some scholars and activists (particularly in the Tamil context) as a self-chosen politicized term of caste opposition. However, in common usage, Dalit is often glossed as outcaste, untouchable, or those designated scheduled caste under India's governmental affirmative action system.

such as the landowning Kallar caste, traditionally live lives more focused in domestic, private spheres, and have fewer opportunities for public expression. Through *oppari*, they can voice personal concerns and protest unfair conditions and injustices. Successful *oppari* performances by women often function not only as cathartic release but also as vehicles of protest and appeals for sympathy, reaching many ears in a village or neighborhood, including those of higher castes. At a funeral, an *oppari* performer also can make claims to the deceased's belongings. *Oppari*, especially when overheard, is therefore a significant expressive opportunity for many rural Tamil women.

Professional male *oppari* performers encroach upon this female expressive space at funerals. As Louis Dumont observes at a Tamil funeral, a purpose of drum music is to "distract" participants with "lively and even tempestuous" sounds (1986, 272). In many cases, male singers, who are often also *parai* (*paṛai*) drummers, are hired to perform the persona of a grieving woman, and possibly also other personae (see Sherinian 2011). As a distraction, this professional *oppari* can become spectacular, involving dramatic buildups of emotional expression, dancing, and buffoonery. This is not to say that the professional *oppari* performer's role is "inauthentic": like women's *oppari*, professional men's *oppari* has a long-standing practice behind it. But I find that professional *oppari* can function to marginalize women's *oppari*, to steal its thunder, and to erase its protest function.

A professional *oppari* musician finds himself in a double bind. On the one hand, he is charged with performing in a way that sounds like the intense, personal, spontaneous expressions of a woman grieving over death. This role in the funeral is a source of income, and also cultural pride for him (see Moffatt 1979, 201). On the other hand, death and widowhood are typically considered dangerous (Wadley 1980, 155). Widowhood has even been called "the most inauspicious of inauspicious things" (Reynolds 1980, 36). Furthermore, spontaneous, personal, intense emotional expressions, although highly valued in certain contexts of Hindu devotion, are more commonly considered "solitary emotions" (Brenneis 1990, 119–121), and their public expression can be taken to indicate "weakness" (Greene 1995, 79–85, 98–106). Thus, professional, male weepers distance themselves from widowhood, death, and emotional spontaneity by performing in ways that are controlled, deliberate, patterned, and "musical"—and thus more reputable. Whether or not an *oppari* performance is considered music is therefore not merely a question for intellectual musing; this is also a highly-loaded question among Tamils, and the performer's social standing is at stake.

There are relatively few studies of lament in ethnomusicology (see Wilce 2009). This may be in part because sounds such as wails, breathy intakes, and sobs tend to be dismissed as non-musical, especially from pitch-based perspectives common in musical analysis (see Box 7.1). For *oppari* more specifically, some Tamil listeners dismiss the performance as emotional outburst, not music. But such assertions, as Raheja and Gold would warn us, can be a means of marginalizing important voices in a society, in this case the voices of women and low-caste men (1994).

As a man writing about an expressive genre that is primarily by and about women, I follow the lead of feminist writers like van Oostrum (1995): I seek not only to analyze, but also to critically reflect on practices in which representations and enactments of women are put forward by men. A deconstruction of professional *oppari* can expose mechanisms by which the traditional form and practice marginalizes women. Professional *oppari* can function as a spectacular, but socially inert, distraction from socially charged expressions of women. Further, the sounds of weeping can be so exaggerated as to become comical. A professional wail can even be subtly crafted to resemble laughter, creating a sonic and emotional double-entendre.

Box 7.1 Exercise 1

In many human societies, a distinction is drawn between activities that can be called "singing" and those that can be called "crying" (Tamil: *pāṭṭu* and *ayira/ararru*, respectively). But the two activities can be understood to be parts of a continuum. Listen to Audio example 7.1, an excerpt of *oppari*. Does this seem to you to be song? Describe how or how not using timbre or other musical concepts and terminology. Does the emotional expression you hear disqualify it as "music"? Explain why or why not. Many music traditions are quite emotional (country, blues), and some songs even include the sounds of actual crying (such as "Daddy" by Korn [1994]). In your opinion, is it possible to draw a boundary between singing and crying? If so, where would you draw the boundary? Use as much musical and aesthetic terminology as possible in your discussion.

A Funeral

My first encounter of *oppari* was at a funeral that took place outside of Isaikurichi in 1995, a village of approximately 4,000.[2] A man of the Kallar (lower-middle) caste community had recently died. In the early evening I made my way to the site of the ceremony, a collection of five buildings in open fields where about 100 people gathered. Villagers lit firecrackers and launched rockets into the air. Five Paraiyar caste (a scheduled caste) drummers had been hired to play *parai* drum music.

The professional musicians were led by a drummer, referred to here by the pseudonym Raja. The leather *parai* frame drum, also called *tappu*, was commonly used in funerals and thereby was traditionally considered polluted (Figure 7.1). Performance alternated between drum patterns and sung phrases in which Raja sang about the dead man.

After some time, Raja performed solo. He sang a few phrases to a repeating incantation melody, and punctuated them with wails and shrieks. Into these wails he incorporated sobbing, breathy intakes, groans, and falsetto. At several points he shed tears. He performed with captivating stage presence and

Figure 7.1 *Parai* drummers in a funeral procession. Photo by Zoe Sherinian; used with permission.

---

[2] Following common anthropological methods, I use a pseudonym for this village: Isaikurichi combines the Tamil words for "music" and "village."

skill. He swayed and danced, lifted his arms and legs, and grinned at times. Perhaps there was too much showmanship. He and his group performed "Rasati," a love song by popular folk singer Pushpavanam Kuppuswamy, and one of the relatives approached, loudly insisting that he return to the occasion at hand. The relative later complained that Raja was thinking about money and his career.

I became aware of wailing and sobbing coming from mourners gathered behind a white sheet. These mourners were the widow, close relatives, and friends. They were mostly women but also included a few men, all crying in a loosely structured, more spontaneous *oppari*. They cried out that their lives were forever changed, and that they would have difficulty supporting themselves. They made arm and hand gestures of two types: (1) a performer struck her fists against her collarbone, then extended both hands forward (called *maradi* or chest beating, Figure 7.2); and (2) a performer clasped both hands against her collarbone on the left side, then lowered the hands to her lap, then raised them to her right side, then back to her lap.

Mourners did not synchronize their expressions, and the result was unsynchronized heterophonic incantation punctuated by sobbing. They leaned into and hugged each other. The grieving grew in volume. Mourners cried out about the dead person, mentioning personal memories of him, his characteristics, and their relation to him. Their expressions settled on a single

Figure 7.2 Women performing *maradi*. Photo by Zoe Sherinian; used with permission.

incantation pitch, sonically conveying a sense of togetherness and shared grief (see ▶ Video example 7.1 cue point 0:24 for a similar example). Their *oppari* continued for about thirty minutes.

Meanwhile in one of the huts, some of the close male relatives decorated a bier (funeral chariot) with flowers and garlands (Figure 7.3). The drummers started again, playing the *tuki adi*, or body-lifting rhythmic pattern. The mourners processed out of the huts to the accompaniment of fireworks, and the body was placed in the bier. Mourning women walked around the cart clockwise several times, performing *oppari*. The men picked up the bier and carried it to the road with the dead man's eldest son leading the way, carrying a pot of burning cow dung. The women followed the procession only as far as the road. There they stopped, huddled down, and continued to cry and hug each other. The men, led by the deceased's eldest son, proceeded with the bier up a small hill, accompanied by firecrackers and energetic *parai* drumming.

The men carried the bier about a third of a kilometer to a cremation site above the fields. When they reached the site, the drumming and firecrackers ceased. The body, wrapped in a pink cloth, was placed on a pile of cow dung covered with sticks and logs. The men covered the body with rice hay and presented coins and rice near the head. The dead man's son lit the hay. The mourners immediately left, and cremation ran its course. After settling the expenses with the members of various hereditary castes who serve funerals, including the musicians on the road nearby, the mourners returned home

Figure 7.3 Funeral bier. Photo by Zoe Sherinian; used with permission.

and bathed to purify themselves from the spiritual pollution of the funeral. Some poured water on themselves as they were leaving.

Oppari and Women

In rural Tamil Nadu at the time of my fieldwork in 1994, traditional codes of modesty often relegated women to their homes and prevented their concerns from being heard. In Isaikurichi, women were excluded from village meetings at which their own wages were negotiated, and they were paid 60 percent of men's salaries for comparable work. There were few recourses for domestic abuse in rural Tamil Nadu. Under most circumstances, a woman channeled her complaints through her parents' household and hoped that they would be taken up by a male relative. Becoming a widow brought on greater hardships. A widow (especially from middle and upper castes) was conventionally considered inauspicious and dangerous, and was therefore excluded from most ritual functions. In Isaikurichi, a widow was expected to wear uncolored (white) saris and not to adorn herself with jewelry or anything that might draw attention. Widows rarely spoke in or involved themselves in public events. They were usually not expected to remarry.[3]

Thus, *oppari* offered a notable opportunity for a rural Tamil woman to express her concerns, appeal for sympathy, and indirectly protest unfair conditions. Although *oppari* lacked prestige, it still presented a significant opportunity for her to have a somewhat prominent voice. Even when performed at home, a woman's *oppari* carried through open windows and doors and could be overheard. Egnor [Trawick] finds that Tamil crying songs could thus successfully communicate grievances up the caste hierarchy (1986). At the Isaikurichi funeral I attended, women used *oppari* to express grief, call for sympathy, and in some cases, assert claims to the possessions left behind by the dead man.

As Reynolds finds, one reason Tamil women were traditionally so carefully controlled by men is that they were believed to be extremely powerful (1980). In countless Tamil folk epics, a good, chaste woman who suffered was attributed a special moral status. Further, if she was wrongly killed, she might become a deity and exact a terrific revenge. An unmarried goddess was

---

[3] Within the lowest castes there were often exceptions to these practices as women were more often equal partners in the economic lives of the family.

worshipped because her female power—*shakti*—made her unpredictable and dangerous, but also potentially a fierce protector of her devotees (1980, 43–44). Unmarried goddesses were among the most important deities in rural Tamil Hinduism, exemplified in Isaikurichi by the popular, protective, and fierce Muttumariamma. Although *oppari* rarely explicitly emphasized that the performer was a "good woman" in the sense developed by Reynolds, it powerfully expressed a woman's suffering as it brought to light injustices and unfair circumstances. Perhaps those listening could imagine some of these special powers of women being invoked, compelling them to listen more closely.

When a woman became a widow, male control and binding—both symbolic and actual—were broken. Like an unmarried goddess, a Tamil widow represented capriciousness and lack of control (Reynolds 1980, 36). But unlike village goddesses, a widow's presence was considered particularly inauspicious not because she was weak, but because she was dangerous (Reynolds 1980, 56; Wadley 1980, 155).

Double Binds of Death and Emotion

Most *oppari*s were about death, which was something from which purification was needed. After the funeral, the mourners immediately bathed, responding to death in ways that were compatible with anthropologist T. N. Madan's understanding of ritual pollution in Hindu culture (1985, 12–13). In this vein, it was the traditional "caste duty" of the Paraiyars to work with dead carcasses, process cow leather, perform the *parai*, and watch over cremation sites, absorbing the pollution of the upper castes or protecting them from it.[4] Yet, through performing these caste duties (*dharma*), they thereby lowered their status and legitimized their oppression in the caste hierarchy.

Raja, his Paraiyar caste, his *parai* frame drum, and the *oppari* genre were all associated with death. It was difficult for him to shake off the association with death, which kept his social standing—and that of his caste community—at the lowest level. Yet, *oppari* and *parai* drumming were also his sources of employment. This presented a double bind: he had to perform and embody the emotions brought about by death because this was his job; at the same time, he had to distance himself, inasmuch as he could, from death and

---

[4] See Mines, "Caste," in Mines and Lamb 2010, 145–151.

widowhood. So he cultivated an aesthetic professionalism that allowed him to do his job, but also maintain some distance from his own performance. In effect, he asserted that his weeping was professional, not personal.

After the funeral, the son of the deceased man explained to me, "At the funeral I must be strong. A man must show no emotion or sadness, even at a funeral of his father. . . . A man must not show weakness in public." I found that many people in the village also made distinctions between "strong" and "weak" actions or emotional expressions. Although the dead man's son did not say that Raja's performance was "weak," a few others from higher caste communities in the village did. "It is just feeling, not skilled, like making music," one said. Public emotional displays, whether deliberately performed or otherwise, were not fitting for a person of prestige. Raja's critics posited that "with education, he would not cry publicly like this."

The ideals voiced by Raja's critics echoed those in classical *rasa* theory: principles of aesthetics and emotional expression articulated in the texts of the Indian high arts. It is debatable whether *rasa* aesthetics comprise a part of one's cultural upbringing in rural India, or indeed among any but the social elite. However, researchers such as Appadurai (1990), Brenneis (1990), and I (Greene 1995, 79ff) have observed everyday practices that embody *rasa*-like ideals. In *rasa* theory, emotion should be cultivated, or "built" (*bhavan*) through stylized gestures. The audience should be contemplative, not over-emotional. Emotional expression may become intense, but never spontaneous. Ramanujan and Gerow describe the ideal theater actor acting "out the conditions that excite the mood and the responses that follow from it: he shudders or faints or sweats, he weeps and his voice cracks" (1974, 128). "The emotion itself . . . is never real; it can only be suggested. Paradoxically, any eruption of real emotion, which is by its nature grounded in individual awareness, would . . . terminate the drama" (1974, 133). This understanding of emotions seemed to underlie critiques of women's *oppari* as women *expressing* "real," personal emotions rather than *performing* the affective trappings of emotions in specific, prescribed, stylized ways. When I asked a middle-caste man whether he considered Raja's *oppari* to be music, he smiled and said, "you decide." Some others simply said no. According to Raja's critics, his performance failed to exhibit such "built" ideals because it imitated "real" expressions of grieving women too closely.

So, in yet another way, professional *oppari* performers were in a double bind. On the one hand, it was essential to the effectiveness of *oppari* that it should at least appear to be rooted in genuine emotion. Professionals had

> **Box 7.2   Exercise 2**
>
> Raja faced conflicting, contradictory concerns in his role as a professional weeper. Can you think of a situation in your life when you faced a double bind? If so, how did you respond?

to offer expressions that could be accepted by participants as appropriate. If they did not succeed, they were reprimanded, as when Raja sang the popular song "Rasati." Yet at the same time, intense emotional expressions evidenced low social standing, according to some high-status villagers.

Double binds shaped the way professional musicians performed *oppari*, and also how they described what they were doing. I asked Raja how he was able to perform with such emotional intensity, and he brought up concerns of being a "strong" performer (as the dead man's son did). He flatly denied that he was channeling grief from his own life (which would be "weakness"). Instead, he insisted he was a professional musician, and that he drew on *musical* skill to craft his expressions, not emotion. He cited his musical apprenticeship, the many kinds of music he knew, and the many years he had performed professionally. He insisted that he had hardly known the man who had died, so his performance was not rooted in emotional "weakness." To him, *oppari* was a matter of musical craftsmanship, not primarily about being emotional.

It was through the artistry of musical expression that Raja arrived at intense emotional expression, not the other way around. Through careful study of pitch, vocal inflection, and rhythm, he explored musical embodiments of sorrow and wove crafted sounds together into an unfolding musical form. Because he was a musician and a professional, he argued that his performance was prestigious, "strong." Further, Raja insisted that he had not been too close to the dead man during life, so his *oppari* was not personal (see Box 7.2).

Musical and Expressive Features of *Oppari*

Taking as an analytic point of departure Raja's claim that his *oppari* performance grew out of musical craftsmanship, I looked for evidence of artistry

PROFESSIONAL WEEPING   123

> **Box 7.3 Exercise 3**
>
> Listen to Audio examples 7.2–7.9. Consider these phrases together as a whole expression. Does Audio example 7.8 sound like an ending of a phrase (half cadence) or of a longer verse (full cadence)? In what ways does this whole musical unit—Audio examples 7.2–7.9—seem as if it may have been deliberately designed?
>
> Plot out this design with your own form of notation. Are there elements of musical repetition or buildup that suggest deliberate musical craftsmanship?

and deliberate patterning in professional *oppari*s performed in rural Tamil Nadu. Analysis in this section is based on four professional musicians in the region.

⏵ Audio examples 7.2 through 7.9 are typical *oppari* incantation melodies (see Box 7.3). *Oppari* consists of melodically similar incanted phrases, performed on a single breath, punctuated by inhalations, and sometimes also by wails and *parai* drumming. Phrases end in what could be called half or full cadences. Cried-out words bring to mind a spontaneous stream of consciousness (Saraswathi 1982) and often gravitate toward bipartite stanzas (Egnor [Trawick] 1986, 299–300). Periodically, the singer's persona cries out to the dead person, addressing him or her generically as "my dear," "you who I brought up," "sir," or as in Raja's *oppari*, "my dear parrot."

A performer marks the end of a group of phrases with a full cadence, sometimes followed by wails, shrieks, or sobs. *Oppari* professionals described the process of crafting and performing these sounds as a musical one, not an emotional one. The professional's skill was in his ability to observe, reproduce, and perhaps exaggerate the sonic trappings of grief.

In Table 7.1 I identify eight distinct features in the punctuating wails used to varying degrees by different professionals. Professional *oppari* performers insisted that their *oppari* was music (*isai*). Their insistence reveals a central thesis of this chapter: that what is at stake in whether or not *oppari* is music reaches well beyond mere intellectual discussion of the definition of music. The definition of music can be caught up in contestations of social standing and prestige and to define *oppari* as music or non-music is to take sides in ongoing struggles of Dalit musicians over their standing within

Table 7.1 Wail features in professional *oppari* analyzed by the author

Wail Feature		Number of Instances
Respiratory Features		
Sobbing	A chain of "cry breaks," or pulses of air pressure built up and then released behind the glottis (Urban 1988, 389–390). This is heard in almost every wail.	238
raspy intake	The performer voices the intake of air. This is most commonly heard following sobbing.	82
sniffling	If the performer is able to produce tears, phrases can be punctuated by audible sniffling.	2
Vocalization Features		
gritty scream	A low-pitched, throaty shriek, related to "creaky voice" (Urban 1988, 390).	85
falsetto	A performer can allow his or her voice to "crack" expressively between normal and falsetto vocalization.	113
Pitch Inflection Features		
up-down arc	Often followed by sobbing.	103
downward slide	The most common pitch inflection.	148
upward slide	Rare.	1

Tamil society.[5] Although this chapter focuses primarily on professional male performers, one can also see that, for many of the same reasons, at stake in such definitions is also the efficacy of Tamil women's use of *oppari* to protest the social injustices they face.

Perhaps for such reasons, social movements to uplift the standing of Dalits, women, and others in Tamil Nadu often employ polished and professionalized folk expressive forms that are most evidently "music," in public (often "folklorized") performances, as vehicles of ongoing social struggle. This *oppari* study suggests some considerations. For example, if an expression becomes too polished—too removed from genuine emotion—is there a risk that it could lose its expressive efficacy in another way: becoming mere artifice, hollow, empty gesture? Does *oppari*'s emotionality guarantee its authenticity? Or could professional *oppari* reach beyond its rootedness in intense emotion and persuade listeners through other rhetorical means? As these social movements continue, we may hear new *oppari* forms emerging.

[5] Sherinian 2011 and 2014 further engage this debate over the value of Tamil folk arts as music.

We may also hear new arguments voiced by the upcoming generations of *oppari* performers—men and women, professional and not—about whether and why it is or is not music.

Works Cited

Appadurai, Arjun. 1990. "Topographies of the Self: Praise and Emotion in Hindu India." In *Language and the Politics of Emotion*, edited by Catherine A. Lutz and Lila Abu-Lughod, 92–112. Cambridge: Cambridge University Press.
Brenneis, Donald. 1990. "Shared and Solitary Sentiments: The Discourse of Friendship, Play, and Anger in Bhatgaon." In *Language and the Politics of Emotion*, edited by Catherine A. Lutz and Lila Abu-Lughod, 113–125. Cambridge: Cambridge University Press.
Dumont, Louis. 1986. *A South Indian Subcaste: Social Organization and Religion of the Pramalai Kallar*. Translated by M. Moffatt and A. Morton. Oxford: Oxford University Press.
Egnor, Margaret [now Margaret Trawick]. 1986. "Internal Iconicity in Paraiyar 'Crying Songs.'" In *Another Harmony: New Essays on the Folklore of India*, edited by Stuart H. Blackburn and A. K. Ramanujan, 294–344. Oxford: Oxford University Press.
Greene, Paul D. 1995. "Cassettes in Culture: Emotion, Politics and Performance in Rural Tamil Nadu." PhD diss., University of Pennsylvania.
Korn. 1994. "Daddy." On *Korn*. CD. Sony Music Entertainment.
Madan, T. N. 1985. "Concerning the Categories of *Subha* and *Suddha* in Hindu Culture: An Exploratory Essay." In *Purity and Auspiciousness in Indian Society*, edited by John B. Carman and Frédérique A. Marglin, 11–29. Leiden: E. J. Brill.
Mines, Diane P., and Sarah Lamb, eds. 2010. *Everyday Life in South Asia*. 2nd ed. Bloomington: Indiana University Press.
Moffatt, Michael. 1979. *An Untouchable Community in South India: Structure and Consensus*. Princeton, NJ: Princeton University Press.
Raheja, Gloria, and Ann G. Gold. 1994. *Listen to the Heron's Words: Reimagining Gender and Kinship in North India*. Berkeley: University of California Press.
Ramanujan, A. K., and Edwin Gerow. 1974. "Indian Poetics." In *The Literatures of India: An Introduction*, edited by Edward C. Dimock, 115–143. Chicago: University of Chicago Press.
Reynolds, Holly Baker. 1980. "The Auspicious Married Woman." In *The Powers of Tamil Women*, edited by Susan S. Wadley, 35–60. Syracuse, NY: Syracuse University Press.
Saraswathi Venugopal. 1982. *Natappura Patalkal (Folk Songs)*. In Tamil. Madurai, India: Madurai Kamaraj University.
Sherinian, Zoe C. 2011. *This Is a Music: Reclaiming an Untouchable Drum*. DVD, 74 mins. Alexander Street Press.
Sherinian, Zoe C. 2014. *Tamil Folk Music as Dalit Liberation Theology*. Bloomington: Indiana University Press.
van Oostrum, Duco. 1995. *Male Authors, Female Subjects: The Woman within/beyond the Borders of Henry James and Others*. Amsterdam: Rodopi.

Urban, Greg. 1988. "Ritual Wailing in Amerindian Brazil." *American Anthropologist* 90: 385–400.

Wadley, Susan S. 1980. "The Paradoxical Powers of Tamil Women." In *The Powers of Tamil Women*, edited by Susan Wadley, 153–170. Syracuse, NY: Syracuse University Press.

Wilce, James M. 2009. *Crying Shame: Metaculture, Modernity, and the Exaggerated Death of Lament*. Chichester: Wiley-Blackwell.

8
Sindhi *Kafi* and Vernacular Islam in Western India

Brian E. Bond

At an intersection in a Muslim neighborhood in Bhuj—the historic capital of Kachchh, a border region in western India—is a tea shop frequented by villagers from rural settlements to the north (see Map 0.1). To a casual visitor, the shop would appear no different from the other countless tea shops in this small, dusty city. For me, though, this humble shop was an invaluable center of learning and networking during my research (between 2014 and 2018) on Sindhi-language Sufi music and poetry in Kachchh. The shop's middle-aged manager, Abdullah "Attaullah" Jat, is a singer of the Sindhi *kafi* (*kāfī*) genre who has performed for three decades. Over the course of my research, I developed a friendship with Abdullah, who commuted daily from his agricultural village. On most days, I would visit him for an hour or so to chat about poetry and music while he sold tea, cigarettes, and sweets. During these informal sessions, Abdullah might show me a video of a Sufi singer from Pakistan, clarify the meaning of a poem, or explain the finer points of Islamic beliefs about what happens after death.

The textual foundation of the Sindhi *kafi* genre is a body of Sufi poetry based on a diverse collection of metaphorical themes. The most prominent of these themes are regional tales known as *qisso* (*qiṣṣo*) or *dastan* (*dāstān*). Among more than a dozen such stories, Abdullah is especially fond of singing poetry based on the tale of Marui (Māru'ī), a peasant girl who was kidnapped by the lustful king 'Umar. Abdullah is unique among local singers in that he composes his own songs. During one of our first meetings in 2014, he sang me a *kafi* he had composed based on the Marui story (▶ Video example 8.1).[1] My comprehension of Sindhi was poor at the time, so Abdullah made

---

[1] Additional performances of Sindhi Sufi music can be found on my YouTube channel, "Sindhi Sufi Music of Kutch": https://www.youtube.com/c/SindhiSufiMusicofKutch/videos.

sure that I received the composition's emotional impact by inserting Urdu translations. Following earlier poets, Abdullah composed the song in Marui's grammatically feminine voice to name the people and things she missed while imprisoned. Abdullah's touching rendition of his *kafi* that day is one among many reasons that I too developed an affinity for the Marui story.

In this chapter, I argue that the interplay between vernacular stories and Islamic meaning in *kafi* generates an emotionally powerful and symbolically rich experience for singers and enthusiasts alike. Focusing on the Marui story, I show how, for men like Abdullah, *kafi* songs are a repository of Sufi philosophical knowledge, references to local lifeways and geography, and moral lessons. Abdullah's musical and poetic journey is also demonstrative of how the contemporary practice of *kafi* in Kachchh emerged from the rise of the audiocassette in the late 1970s and 1980s. Like all *kafi* singers in Kachchh, he was raised in a family of agriculturalist-pastoralists and learned to sing by imitating singers he heard on Pakistani radio and cassettes. As speakers of Kachchhi—an unwritten dialect of Sindhi not officially recognized in India—Muslims in Kachchh have utilized media from Pakistan as a means to increase and sustain their knowledge of Sindhi poetry and music, and of Islamic history and belief. Present-day *kafi* performers in Kachchh continue to transmit this knowledge to their rural Muslim audiences.

The *Kafi* Genre

Indus Valley stories have been kept alive for centuries through melodic poetry performance, and this is still the case today in Kachchh, where *kafi* is the most popular Sufi performance genre. Sindhi Sufi poetry is also performed in the *shah jo rag* (*shāh jo rāḡ*) musical genre and in melodic vocal recitation, which is not considered "music" in Islamic terms because it does not utilize instrumental accompaniment.[2] The *kafi* genre is named after the *kafi* poetic form, which is characterized by monorhyme, in which poetic lines share the same end rhyme. Numerous substyles of *kafi* are popular in Pakistan and western India, and *kafi* compositions are sung in the Sindhi, Punjabi, Kachchhi, and Siraiki languages.

---

[2] See al-Faruqi (1985) for a discussion of the moral parameters of sonic practices in Muslim societies and Shiloah ([1995] 2001) for an overview of debates on the permissibility of music in the Islamic tradition.

The style of *kafi* performed in Kachchh was popularized in the 1970s and 1980s in Pakistan, especially by the singer Ustad Mithoo Kachi and his brothers, the singer Haji Usman Kachi and Hashim Kachi, a *dholak* (*ḍholak*, barrel drum) player. The Kachi brothers were born in Kachchh to a family of Langa hereditary musicians and migrated to Sindh around the time of India's Partition in 1947. From the 1970s onward, many Muslims in Kachchh became ardent fans of Mithoo Kachi. The Kachi brothers' fame was made possible due to the explosion of cassette releases in South Asia during this period (see Manuel 1993). Muslim Kachchhis listened avidly to Pakistani cassettes that were smuggled across the border into India and played on Pakistani radio.

Performances in this style of *kafi* feature a lead vocalist along with one or two backing vocalists and accompanists on harmonium and *dholak*. In Kachchh, all *kafi* singers are non-professional performers from agriculturalist and pastoralist castes/communities,[3] while their *dholak* accompanists belong to the Langa caste/community of Muslim hereditary musicians. Harmonium accompanists include non-professional agriculturalists as well as professional Langa musicians. These caste/community distinctions of musical labor reflect the fact that Langa professional musicians do not view *kafi* singing as a lucrative pursuit, whereas performers from agriculturalist communities can afford to pursue *kafi* singing as a hobby. Langa musicians focus on developing instrumental skills that will serve them in a variety of performance contexts, especially Hindu and Jain marriages and religious events from which they draw most of their income.

An important feature of the Mithoo Kachi style of *kafi* is the lead singer's insertion of recited or spoken storytelling and verse explication between sung poetic texts. Singers use storytelling and explication to flesh out the story on which the poetry is based, and to explain the poetry's Islamic meanings. In this way, they act as informal Islamic teachers (see Bond 2020).[4] The cassette medium was well suited to this style because it was a cheap format that could store long performances with storytelling portions. Through repeated listening to cassettes, singers and enthusiasts in Kachchh learned song texts, stories, and the Islamic meanings of poetic texts. By imitating

---

[3] Muslims in Kachchh often use terms such as *qaum* (nation, tribe, people) and *samaj* (society, community) rather than *jati* (caste).

[4] Compare with the similar practice by Marathi *kirtankar*s in Schultz*.

these recordings, singers in Kachchh extend this tradition of musical Islamic instruction.

Kafi singers perform poetry in a variety of melody types, known as *sur* or *ragini* (*rāgiṇī*) in Sindhi and Kachchhi. Some of these melody types are shared with Hindustani music practices, while others are particular to Sindhi repertoire. In some cases, a Sindhi *sur* may share a name with a Hindustani *raga* (*rāga*) but be substantially different (e.g., Tilang). Whereas Hindustani music practitioners emphasize improvisation, *kafi* performers use melody types as vehicles for performing poetry. *Kafi* singers begin a performance with a short *alap* (*ālāp*, exposition of a melody type), and then sing poetic verses and a main song text. Although *kafi* singers do incorporate melodic elaboration into their performances, its primary purpose is to enhance the poetry's emotional impact rather than to explore the contours of the *raga*, as Hindustani singers do in genres such as *khayal* (*khayāl*). And while *kafi* shares aspects of melodic and rhythmic repertoire and technique with Hindustani music, its audience and practitioners do not consider it "classical music." *Kafi* may thus be considered an "intermediate" genre of South Asian music (Manuel 2015).

The Tale of 'Umar and Marui

The 'Umar-Marui story is based on events of fourteenth-century Sindh and has been passed down orally through poetry performance and spoken storytelling. The story unfolds in locales on both sides of the modern-day India-Pakistan border. In this tale, the young man Phogsen asks the father of the beautiful goatherd girl Marui for Marui's hand in marriage. Marui's father declines because he has promised her to another man, Khetsen. Phogsen, angered by the rejection, takes revenge by going to the local ruler 'Umar and tempting him with descriptions of Marui's beauty. With Phogsen's help, 'Umar abducts Marui while she is drawing water from the well and imprisons her in his palace-fort, 'Umarkot.[5] 'Umar tries to tempt Marui with fine foods, clothes, and jewelry in the hope that she will agree to marry him, but Marui resists his temptations. She weeps constantly and expresses her longing to return to her village and be reunited with her people. Marui tells 'Umar that she could never be his wife because she is already married, and because 'Umar is like a brother to her. After some time, a palace

---

[5] 'Umarkot, which means "'Umar's Fort," is the name of a city in southeastern Pakistan.

milkmaid reveals that, by a twist of fate, 'Umar and Marui had suckled side by side at her breast as infants, making them siblings (by milk). When 'Umar hears this, he regrets his actions and returns Marui to her village, Malir.

Because this story has been passed down orally, there are multiple versions of the ending. In one version, Marui, who had refused to eat while imprisoned, dies upon returning to Malir. In another, she returns home only to have her husband Khetsen cast doubt upon her character (Sayed [1988] 2000, 92). To quell Khetsen's suspicions of her infidelity, Marui and 'Umar undergo a test in which they each hold a red-hot iron rod. Both suffer no injury, thus proving their innocence, and Marui lives happily ever after with Khetsen.[6]

Sufi Philosophy and Vernacular Islam

Stories have historically been an important means for conveying Islamic teachings in South Asia. The spread of Islam in this area of the Muslim world was facilitated in part by Sufi poets who composed allegorical poetry based on vernacular romances. Since at least the thirteenth century, Sufi poets disseminated Islamic teachings to populations that were not literate or did not understand Arabic and Persian, the languages in which most classical Islamic texts are written (Eaton 1974; Asani 1988). Sung poetry has thus been integral to the "vernacularization" of Islam in South Asia (Anjum 2017), a process by which Islamic ideas were assimilated to local languages, symbols, and practices.

What is Sufism? As Annemarie Schimmel once observed, "the phenomenon usually called Sufism is so broad and its appearance so protean that nobody can venture to describe it fully" (1975, 3). Schimmel defined Sufism as "Islamic mysticism": a path toward union with the divine that consists not of mere intellectual contemplation, but of the cleansing of one's heart in order to fully realize one's love for God. One shortcoming of this definition is that "mysticism" can suggest a set of spiritual practices not geared toward common people. However, "Sufism—the theory and practice of holistic, experiential knowing of Divine Truth—was, for over a millennium, a foundational, commonplace and institutionalized conceptual and social

---

[6] Readers might productively compare the tale of 'Umar and Marui and the Ramayana, discussed in Morelli*, particularly the experiences of the tales' heroines, Marui and Sita.

phenomenon in societies of Muslims" (Ahmed 2015, 20). The trajectory of Islam changed with the growth of reformist movements in the late eighteenth and nineteenth centuries, which led many Muslims to reject aspects of what we now call Sufism.

Although many South Asian Muslims have adopted reformist perspectives, Sufi Islam remains vibrant (Gillani*). In Kachchh, most Muslims adhere to the teachings of the Ahl-e Sunnat wa al-Jama'at, a Sunni traditionalist movement that remains attached to beliefs and practices associated with Sufism. Most important among these is the belief that holy individuals—living and deceased—can intercede with God on a devotee's behalf. These individuals are known as "friends of God" (Arabic: *auliyā Allāh*).

Shah 'Abdul Latif Bhitai

One such "friend of God," Shah 'Abdul Latif Bhitai (Shāh 'Abdul Laṭīf Bhiṭā'ī; 1689–1752), is also the most significant figure in the history of Sindhi music and poetry. It is difficult to overstate his importance in the cultural world of greater Sindh, where he is known as Shah Bhitai, Shah Latif, Shah *sahib* ("sir, lord"), and by other titles. Greater Sindh includes Sindh, in Pakistan, as well as Kachchh and parts of western Rajasthan in India. Although cross-cultural analogies are always imperfect, one might think of Shah Bhitai as a combination of Saint Francis of Assisi, William Shakespeare, and J. S. Bach to get a sense of his significance as a spiritual, literary, and musical figure in the Sindhi cultural world.

Shah Bhitai composed poetry based on about thirty themes, including but not limited to Indus Valley stories (*qiṣṣo, dāstān*). In doing so, he built on a model established by earlier Indus Valley poets, including his great-great-grandfather Shah 'Abdul Karim (1536–1623), Shah 'Inat (c. 1623–1712), and the Punjabi poet Shah Husain (1539–1599). Shah Bhitai allegorized over a dozen narratives, most of which are tragic romances that feature female protagonists who occupy an inferior social position relative to their male counterparts.

Shah Bhitai's poetic repertoire is intimately linked to musical performance. His poetic compendium *Shah Jo Risalo* (*Shāh Jo Risālo*, "Shah's Treatise") is organized into thematic groupings, each headed by the name of a melody type (*sur*). In Sindhi, *sur* means "melody type" and has a meaning synonymous with *raga*, in addition to its more common meaning of "note" or "tone."

Sur Marui, Shah Bhitai's collection of poetry based on the Marui tale, can thus be translated as "Melody of Marui."

Shah's allegorical approach to these stories is undergirded by the Sufi philosophical distinction between two levels of existence and meaning. One level is *majaz* (*majāz*), an Arabic term meaning "figure" or "metaphor" that refers to the visible, material world. A higher level of existence is *haqiqah* (*ḥaqīqah*), an Arabic term for "truth" or "reality" that refers to divine existence. Put simply, all that we experience and see in our worldly existence is a metaphor for the existential reality of God. In accordance with this distinction, worldly love (*ishq-i majāzī*) is a metaphor for—and a path to developing—"real love" (*ishq-i ḥaqīqī*), or love for God.

The Feminine Voice

Shah Bhitai emphasized women's experiences in his renderings of regional tales. In his poetry, a woman who longs to be reunited with her beloved is a metaphor for the devotee who longs to be close to God (Schimmel 1997; Abbas 2002). Poetry enthusiasts thus understand Marui's painful longing to return to her people to be a metaphor for the human soul's longing for reunion with God. Extending this approach, Shah Bhitai composed much of his poetry in the grammatically feminine voices of female characters. Shah was not unique in this regard, as the trope of the feminine voice had been central to South Asian devotional poetry for centuries prior. Shah's use of this device is one among many examples of how Sufi poets exchanged literary techniques and philosophical ideas with Hindu *bhakti* (devotional) poets, who similarly employed the feminine voice (see Petievich 2007).[7] It is important to note that male poets' use of the feminine voice is not reflective of their gender identity. Rather, the motivation underlying this trope is a notion that females are more emotional and vulnerable than males and thus predisposed to being good devotees (see Hawley [2005] 2012).

This emphasis on female vulnerability and emotionality is evident in Shah Bhitai's Marui-themed poetry, much of which is composed from Marui's perspective during her imprisonment. For example, in the *bait* (verse) below,

---

[7] Feminine-voiced *bhakti* poetry forms the lyrical basis of multiple Hindustani music genres, such as *khayal*, *thumri*, and *dadra* (see Rao 1990).

Marui appeals to God to let her return to her village before she dies. In *kafi* performance, singers perform such *bait*s before singing the main *kafi* composition (see ⏵ Video example 8.2, 0:00–1:12):

VI:5[8]
alā! i'an̠ ma ho'i, ji'an̠ ān̠ marān̠ banda men̠!
juso zanjīrani men̠, rāto ḍīn̠hān̠ ro'i,
paharīn̠ vañān̠ lo'i, po'i maru pujanimi ḍīn̠han̠rā!

Allah! Don't let me die imprisoned!
Body in chains, crying night and day,
First let me go home, then my days can be completed!

Metaphor, Meaning, and Emotion in *Kafi*

Abdullah (Figure 8.1) and I often returned to the topic of Marui in our conversations. In March 2018, we traveled north from Bhuj to attend a celebration of another singer's father's completion of a pilgrimage to Mecca. Abdullah sat on the back of my scooter as I drove through the arid landscape. The greenery lining the road was deceptive: since the 1960s, Kachchh has been overrun by an invasive acacia species known locally as "poisonous acacia" (*jeheri bavar*). When we stopped to rest, Abdullah pointed out an exception: a *Salvadora oleoides* tree, which is known locally as *jar* and produces a fruit called *pirun* that Abdullah mentions in his *kafi* composition. Abdullah pointed out that Shah Bhitai mentions this tree in *Sur Marui* by another name, *khabar*, and recited a verse as an example. This encounter with nature revealed how Abdullah's experience of the landscape is inflected by his knowledge of Sufi poetry. On other occasions, he described how verses from *Sur Marui* that describe pastoralist lifeways reminded him of grazing goats as a boy. When singing Shah Bhitai's poetry, Abdullah draws on these emotional associations and local forms of knowledge as well as from his understanding of Sufi philosophy.

Because Abdullah's own musical training was informal, his strength in teaching me was less in instructing me in vocal technique, and more in

---

[8] All verse numbers correspond to Kalyan Advani's Sindhi edition of *Shāh Jo Risālo* ('Abd al-Laṭīf 1994).

Figure 8.1 Abdullah Jat at his tea shop, 2017. Photo by the author.

stressing the emotive aspects of performance as they relate to poetic texts. He stressed that a singer needs to feel Marui's pain of longing in order to convey that pain to one's listeners. Abdullah said that when he sings Marui-themed poetry, he thinks about how all humans are like Marui, because we are all imprisoned in this world. By this, he meant that all humans must face hardship as embodied inhabitants of the material world, and that, like Marui, who longs to return to her village, we long to be reunited with God after death.

Another topic that Abdullah often raised was how Marui was an exemplary woman because she refused 'Umar's offers of fine foods and jewelry in exchange for marriage in order to preserve the honor of her family. On a recent phone call, he said, "I don't think that there could be any woman like Marui in this day and age. She was ready to die to save her parents' honor. What a courageous woman she was!" (personal communication, December 30,

2020). He went on to lament what he perceived as a lack of modesty (*sharm*) among young women in Kachchh today, saying that they increasingly wear revealing clothing, a trend he blamed on Westernization and Hindi films. These comments reveal how, for Abdullah, the emotional power of Marui as a symbol of vulnerability is inseparable from the patriarchal expectation that women should act as vessels of family honor.

Abdullah's reflections on the Marui story demonstrate how listening to and performing Sufi poetry in the *kafi* genre generates multilayered interpretations and emotional responses. Table 8.1 shows in schematic form how levels of meaning are associated with different poetic interpretations, which in turn encourage different kinds of emotional experience. While this table is useful for visualizing these layers, it is important to stress that there is fluidity between them.

Table 8.1 Levels of poetic meaning in *Sur Marui*

Level of Meaning	Poetic Interpretations	Potential Emotional Responses
"Real" (*ḥaqīqī*) meanings	Marui symbolizes the pure soul (*rūḥ*) longing for reunion with God; 'Umar symbolizes the desiring self (*nafs*); 'Umar's fort symbolizes the human body; Marui's shackles symbolize human desires.	Reflection on mortality and one's relationship with God.
Islamic allusions	Enthusiasts interpret some *Sur Marui* verses to be references to Sakinah, the Prophet Muhammad's great-granddaughter who was imprisoned by Yazid after the Battle of Karbala in 680 CE.	A strengthening of faith through reflection on the sacrifices made by important figures in Islamic history.
"Figural" (*majāzī*) meanings	Marui-themed poetic texts recount emotional episodes from the Marui tale and include references to regional geography and flora.	Sympathy for Marui. Reflection on one's own experiences of loss and longing. Geographical references may inflect how one moves through the landscape. Reflection on moral lessons on gender roles and norms.

A Marui-themed *Kafi*

Although Shah Bhitai's poetry is the foundation of *kafi* singers' repertoire, they also sing compositions by later poets who drew on Shah's poetic model. The *kafi* text below was composed by the twentieth-century poet Haji Shah. The mid-twentieth-century Pakistani singer Noor Banu performed her famous rendition of this *kafi* in Manjh, a melody type particular to Sindh, Kachchh, and western Rajasthan.[9] Although Sindhi *kafi* singers typically follow their introductory *alap* (melodic exposition) with a verse (*bait*) by Shah Bhitai, Noor Banu does not sing a *bait* in this recording. Following a brief *alap*, she sings the refrain (*thalu*) of the composition. After each strophe (*misra'*), she repeats the refrain. In the text below, notice how *mīru* (bolded) in the first line of the refrain rhymes with *taqdīru*, and how the last word of each strophe rhymes with these two words of the refrain.[10] Also, notice how the last word of the first three lines of each strophe share an end rhyme. Another noteworthy feature is the poet Haji Shah's verbal signature (underlined) in the final strophe, a common practice in South Asian poetry.

"Kaḍhu Koṭana Mān̲"

Refrain
kaḍhu koṭana mān̲ 'umaru **mīru** (mūn̲khe)
hiti āndo khaṇī **taqdīru** (mūn̲khe)

'Umar, release me from this fort,
Fate snatched me up and brought me here.

Strophe 1
rāti 'umaru mūn̲ khvābu ladho
mun̲hinje mārana te ḍāḍho min̲han̲ro vaṭho
tun̲hinjī māṛī'a caṛhiyo mūn̲ bīṭhe ḍiṭho
ḍāḍhī thara jī lagī thadaṛī **hīru**

---

[9] Noor Banu's rendition of "Kaḍhu Koṭana Mān̲" is currently available at: https://www.youtube.com/watch?v=1yqI3vISjzQ.

[10] Sindhi is a vowel-ending language, and terminal short vowels are pronounced shorter than medial short vowels.

'Umar, I had a dream last night,
A heavy rain fell upon my people.
I climbed up to the top of your palace and looked out,
I felt a strong, cool wind from the Thar [Desert].

Strophe 2
rāti 'umaru tokhe 'ishqu lağo
ā'ūn thī bhāyān munhinjo bhā ain sağo
hī'a ki'an pāyān tunhinjo vesu vağo
hī'a lo'ī kā abānī līṛa

'Umar, at night you are overtaken by love.
I think of you as my brother and my relation.
How can I wear these fine clothes of yours?
All I want is the tattered woolen shawl of my people.

Strophe 3
cave Ḥājī Shāh kari qyāsi miṭhā
heḍānhan ni'aru ain nimāṇī kaḍahen ki'an na saṭhā
munhinje mārū miṭhā na ta dil tān lahaṇu
virāhe ḍiyaṇu vaṭana men khaṇḍu khīru

Haji Shah says, please respect me,
These chains in which I am humbled here have never suited me at all.
My dear people will never be erased from my heart,
All I want is the bowl of milk and sugar that my people and I split
    amongst ourselves.

Kafi compositions like "Kaḍhu Koṭana Mān" are a fertile field of metaphorical meanings and emotional associations for performers and listening enthusiasts (Box 8.1). Rooted in knowledge of local lifeways and regional folktales, *kafi*s reference aspects of Sufi philosophy and Islamic belief. There are numerous possible interpretations of this *kafi*, some of which are sketched out in Table 8.1. By listening to live and recorded *kafi* performances, and through discussion with knowledgeable elders, Sufi poetry singers and enthusiasts gradually deepen their understanding of these Islamic meanings.

Box 8.1 Song and Reflection

Singing a *Kafi*

1. Find online and listen to Noor Banu's rendition of "Kaḍhu Koṭāna Mā<u>n</u>" while following along with the transliteration and translation provided in this chapter.
2. Prepare to sing the refrain of "Kaḍhu Koṭana Mā<u>n</u>" by counting the seven-beat metrical structure *rupak tal*. You may find it helpful to feel these seven beats in three groupings: 1 2 3 + 4 5 + 6 7.
3. Sing the refrain of "Kaḍhu Koṭana Mā<u>n</u>" using the notation provided in Figure 8.2. This notation is a simplified version of Noor Banu's rendition. If you are not familiar with reading the *sargam* or staff notation provided, try to sing along with Noor Banu's recording. (*Sargam* refers to the syllables Sa Re Ga Ma Pa Dha Ni, which represent scale degrees 1 2 3 4 5 6 7.)

Discussion and Reflection

1. According to Abdullah, the fort in this *kafi* symbolizes the human body and Marui symbolizes the soul. Can you think of an alternative interpretation relevant to your own life? What might the fort symbolize?
2. As you sing from Marui's perspective, consider why Sufi poets chose to compose songs in the voices of young women who occupied a disadvantaged position due to their caste background and gender. Discuss with your classmates: besides those reasons discussed above, why might male poets have composed in the feminine voice?
3. Having reflected on these questions, listen once more to "Kaḍhu Koṭana Mā<u>n</u>" and try singing the refrain again. Has it taken on a new meaning or emotional significance?

Figure 8.2 Refrain of "Kaḍhu Koṭāna Māṅ."

The musical performance of poetry based on narratives like the ʿUmar-Marui story thus serves as an emotionally powerful and entertaining medium for transmitting Islamic teachings about how to conduct oneself in the material world in order to ensure closeness with God after death.

Works Cited

Abbas, Shemeem Burney. 2002. *The Female Voice in Sufi Ritual: Devotional Practices of Pakistan and India*. Austin: University of Texas Press.

ʿAbd al-Laṭīf, Shāh. 1994. *Shāh Jo Risālo*. Edited by Kalyan Advani. Karachi: Kathiawad Stores.

Ahmed, Shahab. 2015. *What Is Islam?: The Importance of Being Islamic*. Princeton, NJ: Princeton University Press.

Anjum, Tanvir. 2017. "Vernacularization of Islam and Sufism in South Asia: A Study of the Production of Sufi Literature in Local Languages." *Journal of the Research Society of Pakistan* 54(1): 190–207.

Asani, Ali S. 1988. "Sufi Poetry in the Folk Tradition of Indo-Pakistan." *Religion & Literature* 20(1): 81–94.

Bond, Brian E. 2020. "Teaching Islam in Song: Storytelling and Islamic Meaning in Sindhi Sufi Poetry Performance." *Asian Music* 51(2): 39–71.

Eaton, Richard. 1974. "Sufi Folk Literature and the Expansion of Indian Islam." *History of Religions* 14(2): 117–127.
al-Faruqi, Lois Ibsen. 1985. "Music, Musicians, and Muslim Law." *Asian Music* 17(1): 3–36.
Hawley, John Stratton. (2005) 2012. *Three Bhakti Voices: Mirabai, Surdas, and Kabir in Their Times and Ours*. New Delhi: Oxford University Press.
Manuel, Peter. 1993. *Cassette Culture: Popular Music and Technology in North India*. Chicago: Chicago University Press.
Manuel, Peter. 2015. "The Intermediate Sphere in North Indian Music Culture: Between and Beyond 'Folk' and 'Classical.'" *Ethnomusicology* 59(1): 82–115.
Petievich, Carla. 2007. *When Men Speak as Women: Vocal Masquerade in Indo-Muslim Poetry*. New Delhi: Oxford University Press.
Rao, Vidya. 1990. "'Thumri' as Feminine Voice." *Economic and Political Weekly* 25(17): 31–39.
Sayed, Durreshahwar. (1988) 2000. *The Poetry of Shah Abdal-Latif*. Jamshoro, Sindh: Sindhi Adabi Board.
Schimmel, Annemarie. 1975. *Mystical Dimensions of Islam*. Chapel Hill: University of North Carolina Press.
Schimmel, Annemarie. 1997. *My Soul Is a Woman*. New York: Continuum.
Shiloah, Amnon. (1995) 2001. *Music in the World of Islam: A Socio-cultural Study*. Detroit: Wayne State University Press.

9
Music, Religious Experience, and Nationalism in Marathi *Rashtriya Kirtan*

Anna Schultz

Throughout the twentieth and twenty-first centuries, India has been marred by waves of Hindu nationalist violence, even as Hinduism has inflected political discourse on the Left, the Right, and everywhere in between. A robust body of scholarship interrogates the politicians and nationalist organizations who use religion to further India's nationalist agendas,[1] but less attention has been given to nationalism as it seeps into ritual contexts. I argue that to understand the emotional registers of Hindu nationalism, we must pay attention to how nationalism becomes religious experience, a process often activated through music. This chapter attends to singer-storytellers known as *rashtriya kirtankar*s (*rāṣṭrīya kīrtankār*) who generate devotion to nationalism (Hindu and otherwise) through spirited ritual performances. Using examples from two *kirtankar*s on different points of the political spectrum, I consider how meanings are shaped and emotions are generated in *rashtriya kirtan* through participation, ritual, and the careful combination of diverse musical signifiers.

Nationalism in India

Historian Benedict Anderson has defined the nation as "an imagined political community—and imagined as both inherently limited and sovereign" (2006, 5–6). Nations are "limited" in that every nation constructs boundaries beyond which there are other nations and are "sovereign" in that they aspire to be freely self-governed. According to Anderson, national identity emerged as a new way of "imagining" connectedness with those one would

---

[1] See, e.g., Hansen 1999; Jaffrelot 1999; Rajagopal 2001.

Anna Schultz, *Music, Religious Experience, and Nationalism in Marathi* Rashtriya Kirtan In: *Music and Dance as Everyday South Asia.* Edited by: Sarah L. Morelli and Zoe C. Sherinian, Oxford University Press. © Oxford University Press 2024. DOI: 10.1093/oso/9780197566237.003.0010

never meet, but with whom one felt a common, almost familial bond. He asks how emotional attachments to community make "it possible, over the past two centuries, for so many millions of people, not so much to kill, as [to be] willing to die for such limited imaginings" (Anderson 2006, 7). In this chapter, I argue that we can understand these attachments only if we take seriously the contexts in which nationalist emotion emerge.

India was founded as a secular nation-state in 1947 following a hard-fought struggle against a century of British rule. In the 1980s and 1990s, Hindu nationalist parties wrenched ethno-religious nationalism from the margins to the center of Indian political discourse. These parties have worked with ostensibly apolitical organizations to reimagine India as a Hindu nation in which religious minorities, especially Muslims, are deemed outsiders.[2]

In 1998 and 2014, coalitions led by the Hindu nationalist BJP (Bharatiya Janata Party, Indian People's Party) won national elections, and 1992 and 2002 saw devastating waves of Hindu nationalist violence, but these flashpoints tell only a partial story. Less extreme nationalist imaginaries continue to live in tension with Hindu nationalism, and nationalist emotion is incubated in everyday contexts regardless of the party in power. In India, as in many locales, religious performance provides an everyday pathway toward "imagined community." Within those contexts, the emotions generated by music's participatory potential and semiotic malleability—the ways in which the meanings of sounds and words can be shaped by a performer—help transform nationalist ideas into religious experience.

Emotion, Religion, and Nationalism in Marathi *Kirtan*

One genre in which music is used to generate nationalist emotion in India is *rashtriya kirtan*, a Marathi Hindu performance genre combining religious discourse, nationalist storytelling, and song. Marathi is the official state language of Maharashtra—a large and politically powerful state in western India. Rather than fracturing the nation into smaller units seeking independence, nationalist songs in regional languages can serve to generate emotions of attachment to the Indian nation. Marathi songs are intertwined with

---

[2] According to the 2011 census, 79.8% of the Indian population was Hindu and 14.2% was Muslim. In Maharashtra, 79.8% was Hindu and 11.5% was Muslim. ("Census Tables," Office of the Registrar General and Census Commissioner, India, accessed June 8, 2022, https://censusindia.gov.in/census.website/data/census-tables#.)

everyday life and religious ritual; when these songs are combined with nationalism, they imbue politics with emotions of family and religion. In other words, they help singers and listeners feel that they not only belong to the Indian nation, but more important, *that the Indian nation belongs to them.*

There are three main genres of Marathi *kirtan—naradiya* (*nāradīya*), *varkari* (*vārkarī*), and *rashtriya* (*rāṣṭrīya*)—each of which indexes a distinct caste complex, style, and religious orientation (see Table 9.1). Since at least the thirteenth century, Marathi *kirtankar*s have combined song and storytelling in ways that move between participation and solo presentation. By the nineteenth century, differences between those performers who emphasized participation and those who emphasized presentation coalesced into distinct performance practices: *naradiya kirtan* and *varkari kirtan* (Schultz 2013, 1–78). Though this chapter is about *rashtriya kirtan*, I begin with brief descriptions of these two genres because the style and form of *rashtriya kirtan* is modeled on *naradiya kirtan*, and *rashtriya kirtankar*s use some conventions from *varkari kirtan*, described below.

Varkari kirtan is the most participatory of the three kirtan genres. The *kirtankar* (usually male, of any caste) is accompanied by a *pakhawaj* (*pakhavāja*, double-headed barrel drum) player, audience, and a chorus of men called *talkari* (*ṭāḷakarī*) who sing, dance, and play small, concave

Table 9.1 Comparison of *varkari, naradiya,* and *rashtriya kirtan*

Varkari Kirtan	Naradiya Kirtan	Rashtriya Kirtan
Male *kirtankar* of any caste	Male or female *kirtankar*, usually Brahman	Male or female *kirtankar,* usually Brahman
Worship of Vitthala and *varkari* saints	Worship of various deities	Worship of various deities, especially Rama
Emphasizes participation	Emphasizes solo performance	Emphasizes solo performance
Songs: *abhanga*s and bhajans	Eclectic array of Marathi songs	Eclectic array of songs, esp. *povada, kattav, rajahan*s ("nationalist")
Soloist and chorus, with *tal* and *pakhawaj*	Soloist with *jhanj*, harmonium, *tabla*	Soloist with *jhanj*, harmonium, *tabla*
Form: Introductory songs + discourse on a philosophical topic + concluding songs	Form: Introductory songs + *purvaranga* (discourse) + interval + *uttararanga* (story on a nationalist hero) + concluding songs	Form: Introductory songs + *purvaranga* (discourse) + interval + *uttararanga* (story on a nationalist hero) + concluding songs

hand cymbals called *tal* (*tāḷa*). *Varkari kirtan* draws inspiration from the *varkari* religious tradition, a Marathi Hindu devotional sect dedicated to Vitthala, a regional incarnation of the God Vishnu.[3] Like other devotional (*bhakti*) traditions, *varkari* philosophy asserts that anyone can reach the divine through accessible, vernacular means (Schultz 2013, 23–24). In *varkari kirtan*, the *kirtankar* initiates the songs that pepper his spoken discourse, while *talkari*s and audience members join him in call-and-response. *Varkari kirtankar*s use two main song genres: *abhanga* (*abhaṅga*) and *bhajan*. In the Marathi *kirtan* context, *bhajan* refers to a sung repetition of the names of the divine, such as "*Jayjay Rāma Kriṣṇa Hari*" ("Glory to Rama, Krishna, and Vishnu"; see Figure 9.1 at the end of this chapter), while each *abhanga* includes at least four distinct couplets, usually in praise of Vitthala. The name of the poet-saint author is woven into the final couplet.

Naradiya kirtan is performed by a male or female vocal soloist (usually Brahmin) who plays *jhanj* (*jhāñja*, small, flat hand cymbals) and is accompanied by a *tabla* player and harmonium player. In contrast with *varkari kirtan*, it is primarily presentational,[4] with participation emerging only briefly during the introductory, intermission, and concluding songs. Some songs in *naradiya kirtan* are informed by Hindustani *ragas* (*rāga*) and performance practices. While *varkari kirtan* has only one section, *naradiya kirtan* is divided into two parts of approximately equal length—the *purvaranga* (*pūrvaraṅga*), a spoken philosophical discourse on a particular theme, and the *uttararanga* (*uttararaṅga*), an illustrative story on that theme from the life of a saint. Speech within the *purvaranga* is occasionally interrupted with a verse in Sanskrit or a short song composed by a Marathi saint, but spoken storytelling in the *uttararanga* is more continuously enhanced by songs drawn from a wide range of Marathi song genres (Schultz 2013, 23, 47–48, 138–139).

Rashtriya kirtan has the same form as *naradiya kirtan*, and like *naradiya kirtankar*s, most *rashtriya kirtankar*s are Brahmin. The main

---

[3] Marathi poet-saints composed *varkari* songs (*abhanga*s) between the thirteenth and seventeenth centuries; these songs and the biannual pilgrimage to Vitthala's temple in Pandharpur comprise the backbone of *varkari* practice (Schultz 2013, 23–24).

[4] I use the terms "presentational" and "participatory" as defined by Thomas Turino: "*participatory performance* is a special type of artistic practice in which there are no artist-audience distinctions, only participants and potential participants performing different roles, and the primary goal is to involve the maximum number of people in some performance role. *Presentational performance*, in contrast, refers to situations where one group of people, the artists, prepare and provide music for another group, the audience, who do not participate in making the music or dancing" (2008, 26).

difference between *naradiya* and *rashtriya kirtan* is that stories of saints in the *uttararanga* are substituted with stories of nationalist leaders. In addition to the regular host of song genres in *naradiya kirtan*, one might hear genres that evoke history, nationalism, and patriotism. Of the three forms of *kirtan* outlined here, only *rashtriya kirtan* is explicitly nationalist.

Most early twenty-first century *rashtriya kirtankars* trace their practice to Dattopant Patwardhan, a homeopathic doctor known for his association with B. G. Tilak, a Maharashtrian nationalist who agitated against British colonialism in the early twentieth century (Schultz 2013, 56–65). Since independence in 1947, the goals of *rashtriya kirtan* have become more diffuse. In 2009, I asked *kirtankar* Sudhatai Dhamankar to define *rashtriya kirtan*. She said, "During [Dr. Patwardhan's] time, *rashtriya kirtan* was used to awaken the masses and fuel the struggle against the British rulers. But now there are no unwanted rulers or fights. So now *rashtriya kirtan* is used to mold a nation toward development, liberation of the people, introduction of newer philosophies and political awakening" (interview with the author, July 12, 2009).

In other words, India is now an independent state, but concerns of governance and national identity must constantly be negotiated. Which national issues are given importance? What is the identity and character of the nation? To whom should one look for leadership? These questions are at the core of a vigorous debate in which *rashtriya kirtankars* are active participants. Some *kirtankars* draw on Hindu philosophy to support social justice, caste and gender equity, and inter-religious harmony, while Hindu nationalist *kirtankars* seek to form a Hindu "in-group." Today, the majority of *rashtriya kirtankars* fall into the latter category. Even if they are not directly involved with Hindu nationalist parties, their work echoes those parties' efforts to establish caste-based orthopraxis and exclude Muslims, Christians, and other religious minorities from the nation.

Two *Rashtriya Kirtans*

The two *kirtans* discussed below are in some ways typical and other ways extraordinary. Most *rashtriya kirtankars* are men, but both these performers are women: a Muslim named Jaytumbi Maqbulbhai Sayyed (1930–2010) and a Hindu Brahmin named Sudhatai Dhamankar (born in the 1940s). Jaytumbi and Sudhatai have led unconventional lives to pursue religious leadership and performance.⁵ Women of their generation were expected to adopt the roles of wife and mother, but Jaytumbi took a vow of celibacy and founded a religious hermitage. Sudhatai was a married woman and teacher who brought her husband to live with her at the *ashram* (*āśram*, hermitage) of her *guru* (spiritual teacher). Their *kirtan*s tend to emphasize the bravery and everyday experiences of women. As unconventional female leaders who elevate women's issues, Sudhatai and Jaytumbi are feminists, but by telling stories that valorize service to husband and family, they also propagate normative gender roles.

Sudhatai Dhamankar

When I traveled with Sudhatai⁶ Dhamankar and a group of her followers from Pune to Pandharpur in 1998, she was a sturdy, expressive woman in her late fifties. Sudhatai's *kirtan* was held in a semi-outdoor sacred space, with audience members sitting on the ground, segregated by sex.⁷ The performance began when she stood facing the congregation and sang a series of invocatory songs. Except for one *bhajan*, they were all performed as vocal solos with *pakhawaj*, harmonium, and *jhanj* accompaniment. These songs underscored Sudhatai's Brahminness (through singing Sanskrit verses), her devotion to Rama, and her presence at a *varkari* pilgrimage site. In the *jayjaykar*s (*jayajayakāra*, exclamations of praise) with which she concluded the opening songs, she connected devotion to Rama and to the nation by exclaiming in quick succession, "*Rājādhirāj Rāmacandra Mahārāj kī jay!*" ("Glory to the king of kings, King Ramachandra!") and "*Bhārata Mātā kī jay!*" ("Glory to Mother India!"). An incarnation of Lord Vishnu and protagonist of the Hindu epic the Ramayana, Rama(chandra) is framed as an ideal ruler, brother, and husband, and has been appropriated by Hindu nationalists as a defender of Hindu ideals, Hindu space, and feminine virtue. Though devotion to Rama is not necessarily an indicator of Hindu nationalist sensibilities, the proximity of Sudhatai's two *jayjaykar*s encourages listeners hear a connection between Rama and Mother India (see film reference in Sarrazin*).

---

⁵ Few female *kirtankar*s dedicate their performing careers entirely to nationalist *kirtan*s, given the genre's association with a masculine *veer rasa* (*vīr rasa*, heroic mood/sentiment).
⁶ "Tai" is a Marathi term of endearment meaning "elder sister."
⁷ See Schultz 2002 and Schultz 2013, 156–173 for more information on this *kirtan*.

The *purvaranga* of a *naradiya* or *rashtriya kirtan* is structured around the message of a main *abhanga*. In this *kirtan*'s *purvaranga*, Sudhatai expounded on the *abhanga*, "*Sadguru vāconī sāpaḍenā soy*" ("If you want to find happiness, follow a *sadguru*"), by the beloved seventeenth-century *varkari* saint Tukaram. Speaking eloquently on the rewards of finding a *sadguru* ("true guru"), she periodically returned to the *abhanga* in chant or song. "If one dedicates one's self to the right guide with sincerity," she said, "there is no need for ritual or scripture." The focus was on Tukaram, but she also introduced a non-*varkari*, Brahmin saint (Ramdas) and a Hindu king (Shivaji). In an impassioned voice, she politicized this coterie by saying, "Different parts of India were ruled by [Muslim rulers] and Hindus were really suffering. In this adversity, Shivaji became king, but he did not rise alone. He got his strength from Tukaram and Ramdas swami." At the end of the *purvaranga*, she sang Tukaram's complete *abhanga* and was garlanded by the host.[8] Before beginning the *uttararanga*, Sudhatai led the audience in a *varkari bhajan*, "*Jayjay Viṭhōbā Rakhumāī*" in praise of Lord Vitthala and his wife, Rakhumai.

The *uttararanga*'s main story concerned a conflict between Shivaji/Tukaram and a Muslim navab (*navāb*, nobleman) (see ⏵ Audio example 9.1). Sudhatai began the story by repeating the *bhajan* she had sung with audience members earlier, "*Jayjay Viṭhōbā Rakhumāī*" (cue point 0:58–1:36). This time, though, she sang it as Tukaram, signaling that she was embedding a story of his *varkari kirtan* within her own *naradiya*-style *rashtriya kirtan*. By inserting *varkari kirtan* into her *naradiya kirtan*, Sudhatai enlisted the participatory conventions of the former style to generate collective excitement and bring listeners into an embodied experience of her nationalist/devotional narrative.

As Sudhatai sang "*Jayjay Viṭhōbā Rakhumāī*" in call-and-response, excitement grew with each repetition; she built intensity through increases in volume, a gradually ascending pitch range, greater rhythmic density, and quickening tempos. The lyrics described Shivaji entering the temple to listen to Tukaram's *kirtan*. After Sudhatai's congregation had been singing for some time, the text changed; soldiers of the Navab of Chinchwad surrounded the space and trapped Shivaji (cue point 5:34). The fictional and real audiences became immersed in song and Sudhatai was visibly enchanted—her voice became louder and faster, she moved, danced, and spun, and sometimes closed her eyes, seemingly in devotional abandon.

---

[8] When humans are garlanded, they usually remove the garlands immediately. *Kirtankar*s perform as representatives of the divine sage Narad, and thus the garland remains on the body as it would for a deity.

When the music was at its climax, Sudhatai spoke over the audience's singing to narrate the story's denouement (cue point 11:00–12:22). With the Navab's soldiers (and audience members) engrossed in song, Tukaram ordered Shivaji to slip away. At this moment, the participants were engaged in what Norman Cutler calls a "theology of embodiment" (1987, 113). Through song, movement, and storytelling, Sudhatai the performer embodied Tukaram the saint, who in turn embodied the divine through sung poetry. The audience members became part of this chain by embodying the narrated audience at Tukaram's *kirtan*. In this confusion of identities, Saint Tukaram became linked with King Shivaji and religious experience became attached to nationalism. After describing Shivaji's escape, Sudhatai brought down the tempo, dynamics, and musical tension and ended the narrative by warning listeners not to be fooled by political imposters, but to instead look for moral *sadgurus* like Tukaram.

Though she did not explicitly call out Indian minorities such as Muslims and Christians as a threat in her conclusion, by telling a story of Shivaji fighting against a Muslim ruler and by positioning him as a Hindu devotee, Sudhatai reiterated a nationalist imaginary of Shivaji as a defender of Hinduism. In combination with the anti-Muslim rhetoric of her *purvaranga*, the result is a Hindu nationalist story.

By embedding a telling of Tukaram's participatory *varkari kirtan* within the more presentational *naradiya* form of *rashtriya kirtan*, Sudhatai drew a group of singing, clapping, and swaying listeners into Tukaram's imagined experience of devotional embodiment. This heightened experience was invested with meanings and emotions that were simultaneously religious and nationalist.

Jaytumbi Maharaj Sayyid

Most *rashtriya kirtankar*s espouse Hindu nationalist ideologies, but some promote less Hindu-centric conceptions of the Indian nation.[9] Jaytumbi Maharaj began performing *rashtriya kirtan* during the anticolonial movement, before the late twentieth-century Hindu nationalist surge, and her style brought older, more inclusive national imaginaries into the present. Despite these ideological differences, the two *kirtan*s show compelling similarities in performance strategy, inviting us to consider how genres are controlled and combined to promote participation and enhance emotional investment.

---

[9] For more information on this *kirtan*, see Schultz 2013, 124–125, 129.

Of these two women performers, Jaytumbi was clearly the more unusual. First, she was (to my knowledge) the only Muslim performer of Marathi *kirtan*. She combined Hindu and Islamic philosophy/practice in her daily life and performances, doing *namaz* (Muslim prayer) twice a day but also worshipping Krishna. Second, she made the unusual choice to perform *rashtriya/naradiya kirtan* in *varkari* contexts. She lived in the *varkari* pilgrimage town of Alandi, and its participatory ethos reverberated in her *rashtriya kirtans*. Third, her clothing was more male than female and she was known by the Hindu male honorific "Maharaj" (king). Female performers of *varkari kirtan* are rare, and as a Muslim woman, Jaytumbi needed to work even harder than her Hindu counterparts to legitimize her right to perform. Her ascetic, masculine presentation communicated to audience members that she belonged in the ritual space of the temple. Her hybrid identity as a Muslim/Hindu female performer of a male genre made her popular with a wide group of followers—women, men, Muslim, and Hindu—though more orthodox people likely did not seek out her *kirtans*.

It was a cool November evening in 2000 when I joined thousands of pilgrims descending upon Alandi. When I arrived at the temple's concrete stage at around 10:30 P.M. the *kirtan* had not yet begun, but about forty audience members crowded around Jaytumbi, knees touching and voices commingling. People wrapped in shawls and jackets passed the microphone, taking turns singing *abhanga*s in loud, clear voices characteristic of varkari performance. When Jaytumbi began the *kirtan* at around 11 P.M., the crowd was buzzing with energy.

Though small and slight, Jaytumbi Maharaj cut an impressive figure. Hair pulled back tightly and wearing the long white tunic, white pants, and dark vest of Muslim men's fashion, her only gesture toward women's dress was a white scarf covering her hair. She was seventy years old at the time, and her voice had the gravitas of someone who had lived a long, eventful life (see ▶ Audio example 9.2). Like *naradiya kirtankar*s, she held *jhanj*, but like *varkari kirtankar*s her narrative was punctuated by the participatory bhajan, "*Viṭhōbā Rakhumāī.*" Jaytumbi, like Sudhatai, began with a core *abhanga* by Tukaram. In this case, it was "*Hēci thōra bhakti āvaḍatē dēvā. Saṅkalpācī māyā sansārācī*" ("God loves the great devotion of living one's life with conviction"). We heard this song in several forms before she began the narrative: her devotee sang it as a solo; Jaytumbi sang it in call and response with the congregation; and she intoned it as a chant. Throughout the *purvaranga*, she returned to it periodically as a refrain.

For the next forty minutes, Jaytumbi preached about how to fulfill one's duties without attachment to the illusory world of *maya*. During one's life, one should engage in *bhakti* (devotion) through selfless service to family and community. *Bhakti* is open to anyone, she said; God lives in men and women alike. Jaytumbi interspersed her discourse on devotion with illustrative folktales and an episode from the epic Mahabharata. To underline her point about the universality of *bhakti*, she asked the men to sing a *bhajan* and a *qawwali* (*kavvālī*, Muslim Sufi devotional song) with her in call-and-response. When they finished, she invited the women to sing bhajans about the Goddess, a heroic song (*povada* [*povāḍā*]) "Mardānī Jhāṅsīcī Rāṇī" about brave queen (*rani* [*rāṇī*]) of Jhansi, and a genre associated with women's housework (*ovi* [*ovī*]). Here, too, women participated by joining in enthusiastically. These songs were rich in associative meaning (Sufi devotion, Hindu devotion, women's work, heroic storytelling), and their accessible, cyclical melodies invited participation. By singing them in quick succession, Jaytumbi wove together the songs' meanings, and through participation, the congregation embodied a nationalist identity that includes women, Hindus, and Muslims. Though she invited both men and women to sing with her, she spent more time singing women's songs and explaining women's importance in society. She said, "Mothers in the world have done everything.... Therefore, I request that you look at what women are doing today, from Jhansichi Rani to [today]." To conclude the *purvaranga*, she sang the *abhanga* once more.

Following a garlanding ritual, Jaytumbi Maharaj invited the congregation to join in a simple but enthusiastic chanting of "Viṭṭhala, Viṭṭhala, Viṭṭhala!" She then began the *uttararanga* by intoning the first line of the core *abhanga*, after which she said, "How should one do *bhakti*? I will tell you a story." What followed was not typical of *naradiya kirtan*; neither hagiographic nor epic, Jaytumbi narrated an inverted Ramayana-inspired story set in the present day.[10] After about a half hour of storytelling interspersed with song, one of the musicians accompanying Jaytumbi sang a Sufi *qawwali* and she returned to the moral of the story, saying: "Live as God does. Never think of doing anything wrong to others, because God is never on the side of such people." The narrative wrapped up; she sang the core *abhanga* one final time; and the *kirtan* ended with exclamations of praise for saints and deities.

---

[10] The Ramayana is told, written, and performed in many different versions (see Richman 1991 and Morelli*).

> **Box 9.1 Discussion: Jaytumbi and Sudhatai's *Kirtan*s**
>
> 1. How do Jaytumbi and Sudhatai use music and religion to generate nationalist emotion? What nationalist work does music do that would be difficult through speech alone?
> 2. What nationalist visions do these two performances convey? In which ways do they overlap or diverge?
> 3. How do these two performers enact, resist, or comment on gender norms? Would you consider them feminist? If so, in what ways are their feminism(s) particular to South Asia?
>
>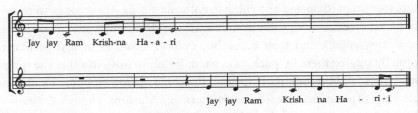
>
> Figure 9.1 *Varkari bhajan* "Jayjay Rāma Krishṇa Hari."
>
> 4. Does this remind you of any ways in which music (religious or otherwise) is used for nationalist purposes in contexts that are more familiar to you?

Reading the description of Jaytumbi's *kirtan*, you may wonder: What makes this nationalist? (see Box 9.1). In addition to the simple fact that Jaytumbi was known as a *rashtriya kirtankar*, seasoned listeners learn to interpret certain genres and signs as nationalist. The historical *povada* about the Queen of Jhansi signaled the presence of a nationalist message. Another clue was Jaytumbi's use of a Tukaram *abhanga* on the spiritual importance of leading an engaged, committed life. Such *abhanga*s are rarely found in non-*rashtriya kirtan*s, which more often emphasize themes of renunciatory spiritual practice. Jaytumbi and other *rashtriya kirtankar*s connect *abhanga*s about service to others with ideas of service to the nation. But what is the nation for Jaytumbi? As a woman who had been active in Gandhian, multifaith, anticolonial resistance, Jaytumbi continued to present a female-centric narrative by incorporating women's folk songs and stories of women's empowerment in her *kirtan*. Furthermore, her performance reflects a vision

> **Box 9.2 Exercises**
>
> 1. Search online for videos using the key terms "Charudatta Aphale kirtan." Aphale is one of the best-known Marathi *rashtriya kirtankar*s. Even if you cannot understand Marathi, the videos you find will give you a sense of how *kirtankar*s move between speech and song and how they use gesture to punctuate the story. How does the performance you watch illustrate (or not illustrate) the devotional embodiment introduced in the chapter?
> 2. Now do another search using the terms "Ghule Maharaj *varkari kirtan*." Compare the instrumentation, song style, and degree of participation in the videos you find with that of Aphale's *rashtriya kirtan*. How do these differences compare to the information found in Table 9.1?
> 3. As a class, sing the *varkari bhajan* "Jayjay Rāma Krishṇa Hari" (see Figure 9.1).
> a) Try singing in call and response. Caller(s) and responder(s) may sing the same phrase or caller(s) can sing one phrase and responder(s) the other phrase.
> b) Clap first on every other beat and then on every beat.
> c) Increase the tempo.
>
> Discuss your own musical experience(s) in relation to the ideas of devotional embodiment introduced in this chapter.

of a nation that embraces multiple religions, as evident in the inclusion of Muslim devotional song within Hindu *kirtan*.

Conclusion

Nationalism is performed in diverse contexts by subjects who understand the nation to mean different things. *Rashtriya kirtankar*s of Maharashtra use Marathi musical and storytelling resources to imagine an Indian nation in terms that are emotionally resonant for Maharashtrian listeners. They draw on Maharashtrian saints and heroes like Tukaram and Shivaji and use genres like *povada, bhajan, abhanga,* and *ovi* with rich associations for

Maharashtrian listeners. This India may look quite different from an India imagined in some other corner of the nation.

Even within Maharashtra, we see that two *kirtankar*s may use similar aesthetic resources to produce different Indias. Sudhatai's *kirtan* promoted an exclusive idea of India as Hindu, while Jaytumbi's national vision included both Hindus and Muslims. Despite differences in their nationalist imaginaries, both *kirtankar*s enlisted similar strategies to generate nationalist emotion. Both inflected their *rashtriya kirtan*s with the participatory practice of *varkari* performance to bring listeners into a nationalist narrative experienced as embodied religion (see Box 9.2). Audience members sat in temples, singing along to cyclical, call-and-response songs that became faster and more intense until the lines blurred between self and other, nation and religion.

Works Cited

Anderson, Benedict. 2006. *Imagined Communities: Reflections on the Origin and Spread of Nationalism.* 2nd ed. London: Verso.

Cutler, Norman. 1987. *Songs of Experience: The Poetics of Tamil Devotion.* Bloomington: Indiana University Press.

Hansen, Thomas Blom. 1999. *The Saffron Wave: Democracy and Hindu Nationalism in Modern India.* Princeton, NJ: Princeton University Press.

Jaffrelot, Christophe. 1999. *The Hindu Nationalist Movement and Indian Politics, 1925 to the 1990s: Strategies of Identity-Building, Implantation and Mobilisation.* New Delhi: Penguin Books.

Rajagopal, Arvind. 2001. *Politics after Television: Hindu Nationalism and the Reshaping of the Public in India.* Cambridge: Cambridge University Press.

Richman, Paula, ed. 1991. *Many Ramayanas: The Diversity of a Narrative Tradition in South Asia.* Berkeley: University of California Press.

Schultz, Anna. 2002. "Hindu Nationalism, Music, and Embodiment in Marathi *Rāshṭrīya Kīrtan.*" *Ethnomusicology* 46: 307–322.

Schultz, Anna. 2013. *Singing a Hindu Nation: Marathi Devotional Performance and Nationalism.* New York: Oxford University Press.

Turino, Thomas. 2008. *Music as Social Life: The Politics of Participation.* Chicago: University of Chicago Press.

10
Prestige, Status, and the History of Instrumental Music in North India

George E. Ruckert

The image of a *sitarist* and *tabla* player—instrumentalists—on the concert stage became iconic in the global representation of classical Hindustani music by the 1970s. For contemporary Hindustani musicians and connoisseurs, however, *vocal* music—particularly the *dhrupad* and *khayal* (*khayāl*) genres—has held center stage due to long-held beliefs regarding its greater spiritual potency than instrumental music. The *Natyashastra*, *Brihadesi*, and *Sangitratnakara*, Sanskrit treatises, all discuss "music" to be primarily vocal, while instrumentalists are not chronicled to a great extent until the nineteenth century. In the early twentieth century, Amanda Weidman argues, a South Indian elite, upper-caste-led discourse dichotomized and distinguished karnatak "classical" music as primarily vocal from Western classical music as largely instrumental. The voice indexed this fundamental difference, which "came to be privileged as karnatak music's locus of authenticity, the preserver of its tradition in the face of modernity." Yet, as Weidman notes, this "leaves out . . . the fact that there are always other instruments on stage with a Karnatak vocalist" (2006, 51). In a similar vein, twentieth-century discourse about Hindustani music's value has constructed vocal music as the privileged form for "India's long history"; however, instruments and instrumental music have long been present, and hence valuable, as evidenced in treatises, iconography, and depictions of court life. For example, we know that Tansen (sixteenth century) and his progeny were instrumentalists, playing the *Seni rabab* (*senī rabāb*) and *bin* (*bīn*); yet, today we identify them primarily as *dhrupad* vocalists. Niamat Khan of the eighteenth century was reputed to be a virtuosic *bin* player as well, but he is identified as a *dhrupadiya* (dhrupad singer), and more so, as an early composer of the *khayal* vocal genre.

A shift toward greater value and respect for instruments and instrumentalists began in the early twentieth century (McNeil 2004). The revered Allauddin Khan, who played *sarod*, violin, *sitar*, and a number of other instruments, led the way by weaving his extensive knowledge of *dhrupad* and *khayal* into instrumental styles. He had trained with *binkar* (*bin* player) and *dhrupad* vocalist Mohammad Wazir Khan of the court of Rampur. In the early twentieth century, Allauddin Khan adapted the rich, complex rendering of *raga* development to instrumental practice, thereby raising its value to equal that of vocalists and vocal music. He transmitted this knowledge to his disciples, including Ali Akbar Khan, Annapurna Devi, Ravi Shankar, Nikhil Banerjee, and Pannalal Ghosh, who, beginning in the 1950s, became world-renowned ambassadors of Hindustani instrumental music.

In this chapter, I demonstrate through analysis of ancient literature, iconography, instrumental development, and socio-religious forces that instruments have historically held a great deal of spiritual and cultural esteem in South Asian music. Their more overt rise in status in the twentieth century is largely due to technical and stylistic contributions by key musicians such as Allauddin Khan (as well as the impacts of recording technology and globalization, largely outside the scope of this chapter). Through listening to three *sarod* recordings—from Chunnu Khan, the first recorded *sarod* player; Allauddin Khan; and Ali Akbar Khan—we can understand some of the instrument's organological developments and musical innovations. Close listening to these recordings helps readers hear how Allauddin Khan developed *sarod* performance, shifting from using the short syllabic plucking style of his first teacher to applying the *dhrupad* vocal techniques of rhythmic *bol* patterns and more melismatic phrasing (see also Perera 1994). This resulted in the expansion of the musical and technical possibilities for the *sarod* and other instruments, helping raise the status of Hindustani instrumental performance to greater prominence in the twentieth century.

Music and the Vedic Heritage

The Vedas, the orally transmitted scriptures of the Aryan people who settled in the Ganges Plain in around 1500 BCE, reveal beliefs regarding music's spiritual origins. Primary is the idea of *Nad-Brahma*, the concept that sound itself is a manifestation of the Divine. The practitioner of music thus partakes in a divine communication with the cosmos. A correlation between the voice and instruments is similarly ancient, perhaps documented first in the *Aranyaka*s, Vedic commentaries from the eighth century BCE. Lewis Rowell, in *Music and Musical Thought in Early India*, discusses correspondences found in the *Aranyaka*s between the human body and a lute: the body being the sounding board, the tongue a plectrum, and the sinews and veins the strings. He continues, "This is no trivial set of correspondences, and it demonstrates how deeply rooted in Indian tradition is the analogy between the vina (as the prototypical melodic instrument) and its human counterpart" (1992, 115).

Of course, we have no way of knowing how the music of lutes described in the *Aranyaka*s sounded. But we can make some simple deductions from the text: the mention of frets suggests that the pitches were intoned in a stepwise fashion up the neck, making the idea of scales possible. The plectrum implies that the strings may have been struck in rhythmic patterns, possibly early forms of bols, a mainstay of modern instrumental technique. And the idea of sustaining pitches with tremolos, rapid up-down motions with a pick, could have been common.

Other types of instruments have also been held in esteem, and further, the Vedas suggest that the gods themselves played instruments and danced. Shiva, for example, is described as *Nataraj* ("lord of dance"), playing the *damaru* drum in one hand. In the *Ramayana* and *Mahabharata*, great epics from at least as early as the sixth century BCE, dancing is described, doubtless accompanied by drums and perhaps by other string or wind instruments.

Flutes, known as *bansuri* in North India, are among the instruments known to have been played in ancient India. Made of hollowed bones or bamboo, they are associated with the god Krishna, whose melodies charmed the milkmaids of Vrindavan. Until the twentieth century, the *bansuri* was considered a popular folk instrument unsuitable for the subtleties of pitch associated with classical music. However, modern virtuosos, including Pannalal Ghosh and Hariprasad Chaurasia, expanded its use to become one of the most prized of classical instruments (Clements 2011). Similarly, the double-reed *shahnai* was adapted from folk contexts to Hindustani concert halls, especially in the masterful hands of the late Bismillah Khan. Ancient sculptures also show trumpets being played, especially in processional depictions. Through ancient Vedic literature and Hindu epics, we see that instruments have historically held great significance and contributed to Hindustani music culture.

The *Natyashastra* and the Golden Age

We first encounter a complex system of instrument classification in the treatise *Natyashastra* dated from the first to fourth century CE. Instruments are described using the categories of *sushira* winds (aerophones), *tata* strings (chordophones), *avanaddha* drums (membranophones), and *ghana* (idiophones). This system was adopted in the late nineteenth century by Western scholars Curt Sachs and Erich von Hornböstel and is still used today by ethnomusicologists (see von Hornböstel and Sachs 1961). Drums in the *Natyashastra* are described in detail, including accompaniment techniques and material construction using wood and hides. Plucked lutes are also discussed extensively. In a large segment, the author, Bharata, makes a famous experiment comparing the tunings of two harps (*vina*s) positioned a fourth apart from one another.[1] The positioning of their combined pitches produced twenty-two *sruti*s, microtonal divisions of the octave. Although the names and positions of these *sruti*s have been the fodder for much discussion, this aspect of Hindustani melodic refinement would not have been possible without harp instruments providing the demonstrative platform.

Iconography is another significant historical source for ethnomusicologists to understand the value of instruments. Many surviving temple sculptures from as early as the first millennium CE show musical instruments in many contexts, primarily being played in a solo capacity, and occasionally in ensembles (Figure 10.1). Whether these ensembles were only the imagination of the sculptors, or whether ensemble music was a developed art form, is not clear from written sources. In these images, however, musicians often appear to be gathered in order to enhance the depicted magnificence of gods or royalty. Thus, we can surmise that they were valued.

As stated earlier, lutes, especially the *sitar*, *sarod*, and *rudra vina*, have assumed a position as the most prestigious of the modern Hindustani instruments (Figure 10.2).[2] The earliest lute described by various authors is the *ekatantri vina*, a one-string stick lute that may have been the source for the concept of drone accompaniment. The *ravanahatha*, or musical bow, which could have been played by plucking or bowing, is also described in ancient literature as the original string instrument. The sound of the musical

---

[1] Bharata termed these scales *sa-grama* and *ma-grama*.
[2] String instruments might also be considered prestigious because, in a caste-Hindu worldview, they are not considered polluting as are drums or wind instruments (see Sherinian, Section III introduction).

HISTORY OF INSTRUMENTAL MUSIC IN NORTH INDIA   159

Figure 10.1 An ensemble of Shiva's *bhuta gana* musicians and dancers. Bhoganandishwara Temple (ninth to tenth century), Nandi village, Chikkaballapur District, Karnataka. Photo by Zoe Sherinian; used with permission.

bow could be amplified or altered by placing the mouth next to the string, and in some cases attaching a resonating gourd.

In the ninth century, records describe Indian lutes imported to Indonesia along the Indian Ocean trade routes. We also associate this period with the development of the *rudra vina*, the long-necked lute with two resonating gourds.[3] If such lutes do indeed begin to take the place of the earlier *vina*s (primarily harps) during this time, then the idea of a manifest drone sound—open strings of a lute played against the melodies intoned by the other strings (or indeed a vocalist)—becomes viable. Of course, harps are also capable of intoning a drone, but with lutes becoming primary, the concept of a drone, so

---

[3] The *rudra vina* is first described in extant written sources in the eleventh-century treatise *Sangita Makaranda*.

Figure 10.2 Goddess Saraswati playing the *vina*. Kalugasalamoorthy Murugan Temple, Kalugumalai, Thoothukudi district, Tamil Nadu. This is an early Pandian cave temple, likely from the thirteenth century. Photo by Zoe Sherinian; used with permission.

much the backbone of modern classical South Asian music, becomes more tangible. The *rudra vina* was dominant from the Middle Ages to the nineteenth century, and many techniques adopted by the modern *sitar* and *sarod* were developed from it (Miner 1993).

The thirteenth-century *Sangita Ratnakara* describes flutes, drums, and *vina*s as the most important instruments of the day. Flutes are described with hand measurements implying varying lengths and different pitches, but the string instruments are not so detailed. The *vina* therein, besides the *ekatantri vina*, is a three-string fretted stick-zither called the *tritantri vina*, which later authors refer to as a *jantar* and may be the ancestor of the *sitar* (Beck 2013, 5).

The age of the *Sangita Ratnakara* marks the end of the Hindu-dominated kingdoms in North India; the incursions of the Persianate world, which had been occurring for several previous centuries, now begin to take a more permanent course with the establishments of Islamic sultanates. Among the most musically significant sultanates is the kingdom of Sultan Allauddin Khilji, who ruled in Delhi from 1296 to 1316 CE. His court brought together three musical forces that influenced the entire course of music in North India: Amir Khusrau, a musician from Turkistan; Gopal Nayak from Southern India; and Nizamuddin Chisti, a Sufi mystic who prized music as a way toward God and a tolerant incorporator of Hindu theologies into his Islamic roots (Gillani*). Amir Khusrau is thought to have brought *sitar* and *tabla* prototypes to India, and made significant West Asian innovations to the Hindustani musical style that led to the development of the *khayal* and *tarana* genres (Miner 1993). Gopal Nayak was an indigenous musician greatly admired and imitated by Amir Khusrau; perhaps together they sowed the seeds of a new style, drawn from both West Asian and Hindu musical elements. Their cooperation was spiritually anchored in the fusion of devotional ideas that Nizamuddin Chisti espoused in his Sufi vision. Significantly, many Hindu musicians who later rose to prominence in Muslim courts adopted Sufism, a syncretic form of Islam that allowed them to sing Hindu traditional texts and styles while converting to Islam, some in order to gain employment in Muslim courts (where they of took the name of "Khan" to indicate their allegiance to royal patrons).

The Middle Ages and the Mughal Era

The Middle Ages includes the magnificent era of the Mughal Empire from 1526 to 1858. The iconography of the period is alive with miniature paintings showing an elaborate musical life, including detailed images of instruments. One of the most significant personalities of the period was the sixteenth-century musician Miyan Tansen, known as the "Father of Hindustani Music."

In her book on musical iconography, *Imaging Sound*, Bonnie Wade reveals the glorious world of instrumental music depicted in battle scenes, courts, and more private moments in the lives of Mughal-era nobility (1998). Just as temple sculptures provide information about early instruments, so too the iconography of medieval paintings serve as important historical sources. We see elephants, horses, and warriors accompanied by kettledrums and trumpets, suggesting that the instruments' sonic power intimidated enemies while urging on the Mughal armies. The kettledrum was a symbol of royal power; nearly all battle and court scenes show the presence of these drums, played with sticks, which also heralded the emperor's entrance. In places like Delhi and Lucknow, a royal court ensemble called the *naubat* featured nine musicians playing drums, trumpets, and *surna*s (the double-reed ancestor of the *shehnai*), which played at prescribed hours of the day and night.

From the point of view of learning the origins of modern instrumental music, Mughal miniatures provide a mine of information, including a whole galaxy of lutes, bowed and plucked. Many show marked influence from West Asian sources, especially the bowed *rabab*s and long-necked lutes described as *tambur*s. Most of these instruments had dried animal intestines woven into strings, and occasionally silk was used. It would be difficult to imagine the bright sound of modern lutes without their steel strings, although *Seni rabab*s and the bowed *sarangi* still have gut strings. The *jawari* flat bridge that creates the characteristic buzzing sound of the modern *sitar*, *tanpura*, and *vina*s is not yet in evidence in early Mughal paintings. This buzzing timbre was apparently already desirable, however; previously, rings were put on the strings to give a metallic jingle (Miner 1993, 37). Other string instruments in Mughal paintings include the occasional flat zither (*santur*).

Mughal miniatures include a number of court scenes depicting dancers accompanied by a variety of instruments—primarily drums of every description. Along with kettledrums, double-headed drums are often depicted, including the *pakhawaj*, the chosen drum of the Hindustani *dhrupad* tradition. The *da'ira*, a frame drum common to West Asia, is shown in miniature paintings played by and accompanying dancers, both women and men. The *da'ira* is not often seen in modern classical ensembles; however, its contrasting bass and treble sounds can still be heard on the two drums of the *tabla*. While the *tabla* does not emerge as a common drum in India until the eighteenth century, its roots seem to harken back to the West Asian paired *tabl* drums.[4]

The *tabla*'s rise from its development in the Mughal era to become the primary modern Hindustani percussive instrument comes from two aspects of this paired drums' personality: its versatility and its ability to contrast the bass-treble sounds, thus allowing for the development of the *theka* (*ṭhekā*), the basic "signature" rhythmic pattern of the different *tals* (*tāls*), or metrical cycles in Hindustani music. The *tabla* is able to play the rigorous compositional repertoire developed on the double-headed *pakhawaj*. It is also able

---

[4] For more information on the *tabla*, see, e.g., Gottlieb 1993; Kippen 1988, 1989.

to play the many virtuosic patterns of the *dholak, nal, dak,* and other folk-style drums. But it is in the development of the *theka*—rhythmic patterns used to accompany vocalists, instrumentalists, and dancers—that the *tabla* contributed most significantly to Hindustani music. Comprising two separate drums, the *tabla* could produce distinct open and closed sounds that clearly communicated sections of the *tal* cycle through changes within the *theka* pattern. No longer did a vocalist or assistant have to maintain the *tal* patterns with *kriya* claps and waves of the hands (as in karnatak music). This instrumental innovation freed soloists from having to keep track of the time cycle with the hand-counting required in *dhrupad* genres. This resulted in a relaxed, freer melodic relationship to regular pulse in the vocal *khayal* style that was adopted by instrumentalists as well.

Changes in the Mughal Era and Beyond

Miyan Tansen, the great vocalist of the Mughal court of Akbar the Great (1556–1605), performed the *dhrupad* vocal style of music, which placed great emphasis on the slow development of *rag* through four primary stages of performance: (1) *alap*; (2) *jor*; (3) fixed composition; and (4) rhythmic variation (see Ruckert 2003). The *dhrupad* style of performance was dominant through the nineteenth century, and this four-stage performance format continues as the most common in Hindustani music.

Although we identify Tansen and his progeny primarily as *dhrupad* vocalists, they also played string instruments. Tansen played what became called the *Seni rabab* (meaning "*rabab* of Tansen"), shown in many miniature paintings. His son, Vilas Khan, also played this *rabab* and transmitted the *Seni rababiya* lineage. Tansen's son-in-law played the *rudra vina*, and descendants of his tradition are known as *Seni binkar*s.

The Mughal court of a lesser emperor, Mohammad Shah (1719–1748), provided a platform for major changes in Hindustani musical style. The court's leading musician was *Seni binkar* Niyamat Khan. Perhaps his greatest contribution was his composition and presentation of a newer genre of vocal music, *khayal*, which was adapted from the Islamic devotional style, the *qawwal* (*qawwali*) melded with shorter *dhrupad* songs. When the Persian general Nadir Shah sacked Delhi in 1739, many nobles packed up their estates in advance of the armies and headed for the fiefdoms they had earned in service to the Mughals—country estates in Rampur, Gwalior, Lucknow,

Jaipur, and Benares. It was in these regional centers that variations of the new *khayal* style were developed. Known as *gharana*s, these "house styles" are identified by their location, heritage of teachers, and distinct stylistic qualities.

The *sarangi*, which rose to prominence after the 1600s, became an accompanying instrument to dance and vocal music, especially after the development of the *khayal* style. While the *sarangi* has been played by famous virtuosos, it suffered under the stigma of being relegated to a position of accompaniment, particularly for courtesan dancers (see Qureshi 1997; Maciszewski*). Many of its players became respected vocal soloists, both because they wished to rise above the position of accompanist and because hours of accompanying vocalists taught them the art of rendering *khayal*.

In Delhi, Khusru Khan, a nephew of *khayal* inventor Niyamat Khan, is said to have developed the *sitar* in the eighteenth century by taking the long-necked lute (*tambur*) and incorporating certain features of the *rudra vina* (Miner 1993). Prime among these innovations was the placing of the main string down the center of the fretboard, allowing the player to pull the string sideways to produce a characteristic sliding and ornamentation in imitation of vocal styles. Illustrations for the next 100 years show much change and evolution of the instrument into what it has become today, with a wide neck, curved and movable frets, and many more strings. The addition of *chikari*, high paired drone strings, enabled instrumentalists to punctuate their phrasing in slower movements and bring their performances to an exciting conclusion with rapidly repeated strokes (*jhala*). Sympathetic strings (*tarafdar*) were also added in the nineteenth century, which produced the instrument's characteristic lingering echo sound.

Beginning around 1800, several *sitar* masters adapted performance practice by borrowing vocal techniques and adopting others from various lutes. These include Masit Khan, whose basic plan for playing a composition in *tintal* (*tīntāl*) used a metrical subdivision of the sixteen-beat cycle into groups of eight, but melodically phrased on beats twelve through three (of the next cycle), and four through eleven (similar to the phrasing of many Bach chorales). The brothers Rahimsen and Amritsen were said to have included virtuosic *dhrupad* (*vina*) techniques into their playing. The infamous Raza Khan of Lucknow was known both for political shenanigans at the court of

Wajid Ali Shah (Katz*) and his ability to dazzle courtiers with fast and flashy *sitar* playing (especially using *jhala* technique).

In the mid-nineteenth century, a steel fingerboard and steel strings were added to the Afghani *rabab*, creating the *sarod*, a Persian word for "melody." Whether this was first done by Ghulam Ali Khan or another is a point of some debate, but in the late nineteenth century, the *sarod* took root in the court of Rampur, the last of the great courts to patronize music after India officially became a British colony in 1858. In this court were several musicians who represented the *Seni binkar* and *rabab* styles; these two styles meld by the end of the nineteenth century. The court of Rampur's primary instrumentalist was *binkar* Wazir Khan, whose disciples included Allauddin Khan, Hafiz Ali Khan, and Vishnu Narayan Bhatkande—all prominent figures who brought Hindustani traditions into the twentieth century.

The Twentieth Century

Allauddin Khan (1862?–1972) was especially noteworthy for bringing together various strands of Hindustani vocal and instrumental traditions (see Box 10.1). In so doing, he raised the esteem of instruments and instrumentalists, including his distinguished disciples Ali Akbar Khan, Annapurna Devi, Ravi Shankar, Nikhil Banerjee, and Pannalal Ghosh, among others. Allauddin Khan redesigned the *sitar* and *sarod*, adding strings and expanding the range of both instruments so that they could play the extensive *dhrupad*-style exposition of *rag*s. Adapting the *dhrupad* vocal genre to instruments involved playing a *rag* in as many as fifteen predetermined sections, including detailed elaborations of *alap*, *jor*, and *jhala*, with defined breakdowns of slides, ornaments, tremolos, and *bol*s (rhythmic variations with right-hand strokes).

Allauddin Khan also took *bol* patterns and used them as a basis for improvisational expansion. Hence a *bol* pattern such as "da diri da ra" would not be treated as a casual diversion in the music, but rather the subject of extensive musical development. While concentrating on sober and serious *dhrupad* renditions of *rag*, Allauddin Khan also adapted lighter vocal genres to instruments, especially utilizing many types of fast runs (*tan*s) common to *khayal* and the filigree ornaments of *thumri*, short compositions that came to delight audiences at the end of instrumental recitals.

Parallel to Allauddin Khan's innovations on the *sarod* was a developing "vocal style" on the *sitar*, particularly by Imdad Khan, his son Inyayat Khan,

Box 10.1 Exercise

One can hear in early recordings from the first decades of the twentieth century that sitarists and sarodists played a more rhythmic style on their instruments than they do today. At that time, they were not capable of the sustained sounds created on later instruments. In addition to organological developments, recording and concert amplification also began to change the techniques of the *sitar* and *sarod* in the 1930s, allowing them to play more quietly and with more subtlety of slide and ornamentation (McNeil 2004).

The purpose of this exercise is to hear changes in how the *sarod* is played over time, from the earliest recordings to more recent times. As you listen to each recording, describe its musical elements using the following questions as a framework:

A. Describe the sound of the instrument. Qualities may include timbre, sustain, and range.
B. How is the instrument played? You may also discuss range, ornamentation, and vibrato. Is the playing more syllabic (meaning, here, one note per pluck of the string) or melismatic (with multiple notes per pluck)? In what musical elements does virtuosity seem most apparent?
C. What is the length of the recording? How might the recording technology of the time affect the sound quality or other aspects of the performance?

Note: all three performances are in *rag bhairavi* (discussed in Katz*).

Examples
1. Chunnu Khan (1857–1912) ▶ Video Example 10.1
   Chunnu Khan was the first sarod player to be recorded, in 1906, and is the cousin of Ahmed Ali Khan, the first guru of Allauddin Khan.
2. Allauddin Khan (1862?–1972) ▶ Video Example 10.2
3. Ali Akbar Khan (1922–2009) ▶ Video Example 10.3
   Ali Akbar Khan is the son of Allauddin Khan.
   As a bonus exercise, search the internet for "*sarod*" and "*bhairavi*." What contemporary recordings do you find? How do they differ from our three examples?

and grandson Vilayat Khan.[5] In the 1940s, Vilayat Khan introduced what he called the *gayaki ang* or "vocal style" of instrumental performance (see Devidayal 2018). "Vocal style" is somewhat misleading, since Allauddin Khan's style also derives from vocal music, simply an earlier genre. Allauddin Khan based his instrumental innovations on the *dhrupad* vocal genre, while *gayaki ang* refers to the playing of instruments through imitating the *khayal* vocal repertoire, with its slow elaborations (*vistar*s) and fast runs (*tan*s). *Gayaki ang* (*khayal*-style) techniques were then adapted by the sarodist Amjad Ali Khan, becoming a mainstay for many of the younger generation of musicians in the late twentieth and early twenty-first centuries.

Conclusion

The twentieth century saw the production of a nationalist discourse that constructed Hindustani music and karnatak music as "classical" and tantamount to the technical virtuosity of the Western art music of India's former colonial rulers. This process involved highlighting the voice as unique in elite Indian court musics and distinct from the perceived European emphasis on instrumental music (Weidman 2006, 5). Concurrently in North India, Hindustani instrumentalists developed increasingly virtuosic techniques abstracted largely from vocal genres. Sarodist Allauddin Khan and sitarist Vilayat Khan drew on the vocal practices of *dhrupad* and *khayal*, respectively. Their innovations contributed to the greater esteem of Hindustani instrumental music and the worldwide fame of their disciples by the mid-twentieth century.

Although these musicians successfully worked against the twentieth-century discourse of vocal spirituality and authenticity, that narrative discounted and ignored a rich history of instrumental performance. Consideration of a variety of evidence, from ancient Sanskrit treatises, temple iconography, and Mughal court miniature paintings, as well as close listening of twentieth-century *sarod* performances, helps us further challenge the discourse of vocal primacy in the history of Hindustani music. Instead, we may recognize a rich historical context in which vocalists and instrumentalists continually influenced each other.

---

[5] Imdad Khan also played the *surbahar*.

Works Cited

Beck, Guy L. 2013. "Divine Musical Instruments." In *Brill's Encyclopedia of Hinduism*, Vol. V, 1–10. Leiden: Brill.

Clements, Carl. 2011. "Tradition and Innovation in the Bānsurī Performance Style of Pannalal Ghosh." *Analytical Approaches to World Music* 1 (2): 330–379.

Devidayal, Namita. 2018. *The Sixth String of Vilayat Khan*. Chennai: Context.

Gottlieb, Robert S. 1993. *Solo Tabla Drumming of North India: Its Repertoire, Styles, and Performance Practices*, Vol. I: *Text and Commentary*. Delhi: Motilal Banarsidass.

Kippen, James. 1988. *The Tabla of Lucknow: A Cultural Analysis of a Musical Tradition*. Cambridge Studies in Ethnomusicology 5. Cambridge: Cambridge University Press.

Kippen, James. 1989. "Changes in the Social Status of Tabla Players." *Journal of the Indian Musicological Society* 20 (1–2): 37–46.

McNeil, Adrian. 2004. "Making Modernity Audible: *Sarodiya*s and the Early Recording Industry." *South Asia: Journal of South Asian Studies* 27(3): 315–337.

Miner, Allyn. 1993. *Sitar and Sarod in the 18th and 19th Centuries*. Wilhelmshaven: Florian Noetzel Verlag.

Perera, E. S. 1994. *The Origin and Development of Dhrupad and Its Bearing on Instrumental Music*. Kolkata: Bagchi & Co.

Qureshi, Regula Burckhardt. 1997. "The Indian Sarangi: Sound of Affect, Site of Contest." *Yearbook for Traditional Music* 29: 1–38.

Rowell, Lewis. 1992 *Music and Musical Thought in Early India*. Chicago: University of Chicago Press.

Ruckert, George. 2003. *Music in North India: Experiencing Music, Expressing Culture*. Oxford: Oxford University Press.

von Hornböstel, Erich M., and Curt Sachs. 1961. "Classification of Musical Instruments: Translated from the Original German by Anthony Baines and Klaus P. Wachsmann." *The Galpin Society Journal* 14: 3–29.

Wade, Bonnie C. 1998. *Imaging Sound: An Ethnomusicological Study of Music, Art, and Culture in Mughal India*. Chicago: University of Chicago Press.

Weidman, Amanda. 2006. *Singing the Classical, Voicing the Modern: The Postcolonial Politics of Music in South India*. Durham, NC: Duke University Press.

SECTION III
INTERSECTIONAL DYNAMICS
Caste, Class, and Tribe
Introduction by Zoe C. Sherinian

The social identities of caste, tribe, and class are constructed and expressed, as well as subverted and resisted, through music, dance, theater, and associated arts in South Asia. The performance of sound, movement, drama, and ritual offers valuable insights into the ways people understand themselves as individuals and as members of specific communities. Caste-, class-, and tribe-based cultural movements use a variety of aesthetic and affective modalities to fulfill a range of political and ethical ends. Some movements reify and fix caste-based stewardship of the arts (typically by caste elites), while others (such as Dalit-Bahujan[1] activist organizations) produce radical, liberating, and empowering expressions of anti-oppression. An arts perspective offers an understanding of the aesthetic meanings and consequences of difference, hierarchy, degradation, and privilege that the identities of caste, class, and tribe carry.[2] Chapters in Section III explore the power of the performing arts to affirm and naturalize social differences or enable new social collectives to be imagined.

---

[1] Bahujan means the majority of people, but generally refers to lower castes, the Indian governmental designation "most backward castes" or "other backward castes," or the Vedic term Shudra (*śūdra*).

[2] Caste and caste discrimination through the arts were not confronted to a significant degree as a theoretical topic in ethnomusicology and dance studies until the 1980s and 1990s, with the exception of Capwell's (1986) *The Music of the Bauls of Bengal* and Neuman's work on social differences among musicians (1990 [1980]). Other early scholars to seriously address caste and music in South Asia were Babiracki (1991, 2000), Greene (1997), Allen (1997), Terada (2000), and Sherinian (2002, 2005a, 2005b, and 2014).

Caste

Caste is a hereditary, hierarchical system of social and religious identity, historically sanctified by Hindu scriptures and practices (e.g., the *Manusmriti*, circa 100 CE). It is also maintained by members of other religious communities, including Christians, Sikhs, Buddhists, and Muslims in South Asia and its diasporas (see Sherinian, Kaur, Sykes [Section V], and Bond* [Section II]). The term "caste" comes from the Portuguese *casta* (likely introduced by seafarers between the fifteenth and seventeenth centuries). However, in local contexts, the Sanskritic term *varna* (*varṇa*, a division of four ranks with prescribed occupations and duties), along with the thousands of specific local and regional *jati*s (*jāti*s, literally "types," here subcastes), is more commonly used. Caste identity and status is transferred hereditarily; yet, unlike the rigid "scheduled" system produced in the colonial period and used by the government in postcolonial India, caste has changed and been contested throughout history and from context to context. For example, there are caste distinctions between Muslims in Kachchh/Sindh, but they are based primarily on hereditary occupations and are not associated with concepts of pollution (Bond* Section II). They also do not use *jati* to differentiate themselves, but rather *qaum* (nation, community) or *samaj* (*samāj*, society).

In the everyday enactment of "non-Othering" by Sikhs, there is a conscious rejection of social differences of class, caste, race, and religion that is codified in *kīrtan* texts. This leads to open and inclusive actions such as equal reverence for diverse paths to the divine and greater toleration of stylistic differences in *sabad kīrtan* practice (Kaur*). While non-Othering is the goal, many Sikhs still use *jati* designations such as Jat and Chamar. Further, there are "outcaste" Sikhs, converts from Hinduism who continue to be oppressed by stigma, social exclusion, and lack of power.

For many arts communities, especially those of hereditary professionals, art is conflated with caste identity, and performance type is thus treated as a caste designation. Tamil courtesans and their accompanying musicians belong to the Melakkara *jati* (literally "subcaste of performers in troupes") and related *jati*s. In the early twentieth century, they took on a new, "respectable" caste identity, calling themselves Isai Vellalar, "cultivators of music" (Krishnan et al.*). North Indian courtesans (*tawai'f*s) and musicians sometimes refer to themselves as a *biradari*, which Maciszewski* (Section IV) citing Dalwai (2019) describes as "socioeconomic communities" bound by occupation that "can cross specific distinctions of caste and religion."

Other categories, such as "tribe," further complicate the caste system. Babiracki's work with Adivasis (indigenous people, also called "Tribals") in Jharkhand reveals that some Scheduled Castes (the governmental designation for so-called outcastes) are also considered either indigenous (called "regionals") or non-indigenous, based on how recently they migrated to the region. Due to the low status of Scheduled Caste groups in the caste hierarchy, some Adivasis do not consider scheduled castes to be outsiders or exploiters as they do upper-caste Hindus (Babiracki*).

The Brahminical *varna* (literally "color") system of caste rankings prescribes four divisions in this order: Brahmin (*brāhmaṇ*), Kshatriya (*kṣatriya*), Vaishya (*vaiśya*), and Shudra (*śūdra*). Its opposition, or *avarna* (*āvarṇa*), contains the so-called outcaste communities relegated to the bottom of the hierarchy. These four *varna*s are not consistent throughout the subcontinent, however; Tamil and central Himalayan cultures typically prescribe only three. In some locales, such as the Punjab, Brahmins are not above kings and landowning Kshatriyas.

Generally, caste groups were also ranked hierarchically by occupation until the development of democratic political systems, when opportunities for education and greater geographical movement intervened. The *varna/avarna* levels historically designated occupational roles on a continuum ranging from pure and valued to polluting and devalued. This included arts-based occupations, such as instrument making and instrumental or dance performance (Neuman 1980). The hierarchical valuation of different artists and artisans was directly related to the relative purity or pollution of their specific occupation, with those involving the skins of animals (drums) considered among the lowest (see Table III.1). These divisions prescribed codes of artistic activity and were further reinforced by marriage and kinship practices (Jodhka 2012, xi).

The term "Dalit" (Marathi: "broken, crushed") is not a term of caste or *jati* identity; it is a self-chosen politicized term of caste opposition, an anti-caste term meaning oppressed (Appavoo in Sherinian 2014; Zelliot 1978; Paik 2011). Its embrace reflects a political process to humanize both the oppressed and oppressors (Freire 2005 [1970], 43–56). However, in common usage, Dalit is often glossed as outcaste, untouchable, or those designated "Scheduled Caste" under India's governmental affirmative action system. The term

Table III.1 *Varna* hierarchy with corresponding occupations and musical roles

Varna and India's Governmental Caste Designations	Occupation/s	Musical Role/s
Brahmin (Forward Castes) 3% of the population	Priests	Elite music singers, string players
Kshatriya (Forward Castes) 7% of the population	Landowners, kings	Patrons of the arts
Vaishya (Backward Castes) 20% of the population	Merchants, artisans	Instruments involving saliva (flutes and reeds), "folk" string instruments
Shudra (Most Backward Castes) 40% of the population	Servants	Instruments involving saliva (flutes and reeds), idiophones, village/folk instruments.
Avarna (Scheduled Castes), Outcastes, Dalits 17% of the population	Agricultural laborers, cleaners, manual scavengers	Drummers

"Dalit-Bahujan" is a politicized term that refers to caste-oppressed people lower on the hierarchy, who include "Most Backward Caste" and "Outcaste" as well as Adivasi communities—notably comprising a numerical majority of the population (see Table III.1). North American anti-caste activists often use the term "caste-oppressed people," its opposite being "dominant castes" (*sāvarṇa*s. Equality Labs 2018; and Soundararajan and Varatharajah 2015). The term "Dalit" was coined by the caste and gender reformers Jyotiba and Savitribai Phule in 1869 and used by Dr. B. R. Ambedkar (1891–1956), leader of the "Depressed class" movement, in the early to mid-twentieth century. Beginning in the 1970s and 1980s, various cultural movements consciously self-identified as Dalit, thus resisting their "former" characterization as outcaste or untouchable, and often using the arts to do so (see Sherinian 2014). Today, the governmental designation of Scheduled Caste applies to approximately 17 percent of the 1.38 billion people in the Indian population (Jodhka 2012, 81). There are close to 260 million Dalits worldwide, including many in Nepal, Sri Lanka, and Pakistan.

Caste violence and endogamy (marriage within the caste) are the primary means of everyday control and reinforcement of caste hierarchy and segregation (Menon 2006). Untouchability and concepts of relative purity and pollution are primary elements of caste discrimination, while other factors such as economic inequality are as significant. Members of the upper castes who follow this system believe they will be polluted by someone of a caste lower than them if they have physical contact, especially through bodily substances. Thus, there is a prohibition in Hinduism against people of different castes crossing physical boundaries, for example by eating together (for fear of encountering saliva) or marrying. Krishnan et al.* discuss caste discrimination couched as a "difference in temperament" or "taste and corporeal demeanor." Outcaste—typically folk—music also becomes "unhearable," bringing on physical disgust for some upper castes. Untouchability thus removes outcaste agency. For musicians playing in polluting contexts such as funerals, the only subjectivity allowed is of a polluting or inauspicious nature.

The colonial period (1857–1947) saw conceptual shifts in the understanding and organization of caste and untouchability that veiled local heterogeneity and fluidity.[3] These reified constructions ascribed uniformity and obscured diversity across regions that did not previously exist (Charsley 1996, 11 in Jodhka 2012, 75–76). One of the results of colonial perceptions and codification of caste was the greater primacy of "pollution related exclusion as the most distinctive . . . feature of the caste system" (Jodhka, 75). Modern understandings of caste oppression came to focus on belief and behavior, not "poverty . . . or powerlessness deriv[ed] from dependence on those who owned the land in an agrarian society" (Charsley 1996, 12 in Jodhka 2012, 76). Those landowners also had the financial means to patronize the arts (Ayyagari and Katz (Section I), and Krishnan et al.*).

Joel Lee states, "The caste order—like all social hierarchies—structures emotions in particular ways. . . . [C]aste, alongside its ideological and political economic foundations, rests upon and requires *ghṛṇā* (or disgust)" (Lee 2021, 316). In the arts, the affect of disgust as a form of violence, control, and reinforcement of caste hierarchy is anchored in the body and the senses and is expressed through segregation, humiliation, and differentiation, particularly in the devaluing of specific genres, styles, instruments, and artists (Lee 2021, 316). These oppressions manifest through functional associations such as the use of drums in funerals, through artist participation in inauspicious polluting rituals, or in their occupational roles as instrument makers. Such performances are typically required as a hereditary

---

[3] For example, caste in Assam is more fluid and complex than in other parts of India, since elites converted to Brahminical Hinduism at a later stage and practiced a syncretic mix of Ahom spirituality and Hinduism (Sengupta and Bharadwaj 2019, 6 in Kheshgi* [Section IV]).

"caste duty," in which services to the village/locale literally represent the performance of caste. If not fulfilled, the musician/dancer risks violent punishment by upper castes (Sherinian 2011). Ironically, the degree of violence inflicted or threatened coexists with the degree of power that Dalit-Bahujan ritual practitioners hold in these contexts and the spiritual dependency that the higher castes or patrons have on them (Ayyagari* [Section I]). While hereditary performers may be economically poor and powerless against local landowners in agrarian contexts, they embody ritual prestige in the spiritual economy of village Hinduism. In such contexts, many believe, for example, that the sound of (Dalit) drumming is necessary to carry the soul to heaven or for reincarnation (Sherinian*). It is this aspect of power that is controlled and invalidated through the deprivation and humiliation of untouchability.

Class

Systems of economic, occupational, and social prestige or a class hierarchy have been present for thousands of years in South Asia, at least as long as kings and land-owning elites have existed. Furthermore, while caste is not the same as class, caste has always carried class ramifications.

> You can still be poor and have caste privilege. You can also conversely be Dalit and be wealthy. But the reality is that most Dalits, Bahujans, and Adivasis struggle with class ascension because they have to overcome generational disparities of wealth. Remember, caste equates to social as well as economic capital. Caste is also structural and generational. (Soundararajan and Varatharajah 2015)

It is likely that in Southern India from the third century BCE (Sangam period), a hierarchy of occupational distinctions existed that evolved in the ninth to thirteenth centuries (Chola period) into a "mature" caste system "marked by conscious defining and ranking of different castes" (Subbarayalu 2012, 6). This included concepts of untouchability and slavery, as the "feudalization of land relations" (Subbarayalu 2012, 8), social conflicts, and crises developed with sharp distinctions between landowners and serf-like sharecroppers (Subbarayalu 2012, 6). At the village level, this developed into a system of hereditary duty (*kaṭamai*) for low-caste performers who were required to perform for fear of violent reprisal while compensation was in-kind. By the Chola period this codification of caste in Southern India signaled an increase in untouchability applied to both the performers who came from these slave *jati*s and in all likelihood, their instruments. The ritual designation of untouchability and association with polluting occupations such as drumming legitimized their enslavement in the agricultural economy.

In the modern period, the value of lower and outcaste labor, including aesthetic labor, continues to be meager and considered inferior. Non-monetary compensation for a ritual performance by Dalit-Bahujans with only a share of crops, alcohol, and/or other material goods keeps performers at subsistence levels. The hierarchical valuing of the instruments themselves in South Asia has class ramifications, as the musicians who play polluted/polluting instruments such as drums and wind instruments are paid less than most vocalists or string instrumentalists. Today, government welfare boards such as the Ministry of Culture or Department of Art and Culture and labor unions for folk musicians provide artists and their children with access to a range of benefits. Artists have also begun negotiating their prices, hours, and other performance conditions.

The modern classification distinctions of "classical" and "folk" also imply binary upper-lower caste and class statuses. In 1952, the Indian government formed a central arts organization, the Sangeet Natak Akademi, which classified certain arts as "classical" and others as "folk," based largely on social rather than aesthetic distinctions, for purposes such as funding. The paradigmatically "classical" dance form became *bharatanatyam*, which by then had been re-scripted as originating in sacred Sanskrit texts and was practiced by largely "respectable" upper-caste individuals (see Krishnan et al.*). The Akademi has thus far designated nine dance forms as "classical" (*shastriya*), conferring upon them and their performers increased status and prestige, as well as a host of grant, performance, and teaching opportunities.

In the 1990s, middle- and upper-class urban Indians in cities like Mumbai witnessed the consolidation of global capitalism, as well as the emergence of digital technologies as fixtures in the home, workplace, and public sphere. The popularity of Indipop, a non-film popular music genre, flourished in the years following India's economic liberalization. A departure from the cross-class popularity of *filmi* Bollywood culture, Indipop appealed to the wealthy, who benefited most from the privatization of India's economy and experienced music through headphones or in the quiet, air-conditioned interior soundscapes of urban shopping malls. In articulating the privileged experiences of English-speaking cosmopolitans, Indipop provided a sense of "what capitalism *sounds* like" (Kvetko* [Section I]).

"Tribe," Adivasi

The category of people formerly called "Tribals" and today called Adivasi ("original inhabitants") make up 8 percent of the Indian population. As they are culturally marginal and politically underrepresented, the Indian constitution designates them with marginal status and dispensations as Scheduled Tribes. This designation also "created a well-defined labor pool for the plantations in Assam" (Babiracki 2000, 36). Many Adivasi communities have been subject to internal displacement, today and historically. In Northern India, for example, Munda people once lived on the Gangetic Plain but were pushed south by invading Indo-Aryans to the Chotanagpur plateau between 800 and 500 BCE. There, they confiscated land from other small groups, eventually migrating to the hills of Ranchi District, now in Jharkhand state. Their movement from the plains to the hills, while maintaining simple political and economic systems, illustrates James Scott's theory that many Adivasi communities consciously moved to less populated areas to preserve political independence and resist state domination (Scott 2009).

Today, Adivasis live in multiple regions of the subcontinent including Central India, the Western Ghats along the Kerala-Tamil Nadu border, and Northeast India. Most live in the hills and forests, where they practice foraging, small-game hunting, and subsistence farming, thus keeping them independent from the caste economy. While many maintain distinct languages and cultural practices, they have had consistent engagement with other tribes, castes, and religious groups. Music is often central to their identity and history of intercultural contact (Babiracki 1991, 207). Colonial stereotypes associate them and their music/dance practices with nature, the primitive, ahistoricity, simplicity, and infantilization. While "tribe" resonates as a part of the post/colonial imagination and within contemporary Indian media, "Indian tribal people do not actually constitute a historically or culturally meaningful entity" (Wolf 2000/2001, 10).

Regional similarities exist between specific Adivasi performing arts, and between these and lower-caste "folk" practices, distinctive from most upper caste practices (Wolf 2000/2001, 12, 13). Babiracki writes that "In Jharkhand, it is the performance of songs with drumming and collective dance, non-segregated by gender, that most clearly and publicly marks a group as 'tribal,' or ādīvāsīs" (2000, 37). She outlines a generalized list of shared Adivasi music characteristics: "asymmetrical rhythmic structures (including an uneven sub-division of the beat and superimposition of different and independent rhythmic systems or meters); and bitonality, either simultaneously or in antiphonal performance" (2000, 37). Further, as seen in Knight* and Babiracki*, phase-shifting between the melody and dance step or rhythm are common. Thus, relative flexibility and in(ter)dependence seem to be common not only in musical structure, but also in the ability of Adivasi people to maintain their culture despite state and caste encroachment. The essays in this section demonstrate that caste, class, and tribe are still significant identifiers and form the basis for both discrimination and privilege among musicians and dancers in South Asia and its diasporas.

Works Cited

Allen, Matthew. 1997. "Rewriting the Script of South Indian Dance." *TDR: The Drama Review* 41(3): 63–100.

Babiracki, Carol. 1991. "Tribal Music in the Study of Great and Little Traditions of Indian Music." In *Comparative Musicology and the Anthropology of Music: Essays in the History of Ethnomusicology*, edited by Bruno Nettl and Philip Bohlman, 69–90. Chicago: University of Chicago Press.

Babiracki, Carol. 2000. "Saved by Dance: The Movement for Autonomy in Jharkhand." *Asian Music* 32(1): 35–58.

Capwell, Charles. 1986. *The Music of the Bauls of Bengal*. Kent, OH: Kent State University Press.

Charsley, Simon. 1996. "'Untouchable': What Is in a Name?" *The Journal of the Royal Anthropological Institute* 2(1): 1–23.

Dalwai, Sameena. 2019. *Bans and Bar Girls: Performing Caste in Mumbai's Dance Bars*. New Delhi: Women Unlimited.

Equality Labs. 2018. *Caste in the United States: A Survey of Caste among South Asian Americans*. www.equalitylabs.org/castesurvey. Accessed January 14, 2022.

Freire, Paulo. 2005 [1970]. *Pedagogy of the Oppressed*. New York: Continuum.

Greene, Paul. 1997. "Professional Weeping: Music, Affect, and Hierarchy in a South Indian Folk Performance Art." *Ethnomusicology Online* 5.

Jodhka, Surinder S. 2012. *Caste: Oxford India Short Introductions*. Delhi: Oxford University Press.

Lee, Joel. 2021. "Disgust and Untouchability: Towards an Affective Theory of Caste." *South Asian History and Culture* 12(2–3): 310–327.

Menon, Dilip. 2006. *The Blindness of Insight: Why Communalism Is about Caste & Other Essays*. Pondicherry: Navayana Press.

Neuman, Daniel M. 1990 [1980]. *The Life of Music in North India: The Organization of an Artistic Tradition*. Chicago: University of Chicago Press.

Paik, S. 2011. "Mahar—Dalit—Buddhist: The History and Politics of Naming in Maharashtra." *Contributions to Indian Sociology* 45(2): 217–241.

Scott, James C. 2009. *The Art of Not Being Governed*. New Haven, CT: Yale University Press.

Sengupta, Madhumita, and Jahnu Bharadwaj. 2019. "Caste Census and the Impact of Colonial Sociology in British Assam." *Asian Ethnicity* 20: 1–26.

Sherinian, Zoe. 2002. "Dalit Theology in Tamil Christian Folk Music: A Transformative Liturgy by James Theophilus Appavoo." In *Popular Christianity in India: Riting between the Lines*, edited by Corinne Dempsey and Selva Raj, 233–253. Albany: State University of New York Press.

Sherinian, Zoe. 2005a. "The Indigenization of Tamil Christian Music: Transculturation and Transformation." *World of Music* 47(1): 125–165.

Sherinian, Zoe. 2005b. "Re-presenting Dalit Feminist Politics through Dialogical Musical Ethnography." *Women and Music* 9: 1–12.

Sherinian, Zoe C. 2011. *This Is a Music: Reclaiming an Untouchable Drum*. DVD, 74 mins. Alexander Street Press.

Sherinian, Zoe. 2014. *Tamil Folk Music as Dalit Liberation Theology*. Bloomington: Indiana University Press.

Soundararajan, T., and Varatharajah, S. 2015. "Caste Privilege 101: A Primer for the Privileged." *The Aerogram*. Retrieved from http://theaerogram.com/caste-privilege-101-primer-privileged/ January 1, 2022.

Subbarayalu, Y. 2012. *South India under the Cholas*. Delhi: Oxford University Press.

Terada, Yoshitaka. 2000. "T. N. Rajarattinam Pillai and Caste Rivalry in South Indian Classical Music." *Ethnomusicology* 44(3): 460–490.

Wolf, Richard K. 2000/2001. "Three Perspectives on Music and the Idea of Tribe in India." *Asian Music* 32(1): 5–34.

Zelliot, Eleanor. 1978. "Dalit—New Cultural Context of an Old Marathi Word." In *Language and Civilization Change in South Asia*, edited by Clarence Maloney, 77–97. Leiden: E. J. Brill.

11

Mundari Performance after the Revolution

Did Dance Save the Tribe?

Carol M. Babiracki

When I started learning music and dance from the Munda people in 1981 in the state of Bihar in east-central India, their regional cultural revival movement had not yet blossomed into a revolution. The revival's inspirational leaders were professors at Ranchi University in the southern reaches of Bihar; one of them, Dr. Ram Dayal Munda, eventually became Ranchi University's vice chancellor. Some years before, when I was studying literature with Dr. Munda at the University of Minnesota, he persuaded me to join his extracurricular music and dance troupe as a flutist, singer, and dancer. Our troupe went on to perform songs and dances from Dr. Munda's homeland throughout the Midwest, donning costumes of red and white, holding each other closely as we sang and danced around a circle to booming drums and a gentle bamboo flute. Dr. Munda encouraged us, a motley mix of diaspora Indians and white Americans, to see ourselves as an extended family or a small village. That sentiment was not new to me; my international folkdance community operated much the same way. Nothing revolutionary about that, right?

In 1980, when Dr. Munda was hired by Ranchi University to head its new Department of Tribal and Regional Languages (DTRL), he took his Minnesota experiences back home to create a program of performances in his new department that featured a stage music and dance troupe for each of the nine tribal and regional languages taught. Shortly after, I arrived in Ranchi and joined the DTRL myself while conducting research for my dissertation about Mundari music and dance (Babiracki 1991). That year also saw the stirrings of a revolution that would carve out the new state of Jharkhand from southern Bihar, although the grievances were much older (Munda and Keshari 2003). In a conversation with me in 1993, Dr. Munda coined the phrase *"nachi se bachi"* (*nāci se bāci*), "Survive by Dance," as the motto of his cultural and now political movement (Babiracki 2000). He fervently believed that the collective, participatory dance style of his people could advance a political upheaval, model a new egalitarian social order, and thus "save" his people from the flood of neo-colonial, neo-liberal influences overtaking the region.[1] His phrase, and the inspiration behind it, still echo faintly in Jharkhand today. *Nachi se Banchi* (*Dance to Survive*) became the title of a 2017 documentary film by award-winning directors Meghnath Bhattacharya and Biju Toppo about Dr. Munda's time in the United States.[2]

The cultural/political movement for state autonomy, joined by many factions and coalitions, did indeed result in the creation of the state of Jharkhand in 2000. Nevertheless, statehood did not bring about the reformed, indigenous-based society that Dr. Munda envisioned, nor has it brought the indigenous people of Jharkhand the self-governance and political power they had expected. Political betrayal certainly has been a contributing factor, but the staged dance performance in which Dr. Munda placed his faith also let his people down. I believe that the urban staging of Mundari dance as display and entertainment, which is a departure from its social function in villages, left behind the shared leadership and gender balance that characterizes the village experience, disempowering women in the process. On stage, women lose much of the leadership, power, and control they enjoy in social dance. An exercise based on Mundari collective dance will help readers understand the differences in embodied values between staged and social dance better than they can by observation alone.

Dancing for the Revolution

When the Department of Tribal and Regional Languages, a graduate program within Ranchi University, opened for business in 1980, over 200 young people signed up from towns and villages throughout the region. Most came to study their *own* "tribal" or "regional" language so they could teach,

---

[1] The most damaging influences on Jharkhand's indigenous people have been consumerism, individualism, individual land ownership and land grabs, political disempowerment, commercial and corporate exploitation, and intense deforestation, all affecting indigenous livelihoods and traditional ways of life.

[2] Before Dr. Munda's death in 2011, he was awarded the Padma Sri and Sangeet Natak Akademi Awards by the Government of India, after which he was appointed to Parliament's Rajya Sabha and the National Advisory Council.

research, and preserve their local literatures and cultures.³ Students found new pride and eventually political empowerment in identities that were otherwise marginalized by caste society. But statehood attracted waves of non-indigenous, high-caste, and hierarchical corporate interests to Jharkhand, rendering its indigenous people minorities in their own homeland and challenging their egalitarian, collective values and lifestyle.

Let me pause here for a few words about identity and terminology. My term "indigenous," a translation of Adivasi (*ādivāsī*, "original inhabitant"), comprises all people of the Chotanagpur plateau (now Jharkhand) whose ancestors have populated the area for at least several hundred years.⁴ "Tribal," a sub-category of indigenous/Adivasi, refers to those original communities who, in the twentieth century, were officially designated as Scheduled Tribes by the Government of India, granting them priority access to education and jobs. By law, a person is a "tribal" only in the region that was first settled by their ancestors. In Jharkhand, the English designation "tribe" is a badge of honor, not a pejorative as in some places. A majority of non-tribal indigenous people fall into the governmental category of Scheduled Castes. They also enjoy benefits, but they must compete for them with non-indigenous Scheduled Caste migrants to the area.⁵ I use "caste" to refer to the General Castes (sometimes called Forward Castes), a stratified society whose hierarchy is sanctified in Hinduism. In the last available census (2011), Scheduled Tribes comprised some 26 percent of Jharkhand's 32,988,134 people, while Scheduled Castes comprised 12 percent. The subtle negotiations between indigenous, tribal, and Scheduled Caste identities, introduced by outsiders, have fueled conflict among the area's original settlers for generations. The Jharkhand movement successfully united these constituencies to agitate for statehood, though the unity did not last long after 2000.

DTRL graduate students became a new generation of agitators for Jharkhand statehood, arguing, as their professors did, that the region is unified by a unique indigenous culture. By the early 1990s, their cultural revival had exploded into a full-blown insurgency.⁶ The movement brought together

---

³ Tribal languages taught in the DTRL include the Austro-Asiatic languages Santali, Mundari, Ho, and Kharia, and the Dravidian language Kurukh. The regional languages, all Indo-Aryan, include Nagpuri, Panchpargania, Kurmali, and Kortha, each functioning as a lingua franca in some part of multi-lingual Jharkhand.

⁴ Evidence of habitation in the area dates back at least 7,000 years ("Cave Paintings," 2008).

⁵ Scheduled Caste individuals retain their official status, which confers some advantages in education and jobs, even when they migrate away from their ancestral regions.

⁶ Two organizations led the effort: the All-Jharkhand Students Union (founded in 1986) and the Jharkhand Coordinating Committee (1987).

a coalition of laborers and farmers; animists and Christians; the landless and landholders; tribes and a wide range of castes; and the Marxists and the "culturalists," with the latter centered in the DTRL. For professors and students, there were no hard boundaries between education, performance, organizing, and agitating. Just outside the department, Dr. Munda erected a half-circular raised platform designated as the DTRL's *akhara* (*akhaṛa*) or arena.[7] In Adivasi villages, an *akhara* is a special, outdoor, open space that belongs to the village or neighborhood rather than to any individual or family. During the day, the space hosts village events, guests, colloquy, and the work of the village council in governing and settling disputes. At night, the *akhara* transforms into a ground for collective singing and dancing by village men and women circling the space to disciplined drumming by men. Nobody has the right to keep anybody else out of the *akhara* or to bring conflict into it.

In 1981 and again in 1983–1984, I spent whole nights dancing in village *akhara*s south of the city of Ranchi with Mundas who by day cultivated rice and vegetables and herded goats and sheep. In the city, I danced with the DTRL's Mundari dance troupe (see Figure 11.1). At some point, I was asked to choreograph and teach dances for the troupe since I had experience dancing both on stage (with our Minnesota troupe) and in Mundari villages. The department troupe was more diverse than village communities and included many urban and Christian students who rarely danced in their communities.

Tribal Values

Why did the academic leaders of the Jharkhand movement consider staged tribal dances such a powerful display of identity? The department took pains to replicate the village festival/dance calendar, organized by seasonal and agricultural cycles, and celebrated each festival in the *akhara*. Each language troupe took its turn to dance, and knowledgeable village students were put in charge—a radical move in an urban area where they were otherwise considered "backward." For many in the audience, the festivals triggered deep memories of multi-day village festivals: rituals for natural and ancestral

---

[7] The word deriving from the Sanskrit *akhāṛa* is variously pronounced in local languages as *akhaṛa*, *akhṛa*, *akhra*, and *akaṛa*.

Figure 11.1 Mundari dance troupe of the Department of Tribal and Regional Languages, Ranchi University, dancing *jadur*, c. 1986. Photo by the author.

spirits, nearly constant collective dancing, and courtship involving boys from other villages visiting to dance with marriageable girls outside their village family.[8]

Dr. Munda's understanding of the power of Jharkhand's indigenous dances ran deeper still. He knew staged dances would empower tribal students and observers alike, as Jharkhand's collective tribal dances embody, encode, and transmit core tribal values. Dancing offered the Jharkhand movement a model of an ideal tribal-based society, even though real tribal life was a good deal messier. "Tribal values are modern values," he argued in a 1981 speech to Ranchi's Rotary Club (which included no tribals): environment-based religious beliefs; collective cooperation for the common good; equality and reciprocity; shared leadership; a balance of power between men and women; equal value accorded to physical and mental labor; doing rather than observing; and self-sufficiency. Staged dance did manage to recreate the

---

[8] British colonials and upper castes who do not understand tribal social practices have long taken this nighttime dancing as evidence of loose morals (see also Kheshgi*).

Jharkhand movement's ideal tribal-based society; however, the values it displayed were selective and incomplete.

Or Jadur

Let's consider Dr. Munda's tribal values as they are expressed in a particular village music-dance complex. Imagine that it is spring; the work of the day is done, stomachs are full, and at 9:00 pm or so, men and women of the village gather in the *akhara* to sing and dance *jadur, or jadur* ("standing" *jadur*), and *gena*, the genres of planting season (February–April). In April, each village caps the season with a *sarhul* festival, installing *sal* tree (*Shorea robusta*) branches in the middle of their *akhara* for rituals (an environment-based religious system, a core tribal value; see Figure 11.2). *Or jadur*, as a genre, actually refers to a complex of three simultaneous, cyclic units: a flexible melody, the women's fixed step pattern, and the men's fixed drumming pattern. Each of these units is of a different length (6, 4, and 8 beats long, respectively, in our example), so that every time they cycle around, they are in a different relationship to each other. This makes the view from inside the dance something

Figure 11.2 Author dancing *or jadur* with host village family at *sarhul* festival in 1984. Photo by Asrita Purti; used with permission.

like a kaleidoscope and keeps the dance infinitely interesting and complex. The cycle or circle is a central paradigm of Mundari thought, another expression of their environment-based belief system and present-centered sense of time. Predictability makes it possible for men to dance with women of other *akhara*s and for a woman to easily join the *akhara* of her marriage village; collective cooperation (another tribal value) is more important than individual innovation. As in all Mundari dances, women sing and dance together in a tight line, eyes cast downward, circling the *akhara* counterclockwise. Men sing and dance in a freer, less disciplined style in the center of the circle, face-to-face with and following the women, always trying to catch their attention. Men sway from side to side, hopping from one leg to the other, sometimes leaping into the air with a spin. Although they dance more individually than women do, they follow strict rules of disciplined turn-taking (shared leadership and egalitarianism).

The social dynamics of Mundari dance replicate marriage patterns, the most important cycle of life: men display, women choose, and the groom's family pays a price for the bride (the reverse of the caste dowry system). To begin the dance, men summon women to the *akhara* by drumming. Once the dance is underway, small groups of men take turns introducing songs. Women hold the crucial responsibility of responding. If they decide not to answer the summons or not to take up a song, the dance does not happen. Although they use this power sparingly, women have the last word. In the *akhara*, dance models social ideals, including equality, reciprocity, and a balance of power within and between male and female groups.

Leading up to the festival, Mundari villagers dance together several nights a week, creating new songs and polishing their dance and drumming for the big seasonal event. All generations join in, though the elderly drop out after an hour or two, and little children come and go. Dancing requires strength, stamina, coordination, and cooperation. It also requires the mental work of accommodating at least two different cyclic units at the same time (drum + dance, song + dance), not to mention the memory needed to recall several nights of unwritten songs. Dance requires skills in both physical and mental work, and Mundas assume that all people have the capacity; "*senge susun, kajige duraŋ*," they say, "to walk is to dance, to speak is to sing."

It is easy to find costumed stage versions of Mundari *or jadur* on the internet. The YouTube videos "Mundari Or Jadur Dance, Ulihatu-2018" (▶ Video example 11.1) and "Mundari Or Jadur Song" (▶ Video example 11.2) are good examples. In the first, men are dancing a choreographed step pattern, and the voices and flute are amplified in what is clearly a display performance. In the second video, a stage troupe appears to have invited audience participation at the end of a show. Neither is a true social performance, so neither exhibits the intense social interaction between men and women that I found in village social dancing. In the villages, Mundas dance *with* and *to* each other rather than *for* an audience of observers; village Mundas value doing over observing.

Learning *Or Jadur*

Mundas learn dances like *or jadur* by joining their elders. They have no dance schools, gurus, or specialists to preserve and transmit their knowledge; the village is self-sufficient in creating, re-creating, remembering, and transmitting songs. Without *akhara* performance, these songs would have no life. Not surprisingly, most songs are about love, but also current issues like land loss and, more rarely, historical issues such as their hero Birsa Munda's battle with the British in 1900. I recorded the *or jadur* song featured in this chapter in 1984, as it was performed (with the dance steps found in Box 11.1) by the Mundari dance troupe of the DTRL, Ranchi University. The recording (⏵ Audio example 11.1, also found in ⏵ Video example 11.3) includes only the last three couplets of the song, bolded below. In a village *akhara*, a song can go on much longer as boys extend their turn at singing by adding new couplets. In this song (below, translated by Dr. Ram Dayal Munda), mustard is a synonym for young girls, who are in dialogue with boys throughout (reciprocal exchange). Men introduce the first couplet, then women repeat it. After the drums enter, women start dancing, men sing the couplet again, women respond, and the dance is underway. The men decide when to move on to the next couplet.

Buru re buru re mani do	On every hill, (there is) *mani* (mustard)
Beṛa re beṛa re rai	On every plain, (there is) *rai* (syn., mustard).
Limaɲa lomoɲa mani do	The *mani* is dancing,
Kidara kodora rai	The *rai* is swaying.
Okoege hereleda mani do	Who has planted the *mani*?
Cimaege pasirleda rai	Who has sown the *rai*?
Muṇḍako ge herleda mani do	**Mundas have planted the *mani*,**
Santako ge pasirleda rai	**Santals have sown the *rai*.**

Side lege moneña mani do	I feel like plucking the *mani*,
Tusalege sanaña rai	I feel like picking the *rai*.
Alorepe sidea mani do	Please don't pluck the *mani*,
Alorepe toṭaʔ ea rai	Please don't pick the *rai*.
Tire mundam gonaŋte mani do	The *mani* is for the price of a finger ring
Katar pola satite rai	The *rai* is for the price of a toe ring.

The song text underscores courtship's reciprocal nature. Men are attracted to women (the dancing mustard flowers), but women define the terms of the relationship (the mustard is not free). We might recall that marriages are sealed with a gift from the groom's family to the bride's.

The best way to understand the values expressed in Jharkhand's traditional Mundari dance—environment-based beliefs, collective cooperation, equality and reciprocity, shared leadership, a balance of power between genders, the worth of both physical and mental labor, doing rather than observing, and self-sufficiency—is to embody them oneself, to understand the dance as a doer rather than as an observer. In this way, we can come to understand the dance as purposeful action rather than empty representation. So, find a group of friends and give it a try; ▶ Video example 11.3 and the directions in Box 11.1 will walk you through it.[9] I like to teach the women's line dance first to everyone, followed by the men's dancing style, which can be more dramatic, individual, and flamboyant.

If you have been dancing along with the written description in Box 11.1 and/or Video example 11.3, you have learned *or jadur* in much the way that DTRL women did from their village classmates and, on occasion, from me. This is also the way many stage dance troupes master their steps today. The structure of *or jadur*, even this choreographed version, embodies some key tribal values: collective cooperation, the individual's responsibility to the group, reciprocal exchange, the worth of physical and mental work, and self-sufficiency (there are no professional musicians, for example).

---

[9] I thank Shilpa Sharma and Pallavi Salvi of the Leela Institute of Kathak and their two daughters for making this video with me. They knew nothing about *or jadur* or Mundari dance before bravely stepping in.

Box 11.1 Dancing *Or Jadur*

1. Arrange yourselves close together, standing in a semi-circle, facing the center.
2. One or two people should volunteer to lead the line in a circle around the space, making decisions about when to start and which direction (right, left) to move. Just as the men take turns introducing songs, women take turns leading, giving up the lead after a couple of songs (shared leadership).
3. Facing the center of the circle, turn your body about 45 degrees to your right, with your left foot in front of the right, toward the center of the semi-circle. Keeping your feet under your body and about a foot apart at all times will make the dance easier.
4. In this position, wrap your arms around the waists of the people next to you, moving as close to the person on your right as possible. A good line shows no gaps.
5. Developing a sense of working together is key. The line should move as a single body, so individuals must accommodate themselves to the line, to the collective. To practice, leaders can guide the line in bending and straightening their knees, while staying in place: bend, straighten, bend, straighten, etc. Leader(s): use your voice at first, then let your own movements guide the line. Then, everyone: try closing your eyes while bending and straightening (▶ Video example 11.3 begins here). This helps the group focus on how the line feels rather than how it looks. Relax, let go, and move together.
6. Add a step before each bend. Always keeping the left foot in front, gently rock your bodies forward and back: step forward on your left, then bend your left knee; step back on your right, then bend your right knee. Repeat the movement, keeping a steady beat: left (L), bend; right (R), bend; L, bend; R, bend, etc. Keep your feet close together and under your body. Practice until everyone is relaxed and moving as one. Each dancer is equally responsible for maintaining the line.
7. Change the bend to a small hop (or bounce): L, hop; R, hop; L, hop; R, hop, etc. As you hop on your left, bring your right foot to it. As you hop on your right, bring your left foot to it.

8. If your line is strong, solid, and relaxed, try adding gentle body movements. Bend at the waist with a flat back as you step-hop back on your right foot, and straighten at the waist as you step-hop forward on your left. The dance should get easier the more you relax.
9. Hopefully, you have surrendered to the movements of those next to you. If not, you would find it exhausting to do this all night! Now, as you rock forward and back (L, hop; R, hop), the leader(s) can gently pull the line to the right. In a Mundari *akhara*, the pull is transmitted physically, instantly down the line. Followers: when you feel a pull from the person on your right, move right. The leader can then change direction, gently pushing the line to her left. Don't fight it; respond to it.
10. All that remains is to get the line up to speed to dance along as DTRL students drum and sing (▶ Video example 11.3, cue point 8:17). At this performance, the women did not match the drummers beat for beat because the drummers were playing too fast. Instead, the women adjusted, completing their four-beat pattern in the same amount of time as three beats of the drumming pattern, coinciding with the drum and song beats on every sixth step. If we were to notate it (Mundas do not), it might look like this:

Dance steps:	L hop	R hop	L **hop**	R hop	L hop	R **hop**	etc.
Dance beats:	1 2	3 4	1 **2**	3 4	1 2	3 **4**	etc.
Drum beats:	1 2	3 4	5 6	7 8	1 2		etc.
Song beats:	1 2	3 4	5 6	1 2	3 4		etc.

The Munda women didn't do such complex math as they danced, however. The lead women simply settled on a comfortable pace. You should not concern yourself with the math, either. As your leader sets a pace, others down the line should try to feel and match their rhythm. Collective cooperation is more important than how the dance looks. The key is to find a way to dance *with* the drums rather than to follow them. Mundari village women are not followers.
11. To learn the men's steps, watch *or jadur* online, for example, in the YouTube video titled "Mundari Or Jadur Song" (▶ Video example 11.4), and try to copy the men's style as they sing to the women.

Some crucial values are missing on stage, however. Village women enjoy more agency, more leadership than we do when we "follow" on stage. Even among men, only the "best" dancers tend to lead and choreograph stage dance because, above all, it must *look* perfect. Furthermore, on stage, the connection to seasonal rituals (environment-based beliefs) has disappeared. Village gender balance falls away on stage too, since men control the scene; they manage bookings, negotiate prices, choreograph entrances and exits (constraining both men and women), and require all dancers to follow the drums. In other words, the core tribal values of shared leadership, environment-based religious beliefs, and a balance of power between men and women did not make the transition to the stage. Not coincidentally, these values are also not embraced by the General Caste, non-indigenous residents of Jharkhand.

To get closer to the experience of female agency one feels in village dancing, shift your mindset from following to creating, even while in the service of group cooperation. There are no YouTube videos of Mundari village social dancing to follow. Video, like stage presentation, is about display rather than socializing. Instead, ask two others from your group to create a simple, new step pattern, perhaps while singing a familiar song. Then put your arms around the others' waists, sing the song, and dance until it feels like you could do it all night! The better you cooperate and accommodate, the easier and more successful the dance will be. Then, let someone else lead.

Conclusion

For indigenous people in Jharkhand in the 1980s and 1990s, watching village dances newly presented on city stages was uplifting. The urban *akhara* modeled the cooperation needed to unite disparate indigenous factions as a political force. The problem with models, though, is that they atrophy with time, becoming rigid containers rather than dynamic inspirations. Today, over twenty years after statehood, outsiders have flooded into the area, reducing the political power and presence of indigenous people and introducing non-indigenous values. Staged dances are so common, homogeneous, and predictable that they have lost their former impact. Song repertories have shrunk, the social dynamics are entirely different, and thus certain values have been lost. Urban, modern values such as consumerism, hierarchy, patriarchy, and the containment of minorities prevail. Most stage dances function as show pieces, tourist art, or, in government programs, as the Jharkhand state brand. With this, women's agency is greatly diminished in urban troupes, most of which are organized, led, booked, and paid for by men. Staged dance is not the fluid, creative social experience of village dancing. It privileges hollow but perfect display rather than courtship, power sharing, or village cohesion. There is no right of refusal by women on stage if they feel uncomfortable or want to make a statement. Leadership in a stage troupe tends to flow to the "best" dancers and stays there. Everyone must begin dancing on the drummer's cue, essentially *following* the male drummers rather than *accommodating* them, and dancers must follow prescribed choreography. Male stage dancers tend to ignore the women dancers altogether, focusing instead on looking good for the audience. Staged dance stopped empowering women when it stopped being a social creation of shared, reciprocal relations between men and women.

The stage model now reigns supreme in Jharkhand's cities, towns, and even some villages. At the same time, collective dancing grounds are disappearing, even in tribal neighborhoods, as General Caste values increasingly

Figure 11.3 Schoolchildren performing a "tribal" dance for guests, 2010. Photo by the author.

define urban life. Without their embeddedness in village social patterns, the dances have lost their social power. This change really struck me a few years ago as I watched a young Mundari troupe, boys and girls, perform a traditional song, but in a new, utterly unique non-village manner. They danced as individuals in undifferentiated rows, unlinked, ungendered, all facing the audience, as schoolchildren often do, while soloists sang into microphones (see Figure 11.3). It was new, innovative, and interesting, but it embodied a set of values very different from those of village social dance or even of the typical, circular stage dance. Their dance was certainly egalitarian, but the intense cooperation of the village, the corporate group, and even the fiction of reciprocal social interaction between men and women were gone. The circle was broken.

Works Cited

Babiracki, Carol M. 1991. "Musical and Cultural Interaction in Tribal India: The Karam repertory of the Mundas of Chotanagpur." PhD diss. Ann Arbor, MI: University Microfilms International.

Babiracki, Carol M. 2000. "'Saved by Dance': The Movement for Autonomy in Jharkhand," *Asian Music* 32 (1): 35–58.

"Cave Paintings Lie in Neglect." 2008. *The Telegraph*, March 13.

Munda, Ram Dayal, and Biseshwar Prasad Keshari. 2003. "Recent Developments in the Jharkhand Movement [1992]." In *The Jharkhand Movement: Indigenous Peoples' Struggle for Autonomy in India*, edited by Ram Dayal Munda and S. Bosu Mullick, 216–231. Copenhagen: International Work Group for Indigenous Affairs.

12
Systematic and Embodied Music Theory of Tamil *Parai* Drummers

Zoe C. Sherinian

The *parai* (*paṟai*) is a frame drum made of cow or water buffalo skin played with two sticks. In Tamil Nadu, India, as well as in several surrounding southern states, the *parai* has for the last millennium been played as a caste duty (*kaṭamai*) by untouchable/outcaste communities. Today, politicized members of these communities call themselves Dalit—an anti-caste, oppositional term. Some have found pride and solidarity in their caste identity, while others still see themselves as slaves (*aṭimai*). The majority of hereditary performers of *parai* come from the Paraiyar community, whose caste name comes from the drum.[1] The drum is also called *tappu* (related to the frame drum called *dappu* in Telugu and *dap* or *daf* in parts of North India and the Middle East). Etymologically, the word *parai* is drawn from "*paraidal*" (*paṟaidal*), "to speak or announce," reflecting the drummers' function to announce both auspicious and inauspicious ritual occasions within the Hindu life cycle. Hindus consider the power of the *parai*'s sound to be essential to invoke possession by deities and take the soul to the next reincarnation.

The *parai*'s long integral association with Tamil culture is reflected in its appearance in the earliest extant Tamil literature, from the Sangam period (third century BCE to fifth century CE). The word "*parai*" occurs forty-four times throughout Tamil Sangam poetry, as a general term for drum and as a specific drum, possibly with a kettle/bowl shape. Sangam poetry describes a *paraisattru* or announcing drum that was used to lead kings into battle Valarmadi 2009). Dravidian Hindu temple iconography also shows the

---

[1] Other drummers come from the Arundathiyar community. Some may have migrated to present-day Tamil Nadu from Andhra Pradesh or Karnataka in the sixteenth century, likely with Nayak kings, who employed them as leather workers in military contexts (Margu 2001 in S. Gunasekaran 2021, 56–57). Some also migrated to labor on colonial plantations in Sri Lanka in the nineteenth century.

Figure 12.1 Iconography of frame drummer at the Bhogananbdishwara Temple in Karnataka (ninth century). Photo by the author.

presence of a single "faced" frame drum played with two hands from as early as the ninth century (Figure 12.1).

While many of these functions historically gave a valued status to the *parai*, for the last millennium, the drum and its drummers are primarily defined by the *parai*'s function to announce death, a caste duty that degrades its performers because of the Hindu association of death with pollution. Further, the drumhead is made from animal skin considered polluting by caste Hindus. Because middle-caste communities attribute ritual power to the drummers and their performance, these privileged castes are dependent on them to perform this hereditary duty. Yet, they in turn mitigate this power through identifying Paraiyars and Arunthathiyars with stigma and degradation as performers of the drum. The drummers I studied with from the group Kurinji Malar (Kuṟiñci Malar) reject this assessment. They believe themselves worthy of being deemed *isai kalainyar* or "music artists" (Sherinian 2011).

A defining step in the process of shifting identity from outcaste to Dalit (anti-caste) for these drummers is to proclaim the sound of their drum as "music": as Kurinji Malar drummer Amulraj declares, "*ida oru isai!*" ("this is a music!," ⊙ Video example 12.1).[2] While my teachers never had to convince me of the understanding of *parai* practice as "music," they did emphasize theoretical aspects they believe comprise the essence of the art. For example, Essiah described "the *isai*" to be in the left-hand stroke, which functions in the musical texture as a cutting timekeeper against the lower bass accents played with the right hand (Interview with the author, September 2008). Furthermore, he emphasized the importance of dancing (*āṭṭam*) while learning to drum in order to internalize and coalesce the performance aesthetics of the complete, intersectional arts genre. Indeed, today the art is commonly called *parai-attam* (*paṛai-āṭṭam*).

Much of Kurinji Malar's discourse asserting that *parai* is a type of music is a response to others in their village and wider Tamil culture who degrade it as polluting noise (see Greene*). Some villagers have described its sound to me with the dismissive phrase "daba daba," and a classical drummer said its sound makes them feel sick (disgusted) (Aaron Paige, personal communication, 2010). To them, it is not only untouchable but "unhearable." From an analytical perspective, however, *parai-attam*'s organization is consciously systematic and embodied. Furthermore, its aesthetic theory, while unwritten, falls on a continuum with other rhythmic systems in South India, such as the temple and concert practices of the *tavil* (a cylindrical temple drum) and *mridangam* (a barrel drum).

In this chapter, I argue that *parai-attam* encompasses a systematic and embodied music/aesthetic theory. That is, it includes both a quantitative, positivist knowledge that can be understood through notational and descriptive (written) analysis and an embodied qualitative experience as intersectional and intersensorial aesthetic knowledge (Stone 2005). Inherent to both approaches for me as an ethnomusicologist, and as an extension of the concept of intersectional arts, is the necessity to ground *parai-attam* analysis in local, village, and shared Dalit community knowledge systems. To do so, I draw on my fieldwork and experience studying *parai* for four months

---

[2] Video examples in this chapter are excerpted from my documentaries *This Is a Music: Reclaiming an Untouchable Drum* (2011) and *Sakthi Vibrations* (2019).

Figure 12.2 Kurinji Malar troupe with author. Photo by Jaisingh Nageswaran; used with permission.

in 2008 with the nine drummers of the *parai* collective Kurinji Malar in the village of Munaivendri near the town of Paramagudi in southeastern Tamil Nadu (Figure 12.2).

I also draw on my work with, and observation of, politically conscious (Dalit and feminist) NGO groups like Sakthi Kalai Kuzhu (*Kuḻu*) of the Sakthi Folk Cultural Centre, as well as expert performers like Arumugan of Alanganalur and A. Manimaran of Buddhar Kalai Kuzhu, Chennai. My fieldwork with these artists resulted in two documentary films. I argue that the use of film footage as a medium of aesthetic analysis effectively demonstrates the intersensorial, embodied knowledge that *parai* drummers have and the communal pedagogical process of acquiring it.

Quantitative Theory

Today, the *parai* is rarely played by professional troupes without dance. Since the 1990s the art has been called *parai-attam*, reflecting the set of intersectional aesthetic expressions found in most Tamil folk genres. In *parai-attam*, rhythmic timbres, cyclical rhythmic patterns or *adi* (*aṭi*), and tune types (*meṭṭu*), along with their mnemonics (called *vai pāṭṭu, son aṭi,* or *solkaṭṭu*), "step" patterns (choreography), accents, and ritual purpose/function, are experienced as a whole. *Parai-attam*'s purposes are coded in the specific *adi* patterns indexically associated with the genre. An *adi* is played to announce specific ritual events in the village, such as Murugan deity festivals, bullfighting during the Pongal festival, weddings, and funerals.

A quantitative, textual approach to *parai* music theory begins with the concept of *adi* or short, ostinato-like, rhythmic patterns. In my four months of intensive study with Kurinji Malar, I learned more than thirty-five *adi*s associated with sixteen different dance and song genres or ritual events. *Adi*, as a rhythmic pattern, is *not* a counterpart to *tala* in karnatak theory, which is closer to a metrical cycle. *Adi* is also not subject to karnatak music's obligatory consistent tempo.

Kurinji Malar has an extensive repertoire of *parai-attam* genres, including three different deity (*sāmi*) dances, seven fast celebratory *adi* variations called *tappattam* (*tappāṭṭam*) and *temmangu* (*temmāṅgu*), two *adi*s to accompany bullfighting, one *adi* associated with *Kuravanji* (*Kuṟavañci*) or "gypsy" people, "disco *adi*s" inspired by film songs, and *adi*s for weddings, first menstruation, and the return of a pregnant daughter to her mother's house for her baby's delivery (*vaḷaikāppu*). All of these are auspicious. Finally, I learned three *adi*s for various stages in a funeral, the only *adi*s out of likely fifty or more (that exist) to be considered inauspicious (Figure 12.3).

Most *adi*s are in ostinato patterns of six, eight, or twelve pulses per repetition (Figure 12.4). There is often an internal tension between duple and triple metrical accents that divide the six or twelve pulses into two or four beats. Each beat is subdivided into three pulses and includes an accent of three sets of two pulses on top of that ("jen - ja na ku -"). Combining the accents of two simultaneous metrical feels (polyrhythm) gives the music its life and the ritual participants the urge to dance, aiding in the production of trance states (cf. Babiracki, Protopapas*).

I was also taught various cadence patterns used to shift from one pattern to the next, as well as lengthy patterns to begin and end musical sections. These all had three-times-repeated phrases. My teachers referred to them as "*matra* (*māṟṟam*) route *adi*," literally "direction changing rhythm." They understood the function of shifting from one *adi* to the next metaphorically, like how

Kurinji Malar's Repertoire of *Āḍis* and Associated Events

Sāmi Āṭṭam (4): Deity Possession. Several for specific deities
Tappāṭṭam (5): General Celebration
Temmāṅgu (2): General Celebration
Naiyāṇḍi
Māṭṭu Poṅgal (2): Bull fighting for Pongal New Year's celebration
Kuṟavañci: Gypsy Dance
Karagam (2): Pot Dance (carried on the head)
Kāvaḍi (2): Murugan Deity Procession
Oiylaṭṭam/Silambam/Kāvaḍi Sindu (folk dances)
Disco (several based on specific film songs)
Kalyāṇam (2): Wedding (also used for *vaḷaikāppu*, 7th month pregnancy baby shower)
Saḍāṅgu: Female puberty rites
Sāvu: Funeral (3 + variations including *tūkki* or lifting the funeral bier)

Other Events at which *paṟai* is played by *Kurinji* Malar troupe and others

Ear Piercing (*kādukuttātal*)
Christian First Communion procession
Village Announcement
Sapparam (leading a deity or Christian saint chariot)

Figure 12.3 Kurunji Malar's repertoire of *adi*s and associated events.

they changed from one bus (route) to another while traveling from village to town.

An opening pattern, which my teacher Arumugan called *tirmanam* (*tirmānam*), acts much like a karnatak *tirmanam* (lit. "resolution") reduction or a *korvai* (*kōrvai*, "composition"; see Figure 12.5). However, the composition is not framed and restricted by a *tala* (metrical) structure because of its solo improvisational context. The length of each of Arumugan's *tirmanam* phrases, like those of karnatak *tirmanam*s, reduces by taking off material from the beginning of the line. Further, while each line only fully repeats twice, the overlapping of material gives the illusion of a three-times repetition, which is a common compositional procedure in karnatak music (▶ Video example 12.2).

Sami Attam 6 beats

son ādi	jen	na	ji	na	nak	--
hand/stroke	R	L	R	R	L	--
pulses	1	2	3	4	5	6
duple meter	1	2	3	1	2	3
triple meter	1	2	1	2	1	2

Polymeter: two meters played simultaneously (in this case duple and triple meter)

Tappāṭṭam/temmāṅgu: 12 pulses. Tension of triple and duple accent in single *ādi*

son ādi	jen	-	ja	na	ku	di	na	ku	je	na	je	na
hand	2	-	R	L	R	R	L	R	R	L	R	L
pulses	1	2	3	4	5	6	7	8	9	10	11	12
subdivision	1	2	3	1	2	3	1	2	3	1	2	3
phrase/accents	1	2	3	1	2	3	1	2	1	2	1	2

Kuravanji ("Gypsy"): 4 beats/16 pulses

son ādi	jen	-	-	ja	na	-	ka	-	na	-	ka	-	din	-	-	-
hand/stroke	2	-	-	R	L	-	R	-	L	-	R	-	2	-	-	-
beat/pulse	1	-	-	-	2	-	-	-	3	-	-	-	4	-	-	-

key: R = Right hand, L = Left hand, 2 = both hands together.

Figure 12.4 Sample *adi*s in six, twelve, and eight pulses to illustrate polyrhythmic relationships.

Besides their complex musical qualities, the sounded pattern of each *adi* is indexically associated with the event for which it is performed. Those familiar with the art easily hear differences between patterns. However, most villagers today only have a contextual association of patterns with specific events, such as *sami attam* (*sāmi āṭṭam*) played during a goddess festival; distant drumming on a non-festival day usually signals a funeral.

Parai performances at village festivals and funerals, as well as on urban stages, have a consistent choreographed form: circle-line-circle. That is, they move from a circle formation to interacting lines, back to a circle, ending with a fast *tirmanam* or longer three-times-repeated cadential pattern (▶ Video example 12.3). Both subsections of form iconically represent embodied collectivity and community process.

```
Jen - - ja na ku je na  je na ku ju ta ka je na
2      R L R R L  R L R R L R R L
                       je na ku ju ta ka je na
                       je na ku ju ta ka je na  je – na - jen –
                                                 2    L    2
Jen - - ja na ku je na  je na ku ju ta ka je na
2      R L R R L  R L R R L R R L
                       je na ku ju ta ka je na
                       je na ku ju ta ka je na  je – na - jen –
                                                 2    L    2
                       je na ku ju ta ka je na  je – na - jen –
                       je na ku ju ta ka je na  je – na - jen –

                       je na ku ju ta ka je na  jen – ta ka je nu
                                                 2     L R R L
                                                jen – ta ka je nu
                                                jen – ta ka je nu

                                                ki ri dom  (roll or urutu)
                                                ki ri dom
                                                ki ri dom
                                                jen – na – jen
                                                 2    R    2
```

key: R= Right hand, L= Left hand, 2= both hands together.

Figure 12.5 Notation of *tirmanam* performed by Arumugan of Alanganallur in Video Example 12.2. Transcription by the author.

This positivist quantitative ethnomusicological approach to *parai* music theory conveys how the *adi* patterns are structured through mnemonic syllables, their number of pulses, beats, and metrical accents, the form of performance, as well as the ritual and life cycle events with which they are associated. However, this approach does not analyze how the performers and community members experience the flow of the dance or how the music sounds. An alternative, phenomenological analysis would not start with a work, a piece, notation as a generic sign, or a performance, but with the specific *experience* of the embodied subject in music/dance training or performance, not as an object, but as an embodied cultural practice (Butler 1988, 530). An embodied approach to music analysis emphasizing pedagogy, using

Six-beat version of Tappattam

Son Adi	Jen	—	ja	na	ka	—
(alt)	Din	—	ku	ta	ku	—
Pulse	1	2	3	4	5	6
Sticking	2	—	R	L	R	—

Figure 12.6 *Tappattam adi.*

the audiovisual medium of film, can bring insight to these perspectives for *parai-attam* through a focus on timbre, accent, groove, intersensorial experience, and the values and practice of collectivity.

Hearing the *parai* as a young villager may provide a local understanding of the art and its functions; however, the student must first learn the drum technique and proper sound for each hand—the source of the embodiment of the art. There are two primary strokes. The right-hand *adi kuchi* (beating stick) is a thick short stick that plays double strokes, booming accents, and multi-toned articulations in the center and edge of the drumhead. The left-hand grip of the *sindu kuchi* (*cīṇṭu kucci*, small or thin stick) is similar to "traditional grip" on the snare drum. This stick makes a snapping sound that is particularly difficult to master. The left hand also articulates the consistent beat in most *adi*s. Next, one learns the *adi* pattern orally using mnemonic drum syllables, *son adi* ("spoken rhythm") that orally articulate the timbre, accent, and flow.

Next, one learns the sticking patterns associated with the *son adi*: the higher, dry left-hand snap and the lower, resonant right-hand boom. After the drummed *adi* is secure in the hands, kinesthetically habituated in the body, the dance pattern is taught (see Box 12.1). My teacher Ramu taught me that dance should always be learned while drumming, thus emphasizing the interconnected, intersensorial nature of music structure and embodied practice (▶ Video example 12.4).

Parai Music Theory as Embodiment

Not only is *parai-attam* intersectional as part of a larger genre, but it is also intersensorial. The fundamentally interconnected nature of the senses are unified in the body's perception, and the drum becomes an extension of the

Box 12.1 Exercise: Practicing *Tappattam Adi* Hand and Step Patterns

1. Watch ⏵ Video example 12.5, a demonstration of the *son adi*, sticking, accents, dance steps, and feel of the six-pulse version of *tappattam*.
   - The six-pulse *tappattam* pattern is recited as Jen - ja na ka - (or using the alternative standardized mnemonics, Din - ku ta ku -). Note that each dash represents a rest for one pulse.
   - The first stroke in *tappattam adi* (Figure 12.6) is *jen* (or *din*), a loud accented double-stick flam ("2" in the sticking notation means striking both hands almost simultaneously) on the first beat. *This is emphasized in the dance with the cocked right leg making a hard toe stomp behind the body* (⏵ Video example 12.7, cue point 9:25). Its physical grounding is emphasized on the drum with the lower-tone resonant right-hand stroke.
   - If felt in duple meter, the second beat in this six-pulse pattern is *na* (or *ta*), which comes on the fourth pulse after the *ja* (or *ku*) on the third pulse, helps lift and rock the body leftward. *Na* is a dry snap struck alone with the left hand as a secondary accent. At the same time, *the left foot lightly drags to move the body toward the right and the bent knee cocks upward.* Now, try to recite the *adi* clapping on *Jen* and *na*.
   - Finally, the accented *ka* (or *ku*) on the fifth pulse is a lower resonant articulation by the right hand, while its accent emphasizes the polyrhythmic duple-against-triple metrical organization of this *adi*. The sixth pulse is silent, further accenting the fifth, and creating a sense of suspension. Recite the *adi* clapping on *Jen, ja,* and *ka*. Accent the *ka*.
2. Practice reciting the *son adi* (mnemonic syllables) while shifting from clapping the duple to the triple or divide your class into two groups and clap them simultaneously. Try to clap the polyrhythm, practicing with ⏵ Video example 12.5, cue point 6:44.
3. When you can recite and play this pattern with your hands (when it has become a habit), add the step pattern in ⏵ Video example 12.7 and described above in italics. The stepping pattern is also introduced at a slower speed in ⏵ Video example 12.5, cue point 8:29.

> 4. Reflect on and discuss the experience of practicing these polyrhythms through recitation, clapping, and movement. Consider how the parts intersect. Does noticing these intersections help you grasp the patterns in your body holistically? Notice how you feel as you become comfortable with all the parts. Finally, when you feel a sense of "groove" (that the parts have been integrated internally), be sure to look up at others in the group and notice how you are connecting with them.

hands and the feet (Merleau-Ponty [1945] 1962). Ramu exemplifies this as he invokes a sense of *rasa* or mood. "You have to first listen to the sweetness of the beat. Some beats are pleasing, while others bring pathos to the senses [*sohamāna*]. Some beats have to be played loud and rough [*mot aṭi*]. You have to know which beat is appropriate for which dance" (⦿ Video example 12.6). Ramu's timbral reference to the quality of the beat extends the genre's collective nature associating it with the senses. The correlation between accents in the drumming and dance and the accumulative groove creates the mood.

Ramu's lesson also exemplifies what Greg Downey, in his study of the interplay between sound and gesture in capoeira, refers to as "hearing the processes of perception." That is, cultural knowledge and experience of the art is based on perception, which is a cultural process that "condition[s] the ear" (2002, 489). Thus, to understand how musical meaning is perceived in sound through pedagogy, we must analyze how one knows, culturally, "how to hear" (2002, 489). As the quality of *adi* patterns—sweetness, pathos, loudness, or roughness—determines which dance steps (rocking, forward moving, or quick, minimal steps) are most appropriate for the drumming, we see that movement is intrinsic to "hearing" music.

In *parai-attam*, a type of *reorientation* happens when any drummer plays the *matra* (transition or cadential) *adi* to begin a new drum pattern and potentially a new dance. As collective improvisation, other members of the group seamlessly, through visual and kinesthetic clues, reorient their drumming patterns and steps to lock in with the leader (Hahn 2007, 112). How does one learn this? How do one's body, feet, and hands become (re)oriented to engage intersensorially with the other bodies in the group? How can film contribute to the analysis of this process?

Ramu explains the theoretical knowledge necessary to coordinate (or reorient) *parai-attam*, emphasizing the intersectional stance that one has to "listen" to the dance. "Some learn by watching the hands. But, in order to understand the leg movements, you have to listen. You must ask yourself which dance is he dancing, then observe how he lifts his leg and puts it down" (2008; ⊙ Video example 12.7). Downey describes this as "coming to live one's way kinesthetically into a distinctive musical world" (2002, 504). Thus, the body uses all its senses to learn to react to subtle changes when playing *parai*.

Once when I was struggling to learn an *adi* pattern, my teacher Ramu said, "How is the taste of food without salt? That is how your playing is" (September 2008). The quantitative text or graphic notation in Figures 12.4–12.6 are like looking at an image—a drawn sketch—of food. A written description is like bland food. In both, the reader cannot have an embodied firsthand experience of the flavors or how they blend. An embodied analysis and description through film, as I provide below, however, brings the reader closer to the complex, immediate sensation of direct experience. Engaging all our senses helps us understand the flavored essence from which transcriptions and written descriptions of ethnomusicological analysis are abstracted.

Film Analysis: Decasteing and Regendering through *Parai-Attam*

The Catholic nuns at the Sakthi Folk Cultural Centre in Dindigul, Tamil Nadu, use *parai-attam* to empower female high school dropouts from the Dalit community. Their goals are to transform the students' identities from oppressed failures into Sakthi Dalits (empowered female, anti-caste activists) through self-esteem and community building, and to reclaim the value of village folk arts and instruments, considered by many to be degraded (*kochai*, see Paige*). An analysis of their *parai-attam* training, as documented in my film *Sakthi Vibrations* (2019), shows the embodied transformation of these girls as they develop self-respect and reclaim their dignity through learning to perform beautifully choreographed, flawlessly executed dances with straight lines and round circles that represent "collectivity, unity, and equality" (Sr. Chandra, interview with the author, July 2013). Further, they transform their gender—from impish and insecure to emboldened confident young women bringing out their inner *sakthi* or female power—through playing the *parai*, traditionally only performed by men from their communities.[3] Kavitha, one of the trainers, articulated Sakti's intersectional intent: "Some people look down on *parai*. Those who play the *tappu* [another name for *parai*] are also thought of as low. To change that and bring the *parai* to a higher status, we women take the *parai* in our own hands and dance with it" (▶ Video example 12.8). Sister Felci further articulated Sakthi's method in her introduction to the trainees' first public performance in 2013, saying, "All the barriers of caste, religion, and race are shattered by the majestic sound of the *parai*. It allows people to live as human beings, creating empathy in the heart." The students then sang, "The vibration of the *parai* takes away our fears" (▶ Video example 12.9).

In scenes from the documentary analyzed below, one can observe a transformation in the trainees: from their inability to play and lack of self-esteem in their early training to confidence and the embodied expression of community liberation and joy through developing synchronicity in their performances later in the year. I observe and analyze the perceptual process of the trainee bringing the drum, the sound, and the dance into their experience of self-actualization, which involves "listening": an embodied process of perceptually attending to the relationship between the accents and qualities of both the drumming and dance patterns as well as to the other dancing-drumming bodies with which one is in relationship, or intercorporeality (Weiss 1999).

As poor, outcaste, high school dropouts, most girls come to the Sakthi Centre overwhelmed by feelings of failure. At the Centre's yearly opening ritual, instead of showing excitement as a grooving celebratory beat is played on the *tavil* drum, their embodied stance of utter fear and uncertainty about what this experience will bring was palpable as their wide eyes jumped in coordination as the drum strikes (▶ Video example 12.10). On their first day of training in June 2013, they were awkward and lacked seriousness. Some struggled to coordinate their feet following the simple mnemonics of "ta ka di mi," right left, right left (▶ Video example 12.11). Others joked, turned, and playfully moved their upper bodies. Many lacked confidence, shivered, or expressed confusion and passivity.

Two months later, at their first public performance, the tying of ankle bells ritually brought the trainees into the troupe, while their sense of community

---

[3] In turn, they raise the status of women folk artists, typically considered prostitutes, through embracing a middle-class sensibility (Seizer 2005).

in daily life was still forming. Similarly, their lines were still crooked and their circles wobbled. At the beginning of the performance, we notice Reji (▶ Video example 12.12, the second from the left at cue point 0:06–0:13) struggling to articulate the pattern at the shift of the *adi* and to get in sync with the dance pattern as the group moves from line to circle. As they finish playing the opening twelve-pulse *temmangu adi*, "jen - ja na ku di na ku di na ku di," and shift to "jen - - jen - - na ku di na ka -," Reji's attention is forward instead of turned to focus on and follow the dancer to her left. For the next three reiterations of the new pattern, she finds her place in the circle, yet only hits the accented first beat and then the first two beats of the new pattern ("jen - - jen - -"), remaining upright instead of bending into the accents with her upper body (cue point 0:10). She misses the second leg cross and must double-step (0:10), executing the foot pattern correctly only the fourth time (cue point 0:12). Reji's performance foregrounded here deviates from the preplanned "ideal" music and dance choreography that the older students in the group played (the sounds of which dominate the recording, and which would be the focus of a notated text). Instead, film allows us to focus on Reji's experience of negotiating the relationship between her drumming articulations and foot pattern, her shifting attention, and the timing and process of coming into sync with the group.

Film further foregrounds Reji's process of learning, visually distinguishing her articulations (played and missed) by focusing on the relationship between partially performed sequential articulations of the *adi* and danced articulations of the feet. We observe and deduce how Reji may be thinking about the previously played and practiced patterns, those she plays in each frame, those to come when she gets in sync, and how she is able to move through this "mistake" by perceptively striking structural points in the *adi* that also fall on the dance accents. Focusing on Reji's embodiment and intercorporeal alignment with the group, we observe her movement from a self-conscious lack of kinesthetic habituation to a more confident degree of habituated motor intentionality. Through this learning process her body started to memorize the movements. She no longer needed to think about them as she integrated her drum with her body while her body "listened to" the collective body of the group of dancers. She thereby began to express her *sakthi* feminine power and presence through *parai-attam*, constituting herself as part of the community of Dalit women moving toward a greater sense of humanity through the arts.

By the end of the year, Reji and the other students developed their skills to the level at which they had embodied the drum and reclaimed it as empowering. Indeed, Cynthia, another Sakthi trainee, shared that her hands and feet moved more automatically, and she felt great unification and joy from being able to keep up with the older girls.[4] They no longer worried about the learning process of their bodies but focused on synchronicity with the other dancing bodies and exchanging energy with the audience, thereby creating and being fully in community. The *parai* became an extension of their bodies and part of their identity as Dalit-Bahujans. Through practicing these folk arts, they reclaimed the *parai*'s worth, celebrated women's strength, and reoriented their identities toward habits of confidence and practices of community. In so doing, they actively create Dalit/women's liberation.

In conclusion, through case studies of Kurinji Malar and the Sakthi Centre's performance and pedagogy using both a positivist and a film-based, embodied approach to performance analysis, I demonstrate that *parai* drummers have an aesthetic/music theory. Their repertoires of dozens of *adi* rhythmic patterns are associated with the intersectional components of Tamil folk genres—including dance steps and accents, mnemonic syllables, tunes, performance structure, cadences, and *tirmanam*s—through which they play an essential role as announcers of ritual and life cycle events. Film as a medium of analysis effectively demonstrates the relationships between the collective body of players and interactions between music and dance. This is the qualitative intersectional and intersensorial aesthetic knowledge of *parai-attam*.

The political significance of acknowledging *parai* epistemology in these studies is reflected in Amulraj's assertion that "this is a music!," and the Sakthi Centre's goal to reclaim the value of the folk arts. We recognize that caste and casteism still exist within the lives and experiences of these artists as well as the arts institutions of India, functioning to hierarchize the value of different arts and artists: classical as pure and folk as degraded, untouchable, and unhearable. To demonstrate the values of collectivity and embodied empowerment through ethnomusicological analysis of *parai-attam* thus contributes to dismantling this hierarchy.

---

[4] Personal communication, July 6, 2018.

Works Cited

Butler, Judith. 1988. "Performative Acts and Gender Constitution: An Essay in Phenomenology and Feminist Theory." *Theater Journal* 40(4): 519–531.

Downey, Greg. 2002. "Listening to Capoeira: Phenomenology, Embodiment and the Materiality of Music." *Ethnomusicology* 46(3): 487–509.

Gunasekaran, S. 2021. "Documenting a Caste: The Chakkiliyars in Colonial and Missionary Documents in India." *Caste: A Global Journal on Social Exclusion* 2(1): 47–66.

Hahn, Tomie. 2007. *Sensational Knowledge: Embodying Culture through Japanese Dance.* Middletown, CT: Wesleyan University Press.

Margu. 2001. *Arunthathiyar Vazhum Varalaru.* Palayamkottai: St. Xavier College.

Merleau-Ponty, Maurice. 1962 [1945]. *Phenomenology of Perception.* London: Routledge and Kegan Paul.

Seizer, Susan. 2005. *Stigmas of the Tamil Stage: An Ethnography of Special Drama Artists in South India.* Durham, NC: Duke University Press.

Sherinian, Zoe. 2011. *This Is a Music: Reclaiming an Untouchable Drum.* DVD, 74 mins. Alexander Street Press.

Sherinian, Zoe. 2019. *Sakthi Vibrations.* Ethnographic Documentary. Edited by Jeffery Palmer. Unpublished.

Stone, Ruth. 2005. *Music in West Africa: Experiencing Music, Expressing Culture.* Oxford: Oxford University Press.

Valarmadi, Mu. 2009. *Parai: Research on the Musical Instrument.* Chennai: Amruthar Pathippagam.

Weiss, Gail. 1999. *Body Images: Embodiment as Intercorporeality.* New York: Routledge.

Interviews with the Author

Sr. Chandra, Dindigul, July 2013.
Essiah, Munaivendri, September 2008.
Kavitha Kalidass, Dindigul, July 2013.
Ramu, Munaivendri, September 2008.

13

Caste, Class, Aesthetics, and the Making of Modern Bharatanatyam Dance

Hari Krishnan and Davesh Soneji, with a contribution by Nrithya Pillai

Bharatanatyam (*bharatanāṭyam*) dance is perhaps one of the most easily recognizable cultural products of modern India. The iconic image of the bharatanatyam dancer—in exotic postures and bejeweled costumes meant to signal the images found on ancient Hindu temple sculptures—adorns everything from tourism advertisements by the Indian government to Indian restaurant menus around the world. Moreover, the global "industry" of bharatanatyam dance ranges from large-scale transnational arts festivals to the performances hosted by local elite cultural organizations called *sabha*s (*sabhā*s) in South India to typically amateur dance classes held in the basements of homes and temples in almost every city in the United States. Underpinning all of these acts of heritage-making is a complex, modern history of the dance's reinvention, intimately tethered to the forces of Indian cultural nationalism in the early twentieth century. In this process of reinvention, not only was dance recast in terms of its symbolic and technical language, but it was also repopulated by dominant-caste elites and gave rise to an entirely new cultural economy—that of "classical Indian dance"—enabling the global flows of an embodied idea of "India's national classical heritage." Bharatanatyam dance, we suggest, thus became and remains an exercise in embodied nationalism and the caste-based control over culture. This essay contextualizes the caste debate within the context of the reinvention of bharatanatyam that occurred in the 1930s by elite nationalist Brahmins. It argues that expressions of caste- and class-based power were at the heart of the establishment of the aesthetic and social boundaries of the practice of bharatanatyam in its new, urban, middle-class, dominant-caste avatar in cities like Chennai.

A Critical History of Modern Bharatanatyam Accounting for Caste

The city of Chennai presents us with a set of aspirational taste habits around the so-called classical performing arts that have been shaped largely by Brahminic cultural hegemony. The sub-caste known as Smarta Brahmins have wielded disproportionate amounts of power in the life of the modern city, first under British patronage, when they were considered the "indigenous intelligentsia" of South India and placed in positions of civic power in the nineteenth century, then later as "cultural brokers" of nationalist-inflected arts projects that were reconstituted in the 1920s and 1930s at the dawning of independent India (Hancock 1999; Fuller and Narasimhan 2014). Brahminic hegemony in this region also gave rise to the Self-Respect Movement beginning in the 1920s, an emancipatory anti-caste movement that deeply affected the political life of the modern state of Tamil Nadu.[1] Bharatanatyam dance, which was reinvented precisely at the highpoint of these displays of (and challenges to) caste-based power in the civic life of modern South India, bears the deep imprint of these politics.

Before its reinvention at the hands of cultural nationalists in the 1930s, bharatanatyam and its music were the exclusive practice of a hereditary community of professional artists, whose presence is richly documented from the seventeenth century onward throughout the Tamil- and Telugu-speaking regions of South India.[2] The women of this community practiced music and dance in royal courts, some Hindu temples, and at elite social events. It is also significant that these women led non-conjugal sexual lives and typically lived as the "second wives" or concubines of elite (usually married) men. Such a role was tolerated in elite South Indian society on the one hand, yet these women always held a socially ambiguous position. Even in the seventeenth and eighteenth centuries, they were often vilified in literature and the historical record. The English term "courtesan," often used to refer to these women, indexes both their courtly, artistic role as well as their ambiguous

---

[1] The Self-Respect Movement was started by E. V. Ramasami Naicker (1879–1973) (Geetha and Rajadurai, 1998). Male and female members of the courtesan community were at the heart of the movement since its inception, and Naicker himself became a spokesperson for the abolition of these women's lifestyles in 1927 (Soneji 2012, 139–142).

[2] Davesh Soneji shows that dancers, concubines, and female temple-servant figures populate South Indian cultural history from as early as the sixth century CE. But the coalescing of these roles into a single figure—the "*devadasi*-courtesan" of the nineteenth and early twentieth centuries—only occurs in the seventeenth century, especially under the patronage of the Nayaka dynasty rulers in Thanjavur (Soneji 2012).

social status.[3] Indeed, the origins of their music and dance practices are firmly rooted in a courtly telos, and even their temple-based activities ultimately deployed courtly vocabulary and symbology.[4] The bulk of their artistic repertoire revolved around the singing and gestural representation of love poetry (in which the hero of the poem was sometimes a deity such as Krishna [Kṛṣṇa], a king, or other male patron), occasionally interspersed with passages of rhythmic movement. A typical nineteenth-century courtesan love poem looked like this Telugu-language piece in the lyrical genre known as *javali* (*jāvaḷi*):

> *Oho!* Handsome! Why do you keep me trapped in desire?
> Take me in your arms quickly, my love!
> Haven't I suffered long enough
> with love for your glowing body,
> for the game that lovers play,
> your lips drinking from mine?
> Why do you ignore me like this?
> Enough! Get out of here!
> I thought you were an expert at lovemaking,
> so I asked you to match your love to mine.
> Is this the extent of your passion?
> Ah, now I know the man behind the disguise!
> Just go away, since you're leaving me still burning, still unfulfilled!
> *Oho!* Handsome! You are youthful god Krishna of Jagannāthapura,

---

[3] Many scholarly and popular works on *devadasis* and bharatanatyam dance speak of a supposed "golden age" when *devadasis* were universally respected and even worshipped as goddesses. This narrative frames their history as one of a moral "fall," caused by colonialism or sometimes "Muslim rule." We write against this narrative, arguing that *devadasis* were always considered socially ambiguous and marginal women (often because of their non-normative sexuality), even when they were accorded ritual prestige in some Brahmanic temple contexts.

[4] In mainstream writings on *devadasis*, they are largely glossed as "temple dancers," and their origins and practices are seen as inextricably linked to Hindu temples. We write against this narrative, building off the work of Leslie Orr (2000), who clearly demonstrates that "temple women" in early medieval Tamil Nadu were not the same as the *devadasi*-courtesans we encounter in the nineteenth and twentieth centuries. Indeed, later, when dance was incorporated into certain temple contexts, this involved the transposition of courtly technique and vocabulary into the ritual framework of South Indian temples, not the other way around. The popular scripting of bharatanatyam as a "temple dance" is thus an inaccurate representation that does not take into account that all its contemporary technique and repertoire can essentially be traced to courtly roots and systems of patronage.

who protects the poet Nārāyaṇa.[5] (*ohoho sundaruḍā*, Bilahari *rāga*, Eka *tāla*, attributed to the poet Nārāyaṇa Dāsu)

Women in these communities supported their families by working in and/or managing professional performance troupes, known as *melams* (*mēḷams*). In Tamil Nadu, the male musicians in this community played the oboe-like *nagasvaram* (*nāgasvaram*), the cylindrical *tavil*, and the barrel drum *mridangam* (*mṛdaṅgam*) in temple and courtly contexts. Prior to the early decades of the twentieth century, women in this community were known to outsiders by a range of opaque and sometimes pejorative vernacular names—including *dasi* (Tamil: *tāci*, "slave") and *bhogam* (Telegu: "woman of enjoyment")—that indexed their always-already ambiguous social status. In colonial ethnographic writing, these indigenous terms were replaced by the singular Sanskrit term "*devadasi*" (*devadāsī*), which carried with it a history of European Orientalist ideas about the dancers of India being "temple prostitutes" or "brides of the Hindu gods," and also posited temple-based (instead of courtly) origins for their artform. This term, *devadasi*, was then reified by Indian reformers and nationalists. Influenced by Victorian values of propriety, Indian elites were now embarrassed by the "immorality" of these women and began to distance themselves and their families from the long-standing tradition of institutionalized concubinage that these women represented.

In the last decades of the nineteenth century, Indian nationalist elites began a vociferous century-long movement to abolish the livelihood of courtesan artists in South India. The major intervention was made in the late 1920s by a woman reformer, medical doctor, and legislator, Dr. Muthulakshmi Reddy (1886–1968). While many authors, including academics, inaccurately describe her as "a *devadasi*," her mother *was* from a courtesan family. However, Reddy more closely identified with her Brahmin father, under whose stewardship her career developed. Later, she positioned herself at the center of the most powerful political forces of her time: Gandhian nationalism and the Tamil Self-Respect Movement. In 1927, in her capacity as the first female legislator in India, she put forth a bill in the Madras Legislative Assembly to abolish "the *devadasi* system." The bill sought primarily to criminalize the ritual known as *pottukattu* (*poṭṭukaṭṭu*, "the tying of the *poṭṭu* pendant") by

---

[5] This unpublished *javali* was sung by the late Saride Mythili in Duvva village (West Godavari district, Andhra Pradesh) in March 2002. Transcription and translation are by the authors.

which a young woman was marked as a courtesan (and not as a wife).[6] The tying of the *pottu* sometimes carried with it a gift of tax-free land originally owned by royal courts or temples. Ownership was contingent on the women's obligatory music and dance performance in these temples or courts. Reddy's bill also sought, as a welfare gesture, to permanently hand over the entitlement deeds of the gifted lands to these women, without any further obligation. Ultimately, however, these lands were usurped by others.

Many women from these communities staged protests by writing memos to the Madras Government and to Tamil, Telugu, and English newspapers (Figure 13.1). These protests argued the following critical points: (1) that Reddy's proposed bill would end the livelihood of women in the community and terminate their role as breadwinners for their families; (2) that *devadasi* concubinage did not amount to sex-work; (3) that this was a social justice issue they address using the modern English phrase "human rights"; and (4) that men in their own communities would use this opportunity to restore patrilineal inheritance in their families, which would devastate the future of their female descendants (Soneji 2012, 123–129; 227–234).

Despite these efforts, Reddy's "Devadasi Abolition Bill" was passed, and some twenty years later, transformed into law, in the form of the "Madras Devadasis (Prevention of Dedication) Act of 1947." In the interim, however, the controversy around the initial bill afforded social leverage and opportunity to men in the *devadasi* community. They invented a new caste for themselves, Isai Velalar (*icai vēḷāḷar*, "cultivators of music," understood as a "respectable" extension of the *vēḷāḷar* land-owning community), often taking on the surname "Pillai," and thereby inserting themselves into a "respectable" modern caste identity (Soneji 2012, 143–150). This new appellation enabled men from the community to slip easily into spaces of political and civic life that were increasingly being populated by non-Brahmin individuals, due in part to the Self-Respect Movement.[7] While this new caste category afforded social possibility to men in the community, for women, it simply cloaked older stigmas: everyone knew that an "Isai Velalar woman" was a "*devadasi*." Similarly, this label

---

[6] In much scholarly writing about *devadasi*s, they are framed as being "married to god" or "brides of god." This is largely the legacy of early twentieth-century reform debates that emphasized the religious lives of *devadasis*. In pre-reform texts, they are often called kaṇikaiyar (from the Sanskrit gaṇikā, "courtesan") and almost never referred to as wives, let alone brides of god. Even though the ritual of tying the *poṭṭu* pendant was called "temple dedication" in reform debates, it often took place in courtly contexts or the homes of *devadasi* community members (Soneji 2012).

[7] Male Isai Velalar beneficiaries of the reform movement include two of the most powerful and venerated figures in the history of the modern politics of Tamil Nadu, the Chief Ministers C. N. Annadurai (1909–1969) and M. Karunanidhi (1924–2018) (Soneji 2012; Srinivasan 1984).

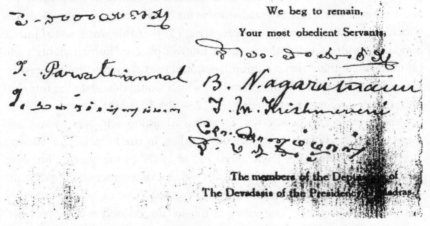

21. Appeal for Justice:—Finally we beg to close this appeal to you not to pass any legislation suppressing or interfering in any manner whatsoever with our dedicating ourselves to a life of religion and service. Kindly consider our great past and the ever brightful future. Do not be blinded away by prejudice and personalities or be guided by impulses. In trying to mend an evil do not end the institution. Remember that every nation is a body politic, that every nation has one life, that neglect of one part injure all. Give us our birth right to live and work for the cause of our country. Encourage and foster our ideals of love and religion and service; and our arts of music and dancing. We are the modern descendants of those who in the past held aloft the torch of civilization. Do not mistake the opinions of the few interested champions for public opinion. You who stood for religion toleration and freedom of religious and philosophical opinions in the past, you who boast of your tender love for small communities we pray that you may allow us to live and work out our salvation and manifest ourselves in the dual aspect of wisdom and devotion, Gnana and Bhakti and show to the world both the aspects of spirituality and the noblest religion enshrined in the sublimest philosophy and that we keep alight the torch of India's religion amidst the fogs and storms of increasing materialism and interpret the message of India to the nations of the world.

We beg to remain,

Your most obedient Servants,

The members of the Deputation of
The Devadasis of the Presidency of Madras.

Figure 13.1 A facsimile of one of the memos signed by members of the Madras Devadasis Association, protesting Muthulakshmi Reddy's Devadasi Abolition Bill of 1927.

too, seems untenable in the modern world, for it carries a deep stigma based on perceptions around these women's sexual immorality, as Nrithya Pillai, a hereditary woman artist from this community, explains in Box 13.1.

The Dominant-Caste Repopulation of Dance and the Sedimentation of Caste-Based Difference

A few years after the "Devadasi Abolition Bill" (1927) was passed, a group of dominant-caste, elite cultural nationalists adopted what they called a "sympathetic" view of the arts. In other words, while they agreed with reformers that

Box 13.1 Nrithya Pillai

I am a dancer, dance composer, singer, writer, speaker, and dance instructor who proudly claims my hereditary, Bahujan courtesan lineage. I am the artistic director of Rajarathnalaya, a bharatanatyam institution founded by my maternal grandfather Swamimalai Rajarathnam Pillai (1931–1994). I consciously preserve and reanimate the rich repertoire, teaching, and choreographic practices of my celebrated ancestors, who include the *nattuvanar*s (*naṭṭuvaṉār*s, dance-masters) Vaitheeswarankoil Meenakshisundaram Pillai, Thiruvalaputtur K. Swaminatha Pillai, and Vazhuvoor B. Ramaiah Pillai. I attempt to carve out my own space as a performer and ultimately hope for a new kind of artistic and intellectual engagement with the troubled history of modern bharatanatyam. I aim to vigorously challenge the power relationships and ideologies that made the form unavailable to women of my community and advocate fiercely for the restoration of credit for bharatanatyam technique, repertoire, and philosophy to the hereditary community of practitioners. My performances and writings about the dominant castes' appropriation of this form—which have evoked both enthusiastic accolades and awards on the one hand and vicious resistance on the other—are at once embodied research, political intervention, and a labor of abiding love toward the traditional custodians of the form, especially my foremothers, who include the remarkable Thiruvalaputtur Kalyani (1873–1958). If the burden of bearing this history were not hard enough, there are some people—usually dominant-caste performers of bharatanatyam—who insist on calling contemporary descendants such as me "*devadasi*s." As a woman who lives with the quotidian stigma of over 180 years of reform and close to a hundred years of the repopulation of our dance by others, I fiercely reject the othering and stigma-laden label "*devadasi*" and choose to be called a "hereditary artist" (*pārampariya naṭaṉa kalaiñar*) from South India.

How does one counter the systemic and institutionalized erasure of hereditary women performers in bharatanatyam that has been described in this essay? Certainly, a change in both the discourse of bharatanatyam and its practice is necessary. We need to foreground the invented nature of the twentieth-century discourse and replace it with real social histories of dance practice. This is a challenge for *all* practitioners of bharatanatyam—whether they are conscious of it or not, whether they deny it or not—they

Figure 13.2 Nrithya Pillai. Photo by Iyappan Arumugam; used with permission.

are all implicated in this problematic history every time they lay claim to this dance and tie bells on their feet. But another major reparation has to do with who gets to speak for bharatanatyam. I come from the erased histories. I represent the remnants of what the state and the Brahminic power structure tried to erase. To my mind, my very presence, my body, my aesthetics, and my reclamation of who I am question and complicate this "clean" history of bharatanatyam. Other women like me, I hope, will also come forward to understand and reclaim our place in these muddied, yet perhaps generative, pasts.

devadasi lifestyles had to be criminalized, they felt that *devadasis* embodied precious music and dance practices that needed to be grafted onto "respectable" women's bodies, and these transformed arts were to be deployed as the heritage of the nation. To this end, beginning in 1933, the Madras Music Academy, an almost exclusively Brahmin organization (established by the Indian National Congress in 1928), began to host a series of performances by women from courtesan backgrounds. These performances, however, held at the very height of the *devadasi* abolition movement, cannot be read as an instance of well-intentioned public patronage of hereditary female artists. On the contrary, as E. Krishna Iyer, the secretary of the Music Academy, explains in a letter addressed to Muthulakshmi Reddy in *The Hindu* newspaper in 1932, their intent was appropriation:

> For my part, it is no question of Art at the expense of morality, or even positive encouragement of the present-day nautch girls as a class and never a justification for the perpetuation of the Devadasi class as such. The Heavens would not fall and morality would in no way be jeopardised if one or two cases of very good Art is reluctantly tolerated in exceptional instances—without the associated vice—as a matter of *temporary evil necessary, pending the coming up of better persons.* (Krishna Iyer 1932, emphasis added)

In other words, the public display of the dance of *devadasi*s (also historically called "*nautch*") at the Music Academy was a "temporary evil"; it was meant to jump-start a process by which dominant-caste elites ("better persons") could practice and steward these arts in the future. Years later, Krishna Iyer makes it clear that an intentional program of appropriation and social engineering was at work on the part of the dominant-caste cultural nationalists through the work of the Music Academy:

> Bharata Natya was still in the hands of exponents of the old professional class, with all its possible and lurking dangers as pointed out by social reformers. The efforts of the present writer were turned towards *steadily taking it out of their hands and introducing it among cultured, family women of respectable classes.* (Krishna Iyer 1948, 24, emphasis added)

While terms like "respectable," "family women," and "better persons" appear as markers of class status, they also reference dominant castes. Iyer's comments are cloaked in the nationalist language of "respectable classes," a euphemism for the dominant-caste, English-educated elite, particularly Brahmins, that formed the intellectual and social backbone of Indian cultural nationalism.

Iyer's vision of the transference of dance knowledge "out of the hands of the old professional class" was realized in the figure of Rukmini Arundale (1904–1986). Rukmini was the daughter of Nilakantha Shastri, a Brahmin engineer and member of the Theosophical Society, a global occult organization headquartered in Madras, populated largely by Tamil Brahmins, and intimately braided with the Indian nationalist movement. The leader of the Theosophical Society at the time was Annie Besant (1847–1933), a British woman who was also president of the Indian National Congress, and mentor to the young Rukmini. At the age of sixteen, Rukmini married George Arundale (1878–1945), who later became president of the Theosophical Society. Together, the Arundales traveled the world as ambassadors for the Society. In 1928, they met the Russian ballerina Anna Pavlova, whom they had previously seen dance in India, and she arranged ballet classes for Rukmini. As a child, Rukmini had also studied "Greek" and "Oriental" dancing, reconstructed forms taught by Eleanor Elder, who staged plays for the Theosophical Society that enacted some of the organization's occult beliefs. The tethering of dance with notions of "metaphysics" and "spiritual enlightenment" from the Theosophists undoubtedly shaped Rukmini's reinvention of bharatanatyam as a "spiritual practice" by the late 1930s.[8]

In 1933, Krishna Iyer invited Rukmini Arundale to a performance of bharatanatyam at the Music Academy, the explicit purpose of which was to inspire "respectable" women to learn the art (Figure 13.3). This performance was by Rajalakshmi (1900–1969) and Jeevaratnam (1905–1933), the young daughters of the highly accomplished courtesan performer Thiruvalapputtur Kalyani (1873–1958), and disciples of the dance-master (*naṭṭuvaṉār*) Pandanallur Meenakshisundaram Pillai (1869–1954). Seeing this performance, Arundale decided she wanted to learn bharatanatyam, fulfilling the vision that Iyer had in inviting these dancers to the Music Academy. A year later, Arundale sought out Pandanallur Meenakshisundaram Pillai and trained with him for about six months. In 1935, she wanted to premiere her version of what he had taught her during this relatively short period at the Diamond Jubilee Celebrations of the Theosophical Society. However, Pillai felt she was not yet ready to perform publicly. Against the wishes of her teacher (a bold challenge to the traditional pedagogical system in which a courtesan studied for many years before publicly performing), Arundale performed an altered interpretation of Pillai's repertoire in December 1935. This first pedagogical encounter set the pattern for decades of extractive

---

[8] Even when bharatanatyam was performed in temples, typically it was the performance of courtly dance genres during festivals in open, public pavilions. The idea that *devadasi*s performed daily temple rituals for the deity in the temple sanctum (as "wife of the deity") is a colonial, Orientalist misreading that was internalized/reified by cultural nationalists and later scholars (Soneji 2012, 6–12).

Figure 13.3 Thiruvalaputtur Rajalakshmi and Jeevaratnam at their 1933 performance at the Music Academy, flanked by Thiruvalaputtur Pakkirisami (clarinetist) and Thiruvalaputtur K. Swaminatha Pillai.

work, in which non-hereditary artists—Brahmin women in particular—mined the bodies and labor of hereditary performers for "rare" repertoire and technique, often without an eye to the well-being, growth, and progress of younger generations within these courtesan communities. In other words, Arundale's project (and the Kalakshetra school she establishes) set into motion the active process of the appropriation of bharatanatyam dance.

The impact of Arundale's interventions in the years that followed rested upon an idea of the recovery of a "golden age" for the dance; in her words, she "had to try to make something new—not with the idea of making it *look* new, but with the idea of making it *look* old." (Arundale 1958a, 62). In practice, she changed several aspects of the dance presentation. First, she collaborated with Theosophists Madame Cazan and Mary Elmore to design the now ubiquitous bharatanatyam costume based on Hindu temple sculptures, or in Arundale's words, costumes that were "in the spirit of what our people wore thousands of years ago" (Arundale 1958a, 62). She also staged her performances against a temple backdrop, squarely locating the dance in a new construction of Hindu antiquity. She placed an icon of the dancing god Shiva-Nataraja on the side of the stage, to lend a transcendental quality to the performance. Most important, she embarked on a project that fundamentally and irrevocably excised the aspects of repertoire and technique that were centered on human love and eroticism, which were at the ontological core of the dance of hereditary courtesan practitioners.

New Aesthetics: Sanskrit, Somatic Pedagogy, and the Regulated Brahminic Body

Rukmini Arundale founded the International Academy of the Arts in 1936, under the patronage of the Theosophical Society. Arundale's vision for the school was modeled after an imagined notion of the *gurukula*, the ancient "schools" for the dominant castes described in Sanskrit literature, in which Hindu males studied scripture, literature, and other forms of knowledge. A kind of asceticism was to pervade the campus, for it is here that the labor of the dancing body was to be yogically *and* scientifically sublimated into transcendent, or "higher" states of consciousness, as per Theosophical thought. Initially, Russian ballet was taught at the Academy, for Rukmini felt this would render the *adavu*s (*aṭavu*s, steps) "accurate in form." The new aesthetic was in large part about an athletic disciplining of the body, an emphasis on the production of "clean" lines and shapes by the dancer, and by extension, an emphasis on the dynamic, movement-oriented aspects of the form, in contrast to the interpretive textual and lyrical aspects of the older courtesan repertoire (*abhinaya*). In 1938, as the ultracosmopolitan Theosophical influence gave way to an emphasis on nationalist discourse around dance, the practice of ballet was dropped, and the institution was crowned with the new Sanskrit name Kalakshetra ("temple of the arts," Figure 13.4). Pedagogy was also governed by references to Sanskrit texts that represented dance as an aspect of the "civilizational glory" of ancient India. Sanskrit verses describing the names of gestures were memorized and ritually recited daily by students, and new Sanskrit terms like *aṅga-śuddham* ("purity of the [lines of the] body") and *manodharmam* ("the *dharma* of the mind," a reference to improvisation) that did not exist earlier became everyday terms used to judge the dancers' abilities. The dance itself was transfigured not only in terms of its optics (athleticism in technique, costume, etc.) but also in its content (the

Figure 13.4 A garlanded image of Rukmini Arundale, enshrined at the entrance of the Bharata Kalakshetra Auditorium said to be built along the architectural guidelines found in the Sanskrit text *Natyashastra*, commissioned by Arundale in 1982. Photo by author, Soneji.

replacement of erotic love poetry with Hindu, largely Sanskrit, mythological stories of deities).

At Kalakshetra, new regimes of Sanskrit intellectualism combined with somatic practices such as yoga, the theatrical and martial arts of Kerala, as well as nationalist practices such as weaving and handicrafts, produced bodies that were marked, discursively and physically, by a new kind of cosmopolitan Brahminic aesthetic. This new dancing body was crafted as a vessel that embodied a kind of "Brahminic Theosophy," in that it simultaneously represented dominant-caste Hindu orthodoxy as well as an internationalism unique to the Theosophical Society in Madras. This was a process that evacuated bharatanatyam of its earlier courtesan aesthetics, especially the expression of female desire and eroticism, and made the new, idealized dance form unattainable for economically, socially, and politically disenfranchised women from courtesan backgrounds and their descendants. While a very small handful of women artists from the courtesan community continued to perform and teach under the rubric of the "reinvented" bharatanatyam, it was mostly at the margins. The best-known exception to this is T. Balasaraswati (1918–1984), from an illustrious courtly dance family of Thanjavur, who received rave praise and patronage from mainstream institutions like the Madras Music Academy and also traveled internationally (Knight 2010). However, this was a true exception, as the vast majority of hereditary women performers did not—and indeed, could not—participate in the new economy of the "reinvented," appropriated bharatanatyam.

Not only did Rukmini Arundale find the bulk of the courtesan repertoire "not good enough" for her vision, but she also expunged aspects of the dance that she felt women of her "temperament" should not perform. For example, Arundale speaks to the audience at the 1958 All-India Dance Seminar in Delhi, when T. Balasaraswati provocatively asked her why she eschews the erotic elements of the dance in her presentations:

> You don't merely teach with what you know, but you also teach with *what you are*. . . . She [Balasaraswati] wants to know when I said that certain aspects of *śṛṅgāra rasa* (the aesthetic expression of erotic love) should not be danced to, and I don't like to dance some of them, she wants to know why. Well, it's very difficult for me unless I'm able to show you what those things are which I don't like [audience laughs]. . . . She says, "can't it be done with dignity and grace?" Of course it can be done. But some songs already have . . . what I consider *not a good enough meaning*. I don't say that, *for a person like her*, she may be able to make it so delicate . . . *she is accustomed to doing it in a particular way*. But . . . for me, *it's a temperamental difference*. I would not be able to do it. There are certain *padas* [songs] I purposely avoid. . . . She [Balasaraswati] says, "such beautiful songs ought not to be discarded; you should do it well." I said, of course, I entirely agree. If you have the genius to do it well, it is alright. But my own experience has been [that] it's not only the songs that I am talking about; there are even *certain suggestive gestures and things* during the interpretation. (Arundale 1958b, transcription of audio recording, emphasis added)

Arundale's body just cannot bring itself to do what the courtesan body did. In other words, the moral and corporeal registers upon which Arundale operates are fundamentally opposed to those of the artform she claims to now embody. The idea of "*difference in temperament*," a coded reference to caste-based differences in taste and corporeal demeanor, is yet another illustration of how the social and aesthetic world of the new bharatanatyam was being redefined through Brahminic stewardship.

Arundale's writings preserve a rich archive of materials, but here we focus on two sets of comments: those that locate non-Brahmin aesthetics as the realm of "the vulgar," and those that explicitly mark her project of reinvention as one of repopulation. First, Arundale depicts the dance of courtesans, which she witnesses many times after 1933 during her travels in the Thanjavur region, as "quite vulgar" (Arundale [1958a] in Ramani 2003, 61). Indeed, she described *devadasi* "costumes" as "very cheap tinsely stuff that did not match the dance," and required "appropriate change" (Arundale 1958a, 62). The solution to the "problem of vulgarity" in the dance was repopulation.

To understand repopulation, we must remember Arundale's relationship with Krishna Iyer, and his vision for the future of dance. Arundale echoes the words of Krishna Iyer cited above, adding that now Kalakshetra, as an institution, enables, through a "reformed pedagogy," what Krishna Iyer earlier referred to as taking dance "out of the hands of the old professional class":

> One great new thing that has come as a result of these difficulties is the complete separation of our work from the traditional dance teachers. It is a well-known fact that they are a small clan of people who have never believed it possible for anybody else to conduct a dance performance. I have always had a determination that this must go. They used to think that, except the *usual class of people*, no one else would be able to dance. Now there are so many *girls from good families* who are excellent dancers. The second aspect is to train Nattuvanars [dance teachers] from good families. I am happy that on Vijayadasami day I was able to prove that *we* could do without *them*. (Arundale in Sarada 1985, 50; Allen 1997, 64–65, emphasis added)

The "us" versus "them" rhetoric here, like her use of the phrase "usual class of people," clearly indexes the deep caste-based hierarchies at work in Arundale's reinvention. Much as nationalist historians (and often practitioners of today's bharatanatyam) may hide or creatively reinterpret passages such as these from Arundale and Krishna Iyer, it is clear that when these facts are considered collectively, they constitute a significant explanation of how Brahmins (and aspirationally Brahminic individuals) came to dominate the aesthetics, sociology, and practice of bharatanatyam.

The "Class" Dimension of the "Classical": Dance, Economy, and Religion

The reinvention engineered by Rukmini Arundale became extremely diffuse and circulated nationally by the 1940s. As dance and music became "respectable" hobbies for dominant castes, schools appeared all over Madras, and then, throughout India. Early representations of the reinvented bharatanatyam also crossed into Tamil cinema, bringing reinvented bharatanatyam to the masses (Krishnan 2019). The popularity of bharatanatyam throughout India by the 1950s gave rise to a new "industry" of classical dance and teaching it as "heritage" became a lucrative business. The aesthetic polish and capital represented by bharatanatyam also became aspirational. Ironically, non-Brahmins, and even some hereditary performers, now sought the patronage of these new Brahmin stewards and the social leverage that came with it. However, they usually remain at the periphery of the dance world. The basic structures of power in the world of bharatanatyam—its flagship cultural organizations (*sabhas*), pedagogy, scholarly representation, and institutions—were from the 1950s, and continue to be, overwhelmingly dominated by South Indian Brahmins.

This new economy of bharatanatyam continued to thrive well into the 1980s, through both state-sponsored and private patronage. Gradually, through immigration to North America, the reinvented bharatanatyam took on an unprecedented transnational presence (Fuller and Narasimhan 2014). The early 1990s saw the revivification of Hindu right-wing politics through the Bharatiya Janata Party (BJP), which espoused a politicized Hinduism known as Hindutva ("Hinduness," cf. Schultz*).[9] Reinvented bharatanatyam's neo-conservativism and orientation as "Hindu spectacle" sat comfortably alongside the Hindutva agenda. Indeed, the cultural arena occupied by today's Hindutva majoritarian politics is the logical resting place for the reinvented bharatanatyam, with its emphasis on public representations of Hindu religious narrative and sacred texts, its valorization of an imagined Brahminic "golden age" for dance, its neo-orthodox forms of bodily comportment and ritual, its moral emphasis on the censure of desire, and its heteropatriarchal gaze. In some instances, the links between right-wing Hindu politics and "classical dance" are explicit (Figure 13.5), and in

---

[9] Critical academic studies of late twentieth and twenty-first century Hindutva as a religious, social, and political phenomenon are ubiquitous. For scholarship on the relationship between the ascent of the Hindu right-wing politics culture, and economy, see Jaffrelot (2009; 2011).

THE MAKING OF MODERN BHARATANATYAM DANCE 225

Figure 13.5 DVD of a "dance ballet" entitled *Hindutva* by Kuchipudi Dancer Swathy Somnath, produced by Moser Baer Entertainment, 2012.

others they lurk in coded religious language, often remaining invisible to the publics who consume the form.

Conclusion

It is through bharatanatyam that troubling politicized religious narratives sit *alongside* an even more troubling casteist legacy of the reinvention that we have discussed (see Box 13.2). Aspects of bharatanatyam in its reinvented form that are definitively associated with Brahminical Hinduism—such as the recitation and choreography of Sanskrit prayers, the ritual worship

> **Box 13.2 Discussion**
>
> Consider the links between economic and social status and prospects to perform in public as a livelihood. How do you think the reinvention and repopulation of bharatanatyam might have affected women from *devadasi* backgrounds for whom dance was a livelihood? Think of the socioeconomic conditions of other disenfranchised artists in the same period (e.g., African American jazz musicians). How might we conceptualize the links between social hierarchy (caste, race, gender, etc.) and performance using the *devadasi* case study?

of images of gods on the stage, government-sponsored dance festivals inside Hindu temples, the legacy of Brahminic stewardship itself, and many other such phenomena—cannot be separated from the aspirations of Hindu majoritarian politics. Bharatanatyam today lives at the heart of complex, transnational Hindu engagements with the logic of global capital. The BJP has foregrounded this association in India through initiatives such as the "Incredible India" tourism campaign, in which "classical dance" occupies a central place. Bharatanatyam is thus also undeniably "mobilized to trademark India as Hindu, stable, strong, and spiritual" (Puri 2019, 331). In its reinvented avatar, bharatanatyam embodies both the affective and material dimensions of caste (see Box 13.3). While on the one hand, its caste-based aesthetics and re-scripted histories enable privilege for dominant-caste performers, it also creates cultures of exclusion that make it nearly impossible for oppressed communities to participate in the fiscal and social cachet represented by the so-called classical arts. The cumulative effects of caste-based power in the arts, which have remained largely ignored by scholars, performers, and policymakers, draw attention not only to the discriminatory, appropriating cultures of classical dance and music, but also to the intergenerational and self-reproducing nature of casteism itself. In today's world, the embeddedness of the classical arts in the world of right-wing Hindu nationalism represents another site void of the possibility for dissent. Critical histories that attend to questions of equity enable us to understand how the arts and social privilege are entangled, along with the politics of nation, the body, and religion. The practice and discourse of contemporary

> **Box 13.3 Exercise**
>
> Search for "Kalakshetra dance" on YouTube. Examine the bodily comportment of the dancers carefully. How would you perform an aesthetic analysis based on movement? "Good" bharatanatyam is often defined today by "clean lines," "straight back," and "deep *aramandi*" (*araimaṇṭi*, half-sitting). Do you see such features in these performances? What other movement qualities/shapes do you recognize? What do such aesthetic signs indicate, and how do you think such bodily comportment and discipline is linked to the story of the reinvention of bharatanatyam in the 1930s?

bharatanatyam dance, therefore, provide a productive space for some of the most crucial conversations for the study of modern South Asia.

Works Cited

Allen, Matthew Harp. 1997. "Rewriting the Script for South Indian Dance." *The Drama Review* 41(3): 63–100.

Arundale, Rukmini Devi. [1958a] 2004. "My Experiments with Dance." In *Some Selected Speeches and Writings of Rukmini Devi Arundale*, edited by Shakuntala Ramani, 1:59–66. Chennai: Kalakshetra Foundation.

Arundale, Rukmini Devi. 1958b. All-India Dance Seminar. Recorded April 3, 1958. Sangeet Natak Akademi Archives, ACD—467, III/37.

Fuller, C. J., and Haripriya Narasimhan. 2014. *Tamil Brahmans: The Making of a Middle-Class Caste*. Chicago: University of Chicago Press.

Geetha, V., and S. V. Rajadurai. 1998. *Towards a Non-Brahmin Millenium: From Iyothee Thass to Periyar*. Bombay: Samya Books.

Hancock, Mary. 1999. *Womanhood in the Making: Domestic Ritual and Public Culture in Urban South India*. Boulder, CO: Westview Press.

Jaffrelot, Christophe, ed. 2009. *Hindu Nationalism: A Reader*. Princeton, NJ: Princeton University Press.

Jaffrelot, Christophe. 2011. *Religion, Caste, and Politics in India*. New York: Columbia University Press.

Knight, Douglas M. 2010. *Balasaraswati: Her Art and Life*. Middletown, CT: Wesleyan University Press.

Krishna Iyer, E. 1932. "A Reply to Dr. Muthulakshmi Reddy." *Madras Mail*, December 17.

Krishna Iyer, E. 1948. "Renaissance of Indian Dance and its Architects." Souvenir of the Sixteenth South Indian Music Conference. The Indian Fine Arts Society.

Krishnan, Hari. 2019. *Celluloid Classicism: The Early Tamil Cinema and the Making of Modern Bharatanāṭyam*. Middletown, CT: Wesleyan University Press.

Orr, Leslie. 2000. *Donors, Devotees, and Daughters of God: Temple Women in Medieval Tamil Nadu*. New York: Oxford University Press.

Puri, Jyoti. 2019. "Sculpting the Saffron Body: Yoga, Hindutva and the International Marketplace." In *Majoritarian State: How Hindu Nationalism is Changing India*, edited by Angana P. Chatterji, Thomas Blom Hansen, and Christophe Jaffrelot, 317–334. New York: Oxford University Press.

Sarada, S. 1985. *Kalakshetra Rukmini Devi: Reminiscences by S. Sarada*. Madras: Kala Mandir Trust.

Soneji, Davesh. 2012. *Unfinished Gestures: Devadāsīs, Memory, and Modernity in South India*. Chicago: University of Chicago Press.

Srinivasan, Amrit. 1984. "'Temple Prostitution' and Community Reform: An Examination of the Ethnographic, Historical and Textual Context of the Devadasi of Tamil Nadu, South India." PhD diss., Cambridge University.

14
Sacred Song, Food, and the Affective Embodied Experience of Non-Othering in the Sikh Tradition

Inderjit N. Kaur

Acute social inequality has been one of the greatest challenges of humanity, throughout history, and around the world. Time and again, expressive practices have arisen to contest and combat this social ill. In this chapter, I discuss an everyday contemporary ritual of non-Othering (rejecting socially created differences such as class, caste, race, and religion) practiced by Sikhs, a small and little-known, but strong faith community born in India about 500 years ago, and today numbering about 25 million people worldwide. For Sikhs, the paired rituals of open-house *sabad kīrtan* (collective singing, pronounced "*keertan*") and *langar* (communal dining) negate social hierarchies and exclusion; this practice of regularly transcending social boundaries (particularly caste and class) aims to habituate equal treatment of all human beings. My claim here is not that Sikhs excel at non-Othering. In fact, like most human beings, they are imperfect in their ability to live up to their ethical ideals in their social and political lives. My purpose is to explicate how the pairing of open-house collective singing and communal dining, as a standard and widespread ritual central to Sikh culture, is embodied action that encourages the everyday practice of non-Othering. I grew up in a Sikh family, and to this day this paired ritual has been part of my everyday life. Further, I have experienced firsthand the special time when social differences and hierarchies recede from one's consciousness.

In Sikh philosophy, the belief in the oneness of humanity is embedded in the idea of the Oneness (all-encompassing unity [*ik*, ੲਿਕ]) of the

---

I am grateful to Dr. Nivedita Singh, Mr. Dil Singh, and the AKJ administration for providing access to their video recordings.

Inderjit N. Kaur, *Sacred Song, Food, and the Affective Embodied Experience of Non-Othering in the Sikh Tradition* In: *Music and Dance as Everyday South Asia*. Edited by: Sarah L. Morelli and Zoe C. Sherinian, Oxford University Press. © Oxford University Press 2024. DOI: 10.1093/oso/9780197566237.003.0015

Divine, and encapsulated in the numeral 1 (੧), the first entry in the primary Sikh scripture. This concept is elaborated upon in the almost 6,000 songs that make up the scripture, through the emphasis on eradicating the conception of the Other (*dūjā*) and of duality (*dubidhā*), and the feeling of Othering (*dūjā bhāu*, lit. "other feeling").[1] Singing and breaking bread together, inclusively and with equal treatment to all, amplifies the ethical meanings in the sacred verses. The oneness within diversity is also manifest in the practice of singing the same scriptural songs in a variety of melodies, rhythms, and styles that appeal to different aesthetic preferences of people with varied lived experiences. While *sabad kīrtan* sung in most styles has some common features, such as the verse-chorus form, the use of melodic instruments and drums, and musical intensification over the course of the song, different musical styles have particular features that heighten the affective impact on and feeling of togetherness in the congregation in different ways.

I focus here on the three main styles in practice, referred to as the "classical,"[2] the "light," and the "AKJ" (*Akhand Kīrtani Jatha*, lit. uninterrupted *kīrtan* singing group). In the classical *kīrtan* style, the pairing of repeated cadential phrases with important textual phrases is a significant means of creating the feeling among participants of arriving at a meeting point. In the light *kīrtan* style, the use of melodies similar to, and often directly drawn from, popular music makes call-and-response participation easier and more enjoyable, deepening a sense of shared appreciation. In the AKJ style, enhanced congregational participation through repeated call-and-response, combined with cyclic musical intensification, brings about an experience of affective cohesion and a feeling of unity among worshippers. These different stylistic aspects of *sabad kīrtan* provide a variety of musical paths to aid the generation of embodied unifying experiences among the diversity of participants, amplifying the theme of non-Othering in the sacred songs.

---

[1] For an excellent exposition of these concepts, see Singh 2021.
[2] While this style shares some features with Hindustani music (see Wade 1987 for details on Hindustani music), the term "Hindustani music" is not used by Sikhs to refer to their *kīrtan*. My interlocutors typically used the English term "classical." Some singers and aficionados use the term *gurmat sangīt* (lit. music according to the Guru's wisdom; see Kaur 2011). Classical style *kīrtan* can be learned, taught, sung, and listened to by people of any social background. Many *gurdware* (Sikh places of worship) and other Sikh institutions offer free lessons as well.

A Philosophy of Oneness or Non-Othering

Othering is a fundamentally divisive and hierarchical process of constructing social groups as we/us versus they/them, where the Other is posited as inferior and even threatening. In South Asia, the Other has been constructed based on many social identifiers including caste, religion, race, class, gender, sexual orientation, and age.

The core philosophy of *Sikhī* (Sikhism; meaning "teachings") is contained in the Sikh scriptures, which are compilations of *sabad* (scriptural verse/s). The congregational singing of these canonized songs, *sabad kīrtan*, is a principal way Sikhs imbibe the ethical values espoused in them. The foremost value is that of non-Othering. The following *sabad* encapsulates the idea of non-Othering in *Sikhī*:

ਦੂਜਾ ਕਉਣੁ ਕਹਾ ਨਹੀ ਕੋਈ ॥	Whom should I call the Other, there
Dūjā kauṇ kahā nahī koī.	is none.
ਸਭ ਮਹਿ ਏਕੁ ਨਿਰੰਜਨੁ ਸੋਈ ॥੧॥ ਰਹਾਉ ॥	The One Immaculate pervades all.
Sabh meh ek niranjan soī. 1. Rahāo.	(Pause [Refrain])
...	
ਧਰਣਿ ਗਗਨ ਨਹ ਦੇਖਉ ਦੋਇ ॥	The earth, the sky see no Other.
Dharaṇ gagan nah dekhau doé.	
ਨਾਰੀ ਪੁਰਖ ਸਬਾਈ ਲੋਇ ॥੩॥	In women, men, all, the divine
Nārī purakh sabāī loé. 3.	permeates. (Verse 3)

(Guru Granth Sahib 1604|1708, 223; Translation by Author)

In this excerpt, the reference to the "immaculate" nature of all human beings speaks against the Indian caste system that is based on the perceived "polluted" nature of people considered to be of low and outcaste. Verse 3 speaks to gender equality. The songs in Sikh scriptures recognize equal dignity and value in all human beings and emphasize that the Other is not a natural construction ("the earth, the sky see no Other") but a social one. They encourage embodiment of non-Othering through actions (*karam*) and activities that are open and inclusive, and support diversity, equality, and service.

The primary Sikh scripture, the Guru Granth Sahib, itself embodies non-Othering in significant ways. It includes hundreds of verses known to be from saint-singers of other faiths, duly ascribed to them. All these canonized verses have sacred status. The *sabad* from the Sikh Gurus (spiritual preceptors) themselves address the divine in devotion using terms from different faiths (e.g., Ram from Hinduism, and Allah from Islam). When Sikhs bow to the Guru Granth Sahib they bow to the wisdom contained in it from all these faiths. Sikh worship thus entails equal reverence for diverse paths to the divine.

Socio-Historical Context

The dominance of the theme of non-Othering in the *sabad* and its musical rendering has much to do with the particular set of socioeconomic conditions in which Sikhī came into being. In the fifteenth century CE, India was severely stratified socially by a deeply entrenched endogamous caste system, by gender, and by sharply divided economic classes deriving from its long political history as a conglomeration of kingdoms, Hindu and Muslim. Problems of social inequality and injustice were pervasive. One of those who spoke up against these societal ills was Guru Nanak (1469–1539), from the northwest province of Punjab, who traveled far and wide voicing his ethics through song. His followers came to be called Sikhs (lit. "students") and the path he led as Sikhī, a way of life committed to oneness. His songs began the practice of *sabad kīrtan*. Guru Nanak also instituted the practice of *langar*. Communal eating while sitting at the same level was a radical practice, especially in the context of the caste system with its strict rules about food sharing between different castes. Directly challenging this belief and hierarchy, Guru Nanak instituted open-house *sabad kīrtan* and *langar*. These have continued as core components of Sikh congregational worship and affective modes of enactment and embodied knowledge of Sikhī.

Open-House Worship and Dining

A Sikh place of worship, *gurdwara* (*gurdwāra*, lit. doorway to the Guru), is open to all irrespective of faith, caste, race, class, gender, and other axes of social identity (see Figure 14.1). No monetary contribution is required to enter a *gurdwara*. The preeminent *gurdwāra*, the Harmandir Sahib, popularly known

Figure 14.1 Congregational worship at Gurdwara San Jose, California. Copyright Gurdwara San Jose Facebook, used with permission.

as the Golden Temple, in Amritsar, Punjab, leads this principle of openness—symbolically with doors on all four sides of the building, and practically, with thousands of daily attendees from diverse social backgrounds. People from all walks of life can enter the worship hall and participate as they wish (respectfully, of course) in rituals such as receiving *parshad* (*parshād*, blessed pudding) and listening to and singing along with the *sabad kīrtan*. Similarly, anyone may enjoy the communal dining in the *langar* hall. No one is questioned, ostracized, or subject to a gaze of Othering based on social difference. On the contrary, the presence of people from different backgrounds is experienced as affirmation that core ethical values are being practiced.

Equality and Service in *Langar*

The principal idea behind *langar* (communal eating) is equality. In addition to opposing the caste system, it also aimed to break hierarchies along the lines of class, gender, and age. As Desjardins and Desjardins note, "In 16th century India, this practice of sharing a meal with anyone constituted a revolutionary idea. For some Indians today it remains controversial" (2009, 11). The practice of equality in *langar* is reinforced through the seating arrangement and

Figure 14.2 *Langar* service at Gurdwara San Jose, California. Copyright Gurdwara San Jose Facebook, used with permission.

the menu. At a *langar*, everyone sits at the same level (typically on the floor), in long rows, and no one is accorded preferential treatment. Everyone is served the same simple vegetarian food in the same serveware (see Figure 14.2). One of my interlocutors put it succinctly, "No one is superior or inferior; all differences end in the *langar*."

The enactment of *seva* (*sevā*, selfless service of all) through *langar* is also salient for Sikhs. Volunteers do all the work involved in *langar*, from food preparation and serving to cleaning up. Most *gurdware* (plural of *gurdwara*, pronounced "*gurdwāray*") with regular congregational worship serve *langar*. The kitchen at the Golden Temple is typically open around the clock; an estimated 50,000–100,000 people from all social backgrounds eat there every weekday, with around 150,000 on weekends and special occasions. The Sikh diaspora worldwide has maintained the *langar* tradition. The *gurdwara* in San Jose, California, the largest in North America, serves about 5,000 congregants every Sunday, and around 15,000 on special occasions. I have also seen on many occasions Hindu visitors enjoying *langar* in an open, inclusive, social, and relaxed environment.[3]

---

[3] Since this *gurdwara* is not in a city center and not easily accessible by public transport, the diversity of the attendees is nowhere what it is at the Golden Temple and many other *gurdware* in India.

The *seva* aspect of *langar* is also manifest in the practice of serving free food to the general community outside the *gurdware*, particularly in places and times of special need. Some *gurdware* in the United States send their extra *langar* to nearby soup kitchens or shelters, often run by Christian organizations, thereby increasing interfaith cooperation. Some have *langar* especially prepared for such deliveries. This arrangement varies from a bimonthly delivery to just special holidays, such as Thanksgiving. Another regular service is increasingly popular via food trucks for the homeless (or anyone). As I write, during the Covid-19 pandemic, *gurdware* around the world have served thousands of free meals, be it on the streets of India for the very poor or drive-through pick-ups in the United States (e.g., Krishna 2020).

In post 9/11 America, using *langar* as a means to spread a message of equality and inclusiveness has taken on special importance for Sikhs. Male members of the community, who wear the turban and beard—articles of faith—have been subject to Islamophobia, targeted as terrorists with hate crimes and racial profiling. Sikh *gurdware* and civil rights groups have used *langar* service as an important means to highlight the message of equality and inclusion. For example, since 2014, Sikhs have organized an annual "Langar on the Hill" on the US Capitol Hill in Washington, DC. Cooking, serving, and eating *langar* collectively, with inclusivity and equality, is thus an embodied, routine practice of non-Othering for Sikhs. The accompanying worship sessions in *gurdware* are similarly free, open, inclusive, and participatory, reflecting these same values through the practice of using diverse musical styles.[4]

Musical Diversity in *Sabad Kīrtan*

Sikh worship is primarily musical, consisting of *kīrtan* (singing) and *patth* (*pāṭṭh*, chanting) of the *sabad*. Musical diversity is a key feature that enacts inclusivity of listeners from different backgrounds with varied stylistic preferences and encourages openness among listeners with respect to these differences (Kaur 2016b). While diversity is found in the musical designations for the *sabad* in the scriptures (which include a variety of regional melodic modes and folk melodic forms [Kaur 2016a, 89–90]), these

---

[4] Unfortunately, at some *gurdware*, though not major ones, Dalit people have felt unwelcome and have turned to developing separate places of worship. Also, some musicians have asserted superiority of the classical style of *kīrtan* (on authenticity debates, see Kaur 2016b).

designations are not worded as restrictive, and practice engages in open choice of style. Musicians sing a given verse not only in different styles and sub-styles, but also in multiple melodies and rhythms within any style. The musical practice is also open to and welcoming of emerging styles, thus keeping the practice dynamic and vibrant. As several Sikh musicians have told me, their primary job is to connect the congregation to the teachings in the *sabad*, and therefore they consider it necessary to employ contemporary and popular musical styles. Most Sikhs enjoy the variety enabled by this flexibility in, and openness to, musical material. In fact, they see open and empathetic listening as an aspect of the ethics of openness and inclusivity espoused in the *sabad* texts. As one interlocutor conveyed, "*jis tarah, koī bōle rām rām, koī khūdāe*" ("Just like [the *sabad*]—Some say Ram Ram, some say Khuda [for the divine]"). In other words, just as the *sabad* emphasize that different faiths are valid means of connecting with the divine, so too different musical styles are valid means of connecting with the *sabad*. In the words of another interlocutor, "*sab nū nāl lai ke chalnā hai*" ("Everyone must be included in the journey"). Thus, musical diversity helps to emphasize the ethics of non-Othering in the sacred texts.

The three main musical styles that practitioners and participants of *sabad kīrtan* currently recognize, the classical, the light, and the AKJ, vary in their ensemble structure, instrumentation, melodic systems, and performance structure (Kaur 2016a, 15). Each also has distinctive performance techniques for heightening the emotional impact of the *sabad* and creating a feeling of togetherness among participants. While call-and-response is featured in all styles, its scope is more limited in the classical style because it uses strict grammatical rules and emphasizes improvisation. These features can make the singing and playing instruments more difficult as well. Consequently, being least accessible to participation, it is the least popular style in the *gurdwara* context. What is important is that within each style, there is an integrated flow of experience from the music and the *sabad* that intensifies (emotional) affect and its circulation among participants, enhancing sensations of interconnection and cohesion.

Classical-Style *Kīrtan*

The classical style is defined by its adherence to the melodic and rhythmic systems known as *rag* (*rāg*) and *tal* (*tāl*) respectively. A *rag* is a melodic framework of a defined set, pattern, and hierarchy of pitches. *Sabad* sung in the classical style are set to melodies with features of particular *rag*. Each performance typically begins with a *manglacharan*—an invocation to the divine and unmetered introduction to the *rag* using a scriptural couplet, or as in this case, the terms used for the divine (▶ Video example 14.1 and Figure 14.3). The introduction is followed by the metered singing of the *sabad*, that is, in a *tal*. A *tal* is a metrical formulation—a rhythmic cycle of a defined number and pattern of beats, with each beat corresponding to a specific drum stroke. The first beat of the cycle, called the *sam*, is the most emphasized drum stroke. A *sabad* melody can begin at any beat in the cycle, and often it does not begin on the *sam*. However, the points at which the melody meets the *sam* are the most important structural and experiential moments in a performance where the release of tension is felt, as also a sense of coming together (*sam* literally means "at par"). In classical-style *sabad kīrtan*, the melody is often composed such that a significant textual phrase in the refrain is sung on

Sabad in *Rag* Bihagda, *tintal* (*tīntāl*, 16 beats)
Lead vocalist: Dr. Nivedita Singh

0:00–0:33	Instrumental prelude on *dilruba*
0:33–1:34	Introductory *manglacharan* using terms for divine: *wāheguru* ("wondrous guide"), *satnām* ("truth by name"); *dilruba* shadows vocals
1:34–1:46	Bridge on harmonium
1:46–2:56	Refrain ("*har ki gat nah koū jāne*"); *tabla* enters with *tihai* (*tihāī*, thrice repeated phrase) meeting the *sam* at 2:05 with the words (the cadential textual phrase "*nah koū*" ("nobody"); responsorial singing by vocal support, one playing *tanpura*
2:56–3:13	Interlude, *dilruba* repeats the melody line; *tabla* plays short pattern variations
3:13–4:45	Verse 1 and refrain; *tabla* variations for rhythmic intensification
4:45–5:55	Interlude; short solo on *tabla* ending on *sam*
5:55–6:42	Verse 2, with melodic improvisation using *sabad* text
6:42–6:59	Refrain; *tabla* executes improvisation ending with *tihai* pattern on *sam* at 6:59.

Figure 14.3 Listening Guide, classical-style *kīrtan* (first seven minutes).

the cadential rhythmic phrase leading to the *sam*, deepening the emotional impact of the *sabad* and the sensation of togetherness among participants. Additional affective techniques include shadowing of the vocals and repeating of melody lines by melodic instruments. The theme of the *sabad* in Video example 14.1 (*har ki gat nah koū jāne*, "The ways of the divine, nobody knows") is the feeling of wonder for the divine. The purpose of generating awe for an ethically conceived divine entity is to engender a smaller sense of the self and all beings, and thereby a greater sense of humility and equality. In this rendition, the cadential textual phrase translates to nobody (*nah koū*), thus emphasizing humbleness.

In addition to the affective impact from its musical features, the classical style of *sabad kīrtan* has emotional weight because the *sabad* in the primary scripture bear *rag* designations. Even though the historical forms of modes, melodies, and manner of singing *sabad kīrtan* from the sixteenth century cannot be precisely ascertained, and more recent systems and styles of singing in *rag* are in vogue, for some Sikhs, historically informed performance practices referentially enhance the sonic presence of the Sikh Gurus. However, a universally held hegemonic status of the classical style is prevented because the repertoire has to be the same sacred *sabad* with the predominant themes of oneness and equality, and as mentioned above, musical sound is not held as sacred. Further, inclusivity of different musical styles has been a practice in Sikh communities throughout their history.

Light-Style *Kīrtan*

In contrast to the classical style, the light style does not follow the strict rules of a *rag*. While the tune and improvisation are still modal in the sense that a particular set of notes are consistently used, these note patterns are not codified as *rag*. The melodies are more easily singable and similar to those of popular (especially Bollywood film) songs. With respect to the rhythmic cycle, while the singing conforms to a chosen *tal*, songs utilize shorter cycles, of six, seven, and eight beats as opposed to ten, twelve, and sixteen typically used in the classical style. The strong downbeat of *sam* is thus felt at shorter intervals compared to the classical style. Additionally, drummers liberally employ a variety of drum stroke patterns to match the rhythmic contours of the melody and the *sabad*-text, and variations on these patterns during instrumental bridges and transitions (see Figure 14.4 and ▶ Video example 14.2

Sabad in ***Keharwa tal*** **(8 beats)**

Lead vocalist: Bhai Harjinder Singh

0:12--2:27	Intro and refrain; tabla flourishes mark line endings for emphasis (e.g. at 0:55 to mark the move to the second line of the song, and at 1:18 to anticipate and signal the return to the refrain)
2:27--2:55	Bridge; complementary melodic material; tabla pattern variations
2:55--4:38	Verse 1 (tabla pattern variations at 3:21; 3:44; 3:50; 4:13; 4:27; 4:35)
4:38--5:00	Refrain; tabla plays the *tal* in *dugun* (double speed), for intensification, starting at 4:40 and ending in a short *tihai* pattern to return to the base speed at 5:00 for the next bridge

Figure 14.4 Listening Guide, light-style *kīrtan* (first five minutes).

for these features in the light style of Sikh *kīrtan*). These performance features have a significant impact on the congregation, increasing their enjoyment and feeling of togetherness. The music thus serves to amplify the meanings of the *sabad*. The theme of the *sabad* in this example is a longing for an experience of union with the divine. The idea is that through merging with a divine, conceived of as the epitome of ethical values, one would begin to embody those attributes, including those of oneness and non-Othering.

AKJ-Style *Kīrtan*

The AKJ, "*Akhand Kīrtani Jatha*" style also uses popular tunes like the light style. Its distinguishing features are its performance setting and structure. *Akhand* means "uninterrupted" and *jatha* means "group." In *kīrtan* sessions, the ensembles and congregations sing the sacred verses continuously without any interruptions by profane sounds such as program announcements or exegeses. AKJ *kīrtan* sessions range from a few hours to all night, often organized over an entire weekend. The ensemble sits surrounded by congregation members, who sing along in call-and-response, and play shakers and cymbals. This engenders active and inclusive participation. Instrumental bridges are minimal or not used at all, to keep the focus on the *sabad* text. Each line of the *sabad* is sung multiple times in call-and-response, whereas in the classical and light styles, each line is typically repeated only twice. The performance proceeds in cycles of increasing intensity in rhythm, tempo, and volume, climaxing with the chanting of the divine name, *waheguru* (*wāheguru*, lit. "wondrous guide"). The communal spirit of call-and-response, simple tunes, and participatory playing of percussion instruments, along with increasing intensity, are important means to create a feeling of togetherness among the participants, and to emotionally amplify the themes of the *sabad* text. For an AKJ performance of Sikh *kīrtan*, see Figure 14.5, ⏵ Video example 14.3. The *sabad* sung here is on the theme of the importance of worship. Devotion to an ethically conceived divine principle intends to engender commitment to those ethics. In addition to these effective musical features, an important affective force in the AKJ community is its special marked love and admiration for the tenth Sikh Guru, who is remembered for his efforts and personal sacrifices for the cause of social justice and liberty.

For Sikhs the three musical styles of *sabad kīrtan* described above, as well as others not discussed here, offer different sonic paths to connect with their sacred verses as well as their shared history. While it is often the case that

Sabad in *Keharwa tal* (8 beats)
Lead vocalist: Bibi Simarjeet Kaur

0:00–2:13	Intro and refrain line 1
2:13–2:42	Phrase from refrain line 1, for intensification
2:42–3:04	Bridge, plays melody of refrain line 2, ushering in the second line of the refrain of the *sabad*
3:04–4:01	Refrain line 2
4:01–4:38	Refrain line 1, *tabla* plays the *tal* in *dugun* for intensification
4:38–5:23	*Waheguru* chant; *tabla* changes pattern with greater emphasis on the bass *tabla* drum; tempo acceleration
5:23–5:53	Refrain line 1; *tabla* maintains intensification
5:53–7:00	*Waheguru* chant; *tabla* changes pattern with open hand resonant strokes on bass *tabla* drum; tempo acceleration
7:00–	New cycle of intensification begins

Figure 14.5 Listening Guide, AKJ-style *kīrtan* (first seven-minute cycle of increasing intensification).

individuals have a favorite or preferred style, the sacred status of the *sabad* texts invites engagement irrespective of musical style, and the process of such inclusive engagement also enlists an ethics of openness and empathetic listening. As in the practice of *langar*, musical inclusivity, openness, and togetherness are multi-sensory, embodied ways of encouraging a habit of non-Othering in everyday life.

Conclusion

When speaking with people about their experience in a *gurdwara* visit, the foremost comment I have received, from Sikhs and non-Sikhs alike,

---

Box 14.1 Exercises

Listening: Which of the three *sabad kīrtan* styles appeals to you more, and why? Can you identify musical features that influence your response?

Collective singing: Sing or hum along with each of the recordings of the three different styles. How does the embodied experience of collective singing change your aesthetic and emotional responses?

Communal dining: Organize a potluck in class and eat in communal spirit after or before a round of collective singing. Do you feel any changes in your aesthetic and emotional responses to the entire sensory experience?

Discussion: Discuss with your colleagues their musical style preferences, and engage in empathetic listening with each other. Think of and/or research additional musical practices that are means of understanding/experiencing non-Othering and discuss them with your peers.

Field trip: Find online the nearest Sikh place of worship using keywords such as Sikh *gurdwara*, center or temple; research *gurdwara* attendance-etiquette; and visit to listen to *kīrtan* and eat *langar*.

Project: Compose your own song on non-Othering and set it to music (in any genre). Discuss the role of lyrics, themes, and music in your experience of non-Othering.

is a feeling of peace they obtain. That people from all faiths, all social identities, and all walks of life can come together and feel welcome in a free and open place of worship where there is equal treatment of all, is a remarkable practice of the oneness of humanity. In *gurdware* around the globe, thousands of *sabad* centered on the Sikh philosophy of oneness are sung in a diversity of musical styles, with *langar* served alongside, open to all without any conditions. Equal treatment is the hallmark of the paired rituals of open, inclusive, and collective musical worship and dining. Importantly, it is an everyday enactment of the philosophy of non-Othering in the Sikh faith.

Works Cited

Desjardins, Michel, and Ellen Desjardins. 2009. "Food that Builds Community: The Sikh Langar in Canada." *Cuizine: The Journal of Canadian Food Cultures, Cuizine:/Revue des cultures culinaires au Canada* 1(2): 0.

Kaur, Inderjit N. 2011. "Sikh Shabad Kırtan and Gurmat Sangıt: What's in the Name?" *Journal of Punjab Studies* 18(1–2): 251–278.

Kaur, Inderjit N. 2016a. "When "Unheard Sound" (Re)Sounds: Affective Listening, Ethical Affects, and Embodied Experience in Sikh Sabad Kīrtan." PhD diss., University of California, Berkeley.

Kaur, Inderjit N. 2016b. "Multiple Authenticities in Motion: Styles and Stances in Sikh Sabad Kirtan." *Yearbook of Traditional Music* 48: 71–93.

Krishna, Priya. 2020. "How to Feed Crowds in a Protest or Pandemic? The Sikhs Know." *New York Times*, 8 June.

Singh, Keshav. 2021. "Vice and Virtue in Sikh Ethics." *The Monist* 104(3): 319–336.

Wade, Bonnie C. 1987. *Music in India: The Classical Traditions*. New Delhi: Manohar.

15
Following in the Footsteps of Muria Music and Dance

Roderic Knight

My first walk through a forest in India was in the moonlight. It was early January 1979, and I was on my way to a village called Remawand. Before the month was out, I would be back on a plane to the United States, but by that time, I had gotten to know some of the Muria people and learned some of their songs. In this chapter, I will teach the song "Marmi Pata," or "Wedding Song," which I learned from the teenage girls in Remawand.

The Muria, numbering perhaps a quarter million, are among the myriad communities designated by the Hindi term *Adivasi* (*ādīvāsī*), or original inhabitants. The Muria homeland is Bastar District, at the southern tip of the state of Chhattisgarh. They are part of the two-million-strong population known as the Gond, spread widely across central India. They speak Gondi, a Dravidian language related to Telugu, and practice a religion resembling Hinduism, but with its own perhaps pre-Hindu deities. The Gond lifestyle is essentially subsistence agriculture by shifting cultivation, gathering forest produce such as ink nuts (*Terminalia chebula*, used in the production of India ink), and small-game hunting. Rudyard Kipling roamed the forests of this area in the late nineteenth century as he gathered ideas for his *Jungle Book*. Perhaps the character of Mowgli was inspired by the Gond men he undoubtedly met.

During my visit, Remawand was a storybook village of whitewashed mudbrick homes like thousands that dot the vast Deccan plain. It had a population of several hundred, in homes clustered close together with sandy paths and a few fences. Some domestic animals wandered about, and a few oxcarts were parked outside. In the middle was a youth clubhouse and hospitality center, called a *ghotul* (*ghōtūl*, Figure 15.1).

The girls who taught me "Marmi Pata" were members of the Remawand *ghotul*. They sang for my tape recorder, but more typically they would have

Figure 15.1 A Muria *ghotul*. Photo by Claudius Nenninger; used with permission.

been singing about an upcoming wedding (Figure 15.2). In the song, the girls, known as *motiari* (*mōtiāri*), lament the departure of one among them, who will soon marry a *chelik* (*chēlik*, boy) from another village and join him there. Why are we interested in this song? I propose that learning a song from another culture, in addition to being enjoyable, holds great potential to increase our cross-cultural understanding and empathy. Learning "Marmi Pata" can help us appreciate how performance of music and dance in the *ghotul* serves to build friendships and develop adult values and character.

My research in Muria country began as an exploratory trip with a broad focus—to learn about the non-classical music of India—but upon my arrival, a librarian handed me a 1947 book by Verrier Elwin titled *The Muria and Their Ghotul*. Encyclopedic at 700 pages and beautifully presented, it quickly focused my attention on the Muria.

As all scholars of South Asia know, to speak of the Adivasi is to speak of Elwin. His twenty-nine books and countless pamphlets, all focused on Adivasi life, were pioneering work. Ironically, despite this output, his reputation in the anthropological world is that of an amateur. Ramachandra Guha, in his excellent book, *Savaging the Civilized: Verrier Elwin, His Tribals, and India*, described an earlier book by Elwin, *The Baiga* (1939), as "the work of a novelist who had strayed into anthropology" (1999, 115). I would refute

Figure 15.2 *Motiari* listening to a recording of their singing. Photo by the author.

this characterization, especially on the basis of the Muria book. Elwin's contributions remain invaluable today, especially in ethnography and ethnomusicology.[1]

Although it had not been part of my plan, in 1983 I released an album on Folkways titled *Tribal Music of India: The Muria and Maria Gonds of Madhya Pradesh*, with "Marmi Pata" included.[2] The title begs an explanation. Before the term "Adivasi" gained currency, Indians typically referred to indigenous people as "tribals." Presumably this stems from the 1952 constitution, in which about 25 percent of the population is identified and recognized in a list called the Scheduled Castes and Scheduled Tribes (SCST). For decades in the

---

[1] Among other scholars who have consulted Elwin are Carol Babiracki (2000/2001) and Richard Wolf (2005).

[2] https://folkways.si.edu. ("Marmi Pata" is item 102.)

West, scholars (myself included) have avoided the term "tribe," because it has taken on too many negative connotations, even though its definition is well established as "human social organization ... defined by common descent, language, culture, and ideology."[3] But, reflective of the Indian usage at the time, the term "tribal music" seemed to fit this collection of recordings.

Who Are the Muria and What Is a *Ghotul*?

The Adivasi people of central India are largely marginalized today, yet most are able to pursue their traditional lifeways while at the same time confronting outside influences (Salopek 2019). In 1968, Elwin published a condensation of the Muria book called *The Kingdom of the Young*. Both his first title and this one are inscrutable, and perhaps Elwin intended it that way. He wanted us to read about something he was onto, the importance of the *ghotul*, and its central role in the transmission of Muria values to young people through music, dance, and other activities, thereby maintaining Muria culture.

Elwin's original title hints at the distinctive nature of the *ghotul*. I described it above as a clubhouse. Think of it as an after-school boys and girls club, except that before marriage they spend the night sleeping there, like a dormitory. Elwin's second title hints at the nature of the organization. It was run and regulated by the young people themselves—the elder teens of the *ghotul*. Girls socialized with their girlfriends, boys with their village comrades, but they were not segregated. Sexual unions were possible, even expected. Elwin hastened, in the preface to his book, to clarify this point for a public that had heard something of the *ghotul*, noting that, "the sexual relation is secondary, and the magical, religious, and social aspects of ghotul life [are] predominant in the Muria's mind." Further, "If there is license, there is also taboo; if youth has freedom it moves on into a life of strictest decorum" (1947, ix; 1968, x). Elwin also urged readers to study his last chapter, "Moral Standards in the Ghotul," in which he emphasized that the *ghotul* was not a recreational free-for-all, but a place where family and kin relationships mattered. He also noted the pervasive positive effect of the institution:

---

[3] *Encyclopaedia Britannica*, 2011 (https://www.britannica.com/topic/tribe-anthropology, accessed June 28, 2021).

In the first place it must be said that the chelik and motiari are wonderfully happy. Their life is full, interesting, exciting, useful. The ghotul is, as they often say, "a little school." ... In the ghotul the children are taught lessons of cleanliness, discipline and hard work that remain with them throughout their lives. They are taught to take a pride in their appearance, to respect themselves and their elders; above all, they are taught the spirit of service. These boys and girls work very hard indeed for the public good. (Elwin 1947, 658)

One of the prime functions of the *ghotul* is as a music academy. The members build their relationships and express their values through singing, dancing, learning drums and other instruments, and by organizing dance expeditions to other villages. Indeed, in Muria culture, music and dance are the province of the young, to be nearly abandoned in adulthood, except on a few festive occasions. Elwin sensed that *ghotul* practices in general were in decline during his lifetime. He lamented later developments he had observed and assessed the *ghotul* as "a unique phase of human development about to disappear" (1968, xiii).

Elwin spent three years, 1939–1942, working with the Muria in his capacity as Honorary Ethnographer and Census Officer. He personally visited 102 Muria villages and listed more than a hundred others that his assistants had researched (1947, 667–682.) He was accompanied by his wife Kosi, herself a Gond woman whom he had met in Mandla District of Madhya Pradesh. In the book, Elwin does not detail his wife's contributions to the research, but an important one would surely have been her access to women and their views. She must have been his primary linguistic assistant also, for he included nearly 100 song texts in Gondi and English. He also had the assistance of Walter Kaufmann (then of All India Radio and later a professor at Indiana University), who accompanied him briefly in 1941 and provided excellent musical transcriptions for the book.

Learning from the Muria People

Every field researcher has stories to tell, but these are typically heard at cocktail parties or in memoirs. I relate mine briefly here to help illuminate my position that participatory learning is a valuable means for cross-cultural understanding. My first research was in Africa, but I have always been equally interested in India. My interest in the non-classical traditions was piqued by the India volume in a 1950s anthology titled *The Columbia World Library of Folk and Primitive Music*.[4] I particularly liked one item, "Gond Song from Nagpur." When a stipend from the National Endowment for the Humanities gave me the opportunity to go to India in 1978, I decided to pursue this as a research lead.

Here serendipity came into play. In that same year I met an Oberlin colleague named Hardarshan Valia. He was from Nagpur! Pocketing his valuable list of contacts, I made my way there. But in Nagpur, I was handed the Elwin book. Immediately I abandoned my search for musicians in Nagpur; I would follow Elwin's footsteps to Muria country.

On December 25, 1978, I boarded an overnight train east to Raipur, and from there, took a day-long bus ride to Jagdalpur, far to the south, in Bastar District. The bus ride took me right past two of Elwin's favorite villages, Remawand and Nayanar (see Map 15.1). I did not know this at the time, but it did not matter. One does not simply show up at a potential fieldwork site and say "Hello!" At the Anthropological Survey in Jagdalpur, I met Vikas Bhatt, who had good news: in many Muria villages, there was a revival in progress. Outsiders, meaning non-tribal Indian officials (himself included) and teachers from nearby towns, had been helping to organize village performers into dance troupes. The troupe from Nayanar had even traveled to Delhi and won an award for their performance at Republic Day in 1975.

Encouraged by this news, on January 2 I boarded the bus back north to the town of Narayanpur, near these villages. Here serendipity helped again. That evening I met a photojournalist named Claudius Nenninger, who had also read Elwin. He was about to travel to Remawand to meet a government forester named Mohamed Rafik, who could serve as our guide. We immediately recognized that our plans could mesh and formed an impromptu team. Thus, as dusk fell on January 3, we boarded the bus for a short ride to an unmarked junction, and here we began the hour-long trek in the moonlight to Remawand.

As arranged, Rafik met us in Remawand, but he escorted us to the next village, Nayanar. It was all a bit unreal. As if by clockwork, the *chelik* and *motiari* of the Nayanar *ghotul* mobilized their prize-winning ensemble in full regalia to put on an impressive show for us, in the dark. Usually fieldwork is

---

[4] This series, put together by renowned folklorist Alan Lomax, had a title that makes us recoil today; in the 1950s, however, the terms "folk" and "primitive" were intended to denote inclusivity and diversity.

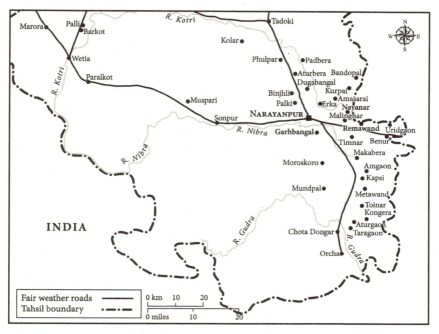

Map 15.1 A portion of Elwin's map of Narayanpur Tahsil, Bastar District, showing the town of Narayanpur and the villages of Garhbangal, Remawand, and Nayanar (1947, 8).

a little more tedious than this! Since the *ghotul* also serves as a guest house, we stayed the night, on cots provided for us in the open courtyard. In the morning, the *ghotul* members performed again (Figure 15.3). We paid them with money, fruits, and *bidi*s (Indian cigarettes). We understood from Rafik that they were pleased. Then we retraced our steps to Remawand. The *chelik* and *motiari* of this village were eager to hear the recording we made at Nayanar and wanted to perform for us in turn. Here we were, outsiders, but the *ghotul* members had immersed us in their music scene and its friendly rivalry between villages.

The Remawand *ghotul* performed for us on January 4, 1979. There is no question that both the Nayanar and Remawand performances were a form of staged folklorization. But the performers could not have suddenly done this if they had not been practicing. They were clearly preparing to participate in religious festivals and trips to other villages for competition and socializing, just as Elwin had described. We saw proof of the ongoing enterprise when,

Figure 15.3 Dancers in Nayanar in full regalia with *jagar*, jingling sticks. Photo by the author.

after two weeks of traveling to other musical events in Bastar, we returned to Nayanar on January 16 to find the *ghotul* deserted. We learned that the troupe would not return for at least two weeks. Plan B was to backtrack to Remawand. This turned out to be most fortunate. The *ghotul* members were ready to spend time with us again, and it was during this visit that I learned to sing and dance "Marmi Pata."

Along with us this time was an assistant named Mohammed Hassan, who could help with song texts and translations. During our four-day stay in Remawand, which was like camping out (no running water, no facilities, but cots and food provided), we developed quite a camaraderie, the two of us, Hassan, and one or two *chelik*, listening to recordings and writing song texts. In the evenings, we sat around a fire of fragrant *saja* wood and were treated to our hosts swapping songs. The girls (maybe aged 12–15) who had sung "Marmi Pata" for me on January 4 were there. Hassan had transcribed the words for me. I asked them if there was a dance associated with the song, and they said yes. I dearly wanted to learn the dance, so we agreed to meet the next day. It still took some cajoling. I got up and started miming some steps, which finally convinced them to humor me. Without a video, I wrote furiously in my logbook. The girls hurried off afterward, but thanks to their willingness and my notes, I had a more complete understanding of "Marmi Pata." I would be able to teach it in turn to my own students.

As our presence in Remawand became more routine for the villagers, some of the people we had not yet seen—grown women and their small children—began to show up. Some of the elder men dropped by as well. One, named Kansai, remembered Elwin's visit from when he was a teen. Kansai was about fifty, married, with five children. He planned to send them all to school and would soon arrange for the marriage of his five-year-old boy with a *motiari* from the *ghotul*, just as his own marriage had been arranged. Kansai asserted that today (i.e., 1979), girls no longer stayed in the *ghotul*. They only came for singing and dancing in the evening. In this statement, I recognized an observation Elwin had made, that Muria men are often inclined to deny the sexual aspect of *ghotul* life when talking to outsiders, presumably in an effort to avoid criticism.

Although Claudius and I spent eleven nights in *ghotul* courtyards in three villages (Nayanar, Remawand, and Garhbangal, close to Narayanpur), I cannot write definitively on the details of *ghotul* life and will leave the question of contemporary practice to future anthropologists. One thing, however, is clear: the *ghotul* is an institution that still generates some controversy. According to an article by Sondeep Shankar in *India Today* (2013 [1997]), the issue of how to run a *ghotul* and whether it is a good institution or not has become a contentious issue in Muria villages themselves. There are groups that call for the *ghotul* to be abolished, basing their argument on mainstream non-Adivasi social values as learned in school, while others with equal vehemence defend the *ghotul* as crucial to indigenous Muria culture. Despite the ongoing debate, one thing is clear: Elwin's fear that the *ghotul* was soon to disappear has not come to pass. An internet search on the word brings up voluminous results and YouTube clips.

I imagine contemporary Muria youth with their cell phones, perhaps using the *ghotul* as a rehearsal space for their next performance, possibly under contract with an agent. If they have not been driven from their villages by political turmoil (such as visited on the area in recent decades by Maoist insurgents known as Naxalites), or their lives disrupted by anti-*ghotul* protests, one might imagine traveling to Remawand today to hear "Marmi Pata" in its contemporary form (see ▶ Audio example 15.1; Knight 1983).

In 1979, "Marmi Pata" was the only wedding song in the Remawand repertoire, but in Muria culture, a wedding is a four-day event. Elwin documented over fifty songs from a wedding he attended in 1941. Is today's "Marmi Pata" one of those? Indeed it is. It appears under Elwin's heading "Preparations for the Marriage." The Remawand version is shorter—only ten lines versus Elwin's twenty-five—but the second line ("*Dindare raju . . .*" see Figure 15.4) is nearly an exact match for one of Elwin's, and the overall theme is the same: girls lament the departure of their friend, the bride (see Figure 15.7).

The Style of Muria Song and Dance

Muria songs commonly feature an opening verse with vocables (non-lexical syllables) such as "re-re lā, relā." For this reason, they are called "*relo*" (*rēlō*) songs. In "Marmi Pata" a fragment of the *relo* verse is repeated at the end of each verse. The song's melody has only four notes, which we may liken to pitches 1, 3, 4, and 5 of a major scale. Rhythmically it may be transcribed with quarter and eighth notes, with sustained notes at the ends of phrases. The dance moves at the quarter-note pace and is a simple line-dance step. In this song, the singers divide into two groups. One sings a verse through, the other repeats it.

As my teachers danced and I took notes, the first thing I noticed was that the dance was twelve counts long, but the song was much longer. I did not try to quantify this at the time, but back home, when I transcribed the song, it spanned twenty-one counts. There was no obvious match between it and the dance. I sought to answer this puzzle without advanced math skills. I strung verses together in my transcription, then underlaid the dance steps. This revealed that the original sync was regained after four times through the song and seven times through the dance ($4 \times 21 = 84$ and $7 \times 12 = 84$).

At first glance it would seem a near-impossible task to keep track of this phase-shifting. A Western music theorist might be inclined to study a full transcription to understand it, while a theorist or performer in the Indian classical traditions might notice a resemblance to the complex temporal calculations that create tension and resolution in *tala* performance. Carol Babiracki reports that Mundari performers in Jharkand delight in paying attention to a similar phenomenon in their dances (Babiracki 2000/2001, Babiracki*, and personal communication, 2020).

Box 15.1 Exercise: Learning "Marmi Pata"

1. Learn the first two lines of the song as given in Figure 15.4 by singing along with ▶ Audio example 15.1. (The vowel sounds are all long.)

1. Rere la- rere- la rela rela, rere la-rere- la re, rela (Chorus) E-he elo, o yo . . .	1. "relo" vocables
2. Dindare raju to raju elo, dindare raju to raju roi. E-he elo, o yo . . .	2. Dear friends [let's sing about] the youth from the kingdom of the young.

Figure 15.4 The first two lines of "Marmi Pata." Translation by Mohammed Hassan.

If you read Western staff notation, my transcription (Figure 15.5) may be helpful.

Figure 15.5 The twenty-one-count vocal line of "Marmi Pata." Transcription by the author; calligraphy by Jean Hasse; used with permission.

2. Now, practice and memorize the dance steps as shown in Figure 15.6. They fall into three groups of four. For the first four, advance (step forward) on the right foot, hop on it, advance on the left foot, hop on

1	2	3	4	5	6	7	clap	9	10	11	clap
Adv	Hop	Adv	Hop	Step	Swing	Step	Swing	Step	Swing	Step	Swing
on R	on R	on L	on L	to R on R	L over R and return	to L on L	R over L and return	(Same as 5–8)			

Figure 15.6 The twelve-count dance step for "Marmi Pata." Transcription by the author.

it. For steps 5 to 8, step on the right foot, swing (or gently kick) the left over it, step back on the left foot, swing the right over it. For steps 9 to 12, repeat steps 5 to 8.

Note that steps 8 and 12 are marked with a clap. This is not in the recording because the girls were not dancing when it was made, but when they taught me the dance, they clapped on these counts, marking a spot where they would ordinarily have stamped the ground with a jingling stick called *jagar* (Figure 15.3). It could be considered an optional detail, but it is helpful since the second clap marks the end of the dance phrase.

3. With the dance steps memorized, it is time to combine the two. To help, here are notes I jotted in my log as the *motiari* of Remawand danced:
   - The girls rock back and forth a little before starting, to make sure they are together.
   - They dance first, then begin to sing.
   - The beat is set by the words at the end of the chorus, "e-he elo," which span four counts.

   Do not think about the dance step starting over on count 13 of your song. You have memorized the dance and it will come naturally.

4. Apply the antiphonal style by dividing your group in two. Although "Marmi Pata" is a song that the *motiari* typically sing among themselves, *chelik* and *motiari* sing together in other songs. So, simply divide your group in two. One group will start; the other will answer. Singing the first two lines of the song in this way will take you through the "four verses/seven dance phrases," and if you continue with the song, you will start in sync again as at the beginning. You are singing like the Muria girls, your song in step with your feet.

Since the *motiari* had hurried off after dancing, I had not been able to question them on the subject, but if I had, I believe their reaction would have been total puzzlement. My reason for believing this is that my own American students, faced with the task of singing a twenty-one-count song while dancing a twelve-count dance, experienced no difficulty. Why? It is the same reason a guitarist can sing while playing the guitar: kinesthetic memory. With chords and fingerings memorized, one can concentrate on singing. In like manner, with the dance steps memorized, singing the song comes naturally.

Marmi Pata

Rere la rere la rela rela, rere la rere la re, rela

Dear friends [let's sing about] the youth from the kingdom of the young.

Dear friends, our king [the groom] has not arrived.

But friends, where is he? Why do you not say?

Dear friends, our queen [the bride] is ready to leave the *ghotul*.

Whether she's had dinner or not, she will leave the *ghotul*.

With cupped hands outstretched toward the road, she walks from the *ghotul*.

Friends, in this manner, she will leave the *ghotul*.

She doesn't know or care about home duties before marriage.

But after marriage, she will do her duties well.

Figure 15.7 English translation of "Marmi Pata." The full Gondi text may be found on this book's accompanying website and in the notes available from Smithsonian/Folkways. Translation by Mohammed Hassan of Narayanpur, with assistance from Dr. Hiralal Shukla, Bhopal University, 1981.

Box 15.2 Questions and Suggestions for Further Study

1. Do an internet search to find YouTube clips of recent performances by young Muria.
2. What difference do you see between what you just practiced and what you find on the internet? Discuss melody, dance steps, and group formations.
3. Are the clips you found formal, informal, or staged events?
4. What other aspects of the event shape the performance?
5. Can you make any inferences about how Muria music and dance has changed since the late 1970s?

As you learn to sing and dance this song, ponder this small glimpse into Muria life. As described in the complete song lyrics (Figure 15.7), the girls are lamenting the departure of their friend. Having learned important life lessons during her years in the *ghotul*, she is ready to join the married adults in her husband's village. She is moving on to raise a family and work cooperatively growing crops and gathering forest produce. She might sing again as part of certain religious events or weddings, but she will not participate in the life of the *ghotul* again.

Works Cited

Babiracki, Carol. 2000/2001. "'Saved by Dance': The Movement for Autonomy in Jharkhand." *Asian Music* 32(1): 35–58.
Elwin, Verrier. 1947. *The Muria and Their Ghotul*. Bombay: Oxford University Press.
Elwin, Verrier. 1968. *The Kingdom of the Young*. Bombay: Oxford University Press.
Guha, Ramachandra. 1999. *Savaging the Civilized: Verrier Elwin, His Tribals and India*. Chicago: University of Chicago Press.
Knight, Roderic. 1983. *Tribal Music of India: The Muria and Maria Gonds of Madhya Pradesh*. LP disc with notes. Folkways FE 4028 (now available as 04028 at https://folkways.si.edu; "Marmi Pata" is item 102).
Lomax, Alan, ed. 1950 (?). *Columbia World Library of Folk and Primitive Music*. Vol. 13, *Folk Music—India*. LP disc with program notes bound in container. Columbia 91A 02021.
Mitchell, A. N. 1947. "The Language of the Muria." Appendix 2 in Elwin, 1947, 683–690.
Salopek, Paul. 2019. "Millions of Indigenous People Face Eviction from Their Forest Homes." *National Geographic*, May 15. Accessed July 30, 2020. https://api.nationalgeographic.com/distribution/public/amp/culture/2019/05/millions-india-indigenous-people-face-eviction-from-forests.
Shankar, Sondeep. 2013. "Controversial Custom of Teenage Mating among Muria Tribals Gains Ground in Madhya Pradesh." *India Today*, June 30, 1997, updated May 3, 2013. Accessed July 30, 2020. https://www.indiatoday.in/magazine/living/story/19970630-controversial-custom-of-teenage-mating-among-muria-tribals-gains-ground-in-madhya-pradesh-832653-1997-06-30.
Wolf, Richard K. 2005. *The Black Cow's Footprint: Time, Space, and Music in the Lives of the Kotas of South India*. Delhi: Permanent Black.

SECTION IV
IDENTITY IN GENDER AND SEXUALITY

Introduction by Zoe C. Sherinian

The chapters in this section explore multiple, varying interconnections between music, dance, gender, the body, and sexuality, as well as their intersectional associations with caste, class, and other aspects of identity.

Gender

South Asian music and dance practices serve as active means to construct and define gendered actions and social norms. Gender is a cultural construction created through performance, or a *"stylized repetition of acts"* (Butler 1988, 519 in Morelli*). Thus, the way gender is "performed" changes historically and from context to context. Further, as an enculturated phenomenon, gendered qualities of music and dance performance are learned, practiced, and transmitted by professionals and amateurs alike.

Early research on gender and music in South Asia focused singularly on the roles of women in musical performance. Lorraine Sakata (1976) examined the connection between musical performance and gender in Afghanistan, and Veronica Doubleday (1990) studied the Afghani and Middle Eastern frame drums. These works depicted male practice as the standard by which others were compared. Women performers who fell outside of normative systems—shamans, prostitutes, midwives, and lesbians—were afforded certain musical freedoms. Thus, these early feminist ethnomusicologists demonstrated that "woman" is not a monolithic category (Koskoff 2014, 26).

In this text, gender in the South Asian context includes qualities of behavior, dress, instrumental sound, and dramatic expression defined as masculine, feminine, androgynous, male impersonation, and transfeminine. One of Jeff Roy's* *thirunangai* research associates declared, "what defines you... is not what is between your legs, but what you do, how you act, who you relate with, who you become." (2015). Gender also includes normative and alternative constructions of the categories "man," "woman," widow (Greene* [Section II]), and transgender (Roy*), as well as conceptions of the divine, including *shakti* (feminine power, Desai* [Section VI]), the bigender deity *ardhanarishwara*, whose right side is masculine and left side feminine (Morelli*), and the transgender deity Krishna-Mohini (Roy*).

Femininity

Femininity in South Asia is a narrowly understood category that defines normative expectations of behavior, dress, and presentation for girls and women. In South Asia's predominantly patriarchal culture and middle class/caste context, much of women's behavior is strictly monitored, as a family's reputation depends on women maintaining the purity of the caste/clan lineage. Underprivileged Dalit-Bahujan women, on the other hand, have more freedom regarding sexual and marital practices and control of their (typically equal) financial and labor contributions to the household (Ilaiah 1996). Similar class and caste distinctions of proper feminine performance are articulated through the arts.

Until the early twentieth century, women who performed publicly, in court contexts, or in private soirées were almost exclusively from hereditary professional performance lineages, carrying caste-like identities and ambiguous social status (Krishnan et al. [Section III], Maciszewski*). Women from higher classes and castes rarely performed publicly, as doing so would tarnish both their reputations and that of their extended families. When upper-caste women received training on socially perceived feminine instruments like the *vina*, they typically played only for family events. Some instruments are considered distinctly *not* feminine because of sexual connotations, such as the flute, associated with the deity Krishna's suave masculinity, and drums, the beating of which is sometimes sexualized. However, during the Mughal period in North India (1526–1858), many Mughal miniature paintings depicted groups of women playing a range of instruments including drums in courtly settings (Wade 1998).

Multiple chapters in this book articulate qualities of ideal femininity. In discussing the kathak dance-drama *Son of the Wind* (based on the Ramayana epic), Morelli describes typical depictions of and conflicted responses to the character Sita. A somewhat naïve martyr-heroine, Sita self-sacrifices for the betterment of her husband and, by extension, for her family and clan. She and her husband Ram "serve . . . as a template for heteronormative gender dynamics and ideals of maleness and femaleness" (Morelli*). However, in contemporary performance, these characteristics are often complicated by actor-dancers who ground their portrayals of Sita in an empowered understanding of her character. Furthermore, kathak dancers themselves often perform multiple gendered roles, broadening their gendered experiences of themselves and the characters they portray (Morelli*).

What the ideal woman should sound and look like and qualities of acceptable feminine behavior—sacrifice, virginity, domesticated naiveté, purity, and modesty—are further codified in the hegemonic Bollywood film industry. Cinematic portrayals of Bollywood actresses are animated by the voices of playback singers like Lata Mangeshkar, sonically indexing these feminine qualities. Sarrazin* (Section V) analyzes the female voices of the Classic Bollywood Era—characterized by a high range with a light, sweet, nasal timbre devoid of excessive sexuality and rarely heard before in South Asian music. These vocal qualities reflected the middle and aspirational middle-class modern femininity of India's Nation-Building period, best portrayed by films like *Mother India* (1957). In the Post-Liberalization era (1990–present), this modern feminine sound has been combined with qualities of local and global pop: a lower range, a belting low chest timbre, and greater sexualization.

In folk and tribal dance contexts (Babiracki*; Knight* [Section III], and Kheshgi*), feminine performance qualities include restraint, coyness, tight dance lines, and graceful arm and pelvic movements. Indeed, these communal dances serve as vehicles for learning proper cisgender performance roles. Stirr's* (Section V) study of change in Nepali popular music in the context of migration reveals a dichotomy between rural and urban women's behavior, the codification of which parallels the contrast of folk and popular music styles.

Shakti/Sakthi is a term that means female power. In the case of the gender constructions of the girls at the Sakthi Folk Cultural Centre in Tamil Nadu, it implies a female masculinity (Halberstam 2019). Sherinian* (Section III) shows the embodied transformation of these empowered female drummers from outcaste "pariahs" to unified anti-caste Dalits through playing the *parai*, a drum traditionally only performed by men in their communities. In turn, they raise the status of women folk artists, typically likened to prostitutes, by embracing a middle-class sensibility in costuming and requiring conditions such as protected dressing rooms, a raised stage, and high fees for their artistry (Seizer 2005).

In Schultz's* chapter (Section II) on Hindu nationalist Marathi *kirtan*, other forms of female androgyny or non-binary gender are performed by female ascetics in service to nationalism. The possibility of female performance in a conservative nationalist religious context requires women to be largely devoid of sexuality. Further, Jaytumbi Maharaj, an older Muslim performer, complicates her gendered self-presentation by wearing the performance attire of a typical Muslim male along with a head covering, while including common women's genres in her repertoire.

Paul Greene's* study (Section II) of Tamil *oppari* (funeral lament) illustrates music of widowed women without outward signs of sexual feminine beauty who lack "male control." A widow's presence at important events is "inauspicious not because she [is] weak, but because she [is] dangerous." Thereby, spiritual power is controlled through the deprivation of femininity (Greene*) and masculinity (Roy*) as well as the humiliation of caste oppression and untouchability (Sherinian* [Section III]). These systems of power differentiation construct and reenact a social order of inequality through aesthetic action (Peiris 2021).

Professional hereditary female entertainers and dancers in this text, called variously courtesans, divas, *devadasi*s and *tawa'if*s, have always had a socially ambiguous status (Krishnan et al.* [Section III]). South Indian courtesan communities did not have a "caste name" because the women were concubines to male patrons; they could never (or rarely) be a "proper" wife, and their children were always of "mixed caste." Maciszewski* writes about the disintegration of the *tawa'ifs'* "once-great artistic tradition" in North India. Today *tawa'if*s lament that clients want overly-sexualized Bollywood-style dancing lacking the "elegance, mine, gestures" of their erstwhile repertoire (Munni Bai in Maciszewski*).

Masculinity

Men, of course, also have gender. Pavitra Sundar's* study of the Bollywood film title track "Rang De Basanti," by composer A. R. Rahman, demonstrates that film music plays an active role in constructing the ideal masculine

Indian citizen. She analyzes how a "hip viral national brotherhood" is constructed using *bhangra*, the Punjabi folk genre turned global pop, with its call-and-response structure and accompanying communal dance. Punjabis, as farmers and military men, were branded a martial race by colonialists. As exemplars of the nation, stereotypical Punjabi rural hypermasculinity was then extended to North Indian men in general.

For gender performance to be successful, it needs to be naturalized. Morelli's* chapter describes techniques cisgender female kathak dancers utilized to move and re/act in masculine ways. In this "naturalization" process, the dancers learn to square and broaden their shoulders, and use wide stances and tall spines. Furthermore, these female performers also needed to develop empathy and understanding of the characters' emotions to embody and portray them convincingly.

Three case studies (Babiracki, Kheshgi, Knight* [Section III]), from tribal/ Adivasi contexts in central and Northeast India, describe dances with strictly dichotomized "male" and "female" parts. These dances teach "proper" cisgender roles yet encourage shared leadership and cooperation between the sexes. In folkorized Bihu of Assam, Kheshgi* shows how elements of music and dance work together to encode values associated with masculinity and femininity. For example, she says:

> Male performers are rewarded for expressing abandon through spontaneous shouts, extended arm gestures, vigorous pelvic movements, and exuberant drumming sequences, while female performers are praised for demonstrating restraint through coy smiles, stylized arm and pelvic movements, and delicate mouth harp percussion. (Kheshgi*)

A conscious sense of gender equity and participation is also seen in Sikh religious performance contexts (Kaur* [Section III]) and the inclusive Sufi *dhammal* dance in ecstasy (Gillani* [Section I]).

Gender Diversity

In South Asia, particularly Bangladesh, India, and Pakistan, gender diversity beyond masculinity and femininity includes communities called *thirunangai, hijra, aravani, Khwaja Sira*, transgender, transfeminine, gender-nonconforming and sometimes third gender (Nanda 1999, Reddy

2005, and Hossain et al. 2022). Roy* emphasizes how such individuals and communities negotiate their self-understandings "along a variety of axes, including religion, sexuality, kinship, class, and caste, in relation to a 'multiplicity of social differences,' languages, and cultural practices" (Reddy 2005, 43 in Roy*). Indeed, they argue, "the emphasis on gender as a defining marker of difference ignores the diversity and fluidity of relationalities that form these communities" (Roy*).

Mid-nineteenth-century British colonial laws limited transgender, *hijra*, *thirunangai* other non-conforming people's "movements, embodiments, and performance practices . . . [including] cross-dressing . . . ritualistic acoustic music and dance known as *badhai*s, the repertoire of devotional prayers, songs, dances, and comic repartee," performed at blessings of fertility, weddings, births, and other auspicious life cycle events (Roy, personal communication, January 2021; see also Hossain, et al. 2022). Interestingly, while the dress and mannerisms of *hijra*s are sometimes hyper-exaggerated feminine, their voices usually do not shift from a normative male or masculine quality/range in performance. *Hijra*s are ideally devoid of maleness; either they are born intersex or go through a castration operation. Yet, they retain the power to bless a baby boy with masculinity to carry on his caste lineage (Nanda 1999). Gender, kinship practices, and pedagogical transmission intersect within *thirunangai* communities; some live in households with *guru-chela* (teacher-disciple or mother-daughter) relationships serving to sustain these practices and the well-being of the community members.

Sexuality

Song and movement are fundamental ways to express sensuality and sexual desire in South Asia. Whether through clearly secular contexts like royal courts, popular films, and labor, or through devotional contexts like Sufi *qawwali*, love is a central theme of life expressed through music and dance. Most of these expressions are heterosexual, while in devotional contexts like Bhakti and Sufism, "Devotees, regardless of their sex, may take on a feminine gender identification in approaching the divine . . . and may use the language and sensibilities of common relationships such as child and mother or lover and beloved" (Morelli 2019, 195). However, in most of the case studies in this book, it is assumed that feminine and masculine expressions are created within heteronormative, patriarchal, gender dynamics. That is, femininity is constructed to serve the pleasure of heterosexual men and vice versa.

Kheshgi* demonstrates how the Bihu genre used during spring planting seasons and celebrations of fertility in Assam serves as a heterosexual mating ritual with songs narrating romantic encounters and drawing on sexual metaphors from nature. Indeed, "Bihu performance builds in intensity and anticipation through cyclical rhythmic and melodic patterns that generate romantic desire, presenting a challenge to the social order that results in inter-caste liaisons and elopements . . . [while] upholding values associated with heteronormative femininity and masculinity" (Kheshgi*). Similarly, Knight* (Section III) shows how for young people in Muria (Adivasi) communities, the performance of music and dance served to build friendships and develop adult values that they carried as they transitioned to marriage and adult responsibilities.

Non-heteronormative expressions of sexuality are also discussed in relation to *thirunangai* people (Roy*). While the traditional ideal is that *thirunangai* are ascetics, they often have sex with men and sometimes engage in sex work. Maciszewski* discusses how *tawa'if*s, who have been deprived of their once culturally sanctioned contexts for music and dance performance, have largely been reduced to sex work. Analogously, Nrithya Pillai, a dancer from the South Indian hereditary courtesan community, expresses how the label "*devadasi*" carries a deep stigma based on perceptions around these women's sexual immorality (Krishnan et al.* [Section III]). In the case of *tawa'if*s, local NGOs have recently developed alternative performance opportunities as a means to livelihood.

Works Cited

Butler, Judith. 1988. "Performative Acts and Gender Constitution: An Essay in Phenomenology and Feminist Theory." *Theatre Journal* 40(4): 519–531.
Doubleday, Veronica. 1990. *Three Women of Herat*. Austin: University of Texas Press.
Halberstam, Judith. 2019. *Female Masculinity*. Durham, NC: Duke University Press.
Hossain, Adnan, Claire Pamment, and Jeff Roy. 2022. *Badhai: Hijra-Khwaja Sira-Trans Performance across Borders in South Asia*. London: Bloomsbury.
Ilaiah, Kancha. 1996. *Why I Am Not a Hindu: A Sudra Critique of Hindutva Philosophy, Culture and Political Economy*. Los Angeles: Samya/Sage.
Koskoff, Ellen. 2014. *A Feminist Ethnomusicology: Writings on Music and Gender*. Urbana: University of Illinois Press.
Morelli, Sarah. 2019. *A Guru's Journey: Pandit Chitresh Das and Indian Classical Dance in Diaspora*. Urbana: University of Illinois Press.

Nanda, Serena. 1999. *Neither Man, nor Woman: The Hijras of India*. Belmont, CA: Wadsworth.
Peiris, Eshantha Joseph. 2021. "Seeking a Ritual Dimension to Historical Caste Structures in Sri Lanka." Unpublished paper. Annual Conference on South Asia. Madison, WI.
Reddy, Gayatri. 2005. *With Respect to Sex: Negotiating Hijra Identity in South India*. Chicago: University of Chicago Press.
Roy, Jeff. 2015. "Ethnomusicology of the Closet: (Con)Figuring Transgender-*Hijra* Identity through Documentary Filmmaking." PhD Diss., UCLA.
Sakata, Lorraine. 1976. "The Concept of Musician in Three Persian-Speaking Areas of Afghanistan." *Asian Music* 8(1): 8–28.
Seizer, Susan. 2005. *Stigmas of the Tamil Stage: An Ethnography of Special Drama Artists in South India*. Durham, NC: Duke University Press.
Wade, Bonnie. 1998. *Imaging Sound: An Ethnomusicological Study of Music, Art, and Culture in Mughal India*. Chicago: University of Chicago Press.

16
Bhangra Brotherhood

Gender, Music, and Nationalism in *Rang De Basanti*

Pavitra Sundar

This chapter discusses the importance of music to Hindi films, specifically to the cinematic representation of nationalism, via an analysis of Rakeysh Omprakash Mehra's 2006 blockbuster *Rang De Basanti/Color My Spring* (henceforth *RDB*). *RDB* was an immediate box office hit and won a slew of nominations and awards. But what really distinguishes it from other blockbusters is the social and political activism it inspired—what came to be known as the "RDB effect." For months, middle-class youth in India mobilized around specific causes and participated in street protests of the kind depicted in the film (Chandra 2010). *RDB* generated much debate in the press as well as in more informal online spaces about nationalism and the responsibilities of citizenship. All the media chatter and scholarly discourse, however, downplayed the film's soundtrack. Even though the songs were immensely popular, they have rarely been incorporated into critical analyses of the film. In this essay, I argue that *RDB* not only offers a compelling model of nationalist agency, but also points to the critical role of film and film music in securing bonds of identity, especially gender, under the sign of the nation. My analysis of the film's hit title track, "Rang De Basanti," demonstrates that music plays an active role in the making of masculine citizen subjects. The iterative, call-and-response structure of *bhangra* (*bhaṅgṛā*), the emphasis on collective dancing, and the genre's dual moorings in Punjabi folk culture and global deejaying culture forge a hip and virile national brotherhood.[1]

---

[1] For a more elaborate discussion of this argument, one that emphasizes the film's treatment of time and history, see my essay "Of Radio, Remix, and *Rang De Basanti*" (2014).

Scholars of Hindi film and music have outlined the substantial cinematic and narrative work that film songs have historically performed, paying particular attention to the cultural politics of the singing voice (see, e.g., Booth 2008; Beaster-Jones 2015; Majumdar 2001; Morcom 2007; Sundar 2023; and Sarrazin*). Song-dance sequences influence the shape, length, and pace of many a mainstream Hindi film. They are powerful star vehicles for the actor, playback singer, and music director. They may be used to comment on filmic themes, elaborate a turn of plot, and reveal characters' feelings. As conventionalized substitutes for romantic interest and lovemaking in Hindi cinema, songs can convey heightened emotional and dramatic tension while avoiding or, at times, deliberately stoking the ire of censors and cultural critics (Mehta 2011). Bollywood soundtracks also function as crucial publicity material: they are released weeks in advance of the film and circulate widely on radio, television, and digital and mobile platforms.

While the new millennium witnessed substantial changes to the form and function of film songs—note, for instance, the rise of the "songless" film—the Bombay film industry has been reluctant to completely shed them (Garwood 2006). This stubborn persistence of musical numbers is partly a function of their financial value. Many contemporary films include "item numbers," elaborately staged song-dance sequences whose value lies in their spectacularity and marketability as isolatable elements of the film. Given the cultural and aesthetic moorings of the Hindi film song and the long-standing discourse on national identity in Hindi cinema (see, e.g., Chakravarty 1993 and Virdi 2003), however, I propose that Hindi cinema's continuing fondness for song-dance sequences is also tied to its ability to make visceral and appealing the otherwise abstract notion of the nation.

RDB makes this point by casting film and film music as the affective apparatus of nation-building. The film's title song enables the heroic national subject and the nation itself—or, more precisely, the "nation-as-audience"—to come into being (Punathambekar 2010, 193). To sing and dance "Rang De Basanti," to be moved by our heroes' boisterous *bhangra*, is to be a national citizen. *RDB* thus reminds us that nation is more than just a literary or linguistic construct (the form it takes in postcolonial studies' favorite genre, the novel) or a visual one (as work in film and South Asian studies suggest). This is an important theoretical intervention into both popular and scholarly understandings of cinema and nation. Music transforms nation into a tangible bodily endeavor, one that is experienced and undertaken in concert with others.

Violence, Past and Present

RDB presents us with two interwoven narratives. One narrative strand tells of the strident protests of Bhagat Singh, Chandrashekhar Azad, and other anticolonial activists of the early twentieth century fighting against the British Raj. Presented partly as a film-within-the-film, these historical events take the form of sepia sequences interspersed throughout *RDB*. The second narrative strand, rendered in color and set in contemporary New Delhi, tells of a group of disaffected college friends who become intensely patriotic over the course of making a film about the aforementioned martyrs. The film project is initiated by a British producer Sue McKinley, who recruits her friend Sonia and four men in Sonia's inner circle, DJ (played by the star Aamir Khan), Karan, Aslam, and Sukhi, to play the roles of the yesteryear revolutionaries. In a controversial move, she also invites Laxman Pandey, a Hindutva activist who routinely voices rabid anti-Western and anti-Muslim views, to join the amateur thespians, teaching them all to embrace the common nationalist creed "unity in diversity."[2] So moved are the young men by the stories of anticolonial struggle that they begin to embody the feelings and perspectives of the characters they play. The increasingly rapid crosscutting as *RDB* progresses blurs the identities, actions, and words of the historical and contemporary actors, suggesting that these characters are one and the same. The audience is thus encouraged to read the story of the past as the story of the present.

The critical consensus on *RDB* was that the film mobilizes a particularly violent, virile image of the past to raise questions about national identity and agency in the contemporary moment. In Neelam Srivastava's words:

> [*RDB*] represents violence as integral to the emergence of national identity.... It rewrites, or rather restages, Indian nationalist history not in the customary pacifist Gandhian vein, but in the mode of martyrdom and

---

[2] Hindutva is the term for Hindu cultural nationalist ideology espoused by several right-wing groups in India. See also Schultz*; Krishnan et al*.

armed struggle. It represents a more "masculine" version of the nationalist narrative for its contemporary audiences. (Srivastava 2009, 703)

What is interesting for our purposes is the role of film and film music, and technologies associated with these media forms (such as radio and television), in inspiring a virile sense of nationalism. When DJ and his buddies embrace the militant tactics of the yesteryear revolutionaries, they are branded terrorists and meet their death at the hands of the state. Their martyrdom inspires a national political awakening across the country. The film's climax has the men broadcasting their crimes over All India Radio (AIR). Their confession calls the nation into being, as other citizens phone in to either applaud or debate their decision to take on the brutality of the state. These final scenes cue us into the relationship between film, film music, and nationalism. Historically, radio as a medium has been crucial to the popularization of film music in India. The state-run agency AIR is famous for having (inadvertently) fostered listeners' love of Hindi film music through its concerted campaign to "ban" film songs from the airwaves in the 1950s (Huacuja Alonso 2023).[3] That said, film and film music play a key role in the emergence of nation and nationalism *throughout RDB*, not just in its climax. With a protagonist named DJ—one, moreover, who plays the role of "Azad" (*Āzād*, the name means "freedom")—how can we not expect music to have deeply transformative power?

Bhangra: Rural India Remixed

The musical centerpiece of *RDB* is an eponymous and rambunctious *bhangra* number (▶ Video example 16.1, "A. R. Rahman" 2015). "Rang De Basanti" documents and *drives* the transformation of carefree college students into serious actors. Over the course of this song, DJ, in particular, goes from being a comic, ethnically marked (Punjabi) character to the revolutionary hero Chandrashekhar Azad. Below I demonstrate how the reference to Punjab via the musical genre of *bhangra* articulates a very specific notion of nationalist agency and heroism.

---

[3] Radio was also the medium that the revolutionary anticolonial activist (and Axis-sympathizer) Subhas Chandra Bose used to broadcast his strident messages while in exile during World War II. Through his short-wave radio station "Azad Hind," he contested the colonial administration's narrative about the war (Huacuja Alonso 2023, 53–81).

While DJ and his friends spend most of their time in New Delhi, "Rang De Basanti" has them traveling out of the capital city and into the rural heartland—specifically, to a village in Punjab. This geographical move is critical to the film's construction of masculinity. In addition to presenting village India as the "real" India, the song highlights Hindi cinema's long history of positioning North Indian men, and Punjabis in particular, as exemplars of the nation (Dwyer 2002, 20). Punjab also enables the song to muscularize its heroes. To the British colonial administration, Punjabis were a "martial race" (Streets 2004). This notion of Punjabis as strong and rugged continues into the present day, with military service and farming being the two professions most closely associated with this community in the public imagination. The journey to Punjab in "Rang De Basanti" confers on our young heroes (who are not particularly tall or muscular in appearance) the strength and authenticity they need to step into their roles as national heroes.

The move to Punjab is signaled aurally by the sounds of *bhangra*, a musical genre close to DJ's heart—and, as we shall see, many a deejay's repertoire. *Bhangra* is traditionally associated with Baisakhi (*baisākhī*), a harvest festival that marks the Sikh New Year. Anjali Gera Roy observes that "the traditional format of the Bhangra boli [*bolī*, a couplet sung in call-and-response] is that of the praise song in which the singer calls out the attributes of the beloved, homeland or the deity in a plain, homespun idiom" (Gera Roy 2010, 41). "Rang De Basanti" employs just such an aural and visual idiom. The song setting appears to be a village fair celebrating Baisakhi. The village dancers are clothed in traditional *bhangra* attire and perform fairly traditional dance moves.[4] Their costumes and movements are in stark contrast to those of DJ and his compadres, who are enthusiastic participants but are clearly marked by their clothes and comportment as city slickers. Indeed, it is this decidedly local, ethnic, and traditional context of the title song that transforms the young men into truly national subjects. As the group traverses the beautiful landscape and cavorts with locals, we understand that for all their "Western" ways, these youngsters are "sons of the soil."[5] They may not (yet) know the history of the freedom struggle or how to tie a *dhoti* (*dhotī*, traditional male

---

[4] As he notes in the Director's Commentary track of the DVD, Rakeysh Omprakash Mehra hired professional *bhangra* dancers from Ludhiana, Punjab, to ensure that the dance looked "correct." The emphasis on realism is key to the film's appeal to the "common man," for it suggests such passion and patriotism can and should be a part of everyone's life.

[5] This accusation of the college students' Westernization is made in *RDB* by the character Laxman Pandey before he joins the film crew.

attire) properly, but they dance with gusto at the Baisakhi celebrations. All this confirms that they are Indian at heart.

If *bhangra* confers on *RDB*'s protagonists a traditional, Punjabi ethos, it also takes them in new directions, linking them to global circuits of musical production and consumption. Beginning in the early 1990s, India was caught up in a version of the *bhangra* revival that had shaken the British music scene a few years earlier. This musical explosion happened in the context of economic liberalization.[6] In 1991, the Indian government introduced sweeping economic reforms with the intent of "opening up" the economy to private and foreign investment. The cultural face of economic liberalization was increased access to films and television shows from around the world via satellite television, and the adoption of various new styles—for example, in dress, movement, and music—once "foreign" to the Indian cultural scene. While *bhangra* per se was not new to Indian ears, it emerged on the (Indian and British) music and club scene in the early 1990s as a racial and cultural hybrid (Gera Roy 2008, 101).[7]

This *bhangra* revival also facilitated, and was facilitated by, the rising popularity of Daler Mehndi. Mehndi's 1995 album *Bolo Ta Ra Ra* was the first regional music album to become a national hit (Gera Roy 2010, 37).[8] Having crossed linguistic and cultural barriers, Mehndi was quickly christened the King of Bhangra-pop. Mainstream Hindi cinema also embraced *bhangra* with renewed vigor. As the format of the Hindi film song shifted toward that of music videos—film songs enjoyed greater presence not only on MTV and VH1, but also on other television channels' film- and music-based programs—Daler Mehndi began to make cameo appearances in several cinematic *bhangra* numbers.[9]

RDB, too, participates in and profits from the craze for Bollywood *bhangra*. Crucially, even as this musical choice grounds the protagonists in Punjab, it keeps them from being parochial subjects. They are not regional exemplars

---

[6] See Kvetko* for discussion of Indipop and economic liberalization.

[7] Even as *bhangra* fused with rap, ragga, hip-hop, and house came to signify a hybrid British-Asian identity and a modern, cosmopolitan sensibility, the genre retained its folk roots with the so-called backlash by musicians who stuck more closely to traditional rhythms and arrangements. See also Bhattacharjya and DJ Rekha.*

[8] Originally from Ludhiana, Punjab, Mehndi sold a million copies of his album in the southern state of Kerala alone.

[9] *Bhangra* has long been one among many styles in Bombay cinema's musical repertoire. What's new since the mid-1990s is that the "naturalization of Punjabi music and dance . . . in Bollywood's song and dance routine in recent Bollywood blockbusters has transformed it into a new Bollywood formula" (Gera Roy 2010, 36).

of masculinity, but modern, cosmopolitan, and national ones. This is because *bhangra* today is embedded in the diffuse, transnational musical circuits that sustain deejaying culture. The genre can no longer be thought of (or even experienced) apart from the remixes that fueled its global popularity beginning in the late 1980s.[10] In fact, it is precisely this simultaneous gesture to the rural *and* the urban, to the regional, the national, *and* the transnational that makes *bhangra* perfect for the film's project of (re)vitalizing Indian nationalism in the contemporary era.

Prasoon Joshi's synaesthetic lyrics for "Rang De Basanti" proffer mixing and melding as key processes in this "modern-day recipe [for] patriotism":[11]

> *Thoḍī sī dhūl merī dhartī kī, mere watan kī* (2x)
> *Thoḍī sī khushbū baurāyī sī mast pavan kī*
> *Thoḍī sī dhauṅkanevālī dhak-dhak dhak-dhak dhak-dhak sānseṅ*
> *Jinmeṅ ho junūṅ junūṅ vo būndeṅ lāl lahūṅ kī*
> *Ye sab tū milā milā le, phir raṅg tu khilā khilā re* (2x)
> *Or mohe tū raṅg de basantī yārā*
> *Mohe (mohe) tū raṅg de basantī yārā* (9x)

> Take some soil of this land
> The scent of this air
> And the breath of my being, the throbbing of my heart
> And the zeal that races through my blood
> Take all of these and stir it, then watch as it brings out the color
> Watch as it brings out the color of patriotism, my friend.

The lyrics of this *mukhra* (*mukhṛā*, "opening stanza and hook"), repeated several times in Daler Mehndi's inimitable and infectious voice, present nationalism as a visceral experience. The song engages our senses of smell, sight, and touch. In the aspirated syllables (*th* and *dh*) of the first line we feel the dry earth (*Thoḍī sī dhūl merī dhartī kī*). We smell the fragrance in the air. We hear our life breath, the constant beating of our heart (*dhauṅkanevālī dhak-dhak dhak-dhak dhak-dhak sānse*). The rhythm, repetition, and onomatopoeia

---

[10] To quote Gera Roy again: "Going by the number of Bhangra remixes circulating globally, one might begin to wonder if any unmixed Bhangra still exists" (2008, 110).
[11] This phrase is director Rakeysh Omprakash Mehra's and is recorded in the Director's Commentary track included in the DVD. English translations are those provided on the DVD as subtitles. See https://www.youtube.com/watch?v=c769V25pX08.

in the above lines—not to mention the driving rhythms on the *dhol* (*ḍhol*, double-headed barrel drum)—make this an eminently danceable song. Anjali Gera Roy reminds us that *bhangra* is "essentially a drumbeat played with or without vocal or visual accompaniment . . . [and its] minimalist formulaic lyrics are set in the *boliyan* format" (2008, 101). This improvisational, call-and-response format—note the address to *yārā* ("friend") in the lyrics—and the genre's characteristic, repetitive rhythmic patterns on the *dhol* encourage audience participation. Thus, in more ways than one, *bhangra* makes nationalism a moving bodily experience, and a collective one at that.

The editing and choreography of "Rang De Basanti" accentuate the sense that nationalism is more than just an abstract concept, something that is disconnected from and irrelevant to lived experience.[12] The sequence is edited thematically, in the style of a music video: images are cut to the rhythm of the song so as to communicate the boisterous mood of the Baisakhi celebrations (Dilip 2008, 95). The constant repetition of the musical hook is mirrored in the visual realm with multiple, sometimes repetitive shots of the *bhangra* dancers in their traditional attire performing a choreographed routine. These are intercut with images of our young heroes entering the arena one by one, led by DJ. The group follows the dancers' moves, mimicking them quite closely at times, and at others repeating the movement, but in their own quirky styles. For example, they might move their heads up and down as if they're in a rock concert or playing air guitar. The rapid cutting and quick movement between different elements in the scene—from the colorful festoons flapping in the wind to the dancers' acrobatic spinning to the friends tussling with wrestlers twice their size—also communicate the joy and energy of the event. The point of this editing technique is not the *bhangra* routine per se, but the joyous bonding the song-dance generates. Accordingly, the camera captures much of the action in close-ups and medium shots, drawing attention to the friends' expressions as they romp around Punjab, DJ's ethnic and cultural homeland.

Lest we get carried away with the dancing and forget that this song is a patriotic *mantra*, "Rang De Basanti" gives us a model of the transformation that the song is meant to effect. While DJ and his friends cheer on the sidelines of the *bhangra* and wrestling matches at first, they quickly jump into the enclosed arena and join in the fun. We witness their transformation from enthusiastic bystanders to active participants. Thus, dancing *bhangra* is not

---

[12] See also Schultz*.

just a means for inciting patriotism, but a metonym for nationalist civic activism: to participate in *bhangra* is to act as a national citizen. The more the young men sing and dance, the more involved they become in the nation. Toward the end of the song sequence, we see the whole group putting on their costumes for Sue's film, trying on mustaches, turbans, and dhotis. Their transformation is complete; all that remains is the shooting of the film.

Even more dramatic is the emergence of DJ as the historical figure of Azad over the course of this song. Three sequences featuring DJ's rehearsals of the role are interspersed with the musical segments of "Rang De Basanti." During these brief rehearsal scenes, the music of the *bhangra* song plays softly, as if waiting respectfully for DJ/Azad to finish speaking. Note that one of the sepia scenes just prior to the title song sequence depicts Azad announcing the plan to loot the train carrying English monies at Kakori. Thus, we have already seen DJ/Azad recite these lines with conviction in the past. "Rang De Basanti" teaches DJ to own those words in the present. The first two scenes are comic, with DJ rehearsing his lines as Azad first in front of a water buffalo at his mother's house (1:30–1:47), and then with a young boy who serves tea in the college canteen (2:45–3:07) (▶ Video example 16.1). In both cases, he replaces some Hindi words with Punjabi ones, and speaks others with a Punjabi accent; he also improvises his lines in a silly fashion. The third instance has him standing in a light T-shirt in front of a projector: black-and-white images from a historical news reel (or a documentary film) wash over him as he recites the same lines, flawlessly this time, in standard Hindi and without the accent of his native Punjab (3:31–3:44). The use of Hindi, one of India's two official languages, nationalizes the performance beyond the local ethnic Punjabi context. We see images of violence and the word "casualties" on his body. The gravitas of this image is unmistakable. DJ is no longer a joking, Peter Pan–ish figure, nor is he an ethnically marked subject, at once a pale shadow and a caricature of Punjabi masculinity. By the end of "Rang De Basanti," DJ's heroic nationalist avatar has fully emerged.

Conclusion

RDB consistently highlights the centrality of film music to nation and nationalism. In essence, it does what scholarship on (Hindi) cinema has not done due to an inordinate emphasis on the visual. In the face of journalistic and scholarly discourse about the death of the film song as we knew it and the irrelevance of the nation as a concept in an increasingly transnational world, *RDB* makes a strong case for the continuing relevance of both nation and Hindi film music (Garwood 2006; Virdi 2017). In enmeshing the two and tying them to heroic masculine avatars, this film not only reminds us of the historical connection between nation and Hindi film music, it also makes music an essential part of the future of the (virile) nation.

This critical intervention notwithstanding, *RDB* is troubling for it leaves us with profoundly masculinist ideas about national citizenship and agency. It is not just that *bhangra* makes national heroes out of DJ and his friends, but that film music and its technologies are themselves masculinized in the process. A film that begins with two women, Sue and Sonia, making a docudrama about the nation's past ends up marginalizing women. Women are sidelined in the title song as well as in the climactic scene. By the end, Sue's

---

Box 16.1   Exercises

1. Watch the three rehearsals that DJ performs in "Rang De Basanti"
   ▶ Video example 16.1:
   a. Rehearsing with the buffaloes (1:30–1:47)
   b. Rehearsing in the college canteen (2:45–3:07)
   c. Rehearsing in front of a projector (3:31–3:44)
   - First, play the sequences with the sound off, watching carefully for differences in the location (setting) of each rehearsal, other figures who are present at or folded into the rehearsal, and the way the camera angles and movement in each shot frame DJ.
   - Next, play these sequences again, this time with the image off and the sound on. Note down what you hear in DJ's pronunciation and the turns of phrase he uses in each of his rehearsals.
   - Finally, prepare a comparative analysis of these three rehearsals that speaks to the ways in which DJ is transformed over the course of "Rang De Basanti."
2. Consider the sequence toward the end of the film when Sue and Sonia sit quietly atop the old fort mourning the deaths of their friends and lovers. In her voice-over in this sequence, Sue says that she and Sonia listen for the sounds of their deceased friends that are occasionally carried in the wind. What does this aural representation of the past (as it returns in the form of sonic fragments) tell us about women's roles in the future of the nation? To what extent does it challenge the argument that women are sidelined in *RDB*?

film project is abandoned, and she and Sonia are left to mourn the deaths of their martyred friends. In bringing film music back into the history of nation and into the cultural discourse of manhood, *RDB* reminds students of South Asian cinema and music to *listen* as closely as we "read" films. But in erasing women's agency, it also reminds us to listen as carefully to film's silences and fissures as we do to its visual and aural representations (Box 16.1).

Works Cited

"A. R. Rahman—Rang De Basanti Best Video|Rang De Basanti|Aamir Khan|Soha|Daler Mehndi." *YouTube*, Uploaded by SonyMusicIndiaVEVO, October 27, 2015. https://www.youtube.com/watch?v=c769V25pX08.

Beaster-Jones, Jayson. 2015. *Bollywood Sounds: The Cosmopolitan Mediations of Hindi Film Song*. New York: Oxford University Press.

Booth, Gregory. 2008. *Behind the Curtain: Making Music in Mumbai's Film Studios*. Oxford: Oxford University Press.

Chakravarty, Sumita S. 1993. *National Identity in Indian Popular Cinema, 1947–1987*. Austin: University of Texas Press.

Chandra, Nandini. 2010. "Young Protest: The Idea of Merit in Commercial Hindi Cinema." *Comparative Studies of South Asia, Africa and the Middle East* 30(1): 119–132.

Dilip, Meghana. 2008. "Rang De Basanti—Consumption, Citizenship, and the Public Sphere." MA thesis, University of Massachusetts–Amherst.

Dwyer, Rachel. 2002. "Indian Cinema." In *Cinema India: The Visual Culture of Hindi Film*, edited by Rachel Dwyer and Divia Patel, 13–41. New Brunswick, NJ: Rutgers University Press.

Garwood, Ian. 2006. "The Songless Bollywood Film." *South Asian Popular Culture* 4(2): 169–183.

Gera Roy, Anjali. 2008. "Bhangra Remixes." In *India in Africa, Africa in India: Indian Ocean Cosmopolitanisms*, edited by John C. Hawley, 95–116. Bloomington: Indiana University Press.

Gera Roy, Anjali. 2010. "Is Everybody Saying 'Shava Shava' to Bollywood Bhangra?" In *Bollywood and Globalization: Indian Popular Cinema, Nation, and Diaspora*, edited by Rini Bhattacharya Mehta and Rajeshwari V. Pandharipande, 35–49. London: Anthem Press.

Huacuja Alonso, Isabel. 2023. *Radio for the Millions: Hind-Urdu Broadcasting Across Borders*. New York: Columbia University Press.

Majumdar, Neepa. 2001. "The Embodied Voice: Song Sequences and Stardom in Popular Hindi Cinema." In *Soundtrack Available: Essays on Film and Popular Music*, edited by Pamela Robertson Wojcik and Arthur Knight, 161–181. Durham, NC: Duke University Press.

Mehta, Monika. 2011. *Censorship and Sexuality in Bombay Cinema*. Austin: University of Texas Press.

Morcom, Anna. 2007. *Hindi Film Songs and the Cinema*. Aldershot: Ashgate Publishing.

Punathambekar, Aswin. 2010. "Ameen Sayani and Radio Ceylon: Notes towards a History of Broadcasting and Bombay Cinema." *BioScope: South Asian Screen Studies* 1(2): 189–197.
Srivastava, Neelam. 2009. "Bollywood National(ist) Cinema: Violence, Patriotism and the National-Popular in *Rang De Basanti*." *Third Text* 23(6): 703–716.
Streets, Heather. 2004. *Martial Races: The Military, Race and Masculinity in British Imperial Culture, 1857–1914.* Manchester: Manchester University Press.
Sundar, Pavitra. 2014. "Of Radio, Remix, and *Rang De Basanti*: Reimagining History Through Film Sound." *Jump Cut* 56. http://www.ejumpcut.org/archive/jc56.2014-2015/RangDeBasanti/index.html. Accessed August 18, 2022.
Sundar, Pavitra. 2023. *Listening with a Feminist Ear: Soundwork in Hindi Cinema.* Ann Arbor: University of Michigan Press.
Virdi, Jyotika. 2003. *The Cinematic ImagiNation: Indian Popular Films as Social History.* New Brunswick, NJ: Rutgers University Press.
Virdi, Jyotika. 2017. "A National Cinema's Transnational Aspirations? Considerations on 'Bollywood.'" *South Asian Popular Culture* 15(1): 1–22.

17
Disrupted Divas

Conflicting Pathways of India's Socially Marginalized Female Entertainers

Amelia Maciszewski

This chapter examines the lives of socially marginalized women singers and dancers in three North Indian communities.[1] These women, known as *tawa'if*s (*ṯavā'if*s), often descend from professional caste or clan lineages and belong to a long tradition of divas: celebrated, controversial entertainers; sought-after court musicians and dancers; and pioneers. Following the partition and independence of India and Pakistan in 1947, members of these communities have, at best, become romanticized archetypes and, at worst, become linked with prostitution and sex trafficking. In the process, their important artistic and cultural roles and contributions have been obscured, co-opted by the mainstream, or silenced. In contemporary India, the disintegration of this once-great artistic tradition has rendered legitimate artistic renown unattainable, negatively impacting *tawai'f*s' social status, artistic development, and economic situation. Are legitimacy and respect still possible, or will these artists remain on the margins of society?

*Tawa'if*s' songs and stories express vivid narratives about history, culture, customs, and life trajectories. Earthy, cryptic, mystical, and double-entendre song lyrics address topics such as birth and marriage, longing and repressed desire, romantic love, and class, caste, and gender discrimination (see also Babiracki 2004). In response to contemporary audiences' rather lowbrow preferences, today *tawa'if*s often sing simple melodies accompanied by relatively unrefined, sexually provocative presentation. Their songs' poignant, raw, and ironic lyrics, nevertheless, both reflect and challenge their contemporary social circumstances.

---

[1] This is a companion text to my ethnographic film *Disrupted Divas, Conflicting Pathways* (Maciszewski 2010).

To contextualize contemporary performance, I begin this chapter by discussing the impact of select twentieth-century *tawa'if*s. Based on my research as participant-observer from 1994 to 2014, I then examine *tawa'if* music-making in three contexts: (1) semiprivate *mujra*s (*mujrās*, soirées mostly for men's entertainment); (2) informal occasions of community music-making; and (3) contemporary *tawa'if* presentations on the global stage, particularly those produced by the Benares-based social service organization Guria Sansthan. Through these specific case studies, I argue that *tawa'if*s still have significant artistic agency despite the substantial discrimination and violence their community has endured. Their performances of light-classical and folk genres of music and dance often involve exaggerated gestures and facial expressions and histrionic vocal techniques to emphasize the lyrics, which are often sexually suggestive or socially critical. I argue that their power is evident through this overt body language, vocal projection, gestures, and facial expression, as they perform their caste (or *biradari* [*birādarī*, community]) role as hereditary dancers and singers despite and as an act of resistance toward a globalized, capitalist market (Dalwai 2019).[2]

*Tawa'if*s, Tradition, and Legislation

On the Indian subcontinent, *tawa'if*s once held allure and commanded respect as divas. They were pioneering women in the theater (where women's roles were previously played by men) and in the twentieth-century recording and film industries (see ▶ Video example 17.1). For example, Gauhar Jan of Kolkata (Calcutta) recorded India's first disc, on His Master's Voice (HMV), in 1902 and became the highest-paid recording/performing artist of her time (Kinnear 1994).[3] Her protégée Indubala recorded for the Gramophone Company in 1916, sang on the All India Radio's first broadcast from Kolkata (1927), and acted in forty-eight films. The renowned vocalist Jaddan Bai was

---

[2] Dalwai examines the caste capital deployed by Mumbai bar dancers, many who are descended from *tawa'if*s. *Tawa'if*s consider themselves members of *biradari*s (lit. "brotherhood"), extended communities generally connected by kinship, occupation, and artistic *gharana* affiliation. While these socioeconomic communities can cross specific distinctions of caste and religion—for example, musician *biradari*s may include Hindus and Muslims (Neuman 1990)—caste-like prejudices may apply to them, their instruments, genres, and performance contexts.

[3] *Vintage Music from India* (Rounder Records 1993) includes rare early twentieth-century recordings of Gauhar Jan, Jaddan Bai, and other *tawa'if*s. Additionally, www.womenonrecord.com contains biographies, interviews, photographs, recordings, and documentaries about South Asian female performers, many from *tawa'if* backgrounds.

one of the first women to produce, direct, and compose music for Bombay cinema; she established her own film production company, in which she and her daughter Nargis (later a Hindi film superstar) acted (George 2007; Shah 2016). Daya Kumari, discussed below, sang, danced, and acted in numerous plays at the Minerva and Starlight Theaters in Kolkata in the late 1940s and early 1950s, recorded on HMV/Calcutta, and toured with the Hyderabad (India) Theatre Company as a singer and actress (personal communication, 1996–2008).

Despite successes of such luminary artists, the forces of colonization, modernization, and globalization made a profoundly negative impact on *tawa'ifs*' status and societal roles. Beginning in the mid-nineteenth century, colonial ethnographers and census-takers listed hereditary female performers as "prostitutes," placing them in the same category as sex workers with respect to colonial public health policies (Oldenburg 1990). This inaccuracy delegitimized *tawa'ifs*' contributions and exacerbated public misunderstandings; legislation emerged that reflected the mainstream public's diminished perception of *tawa'ifs*' morality and artistic value, excluding them further.[4]

Early in the twentieth century, Indian social reformers and reformist music advocates worked to "classicize" musical genres and performance practices. Greater importance was placed on the Hindustani classical genre known as *khayal* (*khayāl*); other light-classical and folk genres commonly performed by *tawa'ifs* were altered to remove any sexual content and their structures were formalized to seem more classical. This process of "sanitization" and "classicization" enabled mainstream performers to co-opt *tawa'if* practices. With these shifts, so-called respectable women (those who lived their lives according to the patriarchally constructed norms of Indian society including entering into and maintaining heterosexual marriages, often arranged by their families) began to perform these genres in socially elite venues such as public concert halls in urban centers. Most *tawa'ifs* who had presented their art in *mujra*s, intimate soirées for the entertainment of wealthy patrons and colonialists, were excluded from this "democratization."

From the early nineteenth until the late twentieth centuries, *tawa'ifs* lived in specific neighborhoods, considered entertainment districts, where they performed *mujra* (see ⊙ Video example 17.2). *Mujra* refers both to intimate

---

[4] Anna Morcom (2018) discusses the complex web of issues and legislation that vilified and dismissed *tawa'ifs* and public/erotic performers as irrelevant at best, at worst, as sociopaths in need of social "rehabilitation" (cf. Krishnan et al.*).

performance events and to the delicately sensuous performance style of the *tawā'ifs'* salon, or *kotha* (*koṭhā*). In *mujra* performance, one *tawā'if*, with a small instrumental ensemble, sings Hindustani vocal music combined with kathak dance and poetry in dialects of Hindi and Urdu. Upper-class men, their sons, and even British colonialists frequented these salons to relish *tawā'ifs'* art, sophisticated conversation, and aestheticized coyness. Art was at the center of these encounters; seduction was a possibility, but not necessarily a given.[5]

In newly independent India, new laws further disenfranchised the already-marginalized *tawā'if*s. The Anti-Zamindari Act of 1952 disempowered landed gentry by reclaiming their lands and titles. As the aristocracy were the traditional audience for Indian classical music and dance, this effected the loss of a major source of patronage for *tawā'if*s. Some *tawā'if*s bore the stigma of having been members of castes or tribes listed in the 1871 Criminal Tribes Act, which arbitrarily designated people of the "independent" trades/professions—including itinerant craftspeople, traders, pastoralists, and entertainers—as "criminal by nature." Although the Act was repealed in 1952, these individuals' caste status was merely changed to "denotified," doing little to erase their markedness and resultant social stigma.[6] Subsequently, the first Immoral Traffic Prevention Act (ITPA), passed in 1956, made it increasingly difficult for *tawā'if*s to prove that salon establishments in which they performed were not connected to prostitution, which was now punishable as a criminal offense. Famous courtesan quarters such as Dalmandi in Benares and Chowk in Lucknow became subject to often-violent police raids. Today, *tawā'if*s still live in some of these quarters, but they are not safe from warrantless searches, arrests, harassment, and evictions sanctioned by the ITPA. Because social reforms and resultant public discourse vilified *tawā'if*s and their artistry, their salon performances have all but disappeared in many former urban centers. The remnants of this tradition remain in a few smaller cities in a degraded form.

---

[5] A hierarchy existed among *tawā'if*s with regard to social/artistic status. At the top were women who only sang; next were those who sang and danced, followed by dancers only. At the lower end were street dancers/singers and acrobats. The higher a woman's social and artistic status, the greater her sexual sovereignty (see Oldenburg 1990, 264; Nevile 1996).

[6] Such people were restricted regarding regions they could visit and social groups they were allowed to interact with. In some cases, entire caste groups were arrested, families were separated, and members were held in penal colonies. They were also denied access to food rations provided by the government to low-caste and low-income people (Morcom 2018; Oldenburg 1990).

One such site of contemporary *tawa'if* performance is Chaturbhujasthan, a red-light district in the provincial city Muzaffarpur, Bihar. Once respected for its art and culture, Chaturbhujasthan has mostly deteriorated into a flesh trade market. Previously, passersby could hear dancers' *ghungroos* (*ghuṅgharū*, ankle bells) and music rehearsals. Now poverty, lack of patronage, and caste/class discrimination have reduced what was a celebrated artistic tradition to little more than an adjunct to the main business of prostitution, in which minimally skilled women and girls dance seductively while lip-syncing to Bollywood tunes. A few *tawa'ifs* living in Chaturbhujasthan continue to perform the *mujra* style they inherited from their foremothers and learned from male instructors.

Music in Everyday Interactions

Teaching and Learning

*Tawā'if*s often lived in matrilineal households and have passed down their artistic practices from mother, aunt, or elder sister to daughter, niece, or younger sister. Following this basic training, adolescent girls typically study to become professional entertainers with a male music or dance instructor (called an *ustad* [*ustād*] if Muslim or *guru* if Hindu). For example, Aruna Devi, a *tawa'if* based in Muzaffarpur's Chaturbhujasthan, trained briefly with an *ustad* and received ongoing coaching from her mother Kali Dasi (Maciszewski 2006, 2007a). Kali Dasi had trained more extensively with the respected Ustad Wajjan Khan (see ▶ Video example 17.3). Kali Dasi was the strongest musical influence on her granddaughter Chandni, who reminisced "*Nānī* taught me *purāne* [old-style] *ghazals*."[7] Another elder in Chaturbhujasthan, Daya Kumari, similarly taught her granddaughter Gunja (Maciszewski 2007a, 2007b, 2010). These women also made music informally at home, where music provided a soundtrack to everyday life. Much of their "practice" happened while doing household chores or socializing (see ▶ Video example 17.4).[8] However, partly due to the convenience and

---

[7] The genre of *ghazal* was commercialized starting in the 1980s; its musical structure and poetic diction were considerably simplified to make it accessible to wider audiences, including Bollywood fans (Manuel 2010, 249). In this interview, Chandni was referring to *ghazal* prior to the 1980s.

[8] Kali Dasi describes women's informal *moqabala* (*moqābalā*, musical duels) in Maciszewski 2007b, 182.

affordability of low-cost technology, live music today faces competition from recorded music, and low-status traditional entertainers find fewer opportunities to perform this traditional repertoire.

Community

The once great variety of traditional songs in North India includes songs for life events such as marriage and the birth of a baby. Such songs are usually sung by women, sometimes elder *tawā'ifs* hired to perform at women's gatherings. For example, *banna-banni* (*bannā-bannī*) are songs performed by women at weddings. *Banni* (lit. "bride") are sung by and/or on behalf of the groom's female family members and friends to describe the beauty of the bride and welcome her with blessings. *Banna* (lit. "groom") are sung by the bride's family as the groom and his attendants arrive at the wedding, to welcome them and describe gifts the bride's family will give him.[9] Wealthier families would commonly employ *tawā'ifs* to entertain at the festivities. Today, *tawā'ifs* are seldom hired to sing *banna-banni* at weddings of "mainstream" people; however, most *tawā'ifs* I spoke with knew such songs and sang them confidently. I suggest that these songs are a part of their caste identity and "cultural capital," or community knowledge (Bourdieu 1984). Today they are shared informally in everyday life and, occasionally, in professional situations (see Box 17.1).

▶ Video example 17.6 shows an impromptu performance of a *banna* by Aruna Devi, Poonam, and their friends in Muzaffarpur celebrating Guria Sansthan founder-director Ajeet Singh's marriage to Santwana Manju Singh. As Poonam provides rhythm on a *dugga* (*duggā*, one-half of a *tabla* drum set), the women express their agency through overt body language, vocal projection in a bold call-and-response style, clapping, and gestures to welcome Ajeet Singh.

Women sing *sohar* in celebration of a birth, inviting everyone to visit mother and baby and offer blessings for a long, healthy, prosperous life.

Erī māī nandjī ke lāl bhaye man rajanā
Oh woman/mother, the son of Nand [the new baby boy] is making my
   heart glad

---

[9] An interesting subset of *banna-banni* is *gali* (*gālī*, "abuse"), songs that complain about or taunt the in-laws' family, particularly from the bride's point-of-view, in a humorous assertion of her refusal to be dominated by patriarchal customs.

> **Box 17.1 Exercise**
>
> The *banna* below was taught to me by my vocal *guru*, the renowned classical "diva" Padma Vibhushan Girija Devi (1929–2017). She had close ties to the community of musicians in Benares that included *tawa'if*s and was a deep repository of such repertoire. See ⓥ Video example 17.5 to sing this *banna* with the me.
>
> *Bannā mhārā phul gulāl bannī ko rang kesariyā*
> *Sone ki pānī mein jīvar paro so*
> *Pī le hmārā bannā ammā lebe bhalāīyā . . .*
>
> Our groom's flowers are pink; bride's color is saffron
> The jewelry is placed in golden water
> Take a drink, our dear groom, while mother blesses you . . .

Chalā ho sakhī mile mangal gāo
Come along, girlfriends, sing his blessings

Chiranjī rahe dūdh pībnā erī dūdh pībnā eri māī . . .
Surround him/her giving him/her milk to drink, oh giving milk to drink, oh woman/mother . . .

ⓥ Video example 17.7, cue point 0:43, shows an informal performance of another portion of a *sohar* by three generations of women: matriarch Kali Dasi (d. 2003), her daughter Aruna Devi, and Aruna's daughter Chandni and niece Shalini, in celebration of the birth of Aruna's older daughter Ragini's (d. 2007) firstborn son in 2000. Similar to other collectively sung traditional songs, the two eldest women take turns introducing a line, echoed in unison by the others. Their vocal timbre is bold, their postures reflect confidence, and their hand gestures either follow the melody or emphasize a turn of phrase in the lyrics.

As in other communities of (often low-status) hereditary professional artisans, *tawa'if*s' music and overall performance style existed both as their (implicit) cultural capital and their (tacit) lifestyle, subsumed under a caste/*biradari* identity. Much like a community's language, their cultural knowledge was shared informally with children from an early age and refined through continuous repetition in a manner that distinguished little between private and public "work." This blurred boundary between informal, private music-making and professional performance, coupled with the morally judgmental conflation of their performance labor with sex work, have contributed to severely disrupting the sustainability of their artistic practice.

Disruptions Described: Caste/Generation/Gender

Today, *tawa'if*s encounter many obstacles that inhibit their ability to make a living as performers. For those who continue to perform in private salons, patrons are often more interested in sex than songs. What were once "entertainment districts" where patrons would go to witness performances by skilled musicians and dancers, listen to and discuss poetry, and practice social graces are now red-light districts, sites of human and drug trafficking and other criminal activity. Women making their living in such spaces struggle with a complex network of crime, exploitation, poverty, and profound social marginalization.

For an example of what life is like now for *tawa'if*s, I share my experience interviewing Munni Bai and Noor Jahan in 2005. Middle-aged at the time of this interview, they lived near Shivdaspur, a red-light area of the city of Benares served by the social advocacy organization Guria Sansthan. Noor Jahan had retired but Munni Bai was still in the "workforce." On the morning of our meeting, Munni Bai complained of feeling so ill after performing all night as singer-dancer with a Bollywood-style wedding band that she had vomited by the side of the road. The hard reality was that at her age, she was offered fewer jobs than before and felt she must accept any engagement offered, regardless of her preferences. Munni Bai said, "In these times . . . this is what is popular among young people": still seated, with chest-thrusting movements and overt facial expressions, she parodied the contemporary Bollywood-style dancing that had become standard in many *tawa'ifs'* performances. She remarked, "But for our generation, well, it's very different.. . . . Elegance, mime, gestures—that's what we prefer." She continued, "People our age don't like to grind and swing our hips. But circumstances have left us no choice. . . . Today's dance style, it's uncouth. But what can we do? It's all what the public wants." When I asked Munni Bai what her favorite song is, she retorted, "My favorite? Ha! What we like means absolutely nothing! It's all about what the customer wants! . . . What I would like is to eat and dress well . . . *when* I earn." She shrugged with a gesture of resignation. Noor Jahan chimed in saying, "It's what the public likes—what we like doesn't matter at all!"

Finally, however, they both shared songs they enjoyed, demonstrating examples from their repertoires (see ▶ Video example 17.8). Each sang sexually suggestive songs in a stylized way, emphasizing the lyrics' double-entendres. Munni Bai began with a Bhojpuri folk song. Fluid in her sassy, provocative gestures, grins, smirks and flirtatious facial expressions, she sang:

> *Indirā mein pānī nahīn̠, nadī nahīn̠ pās bā*
> Lord Indra has no water, the river is not close by
>
> *Hotuwā sukhāilā chalā, kattī nahīn̠ pyāswā*
> My lips are parched, my thirst doesn't subside
>
> *āh re manwā uddāswā*
> My heart is forlorn
>
> *Hotuwā se chal ke more, pīttī nahīn̠ āswā*
> You have left my lips without having drunk
>
> *Bhuāilā bālam*
> Heed this, oh lover
>
> *Apne hotuwā se hotuwā tang satāīlā bālam*
> Touching my lips to yours will refresh me, lover!

Then, Noor Jahan took her turn, singing (cue point 1:14):

> *Lubhāī gāīlā nā, āh re saīnyān̠ more saverīho suratiyā*
> I long for your dark face, my lover
>
> *Bhulāī gāīlā nā*
> I will not forget
>
> *Rātayān dekhlī sapanwā*
> Oh, when I slept, I dreamt
>
> *Saīnyān morā āye anganwā*
> That my lover returned home

Dabaāī dīlā nā ... DABĀĪ DĪLĀ NĀ
He would hold me tight / He would squeeze my breasts

āh re saīnyān more palāī ho jobanawā
Oh, my lover took care of my desire

Historian Veena Oldenburg described a community of *tawa'if*s in Lucknow in the 1970s as living a "lifestyle of resistance," supposedly free from patriarchal constraints (1990). However, by the first decade of the twenty-first century, the "resistance" performed by these women in their suggestive lyrics and dance movements was accompanied by feelings of nostalgia for Noor Jahan and resignation for Munni Bai regarding the economic circumstances of their dying art.

The Politics of Vulnerability

Although women in the *tawa'if* community still wield agency, as seen by the performances described above, they are nevertheless caught in a complex web of patriarchal constraint and interwoven class/caste/gender oppression. Concerns about gossip and social acceptance often result in serious erosion of a young woman's sense of self-efficacy. If a young woman performs too much, members of the extended courtesan community may denounce her for turning into a "singer"—their use of the English word carrying risqué connotations. Such accusations damage her perceived respectability and may hurt her chances of getting married, sometimes considered a step in upward mobility.

In November 2009, I interviewed nineteen-year-old Chandni Kumari about her reluctance to pursue music more deeply. She was trained by her mother and grandmother and had a desire to pursue performance. However, she was unsure whether her mother would allow her to do so. I reminded her that she could pursue music without participating in sexualized salon settings since there is no longer a stigma for women from diverse backgrounds and castes becoming professional musicians. She replied, "Yes. I would like to perform in an *Indian Idol* show.[10] I know that's a good place to get a break."

---

[10] *Indian Idol* is similar to American televised singing competitions *American Idol* and *The X Factor*.

To be considered, she would need to apply; she was waiting for her brother to get the application form and was reluctant to pressure him to do so. When I encouraged her to proceed with applying, her reply clearly demonstrated the patriarchal constraints she felt: "Yes, I'd like to. But just the same, people might talk. And mother and my brothers would like me to get married someday." Although aware and desirous of the opportunities the globalized media might afford her, Chandni was hesitant to act. The tragic irony is that Chandni's elder sister Ragini was married (by familial arrangement) at the age of sixteen to the son of a village attorney and bore a son and a daughter, fulfilling a wife's patriarchal duty. Yet in 2005, Ragini's husband and in-laws, greedy for additional dowry, killed her by poisoning her food then burned her body beyond recognition.[11] Despite this horrific tragedy, Chandni's mother and brothers were considering marriage as one of the options for Chandni's future and to better her marriage prospects, they did not want her to be labeled as a "singer."

A Ray of Hope: Guria Sansthan

One of the most significant contemporary supporters of *tawa'if*s and their traditions is the grassroots Benares-based nonprofit organization Guria Sansthan.[12] Although its primary mission is to fight sex trafficking and prostitution of children, Guria has also provided a forum for members of the *tawa'if* community to reclaim their status as artists by presenting them in public dance festivals. Selected participants can transcend their marginalized status by performing as "legitimate" artists hired for their creative skill, not their sexual availability. On these stages, performers present the best of their repertoire, striving to make their music and dance once again acceptable to mainstream society and, ultimately, financially viable. Guria's 2004 *Dhai Akar Pyar Ka, Pearls of Love* concert series became increasingly successful in subsequent years, riding the wave of India Tourism's "Incredible India" marketing campaign targeting tourist audiences as potential consumers (Edwards and Ramamurthy 2017). Initially marketed as a festival for "Women in Prostitution," a label that made many uncomfortable, *Pearls of Love* was rebranded in 2008 as a festival of "Marginalized Traditional

---

[11] Video example 17.7 documents journalistic evidence (in Hindi) about this tragedy.
[12] www.guriaindia.org.

Artists," which included several other low-caste and socially marginalized communities. Founder/Director Ajeet Singh stated that the role of these festivals is to ignite the spark of co-operative empowerment from within the community and "create a bond of love and understanding among people" (personal communication, 2008).

Longtime Guria performer Poonam Naz, a secular *qawwali* (*qavvālī*) singer-bandleader, participated regularly in the Guria concerts where she performed her cultural knowledge with a distinctly defiant sassiness. Poonam's playfully arrogant gestures, coyly comedic facial expressions, and overall body language communicated a positive embrace of her corpulence. Video example 17.9, shot at the 2009 Pearls of Love outreach concert in Mau (near Benares), documents how Poonam drew both applause and chuckles from the audience as she flamboyantly sang in a husky voice about her conflicted diva-dom, inviting love, acceptance, and, implicitly, remuneration.

> *Dhulī jo urātī hai, urī urāīṅgī . . .*
> *Ham toh sitārā hain*
> *Yūn hī chumkāīṅgī*
> *Ham toh sitārā hain*
> *Jo jag magāeṅgī*

> Whatever dust is stirred up, that dust will fly
> I am a star
> who shines by itself
> I am a star
> who sparkles . . .

> *Aise waqt bhī āigā mohabbat mein,*
> *tum nazar, tum nazar, tum nazar*
> *Tum nazar churāte hai*
> *Ham nazar milāeṅgī*

> Such a time will come in love
> You gaze, you gaze, you gaze
> When you will sneak a gaze
> And I will meet the gaze.

The hope that India's independence in 1947 promised excluded *tawa'if*s who could not gain access to the mainstream because of discrimination that criminalized and then "denotified" them. Today, *tawa'if* is almost synonymous with prostitute, a product of the narratives that eroded their once-respected status. Moreover, the tension between the competing discourses of nationalism and postcolonialism, along with the profound changes caused by globalization, have facilitated a situation in which it is nearly impossible for non-elite *tawa'if*s to earn a living in a non-exploitative manner. Nevertheless, in singing their inherited repertoire, *tawa'if*s continue to express some agency seen in Munni Bai's and Noor Jahan's provocative lyrics and overt body language, Noor Jahan's piercing vocal production, and Poonam Naz's defiantly comedic gestures. There are a few pathways of hope, albeit very fragile, amid this disruption. One of them is Guria's project of building a future for children in red-light areas. The question remains whether this future is one of empowerment or further marginalization. Another question remains, central to the author's positioning as an applied ethnomusicologist, which aligns with Guria's mission: how to empower members of *tawa'if* communities in ways that enable them to take back ownership of their cultural heritage and make it sustainable, thus reversing a process that has essentialized and excluded them from enfranchisement and excised many of their rich music and dance traditions.

Works Cited

Babiracki, Carol. 2004. "The Illusion of India's 'Public' Dancers." In *Women's Voices across Musical Worlds*, edited by Jane A. Bernstein, 36–59. Boston: Northeastern University Press.

Bourdieu, Pierre. 1984. *Distinction: A Social Critique of the Judgement of Taste*. London: Routledge and Kegan Paul.

Dalwai, Sameena. 2019. *Bans and Bar Girls: Performing Caste in Mumbai's Dance Bars*. New Delhi: Women Unlimited.

Edwards, L., and A. Ramamurthy. 2017. "(In)credible India? A Critical Analysis of India's Nation Branding." *Communication, Culture and Critique* 10(2): 322–343.

George, T. J. S. 2007. *The Life and Times of Nargis*. Chennai: EastWest Books.

Kinnear, Michael, 1994. *The Gramophone Company's First Indian Recordings*. Bombay: Popular Prakashan Pvt. Ltd.

Maciszewski, Amelia. 2006. "Tawaifs, Tourism, and Tales: The Problematics of 21st Century Musical Patronage in India." In *The Courtesans' Arts: Cross-Cultural Perspectives*, edited by Martha Feldman and Bonnie Gordon, 332–351. New York: Oxford University Press.

Maciszewski, Amelia. 2007a. "Texts, Tunes, and Talking Heads: Discourses Surrounding Socially Marginal North Indian Women Musicians." *Twentieth Century Music Journal* 3(1): 121–144.

Maciszewski, Amelia. 2007b. "*Nayika ki Yaadgar*: North Indian Women Musicians and Their Words." In *Music and Modernity: North Indian Classical Music in an Age of Mechanical Reproduction*, edited by Amlan Das Gupta, 156–219. Kolkata: Thema

Maciszewski, Amelia. 2010. With ms. mars, Director and Producer. *Disrupted Divas, Conflicting Pathways*. Ethnographic documentary. https://www.youtube.com/watch?v=0CiGtCS_fY4

Manuel, Peter. 2010. "Thumri, Ghazal, and Modernity in Hindustani Music Culture." In *Hindustani Music: Thirteenth to Twentieth Centuries*, edited by Joep Bor, Françoise Delvoye, Jane Harvey, and Emmie te Nijenhuis, 239–250. New Delhi: Manohar.

Morcom, Anna. 2018. *Illicit Worlds of Indian Dance: Cultures of Exclusion*. Oxford: Oxford University Press.

Neuman, Daniel M. 1990 [1980]. *The Life of Music in North India: The Organization of an Artistic Tradition*. Chicago: University of Chicago Press.

Nevile, Pran, 1996. *Nautch Girls of India: Dancers, Singers, Playmates*. New York: Variety Books.

Oldenburg, Veena Talwar. 1990. "Lifestyle as Resistance: The Case of the Courtesans of Lucknow." *Feminist Studies* 16(2): 259–287.

Rounder Records. 1993: *Vintage Music from India: Early Twentieth-Century Classical & Light-Classical Music*. (Audio recording).

Shah, Vidya. 2016. *Jalsa: Indian Women and Their Journeys from the Salon to the Studio*. New Delhi: Tulika Books.

18

"All the Parts of Who I Am"

Multi-Gendered Performance in Kathak Dance

Sarah L. Morelli

Son of the Wind: *April 28, 2018. A narrator introduces the violent scene to come, the abduction of princess Sita. Lights rise to reveal Sita, played by Sonali Toppur, sleeping alone in the forest encircled by a magic ring of protection. A regal-looking man played by Rukhmani Mehta enters the scene.*[1] *His eyes fix on Sita and with mimed gestures he disguises himself, donning the simple clothes and long beard of an ascetic mendicant. Sita greets him respectfully and offers food while standing within her protective circle. He feigns offense. He is a holy man, he emphasizes, and threatens a curse if she doesn't show him proper respect by leaving her circle of protection. As she hesitatingly steps forward, he takes her plate of food, smashes it to the ground, and reveals himself as Ravan, King of Lanka. He invites her to his kingdom. Sita refuses; she is married and devoted to her husband, Ram. Ravan takes Sita by force, dragging her onto his flying chariot. As the pair exits, Sita removes her jewelry, casting each piece into the forest below with hope that someone might discover her trail.*

Some readers may be familiar with this scene, a central, heart-wrenching episode from the Hindu epic Ramayana, or "story of Ram." The Ramayana narrative has been told and retold for centuries in South Asia and beyond, with countless variations in multiple languages and forms—from oral storytelling, poetry, and novels to plays, television, and film to songs, paintings, and dance (Ramanujan 1991; Richman 1991). The Ramayana performance described above, titled *Son of the Wind*, was presented through the *kathak* dance form. Considered a "classical" dance in India, kathak was once performed by courtesan "divas" in elite salons (Maciszewski,* cf. Krishnan et al.*).[2] Today, various styles of the dance are taught in studios, performed

---

[1] At the time of this performance, Mehta danced under her given name, Rina, but has since taken the stage name Rukhmani.

[2] For more on the multifaceted history of kathak, see Chakravorty 2008 and Walker 2014.

at community events, and showcased on major international stages. *Son of the Wind* was conceived and choreographed by artistic directors of the Leela Dance Collective: Seibi Lee, Rachna Nivas, and Rukhmani Mehta. At the time of this writing, Leela's members included first- and second-generation South Asian American dancers, whose families mostly hail from various regions of India, as well as non–South Asian dancers, including me, this chapter's author. We were all trained by virtuosic kathak master Pandit Chitresh Das.[3]

Son of the Wind was relatively distinct in employing an all-female cast to play mostly male parts, particularly highlighting "martial mood (*vīra rasa*)" through scenes of war and conflict (Lutgendorf 2017, 222). The dance-drama provided a valuable context for contemporary women of the South Asian American artistic diaspora[4] to work through challenges associated with performing specific Ramayana characters. While some characters generated unease for performers, as discussed below, it is worth noting that no dance collective members experienced gender dysphoria or communicated qualms about performing both male and female characters more generally. In kathak, a dancer is expected to play any and all characters, regardless of their own sex and gender identification. Multi-gender performance, thus, becomes a naturalized aspect of a dancer's *habitus* (embodied set of practices) and an essential element of one's sense of self (Bourdieu 1977).

Most kathak dancers would agree with scholar Judith Butler's contention that gender is created through performance. As they argue, gender is "an identity tenuously constituted in time—an identity instituted through a *stylized repetition of acts*" (Butler 1988, 519). While Butler notes that gender performance generally serves to "constitute the illusion of an abiding gendered self," members of this community experience various forms of gender performance that complicate a simplistic sense of gender identity. Most members of my kathak community perform cisgender female identities in our everyday lives ("performativity," in Butler's terminology [Stone 2008, 136]). In kathak spaces, however, we develop a broader, what Roy* calls "gender-expansive" sense of self through years of practicing

---

[3] Morelli 2019 provides a detailed examination of the dance culture and style of kathak Pandit Chitresh Das developed in the US diaspora. *Son of the Wind* was the first full-length dance-drama created by the Leela Dance Collective following Pandit Das's death in 2015. Thanks to the following kathak artists who generously shared their insights and input for this chapter: Seibi Lee, Rachna Nivas, Rukhmani Mehta, Anjali Nath, Poonam Narkar, Sonali Toppur, and Ria DasGupta. Unless otherwise noted, all quotes are drawn from conversations with the author.

[4] I employ "artistic diaspora" to refer to this community, which includes both "heritage practitioners" and "affinity practitioners" (Shelemay 2011; Morelli 2019, 20).

abhinaya (character portrayal), becoming intimate with many characters (cf. Shah 1998).

Perhaps kathak dancers feel relative ease embodying variously gendered characters because the "frame" of dance practice differs from everyday life (Goffman 1974). But this comfort is also based in a belief that masculine and feminine energies are always present within everyone—a conviction tied to the Hindu concept of *ardhanarishwara*, the "lord who is half woman," for whom the right is masculine (Shiva) and the left is feminine (Parvati) (Goldberg 2002, 1; Morelli 2019, 101). Pandit Das emphasized this concept, sometimes telling his dance disciples, "you are the masculine; you are the feminine." Kathak thus provides the opportunity—and a safe context—to explore a broader spectrum of gendered ways-of-being: role by role, story by story. My dance colleagues have described this practice as healthy and beneficial, even as a form of "psychotherapy" (Lee, November 23, 2021).[5]

Although dancers generally embrace their experiences of taking on various characters, some characters seem to challenge an overarching narrative of health. This chapter examines the complex experiences of portraying Ram, Sita, and Ravan, three central Ramayana characters, by members of the Leela Dance Collective. To connect with and portray characters, including these powerful, archetypal roles, dancers utilized multiple techniques including observation, introspection, and embodiment. I consider examples of each technique, in particular, arguing that the process of *physically embodying* a character, combined with examining the character's motivations, helps dancers generate the empathetic connection that is crucial for creating compelling art.

Questions and Variations in Ramayana Performance

Among the many ways the Ramayana has been influential, it serves as a template for encoding norms of gendered action and interaction. Ram is upheld by many as *maryada purushottam*, "the supreme exemplar of good [male] conduct" (Hess 2001, 33).[6] Similarly, Sita is idolized as a *pativrata*, a devoted,

---

[5] The therapeutic benefits of an expanded self are also explored in Drama Therapy practices (e.g., Sajnani et al. 2014). Cross-gender performance in North American theater is less common than in kathak.

[6] Ram's positioning as *maryāda puruṣottam* has ramifications that extend beyond gender norms, suggesting proper behavior between groups differentiated by caste, class, religion, age, and more (Richman 2001, 6). Ram has also been appropriated by Hindu nationalist groups (see, e.g., Sarkar Munsi 2021; Schultz*).

"perfect" wife.[7] Together, the couple serves as a template for heteronormative gender dynamics and ideals of maleness and femaleness. However, their actions also generate ambivalence and intense debate.

In some versions of the Ramayana, Ram (considered both human and divine) rescues Sita from Ravan's kingdom only to oblige her to undergo a trial by fire to prove her chasteness. Despite proving herself, he still banishes her, alone and pregnant, to the forest. As Vidyut Aklujkar writes, "generations of poets have felt compelled to sing the glories of [Ram,] the most beloved incarnation of God in human form. Many have also felt the need to question earlier accounts of his exploits in order to raise doubts, accuse, explain, justify, and contextualize them" (2001, 83). And although Sita is admired, many dismay at her seeming submissiveness and lack of agency (Kishwar 2001). She did not free herself from captivity although she was capable, waiting instead for her husband to do so. She did not speak up to defend herself from attacks on her virtue. Even after proving herself time and again, Ram asked her to undergo a second trial by fire, at which point Sita took her own life by asking Mother Earth to swallow her.

Questioning Ramayana characters (even on the part of ardent devotees) and debating the values their actions communicate is perhaps central to the epic's continued relevance in contemporary times (Richman 2001). Because the Ramayana tradition encompasses multiple plots and sub-plots, with no original (*Ur*) text, the choices of which scenes to include in a specific production can profoundly impact audience understandings of the characters' personality traits and motivations. *Son of the Wind* and previous productions by this cast and others have worked to complicate stereotypical character presentations, for example, by downplaying Ram's "heroism" and resisting depictions of Ravan as purely malevolent.[8]

In kathak, there are two basic ways to present stories: as solos and dance-dramas. In solo performance, one person portrays all the characters. The soloist wears one costume throughout and changes characters as the story necessitates (often with a turn, or *palta*), communicating each distinct character through facial expression and body language. By contrast, multiple kathak dancers work together to create dance-dramas like *Son of the Wind*. In such productions, each dancer portrays a discrete character throughout,

---

[7] *Pativratā* literally means "she whose husband is her religious vow" (Sutherland Goldman 2001, 390 fn. 2).

[8] See Part III of *Performing the Ramayana Tradition*, which discusses Kathakali dance and theater productions that situate Ravan as an "anti-hero" (Richman and Bharucha 2021, 97–160).

utilizing specific makeup and costuming to enhance their role. Whereas in some dance communities, one exceptional performer may be showcased in a specific part for years (e.g., Sarkar Munsi 2021), our community privileged the learning opportunities that come from dancing different roles. As Rachna Nivas states, "Guruji [Pandit Das] really instilled that you shouldn't get typecast. You have to extend your range because, ultimately, you have to be able to do *every* character. That's mastery and that's what you're striving for" (September 23, 2018). Thus, one of the primary casting considerations is how a role will challenge and help one grow as an artist. Let us now take a step back: whether dancing in a solo or dance-drama format, how does one learn the skills to portray characters (*abhinaya*)?

"*Abhinaya* Cannot Be Taught"

Kathak scholar Purnima Shah defines *abhinaya* as "the art of creative, imaginative, mimetic portrayal of the narrative theme through facial and bodily expressions," citing the etymology of the term, which implies "the translation of 'knowing' into 'telling'" (1998, 14 fn. 1). In some South Asian dance practices, techniques used in storytelling are more codified than in kathak.[9] Rachna explains that in kathak, "the *abhinaya* is *natural*." This, she asserts, "makes it more challenging, because there is not a codified way to show [for example] sadness—what your face should look like and . . . the motions that you should do when you are conveying sadness. In kathak, we have to figure out how to inspire the dancer to show it with the correct vocabulary of kathak . . . but it also has to be natural to that person, and to their own spirit" (September 23, 2018). This lack of codification provides kathak dancers with both the challenge of determining how to technically communicate a character and the freedom to explore possibilities.

While our guru, Pandit Chitresh Das, often provocatively proclaimed that "*abhinaya* cannot be taught," he did provide some guidance on how to develop this skill, primarily by emphasizing observation and imitation. For his advanced students, he would dance specific characters, usually in spontaneous mid-class demonstrations. Without the assistance of video recording,

---

[9] For example, kutiyattam's *attaprakaram*s ("acting manuals") "provide a notation of how a performance should be structured through the use of specific gestures, movements, and emotions" (Bharucha 2021, 43).

> **Box 18.1 Exercise: Observation and Imitation**
>
> 1. With the sound off, watch a scene from an unfamiliar film or television show in which two characters are interacting. What can you ascertain about the characters' personalities through their body language and facial expression? What do your observations tell you about the nature of their exchange?
> 2. Next, re-enact the interaction yourself, without dialogue.
> 3. Discuss: How did you get into character? What did you need to do to generate the emotions you had witnessed? Did doing so make you feel more or less empathetic to their experiences?

Rukhmani recalled, "you had to absorb and remember as much as you could!" (September 23, 2018). Pandit Das also encouraged imitating everyday interactions. For example, he often recounted exchanges he witnessed between students at San Francisco State University, where he taught kathak classes for several years. Describing and immediately acting out such informal interactions was an indirect way of teaching his dancers that they, too, should observe and imitate (see Box 18.1).

Beyond observing everyday interactions and other dancers' character portrayal, kathak artists might engage in additional practices to deepen their understanding of a character's personality and motivations: (1) read/watch other versions of the story; (2) journal or do other internal work; and (3) practice specific physical movements appropriate to the character. In my experience, practicing physical techniques—stances, gestures, and facial expressions—provides a particularly important affective sense of affiliation with the character. I have found this "outside-in" approach to be especially useful in portraying challenging characters.

Participant-Observation, Resisting Ram

Like many ethnomusicologists, my research involves "participant-observation," active engagement in a community with the goal of gaining "experientially based musical [and dance] knowledge" (Titon 1995, 287). My involvement in this kathak community has spanned more than twenty years of training, teaching, musically accompanying kathak performances, and performing. While I had performed several solo and ensemble concerts before *Son of the Wind*, I had not played a role in a major dance-drama. Thus, I was surprised to be cast in the critical role of Ram. As Titon argues, in active participation in an arts community, "differences are thrust upon us, not simply because we 'notice' them as observers close to the action, but because we live them, we 'experience' them" (1995, 289). In this case, I would not have understood the complex experience of portraying a character like Ram had I not been asked to do so myself.

When cast as Ram (in 2016), I felt I was being asked to play the role that exemplified male privilege, to embody patriarchal forces then increasingly being called to task by the growing #MeToo movement. I was suddenly, it seemed, "the Man," and a white one at that, among a cast of mostly South Asian American dancers. In discussing this choice with the artistic directors, Seibi Lee told me I was cast as Ram for several reasons, including my height, body type, and personality. For one, I had a frame that lent itself to a male presence relatively naturally. Further, she explained, casting is an intricate process in which each part impacts the others. For this production, I would perform alongside Rachna Nivas, who would play Ram's feisty and fearless brother Lakshman. My quieter, more reflective confidence would complement Rachna's charismatic presence, and our similar body types would facilitate synchronized movements (Figure 18.1).

I shared my unease with Rukhmani Mehta, who would play Ravan in *Son of the Wind*, but was Ram in the 2010 production *Sita Haran* ("Sita's Abduction"). As I learned techniques for embodying Ram from Rukhmani, I also became aware of her internal struggles with the character, about which she later wrote:

> When I was cast as [Ram], I was speechless.... Every bone in my body resisted working on the role. It was as if [in] playing the role ... I was complicit in his actions. I was condoning every man's mistreatment of and an entire society's subjugation of women. I was betraying my own being, my mother, my grandmothers, and all the girls and women I felt such kinship with. (Mehta 2019)

In order to play the role successfully, we both had to develop nuanced understanding and empathy for the character through a process that was emotional as well as physical.

298   MUSIC AND DANCE AS EVERYDAY SOUTH ASIA

Figure 18.1 Sarah L. Morelli (the author, left) and Rachna Nivas as Ram and Lakshman in *Son of the Wind*. ODC Theater, San Francisco, April 28, 2018. Photo by M. N. Prasanna Ranganathan; used with permission.

With some ambivalence, I dived into the part. My process began with observation. I watched TV and film versions of the Ramayana, consciously adopting Ram's perspective and working to empathize with him. I studied the beatific expressions of actors who had played him and looked for other heroes with similar emotional makeup. I watched videos of *Sita Haran*, analyzing Rukhmani's body language as she danced Ram and taking screenshots of specific moments in order to study and imitate her stance.

As rehearsals began, our artistic directors corrected basic ways I held and moved my body. Some adjustments—such as to stand flat on both feet and lead from the sternum rather than the hips—were common for dancing many male roles. When Rukhmani previously worked on the role, she had to develop the same body language, as she described, "square and broad shoulders, wide stance, tall spine." On Seibi's advice, Rukhmani even practiced walking with her arms wrapped around a pole nestled behind her neck to broaden her shoulders.

My first scene in *Son of the Wind* introduced Ram and Laskhman searching the forest for Sita (⏵ Video example 18.1). While developing the character, I needed to constantly think about Ram's movement qualities while portraying his search and communicating his dismay to Lakshman. Once I had achieved some level of physical ease, Seibi told me to "try to be *natural* about your maleness." When observing our guruji demonstrate Ram, Rukhmani noticed that moments when he broke the rules of stereotypical masculine movement—particularly drooping his shoulders in despair—were the most impactful (described in ⊙ Video example 18.2). Such intense emotion, communicated even briefly through subtle physical cues, complicates a normative masculinity constructed through the controlled movements we were practicing; as such, they stood out as particularly meaningful.

In Rukhmani's experience, detailed physical study of Ram's character was also complemented by reflection on the men in her life:

> In order for me to enter the character, I was going to have to let go of judgement . . . I began by observing the men in my life—my father, my Guruji and some of my closest friends . . . I saw—more deeply than ever before— . . . how they wrestled with and accepted responsibility. How at times the choice to fulfill one's duty as a father, a teacher, a son was more important than pursuing one's dreams. . . . How at times weakness was strength and strength was compassion. (Mehta 2019)

While learning a character requires individual reflection, Rukhmani and I shared some similar experiences in this process. We first worked on basic physical techniques to move in ways that would be read as "masculine." However, observing and practicing movements that took us beyond gender stereotypes was crucial to communicating not just an empathetic character, but also a more accurate one.

Sita and Ravan, Rehearsing Victim and Perpetrator Experiences

Sita's abduction, which begins this chapter, is central to helping audience members understand Ram's motivation to find Sita and kill Ravan, whose death is crucial to the Ramayana narrative. Like me, Sonali Toppur, who played Sita in *Son of the Wind*, expressed some initial reluctance at her casting. Sita symbolized for her "the silent and subdued heroine," idealized in classical Sanskrit texts as well as more contemporary retellings like the 1987–1988 *Ramayan* television series (Sutherland Goldman 2001, 229).

Sonali's challenge lay also in her high regard for Sita: "She was young and was leaving everything she knew; and yet, she had no doubts about following her husband to the forest. It was intimidating for me to think about having that much faith and confidence" (August 6, 2021). But, as she noted, "Sita lets herself be used as a pawn in this conflict that is really not about her . . . It's a complex character."

The physicality of rehearsals helped Sonali challenge feminine stereotypes and ultimately unlock an interpretation of Sita that was more acceptable to her. She described, "I would go high on my toes because I wanted to step lightly. Seibi-*didi* told me, 'stop going on your toes—you lose all of your grounding.' " The experience of dancing the same choreography on flat feet helped her realize that "Sita is a very grounded person; she knows exactly who she is and what she believes."

While the dance collective practiced scenes like Sita's abduction in a safe environment, experiencing and processing such scenarios is not easy (Figure 18.2, Box 18.2). As Sonali shared, "the kidnapping of Sita is a *very* challenging scene on so many levels." When I asked her what it was like to rehearse and perform the scene repeatedly, she reflected, "I would fall into some pretty negative spaces . . . it was definitely very emotional, [speaking more slowly]

Figure 18.2 Rukhmani Mehta (left) and Sonali Toppur as Ravan and Sita in *Son of the Wind*. ODC Theater, San Francisco, April 28, 2018. Photo by M. N. Prasanna Ranganathan; used with permission.

> **Box 18.2 Exercise: Perceiving Kathak *Abhinaya* in Dance-Drama**
>
> 1. Re-read the description of Sita's abduction that begins this chapter.
> 2. Watch ▶ Video example 18.3, a performance of this scene, looking for the following:
>   **Gestures:** Try to discern and describe specific gestures such as Ravan showing hunger and Sita preparing food.
>   **Stance:** How does Rukhmani Mehta as Ravan hold her body differently from Sonali Toppur playing Sita?
>   **Facial expression:** How does your understanding of the characters' internal motivations deepen when studying facial expression?
>   **Kathak footwork:** Note and describe specific footwork patterns and percussive accents created by the dancers' feet. How does their footwork contribute to specific dramatic moments?
>   **Costuming and makeup:** In what ways do these elements add to or detract from the scene?
> 3. Discuss your observations.

because you're tapping into a systemic, rooted issue that has existed for hundreds of thousands of years . . . and nothing really has changed. It is very defeating" (August 6, 2021).

We all experience being victim and perpetrator at various times in our lives, to varying degrees. Rukhmani Mehta, who has performed all three characters discussed in this chapter during her career, acknowledged connecting with the experiences of both Sita and Ravan—the victim and the perpetrator of violence. She recognized parts of herself with less agency, noting that "as feminists," we might "judge" the "helpless" parts of ourselves reflected in Sita's abduction. She also acknowledged everyone's potential for violence, continuing, "We all have shadows and dark sides."[10] By exploring these aspects of specific characters, we work to recognize and empathize with these aspects of ourselves, creating an expanded internal landscape, and thus doing a form of embodied psychotherapy. Rukhmani reflected, "I

---

[10] Jungian psychologists call aspects of our personalities with which we do not consciously identify the "shadow."

actually really appreciated the opportunity to explore those aspects of myself." However, such work is demanding. Describing performing the abduction as Ravan, she stated, "you have to fully inhabit your violence, which is extremely challenging."

As with any character, Rukhmani also had to find some justification for Ravan's actions such that she could understand his motivation. As we spoke, she laughingly asked, "who wants to be the bad guy—in any story?" While she acknowledged it was difficult for her to "find his goodness," she reported, "I actually learned a lot about Ravan *doing* Ravan." In comparison to her experience finding a connection with Ram by observing the men in her life, it was through embodying the role that she found a strong connection to the character. That is, *dancing* the part of Ravan brought Rukhmani an embodied understanding of what spurred Ravan to abduct Sita. As those acquainted with the epic well know, Ram's brother mutilated Ravan's sister by cutting off her nose. After our last performance, she reflected, "if you think about it, Ravan is the man we wish Ram would have been. Ravan stood up for his sister. He defended her honor." I pressed her, asking, "He defended her honor by abducting another woman?" She acquiesced, "Sure, women are getting screwed in the equation; but still, he still did *something*! In the context of that time—women were being treated like property; men's wars were being fought on women's bodies—but within that context, there is an argument to be made that Ravan wasn't weak. At least he did *something*. There's dignity and honor in that" (August 18, 2021).

The final example, ▶ Video example 18.4, features Sita's abduction performed by Rukhmani Mehta in a solo format. While dance-drama provides the opportunity to deepen one's relationship with a specific character over months or years of rehearsals and performances, the challenge of solo performances is to transition quickly between and convincingly communicate all of the characters (see Box 18.3).

Conclusion

Kathak dancers utilize various techniques to learn a new character including observation, physicality, and emotion; each assists in understanding and developing empathy for a character. Although Ram, Sita, and Ravan can be difficult characters, the process of performing them—along

> **Box 18.3 Exercise: Perceiving Kathak *Abhinaya* in Solo Performance**
>
> Watch the scene of Sita's abduction in Rina Mehta's solo performance (▶ Video example 18.4). How does your experience differ when the drama is enacted by one dancer? How do the dancer's facial expressions, stances, and gestures change with each character? Are the dancer's footwork patterns similar to those you discovered in the dance-drama version of this scene? Does the lack of character-specific costuming impact your understanding of which character is being depicted?

with myriad other characters—can become internally liberating for dancers as they progress in their training. As Rukhmani reflected, "I am grateful to have a container that allows me to explore all the parts of who I am" (August 18, 2021). Through this practice, each character provides new opportunities for kathak artists to move beyond gender-restricted, essentialized ideas of the self.

Works Cited

Aklujkar, Vidyut. 2001. "Crying Dogs and Laughing Trees in Rāma's Kingdom: Self-reflexivity in *Ānanda Rāmāyana*." In *Questioning Ramayanas*, edited by Paula Richman, 83–104. Berkeley: University of California Press.

Bharucha, Rustom. 2021. "Thinking the Ramayana Tradition through Performance." In *Performing the Ramayana Tradition*, edited by Paula Richman and Rustom Bharucha, 29–49. New York: Oxford University Press.

Bourdieu, Pierre. 1977. *Outline of a Theory of Practice*. Cambridge: Cambridge University Press.

Butler, Judith. 1988. "Performative Acts and Gender Constitution: An Essay in Phenomenology and Feminist Theory." *Theatre Journal* 40(4): 519–531.

Chakravorty, Pallabi. 2008. *Bells of Change: Kathak Dance, Women and Modernity in India*. Calcutta: Seagull Books.

Goffman, Erving. 1974. *Frame Analysis: An Essay on the Organization of Experience*. New York: Harper & Row.

Goldberg, Ellen. 2002. *The Lord Who Is Half Woman: Ardhanārīśvara in Indian and Feminist Perspective*. Albany: State University of New York Press.

Hess, Linda. 2001. "Lovers' Doubts: Questioning the Tulsi *Rāmāyan*." In *Questioning Ramayanas*, edited by Paula Richman, 25–47. Berkeley: University of California Press.

Kishwar, Madhu. 2001. "Yes to Sita, No to Ram: The Continuing Hold of Sita on Popular Imagination in India." In *Questioning Ramayanas*, edited by Paula Richman, 285–308. Berkeley: University of California Press.

Lutgendorf, Philip. 2017. "Two Dances and a Conference." *South Asian Popular Culture* 15(2–3): 217–223.

Mehta, Rukhmani. 2019. "Unexpected Lessons from Sri Ramchandra." Blog post, July 14, 2019. Accessed December 14, 2023. https://www.rukhmanimehta.dance/post/unexpected-lessons-from-sri-ramchandra.

Morelli, Sarah. 2019. *A Guru's Journey: Pandit Chitresh Das and Indian Classical Dance in Diaspora*. Champaign: University of Illinois Press.

Ramanujan, A. K. 1991. "Three Hundred *Rāmāyaṇas*: Five Examples and Three Thoughts on Translation." In *Many Rāmāyaṇas*, edited by Paula Richman, 22–49. Berkeley: University of California Press.

Richman, Paula, ed. 1991. *Many Rāmāyaṇas: The Diversity of a Narrative Tradition in South Asia*. Berkeley: University of California Press.

Richman, Paula, ed. 2001. *Questioning Ramayanas: A South Asian Tradition*. Berkeley: University of California Press.

Richman, Paula, and Rustom Bharucha, eds. 2021. *Performing the Ramayana Tradition: Enactments, Interpretations, and Arguments*. New York: Oxford University Press.

Sajnani, Nisha, David Read Johnson, et al. 2014. *Trauma-Informed Drama Therapy: Transforming Clinics, Classrooms, and Communities*. Springfield, IL: Charles C. Thomas Publisher.

Sarkar Munsi, Urimala. 2021. "Revisiting 'Being Ram': Playing a God in Changing Times." In *Performing the Ramayana Tradition*, edited by Paula Richman and Rustom Bharucha, 281–297. New York: Oxford University Press.

Shah, Purnima. 1998. "Transcending Gender in the Performance of Kathak." *Dance Research Journal* 30(2): 2–17.

Shelemay, Kay Kaufman. 2011. "Musical Communities: Rethinking the Collective in Music." *Journal of the American Musicological Society* 64(2): 349–390.

Stone, Ruth. 2008. *Theory for Ethnomusicology: Histories, Conversations, Insights*. Upper Saddle River, NJ: Pearson Prentice Hall.

Sutherland Goldman, Sally J. 2001. "The Voice of Sītā in Vālmīki's *Sundarakāṇḍa*." In *Questioning Ramayanas*, edited by Paula Richman, 223–238. Berkeley: University of California Press.

Titon, Jeff Todd. 1995. "Bi-Musicality as Metaphor." *Journal of American Folklore* 108(429): 287–297.

Walker, Margaret. 2014. *India's Kathak Dance in Historical Perspective*. Surrey: Ashgate.

19
Music and the Trans-*thirunangai* Everyday at Koovagam, Tamil Nadu

Jeff Roy

In Tamil Nadu, the religious festival known as the Kuthandavar-Aravan—or Koovagam—festival has become a contested site for the celebration of transgender and *thirunangai* (*tirunaṅkai*) self-determination since the 1980s, when the communities were "incorporated as a vital constituency of devotees" in significant ways (Hiltebeitel 1995 [2010] in Vasudevan 2020, 15). Occurring annually in Villupuram District on the full moon of the *Chithirai* (fourth) month of the Tamil calendar (generally late April or early May), the festival draws thousands of transgender and *thirunangai* (also known as *Aravani*) devotees to participate in the re-enactment of Mohini's wedding to Koothandavar, or Aravan, from the Mahabharata epic. This chapter explores the variable music and sonic landscapes of performance within imagined traditional spaces and professionally staged contexts known as the "Miss Koovagam" talent competition. Through narrative modes of reflexivity and non-linear storytelling accented by three short films I created while attending the 2013 and 2014 Koovagam festivals, I explore how music and sound form a generative part of transgender and *thirunangai* selfhood and community-building in ways that account for multiple possibilities of feeling, acting, being, and belonging in the everyday.

Connections that transgender, *thirunangai*, and gender-expansive people form to music often emerge from resurgent knowledges of which non–South Asian, cisgender, and/or non-*thirunangai* students and scholars have limited embodied access. Drawing inspiration from interdisciplinary, decolonial writings (Cervantes and Saldaña 2015; Prasad and Roy 2017; Ndaliko 2019), the pedagogical exercise included in this chapter (Box 19.1) facilitates an examination of the relationships between music, gender, sexuality, and selfhood situated both in the sociological and political histories and conditions of a place as well as within the context of our own lives. Rather than focusing exclusively on music's immutable qualities, what music *is* or how music is structured, I wish to draw attention to what music *does* for the people who perform it. This lesson provides opportunities to learn some musical principles not for the purposes of achieving musical proficiency for the sake of musical fluency, but to engage readers' capacities for critical and creative action so that they may be able to apply what they learned to envision and enable entirely different possibilities of living with, listening to, and playing music in the world.

The Everyday

In South Asia, "trans" as it is attached to "gender" is a simultaneously enabling and limiting term. "Transgender" is marked by class and caste, employed in nationalist policy, and circulated by non-governmental organizations that are invested in transnational (as opposed to Indigenous) categories of gender and sexual identification (Dutta and Roy 2014; Khan 2016, 2019; Roy 2016). In Tamil Nadu, transgender's ideological distinction from *thirunangai* reproduces binaries and hierarchies of power such as those that emerge between the rural and urban, rich and poor, Tamil and English languages, "traditional" and "globalizing" divides (Craddock 2018). While there are varying degrees of access depending on socioeconomic background, educational background, and location, these binaries do not reproduce themselves as experientially fixed for transgender and *thirunangai* people. Moreover, the emphasis on gender as a defining marker of difference ignores the diversity and fluidity of relationalities that form these communities, including those that move across their porous boundaries and/or entirely evade contemporary concepts of identity circulating across trans/national discourse. Transgender, *thirunangai*, and gender-expansive people negotiate their self-understandings along a variety of axes, including religion, sexuality, kinship, class, and caste, in relation to a "multiplicity of social differences," languages, and cultural practices (Reddy 2005, 43, in reference to *hijra* communities). As a prominent *hijra guru* and Koovagam participant once told me, "What defines you . . . is not what is between your legs, but what you do, how you act, who you relate with, who you become" (Roy 2015). Similarly, experiences and expressions of selfhood are relational, formed through networks of belonging, and as Adnan Hossain writes in reference to *hijra* communities in Bangladesh, "processual and best understood . . . as emerging in practice [or] as part of the process of doing and becoming" (2012, 496). Such processes of becoming do not necessarily lead to a fixed destination, nor do they signal absence or loss in ways they are normatively understood. Rather, they are indeterminate, unfinished, moving, and filled with possibilities of abundance (Arondekar 2023) through which music and sound play generative roles.

In this chapter, I am not concerned with how performance facilitates the formation of state policy, the mobilization of voting blocs, or the defining of transgender for the purposes of bill formation—although this is indeed happening in certain community circles, particularly in South Asia's metropolitan areas (Roy 2015, 2016; Hossain et al. 2022). Rather, I examine the musics that constitute "the activities of ordinary citizens who, through the exercise of their agency in contexts of public interaction, shape the conditions of their collective existence" (Arendt 1958, in Hirschkind 2006). The everyday here does not imply fixity, but movement, improvisation, and even disruption. As Vasudevan notes, our relations "are part of our everyday, but that does not mean everyday signifies a givenness, a stable ground of action—whether of social reproduction, or resistance, or simply making the best of, or just drifting along" (2020, 30). Through sparing use of the term trans-*thirunangai*, I therefore wish to account for the everyday trans-ing of *thirunangai* experiences, self-/understandings, emotional and sensorial registers, navigations, and movements, as well as to locate the possibilities of resistance, subversion, and playfulness across the boundaries of identity. I am particularly interested in how music and sound cruise through fleeting spaces of inter-subjective knowing, compelling us to think, feel, act, and relate in different, everyday ways. The following sections trace these movements in two different scenes made available through "wispy registers of memory and intimacy" (Kasmani 2021, 163) as well as short films made while attending multiple Koovagam festivals. The first centers the imagined traditional space of the temple grounds, while the second covers public performances staged at the Miss Koovagam talent show in the neighboring city of Villapuram.

Koovagam

You know you have found yourself in Koovagam when the scent of jasmine, filter coffee, and motorcycle fumes enters your nostrils and a smattering of bright color enters your field of vision. A twenty-minute walk from the bus stop takes you down a dirt road lined with food stands, *prasadam* (sanctified food offerings), idols, and souvenir displays. Bright orange and red miniature replicas of Lord Aravan's head sprawl on blankets as though they were sunbathing. The soft drone of human chatter undergirds other sounds entering the place, such as the fleeting rumble of rickshaws and buses, whimpering dogs, children laughing, and *thirunangai* singers singing. One group takes turns jamming the lyrics of popular Tamil *filmi* songs in a call-and-response fashion, while competing to see who can add the most double-entendres. Other sounds from near and far get folded into the soundscape, which trigger or get triggered by the sounds of song and banter.

Crowds amass at the convergence of several dirt roads where the temple sits surrounded by a small collection of modest homes and stores. On the eve of the Koovagam festival, the place turns into the center of the universe for thousands of men, women, children, and *thirunangai* devotees wishing to make offerings to the temple's Lord Aravan. While men (and their young sons) from upper-caste Vanniyar and other caste communities have historically gathered for such rituals, the transformation of the festival into a revered, imagined tradition for *thirunangai* people began when transgender rights activism and self-determination unfolded (Vasudevan 2020, 18). Over the course of two days, participants join to celebrate in varying capacities, followed by the many local and national news media reporters, student researchers, and foreign documentarians.

Drawn to Koovagam by friends and colleagues from my temporary home of Mumbai, I am no exception to the rule. On my first trip there in 2013, I meet with an NGO employee and trained Mohiniyattam dancer from Chennai who recites their version of Lord Aravan's story through poetry and gesture (see ▶ Video example 19.1). It is a harrowing tale of a man who agrees to sacrifice himself to end the devastating war between the Pandava and Kaurava factions on the condition that someone marry him and become his widow so that his death could be mourned. After no one volunteers, Lord Krishna steps forward and on the day of the wedding, transforms into Mohini. Following their marriage, Aravan is executed by the goddess Kali and Mohini mourns as a widow before eventually transforming back into Krishna.

At Koovagam, Aravan's marriage and sacrifice are re-enacted by the townspeople and *thirunangai* devotees, the latter taking Mohini's role. On the first day of the event, devotees visit the temple to make their offerings and celebrate the marriage. In the evening, families return to their hotels and homes while some participants remain overnight to continue rejoicing in Aravan and Mohini's union. The next day, Aravan's sacrifice is marked by a large and colorful procession in which parts of his body—representations of the arms, legs, torso, and head—are paraded in separately from the temples of neighboring towns and reassembled onto a large moving altar. Thousands come to dance, take pictures, make offerings, and participate in song and dance. During the procession, the sounds of the crowd are accented by drum beats as several performance groups offer competing rhythms to accompany rehearsed choreography. A sea of people parts to offer spaces for friendly dance competition between *thirunangai* elders and other devotees. Groups of youth cheer on their elders like front row fans at a boxing match, while several onlookers dangle from nearby trees clapping for their favorites.

Once the procession begins to lose steam around the temple, devotees descend to an adjacent town across the rice field where pop-up restaurants, food carts, souvenir stands, and carnival rides stand ready to receive the masses. Outside the grounds is a large watering hole where *thirunangai* devotees customarily bathe and dress in white *sari*s to mark their transition to widowhood. The festival is simultaneously a place of celebration and mourning, throughout which the melodious, somber sounds of *oppari*—songs of lament performed in local Tamil dialects—diffuse like camphor. *Oppari* is conventionally performed by relatives for the death of a loved one (see Greene*), and at Koovagam, *thirunangai* devotees practice the ritual openly, sometimes in large groups.

On the edge of the festival grounds, in the middle of a large patch of tall, dry grass, I encounter a *thirunangai* elder crouched on the ground by herself in mid-song:

> *I used to own many fields of turmeric and ginger,*
> *But I sold them all to save my husband's life;*
> *I broke coconuts and offered prayers,*
> *Still, I have no place to go;*
> *I sold my jewelry on the side of the road.*
> *Oh, my lord!*
> *Now that he is dead,*
> *I have nowhere to go;*
> *All my desires are gone.*
> *The time has come to break the* thāli.
> *When will you come back?*
> *You came searching for me,*
> *But no one is there for me now.*

The lyrics (translated by my Mohiniyattam friend) reference events in the Mahabharata while also signaling the poverty and injustice that trans-*thirunangai* communities regularly endure. In the time and place of this performance, the words glide across many possible significations, exploring the worlds of the symbolic and the material everyday, in which the shared experience of loss gives way to resilience, pride, togetherness, and joy.

The performance's many meanings help to bring about a shift in affect, momentarily reorienting the attention of nearby festival participants away from the loud noises of screaming and laughter. Beyond the song lyrics, the sonic arrangement itself makes a difference in this situation, from the *oppari* vocalist's rich timbre, bass register, and vocal articulations, inflected by fits of coughing, to the production of place-specific sonic forms, such as the disruptions of the mobile phone ring and interactions with melodious and dissonant sounds. Understated yet pronounced, random and intentional, these sounds compel a growing crowd of attentive listeners to feel, imagine, and act in multiple ways that draw on and shape the social, physical, and spiritual connections people have to the place. Some listeners cry softly, crouched in the grass alongside the elder, while one middle-aged couple, standing somewhat on the outer perimeter of the circle, rests their heads on one another's shoulders. Student researchers in deep concentration, with audio recording devices in outstretched hands, shift their gaze from the performer to a notepad and back again in an attempt to capture clear sound. Multitasking parents struggle to rein in their young children while anchoring their attention to the elder, sending subtle yet powerful affirmations of respect. No one smiles or laughs, because that is the domain of activity just beyond the threshold of audibility. In this place, everyone is transported elsewhere.

Miss Koovagam

On the days leading up to the ceremonies and celebrations in the neighboring town of Villapuram, trans-*thirunangai* community members take the stage for a series of town hall meetings and talent contests in which a "Miss Koovagam" is crowned. The town hall meetings have become a site in which a significant number of reforms and other measures of state-sanctioned visibility have been debated. They also mark a series of performance-based competitions for participants to showcase their talents in front of a network of trans-*thirunangai*-operated NGOs, communities, celebrities, local politicians, government leaders, and media networks. At the 2013 Miss Koovagam competition, I had the fortune of meeting author A. Revathi, activist Malaika, new longtime film companion/friends, and Gopi (▶ Video example 19.2).

Originally from Puducherry, Gopi has been singing professionally for over thirty years (twenty at the time of our filming; see ▶ Video example 19.3). A playback singer (see Sarrazin*) known for an extensive vocal range, versatility, and ability "to sing over 5,000 songs from memory," Gopi is called upon every year by trans-*thirunangai* community members to perform as an invited guest at the talent contest. In our interview, conducted backstage in a literal closet, Gopi spoke in code about the relationship music has to define a sense of purpose on stage:

> My family doesn't know that I'm like *this*, but I am participating in Koovagam for my happiness as well as everyone else's. . . . At home and in public, I've faced a lot of hurdles, tortures, insults, and shame. But I don't care about any of that stuff. I stand firm in what I believe in my heart. And, now my parents are proud of my singing. (▶ Video example 19.3, cue point 2:15)

Music not only plays an integral role in Gopi's self-understanding but also serves as the vehicle through which to communicate to those in close relation. In performance, Gopi interweaves through multiple, if not conflicting, relationalities as a somewhat peripheral trans-*thirunangai* community member and celebrated son of his natal parents. Gopi's talent facilitates his parents' acceptance and pride, though Gopi's onstage personae are held at arm's length in the authentication of his offstage identities (Roy 2019).

Drawn to melodious songs of idols Janaki Amma and Swarnalatha, Gopi has worked hard to emulate the voices of his musical heroines. In "Kotta Paakkum" ("Betel Nut"), Gopi follows the exact contours of the original singer Madhumitha's voice in her register while his male-bodied duet partner performs in a lower register. In the middle of the performance, Gopi appears to coach his partner to switch their lyrical parts while continuing to sing in their respective registers. In the lines below (translated by my friend), Gopi sings his partner's lines in the upper register while his partner sings Gopi's lines in the lower register (▶ Video example 19.3, from cue point 1:00):

> Duet partner (middle octave): *On the tree there is a lotus and sandal flower. Should I get one or the other?*
> Gopi (upper octave): *You have a perfect imagination. I will enjoy anything that you get for me.*
> Duet partner (middle octave): *These desires are covered by my* sari. *My* bindi *is about to come off.*
> Gopi (upper octave): *Like the hot summer, I've got a fever in my upper body.*
> Duet partner (middle octave): *In the lower part (of the body), that's where love is born.*

In the middle of their final verse, Gopi gestures directly into the camera with his left arm raised, palm up. Gopi scoops and then throws the arm into the air as if to follow the upward contour of the melody.

> Duet partner (middle octave): *Betel nut and tender betel leaves, chewing them turns my mouth red.*
> Gopi (upper octave): *You are my love, and I am yours.*
> Together: *When we come together, it's a celebration.*
> Gopi (upper octave): *When we come together, it's a celebration.*
> Duet partner (middle octave): *When we come together, it's a celebration.*

When the song's final chorus arrives, Gopi and his partner return to their former musical parts. With a glance to the camera, a light-hearted giggle marks the song's conclusion. This playful subversion of normative gender roles enacts an intentional misreading of the original piece to liberate audience expectations (see Box 19.1). In their reproduction of Madhumita's voice through skillful manipulations of the falsetto range (a method of vocal production using the "head voice"), Gopi's intonation and timbre reflect a virtuosic sensitivity to mimetic accuracy as a means of queering the sonic recognition of gendered belonging (Roy 2019). Gopi plays with and against audience expectations by reproducing a kind of attunement to vocalizing what is famously recognized, conventional, and pleasing to audiences in Tamil film and music culture, while subverting scripts of gender and sexuality in more ways than one—particularly as they are rehearsed through the singing parts, lyrics, registers, intonations, and timbres.

This act of joyful transgression leads to a shift in affect in the performance hall, pulling its audiences away from experiences of the mundane to the more fantastical. The performance—inflected by offstage sounds of chatter, the

Box 19.1   Exercises

In the following exercises, I seek to guide readers to explore the many possibilities of listening to and playing music in the world through learning Gopi's revisioning of "Kotta Paakkum" and exploring possibilities of playful subversion of conventionally gendered musical roles. We will learn the song "by ear," since this is an important approach to music pedagogy across parts of South Asia and the world.

Part 1: Learn the Ropes

1. Form small groups (of two, three, or four), standing close to and/or facing one another.
2. Familiarize yourself with the lyrics (which can be found online) and melody of "Kotta Paakkum" (▶ Video example 19.4), starting with the chorus and moving to at least one verse. Cover all singing parts in the range that is most comfortable to you.
3. Consider these guiding questions: In your view, what meanings are generated by the aural/oral aspects of the music (pitch, tone, intonation, timbre, etc.)? Which are the most powerful aspects? What do you suppose are the intended impacts for the listener? What cultural myths or constructs about gender and sexuality do you suppose this music reinforces or complicates?

Part 2: Playfully Investigate

4. Once you are comfortable, separate your parts into a formal duet or small ensemble. Take turns singing all vocal parts in the song. Attempt to sing one octave above or below the one in which you have been singing, and practice sustaining it throughout the duration of the chorus and verse of your choosing. Then, switch parts.
5. Consider these guiding questions: In your view, what specific meanings are changed through this playful subversion of roles? What do you suppose are the intended impacts for the viewer/listener? What cultural myths or constructs does this music now complicate or challenge? How does switching vocal parts change the way you relate to the music and to your performance partner(s)? What

other ways can you play with the music and how would this change the performance for you and your audience?

Part 3: Create

6. In this step, you can change, modify, and/or revamp an original song to change its meaning and form for yourselves. With your partner(s), identify a popular duet or multipart song you both enjoy. Complete the same activity for this song to explore possibilities of playful subversion in music that may be more familiar to you.
7. Now, craft a performance that creatively offers something new. Perhaps, rewrite the lyrics to the same musical melody by changing the character referents and their story, or change the melody and/or rhythmic articulation to create something entirely out of the box. Your performance can be ironic, funny, serious, understated, or spectacular. Consider these guiding questions as you explore the many possibilities of living with, playing, and enjoying music in the world: What specific meanings, cultural myths, or constructs are complicated or challenged through your performance? What are the intended impacts of your musical choices for the listener? Do we learn something new or hear things differently as a result? Does the music encourage us to find out more or to engage with others and/or the world in a new way? What would *you* like this music to communicate to its audience?

larger social and cultural context, and their political, symbolic, social, and cultural significances—compels the attentive audience to feel, imagine, and act in multiple ways. *Thirunangai* elders, some visibly moved and shaken, praise Gopi by showering the performer with money. One or two younger audience members holler and clap so loudly as if to draw attention to themselves. Others just sit, quietly stunned. In the back corner of the room, at a significant distance from the stage, the *oppari*-singing elder stands silently, as if transported to another place in another time.

Further Thoughts

Koovagam has played a significant role to help make visible trans-*thirunangai* lives and advance state-sanctioned reforms, many of which have come before those in other Indian states and South Asian nations. Some of these reforms include the establishment of a welfare board focused on social issues, the availability of gender confirmation surgeries (also known as sex reassignment surgery, or SRS) free of charge in government hospitals, and reserved seats in colleges and universities (Craddock 2018). Trans-*thirunangai* people are also able to acquire legal identification documents, which, among other things, provide access to government-sponsored services and jobs. While transformative for many, the framing of such state measures also "risks erasing the fluidity and multivocality that are integral to [trans-]*thirunangai* lives and community" (Craddock 2018, 115). This, as Govindan and Vasudevan note, "reconstitutes a transgender identity and experience away from its more liberatory possibilities and towards a new order of integration into a social structure that is still heterosexist and patriarchal, on the condition of granting certain partial privileges and recognition" (2011, 104). Moreover, the efforts of some to seek a more conciliatory tone in the face of cultural nationalism enact further constrictions, particularly for Muslim and Christian people, as trans-*thirunangai* communities continue to navigate, adapt to, resist, and/or challenge forces of post/colonial modernity.

The many performances that have emerged over the past forty years in and around the Koovagam festival attest to the trans-*thirunangai* communities' capacity to do multiple things and act in multiple ways, generating abundant possibilities of meaning that give life to the trans-*thirunangai* everyday. They form and fortify, among other things, powerful connections between people in shared celebration, affirming a sense of self in relation to the community, while also creating movement toward the advancement of policy, engagement, and political capital. The examples of performance above merely scratch the surface of a vast and complex set of cultural practices at Koovagam, such as the performances of non-Hindu transgender, gender-expansive, transmasculine, Dalit people and others. More work can and should be done on how else music and sound can further self-determination, resistance, and liberation for the communities that actively strive for them every day.

Works Cited

Arendt, Hannah. 1958. *The Human Condition*. Chicago: University of Chicago Press.
Arondekar, Anjali. 2023. *Sexuality's History*. Durham, NC: Duke University Press.
Cervantes, Marco Antonio, and Lillian Patricia Saldaña. 2015. "Hip Hop and Nueva Canción as Decolonial Pedagogies of Epistemic Justice." *Decolonization: Indigeneity, Education & Society* 4(1): 84–108.

Craddock, Elaine. 2018. "Recalibrating (Field)work." *QED: A Journal in GLBTQ Worldmaking* 5(3): 100–116.

Dutta, Aniruddha, and Raina Roy. 2014. "Decolonizing Transgender in India: Some Reflections." *Transgender Studies Quarterly* 1(3): 320–337.

Govindan, Padma, and Aniruddhan Vasudevan. 2011. "The Razor's Edge of Oppositionality: Exploring the Politics of Rights-Based Activism by Transgender Women in Tamil Nadu." In *Law Like Love: Queer Perspectives on Law*, edited by Arvind Narrain and Alok Gupta, 84–112. New Delhi: Yoda Press.

Hiltebeitel, Alf. [1995] 2010. "Dying before the Mahābhārata War: Martial and Transsexual Bodybuilding for Aravan." In *When the Goddess Was a Woman: Mahabharata Ethnographies—Essays by Alf Hiltebeitel*, edited by Vishwa Adluri and Joydeep Bagchee, 207–393. Boston: Brill.

Hirschkind, Charles. 2006. *The Ethical Soundscape: Cassette Sermons and Islamic Counterpublics*. New York: Columbia University Press.

Hossain, Adnan. 2012. "Beyond Emasculation: Being Muslim and Becoming Hijra in South Asia." *Asian Studies Review* 36(4): 495–513.

Hossain, Adnan, Claire Pamment, and Jeff Roy. 2022. *Badhai: Hijra-Khwaja Sira-Trans Performance across Borders in South Asia*. London: Bloomsbury.

Kasmani, Omar. 2021. "Thin, Cruisy, Queer: Writing through Affect." In *Gender and Genre in Ethnographic Writing*, edited by E. Tauber and D. L. Zinn, 163–188. London: Palgrave Macmillan.

Khan, Faris. 2016. "Khwaja Sira Activism: The Politics of Gender Ambiguity in Pakistan." *Transgender Studies Quarterly* 3(1–2): 158–164.

Khan, Faris. 2019. "Translucent Citizenship: Khwaja Sira Activism and Alternatives to Dissent in Pakistan." *South Asia Multidisciplinary Academic Journal* 20: 1–23.

Ndaliko, Chérie Rivers. 2019. "Decomposing the Colonial Gaze: Aesthetics as Activism." Paper presentation. Society for Ethnomusicology Pre-Conference Symposium "Film as Ethnography, Activism, and Public Work in Ethnomusicology." Nov. 6.

Prasad, Pavithra, and Jeff Roy. 2017. "Ethnomusicology and Performance Studies: Towards Interdisciplinary Futures of Indian Classical Music." *MUSICultures* 44(1): 187–209.

Reddy, Gayatri. 2005. *With Respect to Sex: Negotiating Hijra Identity in South India*. Chicago: University of Chicago Press.

Roy, Jeff. 2015. "Ethnomusicology of the Closet: (Con)Figuring Transgender-Hijra Identity through Documentary Filmmaking." PhD diss., UCLA.

Roy, Jeff. 2016. "Translating *Hijra* into Transgender: Performance and *Pehchan* in India's Trans-Hijra Communities." *Transgender Studies Quarterly* 3(3–4): 412–432.

Roy, Jeff. 2019. "Remapping the Voice through Transgender-*Hijra* Performance." In *Remapping Sound Studies*, edited by Gavin Steingo and Jim Sykes, 173–183. Durham, NC: Duke University Press.

Vasudevan, Aniruddhan. 2020. "Between the Goddess and the World: Religion and Ethics among Thirunangai Transwomen in Chennai, India." PhD diss., University of Texas at Austin.

20
Performing Youthful Desires
Bihu Festival Music and Dance in Assam, India

Rehanna Kheshgi

In the northeastern Indian state of Assam, the Bihu festival commemorates the New Year during the mid-April month of Bohag to mark the beginning of spring, to usher in a new planting season, and to celebrate fertility. While Bihu music and dance have a long history of performance in ritual contexts during Bohag in the eastern Brahmaputra Valley region known as Upper Assam (Map 20.1), the transformation of Bihu music and dance into a statewide folkloric genre representing Assamese cultural heritage began in the early twentieth century (Goswami 2003 [1988]). Since the 1980s, folklorized Bihu music and dance has become iconic of Assamese identity within the northeast region of India, nationally, and abroad. This chapter introduces readers to Panchasur, an urban folk school that provides instruction in folkloric Bihu performance. By examining Panchasur's 2016 performance of the play *Dikhour Gorāt Roi*, I demonstrate how Bihu's melodic, rhythmic, lyrical, and movement-oriented structures work together to encode values associated with heteronormative masculinity and femininity. For example, male performers are rewarded for expressing abandon through spontaneous shouts, extended arm gestures, vigorous pelvic movements, and exuberant drumming sequences, while female performers are praised for demonstrating restraint through coy smiles, stylized arm and pelvic movements, and delicate mouth harp percussion. Idiomatic phrases called *fukora zuzona* that draw meaning from everyday life in rural Assam form the core of Bihu song lyrics, communicating values related to gender, caste, and class. Bihu performance builds in intensity and anticipation through cyclical rhythmic and melodic patterns that generate romantic desire, presenting a challenge to the social order that results in inter-class and inter-caste liaisons and elopements. Although the expression of romantic desire in Bihu performance challenges the boundaries of respectability associated with

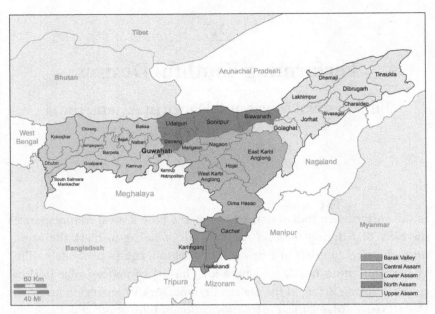

Map 20.1 Map of Assam. Courtesy of Sara Dale at St. Olaf College Geospatial and Data Services.

folklorization in an Assamese context, Panchasur directors have addressed this tension by adopting a narrative from the medieval past to demonstrate Bihu's potential to facilitate the transgression of social norms related to class while upholding values associated with heteronormative femininity and masculinity.

In rural areas of Upper Assam, young people grow up surrounded by Bihu festival rituals that mark seasonal transitions associated with agricultural cultivation. Bihu songs narrate romantic encounters between women and men through idiomatic phrases that encode gendered values. For example, natural metaphors such as a fallen ripe lemon indicate the pressure on young women to marry before a certain age. The sound of the Assamese *dhul* (*ḍhul*) drum evokes the thunderous rainstorms that promise a prosperous harvest as dancers step rhythmically on the bare earth. Rain penetrating fertile soil links seasonal environmental changes with human desire, culminating in songs that recount elopements between young lovers who abscond despite societal opposition to their unions. Through Bihu performance, young people are allowed to be physically close without touching by dancing in sync and singing romantic lyrics while catching each other's gaze.

Village communities with intergenerational households, or "joint families," share, learn, and critique Bihu performance as a part of daily activities such as food preparation and weaving. The shift away from joint-family living arrangements in urbanizing areas of Assam has decreased the frequency of intergenerational and community knowledge sharing. Faced with such shifts in transmission, Assamese folklorists, performers, and cultural authorities distilled disparate performance practices that vary from one village to the next in ritual contexts in order to create performance pieces for urban institutions (Khagen Mahanta, personal communication, April 11, 2009). Bihu folklorization is visually evident in matching costumes, fixed choreography as opposed to spontaneous movement, and performers facing outward to a seated audience instead of the inward-facing circular orientation of participatory ritual performances (Turino 2008; Babiracki 2000). "Now we *perform* Bihu. Before, Bihu was never *performed*. Before, it was among themselves, to enjoy. Now we dance Bihu for an audience (Probin Saikia, personal communication, June 15, 2022).[1] Audible markers of folklorization include standardized drum solos, song stanzas of identical lengths, and lyrics performed in polished Assamese with no hint of sexual innuendo.[2]

As many ethnomusicologists have demonstrated, the transformation of participatory folk music and dance practices into staged folkloric presentational performances is closely tied to regional or national identity construction (Babiracki 2000; Fiol 2017; Rios 2020). It is also a highly gendered process that tends to reinscribe norms of masculinity and femininity, and in the Indian context is centered on discourses of respectability regarding the comportment of young women (see Kheshgi 2017). The downplaying of both eroticism and social hierarchy in a folkloric context is designed to mask Assam's troublesome history as a frontier region often stereotyped as uncivilized and barbaric by outsiders (Kar 2007, 2008), as well as a complex mix of caste and tribal affiliations that are not easily compared to other regions of India (Sengupta and Bharadwaj 2019).

Urban youth who lack access to the participatory learning environment of village ritual performance often turn to urban folk schools in preparation for stage performances and competitions. Established in 1999 by Probin Kumar

---

[1] All personal communications were translated from Assamese into English by the author. In this case, Probin Saikia used the English word "perform."

[2] In order to transform Bihu into a respectable folkloric practice, cultural authorities and government cultural institutions have largely erased erotic depictions of sexual desire and encounter, although I was told many anecdotes confirming that these are alive and well in village contexts.

Saikia and Roshmi Rekha Saikia, Panchasur (meaning "five notes" or "pentatonic") is one such school—an NGO that teaches Assamese folk music and dance to students in Guwahati.³ An upper-caste, middle-class husband and wife team, Probin and Roshmi Rekha Saikia moved to Guwahati from Upper Assam to pursue folk music research, pedagogy, and performance. The Saikias note that most Guwahati folk schools are "stage-oriented, admitting students based on their ability to quickly learn and perform for an audience," while Panchasur has a strict rule: "Until we say that you are ready, that you can sing and dance perfectly, you may not share what you've learned" (Probin and Roshmi Rekha Saikia, personal communication, June 15, 2022). In contrast to other teachers, the Saikias narrow the experiential gap between the material students are learning and their everyday lives in urban Guwahati by teaching students about the lived experiences from which folk and devotional songs, dances, stories, and dramas are customarily created and shared. This chapter aims to bring the reader closer to that lived experience as well, by inviting active participation in Bihu music and dance focused on an example that incorporates the main themes of this chapter: the encoding of values associated with masculinity and femininity in a folklorized context that embraces the transgressive potential of Bihu through framing a love affair that crosses class boundaries in a historical narrative.

Written and directed by Probin Saikia with music and choreography by Roshmi Rekha Saikia, the play *Dikhour Gorāt Roi* ("Waiting by the Dikhou Riverbank") is set in medieval Assam during the rule of the Ahom (*Āhum*) Kingdom.⁴ Premiered by Panchasur in 2016, the plot narrates the love story of Hunali, the daughter of a royal officer in the Ahom court, and Dhonbor, a boy from a *Paik* laborer family in a nearby village, who fall in love while singing and dancing Bihu together.⁵ Resistance to Hunali and Dhonbor's relationship is quelled by Dhonbor's skill in Bihu performance, demonstrating the power of Bihu to change hearts and minds. Romantic relationships and marriages that cross class, caste, and ethnic boundaries are still met with

---

³ https://www.facebook.com/panchasur.guwahati/.
⁴ Originally from Myanmar, the Ahoms ruled Upper Assam for 600 years before the British annexation of the region in 1826.
⁵ The term "Paik" was used in medieval feudal society (thirteenth–fifteenth century) to designate one's occupation as an unskilled laborer (Saikia 2001, 77). Probin Saikia noted that "in the past, the royal family did not participate in Bihu performance, especially royal women. Bihu was associated with the everyday people and song narratives came from their experience as farmers, incorporating slang words typical of their everyday speech" (Probin Saikia, personal communication, June 15, 2022).

resistance in Assam today by some families, and couples continue to elope against their families' wishes during the Bihu festival season.

Hunali and Dhonbor first meet during a *rati* (*rātī*, nighttime) Bihu gathering, featuring short Bihu songs performed in a fashion that can continue for hours. Folklorists describe *rati* Bihu as the original form of Bihu, where young, unmarried villagers gathered in the forest late at night in two circular groups, segregated by sex (e.g., Gogoi 1969; Gandhiya 1988; Goswami 2003 [1988]). Although the groups performed separately, they would remain within earshot of one another, keeping in sync by the rhythm of clapping hands, of the young women's *toka* split bamboo clappers and *gogona* bamboo mouth harps, and the young men's cylindrical *dhul* drums. The two groups would sing antiphonally to each other with flirtatious, teasing stanzas. Although Bihu is no longer typically performed in sex-segregated circular formations, the gendered values of masculine abandon and feminine restraint portrayed in *Dikhour Gorāt Roi* are central to the folkloric norms of present-day Bihu performance.

One of the songs featured in the play's *rati* Bihu sequence, "Sotāi Porebotot" ("On the Sotai Mountain"), demonstrates how gendered values are encoded through idiomatic lyrical phrases drawn from rural life (▶ Video example 20.1).[6] Arranged by Probin Saikia, combining two thematically related Bihu songs into one, "Sotāi Porebotot" begins with two stanzas from a male protagonist and ends with a two-stanza response from a female protagonist. The man describes his journey to Sotāi, an imaginary mountain, where he spent the day hunting deer. He speculates about how to tell his friends that the deer he was pursuing escaped from his hunting net. In this song, the deer represents a young woman for whom the "hunter" has developed a romantic interest. Her "escape" from his "hunting net" suggests she has rejected him.

> In Assamese village society, once it emerges that someone is beginning a relationship with another person and their romantic interests have aligned, young men and women won't receive or seek out other proposals. This is the meaning of the first stanza: do things at the right time; don't drag your feet and let the moment pass you by! (Probin Saikia, personal communication, February 14, 2016)

---

[6] Compare the staged spontaneity of the Panchasur school's *rati* Bihu performance here with the fixed choreography in Kāsi Jun Bihu Troupe's competitive performance (▶ Video example 20.2, cue point 1:25).

Follow ▶ Audio or Video example 20.1 along with the song's text below.[7]

Sotāi porebotot, o mur dhon	On the Sotai mountain, o my beloved
Pohu jāl pātilu, o mur dhon	I went deer hunting, o my beloved *[repeat]*
Tātei nu mur godhuli hol	And there I spent the whole evening
Xomonīyā xudhile, o mur dhon	If my friends ask me, o my beloved
Kome kiye buli, o mur dhon	What should I say, o my beloved? *[repeat]*
Jāl phāli horinā gol	The deer ripped my hunting net and escaped.

The young woman's response in the third and fourth stanzas uses a series of idioms that incorporate natural metaphors to explain why the pursuit was unsuccessful. "The ripe lemon fell" incorporates a ripening metaphor often used to refer to sexual maturity, and here indicates unrequited love, as the young woman moved on to another suitor before the man gathered up the courage to declare his feelings for her. Her rejection of a *kopouphul*[8] orchid draws on an understanding of the social pressure young women face to marry before they've "dried up" like the day-old flower. Similarly, when spring draws to a close, the *nahor* blossoms,[9] mentioned in the final line of the song, fall to the ground. By demonstrating that in nature everything has its proper time, the young woman explains to the man that "he'd waited too long, and that girl had been betrothed to another man or fallen in love with someone else" (Probin Saikia, interview, February 14, 2016). Although urban students are familiar with the underlying gendered values communicated by folk idioms, they rely on Panchasur instruction to interpret the poetic settings associated with village life. Follow ▶ Video example 20.1 along with the text below (cue point 00:38).[10]

Poki nemuṭengā, o mur dhon	The ripe lemon, o my beloved
Xoril xomonīyā, o mur dhon	It fell, my friends, o my beloved
[repeat]	
Poki nu nemutengā xoril	The ripe lemon fell

---

[7] The Assamese language includes a voiceless velar fricative that sounds similar to the "ch" sound in the German "acht" and Scottish "loch." I represent this sound in transliteration with the letter "x."
[8] Foxtail orchid (*Rhynchostylis retusa*) worn by female Bihu dancers to adorn their hair.
[9] From the Indian rose chestnut tree (*Mesua ferrea*).
[10] Also ▶ Audio example 20.1, cue point 0:34.

Bohīyā kopouphul, o mur dhon	Yesterday's kopouphul flower
Pelāu doli māri, o mur dhon	I reject it and throw it away
[repeat]	
Nāhore oi jeuti	The nahor flower's bright blossoms
Nāhore oi jeuti soril	The nahor flower's bright blossoms have scattered.

The setting of "Sotāi Porebotot," as part of a sex-segregated performance sequence within a dramatic narrative of social transgression in Assam's distant past, is meant to educate urban audiences about the historical practice of *rati* Bihu while demonstrating Bihu's potential to break down social barriers: "Rich, poor, powerful, powerless, these distinctions become irrelevant. In Bihu, everyone is the same" (Probin and Roshmi Rekha Saikia, personal communication, June 15, 2022). We can gain a critical perspective on how gender norms are upheld even as other social distinctions are transcended by embodying these roles ourselves.

The following analysis and exercises demonstrate how sound and movement emerge simultaneously in the body of the performer, bringing gendered narratives and expectations into being. We may distinguish singing, clapping, playing the drum, and dancing as separate activities or separate elements to analyze. But in practice, these all together form part of a holistic process that takes place in the performer's body. As you listen to Panchasur's audio recording of "Sotāi Porebotot," (▶ Audio example 20.1), notice the minor third in the pentatonic tune, and how the *dhul* drum and *tal* (*tāl*) cymbals emphasize beats 1 and 2 of the three-beat cycle. Next, familiarize yourself with the linear transcription of the first stanza of "Sotāi Porebotot" (Figure 20.1) and listen to the recording again. Each line of transcription contains five dimensions of representation: numbered beats,[11] drum syllables, dance movements, lyrical text, and melodic contour. Notice the relationship between rhythm, movement, and melody depicted in the transcription as you listen. How does this exercise alter your understanding of the recording?

The most iconic Bihu dance movement is *kokal bhangi* (*kokāl bhāngi*) ("waist-break"). *Kokal* refers to the waist and lower back—the fulcrum point

---

[11] Numbered beats (which can also be thought of as pulses at a subdivision level) are derived from my interactions with performers who articulate Bihu's rhythm in three-beat units combined to create six-beat and twelve-beat patterns called *sapor* (*sāpor*) or *seu*. In "Sotāi Porebotot," the three lyrical-melodic phrases are stretched over five twelve-beat rhythmic cycles.

324 MUSIC AND DANCE AS EVERYDAY SOUTH ASIA

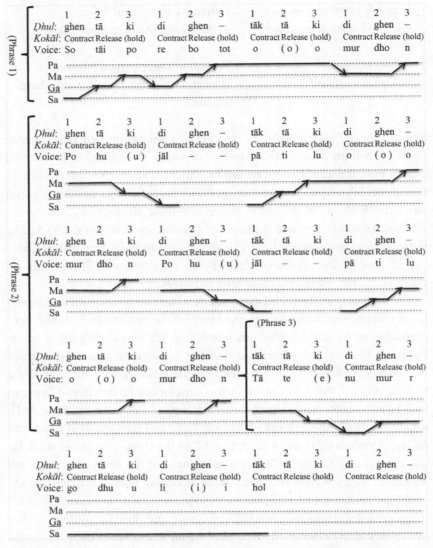

Figure 20.1 Linear transcription of the first stanza of "Sotāi Porebotot" including rhythm, dance movements, lyrics, and melody. Transcription by the author.

around which the performer contracts the abdominal muscles, tucking the pelvis forward and under the upper body without disturbing the straight axis from the lower back to the top of the head. *Kokal bhangi* is performed by both the masculine *bihuwa* (*bihuwā*) role and the feminine *bihuwoti* (*bihuwotī*) role, but *bihuwoti* performance is more stylized and restrained, while *bihuwa*

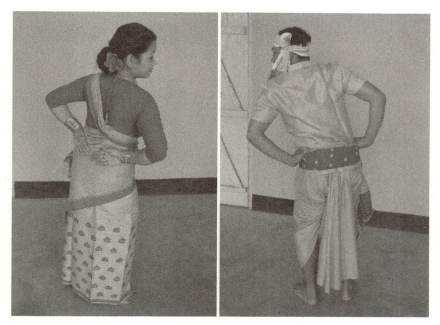

Figure 20.2 Kanika Ingti (left) demonstrates *bihuwoti* posture and Montu Gogoi (right) demonstrates *bihuwa* posture, both with hands at *kokal*. Guwahati, Assam. February 14, 2016. Photo by the author.

performance conveys a sense of abandon. The starting position requires the performer to bend forward slightly at the waist, maintaining a straight axis along the length of the spine (Figure 20.2). Stand up and practice positioning your body as described above in order to prepare for the dance movement exercises that follow.

Aligning movements with each group of three beats, the performer contracts on beat 1, releases on beat 2, and holds the release position on beat 3 (▶ Video example 20.3). Imitate this foot stepping technique as you watch the video clip a second time.[12]

---

[12] Note that the feet are not precisely synched with the beats/pulses. Whichever direction the dancer is going, the right foot touches the ground slightly before beat 1, and the left foot touches the ground slightly before beat 2. No steps happen on beat 3 but the right foot prepares for the next step slightly before the next beat (1). The footsteps are slightly off-the-beat because they are meant to support the body's movements.

Figure 20.3 Kanika Ingti (left) demonstrates *bihuwoti* arm position "breaking" wrists, and Montu Gogoi (right) demonstrates *bihuwa* arm position "breaking" wrists. Guwahati, Assam. February 14, 2016. Photo by the author.

The *bihuwoti* and *bihuwa* also break wrists on beats 1 and 2, and pause on beat 3 (Figure 20.3).[13] You will notice that dancers performing the male role use a full range of motion in the arms to convey a sense of abandon, while dancers performing the female role typically do not extend the elbows above shoulder height. The stylization of movement for female performers in this way is one of the conventions that has become standard practice in Bihu choreography and a marker of contemporary folklorized Bihu performance that conveys a sense of feminine restraint. Another aspect that has become more "refined," as some might say, is the breaking of the waist, which earlier featured more vigorous popping-style movements.[14]

---

[13] In Figure 20.1, only the *kokal*-related (waist) movements are notated, but the same "contract, release, hold" pattern applies to wrist breaks as well.

[14] Some colonial accounts from the nineteenth century described these movements pejoratively as "wanton movements" (Robinson 1841, 269) and "twisting, writhing, wriggling about" (Barker 1881, 176). The stigma associated with Bihu performance in colonial times drove reform efforts by cultural elites who spearheaded the transformation of Bihu into folkloric spectacle featuring stylized, "refined" movements, especially for female performers (Krishnan et al.*). Even in rural areas of Upper

The voice in Bihu is both a melodic and rhythmic instrument. The voice percussively marks the Bihu rhythm through the application of breath pressure (*hesa*). This normally takes place when a sung vowel is extended over multiple beats in a phrase, and a slight glottal stop or "h" is applied on each beat to rearticulate the vowel. During the first stanza of ⏵ Audio example 20.1, *hesa* can be heard in the rearticulation of the "o" vowel on beat 2 in each phrase (cue points 0:09, 0:12, 0:16, and 0:22, 0:26, 0:29). Locate these moments in the music example and imitate the application of *hesa* with your own voice.

Experiencing and analyzing the interconnected melodic, rhythmic, and movement-oriented conventions of Bihu performance (Box 20.1) reveals how these elements work together to create a continuous cycle of anticipation that builds to a climax and then starts again, gaining intensity with each cycle. This intensity is connected to Bihu's sensual power and the cosmological forces of seasonal regeneration that performers animate with their voices, instruments, and bodies. In the transcription (Figure 20.1), four dotted lines represent the four scale degrees used in this song, notated with the corresponding Indian solfège syllables: Sa (1), *komal* Ga (flat 3), Ma (4), and Pa (5).[15] Melodies generally begin at home (Sa), move away (Pa), and return home by the end of the stanza. The coming together of a descending melodic contour back to home, a rhythmic cycle ending only to begin anew, and performers' bodies pausing on the last beat in sync, create an ecstatic convergence of energy, tied to romantic desire through the song text.

As you progressed through the exercises in Box 20.1, you may have recognized one of the key differences between the *bihuwa* and *bihuwoti* roles: abandon vs. restraint. This distinction is the product of folklorized choreographic norms in which men are expected to perform in a boisterous, jovial manner, and women are expected to contain their excitement within a composed demeanor. In contrast, in participatory village ritual celebrations, I have observed people of all ages dancing with abandon regardless of sex. This is because urban folklorized performances are meant to promote socioculturally constructed ideals of heteronormative femininity and masculinity that are a reaction to colonial portrayals of Assamese women as sexually insatiable (Kar 2008) and Assamese men as lazy and uncivilized

---

Assam, young women were cautioned against performing Bihu beyond their own village ritual contexts until the 1980s for fear of stigma (see Kheshgi 2017).

[15] Panchasur classes use rote learning without notation. In discussing music theoretical elements with me, the Saikias often referred to the Indian solfège syllables to clarify melodic contour.

Box 20.1   Exercises

Vocalization Exercise

(1) First, listen to Panchasur's recording of "Sotāi Porebotot" (▶ Audio example 20.1) while following along with the transcription (Figure 20.1).
(2) Listen again while reciting the beats, "one, two, three, one, two, three," along with the recording of the song's first stanza.
(3) Listen again, starting from the beginning of the first stanza, while reciting the simplified drum syllables as notated in the transcription.
(4) Listen again while singing the scale syllables Sa Ga Ma Pa.
(5) Listen again while singing the text of the first stanza along with the recording.

After completing these five steps, you should be able to recognize and feel the Bihu rhythm. Try clapping along on beats 1 and 2 while the recording is playing, without looking at the transcription. Now that you have activated your voice and sense of rhythm, it is time to incorporate dance movements.

Dance Movement Exercise

In preparation for this movement activity, watch ▶ Video example 20.4, noticing any differences between the dance movements performed by the men and women in the video. Follow the instructions below, referring to the transcription (Figure 20.1) for guidance when necessary.

Solo Exercises

(1) First, refer back to ▶ Video example 20.3 for a close-up of the Bihu step technique. Watch a second time while trying out the stepping pattern yourself.
(2) Next, choose either the *bihuwoti* or *bihuwa* role, regardless of your own sex or gender identification. As you move through the stages below, replicate the movements as closely as you can, and then try the other role as well. Pay attention to the differences in how the two roles are embodied, and to how you feel performing both of them.

(3) Play ▶ Video example 20.4 and practice the stepping pattern as you watch and listen. Notice how the dancers move around in the space. Try to imitate their movements, focusing mainly on your feet this time.
(4) Watch, listen, and try again, adding the *kokal bhangi* waist-break movement described in detail above.
(5) Watch, listen, and try again, adding wrist-breaks.

Pair Exercises

Now that you've become familiar with the alignment of dance movements to the Bihu song's melody and rhythm, try dancing in sync with a partner to ▶ Audio example 20.1.

(1) First, both partners try dancing as *bihuwoti* together.
(2) Next, both partners try dancing as *bihuwa* together.
(3) Then, partners dance together as a *bihuwoti-bihuwa* pair.
(4) After that, partners switch roles.
(5) The final step is to combine singing and dancing together in your own body.
   a. Refresh your memory of the meaning of the song lyrics and discuss them with your partner.
   b. Sing the first stanza with your partner and the recording while marking the beat with your feet, waist, and wrists, each according to the gendered conventions of the roles you have chosen.
   c. Consider the hunting metaphor in the song's first stanza as you sing. Reflect on how your perspective on its meaning might change based on whether you embody the *bihuwoti* or the *bihuwa* role.

Discussion

The following discussion questions are designed to help you draw connections between your own embodied performance and the themes addressed in this chapter. Reflect on these questions, jot down some thoughts, and share them with your classmates in a group discussion. You may wish to discuss with your partner before sharing with the larger group.

(1) How did you feel while portraying the *bihuwoti* and *bihuwa* roles? Describe both physical and emotional sensations.
(2) Reflect on your interaction with your partner while portraying each role. How did you connect with your partner during these experiences? Did this connection change when your roles changed? How?
(3) How did singing affect your experience of dancing and vice versa?
(4) How did the song's meaning impact you as you sang and danced? Did your perspective on the song's meaning change depending on which role you performed?

(Kar 2007). Colonial stereotypes live on in discriminatory policies and bigoted interactions against Assamese people by Indians from other states (Kar 2008; McDuie-Ra 2015). The urban folk school Panchasur's portrayal of the power of Bihu to transgress social norms by depicting a liaison between a royal woman and a male laborer ultimately remains within the folkloric frame of respectability by resolving this tension in marriage. Their performance normalizes the narrative that Bihu was historically performed in gender-segregated spaces in order to quell romantic attraction between young women and men. Hunali and Dhonbor's desire for each other challenged the norms of the historical period portrayed in *Dikhour Gorāt Roi*. Although gender-segregated Bihu performance is no longer common practice beyond contexts of historical re-enactment and contemporary Bihu performances are primarily mixed-gender, the passion this arrangement was designed to control is addressed by other means. In a mixed-gender context, the erotic force of Bihu is muted for the stage through the removal of sexual innuendo from lyrics, the standardization of choreography, the adoption of matching dress, and other hallmarks of folklorized spectacle performance.

Works Cited

Babiracki, Carol. 2000. "'Saved by Dance': The Movement for Autonomy in Jharkhand." *Asian Music* 32(1): 35–58.
Barker, George M. 1881. *A Tea Planter's Life in Assam*. Calcutta: Thacker, Spink & Co.
Fiol, Stefan. 2017. *Recasting Folk in the Himalayas: Indian Music, Media, and Social Mobility*. Champaign: University of Illinois Press.

Gandhiya, Jayakanta. 1988. *Bihu-Samskritra Ruparekha Samgrahaka*. Guwahati: Pariwesaka Shanti Prakashana.
Gogoi, Lila. 1969. *Bihu: Eti Samiksha*. Dibrugarh, Assam: Dibrugarh Book Stall.
Goswami, Prafulladatta. 2003 [1988]. *Bohag Bihu of Assam and Bihu Songs*. Guwahati: Publication Board Assam.
Kar, Bodhisattva. 2007. "The Assam Fever: Identities of a Disease and Diseases of an Identity." In *Of Matters Modern: The Experience of Modernity in Colonial and Postcolonial South Asia*, 78–125. Edited by Debraj Bhattacharya. New York: Seagull Books.
Kar, Bodhisattva. 2008. "Incredible Stories in the Time of Credible Histories: Colonial Assam and Translations of Vernacular Geographies." In *History in the Vernacular*, edited by Partha Chatterjee and Raziuddin Aquil, 288–321. New Delhi: Permanent Black.
Kheshgi, Rehanna. 2017. "Navigating Generational Frictions through Bihu Festival Performance in Assam, India." *MUSICultures* 44 (2): 48–73.
McDuie-Ra, Duncan. 2015. *Debating Race in Contemporary India*. New York: Palgrave Macmillan.
Rios, Fernando. 2020. *Panpipes & Ponchos: Music Folklorization and the Rise of the Andean Conjunto Tradition in La Paz, Bolivia*. New York: Oxford University Press.
Robinson, William. 1841. *A descriptive account of Asam: with a sketch of the local geography, and a concise history of the tea-plant of Asam, to which is added, a short account of the neighbouring tribes*. Calcutta: Ostell & Lepage.
Saikia, Yasmin. 2001. "Landscape of Identity: Transacting the Labels 'Indian', 'Assamese' and 'Tai-Ahom' in Contemporary Assam." *Contemporary South Asia* 10(1): 73-93.
Sengupta, Madhumita, and Jahnu Bharadwaj. 2019. "Caste Census and the Impact of Colonial Sociology in British Assam." *Asian Ethnicity* 20: 1–26.
Turino, Thomas. 2008. *Music as Social Life: The Politics of Participation*. Chicago: University of Chicago Press.

Interviews and Personal Communications with the Author

Mahanta, Khagen (Assamese folk singer). April 11, 2009.
Saikia, Probin (Assamese folk singer). June 15, 2022.
Saikia, Probin, and Roshmi Rekha (Assamese folk singers). June 15, 2022.

SECTION V
TECHNOLOGY, MEDIA, AND TRANSMISSION

Introduction by Sarah L. Morelli

How is music and dance knowledge passed from one person or group to another, and what are the ramifications of these exchanges? This is the study of transmission (Shelemay 1996). Pedagogical techniques, musical gift offerings, and uses of media and technology, all topics considered in this section, fall within this broad category. Artistic transmission can take place through a variety of processes, from the relatively long-term, intensive training typically experienced in South Asian guru-disciple relationships to the mass communication enabled by audio, film, and internet technologies.

The South Indian and Sri Lankan drumming practices discussed by Groesbeck* and Sykes* are typically transmitted from gurus (here, *ashan* or *gurunnanse*) to disciples (*shishyan*). In the beginning stages of *chenda* temple drum training at the Kerala Kalamandalam, musical knowledge is nonverbally taught and practiced through rote exercises. Groesbeck argues that practice (*sadhakam*) sessions serve not only to develop skill, but equally important, to help shape the student's identity into a particular type of person: "austere, disciplined, . . . obedient, and attentive" and best-suited to absorb embodied musical knowledge. While at Kalamandalam, training fees and teacher salaries are subsidized by the state government, the economic relationships between "tradition bearers" and learners are not always so straightforward (Slawek 2000). These dynamics, along with myriad other economic concerns, are an area of growing ethnomusicological interest (Morcom and Taylor, 2020–). Such considerations include the profound impacts of capitalist and neoliberal economies on music and dance, including their increased commodification and materiality—their "transformation . . . from *something that someone does* into *something that someone* *owns*" (Beaster-Jones 2014; see also Taylor 2007). Sykes* contributes a different perspective on music's value, examining performance as a form of ritual gift-giving. In Sri Lanka's low country, where Berava drummers present sonic gifts to the Buddha, deities, and demons, the value of a drum offering is in inverse relationship to its "musicality." Offerings to the Buddha most closely approximate sacred speech and, as such, consist of unmetered drum phrases. Offerings to demons, on the other hand, include short, temporally regular phrases; their musicality is intended to appease demons and trick them into thinking they are receiving the ritually efficacious "real thing."

The transmission of recorded and mass-mediated musics in South Asia is a vast area of study. In colonial India, the history of recorded music began soon after the invention of the wax cylinder (Kinnear 1994). As Maciszewski* notes (Section IV), professional female entertainers known as *tawa'ifs* helped pioneer music and film industries, beginning with Gauhar Jan, who in 1902 performed for India's first recording sessions. For decades, the recording industry was dominated by the HMV (His Master's Voice) label. Due to the diversity of regional languages and musics, record companies focused on genres appealing to the broadest audiences, such as Urdu-language *ghazal* and *qawwali* (Manuel 1993). Music broadcast on Indian radio, first controlled by the British colonial government and then by the Indian government, was likewise limited to particular, mostly elite genres. Some Indian audiences were able to broaden their listening by tuning in radio stations from Pakistan and Sri Lanka—the site of Asia's first radio station, built in 1925. As Manuel discusses in his seminal monograph, *Cassette Culture*, cassette technology transformed the music industry in North India (and the rest of South Asia), enabling musicians and music producers to affordably produce and distribute regional genres and styles previously not considered profitable (1993).

Scholarly interest in recording technologies developed in tandem with increased engagement with popular music and dance forms. In the twenty-first century, ethnomusicologists turned greater attention to music studios as sites of cultural production variously reflecting, contesting, and reshaping the cultural norms of the communities outside their acoustically treated walls (e.g., Greene and Porcello 2004; Meintjes 2003). A central concern for scholars such as Fiol* has been the power dynamics between studio producers, musicians, and audiences. Fiol's study of folk music (*lokgeet*) in the North Indian state of Uttarakhand considers the differing aesthetic preferences of rural cultural insiders and urban studio producers in the production of one song and accompanying video. The producer's choice of tempo resulted in a recording that was ultimately unsatisfying for its primary audience, villagers dancing at Uttarakhandi festivals. Scholars of popular music sometimes focus on superstars who use their fame, status, and platform to critique social and political issues of the day. Stirr's* chapter examines multiple releases of one album by popular Nepali *lok dohori* singer Badri Pangeni. Each of the three versions of this album highlighted a different song and became increasingly direct in confronting social and political issues during the years immediately following Nepal's ten-year civil war (1996–2006).

Bollywood is a relatively new but ubiquitous term for the Hindi-language film industry based in Mumbai. As the predominant South Asian film industry, many of its aesthetic elements, including lavish song-and-dance sequences, are found in other film industries of the region based in Lahore, Chennai, Kolkata, and elsewhere (Gehlawat and Dudrah 2020). Recent years have seen a proliferation of scholarship on Bollywood and regional cinemas from a variety of disciplines including dance studies, ethnomusicology, history, and theater, film, and media studies. Sarrazin* takes a diachronic ethnomusicological approach in her chapter, analyzing the vocal timbre, register, and ornamentation of select female voices in Bollywood songs. Comparing vocal techniques with other filmic elements, she traces changes in constructed notions of Indian femininity through films from the 1930s to the 2010s.

Today, Bollywood is a multibillion-dollar industry with studio empires, superstar celebrities, and depictions of wealth most audience members can only dream about. While Bollywood may reflect growing global economic disparity, *filmi* song and dance simultaneously invites participation by millions, in South Asia and abroad, who will never be on the silver screen themselves. Its songs are sung in family settings, and its dances are imitated and re-choreographed for community events. Bollywood songs and dances are performed on reality programs such as *Indian Idol* and *Dance India Dance* (Chakravorty 2017; Desai-Stephens 2017) and repackaged for dance and exercise classes (Nimjee*, Section VI). In the 2020s, everyday people create music and dance videos on their cell phones and share them with millions of potential viewers through YouTube and social media apps. Further, the growing practice of virtual and online learning enables expanded opportunities for artistic transmission, unconfined by geographic locale. The democratization of music-making and consumption described by Manuel (1993) seems, in some areas, to have increased exponentially. Still, unequal access to and control of technology enables some voices to be amplified (or liked, reposted, reshared) more than others, regardless of the perpetually changing hardware and software. Although the specific forms of media discussed in this section may not be the technologies-of-choice for future audiences, its questions regarding the dynamics of transmission and the relationships between technology and individual/group agency presumably will remain central scholarly concerns.

Works Cited

Beaster-Jones, Jayson. 2014. "Beyond Musical Exceptionalism: Music, Value, and Ethnomusicology." *Ethnomusicology* 58(2): 334–340.

Chakravorty, Pallavi. 2017. *This Is How We Dance Now!: Performance in the Age of Bollywood and Reality Shows*. Oxford: Oxford University Press.

Desai-Stephens, Anaar. 2017. "Tensions of Musical Re-animation from Bollywood to Indian Idol." In *Music in Contemporary Indian Film*, edited by Jayson Beaster-Jones and Natalie Sarrazin, 76–90. New York: Routledge.

Gehlawat, Ajay, and Rajinder Dudrah. 2020. *The Evolution of Song and Dance in Hindi Cinema*. London: Routledge.

Greene, Paul, and Thomas Porcello, eds. 2004. *Wired for Sound: Engineering and Technologies in Sonic Cultures*. Middletown, CT: Wesleyan University Press.

Kinnear, Michael. 1994. *The Gramophone Company's First Indian Recordings, 1899–1908*. Bombay: Popular Prakashan.

Manuel, Peter. 1993. *Cassette Culture: Popular Music and Technology in North India*. Chicago: University of Chicago Press.

Meintjes, Louise. 2003. *Sound of Africa!: Making Music Zulu in a South African Studio*. Durham, NC: Duke University Press.

Morcom, Anna, and Timothy D. Taylor, eds. 2020–. *The Oxford Handbook of Economic Ethnomusicology*. Oxford University Press.

Shelemay, Kay Kaufman. 1996. "The Ethnomusicologist and the Transmission of Tradition." *Journal of Musicology* 14(1): 35–51.

Slawek, Stephen. 2000. "The Classical Master-Disciple Tradition." In *South Asia: The Indian Subcontinent*, vol. 5 of *The Garland Encyclopedia of World Music*, edited by Alison Arnold, 457–467. New York: Garland.

Taylor, Timothy D. 2007. "The Commodification of Music at the Dawn of the Era of 'Mechanical Music.'" *Ethnomusicology* 51(2): 281–305.

21

"We Know What Our Folk Culture Is from Commercial Videos"

Rethinking the Popular-Folk Dynamic in the Indian Himalayas

Stefan Fiol

The concept of "folk" typically brings to mind an older way of life, one that emphasizes community and continuity. Usually not far behind is the idea that folk culture is in decline, or surviving at the margins of a globalizing popular culture that slowly cannibalizes it. In Sanskrit-derived languages in South Asia, the term *"lok"*—for instance, *lok sanskriti* for "folk culture," *lokgeet* for "folksong"—has a long and varied set of cultural associations (Chalmers 2004). In contemporary usage, *lok* has been part of the discourse that South Asian social elites use to mark the cultural practices of "others" within the society, typically Dalits, women, hereditary artisans, *Adivasi*s ("original inhabitants"), and the rural masses. The term *lok* is ambiguous because it can simultaneously signify a shared inheritance belonging to everyone and a more restricted birthright of marginalized social groups.

A premise of this chapter is that the "folk" construct is only intelligible within a discourse that sets it in opposition to some other cultural construct, like "classical" or "popular." In the early twentieth-century American music industry, the term "folk" emerged as a commercial genre designation in the context of a growing popular music industry that contributed to anxiety about the survival of "pure" folk forms, even as the music industry itself helped to reify the idea of authenticity in "folk" and "roots" music for its own commercial purposes. In South Asian contexts, the idea that film

---

Research for this article was generously supported by fellowships from the American Institute of Indian Studies and Fulbright-Hays. All interviews were conducted in Hindi and translated into English by the author. I am grateful to Mehindra Singh Chauhan, Balraj Negi, and the late Patti Ram for their participation.

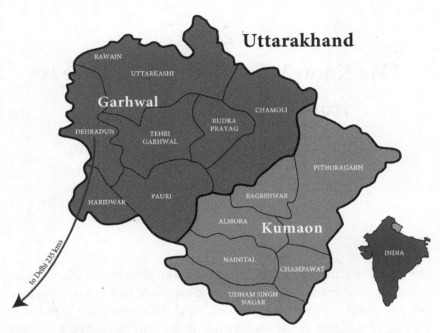

Map 21.1 Map of Uttarakhand's two regions, Garhwal and Kumaon. Photo by Natalie Fiol; used with permission.

music—which incorporates Western instruments and tuning systems—is a direct threat to the survival of folk culture has also been prevalent (Blackburn and Ramanujan 1986, 266). In Uttarakhand, a state located in the Indian Himalayas (Map 21.1) where my research takes place, some scholars have blamed the popular music industries for the decline of "folk" practices in the mountains, arguing that the rise of commercial entertainment has given residents cheap and rootless mass-mediated alternatives (e.g., radio, television, videos, DJs at weddings) to dancing and singing collectively, or to hiring hereditary drummers, dancers, healers, and entertainers from lowered-status hereditary communities (Chandola 1977).

To adequately explain the erosion of participatory musical performance in Uttarakhandi villages requires a broad perspective that includes other intersectional variables such as caste stigma, social restrictions on public female performance, mass out-migration, environmental exploitation, and the predominance of a capitalist, cash-based economy. Even if the growth of the vernacular music industry may be partly to blame for the decline of participatory music-making in rural areas, it is also true, if less acknowledged, that the interest of social elites in studying, celebrating, and codifying folk culture has never been stronger in this region, and that the commercial music industry has played a significant role in bolstering interest in folk culture (Bharucha 2003).

In India, as in North America, many people tend to associate "folk music" and "popular music" with distinct spaces (the rural festival and the urban recording studio, respectively) and sonic codes (e.g., the sound of a *dhol* barrel drum and a synthesizer, respectively). Nevertheless, this habit of categorizing culture into discrete and opposing boxes labeled "folk" and "popular" is part of a particular discourse and a way of being in the world that Turino describes as part of the "modernist cosmopolitan formation" (2000). In North India, individuals socialized within a cosmopolitan formation almost uniformly exhibit a high level of education and social mobility, use Hindi and English, transact through the cash economy, and value individual autonomy. Such individuals are also prone to conceptualizing commercial music as harmful to the survival of regional "folk," even as such commercial productions seek to reify, and in some cases revive, "folk culture."

In contrast, people who attend rural Himalayan festivals correspond to a wide range of caste, class, and gender positions, and draw upon a more heterogeneous set of habits. Festival dancing exposes underlying social boundaries within rural life, as perceived dominant caste singers and dancers group themselves based on age, gender, and residence, and lowered-caste hereditary musicians provide drumming accompaniment but do not dance with others. As compared to urban cosmopolitans, rural residents are generally far less concerned with the loss of folk music or the threat of "popular culture" on local lifeways. Instead, they tend to be engaged in a fluid exchange of songs and dances that may originate in local performance practice *or* mass-mediated sources. Many rural residents are avid consumers of vernacular popular music on their mobile phones, video compact discs, radio, and regional television stations; festival dancing and singing became a means of incorporating these influences and enjoying them communally. The crucial point is that the habit of opposing folk/popular or traditional/modern binaries is not shared by those who are not socialized within a cosmopolitan formation.

This chapter exposes some of the risks involved when high-status culture brokers are involved in sonically engineering "folk culture" for local consumption. I describe the negotiation of tempo in studio and village performances of Mehindra Chauhan's song "Rāsau Lāno" as a means to demonstrate how power is unequally distributed in the production process. Commercial music from Uttarakhand draws from what might be called a distilled Himalayan "pop-folk" aesthetic that includes the preference for high vocal range, free-rhythm cadenzas on the bamboo flute (*bansuri*), pentatonic modes, rhythmical cycles in six (*dadra* and *khemta*) or eight (*kaherva*), binary melodic phrases (*asthai-antara*) separated by instrumental breaks, and a predictable core instrumentation of *dholak*, *tabla*, guitar, mandolin, octopad, flute, electronic samples, and vocals (Fiol 2017).[1] These aesthetic features are not generally derived from village-based musical practices, but for many listeners, they have nonetheless come to signify Himalayan "folk." Regardless of their authenticity, many dance steps, melodic formulae, styles of dress, and artistic motifs are understood to be "traditional" and "folkloric" *as a result of* their circulation through the music industry's channels of production and reproduction.

The Festival Context

In 2005, I attended the annual spring harvest festival Bisu in the Rawain region. Attendees from villages near and far had traveled up to fifteen miles on foot and converged on the open fairground for a full day and night of merrymaking. Urban merchants hauled cases of plastic jewelry, cotton *saris*, and music albums to sell to villagers, as well as gas cylinders and cooking vessels to prepare savory *samosas*, *jalebi* sweets, and endless cups of *chai*. A generator was turned on to power the sound system, which projected the latest commercial songs across the mountain valley.

In the late evening, as the crowd swelled in the courtyard in front of the village temple, circles of anywhere between four to forty dancers began to take shape. As seen in Figure 21.1, dancers in each circle formed an unbreakable chain, weaving their hands and arms around the waists and backs of their neighbors. Some groups sang along with the familiar verses of the recorded music emanating from a sound system, matching the meter of the verse with their footwork patterns as they rotated. Other groups performed idiosyncratic texts and dance steps deriving from their own community, although many of these were similarly learned from viewing commercial videos. Young male dancers directed romantic lyrics toward young women

---

[1] Consider exploring videos of popular music from Uttarakhand—called Garhwali and Kumaoni *geet*—on YouTube channels such as T-Series Regional, Neelam Uttrakhandi, Rama Series, and BK Sangeet.

on the other side of the circle, while mimicking the stylized movements portrayed on video albums. Lowered-caste hereditary drummers (Dhaki) accompanied some of the larger circle dances on the *dhol*, a barrel drum, and the *damaun* (*damaun̠*), a small kettledrum. As this festival was a meeting place for members of many different social groups, round dance-songs were a way for people of a particular locality, gender, age group, or caste to reinforce social boundaries and articulate their in-group identities (cf. Babiracki*).

As I danced and sang alongside friends, I was engulfed by sensations of sound and touch. The group of dancers I had joined was a unit unto itself; individual freedom of movement was not possible, as I was physically carried along by the group in spite of my tentative steps. The entire festival ground was now filled with spinning spheres of dancers, each competing to drown out the sounds of the others and claim the most aural space (see ⏵ Audio example 21.1, ⏵ Video example 21.1, Box 21.1).

As dusk descended, I was introduced to Mehindra Chauhan, a young singer from a perceived dominant Rajput caste and large land-owning family in a nearby village in Rawain who had recorded more than a dozen albums in Delhi. I soon learned that I had just been dancing to several of his

Figure 21.1 Chain of dancers in Rawain. May 13, 2005. Photo by the author.

Box 21.1   Exercise

1. Stand in a tight, inward-facing circle. If the group is big enough and space allows, divide into multiple circles. (If space is limited, create two concentric circles with one moving inside the other.)
2. Listen, practice, and then sing along with the lyrics and melody corresponding to the song "Rāsau Lāno" (▶ Video example 21.3, the studio production) in alternating male-female phrases: Men (cue point 0:23): *Dhākiya dhāke bajāno phāṉo, Dhākiya dhāke bajāno phāṉo* ("Dhākiya [a caste term for drummers] keep playing the drums). Women (cue point 0:31): *Mere bhāī phore rāsau lāno, Mere bhāī phore rāsau lāno* ("My brothers keep dancing *rasau*" [*rāsau*, a dance-song genre]).
3. Repeat the following four-beat stepping pattern moving in a counterclockwise direction: right foot, left foot (crossing over the right foot), right foot, left foot (stepping back to the left and momentarily moving in a clockwise direction) Once you are comfortable with the stepping pattern, try taking bigger steps and bending at the waist with the left foot back-step.
4. Once you have become comfortable with this stepping pattern, put your arms behind the back of the person on either side of you, and hold hands with the person adjacent to your neighbor (see Figure 21.1). You will have created a tightly woven chain that ensures synchronous movement.
5. Next, sing "Rāsau Lāno" again while forming this chain and adding the stepping pattern. Try following ▶ Video example 21.3, noting the tempo of this studio production. Once you get comfortable, try taking bigger steps and bending at the waist. Notice how much harder (and more fun) it is to take big steps and bend at the waist when you are connected to the circle.
6. Now listen to the first 40 seconds of ▶ Audio example 21.1, a different round dance-song recorded during a village festival. Try clapping to the more standard dance tempo of this song. Then try following this recording's faster tempo while dancing the round dance you have learned.

> 7. Which of the song's tempos felt more comfortable to dance to? Try to dance and sing "Rāsau Lāno" at your preferred tempo without a recording. The discrepancy between the slower and faster tempos you have just experienced will be a key consideration later in the chapter.

compositions that had been spontaneously integrated into the dancing by village youth. Mehindra and I exchanged pleasantries and agreed to meet in Delhi during his next recording session.

I began to consider the relationship between village-based dance-songs and regional commercial recordings in a new light. Why did festival goers draw upon commercial recorded music in their participatory dance-song performances? Why, conversely, did recording artists incorporate dance-songs onto their commercial music albums? How does each of these processes challenge the ways that we often think about the relationship between "folk music" and "popular music"? The next section addresses some of these questions by turning to consider the studio context (Fiol 2013).

The Studio Context

From the 1970s through the early 2000s, Delhi was the hub of Garhwali and Kumaoni vernacular music production. Several hundred studios east of the city, from Noida to Ghaziabad across the Yamuna River, catered to musicians coming from Bihar, Haryana, Punjab, Uttar Pradesh, Uttarakhand, and other parts of North India. Real estate rates were historically much cheaper in East Delhi, and this was where a large portion of the Uttarakhandi migrant population lived. This location was also strategically close to the inter-state bus terminal in which artists from Garhwal and Kumaon arrived in the city.

In December 2005, after a seven-hour bus ride from Dehradun, I again met up with Mehindra Chauhan, but this time in a Delhi recording studio. "Is it profitable to be a professional recording artist in Uttarakhand?" I asked him. He smiled and shook his head. "In the beginning, I had to pay out of pocket to rent the studio space and get my albums produced. Now, after a number of my albums have sold well, the company pays me 10,000 rupees [around $225] to make an album, but I can release no more than two or three albums per year. There are no royalties here, so it's hard to make a living from recording. But without the advertising that comes from releasing a new album, I would never get called to weddings and stage programs, and those are the gigs where it is possible to make a decent living." Mehindra's comments pointed to the growth of the entertainment industry in the early 2000s and the primary function of albums as a form of advertisement.

At the studio we met up with Patti Ram, a hereditary drummer whom I had met during the festival in Rawain. Mehindra explained that members of his own Rajput (perceived dominant caste) family had long served as the patrons for Patti Ram and his family, and that as a consequence of this hereditary relationship, he had invited Patti Ram to the studio to accompany him on the *dhol*. It is relatively rare to hear *dhol* in commercial recordings, so I asked Mehindra why he made this decision. "The folk rhythms used in many of my songs are often too difficult for classically trained studio percussionists to play properly. And the *dhol* sounds more authentic in recordings of dance-songs than *tabla* and *dholak*" (two North Indian drums commonly used in regional recordings). Patti Ram explained that even when *tabla* and *dholak* were used in place of *dhol* in the studio, he often had to teach studio percussionists how to perform local rhythmic patterns on their instruments. These statements directly contradict the common misconception that village-based (i.e., "folk") drumming is inherently simpler than classical, *tala*-based drumming.

Once in the studio, Mehindra introduced me to the music director (who was in charge of coordinating all the musical layers on the album), the producer (who was funding the project and ensuring that the album would be distributed to the right areas), and the studio engineer (who sat behind the console and later mixed all the recorded tracks). Once the order of the album's eight songs was agreed upon, the music director worked through the structure of each song on the harmonium, a hand-pumped free-reed organ, deciding how many verses and instrumental breaks to include, what kind of "intro" and "coda" to use, and what rhythmic patterns and instrument combinations to include in each song. Mehindra then recorded a vocal demo track for each of the songs, and one by one, studio musicians came and left, each needing only an hour or less to record successive tracks on *tabla, dholak,* octopad, mandolin, banjo, flute, and synthesizer while listening to the vocal track through headphones.

The music director and producer of this album were both Uttarakhandi men who had spent most of their lives in the urban plains. Both articulated the need for "folk elements" in their recordings as a means of sonically articulating the nostalgia that many migrant listeners might feel when separated from their mountain villages. During the recording of "Rāsau Lāno," the music director requested Patti Ram to slow his performance of the *dhol* rhythm. He felt that the lyrics of the song were becoming too muddled against the reverberations of the *dhol*. Mehindra disagreed, saying that the *rasau* (*rāsau*) variety of round dance-songs needed to be presented in a moderately fast tempo; if the tempo were recorded any slower, people might not recognize it as a *rasau* and would not incorporate the song into their festival dances. But in the studio context, music directors have the last call in such matters, and the song was re-recorded in the slower tempo to privilege the lyrics.

Despite not having ultimate authority in the recording studio, Mehindra stressed the importance of retaining the original character of a folksong as much as possible. Aside from the tempo, he insisted that the audio recording of "Rāsau Lāno" (see ⏵ Video example 21.3) closely follows village dance-song practice. The track opens with the sound of the *ransingha*, an S-shaped copper horn that is used in ritual contexts in Uttarakhand, performing a series of melodic runs drawn from the natural overtone series. The *dhol* and *damaun* drums enter the mix playing a compound meter in six, followed by reedy keyboard samples and a bamboo flute that repeat and embellish the main melody line. This instrumentation remains constant throughout the song, as does the repetition of a single melodic line, even during instrumental breaks between verses. The producers' goal was to mimic and inspire village dance-song performances, rather than to emphasize a variety of sounds and textures.

Mehindra stated that his goal in composing and recording such songs was, in his words, "to make people in Rawain feel proud of their cultural heritage. These songs are gradually disappearing in our villages, but if people hear them on albums, they may begin to appreciate them again. To get the younger generation involved, it is often necessary to make the songs more modern sounding by adding effects on the synthesizer, by making the drum sound heavier in the overall mix. . . . My reason for making these albums is to raise the folk culture of my area to a national level, like they have been able to do in Punjab and Rajasthan." Mehindra articulated a dual desire for his albums to revive music-making and dance in local Himalayan contexts—corresponding to the aforementioned modernist understanding of "folk culture" as something that is dying out—as well as to find commercial success outside the region. He likewise emphasized the use of *dhol* and synthesizer samples in the mix, sonic elements that tend to be associated with folk and pop, respectively.

The Studio Meets the Festival

After mixing and mastering the album in the studio, the producer waited several months for the next festival season to come around before releasing the album on the market. During festivals, people were much more likely to spend their hard-earned money on a new album, especially if it had original dance-songs. Several weeks after releasing the audio recording, I returned to Mehindra's village in Rawain to attend the on-site video shoot. A production team of around fifteen individuals performing various roles—drivers, makeup artists, soundmen, lighting assistants, actors, cameramen, utility men, producer, and director—assembled at Mehindra's village home. It took approximately one week for the production team to record the material that would later be edited into a video album of eight songs. On most days, the team visited spectacular Himalayan locations and recorded the actors dancing and lip-syncing to a song while wearing matching folk dress.[2] At around ten o'clock on the second night, however, the crew set up in front of the temple courtyard in Mehindra's village to record the video for "Rāsau Lāno." The filming did not coincide with any local festival, but the goal of the film crew was to simulate a festival atmosphere. People donned their best clothes and assembled in the courtyard. It took several hours for the director to rein in the dancers' enthusiasm and get them to synchronize their movements with the barely audible playback of the audio coming through a small cassette player (Figure 21.2). As anticipated by Mehindra during the studio session, the tempo of the audio recording was unnaturally slow for a *rasau* dance-song, and many of the dancers found it difficult to move together. To facilitate synchronous movement, many villagers began singing alongside Mehindra's recorded voice, but they were then unable to hear the recorded playback and gradually increased the tempo, to the director's consternation. In ▶ Video example 21.2, the director can be seen cuing spectators

---

[2] These videos somewhat resemble low-budget versions of the dancing and lip-syncing sequences found in Bollywood films. It would be problematic, however, to say that vernacular productions are derivatives of Mumbai-based film industry, not least because many of early Bollywood dance sequences were themselves modeled on village folk practice in the Himalayas and elsewhere.

Figure 21.2 On-site shooting of the video for "Rāsau Lāno." April 10, 2005. Photo by the author.

and dancers to clap in time with the recording. Mehindra also had a difficult time teaching the *dhol* players to mime the action of drumming without actually striking the drum because this too drowned out the cassette playback, making it difficult for the dancers to follow the correct (slow) tempo.

Meanwhile, I asked several older women seated in the courtyard if they were excited to have their village represented on the commercial album. To my surprise, one woman replied that a number of video albums had previously been filmed in this village, and that it was in fact becoming a nuisance, because production teams demanded a lot and never gave anything back. Part of her resentment was triggered by the manner in which the production team interacted with the villagers. Arriving late at night, they set up a noisy generator to power their spotlights, enlisted the help of the village headman to bring the entire village out of their beds and into the courtyard, and then advised many women to clean up and change clothes because they were deemed unsuitable to appear on camera. One woman was told to change her nose ring or leave the scene because it resembled a style of nose ring worn in Rajasthan. The director demanded that only traditional dress and jewelry from Rawain could be shown in the video, because the point was to record "authentic" local folklore. It did not come as a surprise when, after returning to Delhi, the producer told me that many of the sequences recorded in this village would not be used in the final version of the video. Despite the efforts of the crew and the enthusiastic involvement of villagers, his decision was a reminder that the authority over the presentation of "folk" ultimately overwhelmingly rests with the perceived upper caste, male producers and performers in plains-based studios and does not always reflect the fluidity of people's lived experience. For many village participants, this staged festival was a completely manufactured experience of "folk culture" by the video production team.

At the same time, many regarded the video shoot as a truly auspicious occasion. Because of the decline in festival dance-song performances in the region, Mehindra's video album offered a rare opportunity to demonstrate the unity of the village and to celebrate one of their own. Young people were particularly enthusiastic to dance to these songs, and several of them expressed their own desires to release an album. Kusum Negi, a young woman who has recorded several albums in the neighboring Jaunsar region, summed up what she saw as the value of such commercial recordings, saying, "we know what our folk culture is from [commercial] videos."

Conclusion

I now return to my earlier questions: Why, in spite of claims that popular music posed a threat to the survival of folk music, did commercial artists record village-based dance-songs on their albums? And why did villagers incorporate commercial songs into live performances at festivals? I believe that these two processes are part of a single musical production feedback loop that connected the urban plains and the rural mountains, with migrant artists serving as intermediaries. High-status recording artists like Mehindra Chauhan only acquired modest fame and wealth through commercial recordings, but they were able to leverage their gender and caste privilege to become culture brokers between urban and rural contexts. In recording studios, they were valued for their ability to identify and communicate in the local "folk" idiom; in the village, their songs "refined" local elements through studio production.

As we observed when the video director asked Patti Ram to slow the tempo of the *rasau* and when he asked women in the village to change their clothes and jewelry, folk culture was frequently not understood as fluid lived experience but rather as a set of declining cultural resources (musical genres, costumes, dance movements, linguistic idioms, and instruments such as the *dhol*) that were used to stand for an experience of authenticity and originality. Women and lowered-caste residents experienced less agency, and at times alienation, in the process of constructing "folk," even as their participation was deemed essential. This is among the most damaging consequences of folklorization through the music industry.

At the same time, my ethnographic experiences point to the resilience and adaptability of local practices in the face of broader capitalization and cultural homogenization (cf. Ayyagari*). Sonic and visual signs rendered one way in the studio could be drastically altered in festival settings. One recording artist recounted a story of hearing a round dance-song performed at a local festival. The song was his, but it had been transformed so completely that he did not recognize it and had to be informed that it was his own. If the vernacular music industry has disempowered some through its representations, it has also generated interest in local cultural practices and created financial opportunities for hundreds of artists. In spite of the discursive opposition between "popular" and "folk" practices, the fluid refashioning of commercial recordings and festival dance-songs has demonstrated an adaptability of cultural practice that defies reified categories.

Works Cited

Bharucha, Rustom. 2003. *Rajasthan, an Oral History: Conversations with Komal Kothari*. London: Penguin.

Blackburn, Stuart H., and A. K. Ramanujan, eds. 1986. *Another Harmony: New Essays on the Folklore of India*. Berkeley: University of California Press.

Chalmers, Rhoderick. 2004. "When Folk Culture Meets Print Culture: Some Thoughts on the Commercialisation, Transformation and Propagation of Traditional Genres in Nepali." *Contributions to Nepalese Studies* 31(2): 243–256.

Chandola, Anoop. 1977. *Folk Drumming in the Himalayas: A Linguistic Approach to Music*. New York: AMS Press.

Chauhan, Mehindra Singh. 2005. *Meenu Ai* (video compact disc). Devika Cassettes, Dehradun.

Fiol, Stefan. 2013. "Making Music Regional in a Delhi Studio." In *More than Bollywood: Studies in Indian Popular Music*, edited by Gregory D. Booth and Bradley Shope, 179–197. New York: Oxford University Press.

Fiol, Stefan. 2017. *Recasting Folk in the Himalayas: Indian Music, Media and Social Mobility*. Urbana: University of Illinois Press.

Turino, Thomas. 2000. *Nationalists, Cosmopolitans, and Popular Music in Zimbabwe*. Chicago: University of Chicago Press.

22
The Female Voice in Hindi Cinema
Agency, Representation, and Change

Natalie Sarrazin

Indian cinema is deeply connected to India's identity, with cinematic themes and narratives influencing and reflecting cultural behaviors and expectations. After its independence in 1947, India entered a nation-building phase, during which films placed the nation, society, and family (including romance and marriage) at the center of its narratives. Indian constructions of femininity were based on conservative beliefs tempered in Gandhian and Nehruvian visions of a New India. The ideal heroine upheld Indian traditions and was virtuous, self-sacrificing, and pious. This character was imbued with social significance as a potential mother figure and goddess, but whose behavior was controlled through marriage (Babb 1970, 138). She was modeled after Sati-Savitri—a loyal and steadfast wife from the Hindu epic the Mahabharata, who uses the power of her devotion to cleverly rescue her husband from Yama, the god of death.

The majority of India's films are musicals, containing six to eight songs known as picturizations: the film sequence displayed with a song. Film songs are the most popular music in India and dominate the charts via radio, television, and now on streaming platforms. Actors, however, don't sing. Instead, *playback singers* record songs which are then lip-synced on-screen by actors. Only "good" and moral people such as heroes and heroines (and their families) are allowed to sing. Love songs, religious, festival, and celebratory songs are featured, while villains are denied access to musical voice and do not sing.

Female playback singers and songs have varied significantly over the past ninety years. In early pre-Partition years of film (1930s–1940s), for example, playback singers were classically trained or folk singers, and songs had a low *tessitura* (range of pitches in which most notes of a melody fall). Their voices were flexible in terms of ornamentation, warmer, reedy in timbre, with little vibrato and with a nasal vocal production. During the Nation-Building or Classic Bollywood era of the 1950s through 1980s, songs were composed in a higher *tessitura*. The female voice became light, airy, more nasal in production, as exemplified by Lata Mangeshkar (1929–2022), and devoid of excessive sexuality (groans or grunts), although they did include other types of vocalizations (e.g., glides, vocal fry,[1] glottal stops). Contemporary heroine voices in the Post-Liberalization era (1990–present) retained the music core of the Classic era "feminine" vocal production—light, airy, warm, and demure—but also included pop styles including global pop. Songs had a lower *tessitura*, while singers belted in low chest voice, and included sexualized groans, sighs, and grunts.

The voice, as Weidman notes, "is both a set of sonic, material, and literary practices shaped by culturally and historically specific moments and a category invoked in discourse about personal agency, communication and representation, and political power" (2014, 37). The changing female voice tells us two things about India and its perspective on acceptable behavior and cinematic roles: (1) the female voice is highly constructed and representative of the vision and goals of the nation during the Pre-Partition, Nation-Building, and Post-Liberalization eras discussed in this chapter; and (2) female voices in film, for the most part, retained the timbres associated with femininity forged during the Classic, Nation-Building era even as it entered a contemporary "global" one.

In this chapter, I discuss the female playback singer's voice and its relationship to the heroine's on-screen representation. What is the role of music and the voice in representing women's identity and agency? How have song picturizations advanced or limited women's characterizations? Examples from films from three eras of Indian cinema illustrate the negotiation of Indian female identity and femininity in voice and song. Analyses include song *tessituras*, vocal ranges, aesthetics and timbres (e.g., light, airy, reedy, lyrical), vocal production (e.g., nasal, chest, throaty), and stylistic elements such as use of classical ornamentation, pop effects (e.g., glottal stops, vocal fry), or technology (e.g., vocoding, autotune). This analysis will help readers understand India's national ideals and global aspirations as expressed through the female voice.

---

[1] Vocal fry is a deep, creaky sound produced by slow fluttering of the vocal cords.

The Female Voice in Early, Pre-Partition Indian Cinema (1930s–1940s)

Songs in Indian films date back to *Alam Ara* (1931), India's first "talkie." Early female playback pioneers in the 1930s and 1940s include singers such as Rajkumari Dubey, Shamshad Begum, Zohrabai Ambalewali, and Amirbai Karnataki. These women were born in pre-Partition (pre-1947) India under British rule and most were trained in Indian classical or semi-classical singing, or had a folk music background. Despite this training, their sound was relaxed and natural, comfortable in lower ranges (alto, mezzo-soprano) that are accessible for most women. Their voices exhibited a range of production styles (nasal, reedy, chesty), a high degree of flexibility, and some ornamentation.

Two of film's early playback singers, Zohrabai Ambalewali (1918–1990) and Shamshad Begum (1919–2013), were Muslim. Born in British Indian Punjab in present-day Haryana, Zohrabai Ambalewali (1918–1990) was classically trained in the Agra *gharana* (style, lineage) and greatly influenced early cinema's female soundprint. In the film *Rattan* (1944), Zohrabai sang for the character Gauri, a sixteen-year-old girl tragically married off to a fifty-five-year old man and forced to leave her true love and childhood friend, Govind. The song "Rumjhum Barse Badarwa" ("The Clouds Are Drizzling"), for example, is low *tessitura* (ranging from $D\flat_3$ to $G\flat_4$), and Zohrabai's tone is unmistakable as a low contralto with rich overtones (▶ Video example 22.1). Zohrabai has a tight vibrato and thick upper-register sound produced through a relaxed open-throat and focused nasal sound. Her deep and rich voice conveys a seriousness to the on-screen character.

Shamshad Begum's background is in folk music and is also relaxed in timbre and low in range. Begum's voice lent itself to then fourteen-year-old actress Nargis Dutt in *Taqdeer* (1943) ("Destiny, Fate") who played Shyama, a lost child. In the song "O Jaanewale Aaja" ("Oh, You Who Are Going, Come," with a B_3 to D_4 range), Begum alters her voice to represent the lighter, younger sound of the teenage character by utilizing a thin, clear timbre, little vibrato, and a bit of playful vocal fry on the onset of the word *aaja* (*ājā*, "come") (▶ Video example 22.2). Nargis, one of the most famous actresses of her day, sits at the piano acting through expressive facial movements (e.g., she rolls her head and eyes back on the phrase *mere mast javānī*, "my intoxicated youth," and exaggerates the breath on "aahs" of *aaja* (see Box 22.1).

> **Box 22.1 Exercise 1**
>
> Describe the playback singers' voices and actresses' movements in "Rumjhum Barse Badarwa" (▶ Video example 22.1) and "O Jaanewale Aaja" (▶ Video example 22.2) in your own words. What does an ideal woman sound like and look like? How does she behave?

These Pre-Partition era female playback singers sang for female characters that performed acceptable, relatively submissive roles, such as unmarried village girls and children, or as traditional folk/theatrical performers. Their actions and behaviors, particularly in relation to the hero, range from highly reserved to only slightly flirtatious. Their voices—equally reserved, and grounded in folk, semi-classical, and classical music—used low alto ranges and were rich, light, and often unadorned, warm, and flexible, but with distinct timbres (e.g., reedy, nasal).

This female vocal timbre and its accompanying femininity, which was emblematic of this era, significantly changed over the next few years. India's new nation required a new sound and a new femininity to go with it—a sound embodied in playback singer Lata Mangeshkar and her sister, whose timbre would take India to the edge of the millennium.

Nation-Building in the Classic Era

Independence and the partition of East and West Pakistan in 1947 were both devastating and promising for the new Indian nation distancing itself from the British Raj. Prime Minister Nehru's vision modernized business sectors but socially remained rooted in traditional and conservative ideals, especially for women. Men dominated and actively operated in public spaces, while women were invisible or contested and remained relegated to private, household spheres of activity. Women assumed risk when they became "conspicuously visible" in public spaces (Rajan 2001, 11). "Home" became a spiritual space, influenced by Gandhi's ideals, and became the focal point for women's issues in the postcolonial nation (Chatterjee 1993, 133). Home and family were the cultural and social heart of the new middle-class women and were central themes in film.

Partition also directly impacted the film music industry, in that many Muslim playback singers moved to Pakistan. Ready to fill the void were Lata Mangeshkar and her sister, Asha Bhosle, who became the voices of the Classic era of Bollywood (late 1940s to 1980s). Lata's voice, in particular, became synonymous with India's new vision and nation-building efforts.

Lata Mangeshkar and Asha Bhosle

Lata and Asha's voices dominated the next four decades of Indian cinema, eclipsing other timbres and standardizing the sound of purity, modesty, and Indian femininity. Other female vocalists had to conform to and imitate their sound in order to succeed in the business. Lata's soundprint is unique and unmistakable: light and sweet, with an adolescent-girl falsetto, a tight vibrato, and bright, nasal overtones. Above all, her voice was "de-sexualized" and perceived as pure. As such, she sang mostly for heroines, while Asha's more sensually perceived voice accompanies heroines, cabaret dancers, and vamps.[2] Lata's voice differed in timbre and style from pre-Partition singers. Ethnomusicologist Peter Manuel notes that her distinct vocal style is not found in earlier North Indian genres (1993, 53). In addition, her high soprano range shifted film song *tessitura significantly* higher. She easily reached high pitches such as F_5 with lowest pitches hovering around G_4, a pitch that was routinely found in the middle to upper ranges in pre-Partition songs.

The differences between the early singers such as Shamshad Begum and Lata Mangeshkar can be heard in the song "Teri Mehfil Mein," from *Mughal-e-Azam*, one of India's most beloved and iconic films (▶ Video example 22.3, Box 22.2).

Mother India is one of India's most powerful and iconic films of the new nation and cemented women's roles as representative of the motherland. Radha, the heroine, is a married mother of three boys who is strong, willful, and long-suffering as she fights for her family's survival after her husband deserts her. The character upholds tradition and nation, defining femininity, motherhood, and acceptable spheres of power and agency for women of that era and beyond. Rosie Thomas, anthropologist and South Asian film scholar, notes that women can tap into the power of the goddess, but only when saving her husband/family from calamity (a Sati-Savitri)—even at risk of her

---

[2] The vamp played an increasingly significant role in the 1960s and 1970s.

> **Box 22.2 Exercise 2:** *Mughal-e-Azam* (1960)
>
> Mughal-e-Azam ("The Great Mughal") is a love story set in the sixteenth century during the reign of Emperor Akbar. Bahar Begum, a tawa'if (ṭawā'if, courtesan), is in love with Prince Salim, Akbar's son. Salim, however, has fallen in love with Anarkali (also a tawa'if) and has a secret relationship with her. Jealous, Bahar exposes the forbidden relationship between Anarkali and Salim, who amasses an army against his father for the right to marry her. Salim loses and is sentenced to death. Anarkali, however, sacrifices herself in his place. The duet "Teri Mehfil Mein" ("In Your Gathering") is sung by Anarkali and Bahar Begum, the two females in the love triangle, as they debate the nature of love.
>
> Listen to "Teri Mehfil Mein" (▶ Video example 22.3). Bahar Begum (sung by Shamshad Begum) is the first singer pictured and Anarkali (sung by Lata Mangeshkar) is the second.
>
> (1) Compare vocal timbres, gestures, and actions. What are the similarities? Differences?
> (2) Discuss how their vocal timbres, gestures and actions represent ideals of feminine behavior. Which of the women do you believe is "good?" Which is "bad?" How do their voices and movements encourage your conclusions?

own life (1995). Radha in *Mother India* is just such an archetypal mother-in-jeopardy, who goes to great lengths to save her family (Box 22.3).

Another iconic example of a Sati-Savitri or devoted wife who saves her husband occurs in the film *Sholay* ("Embers"). Basanti, played by Hema Malini, uses her dancing talent to save her would-be husband from death (Box 22.4).

1970s Changes

The heroine's image changed slightly during the political and cultural disillusionment of the 1970s. Women worked outside of the house, had some agency, wore non-traditional clothing, and were marginally in control of

> **Box 22.3   Exercise 3: *Mother India* (1957)**
>
> *Mother India is a landmark film telling the story of a poor devoted mother and wife named Radha, who fights for her family against twists of fate (poverty, abandonment by her husband, sexual predators) and perseveres. At the end of the film, she makes the ultimate sacrifice and kills her son, who is a wanted bandit—an action that upholds the laws of the nation over family ties. In the song "Duniya Mein Hum Aaye Hain" ("We Have to Live as We Have Come in This World,"* ▶ *Video example 22.4), Nargis plays the role of Radha (sung by Lata Mangeshkar) shown with her two sons (sung by Usha Mangeshkar and Meena Mangeshkar) as they perform hard agricultural labor, emphasized through dramatic cinematography.*
>
> (1) Describe Lata's vocal timbre and sound. Describe the character Radha's activities, her clothes, and facial appearance, and especially the camera angles used to frame her. How does she represent the idea of a sacrificing and suffering wife/mother? How does the voice convey ideal femininity? Is the voice consistent with Radha's activities and visual representation?
>
> (2) Compare the voices of Usha and Meena, who are singing for the children, with that of Lata. Which voice(s) seems higher? Lighter? Which is more reedy/focused? Which seems lower in range? What do these ranges say about the characters?

their own sexuality and destiny. An excellent example occurs in the film *Hare Rama, Hare Krishna* (1971, Box 22.5). Asha sang for actress Zenat Aman, known for her sex appeal, who plays Jasbir, a young woman in danger of becoming a degenerate hippie. Lata, in contrast, sang for Mumtaz, who plays Shanti, an innocent shop girl. (Lata also provides the playback voices for children in the film.)

Contemporary Heroines and Voices: 1990s through the 2010s

In 1990, India ushered in neo-liberal economic policies that opened the country to foreign investments and ideas. The film industry, however,

Box 22.4 Exercise 4: *Sholay* (1975)

Sholay is a spaghetti-Western-inspired film. Basanti, one of the female leads, is portrayed as a lively and slightly annoying chatterbox with a vivid personality who relies on her work driving a rickshaw—a traditionally male occupation—to survive, thus giving her character some agency. Basanti falls in love with Veeru (played by actor Dharmendra) and saves his life by dancing in the scorching heat and barefoot on broken glass during the song "Jab Tak Hai Jaan" ("Until There Is Life") to prevent her future husband from being killed by villains.

(1) Watch the video of "Jab Tak Hai Jaan" sung by Lata Mangeshkar (⏵ Video example 22.5). How is Basanti displaying true devotion to her would-be husband? What agency does she have?
(2) Compare Lata's voice with Basanti's dance. Is her voice consistent or inconsistent with Basanti's movements?

Box 22.5 Exercise 5: *Hare Rama, Hare Krishna* (1971)

Compare "Dum Maro Dum" ("Keep Puffing," ⏵ Video example 22.6), sung by Asha Bhosle, with the folk-inspired "Ghungroo Ka Bole" ("What Ankle Bells Speak," ⏵ Video example 22.7), sung by Lata Mangeshkar.

(1) Describe the timbre of their voices and the accompaniment (e.g., distorted electric guitar vs. folk instruments) and compare how the two women are picturized in terms of on-screen behavior.
(2) Next, compare the reaction of Prashant (Jasbir's brother) to the two women in each of the songs. How do his responses reinforce "proper" behavior?

continued to emphasize tradition through family-oriented films that often contrasted positive Indian values with negative Western behaviors. Female characters were given a few modern markers, which sold them as "progressive," such as wearing Western clothing or having jobs, but their agency remained stagnant in neo-traditional tropes. Similar to the 1970s, energetic, quirky female leads amused the hero, substituting personality for true agency while her ambitions were undermined by a narrative ending in marriage. Women's jobs were not depicted, nor did they impact the narrative to any great extent. As with most films in the West, in Bollywood, female heroines rarely existed without a romantic relationship in contrast to their male counterparts who did not require a love interest.[3]

The heroine's love songs were confined to the romantic courtship, but soundtracks also emphasized folk-inspired numbers featuring strong female singers (Sarrazin 2008). In the 1997 film *Raja Hindustani* ("Raja, the Indian"), for example, playback singer Alka Yagnik sings both for heroine Karishma Kapoor as well as for a folk singer. In a "folk-type" number "Pardesi Jana Nahin" ("Foreigner Please Don't Leave"), Raja, the hero, sings with two female folk singers (playback singers Alka Yagnik and Sapna Awasti). Yagnik, the first folk singer, is an innocent girl with demure gestures and movements. Her voice is high, light, and Lata-like in timbre. Awasti, the second folk singer/dancer, however, is depicted as a tough, vulgar woman who is heavily tattooed and drinks alcohol while singing. Her vocal timbre is rough, chesty, unfocused, out of tune, and she belts to the point of yelling—a dramatic (and problematic) misrepresentation of folk music culture.

Global Sounds and Feminist Awareness

Film in the 2000s and 2010s contained further musical expansion. For the first time, female folk singers, submissive heroines, and global pop vamps could coexist in the same film. Films depicted some degree of female agency, relaxed sexual mores, and independence through dress (choice of Western or Indian clothing), employment (although jobs rather than full-fledged careers), and mobility (access to scooters or cars). Musically, Lata and Asha's vocal dominance had waned, creating openings for new playback singers. While many singers continued in Lata-esque vocal purity (e.g., Alka Yagnik, Kavita Krishnamurthy), singers such as Shreya Ghoshal and Ila Arun revived the deeper, folk-like timbre, while Alisha Chinai and Sunidhi Chauhan ushered in a newer pop sound.

---

[3] Indian cinema is not the only cinema with this issue. Note the results of the Bechdel-Wallace test, which measures women's representation in fiction, when applied to Hollywood films.

Hindi film still fell short in terms of including female-driven narratives and female characters. In a 2019 interview, playback singer Shreya Ghoshal opines: "Tell me how many films are happening where the lead is female. Where the story is about her? She is probably a part of the supporting cast. Maybe the times will change but we definitely need female-driven narratives so that there is a female voice also" (Sharma 2019). Gupta notes that even in the 1990s, female characters were traditional and reductive and required a re-examination of female sexual representation, audience assumptions, purity and fate and, of course, song picturizations (2015, 107–108). Instead of any conscious, progressive treatment of the heroine, however, the most significant change in film was that she now performed the sexualized "item number" as well as the love songs.[4] This was met with severe criticism. Chowdhury notes, "The nineties inaugurates the New Women, who in these new films is not only seen in western outfits formerly reserved for vamps, but who also throws herself at the scopophilic gaze even as she openly celebrates her own body with jouissance, without surrendering her claim to the special status as the heroine" (2010, 55). Substituting the docile, submissive heroine with a "bold, uninhibited, skimpily clad, and promiscuous" heroine, however, "does not lead to the empowerment of the women character, but only reduces her to a prop to satisfy the male audience" (Tere 2012, 6–7).

A handful of female-centered narratives have appeared since 2011: *No One Killed Jessica* (2011), *Cheeni Kum* (2007), *Dirty Picture* (2011), *PK* (2014), and *Queen* (2014), while films such as *United 6* (2011) or *Gulaab Gang* (2014) have no male lead at all. Two significant films with female leads as entertainers are *Anaarkali of Arrah* (2017) and *Secret Superstar* (2017). *Secret Superstar* is about an aspiring teenaged Muslim pop singer named Insia, who uses her *niqab* (face-covering) to hide her identity from her strict and abusive father in her YouTube posts. Singing for the character Insia, playback vocalist Meghna Mishra's pop style and techniques are unmistakable. In the "audition" song "Nachdi Phira" ("I Dance Wild and Free," ⏵ Video example 22.8), she uses her chest voice and "belts" as she pushes her voice beyond normal limits, adding glides, vocal fry, strong attacks, and glottal stops (an abrupt stop then release of air by the voice

---

[4] See, for example, Katrina Kaif perform "Sheila Ki Jawani" ("Prime Youth of Sheila") in *Tees Maar Khan* (2010).

as when saying "uh-oh," e.g. in Miley Cyrus's "Wrecking Ball"). The song's wide, two-octave range (G_3 to G_5) contains a distinct vocal break between her chest and head voice (*falsetto*). Likewise, her gestures are familiar in pop as she emphasizes high notes and indicates "feeling" through closed eyes, furrowed brows, and head tilted back while her hands gesticulate the onset of the refrain for emphasis (Box 22.6).

This cursory look at contemporary films indicates slight changes in terms of women's representation (see Box 22.7). On one hand, a few films place women at the center of the narrative, depicting an increased independence and agency. Many heroines have jobs, even though their jobs are not woven into the narrative as deeply as those of heroes, and their desires are occasionally projected as serious and worthy of exploration. However, female desire, agency, and independence remained defined by social, cultural, and family strictures, which were obstacles to self-determination (e.g., careers, pursuits, and life partners). Fathers, in particular, still wield a great deal of power over their daughters, even if the heroine does get the man she desires in the end. Women's singing voices, likewise, carry the same mixed messages. Voices are more aggressive, utilizing global pop vocalizations, techniques, and timbres. Song *tessituras* are in lower vocal ranges and are more natural-sounding in production. Vestiges of Lata's and Asha's timbre remain, a carry-over of the traditional feminine voice of earlier decades, even as the heroine takes on more sensual roles such as the cabaret dancer or vamp—roles that are re-defining the definition of femininity from previous decades.

Box 22.6 Exercise 6: *Secret Superstar* (2017)

Listen to the song "Nachdi Phira" ("I Dance Wild and Free," ▶ Video example 22.8) from *Secret Superstar*. How does Meghna Mishra's voice and behavior differ from earlier playback songs? Find the song's lyrics online. What do the lyrics reflect about the singer's desires? Her sense of agency?

Box 22.7 Culminating Exercise: Analytical Model, the Female Voice in Hindi Film Song

As we have seen, playback singers' voice qualities plus on-screen behaviors delineate the ideals of femininity, agency, and representation. The exercise below analyzes the heroine's voice (range, vocal production, and style) across several time periods and deconstructs the female's narrative context, gendered on-screen representation (movements, dress, gestures) in relation to "femininity," and changing Indian ideals as outlined in this chapter.

(1) Select three Indian film songs by female protagonists, one from each of the three different eras (Pre-Partition era [1930s–1940s], Classic or Nation-Building era [1940s–1980s], and Post-Liberalization era [1990s–present]). Answer the following questions about each song to the best of your ability.

  (A) Background: Compile information relevant to each song, including the movie's title, music director, date, the era to which it belongs, the song's lyrics and translation, the playback singer's name, on-screen actress's name, and context of the song in the narrative (e.g., is it a heroine's love song, vamp's dance song).

  (B) Vocal Description:

   (i) Timbre. Describe the vocal timbre using adjectives and metaphors (e.g., rich, smooth like chocolate, rough like sandpaper, etc.) and indicate the vocal quality (nasal, reedy, throaty, chest, and head).

   (ii) Song range and vocal type. If possible, find the pitch range of the song (e.g., C_4 is middle "C"). Is it in a lower range, middle, or high? Based on this range and vocal quality, try to identify the vocal type: contralto (with a typical range of F_3–D_5), alto (G_3–E_5), mezzo-soprano (A_3–F_5), or soprano (C_4–A_5). Describe what seems to be the most comfortable range for the singer (*tessitura*). Are these notes in the lower range? Higher?

      (iii) Breathiness. How breathy is the voice (on a scale of 1 to 10, 1 being highly focused and not breathy, 10 being the least concentrated and most breathy)? While "breathiness" is not a cultural indicator per se, it may indicate, discreetly, the heroine's level of interest in the hero.

      (iv) Ornamentation. To what extent does the vocalist utilize ornamentation (on a scale of 1 to 10: 1 being no ornamentation, 10 being highly ornamented)? Simple ornaments (e.g., trills) may indicate a folk song or imitation of a child's voice. More ornamentation (including long runs) may reference classical Indian styles of singing.

  (C) Lyrics. What is the subject (e.g., love, separation, celebration)? Whose voice (point of view) is expressed? What emotions are expressed?

(2) Analyze: Use the evidence you discovered above about the voice to reveal aspects of the character. Does the voice match her actions and personality (e.g., demure, shy, aggressive, passive)? Is she highly sexualized? Does she have agency? How is this demonstrated in the voice? What conclusions can you draw about how this type of voice portrays Indian women on-screen more generally?

(3) Extrapolate: Compare your analysis of all three songs. What can you hypothesize regarding how Hindi films have changed in terms of their vocal and visual representation of female characters?

Works Cited

Babb, Lawrence. 1970. "Marriage and Malevolence: The Uses of Sexual Opposition in a Hindu Pantheon." *Ethnology* 9(2): 137–148.

Chatterjee, Partha. 1993. *The Nation and Its Fragments: Colonial and Postcolonial Histories*. Princeton, NJ: Princeton University Press.

Chowdhury, Purna. 2010. "Bollywood Babes: Body and Female Desire in the Bombay Films since the Nineties and *Darr, Mohra,* and *Aitraaz,* a Tropical Discourse." In *Bollywood and Globalization: Indian Popular Cinema, Nation, and Diaspora*, edited by Rini Bhattacharya Mehta and Rand Rajeshwari V. Pandharipande, 51–74. London: Anthem Press.

Gupta, Sukanya. 2015. "*Kahaani, Gulaab Gang,* and *Queen*: Remaking the Queens of Bollywood." *South Asian Popular Culture* 13(2): 107–123.

Manuel, Peter 1993. *Cassette Culture: Popular Music and Technology in Northern India*. Chicago: University of Chicago Press.

Rajan, Rajeswari Sunder, ed. 2001. *Signposts: Gender Issues in Post-independence India.* New Brunswick, NJ: Rutgers University Press.

Sarrazin, Natalie. 2008. "Celluloid Love Songs: Musical 'Modus Operandi' and the Dramatic Aesthetics of Romantic Hindi Film." *Popular Music* 27(3): 393–411.

Sharma, Priyanka. 2019. "Studio for Me Is a Temple: Shreya Ghoshal." *Indian Express*, April 20. Accessed September 15, 2020. https://indianexpress.com/article/entertainment/music/studio-for-me-is-a-temple-shreya-ghoshal-5686109/.

Tere, Nidhi Shendurnikar. 2012. "Gender Reflections in Mainstream Hindi Cinema." *Global Media Journal–Indian Edition* 3(1): 1–11.

Thomas, Rosie. 1995. "Melodrama and the Negotiation of Morality in Hindi Cinema." In *Consuming Modernity: Public Culture in a South Asian World*, edited by Carol A. Breckenridge, 157–182. Minneapolis: University of Minneapolis Press.

Weidman, Amanda. 2014. "Anthropology and Voice." *Annual Review of Anthropology* 43: 37–51.

23
Love, Politics, and Life between Village and City in Nepali *Lok Dohori*
One Album, Three Titles
Anna Marie Stirr

Gāūmai choḍe gharakī sakkalī
Śahar tira bheṭiyo nakkalī

I left my "true one" at home in the village
In the city, I've met a "false one"

This couplet opens Nepali singer Badri Pangeni's 2006 song "Do You Love Me or Not?," a duet in the genre *lok dohori* (*lok dohorī*, lit. "folk duet"). Portraying a flirtation between a married man from a rural village who has come to the city, and a young, urban woman he's met there, this song explicitly and implicitly addresses ideas of what is "true" and "false" (or "real" and "fake") in Nepal today. Musically combining aspects of rural and urban through variations in instrumentation and rhythmic patterns, the song sets the stage for another combination—love and politics—in an album that embodies some of Nepal's recent social and political upheavals.

Badri's album was the first mainstream *lok dohori* album to overtly address party politics; there have been few such albums since. Released right after the end of Nepal's civil war between Maoists and state security forces, it embodies the uncertainty of this political moment. It has had three titles, each increasingly political. Its original title, *Do You Love Me or Not?* ("*Mero Māyā Lāgcha Lāgdaina*, 2006), was taken from a song that took up one side of the cassette. The next run of cassettes highlighted songs on the other side and was released as *Sisters, Wear Vermilion* (*Lāu Celī Sindūr*, 2007), the title of a song promoting widows' remarriage. The following run, released as *People's Rule* (*Janatako Śāsan*, 2007), was more political, using the title of a song that called for democracy and an end to the monarchy. This was a controversial move for any commercial recording in 2006, and even more so for an album in a genre long seen as existing apart from politics. The magazine *Music Diary* satirized Badri and the album, refusing to take the political songs seriously and calling the three titles a ploy to make it look as though he'd released more albums "simply by folding over the flap inside the cassette cover" (2007, 38). But Badri emphasized his wish to make more political statements: "For commercial reasons I have to record a lot of love songs, and I like them, but for a long time I've wanted to sing more progressive songs ... whether we like it or not, everything in our life is connected to politics" (Interview with the author, June 26, 2012).[1] By highlighting disparities between rural and urban life, and mixing love songs with political songs in a rural musical idiom, this album demonstrates how the personal is political in Nepali migrant life.

This album makes a powerful statement about how some Nepali migrants engage with sociopolitical change. They bring rural culture, lifeways, and values into urban areas, while simultaneously participating in a fast-changing political economy that has led them to migrate. In the mid-2000s, economic changes and a ten-year civil war (1996–2006) brought far-flung rural villagers together in movements for a new state structure, the end of a 250-year-old monarchy, and rights for oppressed genders, castes, ethnicities, and linguistic and regional groups. Badri Pangeni's album provides a valuable entry point into the intimate politics of such changes, in the 2006–2007 moment directly after Nepal's civil war.

Lok Dohori and Migration

Lok dohori is a commercial genre category including *dohori* duets (traditionally improvised but composed for studio recordings) and solo folk (*lok*) songs (traditionally unimprovised). *Lok dohori* singers mostly come from the rural areas that are home to the commercially dominant *lok* and *dohori* song styles. *Lok dohori* musicians and fans are part of a migrant working class

---

[1] All research was conducted entirely in Nepali; all translations are the author's.

that remains connected to their rural homes while traveling far and wide for work (Stirr 2017).

Songs marketed as *lok dohori* come mainly from Nepal's central and western hills. Since the mid-twentieth century, they have been promoted by the state and the music industry as symbolizing Nepali national identity (Stirr 2017). Their *tals* (*tāl*s, rhythmic cycles), song structures, melodies, and lyrics all ground *lok dohori*'s version of national identity in rural hill life. Studio recordings and music videos, however, combine prominent sonic and visual symbols of Nepali rurality with foreign and electronic instruments, choreography, and costuming inspired by Hindi films, global pop, and global urban landscapes.

Nepali migrants have experienced such juxtapositions of sensory lifeworlds throughout centuries of mobile livelihoods. Migration's place within social structures, and associated feelings, are described in the thematic genre called *viraha*: songs about love and the pain of separation. While *viraha* songs vary widely in musical form, their lyrical themes paint similar pictures of migrating men and waiting women (Orsini 2006). Songs associate village homes with the feminine, and cities and the wider world with the masculine, expressing love and longing along these gendered lines. The emotional narratives in *viraha* songs situate "what is true" in the village, at home with family; this sense of genuineness is communicated in the sounds of rural folk music and the poetic rhythms and themes of their lyrics. Cities and foreign lands challenge those truths.

Today, these gendered perspectives on love, longing, home, and away are one set of narratives in *lok dohori*. They underlie songs of "remembering the village" and inform songs about new, cosmopolitan possibilities. Badri Pangeni's "Do You Love Me or Not?" combines both. The song's narrator is involved with two women, each representing a different world.

"Do You Love Me or Not?"

At the beginning of the music video for "Do You Love Me or Not?" a young man bids his wife goodbye as he leaves his village (⊙ Video example 23.1).[2] His traditionally dressed wife stands on the porch of the wood-and-adobe house, looking wistfully after him. She wears a modest low ponytail, the part

---

[2] The actors in this video are not the singers on the recording (see Sarrazin*).

of her hair red with vermilion powder indicating that she is married. Her red bangles and many-stranded necklace of tiny red glass beads further indicate her auspicious married status. She is the stock character wife in migration songs: young, beautiful, "traditional," and left behind. On the lyrics "I left my true one at home in the village," the camera cuts back to her, establishing the connection between this image of a woman, and what is "true" (cue points 0:35, 0:40, 0:45).

The song's lyrics continue: "In the city, I met a 'false' one." I've translated *nakkali* (*nakkalī*) as "false" to capture its opposition with *sakkali* (*sakkalī*) as "true," but this is only part of what *nakkali* means. A *nakkali* person is also someone obsessed with looks and fashion. The connotations of "false" and "beauty-obsessed" are both present in these lyrics, and in the video's urban woman. When she first appears on-screen, she walks past the man; he notices her and catches her hand (cue point 0:20). Unlike the man's wife, this "*nakkali*" woman is not sitting and waiting for him; she is going about her life, and he is in her world. This world is symbolized by her modern urban fashion: her short red plaid skirt, tall white boots, red cap, and white shirt with a thin ribbon tied in a bow around the front. Her hair is long and loose rather than tied back in the village style that symbolizes modesty. Her contrast to the hero's wife is clear, emphasizing the second meaning of *nakkali*, falsity, that returns in the refrain (▶ Video example 23.1, cue point 0:55):

> *Eh khyal gara hai māyālu, ekohoro rotī pākdaina.*
> Hey, sweetheart, let's play; bread won't bake on just one side.

This refrain frames their love as "play," just a flirtation in contrast to the true, marital love that waits for Badri's character back in his village. Ten years later, when this video was posted on YouTube, a commenter followed this dominant moral narrative, indicating his preference for the village wife: "we guys don't like ... such girls we appreciate ... cultural wife not show pieces" (2017). Regardless of dominant morality, *dohori* songs often revel in the play of love affairs with little concern for their outcome. The lyrics "bread won't bake on just one side" refer to flat *roti* breads which must be cooked, like pancakes, on both sides. The refrain is saying that it takes both partners' involvement for the affair to be any fun. Similarly, the musical arrangement incorporates elements associated with both rural and urban life, and their juxtaposition sparks listeners' interest.

Rhythmic Associations

Popular folksongs in Nepal rely on scales, melodies, and lyrical patterns drawn from various rural areas. In the translation to the urban studio, more instruments are added. These instruments have rural and urban associations. Rural-associated instruments include the *bansuri* flute, the bowed *sarangi*, and the *madal* (*mādal*) and *dholak* drums. Urban-associated instruments include the keyboard synthesizer and digital drum pad, guitar, saxophone, and other South Asian instruments like the *santur* (a zither) and *tabla*. In *lok dohori*, the *madal*, *dholak*, and multiple drum pad sounds often feature prominently together, combining rural and urban associations. Along with this, the *tal*s and their rhythmic patterns carry specific associations with place.

"Do You Love Me or Not," is in a rhythmic cycle called *khyali tal* (*khyālī tāl*, see Table 23.1, in the final section of this chapter). One cycle in *khyali tal* has four beats. Cycles are arranged into longer phrases whose length depends on song genre, form, poetic meter, and lyrics. Nepali folk *tal*s are closely associated with rural hill life. The two most prominent *tal*s in Nepali folk music are the four-beat *khyali tal* and six-beat *jhyaure* (*jhyāure*) *tal* (Shah 2007), both of which appear on this album. Their associations affect how listeners interpret the songs.

"Do You Love Me or Not" is in *khyali tal*. As musicologist Subi Shah notes, *khyali* is a flexible *tal*, in which a greater variety of musical genres are played (Shah 2007). *Jhyaure*, on the other hand, is probably the most rural associated of all Nepali folk *tal*s (see Table 23.3). "*Jhyaure*" is even used in Kathmandu as an epithet for "country bumpkin" (Greene and Rajkarnikar 2005). *Khyali tal* has no such derogatory associations, and some urban musicians see it as rather classy (Maharjan and Moore 2010, 52). *Khyali tal* bridges rural and urban musical styles. "Do You Love Me or Not" highlights rural hill-area rhythmic patterns in this *tal*, musically reinforcing the lyrics' theme of rural-urban migration.

Politics and Love between Village and City

Rural-urban migration and sociopolitical changes have brought articulations between rural and urban musical styles, and between song themes that had long been kept apart. "Do You Love Me or Not" is of a typical *dohori* length of around thirty minutes, taking up an entire side of a cassette tape (the music video features only five minutes of the song as a teaser to drive cassette sales). The other side of the cassette, with four shorter songs, takes *lok dohori* across a rarely bridged divide in Nepal's popular music world: that between love songs and political songs. This side contains a social-message song, "Sisters, Wear Vermilion"; an overtly political song, "People's Rule"; and two love songs, "In the Morning When I Wake" ("Bihānai Uṭhī") and "One Mistake" ("Euṭā Galtī").

"Love songs" and "political songs" had been separated due to state censorship for almost the entire duration of Nepal's recording industry, which began with Radio Nepal in 1951. From the fall of the Rana oligarchy (1950) until the end of the autocratic Panchayat system (1960–1990), state media would not record songs about party politics, and songs that addressed social issues were closely monitored and censored (Grandin 2005). No one recording for the national radio or performing live at state-sponsored events was allowed to sing about social inequality. The state promoted love songs instead. Underground political parties recorded their "progressive songs" in India. When they tried to sing such songs in Nepal, they faced repression and imprisonment (Mottin 2018).

Within this environment, from the perspective of Nepal's political progressives, love songs came to stand for apolitical, meaningless entertainment. Progressive songs about serious social and political issues could not, therefore, involve love. State censorship ended in 1990, but the ideological division between the two types of songs remains. To release political songs in the mainstream *lok dohori* industry was rare enough; to combine them on one album with love songs is still rare. When Badri was writing these songs in 2006, he expressed some worries about the album—hence its three titles, from the apparently apolitical to the overtly political. Badri told me he led with the love song because he was "worried about sales" (Interview, June 26, 2012), but rumor had it that he was afraid to publicly advocate the monarchy's end. Badri denies this, citing his participation in street protests, facing police and army bullets, as proof of his bravery: "once you get caught up in revolution, you stop being concerned for yourself and family."

Whether Badri worried more about his investment or his safety is hard to tell, but the design of the album is aimed to mitigate potential political backlash against the song "People's Rule." "Do You Love Me or Not" (Side B) was initially marketed as the title song, its related graphics taking up the entire cassette cover. This song emphasizes rural-urban interactions in its lyrics and its music, focusing on flirtation. The social-message song "Sisters, Wear Vermilion," the title song of the album's second edition, comes first on the other side of the cassette (Side A), preparing listeners for a more political message. Then comes "People's Rule," and finally, two love songs that gave the audience more of what they might have expected from a *lok dohori* album. Thus "People's Rule" is nestled among more "acceptable" songs.

The two love songs concluding Side A are about the vicissitudes of life and love, without overt political messages. They do not have accompanying music videos and are set in highly recognizable *jhyaure* song forms. The first is in a medium tempo, associated with tragedy, the second in a fast tempo, associated with rural *jhyaure* dancing. In "One Mistake," a poor man laments marrying a rich woman who wants more luxuries than he can provide (⊙ Audio example 23.1). We can hear "One Mistake" as a cautionary tale for the male narrator in "Do You Love Me or Not," reminding him what might happen if he marries the urban, sophisticated object of his affections. This is the flip side of the uncertainties in the celebratory *dohori* song, and a reminder of what *sakkali*, "real" problems he might have after falling for *nakkali*, artificial promises of love. The last song, "In the Morning When I Wake," is a fast, danceable *jhyaure* song about love between a tax collector's daughter and a captain's son—relative equals in class terms (⊙ Audio example 23.2). Set in a hill village, it celebrates young love and rural life.

In a more political vein, "Sisters, Wear Vermilion" takes on an issue of social reform (see ⊙ Video example 23.2). In *khyali tal*, the song is meant to appeal across regions, taking a stand in support of widows' remarriage. Here, women's rural or urban location makes no difference in terms of "truth" or "falsity"—the video shows all uniting, in different locales, to assert their right to love after loss. Directly addressing a social issue is unusual for a commercial folk song, although the topic of love helps listeners ease into the message of sociopolitical change. Badri calls on widowed women to embrace life and future loves for the sake of their own happiness. This contravenes an orthodox Hindu norm prohibiting widows' remarriage and is thus a political statement. This social-message song expresses the *viraha* theme of love and longing in the context of wartime loss, yet reframes the social underpinnings of its emotional pain, arguing that women can and should love again, with society's blessing. In the context of the album, this strategy can be heard as preparation for the next song, "People's Rule."

The overtly political "People's Rule," again in *khyali tal*, challenges the government-in-transition to uphold promises made during the 2006 People's

Movement that helped bring the civil war and the absolute monarchy to an end (▶ Video example 23.3). The urban-associated digital sound of the drum pad is prominent, in contrast to the other songs in which the *madal* can be clearly heard throughout. Two rhythmic patterns stand out: a simple, regionally unaffiliated *khyali tal* beat (pattern 1A; see below) and another pattern, common in both political and love songs, whose repeating eighth notes on beats 2 and 4 are reminiscent of reggae (pattern 1D). As reggae can be heard in many places in Nepal and carries associations with both love and revolution worldwide (Toynbee 2007), many Nepali listeners would associate this rhythmic pattern with reggae, making the song sound more cosmopolitan.

The music video (Video example 23.3) begins with sounds of bullets being fired and footage of police violence during the 2006 People's Movement. Throughout the video, Badri shows people engaging in undervalued labor and political protest and facing police brutality. Men and women dance together, waving Nepali flags, wearing clothing of various castes and ethnic groups to represent unity in diversity. The lyrics describe the struggles of the laboring classes and demand that the new regime pay attention to their needs. Badri says he was inspired to write the lyrics when he saw people beside the Trisuli river performing the arduous labor of manual sand mining: shoveling loads of sand by hand, straining it through a large screen to separate the finer sand from larger pebbles all day in the blazing sun (Interview with the author, June 26, 2012). These lyrics start the song (▶ Video example 23.3, cue point 0:53):

> *Trisulīko kināraimā bāluwā chalneharu*
> *Solumā bhārī bokī bāl bachchā pālneharu*
> *Ajhai ni niraṅkuś ḍhalyā chaina hai*
> *Janatako śāsan ta calyā chaina hai*

> Those who sift sand on the banks of the Trisuli
> Those who carry loads in Solu to raise their children
> Autocracy has still not fallen
> People's rule has not yet been established

Badri calls for republican democracy in a chorus modeled on a political rally chant, at a time when taking a political stand against the monarchy was uncommon in the mainstream media. He also calls for freedom for indentured laborers and repatriation for Bhutanese refugees—topics rarely addressed in the mainstream music industry. He uses leftist language, calling on the proletariat to fight the final conflict with those who live in mansions and ride in slick cars. Even more unusually, he calls out politicians by name (cue point 5:57):

> Mādhav Nepāl, Girijā, Pracaṅḍa, Bāburām,
> Biśram lina nakhoja, sakieko chaina kām

> Madhav Nepal, Girija, Prachanda, Baburam
> Don't try to rest now, the work is not finished.

Nepali political songs rarely address anyone by name, preferring indirect references or kinship terms. Thus, this was perhaps Badri's boldest step on this album. To Badri's surprise, it brought not controversy, but invitations from these politicians to perform at their events. Flattered, Badri remained unaffiliated, saying, "I don't sing for any political party, I sing for the Nepali people" (Interview with the author, June 26, 2012).

As the post–civil war tension eased, the three releases of Badri's 2006 album adopted increasingly political titles. One result of the considerable "buzz" surrounding the album was to break down the rigid boundaries between contexts for love songs and political songs. The political success of this move, though, depended also on listeners' interpretations. Some listeners heard no beauty or sincerity in Badri's songs, dismissing "People's Rule" with scorn: "those are just slogans, they're not music" (Narayan Gurung, interview with the author, March 25, 2007). More political critics derided Badri for being a "false" (*nakkali*) political singer, given his ongoing position in the music industry mainstream. Even so, many listeners appreciated this juxtaposition of love songs, political songs, and social-message songs, and this showed in the album's sales. Few *lok dohori* albums have more than one edition, yet this one had three.

In this time of uncertainty, increased mobility, and rapid sociopolitical change, Badri's album reflected some of the moment's anxieties and suggested new possibilities. Rural-urban migrants brought their music and cultural sensibilities into urban lifeworlds and recording studios. Likewise, while political songs and love songs had been kept separate for decades, this album showed that they could indeed come together, presenting a picture of life that was perhaps more complete, real, or true than the one-sided alternatives. For the rural dwellers and migrant laborers who heard themselves described in

Badri's songs, combining themes of love and politics may have implied a new era in which the ups and downs of their lives, loves, and travels were linked with political movements for change.

Exercises: Rhythmic Patterns on the *Madal*

The *madal* is a two-headed barrel drum with a large head and a small head, usually pitched an octave apart. It is customarily played lengthwise, held in one's lap by a strap that goes around the legs. One learns different rhythmic patterns through spoken patterns of sounds. The *bol*s, or drum mnemonics used for the sounds produced on the *madal*, are not standardized in Nepal. I use *bol*s taught to me by Khadka Budha Magar, *madal* teacher at the National Dance Theatre. As described below, several *bol*s can be used for the same drum stroke. Try speaking the *madal bol*s aloud.

Dhīn, Ghīn: A resonant, low-pitched sound produced by striking the edge of the large head with the middle three fingers, letting the fingers bounce away from the drumhead so the sound can resonate.

Kha, Phat, Khat: A flat, low-pitched sound produced by striking the middle of the large head with the middle three fingers and leaving the fingers on the drumhead to stop it from resonating.

Tāng, Ti: A resonant, high-pitched sound produced by striking the edge of the small head with the middle three fingers (alternatively, with the side of the index finger only), letting the fingers bounce away from the drumhead so the sound can resonate.

Tak, Na: A flat, high-pitched sound produced by striking the middle of the small head with the middle three fingers and leaving the fingers on the drumhead to stop it from resonating.

In the tables below, each grouping represents one beat, known in South Asian musical terminology as a *mātrā*. A dash (—) indicates a rest. Some basic rhythmic patterns are given below. There are myriad variations of these patterns, along with cadential patterns that indicate the end of a musical phrase. Clap on each beat and speak the *madal bol*s for the patterns below.

Khyali Tal

Some of the basic rhythmic patterns in *khyali tal* are represented in Table 23.1. Pattern A is the first *khyali* pattern most people learn. It is used to accompany songs when the lyrics and melody, rather than the rhythmic patterns, are the main focus, and it is widespread throughout Nepal's hill region. Patterns B and C are more associated with rural performance and the western hills. Pattern D is a reggae-like pattern, associated with no particular region.

Patterns A through D, among others, are all used in "Do You Love Me or Not." Pattern B, a favorite of the song's arranger, Juju Gurung, is especially prominent (see, e.g., ⓥ Video example 23.1, cue point 1:40–1:49, where this pattern occurs, but with the third drum stroke [Dhin] dropped). Syncopated cadential patterns popular in the western hills are used to introduce new musical phrases, like in the third rhythmic phrase of the musical introduction, in Video example 23.1, cue point 0:17–0:19 and reproduced in Table 23.2. In this notation, the double vertical lines indicate the end of a musical phrase. The single vertical lines indicate where the phrase should be subdivided. This phrase is subdivided into two groups of four and ends after the second group.

"People's Rule" uses pattern A of Table 23.1 a great deal (see ⓥ Video example 23.3, cue point 0:28–0:39), along with pattern D (cue point 0:40–0:52), which invokes reggae and its revolutionary associations to some listeners (see Box 23.1).

Table 23.1 Some basic *khyali tal* rhythmic patterns

	Beat (Matra):	1	2	3	4	
(A)	Madal Bols:	Dhin	Kha Ti	Na Kha	Dhi Na	||
(B)	Madal Bols:	Dhin	—Tang	(Dhin)	Tang	||
(C)	Madal Bols:	Dhin	Kha Ti	Na Kha	Tang	||
(D)	Madal Bols:	Khat	Tang Tang	Khat	Tang Tang	||

Table 23.2 Syncopated cadential pattern in "Do You Love Me or Not"

Beat (Matra):	1	2	3	4	|	1	2	3	4	||
Madal Bols:	Tang	-Tang	-Tang	-Tang	|	Dhin	Tang	Tang	—	||

> **Box 23.1 Exercise 1**
>
> Listen for these patterns in the *khyali tal* songs on the album to get an idea of how arranger Juju Gurung uses a variety of rhythms to bring rurality and urbanity to mind. Next, try to speak these patterns using the *bol*s when you hear the patterns played in each of these *khyali tal* songs. Do you begin to get a sense of how the songs juxtapose patterns to create a sense of both rurality and urbanity?

Table 23.3 *Jhyaure tal* rhythmic patterns

	Beat (Matra):	1	2	3	4	5	6	‖
(A)	Madal Bols:	Dhin	—	Tang	Tak	Dhin	Tang	‖
(B)	Madal Bols:	Dhin	—	Ta	Dhin	Tang	—	‖
(C)	Madal Bols:	Dhin	Tang	—	Khat	Tang	Dhin	‖

Jhyaure Tal

Jhyaure tal is strongly associated with rurality. Patterns A and B of Table 23.3 are common in fast *jhyaure* songs, as in "In the Morning When I Wake" (▶ Audio example 23.2). "One Mistake" also uses patterns A and B. It begins with B (▶ Audio example 23.1, cue point 0:35–0:40), followed by A (0:41–0:43). Pattern C is characteristic of the slowest of *jhyaure* songs and shows up for a few seconds at 2:13 in "One Mistake" (Box 23.2).

> **Box 23.2 Exercise 2**
>
> Listen for these patterns in the *jhyaure* songs "In the Morning When I Wake" and "One Mistake." Can you speak the appropriate *bol* patterns while listening to these songs? Taking the lyrics and music together, how might the choice of a *tal* that is strongly associated with rurality affect how listeners interpret the meanings of these songs?

Works Cited

Grandin, Ingemar. 2005. "Music under Development: Children's Songs, Artists, and the (Pancayat) State." *Studies in Nepali History and Society* 10: 255–293.

Greene, Paul D., and Yubaraj Rajkarnikar. 2005. "Echoes in the Valleys: A Social History of Nepali Pop in Nepal's Urban Youth Culture, 1985–2000." *Echo* 7(1). http://www.echo.ucla.edu/Volume7-Issue1/yubakar_greene/yubakar_greene1.html.

Maharjan, Sanuraja, and Robert Moore. 2010. *Mādal: Learn the Most Popular Drum of Nepal*. Kathmandu: Kumari Printing.

Mottin, Monica. 2018. *Rehearsing for Life: Theatre for Social Change in Nepal*. Cambridge: Cambridge University Press.

Music Diary. 2007. "Byaṅgyā: Badri Pangeniko Pachhi Lagāū, Lok Sangitlāī Bachāū" ["Satire: Follow Badri Pangeni, Save Folk Music"]. *Music Diary* 3(5): 38.

Orsini, Francesca. 2006. *Love in South Asia*. Cambridge: Cambridge University Press.

Pangeni, Badri. 2006. *Mero Māyā Lāgcha Lāgdaina* [*Do You Love Me or Not?*]. Kathmandu: Dhaulagiri Cassette Center.

Shah, Surendra Bikram (Subi). 2007. *Mādal*. 2nd ed. Kathmandu: Sajha Prakashan.

Stirr, Anna. 2017. *Singing across Divides: Music and Intimate Politics in Nepal*. New York: Oxford University Press.

Toynbee, Jason. 2007. *Bob Marley: Herald of a Postcolonial World?* London: Polity Press.

24
Pedagogy and Embodiment in the Transmission of Kerala Temple Drumming

Rolf Groesbeck

October 5, 1988: I awoke at 3:45 A.M. and walked from the guest house at which I was staying in Cheruthuruthy, Kerala, India, to the chenda (ceṇṭa, *cylindrical stick drum*) kalaris (kaḷaris, *pedagogical arenas*) *at the Kerala Kalamandalam, a state arts institution located in that village.*[1] *Fourteen teenaged male Malayali (native of Kerala) students, my French classmate, and I arrived at the* kalaris *at about the same time. We divided into groups, each of which went to a different* kalari. *In each* kalari, *the beginning students sat on mats each in front of a block of wood or stone, and the rest stood, each with a* chenda *hanging vertically from his shoulder. Shortly after 4:30, the students at my* kalari *picked up their sticks and played a brief invocatory pattern in unison, and then without a word, we began a pattern called "takitta"* (tākīṭṭā) sadhakam (sādhakam, *"practice, exercise"*), *which I had privately learned from my teacher (*ashan [āšān] *or* guru) *the previous day. The pattern consisted of three strokes, one left-stick stroke and two rights. Each segment was to be repeated indefinitely, as described below. (This pattern is the classroom exercise described at the end of this chapter.) At the beginning of* sadhakam *no teacher was present, but all of the students knew what to do without saying anything.*

All of us began "takitta" in first (slowest) rhythmic density playing the equivalent of quarter notes, but gradually one player accelerated to second density (eighth notes). The player beating second then doubled his speed to third (sixteenths, or quadruple density), while one of the players beating first density accelerated to second. Finally, these two players and another doubled their densities so that one was playing fourth density (thirty-seconds), one third

---

[1] This chapter adapts material from my dissertation (Groesbeck 1995), chapters 7 and 11, and introduces other material. It also expands considerably on Groesbeck and Palackal 2000.

(sixteenths), one second (eighths), and the other two of us first (quarters). After about five minutes the player on fourth density returned to first while each of the others doubled his density. This rotation recurred about every five minutes, so that all the drummers had a chance to play in all four densities, until about 5:30.

At about 5 A.M., the drumming had awakened the chenda teachers, and one came out of his bedroom (adjacent to the kalaris) to sit and observe. At about 5:30, he signaled an overall doubling, and each drummer gradually increased his tempo until all were playing at the next highest density (first to second etc.). Around 6 A.M., the teacher signaled another doubling, and a few minutes later, he did so again. By then, all of us were playing first density at the speed of the former fourth density (i.e., in the equivalent of thirty-seconds). Shortly afterward, the teacher signaled one last time, and we students played a cadential pattern and finished (see ⊙ Video example 24.1).[2]

At various times during the session, the teacher glared at a student who appeared to be relaxing, or the teacher held his wrist up toward the student and bent it back and forth to indicate that the latter was rolling his own wrist with insufficient vigor. One plays the last two, right-stick strokes of takitta sadhakam by means of a forceful rolling wrist movement (uruḷakkai) that enables the performer to strike the stick onto the drum toward and then away from his body. Otherwise, the teacher signaled the changes in tempo and made sure that the students did not stop. The teacher was silent during the session; this emphasis on nonverbal learning and embodiment, as we shall see, is central to pedagogy in Kerala.

After the cadential pattern, and the performance of another exercise, the teacher nodded his head slightly, got up wordlessly, and walked back to his room, and we students played the invocatory pattern again, then left to eat breakfast and go to temple. The sun had just risen. It was 6:30 A.M.

The above describes a *sadhakam* session, central to the training of drummers, dance-drama performers, and singers, in genres such as the dance-drama *kathakali* (*kathakaḷi*) and the solo *chenda* performance *tayampaka* (*tāyampaka*), in Kerala, a state in southwest coastal India. Because *sadhakam* inculcates many of the technical exercises necessary to

---

[2] Video example 24.1 initially demonstrates this exercise on wood blocks, and later orally with drum syllables. See also ⊙ Video example 24.2 and ⊙ Video example 24.3 for examples of *takitta sadhakam* in Kerala.

excel in the above genres (and many others), it constitutes one central part of pedagogy.

In this chapter, I argue that *sadhakam*, and some other aspects of the initial stages of pedagogy on the *chenda*, not only serve to impart musical knowledge, but also, and more fundamentally, instill in the learner the identity of student or disciple (*shishyan*, *śiṣyan*). Much literature on pedagogy has stressed how teachers attempt to transform their students' bodies into near copies of their own, as a means of transmitting a tradition. I combine this focus with a consideration of the identity (embodied and otherwise) of the student to understand how students *become students* through the pedagogical process. My inspiration for this point emerges partly from the life-stage theory found in ancient Sanskrit texts (from the time of the *Manusmriti*, c. 1 CE), specifically that which divides the Hindu high-caste male life into four segments: student or *brahmacharya* (*brahmacārya*), householder (*grihastha*), wandering holy man (*vanaprastha*), and ascetic (*sannyasa*) (Flood 1996, 61–65). Most of this theory is not relevant to the pedagogical experience in Kerala drum studios today, but as I have argued earlier (Groesbeck 1995, 2018), I believe the identity of the student today is in part influenced by the *brahmacharya* concept, specifically in its emphasis on austerity. Although the centrality of celibacy (Flood 1996, 63) is not applicable here, the *brahmacharya* stage does focus on discipline, the attentiveness implicit in rote repetition, and the submission and obedience implicit in the student's learning from the guru. The student's identity is distinct from that of the teacher (today as in ancient life-stage theory); and this identity is incorporated into the student partly by the teacher and partly through the student's own experiences, which take place even in the absence of the teacher, in *sadhakam* and in other aspects of pedagogy. Thus, pedagogy exists not only to teach music (and dance) material, but also to transform the student into a specific type of person—austere, disciplined, separated from the teacher to some degree, submissive, obedient, and attentive to tactile and aural instruction. I will make this argument with data from my own pedagogical experiences involving *sadhakam*, rote repetition, and the *arangettam* (*araṅṅēṯṯam*), a student's ceremonial first performance.

My emphasis on bodily transmission is indebted to the focus on embodiment in multiple works in social theory, phenomenology, dance and theater ethnology, and sociology, particularly that of Tomie Hahn, whose scholarship on the teaching of Japanese *nihon buyo* dance (2007) focuses on four methods of transmission: visual, oral, tactile, and media. The dance student follows her teacher visually in close proximity, responds to her occasional comments, and most crucially, learns to embody cultural knowledge and aesthetic values through her teacher's guiding touch. Throughout, Hahn shows how "culture is passed down, or embodied, through dance" and how "cultural knowledge is embodied" (2007, 1). This emphasis on tactile transmission has inspired my focus on embodiment in the discussions of rote repetition and *sadhakam* below.

The Beginnings of Pedagogy: *Sadhakam*

I can consider the focus on tactile and nonverbal transmission further by examining *sadhakam* in more detail. When I participated in and observed *sadhakam*, it took place almost completely without words. Note this essay's introductory vignette: no one says which *sadhakam* pattern is to be performed at the beginning of a session ("*takitta*" is one of four main *sadhakam* patterns, each practiced on a different day of the week); the senior students know the order as a result of having engaged in these sessions for several years. No one explains the rhythmic structure of the session, not even at the very beginning of the teaching period, and it would be unusual for anyone—teacher or student—to acknowledge that it can be analyzed as such. The limited instruction from the teacher that takes place in *sadhakam* centers on a few gestures, notably the teacher's bending of his own wrist back and forth to show the student that the latter's *urulakkai* (rolling hand technique) is insufficiently vigorous. When I, as student, saw my own teacher looking at me and rolling his wrist in this way, I knew that I had to roll my wrist more forcefully. I experienced this more forceful movement as physically different; I now demanded more of my muscles. My bodily experience was transformed. In this way a teacher's nonverbal gesture helped me accrue bodily knowledge; it helped me approximate the body (the rolling wrist, the strengthened forearm and upper arm) of a mature *chenda* player, in much the same way that Hahn's *nihon buyo* teachers instilled bodily knowledge in her.

Thus, bodily transmission incorporates in the pupil a student-specific identity. Part of this identity involves the gradual achievement of the body of an advanced drummer—that is, the student prepares to take on the identity of a future teacher and professional performer—but part of it defines the student as a type of person distinct from that of the teacher. This shows most overtly in the element of submission, apparent in the *guru dakshina* (*dakṣiṇa*) offering that opens the pedagogical experience. In this ritual, a student bows down before and gives offerings to his teacher; the teacher expects gestures of respect and admiration from his student (Groesbeck 2018). The practices that define one as a student are in some cases distinct from those that define one as a teacher.

This differentiation of student and teacher is also emphasized by the spatial separation between the two in *sadhakam*. As noted above, at Kalamandalam, the students start *sadhakam* on their own before the teacher arrives; the advanced students stand up with their *chenda*s over their shoulders while the teacher sits down at the table, several feet from the students; the teacher walks back to his room before the students finish with the opening invocatory pattern (most of the time that I attended *sadhakam*); and they stay in different places (the students stay in small, crowded dormitories). The students learn through this separation that they and their teachers are different categories of person, as opposed to the student being a younger version of the teacher. Since the teacher does so little during the *sadhakam* session, the students must learn a lot about how to behave in *sadhakam* by observing each other, especially the younger students observing the older students, an example of what I have previously called "horizontal learning" (Groesbeck 2009).

Rote Learning

The theme of nonverbal embodiment also emerges in considerations of the daily practice of pedagogy, specifically how compositions (such as *tayampaka* and aspects of kathakali) are taught. Everywhere I have seen in Kerala, *sadhakam* sessions are distinct from the learning of compositions. Whereas the former typically occur in the early mornings, the latter take place in the late mornings and afternoons, sometimes in the evenings. In classes in which the composition *tayampaka* is taught, a group of boys meets with their teacher in the *kalari*; the teacher sits on a chair in front of a table at one end and the boys mostly sit on a mat on the floor in front of the blocks of wood or stone previously noted, although one often stands up and plays the *chenda*. After the boys all play the invocatory pattern at the beginning of class, the teacher points to one, and usually without a word he starts playing the segments (*eṇṇam*s) of *tayampaka*, the solo *chenda* performance he has already learned. If he is able to reach the last segment without making a mistake, the teacher beats with wooden sticks on his table the first few *tala* (*tāla*, metric) cycles of a new segment, one the student is now learning for the first time, and waits for the student to respond. The student answers by playing the same patterns on his block of wood or stone or his *chenda* drum. If the student plays without a mistake, the teacher plays the next few cycles, and again the student is expected to repeat perfectly. This goes on until they have completed the segment. The student plays the whole segment while the other boys in the *kalari* keep the *tala* with a separate pattern. Typically, the student is unable to play every stroke perfectly; when this happens, the teacher often keeps repeating the segment and the student continues to mimic the teacher. In other instances, a student will stop, frozen in place, when he makes his first mistake, and wait for a nonverbal sign from the teacher before he can resume. Eventually, either the student masters the segment, or far more frequently, after many inadequate attempts, the teacher gives up on mastery for the time being. He then turns to another student to begin the process again, with another segment or composition. In this way, the teacher goes through all the students in the *kalari* one-by-one, over the course of a three- to-four-hour lesson. The next day, for the student who was unable to play his segment accurately the previous day, the teacher will return to the segment and have him repeat it until the student has mastered it. With some students I observed, this would take months; a number never figured out a given segment and consequently were not invited back to study the next year. One of my field consultants, a longtime teacher at the Kalamandalam, described the ideal teaching session:

> One lesson, when taught, should be repeated time and again. The teacher should have a lot of patience.... If an *ennam* [segment] is taught at 8:30 in the morning, it should be repeated until 12:30, to make it thorough. If the student even then can't learn it by heart, the same *ennam* should be taught in the next session. (Achunni Poduval, interview with the author, April 1989; in Groesbeck 1995, 459)

The process is thus largely nonverbal. The consistency of the curriculum ensures that each student knows what he must perform in the class, and convention dictates that he normally starts at the beginning of the composition. Rehearsing individual passages, so common in the Western art music setting, is rare here. The teacher generally does not explain a pattern's form or a technical point, nor does he discuss interpretation or an element of the curriculum with the student. Students are aware of the formal structures of the *ennam*s, but they seem to pick up this knowledge informally over a period of time, rather than having it articulated at any one point. The practice of *tala* keeping—in which the group of students articulates the metric cycle on their wood or stone blocks while another student plays the composition—ensures this process of gradual, corporeal absorption; the students learn both the compositions and the *tala* cycle in this way. My teachers explained the forms of the *ennam*s in class to me, as a Westerner with no previous experience with the genres, but this practice was unusual with the Indian students. Again, this nonverbal aspect foregrounds the tactile, physical nature (as well as aurality) of transmission; when one does not receive a verbal explanation, one must learn by mimicking the teacher's wrist, arm, and hand movements. Thus, tactile transmission, like that described by Hahn, is part of what defines a student's identity.

The *Arangettam*: Ascending the Stage

The *arangettam*[3] is the first time that the teacher permits the student to perform publicly. It demonstrates the student's mastery of his basic lessons and acts as his rite of passage to the teacher/professional performer stage of his life. Yet even as the student reaches this stage, he must acknowledge his submission to his teacher, making the *arangettam* one site in which the student defines his "student" identity as submissive and obedient, distinct from that of his teacher. I will show this in the excerpt below.

Students in private contexts performed their *arangettam*s at ages as young as nine or ten, sometimes even earlier; but in institutions like the Kalamandalam, students undertook this ritual around age sixteen, in their first or second year of study. My own kathakali *chenda arangettam*, scheduled after I had studied about a year, unfolded typically:

> During the day I went to the temple and gave some rupees as an offering for a good *arangettam*. At noon, I bought lunch for all of the Kalamandalam *chenda* students and teachers at a local restaurant. Later, I bought sweets for the students, and some of the teachers. At the performance that night, when the singers in the kathakali ensemble started singing the item before the first item at which I performed, I walked backstage behind the curtain. I was thus in the same physical space as the other drummers, but invisible

---

[3] In Tamil, this debut performance is called an *arangetram*.

to the audience. Someone placed the *chenda* I was about to play between my teacher and myself. I gave my teacher an offering of betel leaf, areca nut, a *muntu* (piece of cloth worn around the waist), and some rupees, the same offering I had given him at the commencement of my lessons (the *guru dakshina* ritual noted earlier), and I dropped down prostrate on the floor. I touched my fingers to my forehead, my chest, and to the floor, and he helped me up. Without a word, he gave me my *chenda* and two sticks. I walked onto the stage and performed the kathakali items, along with the other drummers, singers, and kathakali actors, the latter of whom were all Westerners who were studying at the institution. (Educating foreigners has been part of the Kalamandalam's mission for decades, and our performances were lauded, as is usually the case in these instances.) After I had finished, I walked behind the curtain again and gave the same offerings I had earlier given to my teacher, this time to some other teachers at the institution. After this act had been completed, my *arangettam* was over. (Adapted from Groesbeck 1995: 496–498; see also Groesbeck 2018)

Despite the cursory nature of the *arangettam*, its symbolic significance is great, as it is supposed to end the student stage of the drummer's life and begin the teacher/professional performer stage. (In practice, however, all drummers continue to study after they have had their *arangettam*s, and several have multiple *arangettam*s, one for each genre and for each instrument and vocal style they study.) The ritual is dominated by offerings, many of them like those of the *guru dakshina* noted earlier, and like the earlier ritual, they reinforce the focus on embodiment and submission; the student must drop to the floor, not rising until the teacher helps him up, and then wait for the teacher to hand him his sticks and drum. Even as the student reaches (in theory) the verge of adulthood and the attainment of the role of professional performer and teacher, he must acknowledge his indebtedness to and lowliness before his teacher—qualities, again, which are central to the definition of his identity.

Summary

Embodiment, aurality, discipline, and submission thus emerge as themes throughout the study of Kerala temple drumming: the former two through the emphasis on rote repetition and the corporeal nature of *sadhakam* (see

Box 24.1 Exercises

To what degree do these points, then, have the potential to influence pedagogical processes in Western classrooms? I suggest leaving the question open and encourage teachers and students to try a simplified version of the genre discussed at the beginning of this essay, *sadhakam*. Participation in this exercise can help determine whether students can learn this genre through a tactile and less verbal process, and thus approximate some of the components of the "student identity" described above. The primary learning objective is not to attain a specific skill level, but rather to explore the questions below, possibly in class discussion, possibly in short written assignments. I use *sadhakam* in my own American classes, often with students with no Indian music or percussion background. The exercise may proceed as follows:

(1) To prepare, obtain wood blocks and drum sticks. Substitutes for the *chenda*s and sticks used in Kerala *kalari*s can be purchased from a home improvement store. Rectangular lengths of wood can be sawed into smaller blocks about 5" × 6" × 11" to serve as *chenda*s. Brooms with wooden handles can be fashioned into sticks; cut off the handles and saw each handle into pieces about a foot long. Each student needs two broom handles and a wood block, as does the teacher. The blocks are placed on the floor, and players sit on pillows or mats on the floor to play them; some of my students, however, prefer to sit and place their blocks on a bench. Alternatively, teachers and students can dispense with the blocks and sticks and speak the three syllables of "*takitta*" *sadhakam*: "*ta*," "*ki*," and "*ṭa*." (See Video example 24.1; the last part of it [from cue point 7:00] displays spoken *takitta sadhakam*.)

(2) Practice along with Video example 24.1 to learn the *takitta* pattern in preparation for leading a class exercise. There are four main *sadhakam* patterns, but the easiest is the *takitta* pattern described at the beginning of the chapter. It consists of three strokes: a left-stick stroke straight down onto the wood block (*ta*); a right-stick stroke diagonally onto the block, bouncing up in the direction of the player's body (*ki*); and another right-stick stroke diagonally onto the block, bouncing away from the player's body (*ṭa*). Playing

the latter two strokes in succession requires a rolling of the wrist (*urulakkai*).

(3) *Takitta* is played in four speeds, but the fourth (and possibly third) are usually too fast for beginners. The first consists of the equivalent of quarter notes about one per second (i.e., 60 beats per minute); the second doubles the first rhythmic density (120 bpm); and the third quadruples the first (240 bpm). Start off by asking a third of the students to play the first density, another third the second density, and the remaining the third density. After a few minutes the class rotates; those initially playing first go to second, those playing second go to third, and those playing third go to first, as was described in the chapter's opening section. Keep rotating until all have had the chance to play each speed a few times. Beginners sometimes have difficulty managing the remainder of the performance described at the beginning of this chapter, so the exercise can conclude after several cycles through all three speeds. In Kerala, *sadhakam* tends to last at least two hours, sometimes much longer, but in my classes I spend between five and twenty-five minutes on the exercise.

(4) Teachers are encouraged to try several approaches. First, approximate the Kerala context by refraining from verbal commentary; instead, limit oneself to tactile guidance—clutching the student's wrist, forearm, or upper arm and guiding it while they play (after receiving verbal permission from the student to do so), to produce the necessary rolling hand mechanism. This method can attempt to instill part of the student life stage described above. Second, perhaps interrupt sessions by explaining both the musical structure and the Kerala performance context, of *sadhakam* and its associated genres (for more on these, see Groesbeck and Palackal 2000 or Killius 2006). Third, try stopping the group to work one-on-one with individual students; alternatively, have the entire group go through the exercise without stopping.

Consider the experience and engage with the following questions:

What sorts of knowledge were transmitted respectively through tactile, aural, and verbal methods and experiences? How did the student's behavior and experience change as a result of embodied learning, or from interpolating verbal commentary into an otherwise silent session? Or

> did it change at all? In the context of the session, how did the students and teacher define their respective identities, apart from the patterns they played? For instance, did students experience themselves as any more submissive in this exercise than in any other classroom experience? Finally, what aspects of the Kerala pedagogical experience, as outlined in this chapter, problematize context-sensitive pedagogy in the Western academic setting? Which aspects of the experience, as explained in the opening segment, did they feel could not be easily replicated in a university setting, and why? In other words, what elements are more difficult to transport across cultural boundaries? What adjustments need to take place?

Box 24.1), and the first and last through the offerings and prostration associated with the *arangettam*. But I also want to emphasize another point regarding the differing role expectations of teacher and student and their frequent physical separation (at least in the institutional context, less so in private settings). I have mentioned the different expectations for each vis-à-vis attitudes toward punctuality; recall from the opening vignette that students must show up on time to *sadhakam* and classes, whereas teachers can be late without admonishment. The point, as I suggested earlier, is to establish the student not so much as a young version of the teacher, but rather, as a distinct type of person—submissive and disciplined, as well as one who experiences knowledge as embodied and aural—again, corresponding in some ways to the first of the four life stages (*ashrama*s) of ancient Sanskrit theory. I do not deny that part of the purpose of pedagogy in Kerala is to prepare the student ultimately to be a teacher and professional adult performer, but much of it is also to teach the student to be a student, that is, to inculcate him in the responsibilities of his life stage.

Works Cited

Flood, Gavin. 1996. *An Introduction to Hinduism*. Cambridge: Cambridge University Press.
Groesbeck, Rolf. 1995. "Pedagogy and Performance in *Tāyampaka*, a Genre of Temple Instrumental Music in Kerala, India." PhD diss., New York University.
Groesbeck, Rolf. 2009. "Disciple and Preceptor/Performer in Kerala." In *Theorizing the Local: Music, Practice, and Experience in South Asia and Beyond*, edited by Richard K. Wolf, 143–163. Oxford: Oxford University Press.

Groesbeck, Rolf. 2018. "Gift as Devotion, Lesson as Tuition: Transactions among Temple and Dance-Drama Drummers in Kerala." *International Journal of Hindu Studies* 22: 217–233.

Groesbeck, Rolf, and Joseph Palackal. 2000. "Kerala." In *South Asia: The Indian Subcontinent* (*Garland Encyclopedia of World Music*, vol. 5), edited by Alison Arnold, 929–951. New York: Garland.

Hahn, Tomie. 2007. *Sensational Knowledge: Embodying Culture through Japanese Dance*. Middletown, CT: Wesleyan University Press.

Killius, Rolf. 2006. *Ritual Music and Hindu Rituals of Kerala*. New Delhi: BR Rhythms.

25
Sonic Gift-Giving in Sri Lankan Buddhism

Jim Sykes

On Gods, Bananas, and Fieldwork Etiquette

I became aware of gift-giving etiquette in Sri Lanka early on in my fieldwork, when I accompanied a linguist friend to an interview. Noticing that he brought a small box of chocolates with him, I asked how one should give gifts to interlocutors. He remarked that one should bring something small like fruit, candy, or chocolate; the gift does not have to be expensive, for it is just a token of appreciation. Therefore, it is not the content of the gift that matters but the act of giving itself. He said it is customary for the interviewee to refrain from acknowledging the gift, that it will typically be whisked away to a back room and remain out of sight for the duration of the interview. But the hiding of the gift does not mean it goes unappreciated, nor does it mean it is a needless formality—rather, the gift is the action that opens doors. For to not give at least a small token of one's appreciation could come off as rude, and this might seriously curtail the amount of information the person is willing to give.

Although I "knew" this information already, I was struck by how quickly I had forgotten it in the field. By this time, I had been in Sri Lanka for a few weeks and attended lessons with several Sinhala Buddhist drummers.[1] Not once had I brought anyone a gift. I had been to one drummer's house in particular on a few occasions, and while I sincerely appreciated his help and had paid him for each lesson, my lack of a gift meant that I had yet to show real gratitude. My friend's reminder of the gift thus left me feeling embarrassed.

---

[1] The Sinhalas are Sri Lanka's ethnic majority, roughly 75 percent of the population; most identify as Theravada Buddhist, the type of Buddhism that is prevalent in Sri Lanka and mainland Southeast Asia.

So the next day I went to a store and bought bananas, for I remembered that my friend said fruit would make a suitable gift. When I got to my teacher's house, he greeted me with a warm smile and gave the bananas to his wife, who surely brought them to the kitchen (for they later wound up on a plate as an offering to me, accompanied by the requisite cup of tea). I must admit that I felt some relief: it was as if, during this initial research trip filled with numerous gaffes and blunders, I was starting to get this "fieldwork thing" right.

After my teacher and I conversed for some time, I began demonstrating my knowledge of the basic drum exercises (*harambas*) on the *gäta beraya*,[2] the drum associated with Sri Lanka's "up country" (central hill country region). All was going well until my eyes wandered around my teacher's yard to be met with a startling discovery: *his yard was filled with banana trees*! Indeed, my teacher could have obtained my "gift" by walking a few feet from his front door and plucking bananas off a tree. I put my head down and kept drumming, reminding myself that it is the gesture and not the content of the gift that matters, but I could not help but feel ashamed, sure that my "gift" must have caused laughter in the kitchen followed by the Sinhala equivalent of "isn't that cute."

I forgot about this event for some time since the life of an ethnomusicologist is filled with such mistakes. I remembered it only years later when, after spending what was by then a considerable amount of time studying Sinhala Buddhist drumming, it dawned on me that it, too, is a gift. Drumming is offered in a range of Sinhala ritual practices to the Buddha, deities, beings of low karmic standing (*yakku* or "demons"), and prominent "VIPs," such as politicians and visiting dignitaries. In many of these contexts and parades (*peraheras*) held in conjunction with Buddhist temples on full-moon nights, drumming is *sabda pujava* (*sabda pujāva*), a "sound offering." Traditionally, ritual drumming was the duty of the Berava (*Beravā*) caste (*bera* means "drum"), who are not only (nor always) drummers but also dancers, singers, flame-throwers, herbal medicinal specialists, astrologers, altar-makers, and teachers. They are best thought of as practitioners of Ayurveda—the traditional medicinal system found throughout South Asia. During the Kandyan Kingdom (1473–1815), drumming in Buddhist temples was a caste duty of the Berava, their "offerings to the king" (*rajakariya*). The Berava are a historically low, stigmatized caste, akin to the Paraiyars in Tamil society (though

---

[2] The "ä," akin to the vowel in the English word "bat," will be retained in Sinhala terminology throughout this chapter to assist in pronunciation.

not nearly as stigmatized)—from whom the term "Berava" is thought to have derived. Many prefer to call themselves *Näketi* (astrologer caste).³ Large-scale, all-night rituals performed mainly by the Berava combat a variety of problems and fears, such as illness, starvation, drought, pestilence, complications from pregnancy, chickenpox, and sorcery (Kapferer 1983, 1997; Obeyesekere 1984; Scott 1994). Nowadays, each ritual runs all night, but in the past they were longer and could be combined so that a single event might go on for days (Wirz 1954).⁴ In these rituals, the Buddha receives offerings, but he is not the focal point since he has achieved nirvana (Pali: *nibbana*), is beyond the round of rebirth (*samsara*), and is not around to witness the offerings.⁵ Rather, the focal points of the rituals are a range of deities, who graciously receive offerings such as fruit, betel nut, incense, sung poetry, dancing, and drumming.

Suffice it to say that the deities do not *need* Berava drum offerings, for the world is very much their front yard. But while it surely is the respectful gesture of the drum offering that pleases the gods, it turns out—unlike my choice of bananas—that the content of the drumming matters: the proper performance of drum phrases (*padas*) is necessary for the offering to be accepted. In some circumstances, an inadequate performance might lead to the wrathful vengeance of the gods upon the drummer or community, on behalf of whom the drummer offers his sounds. In traditional Sinhala belief, the ordering of sounds may be auspicious or inauspicious, so drummers take precautions to perform the correct drum stanzas at the right moment in rituals. Like a gift offered by a fieldworker to her interlocutor, correctly pronounced *bera pada*s (drum phrases) are gifts that open doors. They are gestures of respect, love, awe, and fear of supernatural power and retribution, and in return for the offering, the deities protect the community from disasters like drought and pestilence. This is the purpose of one set of rituals, *deva tovil*s (commonly known as *santi karma*s or peace-bringing rituals). Another set of rituals, *yak tovil*s, wards off illness brought on by beings of low karmic standing called *yakku* (*yakkha* is the singular). In *yak tovil*s, *yakku* are tricked into believing they are being treated like gods due to receiving similar

---

³ I use the term "Berava" here because it highlights the caste's historical identity as drummers, and I aim to foster greater respect for the community. However, I use the phrase "Sinhala Buddhist drumming" to refer to the tradition as a whole, for today it is also performed by many non-Berava.
⁴ While many Berava have left their traditional caste profession, the community still performs all-night rituals that maintain prominence in Sinhala Buddhist society.
⁵ Pali is the language of the canonic texts of Theravada Buddhism, the *Tipitaka*.

offerings. Indeed, the anthropologist Bruce Kapferer (1983) calls his book on *yak tovil*s *A Celebration of Demons* for this reason.

In this chapter, I argue that because of the doctrinal stipulation in Theravada Buddhism that monks and the laity on specific occasions should not engage in music and dance (known as the "Seventh Precept"), Sinhala Buddhist drumming is structured as sacred speech rather than music so that it will be acceptable to the Buddha and deities (who are *bodhisatta*s or Buddhas-to-be). Focusing on the southern, "low-country" drumming tradition, I show that it consists of the combination of drum syllables (*aksara*) into phrases (*pada*s) mapped onto long and short beats (*matra*s) without reference to a system of meter (what in South Asian classical music is known as *tala* [*tāla*]) or a strict attention to subdivisions of beats. As opposed to classical Indian drumming, in which drum syllables are slotted rigorously into counted subdivisions, Sinhala drumming retains a speech-like character. Much as an English-speaker would not pause after uttering the first syllable of the word "character" (pausing after "char"), so, too, are some Sinhala drum words taken as units that cannot be split up and therefore do not easily fall on subdivisions of beats. My argument is that in Sinhala drumming, to sound "musical" means to disrupt this speech-like foundation by providing shorter, easily countable repetitive phrases—and this is what is avoided in drum phrases (*pada*s) offered to the Buddha and deities. In what follows, I provide three examples that demonstrate a continuum from unmetered drum poetry for the Buddha (Example 1), to unmetered *pada*s for the goddess Pattini set within a section of easily countable drumming (Example 2), to "musical"-sounding *pada*s for a *yakkha* (Example 3).

Sound Offerings (*Sabda Pujava*) as Protection and Healing

There are three regional styles of Sinhala drumming. The up-country tradition from the hill country region of Kandy is performed on the drum *gäta beraya* and is ubiquitous at weddings, parades (*pahera*s), political ceremonies, and other events throughout Sinhala-dominated parts of the island. The low-country tradition is associated with the southern coast up to the capital, Colombo, and is played on the *pahata rata beraya* ("low-country drum"), also known as *yak beraya* ("demon drum") when played in *yak tovil*s. Lastly, the Sabaragamuwa style is associated with the region of that name,

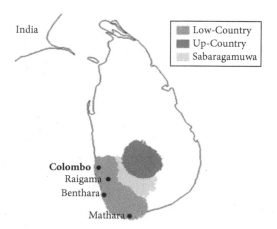

Map 25.1 The three regions of Sinhala Buddhist traditional dance and drumming with the major low country sub-regional styles (*korales*) marked in black along with the country's capital, Colombo. Map from Suraweera (2009); used with permission.

located in between the up and low countries. It uses the drum called *davula*. Each of these regional traditions has a unique drum language, though they also contain sub-regional styles called *korales* (Map 25.1). For example, my drum teacher Herbert Dayasheela is an exponent of the Benthara *korale* (on the southwest coast). The two other major *korale*s of the low country are Raigama and Mathara.

In my story above, I described my initial foray into Kandyan drumming (*gäta beraya*); eventually, I focused on the low-country drum. The two sound radically different: the Kandyan drum is tapered at its ends and produces a high-pitched sound on one side; in the past, it was made with monkey skin (Peiris 2020). By contrast, the low-country drum is a straight (cylindrical) drum with a booming low tone, made of the inside of a cow's stomach. Drummers joked to me that the high-pitched *gäta beraya* sounds like a pesky monkey, while the low-pitched *pahata rata beraya* sounds like a lumbering cow (Figures 25.1 and 25.2).[6]

Besides my love for the sound of the low-country drum, I switched to studying it because of the widely held belief that traditional all-night rituals

---

[6] The *davula* (a fat, cylindrical drum played with one stick and one hand) from Sabaragamuwa is under-researched. I assume it is related to the *dhol*.

Figure 25.1 The Kandyan drum called *gäta beraya*. Photo by the author.

are more common in the south than Kandy. Up-country Kandyan dance and drumming are associated with a ritual found only in that region, the Kohomba Kankariya, which is rarely performed today except as a state-sponsored event (Reed 2010). The style is also famous as a staged tradition ("Kandyan Dance") associated with the annual parade (*Äsala Perahera*) that emanates from the country's most famous Buddhist temple, the Dalida Maligawa (Temple of the Tooth). During that event, the Buddha's tooth relic is taken out of the temple and paraded on the back of an elephant, accompanied by Kandyan dancers and drummers. By contrast, the low country is famous for *deva tovil*s, *yak tovil*s, and a ritual for planetary deities called *bali*.[7] In each of the all-night Berava rituals, offerings are made to the Buddha and "four warrant gods" (*hatara varam deviyo*) who have been given a "warrant" (*varam*) to act on the Buddha's behalf: Natha (the next Buddha), Vishnu (protector of the island), Kataragama, and Pattini. One prominent *deva tovil*

---

[7] These rituals are, or likely once were, also performed in the Kandyan region. However, due to the prominence of Kandyan Buddhism in the national imagination, Kandyan dance and drumming are closely associated with the Dalada Maligawa and its procession the *Äsala Perahera*.

Figure 25.2 The low country drum, *pahata rata beraya*. Photo by the author.

is centered on the goddess Pattini; another is for a god called Devol Deviyo. Dayasheela specializes in the Sanni Yakuma, a *yak tovil* that heals eighteen illnesses brought on by the eighteen *sanni* demons (Sykes 2018a, 76).

Buddhists make offerings for the purpose of accumulating merit (*pin*), which raises one's karma.[8] Berava drumming accompanies some merit-making activities, such as when it is performed at *pirith* (Pali: *paritta*) ceremonies (the chanting of the Buddha's teachings, or Dhamma, by monks). The word *pirith* means "protection." This type of chanting combines syllables in "odd" combinations, through which monks conventionally strive to avoid sounding musical (Kulatillake 1976, 3). In my studies, I came to believe that Berava drumming is structured to mimic the aura of Buddhist chant without appropriating its meters. This is because the origin story about the Berava that Dayasheela told me places drummers at the iconic moment in the Pali Canon (the *Ratana Sutta*) when the Buddha sanctioned monks to use *pirith*

---

[8] The paradigmatic gift in Buddhism is *dana*, the giving of alms to monks.

against disease, demons, and starvation (see Sykes 2018a, 81–82). According to Dayasheela, this event determined the ritualists' division of labor into *deva toyil*s (which alleviate draught and pestilence) and *yak toyil*s (which combat demons who cause illness). Buddhist chant is directly protective; Berava drumming, by contrast, is offered in rituals to honor the Buddha, obtain protection from deities, and trick *yakku* into believing they are being honored like deities (whereupon a ritualist utters *mantra*s to stop them harming the patient). One of my drummer friends, Pabalu Wijegoonawardane, sums it up thusly: "'Sound' or vibrations are a media to convey thoughts and emotions" and this is the "basis of *mantra vidya* known as the science of mantra," which is also "applied in *sabda puja*, a vibrational offering to the Buddha or specific deity."

Sinhala Drumming and Meter

Padaya ("poetic foot") refers to a line of poetry in Sinhala literature. The use of the term for a phrase of drumming does not mean Sinhala drumming is free-flowing poetic speech with no hint of pulse or repetition. Rather, in any given section of low-country ritual, *pada*s are repeated, typically concluding with a through-composed passage called *irratiya*. Many sound as though they are in a six- or eight-beat cycle, but the phrase will go on slightly longer or shorter than what outsiders might expect. Often, a drum stroke will not seem to land on the appropriate subdivision of a beat, and drummers tend not to play in strict unison.

Here's what I learned about these phenomena. First, drummers play slightly off from one another because it makes the drums sound louder. Second, while some patterns are in seemingly countable beat cycles, Sinhala drumming is not conceptualized as having "meter" (or *tala*). Drummers *do* count whether a stroke is of long or short duration, with a number of beats (*matra*s). But what is important is the phrasing of the drum words, not their placement onto a beat's subdivision. Imagine if you spoke a sentence in English over and over: it will start sounding as though it is in a meter, but some words will have characteristic phrasings and pauses learned by convention, which will not fall on a particular subdivision. Similarly, Sinhala drumming is the playing of combinations of drum strokes over beats of long and short duration in which certain combinations must always be played the same way because that is how those "words" are pronounced. Furthermore, the drumming is felt gesturally, with dance, rather than rigorously counted.

Consider the drum word *tari*, which consists of the stroke *ta* (a high-pitched smack on the drum) and a two-stroke phrase, *ri*. Try this out: clap the side of your left leg with your left hand and say "ta". Next, take your right hand, place your middle finger, ring finger, and pinky close together, and hit them against your right leg as your hand swivels upward (palm up); the second stroke then involves hitting your thumb and pointer finger (they do not have to be placed close together) against your leg as your hand swivels back downward. These two strokes together are pronounced "*ri*." All three strokes are played at a fast speed. If you are conversant in Western music, you might call this a triplet, which played at a slower tempo would require that the space *between* the strokes expands. But in Sinhala drumming, *tari* is played the same way no matter the tempo. If the phrase in which it appears is slowed down, the space *around tari* will expand, but *tari* stays the same. Another drum word like this is *dahing*, which is one loud stroke followed quickly by a softer, higher-pitched one played at the edge of the drum. If you elongate the space between those strokes, it is no longer *dahing*.

*Pada*s for deities are often highly poetic-sounding phrases embedded within longer sections of pulsed, metered-sounding (seemingly countable) drumming—I say "seeming" because drummers concentrate on pronouncing the drum words and feel their way through the *padaya* rather than rigorously counting it. The *magul bera* (auspicious drumming) for the Buddha consists of three sections of unmetered drum poetry. At the other end of the spectrum are *pada*s for *yakku* (demons), and "in between" moments of rituals in which drummers perform flashy flips and twirls for the audience, which tend to be more easily felt as having a strong beat. Why? Here is what I concluded from conversations with drummers. All Buddhists adhere to the Five Precepts, a list of injunctions including that one should not kill, steal, commit adultery, use false or malicious speech, or imbibe intoxicating substances. A set of Ten Precepts are followed by monks and serious Buddhists on holy days; the Seventh Precept states that one must refrain from dancing, singing, and music on those days. According to Kulatillake (1976), *pirith* chant is performed in meters that involve auspicious combinations (and additions) of syllables to make the chant avoid having a "regular" rhythm. According to this reasoning, it makes sense that a "musical" meter must be avoided in drum offerings to the Buddha and deities. By contrast, *yakku* became demons on account of bad deeds performed in previous lives; as the epitome of bad Buddhists, they receive more "musical"-sounding *pada*s—and this is considered a bad thing.[9] The following three examples demonstrate this continuum: unmetered drum poetry for the Buddha; *pada*s of unmetered poetry for the goddess Pattini preceded by a passage of repetitive, countable drumming; and an excerpt of shorter, "musical" *pada*s for Riri Yakkha (Red Demon).

Exercises

Example 1: *Magul Bera* for the Buddha

The *magul bera* is played at auspicious occasions in Sinhala society, including the beginning of major Berava rituals.[10] It is unmetered drum poetry; there is a hint of a pulse, but to follow it strongly would be inappropriate and unartful. As I describe above, I argue that the speech-like character of the drumming makes it acceptable as an offering to the Buddha. The *magul bera* is taught by a *gurunnanse* (*gurunnānse*, teacher) at the beginning of a drummer's studies and is memorized. As this is an oral tradition, drummers may inadvertently alter its performance slightly while playing.[11] The content of *magul bera* varies greatly across regional traditions and sub-regional styles (*korale*s). However, while the *magul bera* is auspicious, it is not complex. Playing it well is an art, but the composition is something drummers learn at the beginning of their studies. Figure 25.3 is a transcription of the *magul bera* I learned from my teacher, Herbert Dayasheela, in the low-country "Benthara *korale*" style (see Box 25.1).[12] Each slash (/) represents a repetition of the previous drum words put in brackets {}, but I have also added "X3 etc." to indicate how many times a pattern is repeated in his performance. Each "rrrrr" is a drum roll.

---

[9] *Pada*s for *yakku*, however, are still constructed with the same drum language in which drum stroke combinations do not always match subdivisions of beats. So drumming for *yakku* approximates or hints at a sense of meter that does not actually exist in Sinhala drumming.
[10] The examples in this section are reproduced from Sykes 2018b.
[11] The text presented here is what my teacher performed in the accompanying Video example 25.1. This differs slightly from what he originally gave me. These differences/additions are bolded, and some of the version he gave me is missing at the end.
[12] Longer videos of the drumming in ritual context can be accessed via Sykes 2018b.

Palamu Vattama (first section)

{dahing dit} [**video starts here**] {dahing} X5 (both start slow and speed up)

rrrrrrrim dahingta gata gugu dita gata gugu dang, gata gudang dahing

{din din dahing} X3 (speeds up)

{din gata gati gata gudang dahing} X2

din **gata** gati gata gudang

gati gata gudang X2

{gati gata gunda} X3 (speeds up)

<u>gata gugu dita gata gugu dang, gata gudang, dahing dahing tat gum.</u>

rrrrregata gata gata gata dahing

gat dahing dahing dun dun dahing

dun dun dahing dun dang dun dahing

dunta gatangta gudang taka dita gata

<u>**gata gugu dita gata gugu dang, gata gudang, dahing tat gum.**</u>

Daeveni Vattama (second section, cue point 0:47)

{rrrrregata gatang gati gata gat degata gata du du dung} X3

regata gundang dahing

dahingta gatdirikita gatdirikita gatang

degata gundirikita gundirikita gundang

dahingta gatdirikita gatdirikita gatang

degata gundirikita gundirikita gundang

{rrrrundang gundang dahing} X2

rrrrundang gundang {gati gata gunda} X4 (speeds up)

gatagugu dita gatagugu dang, gatagudang, dahingdahing tat gum.

Figure 25.3 *Magul Bera* as taught by Herbert Dayasheela.

Tunveni Vattama (third section, cue point 1:28)

rrrrrim gata gugu dang, gat **dita gata ku** dum

rrruta [gu] gata gugu dang, gat **dirikita gata ku** dum

rrrrrim gata gugu dang gati gata gugu dang

gata gugu dang, gunda gugu dang, gugu dang

ga ta dit ta gat dita gata gati gata guhadi gadiri kita

dun ta guhi guhi guhi gatang degata

diri diri diri gatang

dun ta guhi guhi guhi gatang degata

diri diri diri gatang

{gunda gunda gunda gata gata gata gata gata} X2 (speeds up)

gaditaka diku dega dahing

gu gunda gunda gundangta gundang gata, gadi gata gata gatangta gatang gata X2

gaditaka diku dega dahing

dum ta gat dahing, regata gat dahing, gat dahing dahing, dun dun dahing, dun dun dahing

dun dahing, dun dahing, dun ta gatangta gundangta ga dita gata

gata gugu dita gata gugu dang, gata gudang, dahing dahing tat gum.

Figure 25.3 Continued

> **Box 25.1 Exercise: *Magul Bera* for the Buddha**
>
> Watch my *gurunnanse* recite this *magul bera*, followed by his performance of it in ▶ Video example 25.1. Then, with the help of Figure 25.3, recite the *pada*s yourself. Do you notice how each section (*vattama*) ends with the same phrase? This drumming should be played expressively, as one would recite a poem.

Example 2: Opening of the *Handa Samayama* (section of a Devol Maduva ritual), including *pada*s for Goddess Pattini

Figure 25.4 presents an example of how drum *pada*s proceed from "somewhat metered" to "free verse drum poetry." It will help to read these with

gati gata gata / gati gata gata / gati gata gatang / gataga dahing
gati gata gunda / gundi gata gunda / gundi gata gunda / gatagu dahing
gati gata gata / gati gata gata / gati gata gatang / gataga dahing

gundang gata gu dahing / gati gata gatang gata gat dahing
rrrregata gata gun / du gata ga ta / gaditeka dikundeku dahing /
gatigata
gundang gata gu dahing / gati gata gatang gata gat dahingta gum
rrregata gata gun / du gata ga ta / gaditeka dikundeku dahing / dahingta gum

rrrrrrrrrrim! gaditekadikundekudom

First pada, Pattini

gadim dim dim (x3)

gatakudom dom dom tagatigatagundang
gatigatagugudagatigatagatakudum dum

Dayasheela says: "This surala"
guhadigadirikiTa / gata gata (x3)
gataku dom

Dayasheela says: "This is long"

guhadigadirikiTa gata gata (x3)
gata ku dom

guhadigadirikiTa gata gata (x2)
gata ku dom

guhadigadirikiTa gata gata (x2)
gata ku dom

gat (this may be an error on Dayasheela's part)
guhadigadirikiTa gataku dom (x2)
gataku dom gundaku dom
dom tat dom takadit tat
takaraka undagat iram (indecipherable)

Figure 25.4 Opening of the *Handa Samayama*.

Second rhythm:
gunda gata gunda gata / gat / dahing
gadi gata /
gunda gata gunda gata / gat / dahing

dom takugundagatagat dit dahing gum
rrrregatat degundeku dom

[A pause, as Dayasheela remembers the *pada*]

Irratiya
regun dang gata gudi tagu dang gata gunda gu gudita gata gata
dom gata gadi gatang gudi gatang / gadi gatang dom gata gahadigadirikiTa (?) gadiku dom

Dayasheela says: "Third One"
gundita gun di dahing
gadita ga din dahing
tat dit ton nang
gundita gun din dahing

rrrrregatagatagatagudigaditekadegundekudom

Irratiya [Conclusion]
gundita dahuragat
gaditada huragat
gundita dahuragata
gu gun ditang gat taga ditagata
gu gun ditang gat rim iram.

Figure 25.4 Continued

▶ Video example 25.2.[13] Can you hear how the first stanza starts off in a seemingly countable six-beat meter, but as it approaches the first *padaya* for Pattini, longer words are added, stretching out the time? Next, can you hear

---

[13] Note on Video example 25.2: the term *surala*, which Dayasheela says after the first few *pada*s ("this is *surala*"), commonly refers to a drum roll; however, *surala* may also refer to a "longer pattern... which consists of technical rhythms and dance steps" (Suraweera 2009, 113), and that is how Dayasheela uses it here.

how the section marked "First Pada, Pattini" loses its sense of beat altogether? Note that the word *dahing* comes often as an exclamation point (of sorts) at the end of phrases; the drum roll, "rrrrrim," is not rigorously counted but felt; and stanzas tend to end with "dom." Farther below, you'll find examples of cadential passages called *irratiya*.

Example 3: *Pada* for Riri Yakkha

Yakku (beings of low karmic standing) are made to think they are being celebrated like gods so that they will appear in the ritual space (as masked dancers), after which ritualists erase their malignant influence on a patient by uttering magic spells called *mantras*. The *pada*s in Figure 25.5 are part of a *yak tovil* in which Riri Yakkha (Red Demon) makes an appearance. In contrast to the previous two examples, this drumming consists of shorter, repetitive phrases that have a strong sense of beat and meter—exactly what you would expect for an "offering" to lowly "demons." However, if you follow how my teacher plays this in the accompanying video, you will hear he is *still* not matching drum strokes to subdivisions of beats exactly. This is because *all* Berava drumming is constructed without reference to meter, and words like *degatang* and *dahing* are felt more than counted (see Box 25.2).

Conclusion

In this chapter, I argued Sinhala Buddhist drumming was constructed as sacred speech so that it would be acceptable as an offering to the Buddha and deities in rituals. This speech-like character is due to the drumming being

---

Box 25.2 Exercise: *Pada* for Riri Yakkha

Recite the drum *pada*s in Figure 25.5 while clapping your hands when you see an "x." As you do this, tap your foot when you see a bolded word. When you reach a place with longer drum words, try to concentrate on saying those words correctly, even if it means slightly delaying your clap. This is what my teacher does in ⊙ Video example 25.3.

Re ga **ta** / de ga **ta** / **gati** gata **gun**dang **de**gatang /
x   x   x   / x   x   x

Re ga ta / **de** gun **da** / dahing (pause) gattang ditagata /
x   x/   x   / x   x   x

re **ga ta** / de ga ta / gati **ga**ta gun**dang** degatang
x   x   x   / x   x   x

Re ga ta / **de** gun **da** / dahing (pause) **gattang** gattaku
x   x/   x   / x   x   x

dom de gat **tang** gattaku   (x4)
x   x   x

dom ta gat ta ku / **dom** gundat ta ku /
x   x   x   x

dom de gat ta ku /**dom gundat** (pause) / regatagundagundagat / regatagundagundagat
x   x   x   x   x   x   x

gundagunda gat / gundagundagatta / gunda gat dita /
x   x   x

gundagahirikitagunda gat / dahing
(indecipherable)   x

Figure 25.5 *Pada* for Riri Yakkha.

constructed as combinations of drum syllables into drum words, some of which cannot be easily split up or conceptualized as falling on a subdivision of a beat. Certain highly auspicious types of Sinhala drumming, particularly the *magul bera* for the Buddha (Example 1), are constructed as drum poetry that, while aligning with long and short beats (and a sense of pulse), must not emphasize the pulse too strongly. By contrast, drumming for *yakku* uses *pada*s (phrases) that are inauspicious, shorter, and more closely emphasize meter (Example 3)—though even in that context, no word for meter is used. Drumming for deities like Pattini (Example 2), I suggest, is in between: the *pada*s for deities are auspicious poetry and free of meter, but they are situated in a longer context of passages with more easily countable drumming.

In recent decades, several outside observers of Berava drumming (including a few non-Berava Sri Lankan musicologists) have insisted that, despite what the drummers say about their drum speech, their drumming can be analyzed through the Indian *tala* system. In my view, applying such foreign concepts to Sinhala Buddhist drumming risks forcing a genre that was conceived as sacred speech to *become* music, potentially invalidating its use as a sacred offering. While that conceptual transformation may seem minor, to an elder drummer I worked with, it is no coincidence that Sri Lanka's civil war (1983–2009) and the 2004 tsunami happened in the decades after Berava ritual knowledge was placed in schools for all castes to learn. Whether we believe in drumming's auspicious power or not, such a belief demonstrates that seemingly benign terms like "music" and "meter" come with conceptual baggage with tangible effects on peoples' lives. As students of the arts, we should stay attuned to the terminology that creators devise for themselves rather than assuming concepts like music and meter have a uniform, universal value.

Works Cited

Kapferer, Bruce. 1991 [1983]. *A Celebration of Demons: Exorcism and the Aesthetics of Healing in Sri Lanka*. Washington, DC: Smithsonian Books.

Kapferer, Bruce. 1997. *Feast of the Sorcerer: Practices of Consciousness and Power*. Chicago: University of Chicago Press.

Kulatillake, C. de S. 1976. *A Background to Sinhala Traditional Music of Sri Lanka*. Colombo: Department of Cultural Affairs.

Obeyesekere, Gananath. 1984. *The Cult of the Goddess Pattini*. Chicago: University of Chicago Press.

Peiris, Eshantha. 2020. "The *Gäta Beraya* Drumming Tradition of Sri Lanka." PhD diss., University of British Columbia.

Reed, Susan. 2010. *Dance and the Nation: Performance, Ritual, and Politics in Sri Lanka*. Madison: University of Wisconsin Press.

Scott, David. 1994. *Formations of Ritual: Colonial and Anthropological Discourses on the Sinhala Yak Tovil*. Minneapolis: University of Minnesota Press.

Suraweera, Sumuditha. 2009. "Sri Lankan, Low-Country, Ritual Drumming: The Raigama Tradition." PhD diss., University of Canterbury.

Sykes, Jim. 2018a. *The Musical Gift: Sonic Generosity in Post-War Sri Lanka*. New York: Oxford University Press.

Sykes, Jim. 2018b. "On the Sonic Materialization of Buddhist History: Drum-Speech in Southern Sri Lanka." *Analytical Approaches to World Music* 6(2): 1–74. http://iftawm.org/journal/oldsite/articles/2018a/Sykes_AAWM_Vol_6_2b.pdf.

Wirz, Paul. 1954. *Exorcism and the Art of Healing in Ceylon*. Leiden: E. J. Brill.

SECTION VI
DIASPORA AND GLOBALIZATION

Introduction by Nilanjana Bhattacharjya
and Sarah L. Morelli

As an appropriate bookend to the volume's first section, "Identity in Place and Community," we now explicitly consider the impact of large-scale transnational movement on people and artistic practices. Humankind has been on the move for tens of thousands of years, taking with them goods, technologies, and cultural practices (Bae et al. 2017). Scholars distinguish between forced and voluntary migration. "Diaspora," the term used for groups who live some distance from a homeland, is paradigmatically applied to Jewish communities throughout the world (Seroussi 2015). In the latter twentieth century, diaspora (uncapitalized) came to refer to any emigrant community with a significant numerical population that maintains a distinct cultural identity affectively tied to an ancestral homeland (Slobin 2011).

Populations have long moved into and out of the Indian Ocean region, by land and sea. Until recently, scholars' understanding of the manifold cultural influences and continuities across the region (especially prior to European colonization) have been obscured by "land-centric" area studies paradigms (Byl and Sykes 2020, 398). From as early as 1500 BCE, predictable monsoon winds and ocean navigability enabled ongoing exchange of goods and ideas between coastal cities from East Africa to the Southeast Asian archipelago. Many communities have settled in South Asia over the centuries, including East Africans who arrived as early as 1100 to form the present-day Sidi community (Catlin-Jairazbhoy and Jairazbhoy 2004) and Zoroastrians (also known as Parsis), who fled religious persecution in Persia in the seventh century. Communal differences are often a significant "push factor" for mass migrations. Beginning in 2017, hundreds of thousands of members of the Muslim Rohingya minority ethnic group fled persecution in Myanmar to refugee camps in neighboring Bangladesh. Simultaneously, climate change—another major cause of mass migration—has forced large numbers of Bangladeshis to leave their country in recent years. Adelaida Reyes's work was among the first to attune ethnomusicologists to involuntary immigrant and refugee issues, including the important roles music and dance often play in experiences of trauma, precarity, relocation, and resettlement (1999).

Beginning in the nineteenth century, we see many cases of people being lured into migration from South Asia under the British colonial regime. When Britain outlawed the slave trade in 1833, they (and later the Dutch and French) turned to a system of indentured servitude to supply laborers to their colonies around the world. Well over a million (mostly lower- and outcaste) people were transported from the Indian subcontinent primarily to work on sugar plantations in the Caribbean, South and East Africa, Malaya, Ceylon, and elsewhere. The vast majority of those who finished out labor contracts were compelled to remain in their worksites abroad. Some scholarship on these long-term diasporic communities has focused on questions of persistence and change in cultural practices (Myers 1998; Manuel 2015), others on twentieth-century artistic fusions, such as *chutney* in Trinidad and Tobago (Manuel 1998). While most Indo-Caribbeans came from the "Hindi belt" of northern India, a majority of indentured workers in present-day Malaysia, Brunei, and Singapore were Tamil speakers from South India. Most Malaysian Tamils continue to face discrimination as a marginalized underclass. Paige's* chapter in this section demonstrates how Tamil-language rappers of Malaysia's *sollisai* movement (which began in 2007) strategically draw on "pure" registers of the Tamil language, poetic literature, and karnatak music to legitimize their claims to representation in Tamil-language media.

South Asian immigration to Canada and the United States began in the late nineteenth century, when primarily Sikh men from Punjab were brought to western regions to work in forestry, agriculture, and building railroads. In the United States, xenophobic legislation banned most immigration from South Asia in 1917. The Immigration and Nationality Act of 1965 reopened immigration but prioritized white-collar workers in select occupations and their families. As such, a disproportionate number of South Asian immigrants came from educated, upper-caste, and upper-class communities, feeding into a "model minority" myth. Hate crimes and racially motivated violence against South Asian Americans increased dramatically following the September 11, 2001, attacks, which spurred political organizing and activism in the community (see, e.g., Kaur* [Section III]). This event, and later, the elections of Donald Trump and Narendra Modi, set the stage for increasingly narrow, rigid conceptions of national identity that in the US excluded South Asian Americans (and others), and in India particularly excluded Muslim, Christian, Dalit, and Adivasi people. Desai,* a second-generation Indian American dancemaker, draws on Gujarati *garba-raas* dance practices to create healing, inclusive spaces for those marginalized and traumatized by the 2016 US presidential election and its aftermath, as well as by the contemporary Hindu nationalist movement (see Jaffrelot 2009; Schultz* [Section II]). In employing *garba*'s egalitarian circle formation and other elements inherent to the dance form, Desai invites people of "all ages, races and ethnicities, religions, caste communities, genders, and abilities," to dance together, embodying a more inclusive vision of American identity.

As we consider diaspora, we inherently consider the nation that engenders its creation. Gopinath's pathbreaking "'Bombay, U.K., Yuba City': Bhangra Music and the Engendering of Diaspora" proposed that diasporic spaces help constitute what we consider as the nation, and in turn, the diasporic space often writes itself into the nation itself (1995). Conventional understandings of diaspora rely on a false hierarchy that privileges the nation as the authentic origin and demotes diasporic cultural practices as illegitimate offshoots. These chapters, instead, consider how musical practices within diasporic spaces highlight relationships and tensions between diasporas and national spaces, and in turn, continuously delineate and challenge our understanding of the borders of the nation as well as of whom it includes.

Bhattacharjya and DJ Rekha* explicitly challenge assumed homeland/diaspora relationships in examining *desi* dance music, produced both within India as well as outside India. Much *desi* dance music also travels from diasporic locations back to India—often via their interaction with other local music scenes—complicating the notion that culture originates in India and then travels outward to diasporic locations in derivative forms. These circuitous pathways redefine both the identity of South Asian music and its legitimate sites of production.

This complex dynamic is illustrative of the flows of global culture described by Appadurai as "scapes" (1990). As he notes, any inflow of global elements into a local space can be potentially homogenizing, and in any location, the balance between local majoritarian practices and identities and the global is constantly shifting to accommodate the continuity of local traditions. Paige's* chapter advances this concept; while examining how the hip-hop genre acquires new forms, meaning, and significance among Malaysian Tamil rappers who use the genre to challenge local hierarchies, he also notes that Malaysia has become a center of authenticity for Tamil-language hip-hop scenes around the world. Nimjee* examines the global Bollywood fitness phenomenon, based on her experiences with BollyX, a company offering online classes throughout the world. She argues that these classes reproduce and disseminate Bollywood *filmi* aesthetics, which, in conjunction with associated films, music, and dance, promote the global Bollywood culture industry. Furthermore, through teaching these aesthetics to a diverse clientele, BollyX classes help *desi* students define their membership both in a transnational cultural community and in the North American mainstream.

As Reed* demonstrates, Kandyan dancemaker Venuri Perera is also a member of a transnational community of artists who self-consciously draw from multiple aesthetic vocabularies and performance histories.[1] Perera integrates her extensive experience in Kandyan dance with her studies of contemporary dance in Pune and London to perform and teach a version of Kandyan dance that eschews some standard practices but is still based on her deeply embodied knowledge of the form. In her strategic departures from "tradition," Perera's work connects to Parijat Desai's gestures toward inclusivity, as Perera seeks to reclaim Kandyan dance from its present service to Sinhalese Buddhist nationalist politics and its associated violence, and to engage the participation of Tamils and other minority populations in Sri Lanka typically excluded from that tradition.

Most of the people featured in this section use the arts to speak out against forms of discrimination, advance a more progressive view of society, or navigate identity in diverse spaces. They also demonstrate a complex relationship to place that is increasingly the norm rather than the exception. Historical studies of the Indian Ocean region and elsewhere show us that globalization is not limited to the twentieth and twenty-first centuries, though what is unique to our contemporary times is the sheer ubiquity and rapid transmission of global influences. Geography often serves to define scholarly activities and specializations, but it serves as a limited frame of reference to understand the "porous boundaries" (Shelemay 1996) of academic disciplines and the cultural practices we endeavor to understand (Wallach and Clinton 2019).

---

[1] This approach, "always simultaneously local and translocal," is sometimes referred to as cosmopolitanism (Turino 2000, 7).

Works Cited

Appadurai, Arjun. 1990. "Disjuncture and Difference in the Global Culture Economy." *Theory Culture Society* 7: 295–310.

Bae, Christopher J., Katerina Douka, and Michael D. Petraglia. 2017. "On the Origin of Modern Humans: Asian Perspectives." *Science* 358(6368): 1269.

Byl, Julia, and Jim Sykes. 2020. "Ethnomusicology and the Indian Ocean: On the Politics of Area Studies." *Ethnomusicology* 64(3): 394–421.

Catlin-Jairazbhoy, Amy, and Nazir Ali Jairazbhoy. 2004. *From Africa to India: Sidi Music in the Indian Ocean Diaspora*. Film. Apsara Media (for Intercultural Education). 74 minutes.

Gopinath, Gayatri. 1995. "'Bombay, U.K., Yuba City': Bhangra Music and the Engendering of Diaspora." *Diaspora: A Journal of Transnational Studies* 4: 303–321.

Jaffrelot, Christophe, ed. 2009. *Hindu Nationalism: A Reader*. Princeton, NJ: Princeton University Press.

Manuel, Peter. 1998. "Chutney and Indo-Trinidadian Cultural Identity." *Popular Music* 17(1): 21–43.

Manuel, Peter. 2015. *Tales, Tunes, and Tassa Drums: Retention and Invention in Indo-Caribbean Music*. Urbana-Champaign: University of Illinois Press.

Myers, Helen. 1998. *Music of Hindu Trinidad: Songs from the India Diaspora*. Chicago: University of Chicago Press.

Reyes, Adelaida. 1999. *Songs of the Caged, Songs of the Free: Music and the Vietnamese Refugee Experience*. Philadelphia: Temple University Press.

Seroussi, Edwin. 2015. "Jewish Music and Diaspora." In *The Cambridge Companion to Jewish Music*, edited by Joshua S. Walden, 27–40. Cambridge: Cambridge University Press.

Shelemay, Kay Kaufman. 1996. "Crossing Boundaries in Music and Musical Scholarship: A Perspective from Ethnomusicology." *Musical Quarterly* 80(1): 13–30.

Slobin, Mark. 2011. "The Destiny of Diaspora." In *The Cultural Study of Music: A Critical Introduction*, edited by Martin Clayton, Trevor Herbert, and Richard Middleton, 284–296. New York: Routledge.

Turino, Thomas. 2000. *Nationalists, Cosmopolitans, and Popular Music in Zimbabwe*. Chicago: University of Chicago Press.

Wallach, Jeremy, and Esther Clinton. 2019. "Theories of the Post-colonial and Globalization: Ethnomusicologists Grapple with Power, History, Media, and Mobility." In *Theory for Ethnomusicology: Histories, Conversations, Insights*, edited by Harris M. Berger and Ruth M. Stone, 114–140. New York: Routledge.

26

Contemporizing Kandyan Dance

Susan A. Reed

Seated cross-legged in the light-filled seaside apartment she shares with two visual artists in the Colombo neighborhood of Wellawatte, dancemaker Venuri Perera demonstrates a gesture from her first contemporary piece, *Abhinishkramanaya*: a "melting" of the *namaskaraya* (*namaskāraya*), a traditional salutation dancers perform for their teacher, the gods, and the Buddha. As she explains, *Abhinishramanaya*—a word that refers to Prince Siddhartha's renunciation of the world in order to become a Buddha—was created to express her departure from Kandyan dance: the traditional Sri Lankan dance form she had performed for years as a member of the famed Chitrasena Dance Company, the island's best-known professional troupe.[1]

Like other contemporary choreographers in Sri Lanka, Venuri seeks to draw from her deep, embodied knowledge of a "classical" form to create new dance works that speak to the contemporary moment.[2] Yet for her and other dancemakers, this process is challenging and often fraught, given the status of Kandyan dance as the national dance of Sri Lanka and symbol of the traditional culture of the Sinhalas, the island's majority ethnic group. The roots of Kandyan dance are in rituals performed for local deities by hereditary male dancers of the Berava (*beravā*, drummer) caste. Kandyan stage dances that drew from these rituals were largely created during the nationalist era of the 1940s and 1950s as a sign of Sinhala cultural and national identity.

Hereditary dancers, the state, and the Chitrasena Company all played critical roles in Kandyan dance's development, with the goal of preserving the

---

[1] The word "traditional" in this context refers to the standardized form of Kandyan dance taught in schools, in this case, the Chitrasena School. The Chitrasena School developed its own style of Kandyan dance (see Nurnberger 1998). While there is significant variation among styles of the dance, they share a similar aesthetic, discussed below.

[2] In South Asia the term "classical" denotes complex codified dance forms said to be rooted in the aesthetic theory of the *Natyashastra*. Indian classical dances are, like Kandyan dance, forms that were adapted from ritual practices and "classicized" in the early to mid-twentieth century for the stage. Thus, classical dances reflect values of modernity in terms of staging, costuming, themes, and choreography. For details on the classicization of Kandyan dance see Reed 2010, 152–153.

dance as a traditional form. Though the dance itself has undergone significant changes since the 1950s, the dominant *understanding* of the dance—as a cultural product and sign of Sinhala Buddhist identity that should be preserved and faithfully transmitted—remains.

Since her first performance of *Abhinishkramanaya* in 2008, Venuri has challenged this view of Kandyan dance. Adapting the strictures and structures of the dance and its pedagogy—and articulating this process as "play"—she redefines Kandyan dance as an artistic form that can be used to embody and express contemporary aesthetic and social concerns. This shift in perspective—from viewing Kandyan dance as something "sacred" and unchangeable, to viewing it as a "very rich form" with which one can "play"—is truly radical (Venuri Perera, interview with the author, March 2019).[3] This "play" includes drawing from and altering Kandyan dance movements, as well as utilizing anti-hierarchical pedagogical practices. Venuri's perspective on Kandyan dance has evolved over the course of many years, moving from an earlier struggle to greater confidence in her choices in pedagogy and artistry.

Venuri is a central figure in the development of contemporary dance in Sri Lanka. She is not only Sri Lanka's best-known solo contemporary dancer, but also an influential teacher, mentor, and curator of contemporary dance. Over the last several years, she has been deeply involved in expanding knowledge about contemporary dance in Sri Lanka, largely through her work with the Colombo-based Goethe-Institut. She is dedicated to expanding the contemporary dance landscape in Sri Lanka, drawing from her deep experience with dance education and practice abroad and at home, and as part of an international community of dancers.[4]

Venuri's process in redefining her relationship with Kandyan dance began with recognizing the limitations of her training at the Chitrasena School. During her teens, Venuri was a principal dancer for the company, where she had trained since the age of six. Over time, however, she became dissatisfied with the constraints of the company. As a "city brought-up" young woman, she could not relate to the village dance-dramas that were its mainstay.[5] She wanted something "different," desiring to learn "how to use the things of the

---

[3] Unless otherwise noted, all quotations in this chapter are from interviews I conducted with Venuri in Sri Lanka in March 2019 and personal communications with her in July 2020.

[4] See Reed 2021 for a fuller profile of Venuri.

[5] Since Venuri's time at the school, the Chitrasena Company has significantly changed its choreographic process in large part due to the influence of Nrityagram, the famed Indian dance ensemble, with which the company has had a creative partnership for over a decade.

past to speak to the present" and to employ dance as a means to "imagine a future." She was also unhappy with the hierarchical pedagogical model of the school that replicated the traditional teacher-student relationship, in which the teacher's views are unquestioned and the purpose of training is to transmit knowledge from one generation to the next.[6]

Leaving the country was instrumental in affording Venuri the opportunity to break with the Chitrasena tradition and gain knowledge about contemporary dance. In 2000, at the age of eighteen, she went to India to attend university in Pune, where she lived for five years. In 2007, she left for the UK to pursue an M.A. in dance at the Laban Institute in London. Though she returned to Sri Lanka in 2008—now defining herself as an independent solo performer—she has continued to train and perform on occasion in Asia and Europe. Since 2008, most of her work has focused on social and political issues of nationalism, violence, patriarchy, colonialism, and class. She is well known internationally and among Colombo's tight-knit artistic community for sociopolitical works that provoke and challenge the status quo (Hisano 2017).

In the years since she returned from the UK, Venuri has not performed traditional Kandyan dance on stage, though she still does teach it. Instead she has drawn from it, in varying degrees, to create some of her performance pieces. Though she no longer sees herself as a "Kandyan dancer" in the conventional sense, she acknowledges that Kandyan dance "is my training. That is what I have in my body."

In contrast to her political performances, her current interest in Kandyan dance is in focusing on "form." She wants to now approach Kandyan dance as "art for art's sake" rather than primarily "using" it for sociopolitical commentary. In this phase of her relationship with Kandyan dance, she asserts, "I'm going to start with the body or the form without having a concept and an idea."

Contemporary dancers in South Asia operate within a historical context in which "classical" dances—which are modern forms that were repopulated, reconstructed, renamed, resituated, and restored for the proscenium stage (Allen 1997, 63–64)—remain the touchstone and apex of dance performance among the general public. However, since the mid-1980s in India, the field of contemporary dance—which often draws from classical forms by expanding or extending them—has grown considerably (see Katrak 2011). In Sri Lanka,

---

[6] Compare Venuri's perspective on pedagogy with that discussed in Groesbeck.*

though, for a variety of reasons—including a rigid state dance curriculum and a twenty-six-year civil war that ended only in 2009—contemporary dance is relatively new, and very much in the early stages of its development. A pivotal moment for contemporary dance occurred in 2010, after the end of the war, when the Goethe-Institut inaugurated the biennial Colombo Dance Platform and its accompanying Forum to promote contemporary dance through performances, workshops, and exchanges with Asian, European, and American choreographers. It was at the first Platform in 2010 that Venuri first performed *Abhinishkramanaya* for a Sri Lankan audience.

Play in Performance and Pedagogy

"Playing" with the *form* of Kandyan dance—a process that she initiated with *Abhinishkramanaya*—is now a key focus of Venuri's dance teaching and practice. While at first she had some anxiety about "playing" with tradition, her experiences at the Laban Institute and later with contemporary dancemakers in Asia dramatically changed her perspective. At Laban, in fact, she read a thesis about the modernity of Kandyan dance, and realized that rather than viewing it as something "sacred" that could not be changed, it was actually a "modern" form that could be a source for experimentation. Her experience at Laban, she reflects, "changed the way I looked at my own tradition. . . . Which gave me a sense of freedom, that actually it's a kind of modern form. And actually it's OK to change some things." By "playing," Venuri means taking elements from the form and altering and modifying them significantly, trying out different configurations.

Play also means freedom and release from inhibitions and societal and self-imposed strictures on one's creativity. In discussing the struggles she has had in innovating the Kandyan dance, Venuri noted in 2019 that it has taken her many years to get to the point of feeling free to play with the form due to "mind blocks." Some of these blocks are societal—concern about "what will people say?"—while others are "self-imposed."

One of these "mind blocks" is the idea that Kandyan dance is essentially tied to Sinhala culture and identity. One of Venuri's most ambitious—indeed radical—ideas is to see if it is possible to divorce Kandyan dance from concepts of, as she says, "nation and culture and preservation" as well as "respect [and] the sacred," which have been central to its identity since its inception. In part, she wants to remove these "labels" so that the form can be made available to Tamils and members of other ethnic groups in Sri Lanka: "I am wondering if we can look at it as something that can be removed from this identity as Sinhalese, and can we just look at it as a form. There is so much in it that can be used. Such an interesting form. So how can you play with it in that way? Removing all these other labels that have been put on it."

The freedom to question and challenge the status quo is central to Venuri's style of teaching, as it is for her performances. She abhors authority and rigid structures: "Even when I'm in class, when I'm put into structures, I don't want to do it anymore.... I have this thing of challenging authority." In workshops and classes, she strives to create a climate of questioning and openness with her students. For example, Venuri does not allow her students to touch her feet (a common practice in dance classes), seeing this as a gesture of deference and subservience that is anathema to her philosophy of teaching. At times, Venuri even hesitates to call herself a teacher, seeing the "teacher" label as implying the kind of hierarchical relationship that she seeks to avoid.

In her teaching, Venuri emphasizes loosening one's ideas about what is "proper" or "correct" in dance to see what possibilities for expression this might open up. Rather than following the rules of dance in a regimented fashion, the idea of play recalls the "spirit of creativity and fun" that was a hallmark of pioneering Indian contemporary dancer Chandralekha (1923–2006), whom Venuri deeply admires (Bharucha 1995, 249). Like Chandralekha, whose roots were in the classical dance *bharatanatyam*, Venuri encourages her students to break the "unspoken rules" of a classical form, such as never showing your back or feet to the audience.

Venuri also encourages her students to think about, process, and question what they are being taught. At a 2019 workshop with young choreographers, I observed how Venuri worked in concert with the dancers, largely through raising questions, to develop a "shared language" to "talk about and do movement." In one such session, she asked the dancers to enumerate the "inherent qualities" of Kandyan dance; what, for example, is involved in thinking about the *lasya* (*lāsya*, gentle/graceful) and *tandava* (*tāṇḍava*, assertive/powerful) qualities embedded in the form? Venuri presented this way of viewing Kandyan dance as a possibility: a new mode of exploration, not as prescriptive.

At the conclusion of the workshop, Venuri had the dancers sit in a circle on the floor, where she asked them to share what they had learned, how it felt in their bodies, and the challenges they encountered. Throughout, she made clear that the point of the workshop was to explore, analyze, and "play" with the form to see if this might be something that could be useful for their own choreographic practice. The open, dialogical methods she employed made the workshop a site for the co-creation, not just transmission, of dance knowledge.

Aesthetics of Kandyan Dance

Abhinishkramanaya was Venuri's first exploration in "playing with" the Kandyan dance form. To understand how she drew from and altered the dance for this piece, I provide here a brief introduction to the aesthetics of Kandyan dance.[7]

Within the schema of South Asian classical dances, Kandyan dance is classified as a *nritta* or "pure dance" form, largely devoid of mimetic movement or symbolic gestures.[8] In solo and group performances, the dancer executes abstract movements performed to the rhythms of the *gata beraya* (*gäṭa beraya*), or Kandyan drum.[9] The dances typically build from relatively slow and measured steps to a climax of rapid, athletic, and acrobatic movements such as leaps, turns, and aerial spins. Kandyan dance aesthetics places a high value on the execution of technique: its accuracy, energy, and precision. While dancers may be lauded for their particular strengths, such as graceful arm movements, or powerful, athletic leaps, overall technical virtuosity is paramount.

Kandyan dance is classified as a primarily *tandava* form: powerful, assertive and vigorous. When the form was adapted for women on stage in the 1940s and 1950s, it was modified and made more *lasya*: gentle and graceful. However, the fundamentally *tandava* character of the dance remains, even for women, as evident in the basic, foundational position of the dance, the *mandiya* (*mäṇḍiya*), as shown in Figure 26.1.

The demeanor of a Kandyan dancer, regardless of gender, should be regal and proud; this is rooted in the ritual of the dance's origin, the *Kohomba kankariya* (*Kohoṁbā kankāriya*), in which dancers play the role of a healer-king. The iconic male Kandyan dancer wears an elaborately ornamented costume, known as the *ves*, which is derived from that of ritual performers.

---

[7] This sketch of Kandyan dance outlines basic aesthetic principles applicable to most dances. For a more comprehensive analysis, including modifications and changes in the dance, see Reed 2010.

[8] When Kandyan dance began to be performed for foreigners in the mid-twentieth century, however, mimetic elements were introduced and are now frequently seen especially in performances of the *vannama* dances described below.

[9] See Peiris 2018 for an analysis of the rhythms of Kandyan (up-country) drumming.

Figure 26.1 Kandyan dancer and ritualist Tittapajjala Samaraweera in the *mandiya* position, wearing the full *ves* costume. Photo by the author.

Women's costumes typically include modified elements derived from the *ves* costume such as a headpiece, arm and wrist ornaments, a softly draped garment for the lower body, and anklets.

The *mandiya* position is an essential element of Kandyan dance. Some semblance of the *mandiya* should be maintained throughout a dance, even when one is performing the most athletic movements or jauntily walking to the rhythms of the Kandyan drum. Like other South Asian classical dances, the traditional dance is structured to emphasize symmetry, with many movement phrases performed first to the right, then to the left, and then to the center. On stage, dancers often move in a linear fashion, forward and back, facing the audience. However, in some dances, such as the popular *Kuveni Asna* (shown in ⊙ Video example 26.1), dancers also perform in circular patterns.

The gaze of the dancer should be focused on the hands, following a common aesthetic principle of South Asian classical dances that states "where the hand goes, the eyes follow" (Reed 2010, 45). According to hereditary dancers, the facial expression should be neutral, but pleasant. However, smiling is now a common feature of staged performances of Kandyan dance, especially for women.

Kandyan dance is accompanied musically by the *gata beraya*, a double-headed wooden barrel drum tied to the waist (see Sykes*). The drum is played vigorously, and in a theater or other enclosed space can be thunderous. Drumming and dancing are closely coordinated, and the dancer's movements are often synchronized with the drum rhythms.[10] Singing can be a part of some dance performances, such as *vannama*s, among the most popular of the staged Kandyan dances.[11]

The *vannama*s are a group of eighteen dances whose songs describe gods, mythical figures, animals, and aspects of the Buddha's life. The songs are usually performed by a solo singer, who may also play the small cymbals (*talampota*). The traditional style of a *vannama* dance does not depict what is described in the song, but rather may suggest some aspect of it through the rhythm. Modernized versions of *vannama*s, which now predominate, often add mimetic elements through movement and/or costume. For example, in the *Gajaga* (elephant) *Vannama* a dancer may depict the waving of an elephant's trunk, or the flapping of its ears.

Namaskaraya

While Venuri plays with elements of Kandyan dance throughout *Abhinishkramanaya*, another element she incorporates is not strictly part of the dance, per se. This is the *namaskaraya*, a ritual salutation that Kandyan dancers perform to honor one's parents, dance teacher, the gods, and the

---

[10] For more on the relationship of dancing and drumming see Reed 2010, 39–40.
[11] See Jayaweera 2004 for a detailed description of the musical structure of a *vannama*.

Buddha at the beginning and end of every dance class.[12] The *namaskaraya* is a feature of most, if not all, South Asian classical dances though *how* it is performed varies according to dance genre.

The traditional *namaskaraya* of hereditary dance lineages has four parts. In the first three parts the dancer, while crouched on her heels, recites the phrase, "teiyat, teiyat, teiyat, tam." With each of the first three beats ("teiyat"), she crosses her hands and touches the earth with her fingertips. On the fourth beat ("tam") the dancer presses her palms together in a worshipping gesture. In the first part, the dancer then brings her hands together to her forehead, paying homage to her parents; in the second part she repeats this gesture for her teacher. In the third part, she brings her hands to her chest, honoring the gods. In the fourth part, she recites a different rhythmic phrase, "tei tei, ta ta, teiyat tam" with her hands in front of her chest and slowly moves into a standing position, in homage to the Buddha, ending the movement with a slight bowing of the head (see ⏵ Video example 26.2, cue point 0:22).

Dancers who studied with the Chitrasena Company enact the *namaskaraya* differently, in reverse order from that of many hereditary dancers. In addition, the Chitrasena-style *namaskaraya* begins with the hands held well above the head (for the Buddha), then move in front of the forehead (for the gods), and then to the chest (for the teacher) (personal communication with Venuri, July 30, 2020; see also Nurnberger 1998, 186–187). As Venuri was trained in the Chitrasena style, this is how she performs the *namaskaraya* (⏵ Video example 26.3).

Abhinishkramanaya

Abhinishkramanaya is Venuri's first contemporary solo work, as well as her first "personal" piece, marking her "point of departure" from the Kandyan dance tradition. In this piece, Venuri reworks several elements of traditional Kandyan dance, such as the *namaskaraya* and *mandiya*, to depict her struggle in breaking with tradition. For choreographing *Abhinishkramanaya*, Venuri was awarded the Laban Institute's Simone Michelle Award for Outstanding Choreography in 2008. She subsequently performed the piece in Colombo (2010) and at the Attakkalari India Biennial in Bengaluru

---

[12] Not all dance lineages (*parampara*) include honoring parents in the *namaskaraya*; this varies by lineage. In some contexts, non-Buddhist dancers may choose to honor beings other than the Buddha in their *namaskaraya*.

(2011). In *Abhinishkramanaya* Venuri draws from two very different movement vocabularies, Kandyan and contemporary (Western) dance: "During the process I wanted to use Sri Lankan dance style as it is so much embedded in me, but create/find my own vocabulary incorporating my contemporary training."

For the performance at the Attakkalari Biennial, she provided a note describing the work as one which "depicts the mental struggle felt at the moment of departure from the learned, honoured and familiar to the new, unknown and unfamiliar. A beginning of a journey." A major inspiration for the piece was the *Thuranga Vannama*, one of Venuri's favorite Kandyan dances. The song of the *vannama* describes Prince Siddhartha's departure from his royal home—symbolizing the worldly life—on his treasured horse, Kanthaka. In the context of the Buddha's life, the Sinhala word "abinishkramanaya" means the "going forth from home."[13]

In contrast to the assertive, energetic, and vigorous movements of Kandyan dance, *Abhinishkramanaya*, is slow, meditative and minimalist (see Box 26.1). A solo work of about nine minutes, the piece is dense with meaning. As Venuri notes, "I tried to do only what was necessary, and not do any extra movement. This was a very personal process/journey for me and a very difficult one." *Abhinishkramanaya* shows Venuri "playing with" Kandyan dance in new ways to show "the struggle of trying to move away and coming back." In creating the work, Venuri was inspired by the idea of "not *performing* a piece but being in the moment, while 'inviting to be seen'"—a concept that she had learned at Laban from Genevieve Grady, a student of pioneering American experimental dance choreographer Deborah Hay.

As *Abhinishkramanaya* is a solo dance, she has to show "everything in one body." Though not by deliberate choice, she found herself using her right hand "to symbolize breaking away (or trying to) in different ways." In terms of Kandyan dance, Venuri plays with three aspects of movement and sound: arm and hand gestures, the spine, and the voice. This is most clearly demonstrated in the ways in which she modifies the *mandiya* and the *namaskaraya* throughout the performance (Figure 26.2). The staging and dress of *Abhinishkramanaya* also deviates from a typical performance. The piece has no musical accompaniment, and in contrast to the heavily ornamented Kandyan dance costume, Venuri wears a simple red tunic and black tights.[14]

---

[13] Patrick Olivelle, personal communication, June 3, 2020.
[14] This description is of the 2011 performance of *Abhinishkramanaya* at the Attakkalari India Biennial (▶ Video example 26.4).

Figure 26.2 Venuri performs the *namaskaraya* in *Abhinishkramanaya*. Photo credit: Attakkalari India Biennial; used with permission.

Box 26.1 Exercises

(1) Watch the *Kuveni Asna* ("Lament of Kuveni"), a traditional Kandyan dance, performed by students from the Risikala Aesthetic College, Kandy (▶ Video example 26.1).
  (A) Reflect on your response to the performance as a whole.
  (B) Try to imitate the *mandiya* position, as shown at cue point 0:34.
  (C) Observe how dancers employ the *mandiya* in a variety of movements. Describe the movements, as well as which elements of the *mandiya* are retained, that begin at the following cue points: 0:47, 1:01, 1:23, 2:54, 3:15, 3:23, 3:44, 5:38, 6:34, 7:43.

(2) Observe these two performances of the *namaskaraya*:
   (A) *Namaskaraya* of hereditary dancers, as performed by students in a dance class taught by the legendary ritualist and dancer, Tittapajjala Suramba (▶ Video example 26.2, cue point 0:22–0:36)
   (B) Chitrasena-style *namaskaraya* performed by Venuri Perera (▶ Video example 26.3)
(3) Watch the full performance of *Abhinishkramayana* (▶ Video example 26.4)
   (A) Reflect on your response to the performance as a whole.
   (B) Keeping in mind that the *namaskaraya* and *mandiya* represent the Kandyan dance tradition, how is Venuri's struggle to move away from tradition depicted?
   (C) Watch the following sections of *Abhinishkramayana* again and describe how Venuri modifies the *namaskaraya*:
   Variation 1: 3:52–4:58
   Variation 2: 5:19–6:25
   Variation 3: 8:52–9:12
   (D) Describe how Venuri "plays with" the *mandiya* in these examples:
   Variation 1: 1:35–3:42
   Variation 2: 3:43–3:55
   Variation 3: 7:28–7:35

Discussion: Reflect on and compare your responses to the two performances: *Kuveni Asna* and *Abhinishkramanaya*. How does a focus on Kandyan dance as "form" open it up for creating new aesthetic possibilities for the dance? How does a focus on Kandyan dance as "form" present the potential for expanding it to new groups of dancers within Sri Lanka? What is the relationship between a dance form and the practices used to teach that form in terms of how dance and knowledge of dance are understood and constructed? Compare the traditional teaching methods of Kandyan dance to the methods employed by Venuri.

Conclusion

Contemporary dancers in South Asia grapple with questions of how to make classical dance forms relevant for current times. Answers to these questions, as many as they are varied, constitute heated subjects for debate in the dance world. In this chapter, I have focused on the work of Venuri Perera to illustrate how one South Asian dancemaker seeks to challenge the dominant conception of classical dance as a venerated cultural object to be preserved by viewing it as a rich form that can be reworked for a myriad of artistic purposes. For Venuri, a central method of "contemporizing" the Kandyan dance is through "play"—the freedom to adapt and alter dance movements and combine them in new configurations. This philosophy of play is also central to her dance teaching. Eschewing the hierarchy embedded in the traditional teacher-student relationship, she creates a climate of openness with her students, encouraging them to question and engage in dialogues about their process and practice.

Venuri also seeks to challenge the idea that dance must be integrally tied to ideas of nation, culture, and Sinhala ethnic identity. In the current ultra-nationalist climate in which Kandyan dance continues to be promoted as a key symbol of Sinhala Buddhist culture and nation, the idea that the dance can be seen solely as "form" is both aesthetically and politically provocative. As Venuri continues to work as a dancemaker and performer, and as a mentor and teacher to the next generation of Sri Lankan choreographers, these radical perspectives will no doubt continue to shape the emerging field of contemporary dance in Sri Lanka.

Works Cited

Allen, Matthew. 1997. "Rewriting the Script for South Indian Dance." *TDR: The Drama Review* 41(3): 63–100.

Bharucha, Rustom. 1995. *Chandralekha: Woman Dance Resistance*. New Delhi: Indus.

Hisano, Atsuko. 2017. "The Body as Provocateur: The Changing of Dance in Sri Lanka." Japan Foundation Asia Center. https://jfac.jp/en/culture/features/asiahundreds021/.

Jayaweera, Almut. 2004. "Vannama: A Classical Dance Form and Its Musical Structure." *World of Music* 46(3): 49–64.

Katrak, Ketu H. 2011. *Contemporary Indian Dance: New Creative Choreography in India and the Diaspora*. New York: Palgrave Macmillan.

Nurnberger, Marianne. 1998. *Dance Is the Language of the Gods: The Chitrasena School and the Traditional Roots of Sri Lankan Stage Dance*. Amsterdam: VU University Press.

Peiris, Eshantha. 2018. "Changing Conceptualizations of Rhythm in Sri Lankan Up-Country Percussion Music." *Analytical Approaches to World Music* 6(2): 1–31. https://www.aawmjournal.com/articles/2018a/Peiris_AAWM_Vol_6_2.html.

Reed, Susan A. 2010. *Dance and the Nation: Performance, Ritual, and Politics in Sri Lanka*. Madison: University of Wisconsin Press.

Reed, Susan A. 2021. "Bathed in Blood: Ritual Performance as Political Critique." *Asian Ethnology* 80(1): 165–198.

27

Desi Dance Music

A Transnational Phenomenon

Nilanjana Bhattacharjya and DJ Rekha

The genre of *desi* dance music offers us new ways to understand how music travels from one place to another, as well as how and why we label this music as South Asian at all. The word *desi* (*desī*, pronounced "deh-see" or "dé-see") comes from the Sanskrit term *des* meaning "land" or "country" and is often used to convey a shared sense of culture and identity based on people's heritage in India (particularly Northern India), Bangladesh, and Pakistan. In many accounts of *desi* dance music's historical development, scholars identify its origin within South Asia and trace its dissemination from there to other locations in the South Asian diaspora, that is, those locations outside South Asia where people of South Asian heritage have settled and formed new communities (see Banerji and Baumann 1990). Some forms of music in the South Asian diaspora utilize sonic elements associated with South Asian classical, folk, and popular traditions—whether it is the incorporation of the Hindustani classical *sitar*, folk drumming on the *dhol*, or the high-pitched voices of playback singers Lata Mangeshkar and Asha Bhosle—and thus directly communicate a relationship to South Asia. But today, many forms of so-called *desi* dance music do not contain such readily discernable, regionally specific codes.

Within this chapter, we argue that (1) *desi* dance music is produced in South Asia and in multiple locations throughout the world, from which it travels in different directions through transnational networks; (2) the various national identities and roles of musicians as producers, guest artists, and/or music directors further complicate how these songs travel through transnational networks of production across Great Britain, the United States, Latin America, and South Asia; (3) how these songs define and express a *desi* identity through their sound elements may at times relate less to South Asia itself, and much more to how people of South Asian heritage distinguish their own identities from those of other people where they live; and (4) *desi* dance music often reaches its listeners through film music. To illustrate these four points, we analyze the songs "Push It Up" (2006) by Rishi Rich, "Tha Kar Ke" from the Bollywood film *Golmaal Returns* (2008), and "Baamulaiza" from the Bollywood film *De Dana Dan* (2009). These three examples demonstrate the influences of American hip-hop and R&B, Caribbean and Latin music, and specific individuals, locations, and media on *desi* dance music. In drawing from multiple genres and styles, *desi* dance music is a creative expression that flows against an essential sense of national, regional, or diasporic identity.

Desi Dance Music and the Question of Origins

Scholars have often focused on *bhangra*, a Punjabi music and dance genre popular in the diaspora, to narrate how South Asian music transforms as it travels from the homeland to diasporic locations. In this history, *desi* dance music begins with *bhangra*'s roots in the Punjabi heartland of Northwest India and Pakistan. From there, it migrates to Britain, where artists like Bally Sagoo and Apache Indian in the 1980s and 1990s integrate it with Afro-Caribbean dancehall music. Finally, during the late 1990s and early 2000s, *bhangra* artists such as Panjabi MC begin to incorporate hip-hop into their songs.[1] This version of history suggests that *desi* dance music originates in South Asia and then develops in South Asian diasporic communities in Britain and the United States. But this narrative does not explain the presence of Caribbean and Latin American influences and sonic elements encountered in contemporary *desi* dance music, such as the incorporation of reggae in the song "Baamulaiza," "Tha Kar Ke"'s riff on Daddy Yankee's Spanish-language *reggaeton*, or images found in the music video for "Push It Up," filmed on location in Puerto Rico.

A closer look at the historical trajectory of *bhangra* and *bhangra*'s identity reveals that the narrative outlined above cannot contain what we see. Although many identify *bhangra*'s deep historical roots in the Punjabi heartland, Gibb Schreffler notes that *bhangra* is only documented as a distinct,

---

[1] Panjabi MC remixed his 1998 song "Mundian to Bach Ke" in 2003 to include a rap by Jay-Z, "Beware of the Boys."

recognizable form in 1920, when a local newspaper describes a community-oriented dance performed by Punjabis of the Jatt caste around harvest time (2013, 390). The Partition of India in 1947, which split the region of Punjab between India and Pakistan, displaced many of *bhangra*'s performers from their ancestral lands. After Partition, Punjabis began to perform *bhangra* within the context of "folkloric reconstructions" produced for film music and other popular genres. Beyond Punjab, the performance of *bhangra* served to define Punjab's identity within a postcolonial context (Schreffler 2013, 393). Schreffler argues that it is the popular construction of the *bhangra* folk dance after Partition that serves as the basis for *bhangra*'s next well-documented transformation by South Asian migrants to Britain during the late 1970s and 1980s (2013, 393). In this transformation, drum kits, bass guitars, lead guitars, and synthesizers are used alongside, or replace, more traditional Punjabi folk instruments such as the *tumbi, algozeh, and chimta,* and even the *dhol,* a barrel-shaped drum whose swinging rhythm often dominates *bhangra.* We should not assume, however, that traditional Punjabi instruments come from South Asia, while the other sounds come from Europe. South Asian film music from the 1940s onward regularly drew from swing, rock and roll, and other popular music practices, often associated with Europe and the United States, but simultaneously enjoyed throughout the world. Anjali Gera Roy in her book *Bhangra Moves: From Ludhiana to London and Beyond* rightly observes that *bhangra* scholars thus far "have all studied Bhangra in a diasporized domain ignoring that Bhangra now flows in multiple directions, which calls for a transnational framework" (2011, 3).

To illustrate how *desi* dance music, including *bhangra*, flows in multiple directions and incorporates influences from African American and Afro Caribbean music, we draw on Paul Gilroy's theorization of the African and African diasporic transnational framework, as described in his seminal book *The Black Atlantic* (1993) to apply to *desi* dance music. Gilroy asks, "What special analytical problems arise if a style, genre, or particular performance of music is identified as being expressive of the absolute essence of the group that produced it?" (1993, 75). In relation to *desi* dance music, we need to consider how musical transmissions and adaptations by respective diasporic populations sometimes contradict what's been produced so far, and how scholars should go about resolving those contradictions. We must reconsider the value we so often place on music's origins—as opposed to that music's subsequent transformations. Finally, if we acknowledge that music both constitutes and signifies difference, we must also consider how any engagement with this music relates to the self-identity of the group producing that music. Any attempt to answer these questions will, and should, complicate any claim that music expresses a unified, essentialized sense of identity.

With respect to cultural heritage, racial authenticity, and the valuing of origins, in *The Black Atlantic*, Gilroy explicitly criticizes accounts of diasporic cultural production that privilege the homeland as the source of the most authentic version of black culture. He also criticizes accounts of the expression of black traditions in diasporic locations that reduce them to "crises of self-belief and racial identity" (1993, 194). In doing this, he questions the tendency to associate the homeland with tradition, and diasporic locations with modernity (1993, 194–197). He argues, instead, that there has long been "two-way" traffic between African cultural forms and diasporic populations, which he conveys, in part, by citing the African American musician James Brown's description of his band's relationship to Nigerian Afrobeat pioneer Fela Kuti: "[Fela would] come to hear us, and we came to hear him. . . . He was kind of like the African James Brown. His band had strong rhythm. I think Clyde [Stubblefield] picked up on it in his drumming, and Bootsy [Collins, the bassist] dug it too. Some of the ideas my band was getting from that band had come from me in the first place, but that was okay with me. It made the music that much stronger" (Brown and Tucker 1986, 221 in Gilroy 1993, 199). Gilroy offers additional examples of this "two-way" traffic as he describes how South African townships have adapted jazz and other African American influences, and how Rastafari culture in Zimbabwe has incorporated Caribbean and British reggae. These examples illustrate how black music exists and is produced outside any single unidirectional line of transmission from the homeland to the diaspora. If we consider the British origins of the musicians and producers Rishi Rich, Juggy D, and Jay Sean who produced "Push It Up" in the late 2000s alongside the origins of the more recent Caribbean-influenced Hindi film songs "Tha Kar Ke" and "Baamulaiza," we can trace similar multidirectional networks.

Transnational Connections: Apache Indian and Panjabi MC

By the late 1990s, the British Punjabi musicians Apache Indian and Panjabi MC had released songs that drew on dancehall, reggae, and hip-hop, which became popular hits throughout Britain. In 1993, Apache Indian, born in

Birmingham, England, released "Arranged Marriage," a collaboration with British Jamaican reggae musician Maxi Priest, as well as "Boom-Shack-A-Lack," a collaboration with African American rapper Tim Dog (▶ Video example 27.1). He described his music as *bhangramuffin*, a fusion of *bhangra* with *ragamuffin* ("*ragga*,") a subgenre of Jamaican reggae and dancehall. As one critic writes, "Apache's music combines traditional Eastern instruments with ragga's state-of-the-art digital crunch, and his language is a spectacular collision of British Caribbean and Punjabi street-slang—'Straight from Delhi on a flying carpet, with a million watts of hockey stick'" (Thompson 1993). Apache Indian's music also circulated in India, even if at first some Indian music critics dismissed it:

> If Apache is big in Britain, he is massive in India. His album has sold nearly 200,000 copies and his tour in June, with all proceeds going to India's National Association of the Blind, threatened to make sense of his questionable sobriquet "The Gandhi of Pop." There was the occasional dissenting voice—"Most of his songs have almost an identical beat," carped *Delhi Midday*; and the *Pioneer* railed against "insipid lyrics, canned music and nonsensical rap" . . . The President of India wanted to meet him, so did Gandhi's granddaughter, and the Governor of Bombay called him a national hero. (Thompson)

Although critics link Apache Indian's music to "traditional Eastern" sounds, as he produced this music, he actually engaged more substantively with British Jamaican culture and African American hip-hop than with anything connected to South Asia itself—something that explains Indian music critics' mixed reactions to his music.

Apache Indian's collaborations with British Jamaican reggae and dancehall artists stem from the history of South Asian and Jamaican immigration to Britain after World War II, and more specifically, the close contact between those communities in British industrial cities. After the war, Britain's factories struggled to meet their labor demands, so a wave of immigrants from newly independent India, Pakistan, and later Jamaica arrived to work in the factories, particularly in cities like Birmingham, Apache Indian's hometown. Many South Asian immigrant families to Britain were working-class and could not afford to visit India; thus, children born into these families had only a tenuous relationship with a country they may never have visited. As a result, Apache Indian's music likely stems more from his identity as a non-white British person growing up in Birmingham than from South Asia itself.

British Asian *bhangra* producer Panjabi MC's 1998 song "Mundian To Bach Ke," featuring the voice of Punjabi folk singer Labh Janjua, outlines transnational connections that intersect with Punjab, but also intersect with African American hip-hop—and as depicted in the song's video shot in Kuala Lumpur, Malaysia, bypass the South Asian diaspora in the United States (⏵ Video example 27.2). In 2002, Panjabi MC issued a new remix of "Mundian To Bach Ke" as a single featuring the American rapper Jay-Z. This remix, "Beware," begins with Jay-Z's distinctive voice rapping over a looped sample of the twangy *tumbi*, a Punjabi single-string folk instrument typically identified with bhangra, accompanied by the characteristic rhythms of the *dhol* (⏵ Video example 27.3). Labh Janjua starts singing at 0:12 and at 0:29 the booming bassline appears, inspired by the bass of the theme song to the 1980s American television show *Knight Rider* (Panjabi MC 2009). The juxtaposition of a sample of the *tumbi*, an acoustic folk instrument, and Labh Janjua's traditional Punjabi singing against the booming bass associated with contemporary American hip-hop marks this song's departure from the *bhangra* fusion with drum sets and rhythm guitars prevalent in the 1980s— as well as from earlier integrations of *bhangra* and British Jamaican music. As Jay-Z raps "live from the United States, Brooklyn," his deep, resonant voice presents a marked contrast to the more acoustic, nasal, folk-oriented foundation. While Apache Indian's songs integrate British *bhangra* with Jamaican influences via his location in Birmingham, Panjabi MC skips referring to Jamaica and instead outlines a different network that via his role as a producer in Britain connects Punjab to New York City.

Analyzing Three Examples of *Desi* Dance Music

The song "Push It Up" (2006) released by producer Rishi Rich with guest singers Juggy D and Jay Sean extends the exchanges between India, Britain, and the continental United States to include Puerto Rico, in the Caribbean (⏵ Video example 27.4). While the connections between India and Britain are long-standing, the music's Puerto Rican influences do not draw on connections between the diaspora and South Asia so much as forge new links with African American music genres, including R&B and hip-hop. The musicians, all British-born and of Punjabi heritage, had already collaborated on several *bhangra*-inflected R&B tracks, such as "U'n'I (Mere Dil Vich Hum Tum)" for the 2004 Bollywood film *Hum Tum*. The video for "Push It Up (Bhangraton Version)" was filmed on location in Piñones, San Juan, far away from Britain or South Asia—with the term *bhangraton* nodding cheekily toward the Puerto Rican genre *reggaeton*. As 2Point9 Records describes on the video's YouTube page, " 'Push it up' was shot on the beautiful island of Puerto Rico . . . Sun . . . sea . . . sand . . . party people . . . and loads of cocktails. A hook up with the Luny Tunes crew . . . [resulted in a twist—] bhangra meets reggaeton (bhangraton)" (2Point9 2007).

"Push It Up" brings together Punjabi language vocals, R&B, and sonic elements associated with North Indian classical and folk music traditions—but in terms of its sound, it has nothing to do with *reggaeton*. The song begins with Juggy D's softly sung vocals in Punjabi, which begin to stutter before another loop sample of a male voice reciting *bol*s, Indian rhythmic syllables, at 0:19, and a few notes of the *bansuri*, a bamboo, side-blown flute, both commonly heard in South Asian classical and folk music. Jay Sean's light R&B style vocals then sing the first verse in English before they mesh with Juggy D's Punjabi vocals over an upbeat hip-hop groove. Their voices share such similar timbres, ranges, and melodies that they almost blend into one another.

These British Punjabis' decision to film a video in Puerto Rico does not follow previous itineraries of music traveling from Punjab to communities in the South Asian diaspora—in the United Kingdom, United States, or in the case of the "Mundian To Bach Ke" video, Kuala Lumpur in Malaysia, the home of a large South Indian Tamil population exoticized within the video (see Paige*). In depicting the three musicians relaxing, dancing, and grinding with attractive Puerto Rican women on a beach, "Push It Up" adopts the American touristic idea of Puerto Rico as an exotic fantasy. The video focuses on sexually suggestive shots of women's bodies and ignores the region's more troubled history as a European colony and the United States' unincorporated territory. The Puerto Rican beach may have been chosen as the location for the music video due to the relatively recent mainstream commercial success of the genre *reggaeton*. A Spanish-language reggae and hip-hop fusion, *reggaeton* emerged in Puerto Rico during the late 1990s, making its way to the US mainland in mid 2000s with Daddy Yankee's massive hit "Gasolina" (2004). "Push It up" 's "*bhangraton*" mix capitalizes on *reggaeton*'s established popularity through this visual reference to Puerto Rico.

The Hindi film song "Tha Kar Ke," from the 2008 film *Golmaal Returns*, was composed by Ashish Pandit and features Hindi film stalwart vocalist Neeraj

Shridhar (▶ Video example 27.5). As a dance number depicted in a film, we may not expect it to make its way onto the dance floor, but many songs from popular films do, as they take on multiple roles beyond films in music videos, and dance music mixes and remixes. This song presents the broad range of genres listeners have come to expect of film music, but adds a new sound drawing idioms from *reggaeton*. In this case, there are no collaborations or visual, sonic, or thematic elements gesturing specifically toward Puerto Rico, but simply appropriation of what is recognized as a commercially popular style. This fantastical song sequence features black leather clad gangs running and dancing amid over-the-top special effects (including flying guns, somersaulting vehicles, and explosions) in a Wild West–inspired set shot at Ramoji Film City in Hyderabad. References to somersaulting vehicles and flying guns appear to parody music director A. R. Rahman's "Athiradee" song sequence from the 2007 Tamil action film *Sivaji*, starring action superstar Rajinikanth. And yet, the song's very first bars recall the male chorus of "Oohs" and the grooves from *reggaeton* singer Daddy Yankee's 2007 hit "Impacto," as well as "Gasolina." At 0:17 a digitized auto-tuned female voice singing in English enters over the background synth and thumping bass, and at 0:40, the male chorus enters atop the trademark "boom--cha boom-chick-" beat associated with *reggaeton* hits, including "Gasolina."

As one of many *desi* dance songs that originated within the Hindi film industry, "Tha Kar Ke" exemplifies film music's continuing dominance within the sphere of South Asian popular music. Typically, a single composer, called the music director, writes a film song in collaboration with a lyricist. However, soundtracks to more recent films sometimes feature guest artists. In this vein, Ashish Pandit composed "Tha Kar Ke," while the established music director Pritam composed the rest of *Golmaal Returns*. As an action comedy, many song sequences within the film feature elaborate choreography, foreign locales, and special effects, and songs are sometimes structured to support the choreography on-screen. Amid their energetic, upbeat grooves, such songs sometimes explicitly feature South Asian sounds alongside their Hindi lyrics, which often integrate English. Yet we do not hear any traditional South Asian sonic elements within "Tha Kar Ke"'s studio-produced synthesized tracks, beyond the different vocal types featured in the song, offering clues about its South Asian origins. What we do hear is a series of discrete sections arranged in varying styles (Box 27.1), which might not make sense in other contexts but is a standard feature in film music. Further,

Box 27.1 Exercise

Ensemble dance songs are usually composed in discrete sections of form. In "Tha Kar Ke," some sections sound like those from other contemporary Hindi film songs, but other sections explicitly incorporate elements from *reggaeton*, including the "boom--cha boom-chick-" beat and a male chorus chanting. In the following exercise, familiarize yourself with the groove of contemporary *reggaeton*, then follow the discrete sections of "Tha Kar Ke" to mark where and how the song does and does not refer to *reggaeton*. Consider how the sections' music changes from one style to another, and how those different sounds support the respective choreography and other visual elements.

(1) Familiarize yourself with the sound of *reggaeton* referenced in "Tha Kar Ke"
   (a) Listen to Daddy Yankee's "Gasolina" (2005), the first *reggaeton* hit in the US mainstream (⏵ Video example 27.6). Identify the "boom--cha boom-chick-" beat. Describe the timbre of Daddy Yankee's voice and of the male backup voices.
   (b) Listen to the first few minutes of Daddy Yankee's song "Impacto" (⏵ Video example 27.7). Note the repeating four-note ascending bass and melodic motive at the start, as well as the "oooh" male chorus vocals and the entry of the "boom--cha boom-chick-" rhythm (cue point 0:24).
(2) Watch the video for "Tha Kar Ke" (⏵ Video example 27.5). Note how it is marked by a series of sections distinguished by the elements below. Try to identify where in time (minute:second) the different sections begin and end:
   (a) Opening male chorus shouts and ascending four-note motive evoking Daddy Yankee's "Impacto"
   (b) Instrumental interludes
   (c) Autotuned female digitized female vocals (in English) (e.g., 0:18–0:39)
   (d) Male chorus chanting in Caribbean-inflected English ("Say hey, as you move to the beat") and the entry of the *reggaeton* "boom--cha boom-chick-" beat

(e) Nasal, solo male voice toasting in English patois ("shake it down, to the body down"), evoking dancehall
(f) Male voices chanting in Hindi ("*chal haṭ jā re ...*").
(g) Solo male voice singing the chorus in Hindi (e.g., 0:57–1:14).
(h) Verses sung by the same voice as the solo male voice in the chorus, in Hindi, and its answer from a breathy, more nasal, higher-pitched solo female voice, singing in Hindi.
(i) Lower-voiced female voice rapping in American-accented English.

(3) Watch "Tha Kar Ke" again, and identify as many of the different sections above as you can, and the order in which the different elements occur.
   (a) Draw a table. In the first column, note the sections and their sound elements—and the time elapsed for each. In a second column, note what is happening in the visual setting of the song and the narrative.
   (b) How do the different sections and different sound elements correspond with what we are seeing on-screen? What, if anything, happens on-screen during vocal interludes?
   (c) Are the sections interchangeable, or do they occur in a particular sequence? Why and how does the song sequence retain the viewers' attention?

(4) Finally, *listen* to the song without watching the video and consider how it may work differently as a dance song played in a club or at a party. Does it build toward a single climax or have multiple arrival points? How might the physical dancing body make sense of these shifting styles when our ears do not necessarily connect them?

given film music's dominance in the *desi* dance music genre, such arrangement can also be heard as a standard feature in *desi* dance music.

As we conclude our discussion, we consider one more Bollywood song from the 2009 film *De Dana Dan*. "Baamulaiza," composed by Pritam, is a festive ensemble dance number that once again integrates Caribbean influences with more local South Asian influences (▶ Video example 27.8). The actors on-screen describe its having alternately a "ragamuffin, reggae feel," a "party feel," evoking carnival music, and *baila* music (▶ Video example 27.9, Eros International 2009).[2] The song sequence "Baamulaiza," shot on the grounds of a luxury hotel in Singapore, begins with a scene featuring non–South Asian musicians, likely of Malay and Chinese descent, at a pool party, before moving to an interior set with backup dancers in elaborate Caribbean Carnival-influenced sequined costumes with giant hats and headdresses. The female voices in English use timbres more typical of Caribbean *chutney* and *soca* than Hindi film music (0:01–0:13). A nasal male voice follows in Jamaican-accented patois sung by the Indian "Style Bhai." At 0:35 a male voice in Urdu-inflected Hindi sings in a nasal quality typical of South Asian films. The other vocals, however, in combination with the Caribbean-influenced rhythm and brass riffs, mark the song as a Hindi film "party song." The song seamlessly incorporates influences from the Caribbean and the western Indian tourist beaches of Goa alongside the sights of the Indian tourist destination of Singapore to evoke a sense of "island music," unmoored from its implied Caribbean location. Indeed, the Caribbean is relocated and appropriated within the imagined international geography of Bollywood through *desi* dance music broadcast on dance floors in India and its diasporas.

To summarize, in considering *desi* dance music songs' origins and production in Punjab, Mumbai, the United Kingdom, and the United States, we do not limit *desi* dance music to music from so-called authentic sites within South Asia. This genre is produced in multiple locations throughout the world, where different producers, vocalists, instrumentalists, and/or music directors work within transnational networks that determine how these songs cross Great Britain, the United States, the Caribbean, Central America, and South and Southeast Asia. Some so-called *desi* songs such as "Tha Kar Ke" sound more like *reggaeton*, R&B, and hip-hop and may outwardly have very little to do with recognizably South Asian sonic elements—and they need not sound some "essential" quality of South Asianness to be considered *desi* dance music (Gilroy 1993, 75). However, many *desi* dance music songs reflect and communicate how people of South Asian heritage distinguish their own identities against and amid those of other people where they live—in this case, music produced by Europeans, African Americans,

---

[2] "Baila," from the Portuguese *bailar*, to dance, is wedding and party music performed in Sri Lanka, Goa, and Mangalore—areas colonized by the Portuguese. In this case it reflects the mixing of popular Portuguese rhythms with local folk music.

British Afro Caribbeans, and Central Americans. As an example of one of the most watched and listened to music genres in the world, "Tha Kar Ke" demonstrates how Bollywood's extensive networks of production and distribution also provide the means through which *desi* dance music travels. To conclude, the category of *desi* dance music is defined more by its itineraries of production and consumption than any other essential quality, including this music's sound.

Works Cited

2Point9 Records. 2007. "Rishi Rich, Jay Sean and Juggy D—Push It Up." YouTube, Last Modified November 1, 2017. https://www.youtube.com/watch?v=VBWk3Do_5IU.

Banerji, Sabita, and Gerd Baumann. 1990. "Bhangra 1984–8: Fusion and Professionalization in a Genre of South Asian Dance Music." In *Black Music in Britain: Essays on the Afro-Asian Contribution to Popular Music*, edited by Paul Oliver, 132–152. Milton Keynes: Open University Press.

Brown, James, and Bruce Tucker. 1986. *James Brown: The Godfather of Soul*. New York: Macmillan.

Eros International (Firm). 2009. "Making of Baamulaiza Video." YouTube. https://www.youtube.com/watch?v=h5y6L9NgFzc.

Gilroy, Paul. 1993. *The Black Atlantic: Modernity and Double Consciousness*. Cambridge, MA: Harvard University Press.

Pandit, Ashish, Neeraj Shridhar Sameer, Aakariti Anvesha, Earl, and Indie. 2011. "Tha Kar Ke [Full Song] Golmaal Returns." T-Series. Accessed July 31, 2019. https://www.youtube.com/watch?v=AK2upOdOtek.

Panjabi MC feat. Jay-Z. 2009. "Beware." [Video]. Ultra Music. Accessed July 31, 2019. https://www.youtube.com/watch?v=wke0-lj2wzw.

Pritam, Irshaad Kamil, Mika Singh, Dominique Cerejo, and Style Bhai. 2014. "Baamulaiza (HD) Full Video Song | De Dana Dan." [Video]. Eros International (Venus Records and Tapes). Accessed July 31, 2019. https://www.youtube.com/watch?v=6YWdFEzFFIU.

Rich, Rishi. 2007. "Rishi Rich—Push It Up (Aaja Kurieh) [Bhangraton Version from The Project]." [Merlin] Absolute Label Services (on behalf of 2point9); BMI—Broadcast Music Inc., LatinAutor. Accessed July 31, 2019. https://www.youtube.com/watch?v=XeI0vg7rM0A.

Roy, Anjali Gera. 2011. *Bhangra Moves: From Ludhiana to London and Beyond*. Burlington, VT: Ashgate.

Schreffler, Gibb. 2013. "Situating Bhangra Dance: A Critical Introduction." *South Asian History and Culture* 4(3): 384–412.

Thompson, Ben. 1993. "ROCK / Tales of the Wild West Midlands: Ragga, Bhangra, Pop, Fame, Fortune, a Brummie Accent—Apache Indian Has It All. Ben Thompson Meets Him." *The Independent*. Accessed November 1, 2021. http://www.independent.co.uk/arts-entertainment/rock-tales-of-the-wild-west-midlands-ragga-bhangra-pop-fame-fortune-a-brummie-accent-apache-indian-1464149.html.

28

Dance In The Round

Embodying Inclusivity and Interdependence through *Garba*

Parijat Desai

A Night in Texas.[1] *Gymnasium. Piles of shoes outside. Throngs—sitting, standing, milling, darting. Nasal announcements. A lone voice sings out, and a chorus responds, repeating her lyrics. A pioneering woman goes forth, dipping low to swing her arms up in a clap: she is a particle traveling down an unseen arc. She attracts others to her curving path, traces of herself, together punctuating the downbeat with each clap. Chaos organizes into a comet of women. As more people join the comet's tail, its arc becomes a semi-circle, then a circle. Concentric circles materialize and dissipate tonight. Players notice each other, old and young, graceful and awkward—no judgment. The whole community is alive with rhythm, manifesting some shared inner pulse that takes us to a collective crescendo.*

Feel like joining? Not surprising! The energy generated at a *garba* dance event is infectious (Figure 28.1). Those who "play" *garba* (*garbā*) perform sweeping arm movements and claps as they travel primarily counterclockwise around the perimeter of a circle. At community events, participants of all ages dance *garba* and a related form called *raas* (*rās*) played with sticks (together called *garba-raas*). The dances originated in multiple regions within the state of Gujarat in western India and today are practiced in South Asian communities around the world, including Turtle Island (North America). In 2023, *garba* was added to UNESCO's Intangible Cultural Heritage list, which brings awareness to humanity's living and inclusive traditions (UNESCO 2023).[2]

---

[1] I dedicate this chapter to my great-grandmothers Sushil, Chandrakanta, Pushpavati, and Nirmala.

[2] Folk scholar Utpala Desai (who is also my aunt) was instrumental in building the dossier to nominate *garba* for this recognition.

Figure 28.1 Rohan Sheth (left) and Parijat Desai (the author), reprinted from *Dance Teacher* magazine, September 2017. Photo credit: Kyle Froman; used with permission.

Beyond the appeal of the dance steps, *garba* events offer a template for contemporary community ritual that welcomes each person to enter in whatever manner suits them and a structure that transforms energy and space. These community dances have shaped my life and career as a dancemaker and educator. In this chapter, I share principles I have observed at the core of *garba-raas*: inclusion, egalitarianism, individual and collective expression, interdependence, repetition, and transformation. These elements and others motivated me to begin "Dance In The Round," a program that highlights these *garba-raas* principles as powerful tools for practicing, experiencing, and literally dancing into existence a more inclusive vision for the United States and beyond.

In 2016, alarmed by anti-democratic, anti-immigrant forces in the United States and inspired by the multifaceted benefits of *garba-raas*, I created Dance In The Round while based in New York City, ancestral lands of the Munsee Lenape, to facilitate new movement experiences modeled on principles from this evolving tradition. No doubt *garba-raas* can be experienced as fun, rhythmic dances or workouts. But I seek to access the inner wisdom of *garba*, to help us move through our current challenges of disconnection, disembodiment, and collective trauma. In my view, *garba*'s form and structure—its circular formations and shifting spatial relationships between people—express and support social values of inclusion, individual expression, and interdependence. Mobilizing the egalitarian and porous circles of *garba* and emphasizing the intention to *welcome*, I aspire to create inclusive spaces, and to use *garba*'s format of repetitive rhythms and claps, spiraling motions, and building tempos to energize participants. Dance In The Round intentionally repurposes Gujarati community dance practices to address isolation and woundedness, and to support individual and collective well-being and empowerment. As a longtime educator and trainee in expressive arts therapy, I am beginning to understand processes of healing, and see that *garba* offers a community-ritual template that can aid us on our individual and collective journeys.

I root Dance In The Round in my family and ancestral practices. As a South Asian American dancemaker, I also frame what I do as contemporary, to assert that we are part and parcel of American cultural life, not perpetually foreign and other. I resist rubrics of authenticity and purity adopted by some producers and artists, including American competition/collegiate dance groups who have "often falsely constructed [*garba*] as a pure, unchanged form that has belonged to Gujaratis from time immemorial" even as they "altered, cleansed, dehistoricized" it (Falcone 2013, 59). I oppose the nationalist and exclusionist politics I witness in the United States and India, and approach *garba-raas* not as static artifacts that demonstrate one group's superiority, but as living, malleable practices we can harness to support human well-being. I aspire to repurpose *garba-raas* to create a space inclusive of all ages, races and ethnicities, religions, caste communities, genders, and abilities.

Contextualizing *Garba*

Garba and *raas* are just two of the diverse folk dance and theater forms originating in the broad region of Gujarat. *Hudo, tippani*, and *talwar* dances come from particular regions and communities, while *garba-raas* are practiced across modern-day Gujarat, the state's borderlands, and South Asian diasporas. Within *garba-raas* are multiple forms and approaches—*garba, dandiya raas, raas garbi*—and though related, these are practiced differently depending on local custom, community resources, and social hierarchy. So each person's experience of *garba* depends on age, caste, religion, and the geographical locations where they have "played." And the dances are ever-changing because all humans are evolving and creative.

My first experience of *garba* was while curled up in my mother's womb. My family is of the Gujarati caste called Nagar Brahmans. Historically, we have been city dwellers and worked in bureaucratic and educational spheres; a few are literary figures. I am aware of my caste and economic privilege inside a brutal, oppressive system, and that this colors my experience of the dance. The *garba* I describe reflects my experiences from 1970 to the present at family events in the United States and Mumbai; in Houston, Aurora (CO), Los Angeles, and Jersey City immigrant communities; through field research in rural Gujarat; and at neighborhood gatherings and public events in Ahmedabad, India. My work with Dance In The Round is informed by these experiences.

"*Garba*" is an old word referring to sung poetry and dance, typically in worship of Amba Mata (the primordial mother) or Shakti (divine feminine energy). Utpala Desai finds that the word "*garbe*" first appears in a fifteenth-century poem by Narsinh Mehta, referring to circle dances,[3] and "*garbo*" in a seventeenth-century song by the poet Bhandas, describing a dance celebrating Shakti (Desai 2020). Many such songs were likely created prior to these written sources, and innumerable songs are in circulation today. Based on my own field research and a lifetime of observation, I speculate that *garba* as a dance form has its roots in groups of women singing and clapping as a form of social bonding and worship. My family hails from the Saurashtra/Kathiawad, central Gujarat (Anand), and Kachchh regions. Our female relatives and Nagar family friends talk about and still host a

---

[3] The dances in Narsinh Mehta's poem are called "*tal rasak*" and "*dand rasak*"—in which rhythm is marked with claps (*tal*) and with sticks (*dand*), respectively (Desai 2020, 138).

community-specific practice, *betha* (seated) *garba*, in which participants sit to sing *garba* songs and sometimes dance. When I conducted fieldwork in a rural Patidar community in Kathiawad, I observed that during the women's nightly post-dinner hangout, they would stand in a circle, sing, clap, and sometimes travel around the circle with a simple step. Their focus was singing; they did not participate in the *raas* choreographies performed by the village's men in festivals and competitions.[4] In both cases, women shared *garba* songs and body movements with each other informally, along with social interaction.

Garba-raas singing and dancing practices span multiple caste and religious communities in Gujarat. Nagars are considered "upper caste," and "Patidar" is a term for both people who work the land and landowners, encompassing both "lower" and "upper" caste communities (Sheth and Yagnik 2005). Indigenous and Dalit Gujaratis play *garba*, and two of *garba*'s iconic vocalists—Diwali Behn Bhil and Hemant Chauhan—are of Adivasi and Dalit communities, respectively. On the outer edges of Ahmedabad city, I have witnessed Bahujan[5] people dancing *garba* and playing the double-headed *dhol* drum. Gujarati Muslims, Christians, and Parsis also play *garba* in their communities, including in East Africa and the United Kingdom. Although the forms are practiced by nearly all Gujaratis, they typically only play within their own community/caste formations because of entrenched social/religious divisions in Gujarat and the diaspora.

Most *garba* dancing takes place during the fall festival of Navratri. For nine nights, Hindus gather to play *garba-raas* in worship of Jagadamba (Mother of the Universe). Others dance in praise of Allah or Ambedkar, or to boogie. The word *garba* comes from *garbh* ("womb"); *garbo* and *garbi* are variants referring to earthenware pots with designs cut out of the sides (Figure 28.2). One practice during Navratri has been to light small oil lamps (*divo*) and place them inside *garbo* pots, a symbol of life resting in the womb, or the lifeforce in each body. My mother Meena Desai throws *garbo* pottery and told me clay pots used to be placed in the center of the dancing.

People of all ages attended the Navratri events I experienced growing up, and most danced at least briefly. For two-thirds of the event, participants played

---

[4] The men of Mandan Kundla, the village I stayed in, danced complex *raas-garbi* and *dandiya-raas* choreographies as part of their performing group (*raas mandali*; see Desai 2017). They performed at folk festivals and competitions organized by Gujarat Tourism.

[5] "Bahujan" is a Pali term used by anti-caste activists meaning "people in the majority." It refers to diverse caste-oppressed peoples including Dalit, Adivasi (Indigenous), and Shudra (laborer) communities.

Figure 28.2 *Garbo* pots made by Meena Desai. Photo by the author.

garba, and the evening concluded with *raas*. *Garba* was ostensibly open to all, but participation tended to be gendered: women and girls often began the dancing and were eventually joined by some men. Music was played live by a group of community musicians (today, there might instead be a professional band or DJ). A music set lasts for 25–30 minutes, and in one Navratri night, there are usually three to four sets. Within a set, several *garba* songs (old and new) are sung back-to-back, beginning slowly and increasing in tempo gradually. As the night continues, each set starts a little faster than the previous, culminating in a vibrant climax of speed and rhythm. After *garba* comes a ceremony (*puja*) for Amba Mata (another name for the primordial Mother): a tray of *divo* (fire lamps) is circled before the goddess, and sweets and food are distributed. The exciting finish to the night is *raas*, and the whole community plays.

Moving in a *Garba* Event

The most common *garba* steps include *be-tali* (*be-tāḷī*), *tran-tali* (*trāṇ-tāḷī*), and *dodhiyu* (*doḍhiyu*). I consider *be-tali* or "two-clap" to be the quintessential *garba* step. Arms swing forward into a clap to the right, then back and open (with optional snap), and again forward to clap to the left, then back and open, with players traveling counterclockwise to the lilting rhythm "dhin – thra ki ta – / dhin -dhin thra ki ta –." Another main step is *tran-tali* or "three-clap." To the four-count rhythm "dhin trak / dhin trak / dhin traka / dhin trak," players clap three times: (1) right hand on top, (2) left hand on top, and (3) clap, then swing the arms down and back. They can choose to step lightly or with great bounds of energy. *Dodhiyu* is a stepping pattern: players mainly use the step-together-step (or gallop) to travel, alternating between right and left feet. Over this stepping, they swing, slice, or row their arms in a figure eight. In the past, *dodhiyu*s were fairly standard six- to fourteen-count patterns. Today, the doors of creativity are open: *dodhiyu*s incorporate *garba* and non-*garba* moves. It has become so popular that nowadays *dodhiyu* is synonymous with *garba*. But I also love the simple clapping steps I learned as a toddler and that grandmas still do. Try them out with ▶ Video example 28.1 and the exercise in Box 28.1 focusing on *be-tali*. *Raas* is similar to *garba* in its swinging arm motions and footsteps but is played with a *dandiya* (*dāṇḍiyā*, stick) in each hand. The sticks extend dancers' movement, and their tapping sound accentuates the music's rhythm.

Dance In The Round: An Offering

In developing Dance In The Round, I draw on dance forms I have inherited, as well as principles I have observed in those forms, to craft dance and movement experiences that might serve us in our contemporary and political life. I initiated Dance In The Round in 2016 to address exclusionary and anti-democratic forces I witnessed in the United States and India. As I watched Donald Trump's attacks on people of color and immigrants during his presidential campaign, I sensed growing anxiety and disempowerment within myself and the progressive, immigrant, and artist communities I am connected to. In India, I see a Hindu majoritarian, fundamentalist movement that harkens back to an imagined pure Hindu society, rejects "outside" influences, and allows caste/gender-based violence to occur with impunity.[6] Globally, social media and texting sometimes replace in-person and

---

[6] See the Dalit Human Rights Defenders Network, https://www.dhrdnet.org/.

> **Box 28.1 Exercise: Dancing *Be-Tali*, "Two-Clap"**
>
> Form a circle with each participant standing at a slight angle toward your neighbor to the right (R), with your left (L) foot stepped forward, across the body.
>
> Orientation: Before trying the steps described below and demonstrated in ▶ Video example 28.1, I suggest participants familiarize themselves with one another and the circle formation:
>
> - Stand shoulder-to-shoulder in a circle. Notice where people are placed, and get acquainted with your neighbors.
> - Let's say your neighbor to your R is Riz and your neighbor to your L is Leia. Angle your body a bit toward Riz (to your R). Notice how that affects the shape of the whole circle. If the group is okay with it, have each person place their R hand on their R neighbor's shoulder and notice what happens to the group shape.
> - Try the same to the L: Turn slightly toward Leia. If the group is willing, place your L hand on your L neighbor's shoulder.
>
> Note: You'll be traveling counterclockwise. Swing your arms on the "and-uh" and clap on the downbeat.
>
> (1) Swing your arms forward (toward your R), shifting your weight onto your front/L foot.
> (2) Clap as you bring your back/R foot in toward the L and tap your R toe.
> (3) Swing your arms back, stepping back and slightly to the side on the R foot. (As you step back, pivot or rotate your body slightly L.)
> (4) Bring the L foot in, tapping the L toe and suspending the arms back (optional: snap your fingers).
> (5) Swing your arms forward (toward your L), stepping onto your front/L foot.
> (6) Clap as you bring your back/R foot in toward the L.
> (7) Swing your arms back, stepping back and slightly to the side on the R foot. (As you step, pivot or rotate your body slightly R.)
> (8) Bring the L foot in, suspending the arms back (optional: snap your fingers).

(9) Repeat the steps described in 1–8. Once the group is relatively comfortable, choose a song with a comfortable tempo and enjoy the dance!

Discussion: When in the circle, what did you notice about the people standing and moving next to you, versus those across the circle from you? What did you observe about how movements shaped the circle or the group? What did it feel like to be conscious of the circle? What felt good and what was challenging? What did you think about while moving? How did you deal with rhythm? Did you have any realizations about rhythm? Did your group experience failure? Did you try to solve the problem? If so, how?

real-time interaction, leading to social fragmentation, isolation, and disembodiment. In today's larger urban *garba-raas* events, the intergenerational inclusiveness and primacy of the circle I grew up with have eroded. And though the form is danced by many kinds of people, it still reflects caste dynamics of South Asian society in India and in the diaspora.

Through Dance In The Round, I strive to create new dance spaces that allow for wider participation in *garba*, as an antidote for separateness and exclusion, and as a vehicle for individual and community well-being. I seek to support people to reconnect with their bodies, express themselves, and experience that self as part of a larger whole. Although *garba-raas* do embody values of inclusion, egalitarianism, self-expression, interdependence, and transformation, these values are rarely made explicit—and are sometimes blatantly violated. For that reason, in my evolving pedagogy for Dance In The Round, I foreground these values and practice them intentionally by modifying or emphasizing particular elements of *garba* and *raas*.

Inclusion and Egalitarianism

The circle is a potent spatial formation for humans; we gravitate toward it in social, professional, and dance realms. The curve of the circle embraces participants: no one is in front or back; we are equal. When we dance in a circle, we can enact and physically experience the inclusion and egalitarianism the circle represents. The alive-and-morphing *garba* circle can expand to accommodate people; and if necessary, a new circle can be formed inside the first one.

Despite these appealing attributes, I suspect that *garba* and *raas* were not born "inclusive" (in the modern sense of the word); singing and dancing probably happened within caste/community groups. But in the late 1950s, a group of artist-scholars at Maharaja Sayajirao University/Baroda spawned a new movement, hosting departmental and, later, public Navratri *garba* events, which began *garba*'s transformation from a community-specific activity to one in which a more diverse body of people come together. The Baroda organizers' explicit intent was to create a participatory dance space, initially through campus events with students hailing from different parts of India, and later in public events. These efforts made Baroda *the* town for Navratri *garba*. They also likely spawned the multi-generational community events I experienced growing up, and the massive urban *garba*s of today (Bhatt 2016; Shwetal Bhatt, personal communication October 18, 2021, and January 3, 2024).

Though the implication today is that anyone is welcome to join a *garba-raas* event, there are barriers to participation, which I try to address through Dance In The Round. For one, instruction is rarely offered. Most players learn movements informally as children or young adults. Offering instruction is one way I try to realize inclusion. Formats I use include: (1) mixed-level community workshops open to all ages and levels, modeled on the Navratri experience; (2) classes for age-specific groups like elementary school kids and older adults; and (3) dance experiences as part of public-space and private events where participation is spontaneous. During the COVID-19 pandemic, I produced virtual dance parties and online *garba*-based classes.

Further, I consider inclusion in the way I teach. I begin Dance In The Round workshops by inviting participants to stand shoulder-to-shoulder for a greeting, conversation, and/or warmup. Facing into the circle, we see one another, and the circle becomes even more intentional than if we had just launched into "steps." Basic *garba* steps are loose-limbed and swingy, and are more doable by a wider range of people than sculpted, stylized classical dance movements. I believe that with support and preparation, anyone can do some version of these steps. *Garba-raas* movements do have specificity—how you lean, how you step, what beat you emphasize—especially when choreographed for performance. But when I teach them as social forms, my emphasis is on helping people feel safe to participate and express their individuality. I also draw on practices such as *qi gong*, contemporary dance, conscious breath, and imagery to assist with warming up and cooling down. These elements help participants access their inner and creative resources. In our workshops, after my colleagues and I[7] teach steps and phrases, we facilitate free-flowing dance circles—as might occur at a Navratri event—so participants experience the choice and play of it.

But circles can also exclude, and *garba* is no different. Today, Navratri events in India and the diaspora tend to be very large and privilege young, non-disabled people because of the hectic environment and fast tempos. Through Dance In The Round, I strive to counteract casteism, racism, ageism, ableism, and even cliques, by inviting people of all communities and supporting the participation of people of varying ages and dance levels. I also make Dance In The Round available at different times of the year, rather than only during Navratri season (fall), and through outdoor events where passersby can join. For kids, I use creative movement to warm up, and simpler vigorous movements. For older adults, I teach with lower impact and offer seated options. I also draw on my experiences with injury to modify movements for participants whose mobility is constricted. For mixed-age groups, I take advantage of concentric circles to offer options: simpler sequences for one circle and more complex ones for the other, and place chairs in the circle for those who want to participate seated. Making the practice accessible to people with disabilities is my intention, but proper implementation requires more research, resources, and learning.

A disturbing trend away from inclusion is that, since the 1990s, *garba* has been employed by Gujarati political leaders to promote Hindutva ideologies, including by working aggressively to ban non-Hindus from *garba-raas* events and stop the dance from being played in churches (Falcone 2016). In 2017, three years after right-wing political leaders from Gujarat came to national power, a Dalit youth was lynched for going to watch a *garba*. If we seek to engage with cultural practices in a meaningful way, we must face these horrors and reckon with how the arts are used as "soft power" to legitimize majoritarian hate. I firmly reject these moves to exclude, and refrain from deploying my practice as an expression of caste or cultural pride. Rather, I seek to realize the philosophy, reverence, and power of the dance by encouraging greater inclusion. Even as I embrace the roots of this dance in my homeland, the immigrant in me also joyfully blends and bastardizes,

---

[7] I often invite dancers to help me demonstrate or to co-teach.

dialoguing *garba* with everything from contemporary dance to Sufi *qawwali* to house and Afrobeat. I acknowledge my caste privilege in this endeavor, having materially benefited from an exploitative hierarchy. Through this work, I seek to support marginalized communities' dance practices and their struggles for liberation.

Individual Expression inside of Unity

Garba-raas can express unity through the circle and the repetitive rhythm and movements, which create a group heartbeat. Yet, the movement is not a forced unison. In some tight-knit communities, participants may all seem to dance in the same way, but at most *garba* events, people show off individual styles or new steps while maintaining the circle. Players also make their own decisions to follow or change the movement, to start a new circle in the center or on the outer perimeter, to join or not, or to pause for a while. At the same time, everyone is tuned into the shared rhythm—in sync with each other, but free. This choreographic framework sets up a powerful experience of collectivity for participants.

As facilitator, I impart instruction on how to step, swing the arms, and tilt the body, but I also encourage people to move in a manner that feels natural—making sure my teaching does not enforce an oppressive conformity. When we first begin the open circle, participants apply what I have taught. Eventually I offer more movement choices, encouraging students to be aware of and responsive to others in the circle. The goal is to allow people to find their own freedom, while maintaining the rhythm and connection to each other.

Interdependence

Interdependence, a reality of human existence and the natural world, is also a feature of *garba* and *raas*. Participants must work together to create and maintain the circle. They must be aware of what they are doing, where their own bodies are in space, and where fellow dancers are. If someone leaves, the remaining players adjust to fill the gap; if someone starts a new circle, others might switch to support that one, creating a new arc that may or may not grow into a new circle. *Raas* involves even more shared responsibility because participants contact each other by tapping sticks. As a *raas* facilitator, I teach a pattern, emphasizing that each person is needed to maintain the group rhythm. If participants don't maintain the tempo, we get cacophony and eddies of confused people swirling around each other. So participants work to tap in time, staying aware of each other as they move from partner to partner. Eventually, newbies figure it out, and I get out of the way! Once anchored in the collective beat, each person twirls their *dandiya*s as they please.

Repetition and Transformation

In *garba-raas*, individual steps and *dodhiyu* sequences are repeated over and over. The movements swing and spiral, so when repeating them one can experience a wavelike flow. In a Navratri event, the rhythm transforms over time. Throughout the night, one hears the *be-tali* and *tran-tali* beats, variations, and new rhythms the band or DJ introduces. The tempo increases steadily in each set. At a good Navratri event—where people are really grooving—the repeating movements and gradual increase in tempo make the space and bodies warmer and warmer. Participants report experiencing a building of individual and collective energy, and in the swirl, a sense of internal centering and letting go (cf. Protopapas*). These changes in heat, energy, and effort indicate that circle-dance practices can be transformative for participants. As a facilitator, I sequence music and instruction following the Navratri structure, preparing people for gradually more complexity and speed, and creating conditions for transformation to occur.

Redefining *Garba*, Redefining America

In Dance In The Round, I am transforming a culturally specific ritual into a secular, inclusive, and cross-cultural project. This is one of the ways I, as an artist, play at embodying a new kind of Americanness. In bringing an ancestral family practice into public space, I assert our presence as immigrants on this cultural landscape, redefining what "American" is beyond whiteness and also beyond a white/Black binary—through music, choreography, and performance. I seek to disrupt the divide between American and foreign, between traditional and modern. These dichotomies may seem innocent, but they support nationalist ideas that simplify, homogenize, and divide humanity. Humanity, like other species, is biodiverse, migratory, and evolving. My practice participates in the evolution of culture, standing in opposition to Hindutva and other nationalist forces. Instead of harkening to an imaginary past glory and selling "authentic" cultural product, I am putting my energy toward learning how to welcome people across various boundaries to the dance. In evolving new methods for old dances and blending forms across cultures, I subvert dichotomies.

The development of Dance In The Round has been moving to witness. It is rare that we come together to dance consciously, in a fluid unity. Participatory dance activates our energies with rhythm and repetition, and my hope is that this process can, in small part, help sustain us in our struggles for justice. When we dance in these ways, we transform ourselves and embody the society we seek to manifest. The time feels ripe to go deep into our roots for old wisdom to create new pathways for healing and transformation.

Works Cited

Bhatt, Shwetal, filmmaker. 2016. *Ramji Thakkar Bhimji Thakkar*. https://www.ramjithakkarbhimjithakkar.com/.

Desai, Utpala. 2017. "Raas Traditions of Gujarat." *Sahapedia*. September 21. Accessed January 5, 2024. https://www.sahapedia.org/raas-traditions-of-gujarat.

Desai, Utpala. 2020. "Garba: A Journey from Streets to Stage." *INTACH Journal of Heritage Studies* 4(1): 137–146.

Falcone, Jessica Marie. 2013. "'Garba with Attitude': Creative Nostalgia in Competitive Collegiate Gujarati American Folk Dancing." *Journal of Asian American Studies* 16(1): 57–89.

Falcone, Jessica Marie. 2016. "Dance Steps, Nationalist Movement: How Hindu Extremists Claimed Garba-raas." *Anthropology Now* 8: 50–61.

Sheth, Suchitra, and Achyut Yagnik. 2005. *The Shaping of Modern Gujarat: Plurality, Hindutva and Beyond*. New Delhi: Penguin India.

UNESCO. 2023. "Garba of Gujarat Inscribed on the UNESCO Representative List of the Intangible Cultural Heritage of Humanity." UNESCO. Accessed January 5, 2024. https://www.unesco.org/en/articles/garba-gujarat-inscribed-unesco-representative-list-intangible-cultural-heritage-humanity.

29
Tamil Rap and Social Status in Malaysia

Aaron Paige

For the last century, Tamil political and academic discourse, as well as much European and American scholarship, has theorized the Tamil language through a framework of "diglossia," the bifurcation of a language into two functionally opposed forms, typically written and spoken. The term *sentamil* (*centami̱l*) is used to refer to a high register of Tamil that is felt and heard to be grammatical, regularized, ancient, classical, and poetic. *Kochaitamil* (*koccaitami̱l*), meaning "bent" Tamil, is sometimes the term used for the everyday colloquial form of the language that is thought to be impure, irregular, and degraded by foreign influence, whether Sanskrit, Hindi, English, or Malay. These two language types, *sentamil* and *kochaitamil*, have historically been used to index particular identities and have long been mapped onto various speech communities and groups to create "definite and hierarchal ordered categories of people" (Bate 2009, 13–17).

Tamil language hierarchies exist both in India and Tamil diaspora communities. In Malaysia, social and political institutions sociolinguistically segregate working-class Tamils in order to preserve purist language standards and by extension class-based, and to some degree, caste-based distinctions. Thought to lack a "proper" Tamil voice, working-class Tamils in Malaysia have routinely been denied representation in private and public Tamil-language media—especially radio and television. In the mid-2000s, however, Malaysian Tamil working-class youth turned to music, specifically rap, I argue, as a strategy to navigate the language hierarchies of the elite and dismantle sociolinguistic stereotypes. They have done so in three ways: (1) by utilizing a verbal aesthetic that recalls the classical and poetic language of Tamil literature; (2) by rapping about Tamil language itself, often in the form of extensive praise; and (3) by drawing upon the rhythmic vocabulary of South Indian classical karnatak music and fifteenth-century devotional Tamil song.

Figure 29.1 Fusion Andavan with Subramaniya Bharatiyar tattoo. Photo by the author.

February 22, 2013. Tonight is the one-year anniversary celebration of Tamil Rhythm and Poetry, or TRAP, a monthly hip-hop gig, which offers underground Tamil rappers in Malaysia a platform to exhibit their skills for friends, family, fans, and fellow musicians. It is one hour before showtime and already dozens of hip-hop makkehs *(bros) congregate in clusters along Ipoh Road, talking shit* (vetti pechu), *and showing off their modified cars and bodies. As I walk through the crowd, Fusion Andavan, a photographer, amateur emcee, and lyricist calls out, "Bro, look here!" He lifts up his black tee shirt, and points to a fresh tattoo on his side depicting the head of Subramaniya Bharati, one of the great Indian Tamil poets and political activists of the early twentieth century (Figure 29.1). "Tamil is with me forever!" he exclaims. When I tell Fusion that I admire his love of the language, two other guys standing with him, both rappers, volunteer their ink. Written across the fingers of one rapper are the three characters that spell out the word Tamil:* தமிழ். *The other extends his wrist (Figure 29.2), upon which the first character/letter of the Tamil language,* ஆ *(ā), is inscribed. Suddenly he breaks into a verse, reciting a line from the Tirukkural*

Figure 29.2 Tattoo of அ (ā), the first letter in the Tamil alphabet. Photo by Stylomannavan; used with permission.

(*tirukkuraḷ*), *a 2,000-year-old text of Tamil poetic couplets, to which he joins a refined and eloquent rap verse of his own. "Just as 'ā' is the first letter in the alphabet, so is god the source of all that exists. So long as Tamil rap thrives, I will never forget my mother tongue. Until my last breath, I will show my skills. Come fellow Tamils, lift and raise up the Tamil language!"* "Mayiru!," "Shit!" *he suddenly blurts out, scolding himself in a mixture of Tamil, English, and Malay: "Sorry bro. I said Tamil. But I should have pronounced it Tamiḻ. There needs to be a* ழ (*ḻa*) *at the end.*[1] *That is respect. Ha! I should not be killing Tamil in a Tamil praise song!"*[2]

Why, in a musical genre like hip-hop, so embracing of the vernacular, would an emcee apologize for his lack of verbal propriety and excuse himself for his slang? Why do Malaysian Tamil emcees describe their street talk as "empty" and "rusty," but on the stage and in their albums strive to embody

---

[1] There are three "L" sounds in the Tamil language. The first one, the most common, uses the same sound as the English "l." The second is a lateral retroflex approximant; the tongue is curled backward, touching the roof of the hard palate, transliterated here as ḷ. The third "l," transliterated ḻ, is a central retroflex approximant; the speaker pulls the tongue slightly backward, curling it a little in the front. In Tamil script, it is written as "ழ."

[2] Translation from Tamil to English by the author.

a Tamil aesthetic of linguistic purity that exudes the literary and learned? In this chapter, I argue that by rapping in linguistic registers that recall several literary genres, Malaysian Tamil youth complicate local and transnational language ideologies of Tamil diglossia that all too often naturalize the relationship between linguistic register and social position.

Historically, Tamil sociolinguistic hierarchies in Malaysia, like those in South India, have been upheld by ideologies of diglossia. Under British colonial rule, between 1834 and 1938, millions of outcaste Pallan, Parayan, and Arunthathiyar Tamils (today called Dalits) from the Indian subcontinent were sent, often coercively, to Malaysia to serve as cheap labor for the growing plantation and railroad industries. Along with this massive low- and outcaste labor force, an educated Tamil- and English-speaking elite of higher-caste Tamils, mainly Chettiyars, Mudaliyars, Kaunthar, and Vellalars, from Sri Lanka and South India were brought to the Malay colonies to work as foremen and British civil servants. They managed and oversaw plantation work and acted as middlemen between the British and the outcaste laborers (Clothey 2006, 7). Although labor recruits were promised a "caste-free" environment in their new lives abroad, this was hardly the reality that they encountered upon arrival. Lee and Rajoo note that higher-caste, upper-class Tamil merchants and civil servants remained largely disconnected, physically and culturally, from the indentured masses, contributing to the reproduction of South India's status distinctions of caste and class in the Malaysian diaspora (1987, 392).

Language education was one of the primary means by which these social differences were perpetuated. Tamils of the social elite attended superior schools where they were often taught Tamil writing, grammar, and literature, in addition to British English. The children of plantation laborers, on the other hand, were provided a rudimentary Tamil-medium education up to the age of ten, in substandard and decrepit facilities with poorly trained teachers (Willford 2006, 19). Historians have argued that this system of education was encouraged by the British and later by Malaysian Indian diaspora leaders because it trapped Tamil laborers in indentured servitude, ensuring the reproduction of a laboring underclass (Muzaffar 1993; Willford 2006).[3]

---

[3] Social hierarchy within today's Malaysian Tamil community is typically framed in terms of class, not caste. Malaysian Tamil rappers, like most Malaysian Tamils, generally distance themselves from any association with the caste system. In my conversations and interviews with young Malaysian Tamils, nearly all framed caste as a backward "Indian" system of oppression that their ancestors purposefully chose to leave behind. Most claimed not to know the caste of their ancestors, and those who did were uninterested in discussing it. The notable exception to caste not having a place in Malaysia

Tamil cultural and political institutions in Malaysia continued to reproduce social divisions through discriminatory language policies that privilege purist language standards over everyday speech. Working-class Tamils in Malaysia routinely have been denied representation in private and public Tamil-language broadcast media—particularly radio and television—both of which remain largely under the control of an English- and Tamil-educated oligarchy. In the following quote, a senior announcer at Minnal FM (formerly known as Channel 6, the sole government radio station for Tamil broadcasting in Malaysia) explains to me why the station's censorship board bans certain kinds of Tamil from the air:

> Estate Tamils are without a proper Tamil education. . . . They brought their village Tamil with them to the cities like Kuala Lumpur. Now their Tamil has mixed with other languages. If they speak a sentence, only a few words will be Tamil. The rest is all Malay. . . . Their pronunciation is bad. "La" sounds like "la." "Da" sounds like "ta." Actually, this is a dangerous situation. Do we want Tamil language to be destroyed in Malaysia? That is why we only select clean Tamil for our broadcasts. (April 6, 2012; translated from Tamil by the author)

Explicit language bias not only is expressed at the individual level but also is reproduced systemically. The following formal guidelines regulating Tamil language usage and pronunciation in the broadcasting of Tamil-language song were distributed to artists by Channel 6, beginning in 1998:

- Non-Tamil words are discouraged and will only be allowed if deemed suitable and necessary by the Channel 6 review board.
- Album titles should be in the Tamil language or another Indian language.
- Songs should be correctly sung in accordance with general pitching and timing rules. The words should be clearly and correctly pronounced with the correct diction in the Tamil language.
- Rap is acceptable provided the meaning is decent and positive, and that it conforms to Malaysian values, and meets the criteria outlined above.

---

was marriage. In keeping with the discourse of Malaysian Tamil rappers, I have chosen to focus this article on class-based, rather than caste-based, social hierarchies.

In a preface to these guidelines, notably written in English, the station writes that "the poor quality of local [Malaysian Tamil] songs contrasts starkly with the high standards of cinema songs from India." It goes on to say that "following these rules and regulations will help improve the public perception of local songs, which now have a serious image problem with a touch of stigma."[4] Undergirding these language policies is a long-standing and deeply entrenched prejudice against everyday working-class Tamil speech, with its non-standard accent, its non-standard grammar, and the frequent mixing of languages.

Pejorative stereotypes of working-class Malaysian Tamil speech circulate within the diaspora and the Indian homeland. Like the voices of non-native English-speaking immigrants or the southern "hillbilly" in American pop culture, the working-class estate Tamilian is marked and stereotyped for his or her speech. Working-class spoken Tamil is commonly referred to as *kambattu pecchu* ("village speech") and *karatana* Tamil (*karatāna*, "rusty" Tamil). *Kambattu* directly links this speech to the provincial and rural, while *karat* (adj.: *karatāna*) suggests speech that has degenerated and deteriorated through the passage of time. Sonically, working-class Tamil speech patterns are characterized by loud volume, more exaggerated intonation, prolongation of vowels at the end of interrogative sentences, truncated verb endings, occasional profanity, and use of Malay-, English-, and sometimes Chinese-language words, phrases, and syntax. Popular representations of Malaysian Tamils in Malaysia, and occasionally in India, often exaggerate these features, turning them into character types and comical tropes. Furthermore, Malaysian public narratives frequently portray urban working-class Tamils as criminals and gangsters and working-class Tamil spaces as chaotic and dangerous. As Richard Baxstrom writes, "The Malaysian-Tamil gangster . . . has often served as a shorthand 'character type' generated by journalists, state officials, and city residents. . . . Tamil gangsterism was so strong in popular accounts of crime that nearly any illegal or violent act was attributed to its pernicious influence" (2005, 209).

It is in direct response to such pervasive and derogatory stereotyping, linguistic and otherwise, that Malaysian Tamil working-class youth began to embrace rap as a strategic weapon—one that could "challenge the sociopolitical arrangement of relations between languages, identities, and power" (Alim

---

[4] From 1998 Radio Televisyen Malaysia (RTM) archival document "Quality of Local Songs Aired on Channel 6."

2009, 13). Frustrated by the exclusion of popular Malaysian Tamil music from radio and television and its displacement by imported films songs from India, Yogi B—popularly dubbed the godfather of Tamil rap—staged an agitation in the spring of 2007. Waging what Samy Alim calls "language ideological combat," he and his crew members challenged private Tamil radio station THR Raaga to premiere their recently produced single, "Hip Hop Era," over the Malaysian airwaves. This song, they asserted, would not only meet the station's language standards, but it would also inaugurate a new genre of pure Tamil language rap music, which they called *sollisai* ("word music"). Yogi B explains:

> "Hip Hop Era" was the beginning of the [*sollisai*] revolution. Writing songs in *sentamil* when you can't even read or write Tamil . . . that is a revolution bro. We picked up the mic with pride. . . . We proved that we are the descendants of great Tamil kings and poets. Just because I cannot read and write Tamil doesn't mean I cannot speak it. They [the station] could not ban me because my Tamil was clean and the themes were inspirational. . . . We became role models for Tamil kids, you know. We showed that it doesn't matter what caste, or class, or country you come from . . . anyone can rap sweetly in Tamil. (Yogeeswaran Veerasingam; interview with the author July 12, 2012)

"Hip Hop Era" was aired on Malaysian public and private radio in 2007, where it quickly became a national, and subsequently an international, hit.

Prior to the rise of *sollisai* in 2007, Malaysian-Tamil hip-hop crews had been cultivating a rapping style that was much more multilingual, colloquial, and interracial—as in the case of "Jokana Cari Makan" by Boomerangx—sometimes featuring Malaysian Chinese as well as Malay hip-hop artists on their albums and in their staged performances (see Figure 29.3, ▶ Video example 29.1).

"In the 90s and early 2000s we thought we were African Americans," Coco Nantha, one of the founding members of Boomerangx, explained to me in an interview in 2013.

> We thought rapping in *karat* Tamil was cool, like mixing languages. We were wearing bling bling, and saying "yo, yo!" We didn't really know what we were doing. Just following. But then *sollisai* came. That's when our Tamil hip-hop journey began. (Coco Nantha, interview with the author July 7, 2012; translated by author)

Joke ஆன *cari makan*, வெட்டி வேலை இங்கே *jangan*
Don't sit around doing nothing, go out and survive,

அப்பா சொத்து இங்கே தப்பா போகுது
If your dad's property is dwindling,

எதற்கு *dua tangan*
what's the point of having two hands?

Ok Mike, *turun jahat* பண்ண
Get down bro (mike)

பயமில்லை வா உள்ள
Don't be afraid, come inside.

இருட்டுல நடந்திடும் ரகசியம் கண்டுக்காத I
I'm gonna tell you a secret in the dark.

அவன் இவன் எவன் <u>backing</u> கொடுத்தாலும் <u>one man show</u> ஆ
Whoever you are, you may get backing (help) from us,

நீ நின்னு எறங்கு
but remember, you are a one man show in life

Puchong, Rrawang, Lobah Samping, JB
(Lists townships and areas closely associated with working-class Tamils)

நம்ம படை எல்லாம் வந்திருங்க <u>peace</u> ஆக
Our entire army has come peacefully

Kampung Lechumana, KKB, Teluk Intan, Masai, Butterworth, Jinjang, Loke Yew
(place names continued)

என்ன பிரச்சனையா? அது *puas* இல்லையா?
What's your problem? Are you not satisfied?

சிறப்பான <u>table talk</u> பண்ண வருயா?
You want to fight/bring this to the table, do you?

<u>Hey,</u> போதும் மக்க போதும்
Hey enough people, enough!

<u>Line</u> எல்லாம் *jaga* பண்ணு
Protect your entire gang.

Mat cai சொன்னபடி <u>plan</u> ஆ முடி
Complete the mission that the boss assigned.

ஒழுங்காக ஒத்துவரும் *budak* மட்டும்
My boys will come together orderly.

Kap cai எடுத்துட்டு <u>follow</u> பண்ணு
Take your bikes and follow.

Figure 29.3 Lyrics from "Jokana Cari Makan" from the 2002 album *Nil Gavanee* by Coco Nantha, Behug Maran, and Jinjang Hari (cue point 1:11–2:13). To differentiate languages, English is underlined, Malay is italicized, Hokkien (a common Chinese language in Malaysia) is bolded. The remaining Tamil text is in Tamil script. Translation by the author.

Sentamiḻ nāṭeṉum pōtiṉilē iṉpa tēṉ vantu pāyitu kātiṉilē
When I say pure Tamil, the sweet flow of honey drips in my ears

Laṭcam varikaḷ koṭṭi kiṭakku tamiḻil
There are hundreds of thousands of verses in Tamil

Paṭikka teriyillai oru vari uṉakku
and you claim that you cannot read a single sentence

Eṉṉa koṭumai cār itu putu vaḻakku
What kind of travesty is this?

Accamillaiyē 4x
I have no fear

Uṉ tāy uṉṉai peṟṟatiṉāl nī iṅku tamiḻaṉ illai
Just because your mother gives birth to you doesn't make you a Tamilian

Tamiḻ tāy nī kaṟṟatiṉāl nīyum tamiḻaṉaṭā
If you study your mother Tamil, you are a Tamilian

Figure 29.4 Transcribed Tamil lyrics from "Achamillai" from the album *Satriye Sambrajyem* (cue point 1:56–2:31). Transcription and translation by the author.

In late 2007, Boomerangx released a track entitled "Achamillai" (▶ Video example 29.2). In contrast to the multilingual and highly vernacular tracks like "Jokana Cari Makan" that they were performing just a few years earlier, the rap of "Achamillai" is almost entirely in Tamil, with the exception of the crew's English name Boomerangx (see Figure 29.4). In a voice that recalls the rhetorical flair and didactic style of Tamil nationalist Subramaniya Bharati's poetry of the early twentieth century, Coco Nantha, in this song, calls upon Tamils to overcome stereotypes of linguistic backwardness, to "go out and find a skilled Tamil teacher," to "study your mother tongue, Tamil," and to "discover the flame of Tamil that burns within you."

Like that of many Malaysian Tamil rappers, Coco Nantha's rap recalls the rhetorical conventions of *tamilpattru* (*tamiḻpaṟṟu*), a Dravidian nationalist ideology of Tamil-language devotion. To cultivate *tamilpattru* is to devote one's life, self, and body to Tamil—to see, feel, and hear Tamil in all things and all places (Ramaswamy 1997, 6). In "Achamillai," the rappers not only embrace *sentamil*, using a style of speech that sounds and feels literary, timeless and ancient, they also perform their emotional attachment to the Tamil language itself, in the form of direct and explicit praise. Malaysian Tamil rappers like Ruben Manoharan (aka Dr. Burn), Coco Nantha, and Yogi B have devoted albums, tracks, and hundreds of rapped verses to extolling Tamil's virtues and bring a range of visions to bear on their representations of the Tamil language and its role in their lives.[5] As Dr. Burn explains:

> *Sollisai* is a nation for all devotees of Tamil. It's like an understanding . . . like a movement. . . . Where are the boundaries of this nation? There are no boundaries. There are no divisions in Tamil. Just like that, there are no divisions in *sollisai*. . . . Whoever expresses their love and devotion to the Tamil language is a part of it. It doesn't matter if you are from Malaysia, India, Sri Lanka, Canada, Germany. Birthplace is not important. . . . If you are a member of the *sollisai* nation you raise your head up high and speak Tamil with pride. You must say, "I am Tamil. I speak Tamil. Long live Tamil!" (Ruben Manoharan, interview with the author June 26, 2012; translated by author)

One of the most striking characteristics of *sollisai* is its predominant use of pure Tamil idioms, grammar, and pronunciation, its citations of Tamil literary texts, and the composition of lyrics in the style and meters of those texts.[6] In the song "Kalai Uyaruma," rapper Masta K uses a compositional strategy common to *sollisai*, in which he organizes his verses around quotes from several literary sources (▶ Video example 29.3).[7] As indicated in Figure 29.5, Masta K draws on text from a 2,000-year-old epic poem the *Silappatikaram* (*cilappatikāram*) (cue 1, 0:47–0:52); a fifteenth-century medieval religious treatise titled *Tiruppugal* (*tiruppugaḷ*) (cue 2, 1:06–1:09; and cue 3, 1:11–1:14); a song written by the nineteenth-century poet Nilakantha

---

[5] In rap verse, Tamil is endowed with many attributes. It is likened to sweet honey and milk. It is personified as a nurturing mother, it is described as a life force, and it is bestowed with qualities of antiquity and timelessness, as well as globality and universality.

[6] After 2007, the majority of Malaysian Tamil rappers joined the *sollisai* movement and began experimenting with a literary *centamil* voice. Notable exceptions include Psycho Unit, who rather than embrace *centamil*, purposefully and strategically combined Tamil folk rhythms, sexually explicit and violent themes, and Tamil profanities to incite and provoke listeners—giving the proverbial middle finger to the purist language standards of Tamil middle and upper classes.

[7] The translated section in Figure 29.5 is performed from 0:37–1:16 of Video example 29.3.

My sound will penetrate beyond the boundaries of the universe.
My sound will make you dance.
To the one who created the first Tamil *sangam*, I dedicate this song.

1) **Born from the 12 vowels
the 12 colors sa ri ga ma pa da ni were created.**
Mentioned in the ancient Tamil literary treatises,
is the philosophy that the Tamil language itself is music.
Let music overflow. Let worries be pushed aside.
Let the people's applause thunder.
Let art mature like a fruit. Let music win over the world.
Let desires dreamed of become sparks that rain down on the world.

2) **Life is full of deafness, blindness, and ugliness.**
Let music rise above it. Let it provide happiness.

3) Pray **to get the wisdom and grace of the celestial deities.**
Let all bad things pass. Hereafter let victory prevail.

Figure 29.5 Lyrics rapped by Masta K in the song "Kalai Uyaruma" from the 2009 album *Zoorasamharam*. Italicized and bolded text indicate quotes from Tamil literary sources. Translation by the author with the help of B. Balasubrahmaniyam.

Shivan (not included in Figure 29.5); and a speech given by the great politician, language activist, and orator M. Karunanadhi (not included in Figure 29.5).

Weaving his verses in and out of these historically diverse poetic Tamil sources and doing so in accordance with idiomatically appropriate rules of *yappu* (*yāppu*, poetic meter), Masta K demonstrates both his knowledge of *sentamil* and his ability to use it creatively. In tracing the origins of Tamil rap to these very texts, Masta K, claims belonging to and direct descent from a centuries-old lineage of pure literary Tamil sources. Malaysian-Tamil rap, is as he puts it, the "newest manifestation" of a very old art (see Box 29.1).[8]

---

[8] In addition to incorporating *solkattu* (discussed in Box 29.1), Tamil rappers draw upon the rhythms of karnatak music and classical Tamil prosody to structure the flow of their rapped verse. Tamil rap tends to be rhythmically dense, with Tamil rappers claiming to be some of the fastest rappers in the world of hip-hop. For more information on karnatak rhythmic theory see Nelson 2014.

TaKaDiMiTaKiTa - TaLan - GuTa - Tom - TaRiGiDuTa - Tom - KiTaTom- Tom - Ta -
TaKaDiMiTaKiTa - TaLan - GuTa - Tom - TaRiGiDuTa - Tom – KiTaTom- Tom - Ta -
TaKaDiMiTaKiTa - TaLan - GuTa - Tom - TaRiGiDuTa - Tom – KiTaTom- Tom - Ta -
Ta - - - Tam - GiDuDiKuTaKaTaRiGiDuTaKaDi - Tam - GiDuDiKuTaKaTaRiGiDu Tam

Figure 29.6 Transcription of one of the *solkattu* sections from Masta K's verse (cue point 2:32–2:52).

Box 29.1 Exercise

Thus far, I have discussed the significance of language in Malaysian Tamil rap, but what of the music and its significance? Just as the language of *sollisai* draws upon classical literary texts, the sound of *sollisai* is deeply informed by elements common to South Indian classical and devotional musics. For example, many Tamil rappers incorporate *solkattu* (*colkaṭṭu*), the rhythmic language of karnatak classical music, into their rap verse. The Tamil word *solkattu*, meaning "words bound together," refers not to actual words, but to percussive-sounding syllables that are strung together to create rhythmic phrases as well as more complex rhythmic compositions. Creatively borrowing from this rhythmic language and fusing it with their rap verse is yet another innovative strategy by which Malaysian Tamil rappers seek to elevate the status of their art.

(1) Listen to the song "Kalai Uyarma" (▶ Video example 29.3) and see if you can identify where rapper Masta K shifts from rapping in the Tamil language to reciting *solkattu* syllables. There are four occasions in which Masta K utilizes these rhythmic syllables: 2:07–2:14, 2:32–2:52, 4:29–4:49, and a shorter example 0:40–0:42.

(2) Figure 29.6 is a transcription of one of the *solkattu* sections from Masta K's verse, found at 2:32–2:52. Watch ▶ Video example 29.4 and try reciting the *solkattu* syllables below along with me at a slower tempo. In the video, I also demonstrate the relationship between the spoken *solkattu* syllables and the karnatak classical drumming tradition from which the syllables arise.

Discussion: Think of some examples from the hip-hop that you listen to, where rappers draw on or incorporate non-lexical vocal sounds into their performance. How do they use these non-lexical sounds, and why do you think they use these sounds?

Conclusion

Coco Nantha, Dr. Burn, and Masta K represent only a few of many Malaysian Tamil rappers who are challenging the representation of working-class Tamils as culturally and linguistically impure and degraded. Today's Malaysian Tamil rappers are inspiring Tamil diasporic youth globally, in Switzerland, France, Canada, the United Kingdom, and beyond, to experiment with Tamil language in rap—reconfiguring conventions of Tamil diglossia and subverting stereotypes.

Works Cited

Alim, Samy. 2009. "Intro." In *Global Linguistic Flows: Hip Hop Cultures, Youth Identities, and the Politics of Language*, edited by Samy Alim, Awad Ibrahim, and Alastair Pennycook, 1-24. New York: Routledge.
Bate, Bernard. 2009. *Tamil Oratory and the Dravidian Aesthetic: Democratic Practice in South India*. New York: Columbia University Press.
Baxstrom, Richard. 2005. "Wrecking Balls, Recognition, Reform: The Ambivalent Experience of Law, Justice, and Place in Urban Malaysia." PhD diss., Johns Hopkins University.
Clothey, Fred W. 2006. *Ritualizing the Boundaries: Continuity and Innovation in the Tamil Diaspora*. Columbia: University of South Carolina Press.
Lee, Raymond L. M., and R. Rajoo. 1987. "Sansrikritization and Indian Ethnicity in Malaysia." *Modern Asian Studies* 21(2): 389-415.
Muzaffar, Chandra. 1993. "Political Marginalization in Malaysia." In *Indian Communities in Southeast Asia*, edited by K. S. Sandhu and A. Mani, 211-236. Singapore: Institute of Southeast Asian Studies & Rimes Academic Press.
Nelson, David P. 2014. *Solkattu Manual: An Introduction to the Rhythmic Language of South Indian Music*. Middletown, CT: Wesleyan University Press.
Ramaswamy, Sumathi. 1997. *Passions of the Tongue: Language Devotion in Tamil Nadu India 1891-1970*. Berkeley: University of California Press.
Willford, Andrew C. 2006. *Cage of Freedom: Tamil Identity and the Ethnic Fetish in Malaysia*. Ann Arbor: University of Michigan Press.

30
Beyond the Silver Screen
Filmi Aesthetics in Bollywood Fitness Classes

Ameera Nimjee

Dance-based aerobics classes have long been popular in the landscape of North American fitness programs. Jazzercise, Zumba, and ballet barre-based Pilates have become fixtures in the offerings of dance studios, gyms, and the expanding entrepreneurial efforts of dance teachers. This chapter explores a relatively recent addition to dance-based workouts since the 2000s: Bollywood fitness programs. Offered both in-studio and online, classes are usually facilitated by an instructor who leads participants through movement sequences designed to match the rise and fall of a high-intensity, cardiovascular workout. The sequences—"choreographies"—draw from movements one might find in the song-dance numbers contained in films produced by South Asia's many cinema industries. The soundtracks of the classes comprise a series of *filmi* (*filmī*) hits, in addition to remix tracks by *bhangra* (*bhaṅgrā*), hip-hop, and popular recording artists and producers.

Bollywood fitness programs are often advertised as exercise classes with a cultural flair that are open to anyone (see, e.g., bollyx.com). While they offer a cardio workout, I argue that Bollywood fitness classes teach participants to "be *filmi*" by teaching song-dance aesthetics that feature in South Asian cinema. These aesthetics include the iconic hip pops and expressive, spectacular choreographies of Bollywood film scenes, as well as the *masala* (*masālā*, spicy), dramatic, *mastiwale* (*mastīvāle*, mischievous), and *nakhre* (*na<u>kh</u>re*, flirtatious) stylized attitudes that accompany their delivery and mimic character interaction on-screen. In Bollywood fitness classes, student-consumers are taught to embody movements that are taken from or inspired by film scene choreography, performing one- or two-minute cardio sequences to corresponding film songs. *Filmi* aesthetics—in dance vocabulary and stylized attitude—move beyond the silver screen as participants learn to embody Bollywood in the moment of a cardio workout. In the diaspora, the teaching of *filmi* aesthetics in a gym or fitness studio places otherwise-minoritized South Asian culture squarely in everyday life.

As a South Asian Canadian, I was raised on Bollywood. More specifically, I was raised on the idea that consuming Hindi films and performing Bollywood song-dances was a means to locate and reproduce my Indian identity. Bollywood was part of my "everyday South Asia," in a family that migrated from parts of India, Pakistan, and East and South Africa to Canada. During my childhood in 1990s Toronto, I performed various types of South Asian dance. At weddings and variety shows, I restaged dances to the songs of Bollywood hit films *Dilwale Dulhania Le Jayenge* and *Kuch Kuch Hota Hai*, taking choreographic inspiration from their on-screen versions. DJs and bands remixed the same hits at the "music parties" of our then mostly Indo-African Muslim migrant community, where we "played" (danced) *dandiya* (*dāṇḍiyā*) and *raasara* (*rāsara*, *rās*).[1] I joined dance teams in high school and university through which I performed and competed in South Asian culture shows even after I began a more rigorous training in Indian classical *kathak* dance in my late teens. I was initiated into a compartmentalized world shared with other diasporic *desis* (*desīs*),[2] in which we restaged on-screen choreographies into live performances of Bollywood dance. In doing so, I was taught to mimic and value Bollywood's *filmi* aesthetics, delivering its *masala* flare.

Teaching *filmi* aesthetics is central to the Bollywood fitness class, as a culturally inflected, dance-based workout. Fitness programs join an array of activities that broaden the term "Bollywood" beyond the Hindi-language cinema of India (see Rajadhyaksha 2007). Such activities include ritualized performances of song-dance sequences at weddings and cultural shows, and in videos and on social media. In global contexts, these forms of cultural production illuminate racialized and minoritized citizenship experienced by *desis*, who perform their everyday South Asia at home or in places of shared affinity. In the following sections, I analyze my own ethnographic experience with fitness company BollyX in dialogue with scholarship on Bollywood. This is accompanied by an exercise that asks readers to try their own cardio sequence, mimicking its choreography to experience how the combination of

---

[1] *Dandiya* and *raasara* (more commonly referred to as "*raas*") are two forms of Gujarati folk dance, performed in lines and circles. A participant "plays" (dances) *dandiya* with a pair of sticks (*ḍaṇḍās*). Raas is similar to forms of *garba*, performed in revolving, concentric circles or straight lines. See also Desai*.

[2] *Desi* is a term used to refer to a person of South Asian descent, and often in transnational contexts.

movement vocabulary and accompanying attitude encourages an experience of "being *filmi*." Bollywood fitness—and the *filmi* aesthetics taught therein—render *desi* culture visible and even mainstream in North American life.

Bollywood beyond the Screen

The song-dance number endures as one of the most iconic features of South Asia's many film industries (Gopal and Moorti 2008, 1).[3] Song-dance numbers exist within films as elements that "break" narrative, while also continuing it, moving between soundtrack, in-story performance, and dream sequence in modes of "multiple diegesis" (Gehlawat 2010, 39). While these numbers are central features in Indian cinema, their production supports larger creative economies of composers, music directors, producers, editors, musicians, and singers who work in Indian playback recording industries (see Booth 2008; Booth and Shope 2014). Song-dance numbers also create economies for choreographers, dancers, costume and lighting designers, numerous technicians, dramaturgs, and many other creatives, who contribute to the spectacular sequences that feature in a *filmi* number. These sequences become blueprints for repeated performances at weddings and other community events, in touring productions, and on television shows.

The term "Bollywood" is often invoked colloquially to refer to the Hindi film industry. Ashish Rajadhyaksha argues, however, that Bollywood is much larger in scope. He writes, "Bollywood is not the Indian film industry, or at least not the film industry alone. Bollywood . . . might best be seen as a more diffuse cultural conglomeration involving a range of distribution and consumption activities from websites to music cassettes, from cable to radio" (2007, 451). While the Hindi film industry developed during the first half of the twentieth century and was coined "Bollywood" in the 1970s, Bollywood as a culture industry is a more recent phenomenon that began in the 1990s, relying on the transnational dispersion of "distribution and consumption activities" (2007, 453–454). Bollywood dance is one of these manifestations.

Today, these activities continue in a wide variety of contexts: live performances of song-dance numbers in concerts by singers and composers; appearances of Bollywood celebrities at corporate, fundraising, and sporting

---

[3] Ajay Gehlawat and Rajinder Dudrah make a similar rhetorical gesture, stating, "The history of Hindi cinema is in many ways the history of song and dance" (2019, 1).

events; competitions and televised reality shows (see Chakravorty 2017); performances at *desi* weddings (see Mason and Nimjee 2019); and in queer nightlife (see Khubchandani 2020). Bollywood production and consumption activities also involve the exchange of media online, wherein social media personalities, influencers, amateurs, and professionals alike post video content on platforms such as YouTube, Vimeo, Instagram, Facebook, and TikTok. Bollywood fitness programs join this range of activities that construct the culture industry of Bollywood by reproducing and recontextualizing *filmi* song-dance. Bollywood fitness program participants are part of a process of mainstreaming South Asian culture abroad, in classes where student-consumers learn and perform movement sequences to popular hits from South Asian cinema.

Some scholars suggest that off-screen Bollywood song-dance activities have particular currency in and for the diaspora. Sangita Shresthova posits, "live Bollywood dance has become a more formalized cultural movement that is now the dominant influence on the vast majority of staged performances showcasing Indian culture in the US" (2011, 106). Sangeeta Marwah argues that the institutionalization of Bollywood dance in the diaspora "attempts to authenticate [the neoliberal Bollywood song] as a genuine purveyor of Indian culture" (2017, 190).[4] While some scholars concentrate on Indian classical dance communities as critical sites for performing South Asian heritage in the diaspora (see Srinivasan 2012; Thobani 2017; Morelli 2019), it was my experience as a Muslim with diverse South Asian heritage that classical dance was unrelatable compared to Bollywood dance. Further, Bollywood song-dance activities have pervaded the lives of a wider swath of transnational South Asians with a variety of ethnic and religious identities and histories. In effect, the Bollywood culture industry is the quotidian location for performing South Asian heritage.

Bollywood dance has always featured a pastiche of movement vocabulary, whether from South Asian regional dance styles such as *bhangra*, *garba*, *lavani*, and *ghoomar*; or from others like flamenco, disco, hip-hop, and salsa. In Bollywood classes, these dances are typically imbued with the athletic, choreographic, formational, and *nakhre* aesthetics found on the silver screen. Bollywood fitness programs are contiguous with formalized Bollywood

---

[4] Marwah's "neoliberal song" refers to Bollywood production in the early 2000s, in the decade that followed a series of market deregulations as the government of India encouraged more foreign investment during the liberalization of its economy.

dance classes in that the body is trained to perform what can be seen on-screen. While fitness consumers do not necessarily seek to learn forms of Indian dance, nevertheless they are taught to embody *filmi* aesthetics in their delivery of cardio sequences. Both Bollywood dance and fitness curricula circulate ideals of a physically fit body, which are intertwined with histories of class, caste, gender, and consumption.[5] The next section analyzes how the teaching of *filmi* aesthetics in Bollywood fitness offers an opportunity for *desi* culture to move from the racialized periphery of North American life to become mainstream in the moment of a workout.

BollyX: Branding Fitness as Culture

In the diaspora, fitness programs join an array of Bollywood song-dance activities through which many South Asians maintain and enact their *desi* identities. When marketed to demographic groups beyond transnational *desi*s, fitness classes also render South Asian culture visible. In these contexts, the classes are marketed as accented cardiovascular workouts, wherein exercise can be "cultural." The gym or fitness studio becomes transformed into a space where *filmi* aesthetics move past a sharing of racialized affinity among South Asians to everyday, public life.

A simple Google search of the term "Bollywood fitness" in the United States yields numerous in-studio classes, as well as online videos, branded membership programs, and DVD purchases. BollyX is one such company, defining itself as a "Bollywood-inspired dance fitness community" (bollyx.com). The company's growing community includes 4,000 certified instructors, who hold weekly classes in over 100 cities worldwide—and counting. The company's website presents these impressive statistics amid high-res images of instructors and fitness participants, links to its social media platforms, and an interactive map to locate classes around the world, all embedded in persuasive copy text and sleek design. The website also houses the company's "On Demand" portal, a paid-membership zone in which patrons can access

---

[5] Anna Morcom argues that formalized Bollywood dance classes have resulted in a distancing between middle-class professional dancers and communities of hereditary dance professionals, many of whom were lower-class and lower-caste (2013, 120–125). She continues that today's dancers are trained to produce bodies that are physically fit and athletically conditioned, which is reflected in Radhika Parameswaran's cosmopolitan "new Indian woman" (2004, 353). At the same time, Chatterjee and Rastogi point to ways that the politics of beauty and fitness are changing in representations of modern-day film heroines (2020, 297).

hundreds of video workouts. Short excerpts of these workouts feature as presumable enticements on YouTube, several of which garner millions of views.

I attended my first BollyX class in December 2019, following correspondence with the company's cofounder and CEO Shahil Patel. I showed up thirty minutes early to Flow Fitness gym, parking my car in the heart of Amazon corporate territory in Seattle's South Lake Union neighborhood. After paying my $25 drop-in fee to a gym representative, I walked through a sea of gym-goers into a brightly lit, large, open studio featuring a requisite wall of mirrors and barre that jutted out from the wall. It seemed that I was the first to arrive, and I went to introduce myself to BollyX Instructor Tulika Venugopal, with whom I had corresponded the week before.

As people filtered in, I positioned myself "stage right," in what became the first row of students. Tulika said a quick greeting, made a few announcements, and in a few moments, the hit song "Chammak Challo" from the film *Ra. One* (2011) blasted through the studio's speakers. Tulika directed us through relatively simple, symmetrical choreography; if we were directed to perform movements with the right arm and leg, and moving in a rightward direction, I could expect the same on the left in the proceeding musical phrase. Choreography was organized per a predictable sixteen-bar musical organization in a two-minute abbreviated version of the original song. Throughout the short sequence, Tulika interjected exclamations like "hit that pose!" and "give me some attitude!," communicating the importance of not just learning the movements, but also of their *nakhre* delivery.

Most of the fourteen students in the class were *desi*. Each of the eleven songs featured a similar approach to the opening song, "Chammak Challo." We learned four or five movement sequences per song and repeated them in a series, at Tulika's direction. She performed each song-dance sequence along with us, signaling the movements that were to come next, sometimes teaching one or two before a song began, all the while cheering us on. I noticed slip-ins of *filmi* choreography from *Ra.One*, including the mimed shooting of guns and the brushing of shoulders with a swagger that often embellishes the masculine bravado of a story's hero on-screen.

Every three or four songs was a contemporary *bhaṅgra* tune, with the identifiable treble and bass of a digital *dhol* and lyrics sung in Punjabi (see also Bhattacharjya and DJ Rekha*). To these, we performed some of the genre's accompanying large, oppositional, arm movements and jump-skip choreography. Tulika directed us to perform the *bhangra* choreography with the haughty confidence that is attributed to a performance of Punjabi and Jat masculinity (see Roy 2020).⁶ *Bhangra* has become a fixture in Bollywood and *filmi* choreography (see Roy 2014). In my experience among North American *desi*s, Punjabi *bhangra* and Gujarati *garba-raas*, though "folk" dance forms, have circulated under the umbrella of commercialized Bollywood dance in competition circuits and through college dance teams (see Bakrania 2013; Shresthova 2008). It is almost an expectation that fitness classes would teach *bhangra* choreography under the "Bollywood" moniker, demonstrating the fluidity of the term "Bollywood" in *desi* spaces of affinity.

Many of the songs in my BollyX class were "new"—from the 2010s onward. As has always been the case in Bollywood, songs derive from regional styles of South Asian popular music and the pastiche of global trends in production. In these newer, neoliberal songs (Marwah 2017, 190), phrases are arranged in identifiable rises and falls and feature the building of electronic dance music (EDM)-like climaxes in pre-choruses that resolve in refrains. Lyrics are in Hinglish, a mix of Hindi and English, featuring regional slang delivered by male performers in rap-like cadences. Female voices are more varied in timbre, with a hint of the concerted autotune aesthetic of global pop music—a far cry from the childlike falsetto of earlier playback singers Lata Mangeshkar and Asha Bhosle (see Sarrazin*). Although it was my first BollyX class, after years of performing *filmi bhangra* and Bollywood choreography, my body knew what to expect. I followed along easily with the "selectively citation[al]" Bollywood movements (Shresthova 2008, 261) interspersed with original choreography, responding to Tulika's encouragement to do so "with attitude," as actors would dance in films.

In an interview with Tulika Venugopal, she explained that setting up a BollyX class in Seattle was relatively easy for her to do, given the presence of *desi*s who work in tech.⁷ She explained that her *desi* participants often made requests for particular songs, which helped her keep a pulse on what is popular. She added, "just having the familiarity of what 'Bolly' even means makes a lot of them feel comfortable to attend a class like this, right? . . . having the students have that kind of feedback also makes them feel that, 'Oh the instructor is actually listening, and this class is tailored to what we actually enjoy'" (Interview with the author, April 22, 2020). This maintenance

---

⁶ "Jat" (sometimes spelled "Jatt") refers to a dominant caste community of Punjabis.
⁷ Instructors pay a monthly fee to access the BollyX portal with new song/choreography releases. It is incumbent upon instructors to set up their own classes, which usually involve contracts with gyms, fitness studios, or corporate gigs. Correspondingly, all revenues from class contracts are returned to the instructor directly, and none goes to BollyX.

of currency around Bollywood is an example of centering *desi* affinity—privileging those who consume and produce their everyday South Asia at Flow Fitness gym. At the same time, Tulika emphasized in our interview the importance of adhering to the "comfortable and enjoyable experience" promised by BollyX to make fitness and *filmi* aesthetics easy to achieve for anyone, regardless of prior experience with Bollywood.

On December 9, 2018, cofounder and CEO Shahil Patel appeared on an episode of *Shark Tank* to pitch BollyX to the American television show's five "Sharks" for investment in the company. The episode begins with Shahil and members of the BollyX team bursting through the "tank's" studio doors, adorned in sequined *kurta*s, *gagra-choli*s, and *dupatta*s, performing a Bollywood-style choreography to "Say 'Shava Shava'" from the film *Kabhi Khushi Kabhie Gham*. The dancers end their routine by draping *dupatta*s around the necks of each Shark, following which Shahil exclaims, "And we'll be right back after this quick Bollywood scene change." The episode continues with the rest of Shahil's pitch, beginning with the question, "What if we could combine the fun, the energy, the excitement of Bollywood into a workout?" Shahil's dancers return to the studio to lead the Sharks in a BollyX demonstration, teaching a choreography in a style that emulates the company's On Demand videos. Shahil narrates his instructions as he and his dancers perform the choreography: "We're gonna bend those knees until your shins are vertical, hands up, alright? We're gonna go: down, two, step-with-the left; Three, two, one, say-HUH! Down, two, three, step-it-back; Three, two, lemme-hear-ya say-HUH!" (*Shark Tank*, Season 10, Episode 8). The Sharks mirror the dancers' movements, laughing along throughout, after which Shahil describes rediscovering his Indian roots by joining a Bollywood dance team in college to "straighten out his two left feet." While Shahil was unsuccessful in securing an investment agreement from any of the Sharks for BollyX, the content of his pitch matches the messaging of the now-successful company, which seeks to appeal to its patrons both physically and emotionally.

I infer that one of the most important features of BollyX, branded as a "Bollywood-inspired fitness platform" and "community" (*Shark Tank* and bollyx.com), is its inclusivity to any and all patrons while teaching *filmi* aesthetics. My class, Tulika's interview, and Shahil's pitch on *Shark Tank* and BollyX's website demonstrate that participating is fun, exciting, comfortable, and can be easy, even though what it teaches may be unfamiliar to some—as evidenced later on in the *Shark Tank* episode, when Shahil and his dancers teach the Sharks a simple choreography. I noted the same during my experience in a BollyX class, wherein student-consumers learned movements that were clearly new—in vocabulary and attitude—but rarely faltered during repeated iterations of the choreography. BollyX offers a forum for a range of activities that support Bollywood as a culture industry. For *desi* clients, its Bollywood aesthetic-inspired movement serves to perform Bollywood in public while, at the same time, offering an easy-to-master sequence that provides an instantly gratifying workout for anyone. It casts a wide patron network while branding fitness as culture in a seemingly saturated market for innovative exercise routines.

Spaces between Dance and Cardio

The BollyX On Demand portal houses hundreds of videos that lead a student-consumer through fitness choreographies. Featuring Shahil and other members of his team, the videos teach movement vocabulary punctuated by exclamations of "yeah, you got this!" and "nice!" as well as "let's go!" (see Figure 30.1 and Box 30.1).

Figure 30.1 The author follows along with a BollyX On Demand video in her living room. Photo by Matthew Del Ciampo; used with permission.

> **Box 30.1 Exercise**
>
> (1) Try your own BollyX routine by navigating to the company's YouTube channel: @BollyX. If the channel is not available, navigate to any video advertised as a Bollywood-style workout. Follow along with one of the sequences available. How does this compare to other kinds of workout classes you have experienced? To your previous experiences of Bollywood culture?
>
> (2) Try the same sequence a second time. Now that you are somewhat familiar with the choreography, pay extra attention to the instructors' non-exercise directives. How do these communicate the *nakhre* aesthetics described in this chapter? Beyond the choreography, what do the instructors ask you to do? Why are these directives important? How do they impact your experience of the workout at large?

Just as I experienced in my live class with BollyX Instructor Tulika Venugopal, peppered throughout the On Demand videos are directions on how to render movements, with calls of "add a little spice to it!" and "a little flavor!" These verbal cues complement the song-dance choreographies, which offer a means to teach Bollywood dance and *filmi*, *nakhre* aesthetics in the process of exercising. Though the goal of BollyX is to facilitate exercise, the attention to pedagogy and style communicates a desire to teach dance while working out, delivering choreographies with *masala*, drama, *masti*, and what Shahil refers to as "cheese" in *Shark Tank* (Season 10, Episode 8). In Bollywood song-dance, the dramatic expression of story is interspersed with other choreographic elements, including gestures that are filled with flavors of mischievous bravado, coquettish attitude, and flirtatious spice.

The aesthetics of Bollywood "cheese"—especially in the song-dance number—have often been sources of patronizing attitudes toward the "frivolity" of the Indian cinema. Tejaswini Ganti argues that an "inferiority complex" on the part of Hindi film directors has resulted in the perception of song-dance numbers as local "cultural baggage" (2012, 350). On the other hand, "cheesy" song-dance numbers and their spicy drama circulate far beyond films to buttress the Bollywood industry at large. Kareem Khubchandani argues that the "excesses" of Bollywood camp define what is meant by the term *"filmi"* (2020, 137).[8] Teaching Bollywood dance is teaching one to be *filmi*. And teaching one to be *filmi* is, in effect, teaching the aesthetic priorities of the Bollywood culture industry, which is reproduced in the Bollywood workout studio.

Conclusion

Bollywood fitness programs contribute to the transnational production of Bollywood by teaching consumers to inhabit *filmi* aesthetics through dance movements organized as exercise routines. Centering on the reproduction and performance of the *filmi* song-dance number, and drawing from adjacent traditions like *bhangra* and *garba-raas*, Bollywood fitness programs sit squarely in the song-dance range of distribution and consumption activities that comprise contemporary transnational Bollywood culture (Rajadhyaksha 2007, 451). The student-consumers who attend Bollywood fitness classes thus become part of a broader exchange of Bollywood culture at large.

Bollywood fitness programs bring to North American mainstream culture the *filmi* aesthetics that are an important part of the everyday life of transnational *desi*s, repackaged as a cardio workout. Fitness classes join an array of activities that center on the reproduction of song-dance numbers to perform this mainstreaming work. The fitness economy maintains Bollywood as a global culture industry by restaging *filmi* aesthetics. What is seen on the silver screen of South Asian cinema enters a world of exchange with what happens beyond it as exercising bodies restage *filmi* drama.

Works Cited

Bakrania, Falu. 2013. *Bhangra and Asian Underground: South Asian Music and the Politics of Belonging in Britain*. Durham, NC: Duke University Press.

Booth, Gregory. 2008. *Behind the Curtain: Making Music in Mumbai's Film Studios*. Oxford: Oxford University Press.

Booth, Gregory, and Bradley Shope, eds. 2014. *More than Bollywood: Studies in Indian Popular Music*. New York: Oxford University Press.

---

[8] Khubchandani continues on to argue that centralizing *filmi* excesses demonstrates the inherency of queer aesthetics in Hindi cinema (2020, 137).

Chakravorty, Pallabi. 2017. *This Is How We Dance Now!: Performance in the Age of Bollywood and Reality Shows.* New Delhi: Oxford University Press.
Chatterjee, Srirupa, and Shreya Rastogi. 2020. "The Changing Politics of Beauty Labor in Indian Cinema. *South Asian Popular Culture* 18(3): 271–282.
Gehlawat, Ajay. 2010. *Reframing Bollywood: Theories of Popular Hindi Cinema.* New Delhi: Sage.
Gehlawat, Ajay, and Rajinder Dudrah, eds. 2019. *The Evolution of Song and Dance in Hindi Cinema.* New York: Routledge.
Ganti, Tejaswini. 2012. "No Longer a Frivolous Singing and Dancing Nation of Movie-Makers: The Hindi Film Industry and Its Quest for Global Distinction." *Visual Anthropology* 25(4): 340–365.
Gopal, Sangita, and Sujata Moorti, eds. 2008. *Global Bollywood: Travels of Hindi Song and Dance.* Minneapolis: University of Minnesota Press.
Khubchandani, Kareem. 2020. *Ishtyle: Accenting Gay Indian Nightlife.* Ann Arbor: University of Michigan Press.
Marwah, Sangeeta. 2017. "*Kehte Hain Humko Pyar Se Indiawaale*: Shaping a Contemporary Diasporic Indianness in and through the Bollywood Song." *South Asian Popular Culture* 15(20): 189–202.
Mason, Kaley, and Ameera Nimjee. 2019. "Sound Unions: The Work of Music Specialists in the South Asian Diaspora." In *Music in the American Diasporic Wedding*, edited by Inna Narodistkaya, 208–230. Bloomington: Indiana University Press.
Morcom, Anna. 2013. *Illicit Worlds of Indian Dance: Cultures of Exclusion.* Oxford: Oxford University Press.
Morelli, Sarah. 2019. *A Guru's Journey: Pandit Chitresh Das and Indian Classical Dance in Diaspora.* Urbana: University of Illinois Press.
Parameswaran, Radhika. 2004. "Global Queens, National Celebrities: Tales of Feminine Triumph in Post-Liberalization India." *Critical Studies in Media Communication* 21(4): 346–370.
Rajadhyaksha, Ashish. 2007. "The 'Bollywoodization' of the Indian Cinema." In *The Inter-Asia Cultural Studies Reader*, edited by Kuan-Hsing Chen and Beng Huat Chua, 449–466. London: Routledge.
Roy, Anjali Gera. 2014. "Filming the *Bhangra* Music Video." In *More than Bollywood: Studies in Indian Popular Music*, edited by Gregory D. Booth and Bradley Shope, 142–159. New York: Oxford University Press.
Roy, Anjali Gera. 2020. "Gendering Dance." *Religions* 11(4): 202–220.
Shresthova, Sangita. 2008. "Dancing to an Indian Beat: 'Dola' Goes My Diasporic Heart." In *Global Bollywood: Travels of Hindi Song and Dance*, edited by Sangita Gopal and Sujata Moorti, 243–263. Minneapolis: University of Minnesota Press.
Shresthova, Sangita. 2011. *Is It All about Hips?: Around the World with Bollywood Dance.* New Delhi: Sage.
Srinivasan, Priya. 2012. *Sweating Saris: Indian Dance as Transnational Labor.* Philadelphia: Temple University Press.
Thobani, Sitara. 2017. *Indian Classical Dance and the Making of Postcolonial National Identities: Dancing on Empire's Stage.* London: Routledge.

Index

For the benefit of digital users, indexed terms that span two pages (e.g., 52–53) may, on occasion, appear on only one of those pages.

Tables and figures are indicated by an italic *t* and *f* following the page number.

Abdullah "Ataullah" Jat 127–28, 134–36, 135*f*, 139
abhanga(s) 144*t*, 145n.3, 148, 150–54
abhinaya 220–21, 292–93, 295–96
Abhinishkramanaya 413, 414, 415–16, 418, 420–23
"Achamillai" 461, 461*f*
activism
  nationalist civic 272–73
  social and political 265
  transgender rights 308
activist(s)
  anticolonial 267, 268n.3
  Hindutva 267
adavu(s) 220–21
adi(s) 91, 196–201, 201*f*, 202, 203, 205–6
  disco 197, 198*f*
  kuchi 201
  son 91, 199*f*, 201
  tuki 118
Adivasi(s) 93, 171, 174, 176–77, 181, 243, 246, 261, 337, 443
  communities 11, 171–72, 176, 263
  music characteristics 176–77
  performing arts 176–77
  villages 181–82
Advani, Kalyan 134n.8
aerobics 466
aesthetic action 260
affect
  shift in 310, 312–14
Afghani 257
Afghanistan 1–3, 257
Africa 58, 247–48
  East 407–8, 443
  South and East 408, 467

African 429–30
  American(s) 430–31, 437–38, 459
  American hip-hop 431, 432
  American jazz musicians 226
  American music 429–30
    cultural forms 430
    diasporic transnational 429–30
    South 430
Afro-Caribbean (dancehall) music 428, 429–30, 436
Afrobeat 430, 449–50
Agawu, Kofi 78
agency 172–73, 190, 282, 286, 288–89, 294, 301–2, 307, 348–49, 356–58, 360
  artistic 278
  female 358
  national 274–75
  nationalist 265, 268
  personal 351
  true 356–58
  women's 274–75, 351, 360
Agra 37
Ahl-e Sunnat wa al-Jama'at 132
Ahmedabad 442, 443
Ahom Kingdom 320–21
Akbar/Akbar the Great 163, 355
akhand 239–40
Akhand Kirtani Jatha (AKJ) 230, 239–40
akhara(s) 11, 181–83, 182n.7, 184–86, 189, 190–91
Akhtar, Begum 37
Aklujkar, Vidyut 294
Aks 24
aksara(s) 392
al-'Arabi, Ibn 45
al-Ghazali 44–45

480 INDEX

Alam Ara 352
Alandi 150
Alanganallur 200f
alap 22–23, 130, 137, 163, 165
algozeh 428–29
Ali, Lucky 13, 20n.7, 22–27, 22n.10
   debut 25–26
   fans 22
   identity 24
   music videos 17, 20, 21–22
   promoters 25
Alim, Samy 458–59
Allah 45n.3, 134, 232, 443
   auliya 132
All India Dance Seminar 222
All India Music Conference 37
All India Radio (AIR) 109n.6, 268, 278–79
alto 352
Aman, Zeenat 355–56
Amazon 471
Amba Mata 442–44
Ambalewali, Zohrabai 352
Ambedkar, B. R. 171–72, 443
America
   Central 437–38
   Latin 427–28
   North 25n.13, 73–74, 224–25, 234, 339, 439
   post 9/11 235
American(s) 432, 451–52
   -accented English 436
   Central 437–38
   choreographers 415–16
   competition/collegiate dance groups 441
   congregational missionary(ies) 97–98, 102
   cultural life 441
   gospel music 109
   hip-hop 432
   hip-hop and R&B 427–28
   identity 98
   missionary 102
   music industry 337–38
   native history 23
   North 3, 171–72, 293n.5, 409–10, 466, 467–68, 469–70, 471–72, 476
   pop culture 458
   rapper 432
   scholarship 453
   southwest 13, 23
   students 254
   touristic idea 433
   white 179
   -ness 451–52
amirtam 99–101
Amritsar 232–33
Amritsen 164–65
Amulraj 195, 207
Anarkali 355
Anaarkali of Arrah 359–60
Andavan, Fusion 454–55, 454f
Anderson, Benedict 142–43
androgynous 257–58
androgyny, female 260
anga-suddham 220–21
Anglican
   liturgical practices 106
   mission societies 99
   missionary 109
   missions 105–6
   preference 106
Anglicizing 106–7
animist(s) 181–82
Anthropological Survey 248
Anti-Zamindari Act of 1952 280
anticolonial
   movement 149
   nationalist movement 36
   rebellion 36
   resistance 152–53
   struggle 267
antiphonal 176–77
anupallavi 101n.4, 107
Appadurai, Arjun 121, 409–10
Appavoo, Rev. J. T. 93–94, 103–4, 105, 113
Arab culture 43–44
Arabic 131, 133
aramandi 227
arangettam(s) 379, 383–87
   chenda- 383
*Aranyaka*s 156–57
Aravan 305, 307–9
Aravani 261–62, 305. *See also thirunangai*
Arba Sangeet Club 80n.1
ardhanarishwara 257–58, 293

INDEX   481

Arizona 23
"Arranged Marriage" 430–31
Arumugan 196, 198, 200f
Arumugan, Iyyapan 215b, 216f
Arun, Ila 358
Arundale, George 217–18
Arundale, Rukmini 92, 217–24, 221f
Arundathiyar/Arunthathiyar(s) 194–95, 456
Aruppukkottai 102
Arya Samaj 57
Aryan
   Indo-Aryan(s) 176, 181n.3
   people 156–57
   -Vedic high civilization 4–5
Asghar 50
ashram 147 146–47
Asia 3, 415, 416
   -n 415–16
Asiatic Society of Bengal 4–5
Assam 176, 261, 263, 317–18, 318f, 319–21, 323, 326f
   Upper 317–18, 319–20, 320n.4, 326–27n.14
   -ese 317–21, 322n.7, 327–30
asthai-antara 339–40
"Athiradee" 433–34
Attakkalari India Biennial/Attakkalari Biennail 421–22, 422n.14, 423f
attam 195
*attaprakaram*s 295n.9
aurality 384–87
Aurora (CO) 442
Australia 25n.13, 26, 73–74
avanaddha drums 158
avarna 171, 172t
Awadh 32–36
   administration 35
   King 34–35, 38
   masses 35
   Nawabs 33–34
   overthrow 34
   people 34–35
Awasti, Sapna 358
ayira/ararru 115
Ayurveda 390–91
Ayyagari, Shalini R. 12–13
Azad, Chandrashekhar 267, 268, 273

"Azad Hind" 268n.3

Baiga, The 244–45
"Baamulaiza" 427–28, 430, 436–37
Baba Chinda 60, 65–70, 66n.8, 67n.9
Babiracki, Carol M. 4–5, 18n.1, 171, 176–77, 252
"Babul Mora" 13, 29–31, 30f, 33–39
Baburam 372
Bach, J. S. 132, 164–65
*badhai*s 262
Badri 369–73
Bahar Begum 355
Bahujan(s) 97–98, 174, 215, 443, 443n.5
   self-esteem 104–5
baila 436–37, 437n.2
bailar 437n.2
bairag 56–57, 65–66
   -*i* 66–67
Baisakhi 269–70, 272
bait(s) 133–34, 137
Baksh, *pir* Hazrat Farid Shakar Ganj 46, 47–49, 54–55
Balasaraswati, T. 221–22
Balasubrahmaniyam, B. 463f
bali 393–95
ballet 466
Banerjee, Nikhil 156, 165
Bangalore 22
Bangladesh 1–3, 32–33, 261–62, 306–7, 407–8, 427
   -*i*(s) 407–8
banjo 344
banna 282, 283
banna-banni 282, 282n.9
bansuri 157, 339–40, 368, 433
Banu, Noor 137
Barna, Gazi 78–86, 79f, 80n.1
Barna Village 78, 83
Baroda 448
Basanti 355, 357
Bastar 243
Battle of Karbala 136t
Baxstrom, Richard 458
bayan 46
Bechdel-Wallace test 358n.3
Becker, Judith 67–69
Begum, Shamshad 352, 354

"being *filmi*" 467–68
belonging 54–55, 305, 306–7
  gendered 312
  inheritance 337
Benaras 163–64, 280, 283, 284–85, 287–88
Benegal, Uday 25
Bengal
  Army 36
  -i Hindus 95
  -i social elites 93
Bengaluru 109
Berava 390–92, 391n.3, 391n.4, 395–96, 398, 405, 413
Besant, Annie 217–18
be-tali 444–45, 451
"Beware" 432
"Beware of Boys" 428n.1
Bhaini Sahib 58, 58n.2, 58n.25, 60
bhairvin 32n.2
bhajan(s) 46, 144–45, 144*t*, 147, 148, 150, 151, 153–54
bhakti 53–54, 99–101, 144–45, 151, 262–63
Bhandas 442–43
bhangra 260–61, 266–67, 268–75, 270n.7, 270n.9, 271n.10, 428–31, 432–33, 466, 469–70, 471–72, 476
  artists 428
  attire 269–70
  boli 269–70
  Bollywood 270–71
  British 432
  dancers 269n.4, 272
  fusion 432
  historical trajectory 428–29
  identity 428–29
  -inflected R&B Tracks 432–33
  music 432
  number 268
  performance 428–29
  -pop 270
  remixes 271n.10
  revival 270
  scholars 428–29
  sounds 269
  structure 265
  -'s performers 428–29
Bhangra Moves: From Ludhiana to London and Beyond 428–29

bhangramuffin 430–31
bhangraton 432–33
Bharata 158, 158n.1
Bharata Kalakshetra 216*f*, 221–22
Bharata Natya 217
Bharatanatyam 91–92, 175, 209, 211n.3, 211n.4, 215–16, 217–20, 218n.8, 221–27, 417
Bharati, Subramaniya 454–55, 454*f*, 461
Bharatiya Janata Party (BJP) 143, 224–25
Bhatkande, Vishnu Narayan 165
Bhatt, Vikas 248
Bhattacharjya, Nilanjana 409
Bhattacharya, Meghnath 179–80
bhavan 121
Bhil, Diwali Behn 443
Bhitai, Shah 'Abdul Latif 132–34, 137
bhogam 212
Bhogananbdishwara Temple 159*f*, 194*f*
Bhojpuri 285
Bhopal University 255*f*
Bhosle, Asha 354, 360, 427, 472
Bhuj 127, 134
bhuta gana 159*f*
Bhutan 1
  -ese 371–72
bidi(s) 248–49
Bihagda 237*f*
Bihar 179, 280, 343
Bihu 317–25, 319n.2, 320n.5, 322n.8, 326–30, 326–27n.14
  festival rituals 318
  folkloric 317–18
  folklorization 319
  folkorized 261, 317–18, 326
  genre 263
  music and dance 317–18, 319–20
  performance 263, 317–21, 320n.5, 326, 326–27n.14, 327–30
  rati 321, 323
  rhythm 323n.11, 327
  songs 318, 321
bihuwa 323–25, 325*f*, 326, 326*f*, 327–30
bihuwoti 323–25, 325*f*, 326, 326*f*, 327–30
bin 155
  -*kar* 156, 165
biradari 170–71, 278, 278n.2, 283–84
Birmingham 430–32

Birsa Munda 186
Bisu 340
bitonality 176–77
BK Sangeet 340n.1
Black Atlantic, The 429–30
BMG 17, 25
    Crescendo 22
bodhisatta(s) 392
Bohag 317–18
bol(s) 91, 157, 165, 373–75*t*, 433
    patterns 156, 165
boliyan 271–72
Bollywood 25, 260–61, 335–36, 356–58, 436–37, 466–68, 471–74
    actresses 259
    aesthetic-inspired 473–74
    camp 475–76
    celebrities 468–69
    "cheese" 475–76
    choreography 472
    cinema 22–23, 26, 335
    classes 469–70
    Classic Era 259, 350–51, 354
    connections 22–23
    culture 175–76, 476
    culture industry 409–10, 468–69, 473–74, 475–76
    dance 467, 468–70, 470n.5, 471–72, 473, 475–76
    dance sequences 346n.2
    fans 281n.7
    film(s) 346n.2, 427–28, 432–33
    filmi 409–10, 467–68
    film music 95
    film scenes 466–67
    film songs 238–39
    fitness 467–68, 469–71
    fitness class(es) 466–68, 476
    fitness programs 466–67, 468–69, 476
    industry 26n.14, 259, 475–76
    -inspired dance fitness community 470–71
    -inspired fitness platform 473–74
    listener 95
    masala 5–6
    movements 472
    producers 25
    production 469n.4, 476

production and consumption activities 468–69
singers 91
song(s) 335–36, 436–37
song-dance(s) 467, 469, 470
sound 95
soundtracks 266
style 91, 95
-style choreography 473
-style dancing 260, 284–85
-style wedding 284–85
tunes 281
workout studio 475–76
's extensive networks 437–38
BollyX 409–10, 467–68, 470–75, 472n.7, 474*f*
bollyx.com 466–67
Bolo Ta Ra Ra 270
Bombay 32–33
    cinema 270n.9, 278–79
    film industry 266
    Governor 431
" 'Bombay, U.K., Yuba City': Bhangra Music and the Engendering of Diaspora" 409
"Boom-cha boom-chick-" beat 433–34, 435
Boomerangx 459, 461
"Boom-Shack-A-Lack" 430–31
Bose, Subhas Chandra 268n.3
Bose, Sugata 36
brahmacharya 379
Brahmaputra Valley 317–18
Brahmin (s) 92, 171, 172*t*, 212–13, 214–17, 223, 224
    female vocal soloist 145
    Hindu 146–47
    Nagar 442, 443
    rashtriya kirtankars 145–46
    saint 148
    South Indian 224
    Smarta 210
    women 92, 218–19
    -ic 210, 215–16, 221–23, 224–25
    -ical Hindu images 99–101
    -ical Hinduism 225–27
    -ical Saivite music culture 99–101
    -ical upper-caste cultural hegemony 101
    -ization 5–6
    -ness 147

Brenneis, Donald 121
Brihadesi 155
Britain 408, 428–29, 430–31, 432–33
British 27, 34, 56, 57, 58, 59, 456
   Afro Caribbeans 437–38
   Asian 270n.7, 432
   -born 432–33
   civil servants 456
   colonial centers 32–33
   colonial laws 262
   colonial regime 408
   colonial rule 33, 456
   colonialism 29, 146
   colonialists 279–80
   colonizers 14, 35
   colony 165
   cultural elites 3
   East India Company 33–35
   empire 34, 37–38
   English 456
   government 34–35
   governor-general 34
   hymnody 105–6
   imperialism 34–35
   Indian Punjab 352
   Jamaican 430–31
   missionaries 3
   music scene 270
   non-white 431–32
   occupation 57, 59
   officials 35
   origins 430
   Punjabi 430–31, 433
   Raj 267, 353
   reggae 430
   residents 34–35
   rule 37–38, 143, 352
   rulers 146
   social elites 93
Brown, James 430
Brunei 408
Buddha 390–91, 392, 393–98, 403–5, 413, 420–21, 421n.12
Buddhism 389n.1
   Theravada 391n.5, 392
Buddhist(s) 170, 395–96, 397–98
   chant 395–96
   drummers 389
   drumming 390–91, 392, 393–95
   Sinhala 389, 390–91, 392–93, 393*f*, 403–5
   temples 390–91
   Theravada 389n.1
   Traditional dance and drumming 393*f*
Burma 58, 61*f*, 65–66
Butler, Judith 257, 292–93

call-and-response 46, 60–61, 65, 90, 104, 144–45, 148, 151, 154, 230, 236, 239–40, 260–61, 265, 269–70, 282, 307–8
Calcutta 32–33, 34, 278–79
   HMV 278–79
   Kolkata 278–79
California 233*f*, 234
Calvinist CMS Missionaries 105–6
Canada 1–3, 58, 408–9, 462, 465, 467
   -ian 20n.6, 467
capitalism 20, 36, 175–76
   global 17, 175–76
Caribbean(s) 1–3, 408, 427–28, 430, 432–33, 436–38
   Carnival 436–37
   chutney 436–37
   Indo- 408
   inflected 435
   soca 436–37
caste(s) 93, 119–20, 129, 169, 169n.2, 170–74, 172*t*, 173n.3, 209, 210, 231, 257, 258, 261–62, 277, 280, 293n.6, 306–7, 317–18, 319, 320–21, 338–39, 365, 443n.5, 469–70
   anti- 98n.1, 105, 171–72, 193, 210, 443n.5
   based patronage 73–74
   based power 210
   community(ies) 113–14, 308
   discrimination 12–13, 105, 169n.2, 277, 281
   distinctions 92–93, 129, 170–71, 258, 453
   dominant 209, 214–17, 220–22, 224, 225–27, 341–43, 344
   duty 120, 173–74, 193, 194–95, 390–91
   Forward 181
   General 181, 190, 191–92

INDEX 485

high 75–76, 85, 180–81, 379
identity 170–72, 213–14, 282, 283–84
inter- 263, 317–18
lineage(s) 258, 262, 277
low 58, 74–75, 82–83, 93, 115, 280n.6, 287–88, 390–91
lower(ed) 102, 169n.1, 176–77, 340–41, 348–49
middle 119, 121, 194–95, 258
most backward 169n.1, 171–72, 172t
"oppressed people" 171–72
oppression 260, 286
other backward 169n.1
role 278
scheduled 113n.1, 116, 171–72, 172t, 181, 181n.5, 245–46
society 180–81
status 280
system 171, 173, 174–75, 231, 232, 233–34
upper 92, 97–99, 101, 102, 104–5, 106–7, 108, 119, 120, 155, 172–74, 175, 183n.8, 258, 308, 443
-ist 94, 225–27
"caste-free" 456
Catholic 204–5
Catholicism 105–6
Cazan, Madame 219–20
Celebration of Demons, A 391–92
Census 247
Ceylon 408
cha-cha-cha 109
chai 20
Chamar 170
"Chammak Challo" 471
Chandler, John 102
Chandralekha 417
charanam 99–101
Chatterjee, Partha 105–6
Chatterjee, Srirupa 470n.5
Chaturbhujasthan 281–82
Chauhan, Hemant 443
Chauhan, Mehindra Singh 339–40, 341–48
Chauhan, Sunidhi 358
Chaurasia, Hariprasad 157
Cheeni Kum 359–60
chelik 243–44, 247, 248–51, 254
chenda 333–34, 377–84, 385

Chennai 92, 209, 210, 308
Cheruthuruthy 377
Chhattisgarh 243
Chicago School 12, 18–19
chikari 164
Chikkaballapur 159*f*
chimta 60–61, 67–69, 428–29
Chinai, Alisha 25, 358
Chinese 436–37, 458, 460*f*
Chishtiyya 46, 48n.5
  beliefs 48
  poem 42
  Sufi saint 42, 47
  understanding 48
Chisti, Nizamuddin 160–61
Chitra 109
Chitrasena 415, 421
  Dance Company 413, 414n.5, 421
  School 414–15
Chola 174–75
Chotanagpur 176, 181
Christian(s) 5, 95, 98, 99, 101, 102, 104–5, 106–11, 146, 149, 170, 181–82, 314–15, 443
  bhakti 99–101, 104–5
  class, caste and cultural identity 109–11
  context 90
  converts 5n.5
  evangelism 97–98
  institutions 106
  kirttanai-oyilattam tune 104
  kirttanai tunes 105
  liturgical content 109–11
  liturgy 113
  message 98–99
  missionaries 57
  monks 45
  music 97–98, 99, 103–4, 108–9
  musical agency 108
  musical and theological expressions 98–99
  musical localization 99
  practice 97
  ritual 102
  songs 3–4
  songs and liturgies 111–12
  theology and hymnody 104–5
  worship 102, 104
  -ity 97, 98–99, 105, 111–12

Christian Lyrics for Public and Social Worship 97–98
church(es) 95, 105, 449–50
  service(s) 107
Church Mission Society 105–6
Church of South India 102, 106
  congregational parish 106
  Methodist parish 106
chutney 408
Cinema
  Hindi 265, 266, 269, 270, 468n.3, 476n.8
  Indian 320n.3, 350, 351, 354, 468, 475–76
citizen subject
  masculine 265
citizenship
  responsibilities of 265
class(es) 93, 169, 257, 261–62, 277, 293n.6, 306–7, 317–18, 320–21, 415, 469–70
  conscious 105
  discrimination 281
  distinctions 92–93, 258
  inter- 317–18
  low 73–74
  lower 93, 97–98
  middle 92, 93, 108, 109–11, 258, 265
  oppression 286
  upper 99, 101, 279–80
classical 4–5, 12, 43–44, 90, 91–93, 94, 175, 427
  arts 5, 92–93
  audiences 29
  dance 91–92
  Indian music 5
  instruments 157
  light 29, 98, 278, 279
  music 38, 92, 130, 157, 167
  musicians 29
  "non-" 12–13, 244, 247–48
  rasa theory 121
  realm 1–3
  singers 29
  systems 3–4
  tradition 92
"classicized" 98, 279, 413n.2
  -ation 84–85, 279, 413–14
code(s)
  indexical 90–91
  musical 90–91
  semiotic 90–91
  sonic 339
codification 295
Coke Studio India 73–74
cold war 17
Collins, Bootsy 430
Colombo 392–93, 393f, 413–15
Colombo Dance Platform 415–16
colonial 173, 218n.8
  agency 111–12
  ambition 18
  centers 32–33
  coup 35
  dominance 93
  ethnographers 279
  history 93
  imagination 176
  initiatives 4–5
  knowledge 3
  period 173
  portrayals 327–30
  power 34–35
  public health policies 279
  records 73–74
  rule 35
  rulers 167
  stereotypes 176, 327–30
  -ism 3, 11–12, 36, 37–38, 91–92, 414–15
  -ist construction 94
  -ist discourse 92
  -ists 3, 279
Colonial Cousins 20n.7, 25
colonization 279
Columbia World Library of Folk and Primitive Music, The 247–48
"communitas" 13–14, 67–69
community-building 305
cosmopolitan(s) 85–86, 175–76, 270–71, 339, 370–71
  fans 22
  formation 339
  "indigenous cosmopolitanism" 12–13
  lens 86
  Manganiyar musicians 74–75
  middle and upper class urban 20
  positioning 86

INDEX 487

possibilities 366
sensibility 270n.7
subject 92
ultra- 213
upper middle class audience 26
urban cosmopolitanism 26–27
-ism 410n.1
courtesan(s) 210–11, 212–13, 213n.6,
  214–17, 218–23, 260, 355
  community(ies) 210n.1, 218–19, 221–
    22, 260, 263, 286
  "divas" 291–92
  quarter(s) 280
Covid-19 235, 448
Criminal Tribes Act 280
criminalized 288–89
cross-dressing 262
Cuba 24
-n 109
cultural capital 282, 283–84
cultural gray out thesis 17–18
cultural politics of the singing voice 266
cultural tourism 83–85
Cutler, Norman 149
cymbal(s) 59, 60–61, 102–3, 144–45, 239–
  40, 323, 420
Cynthia 207
Cyrus, Miley 359–60

"da diri da ra" 165
dahing 397, 400–3
da'ira 157
dak 162–63
Dalada, Maligawa 394n.7
Dalit(s) 97–98, 103–4, 109–11, 113n.1,
  124–25, 171–72, 172*t*, 173–74,
  211n.4, 315, 337, 443, 443n.5,
  449–50
  anti-caste 98n.1, 171–72, 193, 195,
    204–5, 259–60
  Christians 104–5
  community (ies) 113, 204–5
  community knowledge systems 195–96
  drumming 173–74
  folklorist 93–94
  Human Rights Defenders
    Network 445n.6
  music and dance form 104

musicians 113, 123–24
NGO groups 196
self-esteem 104–5
women 113–14, 206
women's liberation 207
Dalit-Bahujan(s) 5, 93, 171–72, 207
  activist-organizations 169
  artists 8
  communication 93–94
  communities 13
  ritual performance 175
  ritual practitioners 173–74
  women 258
Dalmandi 280
Dalwai, Sameena 170–71, 278n.2
damaru 157
damaun 340–41, 345
dana 395n.8
dancehall 430–31
Dance In The Round 436–38, 440–42,
  445–47, 451–52
dance-song(s) 33, 340–41, 343–49
  participatory performances 343
  performances 348
  village 345
  village-based 343, 348
Dance Teacher magazine 440*f*
dandiya 467, 467n.1, *See also* raas
dand rasak 442n.3
darshan 53–54
Das, Pandit Chitresh 291–92, 292n.3, 293,
  294–96
dasi 212
dastan 127–28, 132
davula 393–95
Dayasheela, Herbert 392–96, 398, 399*f*,
  401*f*, 402n.13
decaste 8
Deccan 243
declass 8
decolonial writings 305–6
decolonization 8
De Dana Dan 427–28, 436–37
deejaying culture 265, 270–71
degatang 403
Dehradun 343–44
"Dekha Hai Aise Bhi" 13, 23
Del Ciampo, Matthew 474*f*

Delhi 32–33, 156–64, 222, 248, 341–44, 347–48, 430–31
 East 343
 Midday 431
democratization 279, 335–36
"denotified" 280, 288–89
des 427
Desai, Meena 443, 444*f*
Desai, Parijat 408–9, 410, 440*f*
Desai, Utpala 439n.2, 442–43
"Desert Symphony" 79*f*, 84
desi(s) 427, 467–68, 467n.2, 470, 471, 472–73
 affinity 472–73
 clients 473–74
 culture 467–68, 469–70
 dance music 409, 427–30, 434–38
 identity(ies) 427–28, 470
 music 12–13
 North American 471–72
 participants 472–73
 songs 434–36, 437–38
 spaces 471–72
 students 409–10
 transnational 470, 476
 weddings 468–69
de-sexualized 354
deva tovils 391–92
Devadasi
 Abolition Bill 213–17, 214*f*
 Abolition Movement 214–17
devadasi(s) 7, 210n.2, 211n.3, 211n.4, 212–17, 213n.6, 218n.8, 223, 260, 263
Devi, Annapurna 156, 165
Devi, Girija 30, 31
Devol Deviyo 393–95
Dhai Akar Pyar Ka 287–88
Dhaki 340–41
dhamal 42–43, 50, 52, 53–55
Dhamankar, Sudhatai 146–50, 154
Dhamma 395–96
Dharavi 18
dharma 120
dhikr 42–43, 44–45
dhol 46, 52, 271–72, 340–41, 344–47, 393n.6, 427, 443
dholak 60–61, 75, 76*f*, 84, 128, 129, 162–63, 339–40, 344, 368

dhrupad 90, 155–56, 158, 162, 163–65
 -style exposition of *rags* 165
 -*iya* 155
dhul 318, 321, 323
diaspora(s) 170, 176–77, 407, 409, 443, 466–67, 469, 470
 artistic 292
 Indians 179
 Malaysian 7–8
 South Asia(n) 1–3, 6, 8, 427, 432, 433, 442
 South Asian American 292
 US 292 292n.3
 -ic 58, 409, 427–28, 429–30
didar 53–54
diglossia 453, 455–56, 457
Dikhour Gorāt Roi 317–18, 320–21, 327–30
dilruba 237*f*
Dilwale Dulhaniya Le Jayenge 26n.14, 467
Dindigul 204–5
Dirty Picture 359–60
disco 469–70
discrimination 176–77, 288–89, 408, 410
diva(s) 260, 277, 278–79, 283, 291–92
 -dom 288
divine 257–58
dodhiyu 444–45, 451
Dog, Tim 430–31
Doha(s) 82–83
 Manganiyar 83
 preservation project 83
 texts 83
 value 83
dohori 367, 368–70
Doubleday, Veronica 257
Downey, Greg 203, 204
dowry 185, 286–87
"Do You Love Me or Not?" 364–65, 366–67, 368–70
Dravidian 462 193–94, 243, 461–62
drug trafficking 284
drumkit(s) 428–29
Dubey, Rajkumari 352
Dudrah, Rajinder 468n.3
dugga 282
dugun 240*f*
"Dum Maro Dum" 357

INDEX 489

Dumont, Louis 114
"Duniya Mein Hum Aaye Hain" 356
*dupatta*s 473
Durkheim, Emile 12, 22n.9
Dutch 408
Dutt, Nargis 352, 356

eclecticism 5-6
ecological
   change 79-80
   model 18-19
Egnor (Trawick), Margaret 119
Egypt 22
Elder, Eleanor 217-18
electronic dance music (EDM) 472
Elmore, Mary 219-20
Elwin, Verrier 244-45, 246-50, 249*f*, 251
embodied 18, 149, 151, 195, 207, 214-17,
      221-22, 235, 353, 379-80, 384-87
   access 305-6
   action 229
   analysis 204
   approach 200-1, 207
   collectivity 199
   cultural practice 200-1
   empowerment 207
   experience 6-7, 26-27, 148
   expression 205
   firsthand experience 204
   idea 209
   inhabitants 134-35
   knowledge 196, 232, 410, 413
   music/aesthetic theory 195-96
   musical knowledge 333-34
   nationalism 209
   practice 18, 19-20, 21-22, 201
   process 205
   psychotherapy 301-2
   qualitative experience 195-96
   religion 154
   research 215
   stance 205
   subject 200-1
   transformation 204-5, 259-60
   understanding 302
   unifying experiences 230
   values 180
   ways 240-41

embodiment 149, 293, 384-87
embodying 149, 293, 302, 323, 451-52
   physically 293
emotion 302-3
empowerment 287-89
endogamy 172-73
England 430-31
English 306-7, 339, 396-97, 433-37, 453,
      454-55, 455n.1, 458, 460*f*, 461, 472
   -educated elite 217
   hymnody 105-6
   -language 458
   -language recordings 25n.13
   newspapers 213
   song texts 247
   -speaker 392
   -speaking 20, 92, 175-76, 456, 458
   -and-Tamil educated 457
ennam 382
entertainment districts 279-80, 284
epistemology 207
ethnographer 247
   colonial 279
ethnography 244-45
   -ic 1, 12, 20n.7, 42, 85-86
ethnology 379-80
ethnomusicological 200-1, 204
ethnomusicologist(s) 3, 70, 158, 296-97,
      319, 390-91, 407-8
   applied 288-89
   feminist 257
   proto 4-5
ethnomusicology 3
   Indic 3
   South Asian 3-4, 5-6
Eurocentric
   fine arts department 3
   hegemony 3
Europe 18-19, 25n.13, 73-74, 415, 428-29
   western 12
European(s) 415-16, 433, 437-38
   colonization 407-8
   emphasis on instrumental music 167
   ethnomusicologists 3
   protolanguage 3
   string instruments 95
evangelical
   Christians 109-11

evangelist(s) 109–11
everyday 305, 307, 315
  symbolic and material 310
everyday South Asia 1
  -ns 38–39

Facebook 233*f*, 234*f*, 468–69
falsetto 305–6, 354, 359–60
fana 48
Farsi 43
Feld, Steven 17–18
femaleness 258–59, 293–94
feminine 257–58, 259, 262–63, 321, 323–25
  stereotypes 300
  trans- 257–58, 261–62
femininity 258–63, 319–20, 350, 351, 353, 354–55, 360
  heteronormative 263, 317–18, 327–30
feminist(s) 196, 301–2
filmi 22–23, 95, 175–76, 466–67, 475–76, 476n.8
  aesthetics 409–10, 466–68, 469–70, 472–74, 475, 476
  bhangra 472
  choreography 471–72
  drama 476
  hits 466
  models 25
  number 468
  song(s) 52, 307–8, 335–36
  song-dance 468–69, 476
  style 94
Fiol, Natalie 338*f*
Fiol, Stefan 93, 334–35
flamenco 469–70
Flow Fitness gym 471, 472–73
Flute(s) 157, 160, 172*t*, 179, 185–86, 258, 339–40, 344, 345, 368
folk 92, 93, 94, 99, 101, 175, 259, 278, 279, 319, 337, 339, 344, 346, 348 92–94, 99, 101, 175, 259, 278, 279, 319–20, 337–38, 339, 344–46, 347–49
  artists 93, 94
  culture 93, 337–40, 345–46, 347–49
  dance 259
  drumming 427
  female/women folk artists 93, 259–60

idiom(s) 322, 348
lower-caste practices 176–77
music and dance 93, 319–20
musicians 94, 175
practice(s) 94, 337–38
Punjabi 260–61, 265
roots 270n.7
school 317–18, 319–20, 327–30
song 285
South Asian traditions 427
-ifying 94
-lore 347–48
-loric 317–18, 319, 319n.2, 321, 326–27n.14, 327–30, 339–40
-lorist(s) 319, 321
-lorization 5–6, 11, 93, 249–50, 317–18, 319, 348–49
-lorized 124–25, 261, 317–18, 319–20, 327–30
folksong 337
Folkways 255*f*
Fort district 18
Fox Strangway, A. H. 3–4
frame drum(s) 91, 116, 120–21, 162, 193–94, 194*f*, 257
France 465
freedom struggle 37–38, 269–70
French 377, 408
Freud 12
Froman, Kyle 440*f*
fukora zuzona 317–18

*gagra-choli*s 473
Gajaga Vannama 420
gali 282n.9
gamaka 101, 103–4, 106–7, 106–7n.5
Gandhi 353
  -an 152–53, 212–13, 267–68, 350
  -'s granddaughter 431
"The Gandhi of Pop" 431
Gangetic Plain 176
Ganti, Tejaswini 475–76
garba 408–9, 439–51, 439n.2, 469–70
  betha 442–43
  -*raas* 343, 408–9, 439–42, 443, 445–47, 448–50, 451
garbe 442–43
garbh 443

garbo 442–43, 444*f*
Garhbangal 249*f*, 251
Garhwal 338*f*, 343
 -i 3–4, 340–41, 343
"Gasolina" 433–34
gata beraya 390, 392–93, 394*f*, 418
 pahata 393
gayaki ang 165–67
Geertz, Clifford 13–14
Gehlawat, Ajay 468n.3
Gemeinschaft 18–19, 19n.2, 19n.3, 20, 20–21n.8
gena 184–85
gender 176–77, 190, 204–5, 231, 257–58, 260–62, 265, 292–93, 305–7, 312, 317–18, 469–70
 bi- 257–58
 cis- 259, 261, 292–93
 confirmation surgeries 314–15
 constructions 259–60
 cross- 293n.5
 discrimination 277
 diversity 261–62
 dynamics 262–63
 dysphoria 292
 equality 231
 equity 261
 expansive 292–93, 305–7, 315
 heteronormative dynamics 259, 293–94
 identification 262–63, 292
 -identity 292–93
 non-binary 260
 -nonconforming 261–62
 normative 312
 norms 293n.6, 323
 oppression 286
 participation 261
 performance 261, 292–93
 -restricted 302–3
 stereotypes 299
 third 261–62
gendered
 action 257, 293–94
 characters 293
 experiences 258–59
 musical roles 313
 qualities 257

 roles 258–59
 self 292–93
 self-presentation 260
 values 318, 321, 322
 ways-of-being 293
Germany 462
Gerow, Edwin 121
Gesellschaft 18–20, 19n.2, 19n.3, 20–21n.8
ghana (idiophones) 158
gharana(s) 13, 278n.2, 322
 Agra 352
 Lucknow 13
ghazal(s) 22, 281–82, 281n.7, 334
Ghaziabad 343
ghoomar 469–70
Ghosh, Pannalal 156, 157, 165
Ghoshal, Shreya 358, 359
ghotul 243–44, 244*f*, 246–51, 255–56
*ghungroo*s 281
gift-giving 389
Gillani, Karim 14
Gilroy, Paul 429–30
giramiya 6, 6n.6
 pattu 93
gitam 6
global
 Bollywood 409–10
 connectivity 38–39
 imagination 25
 industry of bharatanatyam 209
 local and global pop 259
 pop 260–61, 350–51, 366
 pop vamps 358
 pop vocalizations 360
 South 77–78
 urban landscapes 366
 -izing divides 306–7
globalization 11–12, 17–18, 156, 288–89, 410
gnostics 45
Goa 95, 437n.2
 -ns 95
Goethe-Institut 414, 415–16
gogona 321
Gold, Ann G. 115
Golden Temple 231, 234
Golmaal Returns 427–28, 433–36

Gond(s) 243, 247–48
　lifestyle 243
　Muria 13
　woman 247
　-i 243, 247, 255f
Google 470–71
Gopinath, Gayatri 409
Govindan, Padma 314–15
gramiya isai 93
Great Britain 427–28, 437–38
"great tradition(s)" 4–5, 12–13, 12n.1
"Greek" dancing 217–18
Greene, Paul D. 260
grihasta 379
Groesbeck, Rolf 333–34, 377n.1, 415n.6
Guha, Ramachandra 244–45
guitar(s) 109n.6, 254, 339–40, 368
　acoustic 22–23
　air 272
　bass 428–29
　lead 428–29
　rhythm 432
Gujarat 439, 442, 443, 449–50
　central 442–43
　Muslims 443
　Tourism 443n.4
Gujarati(s) 441–43
　community dance 441
　Dalit 443
　folk dance 467n.1
　garba raas 408–9, 471–72
　political leaders 449–50
Gulaab Gang 359–60
Gur Gaddi 67–69, 68f
Guria Sansthan 277, 282, 284–85, 287–89
guru(s) 3–4, 59–60, 69–70, 146–47, 186, 230n.2, 281–82, 283, 295–96, 333–34, 377, 379
guru dakshina 380–81, 383–84
gurdwara(e) 230n.2, 232–33, 234–36, 234n.3, 235n.4, 241–42
Gurdwara San Jose 233f, 234f
guru-chela 262
Guru Granth Sahib 60, 231, 232
Guru Nanak 232
guru-sisyan 7–8
gurukula 220–21
Gurung, Juju 375

Gurung, Narayan 372
gurunnanse 398
Guwahati 319–20
Gwalior 163–64

habitus 292
　of listening 70
Hahn, Tomie 379–80
hal 44–45, 67–69
hale da divan 56–57, 58, 59, 59n.6, 60, 61–65, 67–69, 70–71
　origin 59
　service(s) 14, 56–57, 59, 67, 69, 70
Hamira Village 73, 74f
Handa Samayana 400–3, 401f
Hanson, Thomas Bloom 4–5
haqiqah 133
haqiqi 136t
*haramba*s 390
Hare Rama, Hare Krishna 355–56
Hari, Jinjang 460f
Harmandir Sahib 232–33
harmonium 3n.3, 29, 46, 56–57, 60–61, 65, 67, 75, 76f, 84, 91, 103–4, 105, 129, 144t, 145, 147, 344
Haryana 343
Hassan, Mohammed 250–51, 253f, 255f
Hasse, Jean 253f
Havana 24
Hayes, Captain Fletcher 34
heritage, cultural 288–89, 317–18
heroism 59, 268, 294
heteronormative 262–63
hijra(s) 261–62, 306–7
　guru 306–7
"hillbilly" 458
Himalaya(s) 346n.2
　Indian 337–38
　-an 171, 339–40, 345–47
Hindi 6, 21–22, 43, 93, 243, 273, 287n.11, 339, 436, 453, 472
　belt 408
　cinema 266, 269, 270, 273–74, 468n.3, 476n.8
　dialects 279–80
　film(s) 29, 135–36, 265, 266, 278–79, 359, 366, 433–34, 436–37, 467, 475–76

film industry 434–36, 468
film music 268, 273–74, 436–37
film song(s) 22, 266, 270, 361*b*, 430, 433–34, 435
-language 17, 335, 467–68
lyrics 434–36
music 266
pop 25–26, 25n.13
songs 25n.13
words 273
Hindu(s) 58, 98, 99–101, 143–44, 143n.2, 148, 150, 151, 154, 193, 194–95, 219–21, 225–27, 278n.2
bhakti poets 133
-centric conceptions 149
contexts 90
counterparts 150
culture 120
devotee 149
devotion 114–15, 151
-dominated kingdoms 160–61
epic(s) 147, 157
female performer 150
folk songs 23
fundamentalist movement 4–5
ideals 147
in-group 146
king 148
kirtan 153 152–53
life cycle 193
majoritarian 225–27, 445–47
marriages 129
music 97
musical elements 160–61
musicians 160–61
nation 143
nationalism 5, 142, 143, 225–27
nationalist(s) 143, 147, 260, 293n.6
nationalist ideologies 149
nationalist parties 143, 146
nationalist sensibilities 147
nationalist story 149
nationalist surge 149
nationalist violence 142, 143
origins 102
orthodoxy 221–22
patrons 75
philosophy 146

philosophy/practice 150
playback singer(s) 98, 109
pre- 243
religious musical practices 4–5
right-wing politics 224–25, 224n.9
ritual praise 99–101
space 147
spectacle 224–25
theologies 160–61
traditional texts 160–61
-ism 4–5, 75, 105–6, 119–20, 142, 149, 170, 172–73, 173n.3, 224–25, 243
Hindustani
classical 33, 84, 89, 427
concert halls 157
dhrupad tradition 162
improvisation 90–91
instrumental 156, 167
instrumentalists 167
instruments 158–59
melodic refinement 158
singers 130
style 91
systems 3–4
traditions 165
vocal and instrumental traditions 165
vocal genres 90
Hindustani music(s) 4–5, 13, 29, 32, 33, 43, 70–71, 90, 91–92, 130, 133n.7, 155, 161, 162–63, 167
culture 157
practitioners 130
-al style 160–61, 163–64
-ians 155
Hindutva 4n.4, 224–25, 224n.9, 225*f*, 267
hip-hop 409–10, 428, 430–31, 432–33, 455–56, 469 , –55
*makkeh*s (bros) 454–55
"Hip Hop Era" 459
hippie 355–56
His Master's Voice (HMV) 278–79, 334
Hokkien 460*f*
Holla Mohalla 60
Hollywood 358n.3
homeland 272
honor 302
Hornböstel, Erich von 158

494 INDEX

Hosain, Attia 37–38
Hossain, Adnan 306–7
Houston 442
hudo 442
Hum Dil De Chuke Sanam 26n.14
Hum Tum 432–33
human trafficking 284
Husain, Shah 132
Hyderabad 433–34
Hyderabad (India) Theatre
    Company 278–79

iconography 155, 156, 158
    Dravidian Hindu temple 193–94
    frame drummers 194*f*
    medieval paintings 161–62
    Mughal period 161
    musical 161–62
    temple 167
identity(ies) 5–6, 11–12, 14, 17–18, 42,
    85–86, 89, 95, 97, 105, 146, 149,
    170, 176, 180–81, 182–83, 257,
    265, 267, 292–93, 306–7, 317–18,
    380–81, 429–30
    British-Asian 270n.7
    caste-like 258
    cisgender female 292–93
    cultural 91–92, 97–98, 109–11, 407
    gender 133
    hybrid 150
    India's 350
    musical 89
    national 142–43, 146, 266, 267
    nationalist 151
    offstage 311
    racial 430
    Scheduled Caste 181
    social 6, 26–27, 98, 101, 111–12, 169
    socio-religious 98–99
    sound 99n.2
    South Asia 11–12
    student 379
    transgender 314–15
Ilaiyaraja 109
imagined
    Brahminic "golden age" 224–25
    community(ies) 14, 36, 143
    experience 149

international geography 436–37
notion 220–21
political community 142–43
pure Hindu society 445–47
tradition 308
traditional space(s) 305, 307
Imaging Sound 161–62
The Immigration and Nationality
    Act 408–9
Immoral Traffic Prevention Act
    (ITPA) 280
"Impacto" 433–34, 435
"In the Morning When I Wake" 368–69,
    370, 375
'Inat, Shah 132
inclusivity 235–36, 238, 248n.4, 473–74
"Incredible India" 287–88
India Today 251
India(s) 1–3, 3n.2, 4–5, 18, 20, 21–22,
    26–27, 26n.14, 29, 32, 33, 34, 35,
    36, 37–38, 41, 57, 75–76, 77–78,
    93, 128, 129, 132, 142, 143–44,
    143n.2, 146, 148, 153–54, 160–61,
    162, 165, 173n.3, 212–13, 217–18,
    224, 225–27, 229, 232, 233–34,
    234n.3, 235, 243, 244, 247–48,
    261–62, 265, 270, 291–92, 317–18,
    319, 339, 350, 351, 353, 356–58,
    409, 415–16, 427, 428–29, 430–33,
    436–37, 442, 445–47, 448, 449,
    453, 458–59, 462, 467
    ancient 157, 220–21
    arts institutions 207
    Central 176, 243, 246
    cinema 467–68
    classical dance 291–92
    Coastal 378–79
    colonial 334
    dancers 212
    diasporic spread 58
    east-central 179
    economic liberalization 77–78, 175–76
    economy 17, 20, 175–76
    film music 268
    Government 180n.2, 181, 469n.4
    independent 37–38, 210, 280, 431–32
    ink 243
    modern 36, 209

modernity 36
nationalist consciousness 36
New 350
new nation 353
North 22–23, 32–33, 36, 157, 160–61, 167, 258, 260, 282, 343
Northeast 176, 261
Northern 176, 339, 408, 427
Northwest 7–8, 428
-Pakistan border 43, 130–31
politics 441
President 431
progressive songs 369
"real" 269
right wing groups 267–68
rural 121
South 7–8, 105, 195, 209, 210–11, 408, 456
Southern 160–61, 174–75
village 22
volume 247–48
western 127, 128, 143–44, 439
India's
 central arts organization 92–93
 classical heritage 92
 embrace of western modernity 38–39
 films 350
 first disc 278–79
 first recording session 334
 first talkie 352
 governmental affirmative action system 113n.1, 171–72
 governmental caste designations 172*t*
 independence 26–27, 58, 277, 288–89
 long history 155
 musical heritage 38–39
 Nation-Building period 259
 National Association of the Blind 431
 national classical heritage 209
 nationalist agendas 142
 nationalist ideals 351
 neoliberal transformation 20
 new vision 354
 struggle for freedom 38, 56
Indian(s) 3n.3, 25n.13, 38, 233–34, 245–46, 248, 260–61, 327–30, 405
 American 408–9

arts 92
audiences 84–85
cinema 354
classical dance 92
classical music and dance 280
constructions 350
court musics 167
farmers' protest 13
femininity 354
feudal aristocracy 37–38
high arts 121
history 35, 267–68
identity 467
lutes 159–60
masses 38
minorities 149
music 30–31
music and dance 84–85, 92
music critics 430–31
music scholars 32
musicians 95
nation 5, 14, 143–44, 149, 153–54
non- 84–85
North 3–4, 29, 35, 170–71, 260–61, 269, 277, 334–35, 344, 354, 433
Ocean 18, 159–60, 407–8
People's Party 143
performing arts 91–92
political discourse 143
population 143n.2
practitioners 4–5
record companies 25n.13
roots 473
scholars 4–5
social reformers 279
solfège syllables 327, 327n.15
South 29, 92, 113, 155, 210–11, 210n.2, 211n.4, 260, 263, 333–34, 433, 453, 464
spiritual values 57
state(s) 59, 314–15
styles 362
subcontinent 13, 408
tradition(s) 156–57, 350
-ness 92
Indian, Apache 428, 430–32
Indian Idol 73–74, 286–87, 286n.10
Indian National Congress 214–18

Indian Ocean 18, 159–60, 407–8, 410
Indiana University 247
indigenous 109, 171, 181, 306–7
    aesthetic elements 6–7
    alternative to western hymns 99–101
    -based society 180
    Christian music genre 97
    communities 11
    culture 181–82
    factions 190–91
    Gujaratis 443
    hymnody 102
    intelligentsia 210
    kirttanai 106
    livelihoods and traditional ways of life 180n.1
    musician 160–61
    non- 171, 180–81, 190
    people 171, 180–81, 180n.1
    performance idioms 97–98
    South Asian 12–13
    styles 108, 111–12
    understandings of Christianity 98–99
    terminology 93
    terms 212
Indipop 13, 17–18, 20, 20n.7, 21–23, 25, 25n.13, 26, 175–76
Indo-
    African Muslim 467
    European 93
    Gangetic Plain 32–33
Indology 3
Indomania 3, 3n.2, 4–5
Indonesia 159–60
"Indophobia" 3, 3n.2, 3n.3
Indubala 278–79
Indus Valley 128
    poets 132
    stories 132
Instagram 468–69
intentionality 206
interconnectedness 56–57, 67
intercorporeality 205
interdividual
    experience 14
    -ity 56–57, 67, 388
International Academy of Arts 220–21
Ipoh Road 454–55

Iran 1n.1, 41
irratiya 396
isai 123–24, 195
isai kalainyar 194–95
Isai Velalar 213–14
Isaikurichi 116, 116n.2, 119–20
ishq-i ḥaqiqi 133
ishq-i majazi 133
Islam 41, 42, 45, 45n.4, 75, 131, 160–61
    conservative practices 54
    messages 43–44
    musical instruction 129–30
    orthodox 43–44
    sects 42–43, 42n.1
    trajectory of 131–32
    vernacularization of 131
    -ophobia 41, 235
    -'s belief systems 42
    -'s devotion and piety 41
Islamic
    allusions 136*t*
    belief(s) 127, 138–40
    devotional style 163–64
    history 128, 136*t*
    ideas 131
    India 41–42
    influence 4–5
    meaning(s) 128, 129–30, 138–40
    mysticism 23, 43–44, 67–69, 131–32
    philosophy/practice 150
    roots 160–61
    sultunates 160–61
    teachers 129–30
    teachings 131, 138–40
    terms 128
    terrorism 41
    texts 131
Ismaili *ginan* 53–54
item number(s) 266, 359
Iyer, Krishna E. 92, 214–19, 223

"Jab Tak Hai Jaan" 357
Jaddan Bai 278–79
jadur 183*f*, 184–86, 187, 189
Jagadamba 443
Jagannathapura 211
jagar 250*f*, 254
Jagdalpur 248

Jaipur 79f
Jairazbhoy, Nazir 80n.1
Jaisalmer 78, 83
Jalal, Ayesha 36
jalebi 340
Jamaican 430–32
    reggae 430–32
Jan, Gauhar 278–79, 334
Jan, Malka 37
Janjua, Labh 432
jantar 160
Japanese 379–80
jar 134
Jat/Jatt 170, 428–29, 472n.6
Jat, Abdullah "Ataullah" 127–28, 134–36,
    135f, 139
jatha 239–40
jathedar(s) 59–61
jati 170–71
    Melakkara 170–71
Jaunsar 348
javali 210–11
jawari 162
Jayaweera, Almut 420n.11
"Jayjay Rama Krishna Hari" 144t, 152f, 153
"Jayjay Vithoba Rakhumai" 148
*jayjaykar*s 147
Jay-Z 428, 432
jazz 226, 430
Jazzercise 466
Jeevaratnam 218–19
jeheri bavar 134
Jersey City 442
Jesus 99–101, 104
    baby 99–101
    love 99–101
    lower class status 99–101
Jewish 407
jhala 164–65
jhanj/jhanja 144t, 145, 147, 150
Jharkhand 171, 176–77, 179–84, 180n.1,
    181n.3, 181n.6, 187, 190–92, 252
Jikki 109
"Jokana Cari Makan" 459, 460f, 461
Jones, William 3, 4–5
jor 163, 165
Joshi, Prasoon 271
jugalbandi 84

Juggy, D. 430, 432–33
Jungle Book 243

Kaaba 45, 47, 48
Kabhi Khushi Kabhi Gham 473
Kachchh 127, 128–30, 132, 134, 135–36,
    137, 170, 442–43
    kafi performers 128
    Muslims 128, 129
    singers 130
    -i 128, 130
kacheri 82
Kachi brothers 129
Kachi, Haji Usman 129
Kachi, Hashim 129
Kachi, Ustad Mithoo 129
"Kadhu Kotana Man" 137, 137n.9,
    138–40
kafi 43, 90, 127–30, 133–34, 136, 137,
    138–40
    composition(s) 128, 133–34, 138–40
    Kachchh 129
    Mithoo Kachi style 129–30
    performances 138–40
    performers 90, 128, 130
    poetic form 128
    Sindhi genre 127–28
    Sindhi singers 137
    singers 130, 137
    songs 128
Kaif, Katrina 359n.4
Kakori 273
"Kalai Uyaruma" 462–63, 463f
Kalakshetra 218–19, 220–22, 223, 227
Kalamandalam 333–34, 381–82, 383–84
kalari(s) 377, 381–82, 385
Kali 308
"Kali Kambli Waliya Kadon Ku Fera
    Pavenga" 56–57, 60–61, 62f, 65
Kallar 113–14, 116
Kalugasalamoorthy Murugan
    Temple 160f
Kalugumalai 160f
Kaluli 17–18
kalyanam 197–98
Kalyani, Thiruvalaputtur 215, 218–19
kamaicha 73, 74f, 75, 84
kambattu pecchu 458

498 INDEX

Kandy 392–95, 423
  -an 394n.7, 410, 413
  -an dance(r) 7–8, 393–95, 394n.7, 410, 413–15, 413n.1, 416–17, 418–22, 418n.7, 418n.8, 423, 424, 425
  -an drum(ming) 390–91, 393–95, 394n.7, 394f, 418n.9
  -an Kingdom 390–91
Kanoi Village 76f
Kansai 251
Kapferer, Bruce 391–92
Kapoor, Karishma 358
karagam 198f
karatana 458
Karim, Shah 'Abdul 132
Karnatak 198, 453, 463n.8, 464
  bhairavi 101, 108
  Brahminical culture 108
  characteristics 103–4
  classical music 155
  classicized 98
  hymnody 97–98
  idioms 99–101
  music(s) 4–5, 29, 30–31, 91–92, 102, 106–7, 106–7n.5, 155, 162–63, 167, 408
  music contexts 97
  music theory 105, 106–7
  ragas 97
  songs 106–7
  style 91, 99, 101, 102, 103–4, 111
  systems 3–4
  Tamil-Christian compositions 99
  training 98
  vocalist 155
Karnataka 159f, 193n.1, 194f
Karnataki, Amirbai 352
kartal(s) 60–61, 67–69, 70–71
Karunanidhi, M. 213n.7
kasam 22
Kāsi Jun Bihu Troupe 321n.6
Kasur 52
katamai 174–75, 193
Kataragama 393–95
kathak 13, 91–92, 258–59, 261, 279–80, 291–93, 291n.2, 293n.5, 294–97, 301, 302–3, 467
kathakali 294n.8, 378–79, 381–82, 383–84

Kathiawad 442–43
kattav 144t
Katz, Max 13, 101n.3
Kaufmann, Walter 247
Kaur, Bibi Simarjeet 240f
Kaur, Inderjit N. 89n.1
Kaurava 308
kavadi 198f
Kavitha 204–5
Kent, Eliza 105–6
Kerala 97, 270n.8, 377, 378–79, 378n.2, 381–82, 385, 386
  drum studios 379
  pedagogy 386–87
  -Tamil Nadu border 176
  temple drumming 7–8, 384–87
  theatrical and martial arts 221–22
Kerala Kalamandalam 333–34, 377
kettledrum(s) 161–62, 340–41
khabar 134
Khan 160–61
Khan, Aamir 267
Khan, Ahmed Ali 166
Khan, Akbar 80n.1
Khan, Ali Akbar 156, 165, 166
Khan, Allauddin 156, 165–67
Khan, Amjad Ali 165–67
Khan, Asadullah Kaukab 32
Khan, Bismillah 157
Khan, Chugga 79
Khan, Chunnu 156, 166
Khan, Faiyaz 37
Khan, Ghewar 73
Khan, Ghulam Ali 165
Khan, Hafiz Ali 165
Khan, Imdad 165–67, 167n.5
Khan, Inyayat 165–67
Khan, Khusru 164
Khan, Masit 164–65
Khan, Mohammad Wazir 156
Khan, Niamat 155
Khan, Niyamat 163–64
Khan, Raza 164–65
Khan, Thanu 82
Khan, Ustad Wajjan 281–82
Khan, Vilas 163
Khan, Vilayat 165–67
Khan, Wazir 165

INDEX   499

khartal 75, 76*f*, 78, 84
Kheshgi, Rehanna 261, 263
Khetsen 130–31
Khilji, Sultan Alauddin 160–61
Khubchandani, Kareem 475–76
Khusrau, Hazrat Amir 42, 53–54, 160–61
Khwaja Sira 261–62
khyal/khayal 90, 130, 155, 156, 160–61, 163–64, 165–67, 279
King Ramachandra 147
Kingdom of the Young, The 246
kinship 261–62, 306–7
Kipling, Rudyard 243
kirtan(s) 46, 90, 144–47, 147n.5, 147n.7, 148, 149, 150, 151, 152–53, 154, 230, 230n.2, 235–36, 235n.4, 239–40
   Marathi 144–45, 150, 260
   naradiya 144, 144*t*, 145–46, 148, 149, 150, 151
   naradiya-style 148
   non-*rashtriya* 152–53
   rashtriya kirtan(s) 142, 143–44, 144*t*, 145–46, 148, 149, 150, 153, 154
   varkari 144–45, 144*t*, 148, 149, 150
kirtankar(s) 142, 144–45, 144*t*, 146, 147n.5, 148n.8, 153, 154
   naradiya 145–46, 150
   rashtriya 14, 142, 144, 145–47, 149, 152–54
   varkari 144–45, 150
kirttanai 90, 97–99, 101, 102, 103–5, 106–7, 106–7n.5, 108, 109–12, 109n.6
   Christian 97–98, 104, 105, 106–7, 109–11
   composers 99–101
   concert-style 98
   congregational style 106–7, 108–9
   karnatak 104–5
   karnatak style 101, 102
   localization 98–99
   performance 97, 98
   performance style 102
   texts 104–5
   transmission 98
Knight, Roderic 13, 176–77, 263
Knight Rider 432
knowing, inter-subjective 307

knowledge
   community 282, 319
   cultural 283–84, 288
Kohomba kankariya 393–95, 418–19
kokal 323–25, 325*f*, 326n.13
   bhangi 323–25, 329
kolam, Christian 108
Kolkata 278–79, 335. *See also* Calcutta
Koovagam 305, 306–9, 311, 314–15
   "Miss" 305, 307, 310–11
   See also Kuthandavar-Aravan
kopouphul 322
Koppuchittampatti 102
korale(s) 392–93, 393*f*, 398
   Benthara 392–93, 398
Koran 45
Kosi 247
kotha 279–80
Kothari, Komal 75–77, 78–81, 83, 85–86
"Kotta Paakkum" 311, 313
Krishna 23, 144–45, 150, 157, 210–11, 258, 308
Krishna-Mohini 257–58
Krishnamurthy, Kavita 358
Krishnan, Hari 172–73
kriti
   composers 99–101
   Karnatak 106–7
   three-part form 97
kriya 162–63
Kshatriya 171, 172*t*
Kuala Lumpur 432, 433, 457
Kuch Kuch Hota Hai 467
Kuka(s) 56, 58
   identity 58
   movement 57, 58
Kulatillake, C. de S. 397–98
Kumaon 338*f*, 343
   -i 340n.1, 343
Kumari, Daya 278–79, 281–82
Kuppuswamy, Pushpavanam 116–17
Kuravanji 197, 198*f*
Kurinji Malar 194–96, 197, 207
kurtas 473
Kuthandavar-Aravan 305. *See also* Koovagam
Kuti, Fela 430
kutiyattam 295n.9

Kuveni Asna 419–20, 423, 424
Kvetko, Peter 13, 270n.6

Laban Institute 415, 416, 421–22
Lakshman 297, 298–99, 298f
landscape, expanded internal 301–2
Langa 129
langar 48–49, 50–51, 229, 232–35, 240–41
Langar on the Hill 235
language ideological combat 458–59
Lanka 291
lasya 417, 418
Latif, Shah 132
Latin 427–28
lavani 469–70
Lee, Joel 173–74
Lee, Raymond L. M. 456
Lee, Seibi 291–92, 292n.3, 297, 298–99, 300
Leela Dance Collective 291–92, 292n.3, 293
legitimate artists 287–88
liberalization 17, 270, 270n.6, 469n.4
  Post- 259, 350–51, 361
liberation 315
liminality 13–14
lineage(s)
  caste/clan 258, 262, 277
  hereditary professional performance 258
"little traditions" 4–5, 12–13
lok 6, 93, 337
lok dohori 364–66, 368–70, 372
lok sanskriti 337
lokgeet 93, 334–35, 337
Lomax, Alan 248n.4
London 34–35, 410, 415
Lord Dalhousie 34–35
Lord Vishnu 144–45, 147, 393–95
Los Angeles 442
Lucknow 13, 32–33, 34, 37–39, 161–62, 163–65
  chowk 280
  colonial 13
  court 32–33, 34–35
  gharanas 13
  resident 34
  royal courts and salons 33
  tawa'ifs 286

Lucknow: The Last Phase of an Oriental Culture 32
Lutheran Mission Society 99

Maciszewski, Amelia 170–71, 260, 263, 334
madal 368, 370–71, 373, 374t–75t
Madan, T. N. 120
Madhya Pradesh 247
Madinat al-Awliya 41–42
Madras 32–33, 92, 217–18, 224
  Devadasis Association 214f
  Devadasis (Prevention of Dedication) Act 213–14
  Government 213
  Legislative Assembly 212–13
  Music Academy 214f, 214–17, 218–19, 221–22
Madras Theosophical Society 92, 221–22
Madurai 108
Magar, Khadka Budha 373
Magul Bera 397–98, 399f, 400, 403–5
Mahabharata 151, 157, 305, 310, 350
"Maharaj" 150
Maharaj, Jaytumbi 149, 150, 151, 260
Maharaja Sayajirao University 448
Maharashtra 143–44, 143n.2, 153–54
Maharashtrian
  listeners 153–54
  nationalist 146
  saints and heroes 153–54
majaz 133
  -i 136t
majbur 22
majoritarian 409–10
makkal isai 93
Malay 436–37, 453, 454–55, 456, 457, 458
  hip hop 459
Malaya 408
Malayali 377
Malaysia 1–3, 408, 409–10, 432, 433, 453, 454–55, 456, 456–57n.3, 457, 461–62
  -n 409–10, 457, 458–59
  -n Chinese 459
  -n diaspora 7–8, 456
  -n Indian diaspora 456
  -n Tamil 408, 453, 455–56, 456–57n.3, 457, 458–59, 463, 464

INDEX 501

-n Tamil gangster 458
-n Tamil rappers 409–10, 456–57n.3, 461–62, 463n.8, 464, 465
Maldives 1–3
male control 120, 260
male impersonation 257–58
male privilege 297
maleness 258–59, 262, 293–94, 298–99
Malerkotla 58
Malini, Hema 355
Malir 130–31
Mandan Kundla 442n.3
mandiya 418, 419–20, 419f, 421–22, 423, 424
Mandla 247
mandolin 339–40, 344
Mangalore 437n.2
Manganiyar(s) 75, 76–77, 76f, 81, 82, 84, 85, 86
  brand of development 80
  children 80–82
  community 73–74, 75–77, 78, 79–80, 80n.1, 81, 82, 83, 84, 85–86
  contemporary musicians 86
  culture 80
  *doha*s 83
  lexicon 78
  music 83–84, 85
  musical discourse 78
  musical knowledge 80, 82
  musical repertoire 73
  musician families 75–76
  musicians 12–13, 73–75, 76–77, 78, 82–83, 84–85, 86, 90
  oral history 82
  organization 80n.1
  patronage 77
  school 80–81
  sung poetry 82
  voices 73–74
Manganiyar, Sakar Khan 73
Mangeshkar, Lata 91, 259, 350–51, 353, 354, 355, 356, 357, 427, 472
Mangeshkar, Meena 356
Mangeshkar, Usha 356
manglacharan 236–38
manhood 274–75
Manjh 137

manodharmam 220–21
Manoharan, Ruben (Dr. Burn) 461–62, 465
mantra(s) 395–96
Manuel, Peter 94, 354
Manusmriti 170, 379
Maoist(s) 251, 364–65
maqam 44–45
  -at 44
maradi 117
Maran, Behug 460f
Marathi 143–44, 153
  Hindu devotional sect 144–45
  Hindu performance 143–44
  kirtan 144–45, 150, 260
  *kirtankar*s 144, 153
  musical and storytelling resources 153–54
  saint 144–45
  song genres 145
  songs 143–44, 144t
"Mardani Jhansici Rani" 151
marga 12–13
marginalization 73–74, 288–89
  social 284
marginalized 408–9
  Adivasi 246
  communities 134
  historically 19n.3
  identities 180–81
  Sikh community 14
  social groups 337
  socially 287–88
  societally 73–74
  status 287–88
  *tawa'if*s 280
  underclass 408
  women singers 277
  women's *oppari* 114
Marmi Pata 243–44, 245–46, 249–52, 253f, 254, 255f
"martial race" 260–61, 269
Martin, Ricky 25n.13
martyr(s) 267
  -dom 56–57, 60, 69, 71, 267–68
Marui 127–28, 130–31, 131n.6, 132–36, 136t, 138–40
Marwah, Sangeeta 469

Marx 12, 20–21n.8
Marxist(s) 182
maryada purushottam 293–94
masala 95, 466–67, 475
masculine 257–58, 261, 262–63, 267–68, 293, 298–99, 321, 323–25, 366
  citizen subjects 265
  ideal 260–61
  presentation 150
masculinist 274–75
masculinity 258, 260, 261–62, 269, 270–71, 319–20
  female 259–60
  heteronormative 263, 317–18, 327–30
  hyper- 260–61
  normative 298–99
  Punjabi 273, 471–72
masculinized 274–75
mast 56–57, 59, 65–66, 67–69, 70
  -i 65–66, 475
Masta K 462–65, 463*f*, 464*f*
mastana(s) 56–57, 65–66, 67, 70
mastani 50–52, 51*f*, 54
masti birthi 61–65
mastiwale 466–67
Mathara 392–93
matra(s) 197–98, 203, 373, 374*t*–75*t*, 392, 396–97
matrilineal households 281–82
Mattu Pongal 198*f*
Mau 288
maya 151
McKinley, Sue 267
Mecca 47, 48, 134
Meerut 36
mehfil-e sama' 42
Mehmood 22–23
mehndi 53–54
Mehndi, Daler 270, 270n.8, 271–72
Mehra, Rakeysh Omprakash 265, 269n.4, 271n.11
Mehta, Narsinh 442–43
Mehta, Rukhmani 291–92, 291n.1, 297, 298–99, 301–3
melam 212
"Melody of Marui" 132–33
"Mere Dil De Sheeshe Wich Sajna" 52
metaphysics 217–18

MeToo movement 297
mezzo-soprano 352
Middle Ages 159–60, 161
Middle Eastern 257
migration 5–6, 11–12, 259, 366–67, 368–69, 407–8
  out- 338–39
mimesis 67
Minnal FM 457
Minnesota 179–80, 182
miru 137
Mishra, Meghna 359–60
misra' 137
Misra, Susheela 37
mnemonic(s) 94, 196–97, 202, 205
  drum 373
  drum syllables 201
  rhythmic 6
  syllables 91, 200–1, 202, 207
modern social theory
  classical period 12
modernity 5–6, 12, 21, 29, 36, 37–39, 92, 155, 430
  critique 38
  India's 36
  post/colonial 314–15
  values 413n.2
modernization 279
Modi, Narendra 408–9
Mohini 305, 308
Mohiniyattam 308
Moinuddin 48
monsoon 407–8
moqabala 281n.8
Morcom, Anna 279n.4, 470n.5
Morelli, Sarah L. 131n.6, 258–59, 261, 292n.3, 292n.4, 298*f*
Moser Baer Entertainment 225*f*
Mother India 147
Mother India (film) 259, 354–55, 356
Mother Mary 100*f*
motiari 243–44, 245*f*, 247, 248–49, 251, 254
Movers and Shakers 24
Mowgli 243
mridangam 195, 212
MTV 17, 270
  India 25

Mughal(s) 163–64
  armies 161–62
  court(s) 33, 163–64
  Empire 32–34, 161
  era 162–63
  miniature paintings 167, 258
  miniatures 162
  paintings 162
  period 258
  -era nobility 161–62
Mughal-e-Azam 354, 355
muhabbat 43–44
mujra(s) 278, 279–80, 281
Mukherji, Prasad Kumar 37
mukhra 30–31, 30*f*, 271–72
Multan 14, 41–43, 45, 53–55
  devotees and listeners 54–55
  Persian saying 41–42
  Sufi saints 42
  shrine contexts 42
  shrines 42, 50, 53–54
  -i culture 42
Multani, Hazrat Bahauddin Zakariya 42, 46*f*, 50–51, 52
  darbari qawwals 52
  mausoleum 46*f*
  shrine 42, 50–52
multiple diegesis 468
multiplicity of social differences 261–62, 306–7
Mumbai 17–18, 20, 22, 25, 26–27, 175–76, 278n.2, 308, 335, 346n.2, 437–38, 442
  bar dancers 278n.2
  history 18
Mumtaz 355–56
Munaivendri 195–96
Munda(s) 176, 179, 182, 185–86, 189
Munda, Ram Dayal 179–80, 180n.2, 181–82, 183–85, 186
Mundari 179–80, 181n.3, 182, 183*f*, 184–86, 187, 187n.9, 189, 190, 191–92, 252
"Mundian to Bach Ke" 428n.1, 432, 433
Munsee Lenape 441
muntu 383–84
Muria 13, 243, 244–46, 244*f*, 247, 248, 251–52, 254, 255–56

Muria and their Ghotul, The 244
murshid 48, 50–51
Murugan 196–97
music
  -making 278, 283–84, 335–36, 338–39, 345–46
  vernacular 338–39, 343, 349
Music and Musical Thought in Early India 156–57
Music Diary 364–65
Music of Hindustan, The 3–4
musicology 3–4
Muslim(s) 5, 41–42, 58, 75, 95, 128, 129, 131–32, 143, 143n.2, 146, 149, 150, 151, 154, 278n.2, 314–15, 359–60
  anti-Muslim 149, 267
  audiences 128
  courts 160–61
  devotional performance 41
  female performer 150
  Indo-African 467
  in Kachchh 128, 129, 129n.3, 170
  men's fashion 150
  navab 148
  neighborhood 127
  orthodox 48, 52
  orthodox understanding 48
  performer 150, 260
  practices 41, 42
  Rohingya minority ethnic group 407–8
  ruler(s) 148, 149
  Shi'a 33–34, 41–42
  society 54, 128n.2, 131–32
  South Asian 132, 170, 469
  Sunni 41–42, 48
  world 131
Muttumariamma 119–20
Muzaffarpur 281–82
Myanmar 320–21, 407–8

"Nachdi Phira" 359–60
Nachi se Banchi 179–80
Nadar(s) 97–98, 105–6, 106–7n.5, 108
  Christians 109–11
  lower-caste urbanites 109–11
  organists 106–7
Nad-Brahma 156–57
nafs 136t

nagasvaram 212
Nagpur 247–48
nah kou 236–38
nahor 322
Naicker, Ramasami E. V. 210n.1
naiyandi 198*f*
Naketi 390–91
nakhre 466–67, 469–70, 471, 475
nakkali 367, 370, 372
nal 52, 162–63
namaskaraya 413, 420–22, 421n.12, 423*f*, 424
namaz 150
Namdhari Sikhs 5, 14, 56, 57n.1, 58, 58n.3, 67n.9, 70
  agitation 58
  children 70–71
  freedom fighters 59
  history 69
  identity 56, 58, 70–71
  *jathedar*s 59–60
  martyrdom 56–57, 60
  musical repertoire 65
  rebels 58
  sense of community 56
  youth 70–71
  See also Kukas
Nandi village 159*f*
Nantha, Coco 459, 460*f*, 461–62, 465
Narad 148n.8
Narayana 212
Narayanpur 248, 249*f*, 251, 255*f*
Nataraj 157
Natha 393–95
nation(s) 1–3, 14, 38, 75–76, 129–30, 142–44, 146, 147, 152–54, 170, 214–17, 225–27, 260–61, 265, 266–67, 268, 269, 272–75, 350, 351, 353, 354–55, 356, 409, 416–17, 425, 462
  building 259, 266–67, 350–51, 353
  history of 274–75
  postcolonial 353
  -state 143
nation-as-audience 266–67
national 270–71, 306–7, 427–28
  agency 267, 274–75
  brotherhood 260–61, 265
  citizen 266–67, 272–73

citizenship 274–75
culture 85
discourse 306–7
groups 5
heroes 269, 274–75
identity(ies) 266, 267–68, 319, 366, 408–9, 413, 427–28
imagination 394n.7
independence 57
music style 95
political awakening 268
spaces 409
subject(s) 266–67, 269–70
vision 154
-ities 1
-izes 273
National Association of the Blind 431
National Dance Theatre 373
National Endowment for the Humanities 247–48
nationalism 5–6, 91–92, 95, 142, 143–44, 145–46, 149, 153–54, 260, 265, 268, 270–72, 273–74, 288–89, 415
  cultural 93, 209, 217, 314–15
  ethno-religious 143
  Gandhian 212–13
nationalist(s) 92, 144*t*, 145–46, 149, 152–53, 212, 260, 267, 273
  agency 265, 268
  avatar 273
  Brahmins 209
  civic activism 272–73
  creed 267
  cultural 210–11, 214–17, 218n.8, 267n.2
  discourse 167, 220–21
  elites 212–13
  emotion 142–44, 154
  era 413
  forces 451–52
  Hindu 260, 267n.2, 293n.6
  Historians 223
  history 267–68
  ideas 143, 451–52
  imaginary(ies) 143, 149, 154
  -inflected arts project 210
  language 217
  leaders 145–46
  message 152–53

INDEX 505

movement 217–18, 408–9
narrative 148, 154, 267–68
organizations 142
policy 306–7
politics 441
practices 221–22
songs 143–44
storytelling 143–44
ultra 425
Nattiez, Jean-Jacques 78
nattupura isai 93
nattuvanar(s) 215, 218–19, 223
naturalization 261, 270n.9
natyam 6
Natyashastra 4–5, 155, 158, 221f, 413n.2
naubat 161–62
nautch 217
Navab of Chinchwad 148
Navratri 443–44, 448–49, 451
Nawab(s) 13, 33–34
Nawab Wajid Ali Shah 13, 34–35, 36–37, 38, 164–65
Naxalite 251
Nayak, Gopal 160–61
Nayaka dynasty 210n.2
Nayanar 248–50, 249f, 250f, 251
Naz, Poonam 288
nazrana 48–49
Neelam Uttarakhandi 340n.1
Negi, Kusum 348
Nehru 353
 -vian vision 350
Nenninger, Claudius 244f, 248
neoliberal 20, 21–22
 song 469, 469n.4, 472
Nepal 1–3, 13, 171–72, 334–35, 364–65, 366, 368–69, 370–71, 372, 373, 374
 -i 259, 334–35, 364–65, 365n.1, 366, 368, 370–71, 372
Nepal, Madhav 372
New Delhi 267, 269
New York City 432, 441
Nigerian Afrobeat 430
nihon buyo 379–80
Nil Gavanee 460f
Nimjee, Ameera 409–10
niqab 359–60

nirvana 390–91
Nivas, Rachna 291–92, 292n.3, 294–95, 297, 298f
Noida 343
No One Killed Jessica 359–60
Noor Jahan 52
NRI (Non-Resident Indian) 25n.13, 26–27
nritta 418
Nrityagram 414n.5
nrityam 6

"O Jaanewale Aaja" 352, 353
"O Sanam" 22–23, 22n.10, 24
Oberlin (College) 248
occult 217–18
octopad 339–40, 344
Oldenburg, Veena 37, 286
On the Musical Modes of the Hindus 3
"One Mistake" 368–69, 370, 375
ontological 219–20
oppari 90, 113–16, 117–18, 119–25, 260, 309, 310
 forms 124–25
 incantation melodies 123
 male performers 114
 performance(s) 113–14, 122–23
 performer(s) 113–14, 121, 123–25
 professional 114–15, 121, 122–25
 singing 312–14
 themes 113
 women 113, 114, 119, 121, 123–24
or jadur 6n.7, 184–86, 184f, 187, 187n.9, 189
Oriental dancing 217–18
Orientalism 3, 3n.2, 91–92
Orientalist 4–5, 91, 92, 212, 217–18
 discourse 92
 European 212
 feeling 91
 imagination 4–5
Orr, Leslie 210n.2
Other(s) 229–30, 231, 337
Othering 229–30, 231, 232–33
 non- 229, 230, 231–32, 235–36, 238–39, 240–42
Oude 34, 35. *See also* Awadh
Oughourlian, Jean-Michel 67

outcaste 97–98, 98n.1, 102, 113n.1, 170, 171–72, 172t, 193, 195, 205, 231, 259–60, 456
   Christians 102
   converts 97
   labor 175, 456
   laborers 456
   people 104–5, 408
Outram, General James 34, 36
ovi 151, 153–54
oyilattam 90–91, 98, 102–3, 103f, 104–5, 198f

pada(s) 222, 391–92, 396, 397–98, 398n.9, 400–5, 402n.13
   bera 391–92
padaya 396, 397–98, 400–3
pahata rata beraya 392–93, 395f, *See also yak beraya*
Paik 320–21
pakhawaj 144–45, 144t, 147, 162–63
Pakistan 1–3, 7–8, 14, 32–33, 37–38, 41–43, 52, 54, 75–76, 127, 128–29, 132, 171–72, 261–62, 277, 354, 427, 428–29, 431–32, 467
   East and West 353
   southeastern 130n.5
   -i cassettes 128, 129
   -i radio 128, 129, 334
   -i singer 52, 137
Pakkirisami, Thiruvalaputtur 219f
Pali 390–91, 390n.2, 395–96, 443n.5
pallavi 99–101, 101n.4, 104, 107
palta 294–95
Panchasur 317–18, 319–21, 321n.6, 322, 323, 327–30, 327n.15
Panchayat system 369
Pandava 308
Pandey, Laxman 267, 269n.5
Pandharpur 145n.3
Pandian cave temple 160f
Pandit, Ashish 433–36
Pangeni, Badri 334–35, 364, 365, 366
Panjabi MC 428, 428n.1, 430–31, 432
parai 91, 120, 193–97, 200–1, 204–5, 207, 259–60
   -*attam* 6, 195–97, 200–3, 204–5, 206, 207

   collective 195–96
   drum music 116
   drummers 114, 196, 207
   drumming 116f, 118, 120–21, 123
   frame drum 97–98, 116, 120–21, 193
   function 194–95
   music theory 197, 200–1
   performances 199
   practice 195
   status 194–95
   See also tappu
paraidal 193
paraisattru 193–94
Paraiyar(s) 97, 98n.1, 109–11, 116, 120–21, 193, 194–95, 390–91
   "caste-duty" 120
   Christians 97–98, 102, 103f
   Christian communities 97–98
   drummers 116
   villagers 102, 106–7n.5, 109–11
Paramagudi 195–96
Parameswaran, Radhika 469–70
"Pardesi Jana Nahin" 358
"pariahs" 259–60
parshad 232–33
Parsi(s) 95, 407–8, 443
participant-observation 296–97
Partition 37–38, 75–76, 129, 277, 353, 354, 428–29
   pre- 350–51, 352, 353, 354, 361
party feel 436–37
party song 436–37
Parvati 293
Patel, Shahil 471, 473
Patidar 442–43
pativrata 293–94, 293n.6
patriarchal 135–36, 262–63, 279, 314–15
   constraint(s) 286–87
   culture 258
   customs 282n.9
   duty 286–87
   forces 297
patriarchy 415
patriotic 267
   mantra 272–73
patriotism 145–46, 269n.4, 271, 272–73
patron(s) 284
patth 235–36

Pattini 392, 393–95, 397–98, 400–5
pattu 115
Patwardhan, Dattopant 146
Pavlova, Anna 217–18
Pearls of Love 287–88
pedagogy 6–8, 200–1, 203, 207, 220–21, 223, 313, 378–79, 381–82, 384–87, 414, 447, 475
  -ical 379, 380–81, 385, 386–87, 414n.5
Pehchan Lok Sangeet Sansthan 79–82, 83, 84, 85–86
Peirce, Charles Sanders 13–14, 90–91
Peiris, Eshantha 418n.9
penal colonies 280
Pentecostal(s) 109, 109n.6
  Ceylon 108–9, 109n.6
"People's Rule" 364–65, 368–71, 372, 374
perahera(s) 390–91, 392–93
  Asala 393–95, 394n.7
Perera, Venuri 7–8, 410, 413, 424, 425
performance(s) 3–4, 5–6, 11–12, 14, 18, 41, 43, 56, 58, 69–70, 84, 89, 90, 94, 97–98, 113, 129, 144, 145, 145n.4, 163, 173–74, 195, 200–1, 236, 238–40, 257, 262, 278n.2, 279, 292–93, 307, 333–34
performative 13–14
"performativity" 292–93
Persia 407–8
Persian 131, 165
  culture 43–44
  extraction 33–34
  general 163–64
  saying 41–42
  -ate world 160–61
Pettigrew, Joyce 59
phantom nostalgia 13, 23
phenomenology 379–80
Phogsen 130–31
Phule, Jyotiba 171–72
Phule, Savitribai 171–72
physicality 300, 302–3
Pilates 466
Pillai 213–14
Pillai, Nrithya 213–14, 216*f*, 263
Pillai, Pandanallur Meenakshisundaram 218–19
Pillai, Swamimalai Rajarathnam 215

Pillai, Tanjore Sathiyanathan 99–101, 100*f*, 101*f*
Pillai, Thiruvalaputtur K. Swaminatha 215, 219*f*
Pillai, Vaitheeswarankoil Meenakshisundaram 215
Pillai, Vazhuvoor B. Ramaiah 215
Piñones 432–33
Pioneer 431
pir(s) 44, 46, 48, 50, 54–55
pirith 395–96, 397–98
pirun 134
PK 359–60
play 414, 416, 417–18, 424, 425, 439
  -ed 442, 467
  -ing 416, 418, 422
playback 346–47, 468
  singers 95, 109, 259, 266, 350–51, 352, 353, 361, 427, 472
    female 350–51, 352
    Hindu 98, 109
    Muslim 354
    pre-partition era female 353
Poduval, Achunni 382
poisonous acacia 134
Pongal 196–97
pop 259, 260–61, 350–51, 359–60, 366, 458, 472
  Bhangra- 270
  -folk 339–40, 345–46
  Hindi 25–26, 25n.13
  music 17, 25n.13
  songs 20, 26
  sound 358
Popley, H. A. 3–4, 101, 101n.4, 101*f*, 102–3
popular 3, 5, 91–92, 119–20, 337–38, 339, 349
  artists 8
  audiences 29
  construction 428–29
  culture 337, 339
  films 262–63
  -folk dynamic 5–6
  imagination 34–35
  music 17, 22–23, 89n.1, 95, 109n.6, 175–76, 230, 259, 334–35, 337–38, 339, 340n.1, 343, 348, 350, 368–69, 428–29, 472

popular (*cont.*)
   music and dance forms 334–35
   musical styles 235–36
   songs 238–39
   style 1–3, 42, 43
   stylistic elements 89n.1
   traditions 427
   understandings of cinema and nation 266–67
porous boundaries 306–7, 410
Portuguese 95, 170, 437n.2
positioning 86, 288–89
positivist ideologies 3
postcolonial
   context 428–29
   economic and political rearrangements 75–76
   India 170
   nation 353
   shifts 77–78
   studies 266–67
   -ism 78, 288–89
Post-Liberalization era 259, 350–51, 361
postmodern 77–78
   -ism 78
pottukattu, pottu 212–13, 213n.6
povada 144t, 151, 152–54
Prachanda 372
practice(s) 1, 8, 18, 20, 90, 121, 144, 229, 230, 281–82, 333–34
   ancestral 441
   anti-hierarchical pedagogical 414
   artistic 1–3, 7–8, 12–13, 145n.4, 281–82, 283–84, 407
   celebratory 105–6
   concert 195
   cultural 43–44, 176, 261–62, 306–7, 315, 337, 349, 407, 408, 409, 410, 449–50
   dance 5, 215–16, 408–9, 449–50, 451
   devotional 44–45
   Drama Therapy 293–94
   elite 6
   emerging in 306–7
   folk 6, 346n.2, 349
   harmonic 3n.3
   hegemonic 7–8
   High-Church 105–6
   Hindu 170
   kinship 171, 262
   "little" 5
   majoritarian 409–10
   male 257
   music and dance 6–7, 8, 11–12, 176, 210–11, 214–17, 257, 319
   musical 77, 80, 235–36, 339–40, 409
   Muslim 42
   performance 3–4, 5–6, 97, 98, 145, 164–65, 238, 262, 279, 319, 339
   religious 75
   ritual 390–91, 413n.2, 469–70
   rural 11, 93
   sexual and marital 258
   stylistic 91–92
   tribal social 183n.8
prasadam 307–8
precarity 407–8
precolonial history 36
President of India 431
Priest, Maxi 430–31
Pritam 434–37
progressive 356–58
proletariat 371–72
Prophet Muhammad 54–55, 136t
prostitute(s) 93, 205n.3, 257, 259–60, 279, 288–89
   temple 212
prostitution 277, 280, 281, 287–88
protest(s) 58, 59, 70, 93–94, 113–14, 119, 123–24, 213, 265, 267, 369, 371
   anti-*ghotul* 251
   Indian farmers' 13
Protestant(s)
   Church of South India 106
   community 105–6
   lower-caste 98
   Lutheran 97
   missionaries 3–4, 97
   missions 97–98
   Tamil 97–99, 109–12
   Tamil Christianity 97–98
   Tamil hymnal 97–98
Protopapas, Janice 14
Psycho Unit 462n.6
psychologist(s) 301n.10
Puducherry 311

Puerto Rican 432–33
Puerto Rico 428, 432–34
Pune 147, 410, 415
Punjab 41–42, 52, 58n.2, 171, 232–33, 268–71, 269n.4, 272, 273, 343, 345–46, 408–9, 432, 433, 437–38
  Dadhi singers 59
  folklore 59
  province 41–42, 52, 232
  rural 59
Punjabi(s) 41–42, 43, 260–61, 269, 270n.9, 273, 428–29, 430–31, 432, 433, 471–72, 472n.6
  accent 273
  folk 260–61
  folk culture 56, 265
  folk melodies 60–61
  folk singer 432
  heritage 432–33
  langauge 128, 433
  masculinity 260–61, 273
  poet 132
  singing 432
  words 273
purity 171, 172–73, 258
  female 258, 259, 354, 359
purvaranga 144t, 145, 148, 149, 150, 151
"Push It Up" 427–28, 430, 432–33
  (Bhangraton Version) 432–33

Qalandar, Hazrat Lal Shahbaz 42, 52
qaum 129n.3, 170
qawwal(s) 42, 43, 44f, 46, 47, 48–49, 50, 51–52, 163–64
qawwali 41, 42–43, 46, 47, 48, 49f, 49, 50, 53–55, 151, 163–64, 262–63, 288, 334, 449–50
  performance 42–43, 45, 48–49, 50, 54
  sama' performance 46, 52
qi gong 448–49
qisso 127–28, 132
"Quality of Local Songs Aired on Channel 6" 458n.4
Queen 359–60
Qureshi, Regula 42–44

R&B 427–28, 432–33
raas 439, 442–47, 448, 450–51

dandiya 442, 442n.3, 444–45, 450–51
  (*see also dandiya*)
  garba- 408–9, 439–42, 443, 447, 448–51
  garbi 442, 442n.3, 443
  mandali 442n.3
raasara 467
rabab(s) 162, 163, 165
  Afghani 165
  Seni 155, 163
race 170, 204–5, 226, 229, 231, 232–33, 260–61
  -ism 3, 449
radio 268
Radio Ceylon 108–9, 109n.6
Radio Nepal 369
Radio Televisyen Malaysia (RTM) 458n.4
Rafik, Mohammed 248–49
rag/a(s) 31–32, 32n.2, 33, 82, 84–85, 90, 105, 106–7, 130, 132–33, 156, 163, 236–39
  -based art music 33
  bhairavi 31–32, 32n.2, 38–39, 101, 101f, 101n.3, 102–3, 107–8, 111
  classical systems 3–4
  dhrupad 165
  folk songs 3–4
  Hindustani 130, 145
  karnatak 97
  kirttanai 106–7, 108
  light-classical style 31
  positivist analysis 5
  "pure" 3–4
  shah jo 128
  sindhi bhairavi 31
  sorath 73
  -specific melodic movement 106–7
  theory 84
ragamuffin 430–31, 436–37
ragini(s) 32, 32n.2, 90, 130
Raheja, Gloria 115
Rahimsen 164–65
Rahman, A. R. 22–23, 260–61, 433–34
Raigama 392–93
Raipur 248
Raja 116–17, 120–22, 358
Raja Hindustani 358
Rajadhyaksha, Ashish 468
*rajahan*s 144t

rajakariya 390–91
Rajalakshmi, Thiruvalaputtur 218–19, 219f
Rajarathnalaya 215
Rajasthan 77–78, 345–46, 347–48
  western 73, 75, 90, 132, 137
Rajasthani
  artists and artisans 75–76
  desert 12–13
  folklorist 75–76
  music 85
  oral textual traditions 75–76
Rajinikanth 433–34
Rajoo, R. 456
Rajput 341–43, 344
Rakhumai 148
Ram/Rama 144t, 147, 258–59, 291–92, 293–94, 293n.6, 296–97, 298–99, 298f, 302–3
Ram, Patti 344–45, 348–49
Rama Series 340n.1
Ramanujan, A. K. 121
Ramayana 147, 151n.10, 157, 258–59, 291–92, 293–94, 298, 299–300
  -inspired story 151
  television series 299–300
Ramdas 148
Ramoji Film City 433–34
Rampur 156, 163–64, 165
Ramu 201–3, 204
Rana oligarchy 369
Ranchi 176, 179–81, 182, 183–84, 183f, 186
"Rang De Basanti" (*RDB*) 260–61, 265, 265n.1, 266–71, 269n.5, 272–75
  effect 265
Rani of Jhansi 151, 152–53
ranj 32
ransingha 345
Ra.One 471
rap 270, 428n.1, 431, 453, 455–56, 457, 458–59, 461–62, 462n.5, 464
rapper(s) 408, 409–10, 430–31, 432, 454–55, 456–57n.3, 461–63, 462n.6, 463n.8, 464, 465
  Tamil 455–56, 458–59, 463, 463n.8, 464, 465
rasa(s) 121, 201–3

aesthetics 121
  bhakti 32
  karuna 32
  -like ideals 121
  theory 32, 121
  shringara 32, 222
  veer 147n.5, 292
"Rasati" 116–17, 121–22
rasau 342, 344–45, 346–47, 348–49
"Rāsau Lāno" 339–40, 342, 343, 344–45, 346–47, 347f
Rastafari 430
Rastogi, Shreya 470n.5
Ratana Sutta 395–96
Rattan 352
Ravan 291, 293, 294, 294n.8, 297, 299–300, 300f, 301–3
ravanahatha 158–59
Rawain 340, 341–43, 341f, 344, 345–48
93.5 RED FM 22
red-light
  area(s) 284–85, 288–89
  district(s) 281, 284
Reddy, Muthulakshmi 212–17, 214f
Reed, Susan A. 410
regendering 204–7
reggae 370–71, 374, 428, 430–32, 436–37
reggaeton 428, 432–34, 435, 437–38
reincarnation 173–74, 193
Reji 205–7
Rekha, DJ 270n.7, 409
relationalities 261–62, 306–7, 311
relo 252
relocation 407–8
Remawand 243–44, 248–52, 249f, 254
Republic Day 248
resettlement 407–8
resistance 56–57, 58, 152–53, 278, 286, 307, 315, 320–21
  lifestyle of 286
revolutionary(ies) 267, 268, 268n.3, 374
Reyes, Adelaida 407–8
Reynolds, Holly Baker 119–20
Rich, Rishi 427–28, 430, 432–33
Riri Yakkha 397–98, 403, 404f
Risikala Aesthetic College 423
ritual(s) 42, 54, 91, 94, 99–101, 102, 142, 143–44, 148, 169, 182–83, 184–85,

190, 224–25, 229, 318, 380–81, 383–84, 390–92, 393–96, 394n.7, 397–98, 403–5, 413, 418–19
 Berava 393–95, 398, 405
 community 440–41
 context(s) 99, 142, 317–18, 319, 326–27n.14, 345, 398n.12
 designation 174–75
 drumming 390–91
 events 196–97, 200–1, 207
 framework 211n.4
 function(s) 6, 119, 196–97
 gift-giving 333–34
 heterosexual mating 263
 musical 109–11
 paired 229, 241–42
 participants 197
 peace-bringing 391–92
 performance(s) 142, 169, 175, 317–18, 319–20, 413
 performer(s) 418–19
 pollution/polluting 120, 173–74
 power 194–95
 practice 44–45, 173–74, 309, 390–91, 413n.2
 practitioners 67–69
 prestige 173–74, 211n.3
 purpose 6, 196–97
 salutation 420–21
 space 150, 403
 Sufi 50
 temple 218n.8
 village 326–27n.14, 327–30
 women's participation 52
 worship 225–27
 -ist 395–96, 403
 -ized 467–68
 -ly 205–6, 220–21, 333–34
ritualistic acoustic music 262
rock and roll 428–29
Rohingya Muslim 407–8
Route 66, 23
Rowell, Lewis 156–57
Roy, Anjali Gera 269–70, 271–72, 271n.10, 428–29
Roy, Jeff 262, 292–93
ruh 136*t*
"Rumjhum Barse Badarwa" 352, 353

Rupayan Sansthan 75–77, 78–79, 85
Russian 217–18
 ballet 220–21

sabad/shabad 61–65, 232, 235–42
sabad kirtan 170, 229–33, 236–38, 240–41
Sabaragamuwa 392–93, 393*f*
sabda puja(va) 390–91, 395–96
*sabha*s 209, 224
Sabzwari, *pir* Shams 42
Sachs, Curt 158
sadangu 198*f*
sadguru 148, 149
"Sadguru vāconī sāpaḍenā soy" 148
sadhakam 333–34, 377–82, 378n.2, 384–87
Sagoo, Bally 428
Saigal, K. L. 29, 37
Saikia, Probin Kumar 319–21, 319n.1, 320n.5
Saikia, Roshmi Rekha 319–21
Saint Francis of Assisi 132
saja 250–51
Sakata, Lorraine 257
Sakinah 136*t*
sakkali 364, 367, 370
Sakthi 204–7, 259–60. *See also shakti*
Sakthi Dalits 204–5
Sakthi Folk Cultural Centre 196, 204–5, 207, 259–60
Sakthi Kalai Kuzu 196
Sakthi Vibrations 195n.2, 204–5
sal 184–85
Salim 355
salon(s) 33, 279–80, 286–87
 elite 291–92
 establishments 280
 performances 280
 private 284
salsa 469–70
Salvadora oleoides 134
sam 236–39, 237*f*
sama 44–45, 46
samaj 170
Samaraweera, Tittapajjala 419*f*
sami attam 198*f*, 199
samosa(s) 340
samsara 390–91

San Francisco State University 295–96
San Juan 432–33
sangam 463f
   period 193–94
   poetry 193–94
sangeet 6
Sangeet Natak Akademi 92–93
Sangitratnakara/ Sangita Ratnakara 155, 160–61
"sanitization" 5, 279
sanni 393–95
Sanni Yakuma 393–95
sannyasa 379
Sanskrit 3, 6, 32, 182–83, 212, 213n.6, 220–21, 337, 427, 453
   intellectualism 221–22
   literature 220–21
   prayers 225–27
   text(s) 4–5, 175, 220–21, 221f, 299–300, 379
   theory 384–87
   treatises 92, 155, 167
   verse(s) 145, 147, 220–21
   -ic 170
   -ized Tamil 101, 102
santur 162, 368
sapor 323–25. *See also seu*
sapparam 198f
Saraiki 41–42, 43
sarangi 162, 164, 368
Saraswati 160f
sargam 30–31, 91
sarhul 184–85, 184f
sarod 156, 158–60, 165–67
   -ist(s) 165–67
Sarrazin, Natalie 259, 335
Sastriar, Vedanayakam 97–98
Satguruji (Baba Ram Singh) 65–67, 70
Sati-Savitri 350, 354–55
satnam 237f
Satriye Sambrajyem 461f
Saurashtra/Kathiawad 442–43
Saussure, Ferdinand de 13–14
Savaging the Civilized: Elwin, His Tribals, and India 244–45
savarna 171–72
savu 198f
sawal-jawab 84

"Say 'Shava Shava'" 473
Sayyed, Jaytumbi Maqbulbhai 146–47, 149–53, 154, 260
scapes 409–10
Schimmel, Annemarie 131–32
Schreffler, Gibb 428–29
Schultz, Anna 14, 260
Scott, James 176
Sean, Jay 430, 432–33
Seattle 472–73
   -'s South Lake Union 471
Secret Superstar 359–60
self 12, 13–14, 48, 53–54, 136t, 148, 154, 236–38, 292, 302–3, 447, 461–62
   -actualization 205
   -chosen 113–14, 171–72
   -conscious 206
   -consciously 410
   -defense 104
   -determination 93, 305, 308, 315, 360
   -efficacy 286
   -esteem 97–98, 102, 109–11, 204–5
   expanded 293n.5
   -expression 447
   -governance 180
   -governed 142–43
   -hood 305–7
   -identified 171–72
   -identity 26n.14, 429–30
   -imposed 416
   -interested 18–19, 19n.3
   -recognized 78
   -reproducing 225–27
   -respect 204–5
   -restraint 105–6
   -rule 29
   -sacrifices 258–59
   -sacrificing 350
   sense of 292–93, 315
   -sufficiency 183–84, 187
   -sufficient 186
   -understanding 261–62, 306–7, 311
   -worth 83
Self-Respect Movement 210, 210n.2, 212–14
Senegal 41
Seni binkar(s) 163–64, 165
Seni rababiya lineage 163

sensuality 34–35, 262–63
sentamil 462n.6
seu 323n.11, *See also sapor*
seva 235
Sewan 52
sex reassignment surgery (SRS) 314–15
sex trafficking 277, 287–88
sex work 213, 263, 283–84
   -er(s) 279
sexist, hetero- 314–15
sexual
   aspect 251
   availability 287–88
   connotations 258
   content 279
   desire 262–63, 319n.2
   feminine beauty 260
   hetero- 262–63, 279
   identification 306–7
   immorality 213–14, 263
   innuendo 319, 327–30
   lives 210–11
   maturity 322
   metaphors 263
   mores 358
   orientation 231
   practices 258
   predators 356
   relation 246
   representation 359
   sovereignty 280n.5
   unions 246
   -ity (-ies) 1, 5–6, 105–6, 211n.3, 257, 259, 260, 261–62, 263, 305–7, 312, 350–51, 355–56
   -ization 259
   -ized 258, 260, 286–87, 350–51, 359
   -ly explicit 462n.6
   -ly insatiable 327–30
   -ly provocative 277
   -ly suggestive 278, 285, 433
Shah, Haji 137, 138
Shah, Hazrat Baba Bulle 52
Shah, Mohammad 163–64
Shah, Nadir 163–64
Shah, Purnima 295
shah jo rag 128
Shah Jo Risalo 132–33, 134n.8

Shah Rukn-e-Alam 42, 44*f*, 46, 47, 49*f*
   darbari qawwals 51–52
Shah sahib 132
shahnai/shehnai 157, 161–62
Shakespeare, William 132
Shakira 25n.13
shakti 119–20, 257–58, 259–60, 442–43.
   See also sakthi
Shankar, Ravi 156, 165
Shankar, Sondeep 251
Sharar, Abdul Halim 32
Shark(s) 473–74
Shark Tank 473–74, 475
sharm 135–36
Shastri, Neelkanth 217–18
sheikh 48
"Sheila Ki Jawani" 359n.4
Sherinian, Zoe C. 116*f*, 117*f*, 118*f*, 124n.5, 159*f*, 160*f*, 169n.2, 259–60
Sherwood, Christopher 100*f*
Sheth, Rohan 440*f*
Shiva 157, 159*f*, 293
Shiva-Nataraja 219–20
Shivaji 148–49, 153–54
Shivan, Nilkantha 462–63
Shivdaspur 284–85
Sholay 355, 357
Shresthova, Sangita 469
Shridhar, Neeraj 433–34
shubhraj(s) 82
Shudra 169n.1, 171, 172*t*, 443n.5
Shukla, Hiralal 255*f*
Siddhartha 413
Sidi 407–8
Sikh(s) 14, 56, 57, 58, 95, 170, 229, 230n.2, 231, 232, 234, 235–36, 238, 240–42
   congregational worship 232
   context 90
   culture 229
   diaspora 234
   Guru(s) 66n.8, 232, 238, 239–40
   faith 241–42
   family 229
   hymns 56–57
   institutions 230n.2
   kirtan 238–40
   men 408–9

Sikh(s) (*cont.*)
  musicians 235–36
  New Year 269–70
  non-Othering 170, 229, 235
  non-Sikhs 241–42
  outcaste 170
  philosophy 229–30, 241–42
  preacher 57
  religious performance 261
  scholar 59
  scripture(s) 229–30, 231, 232
  South Asia and diaspora 170
  worship 232, 235–36
  -i 231, 232
silambam 198*f*
Silappatikaram 462–63
Silicon Valley 26–27
Simmel, Georg 18–20
Simone Michelle Award for Outstanding Choreography 421–22
Sindh 52, 75, 129, 132, 137, 170
  fourteenth-century 130–31
  greater 132
Sindhi 43, 127–28, 130, 134n.8, 137n.10
  cultural world 132
  poetry and music 128, 132
  repertoire 130
  Sufi poetry 128
sindhi bhairavi 31
sindu kuchi 201
Singapore 408, 436–37
Singh, Ajeet 282, 287–88
Singh, Baba Balak 57
Singh, Baba Ram (Satguru) 56–58, 59n.6, 60, 65–66, 66n.8
Singh, Bhagat 267
Singh, Bhai Harjinder 239*f*
Singh, Gurdit 59
Singh, Gurmukh 58
Singh, Musvar Varyam 60
Singh, Rana 60, 65–66, 69–70
Singh, Satguru Hari 58
Singh, Satguru Jagjit 58
Singh Satguru Pratap 58
Singh, Satguru Uday 58n.5
Sinhala(s) 389n.1, 390–93, 390n.2, 396–98, 398n.9, 403–5, 413–14, 425

Buddhist 4, 389, 390–91, 391n.3, 392, 393*f*, 403–5, 413–14, 425
  -ese 416–17
Siraiki 128
"Sisters, Wear Vermillion" 364–65, 368–70
Sita 258–59, 291, 293–94, 298–303, 300*f*
Sita Haran 297, 298
sitar 156, 158–62, 164–66, 427
  -ist 155
Sivaji 433–34
slave trade 408
Sleeman, Colonel William 34–35
Smithsonian 255*f*
social norms 257, 317–18, 327–30
social reproduction 307
Society for the Propagation of the Gospel and Church Mission 105–6
soft power 449–50
sohar 282, 283
solkattu 91, 463n.8, 464*f*
sollisai 408, 458–59, 462–63, 462n.6, 464
Somnath, Swathy 225*f*
Son of the Wind 258–59, 291–92, 292n.3, 294–95, 296–300, 298*f*, 300*f*
Soneji, Davesh 210n.2, 221*f*
"sons of the soil" 269–70
Sony 17
  Music 25
  Music India 23, 24
"Sotāi Porebotot" 321, 323, 323n.11, 324*f*
soundscape(s) 20, 20n.6, 108–9, 175–76
South Asia 23, 41, 43–44, 89, 169, 169n.2, 170, 174, 175, 176–77, 231, 306–7, 335–36, 337, 390–91, 407–9, 413n.2, 427–29, 431–33, 467–68, 472–73
  cassette releases 129
  contemporary dancers 415–16, 425
  femininity 258
  folk music-dance styles 94
  gender and music 257
  gender diversity 261–62
  geography 1–3, 2*f*
  historical narratives 36
  Islam 131
  marriage 38
  mass-mediated musics 334
  modern 225–27
  music pedagogy 313

Ramayana 291–92
scholars 3, 244–45
sensuality and sexual desire 262–63
style categories 91–92
women 53–54
South Asian(s) 1, 25n.13, 37, 427, 469, 470
   aesthetics 6–7
   American(s) 291–92, 297, 408–9, 441
   artists 8
   arts 93
   Association for Regional Cooperation 1n.1
   cinema 274–75, 466–67, 468–69, 476
   classical and folk music 433
   classical dance(s) 418–21
   classical music 392
   communities 439
   context(s) 257–58, 337–38
   cultural values and people 5
   culture 466–67, 468–69, 470
   dance 467
   dancemaker 425
   dance practices 295
   descent 467n.2
   devotional poetry 133
   ethnomusicology 3–4, 5–6, 8
   female performers 278n.3
   film(s) 436–37
   film industry 335
   film music 428–29
   guru-disciple relationships 333
   heritage 427–28, 437–38, 469
   immigrant(s) 408–9, 431–32
   immigration 408–9, 431–32
   influences 436–37
   instruments 368
   listeners 23
   marriage 37–38
   migrants 428–29
   music 1, 12–13, 90, 130, 156, 159–60, 259, 409, 428
   music and dance 11, 95, 257
   music scholarship 3
   musical practices 4–5
   musical terminology 373
   nations 314–15
   non- 291–92, 305–6, 436–37
   origins 434–36
   performance 6
   performing arts scholarship 3n.2, 95
   perspective 8
   poetic traditions 22n.9
   poetry 22, 137
   popular imagination 33
   popular music 434–36, 472
   regional dance styles 469–70
   social elites 337
   society 445–47
   sonic elements 434–36, 437–38
   sounds 434–36
   studies 266–67
   Sufism 43–44
   -ness 437–38
South East Asia 389n.1
   -n archipelago 407–8
Spanish-language 428
spiritual 4–5, 132, 225–27
   advancement 42–43
   arousal 67–69
   classicalness 92
   connections 310
   dependency 173–74
   devotion 50–51
   economy 173–74
   encounters 50
   enlightenment 92, 217–18
   esteem 156
   exegesis 60
   experience 50, 51–52
   goals 48
   guide(s) 44, 48
   importance 152–53
   intoxication 59–60, 67–69
   life 57
   master(s) 46–49, 50–51, 53–54
   origins 156–57
   pollution 118–19
   potency 155
   power 260
   practice(s) 42–43, 131–32, 152–53, 217–18
   prosperity 109–11
   separation 56–57, 65–66
   space 353
   union 54–55
   -ity 27, 52, 173–74
   -lly 44–45, 52, 93–94, 160–61

Sri Lanka 1–3, 7–8, 108–9, 389, 389n.1, 410, 413, 414, 414n.3, 415–17, 437n.2, 462
  civil war 405
  contemporary dance(r) 414, 425
  Dalits 171–72
  up country 390
  -n 405, 413, 415–16, 425
  -n dance style 421–22
Srivastava, Neelam 267
srutis 158
St. Thomas 97
St. Xavier 97
status 109–11, 175, 259–60, 279, 288–89, 334–35
  artistic 280n.5
  caste 170, 175, 280
  class 99–101, 175, 217
  high(er) 37, 121–22, 204–5, 339–40, 348
  low 171, 175, 281–82, 283–84
  lowered 337–38
  marginal 176
  marginalized 287–88
  middle-class 108–9
  moral 119–20
  oppressed 108
  quo 415, 417
  sacred 232, 240–41
  social 95, 210–11, 212, 258, 277, 280n.5
  special 359
stereotype(s)
  feminine 300
  masculine movement 298–99
stigma 93, 164, 170, 194–95, 213–14, 215, 263, 286–87, 326–27n.14, 338–39, 458
  social 280
Stirr, Anna Marie 13, 259, 334–35
Street Singer 29
Stubblefield, Clyde 430
"stylized repetition of acts" 257, 292–93
Stylomannavan 455*f*
Sufi 46*f*
  approach 45
  ceremonies 67–69
  dance 42, 52
  devotion 151
  devotional practices 53–54
  devotional song 151
  dhammal dance 261
  genres 43
  ideologies 43–44
  Islam 132
  master 50
  music 52, 127
  musicians 43
  mystics 41–42
  orders 14, 41, 42, 43
  performance genre 128
  performances 50
  philosophical distinction 133
  philosophical knowledge 128
  philosophy 134, 138–40
  poetry 90, 127–28, 134, 136
  poetry singers 138–40
  poets 131, 133
  practices 42
  qawwali 151, 449–50
  saints 42–43, 48, 54–55
  sama' 42–43
  shrine(s) 14, 43, 46, 52
  shrine devotional practices 54
  singer 127
  songs 52
  soul 45n.3
  tombs 46
  vision 160–61
  -s 43–44, 44*f*, 45, 48
  -sm 41, 42–45, 131–32, 160–61, 262–63
Sufi Music of India and Pakistan 42–43
Suhrawardiyya 46, 47
Sundar, Pavitra 260–61
Sunlight on a Broken Column 37–38
Sunni 132
sur 90, 130
  Sindhi 130
surala 403
Suraweera 393*f*
Sur Marui 132–33, 134, 136*t*
surnas 161–62
sushira winds 158
swadeshi 56
swing 428–29
Switzerland 465
Sydney Opera House 73–74
Sykes, Jim 333–34

synth pad 22–23
Synthesizer(s) 344, 345–46, 368, 428–29
system(s) of power 260

tabla 13, 46, 91, 109, 144*t*, 162–63, 162n.4, 237*f*–40*f*, 282, 339–40, 344, 368
  player 48–49, 145, 155
  prototypes 160–61
tadap 22
tai 147n.6
takitta sadhakam 377–78, 378n.2, 380, 385–86
tal/a 5, 97, 106–7, 144–45, 144*t*, 197, 198, 236–39, 252, 323, 344, 366, 381–83, 392, 396–97
  adi 101
  cycle(s) 162–63, 381–83
  dadra 339–40
  Hindustani music 162–63
  jhyaure 368, 375, 375*t*
  keharwa/keherwa 48–49, 49*b*, 240*f*, 339–40
  khemta 339–40
  khyali 368, 370–71, 374, 374*t*, 375
  partali 60–61
  patterns 162–63
  rupak 139
  system 405
  tintal 164–65
tal rasak 442n.3
talkari 144–45
talkie 352
talking shit (*vetti pechu*) 454–55
talwar 442
tambur(s) 162, 164
tambura 91
Tamil(s) 98n.1, 101, 102, 105, 113n.1, 114–15, 116n.2, 217–18, 306–7, 309, 383n.3, 408, 410, 416–17, 434–36, 453–57, 455n.1, 458–59, 460*f*–63*f*, 461–65, 462n.5
  Chettiyars 456
  Christian(s) 98–99, 101, 105–6, 109–11
  Christian liturgy 113
  Christian music scholars 103–4
  churches 105
  cinema 224
  converts 97
  courtesans 170–71

crying songs 119
culture(s) 171, 193–94, 195
diaspora 453
film and music culture 312
film music 98
film music producer 109
filmi songs 307–8
folk 90, 98, 123–24, 462n.6
folk dances 98, 104
folk epics 119–20
folk genres 196–97, 207
folk music 102–3, 104
funeral 114
Hymnal 97–98, 99
Kaunthars 456
kirttanai 90, 109–11
kochaitamil 453
-language hip-hop 409–10
lay teachers 97–98
listeners 115
literature 193–94, 453, 462–63
Malaysian 408, 455–56, 456–57n.3, 458–59
Malaysian rap(pers) 409–10, 456–57n.3, 461–62, 462n.6, 463, 464, 465
-medium education 456
Mudaliyars 453
musicians 170–71
newspapers 213
oppari 260
Pallan 456
parai-attam 6n.7
Parayan 456
pastors 102
population 433
Protestant(s) 97–99, 109–12
rap(ers) 408, 409–10, 453, 454–55, 458–59, 463, 463n.8, 464, 465
religious and musical context 99–101
Rhythm and Poetry (TRAP) 454–55
rural Hinduism 119–20
Sangam poetry 193–94
Self-Respect Movement 212–13
sentamil 453, 459, 461–62, 462n.6, 463
society 113, 123–24, 390–91
speakers 408
-speaking regions 210–11
widow 120
women 113–14, 119–20, 123–24

518 INDEX

Tamil Nadu 97, 105, 124–25, 160*f*, 176, 193, 193n.1, 204–5, 210, 213n.7, 259–60, 305, 306–7
  early medieval 210n.2, 212
  rural 119, 122–23
  southeastern 195–96
tamilpattru 461–62
tan(s) 165–67
tandava 417, 418
Tanjore 97–98, 99
tanpura 162, 237*f*
Tansen/Miyan Tansen 155, 161, 163
tappattam 197, 202
  adi- 198*f*, 201*f*, 202, 202*b*, 205–6
tappu 116, 193, 204–5
Taqdeer 352
taqdiru 137
tarafdar 164
tarana 160–61
tari 397
tariqah 44, 46, 47, 48
tata strings 158
tattoo 454–55, 454*f*, 455*f*
tauhid 43–44
tavil 102–3, 111, 195, 205, 212
tawa'if(s) 170–71, 260, 263, 277–82, 278n.2, 278n.3, 279n.4, 280n.5, 283–85, 287–89, 334, 355
  community(ies) 286, 287–89
  music 283–84
  music-making 278
  performance(s) 281, 283–85
  practices 279
  songs and stories 277
  -s' salon 279–80
  -s' social status 277, 279
tayampaka 378–79, 381–82
tecikarkal 99–101
Tees Maar Khan 359n.4
Telugu 193, 210–11, 213, 243
temmangu 197, 198*f*
temple(s) 209, 210–11, 211n.4, 212–13, 218n.8, 225–27, 308–9, 465
  -based activities 210–11
  -based origins 212
  Brahmanic contexts 211n.3
  contexts 211n.4, 212
  courtyard 346–47

  cultures 3
  dance 211n.4
  dancers 211n.4
  dedication 213n.6
  drum 333–34
  drumming 7–8, 384–87
  grounds 307
  practices 195
  "prostitutes" 212
  sanctum 218n.8
  sculptures 158, 161–62, 209, 219–20
  -servant 210n.2
  women 211n.4
"Tere Mere Saath" 24
"Teri Mehfil Mein" 354, 355
terrorist(s) 235, 268
tessitura(s) 350–51, 352, 354, 360, 361
Texas 439
"Tha Kar Ke" 427–28, 430, 433–36, 437–38
Thailand 58
thalu 137
Thangaraj, Thomas 106–7
Thanjavur 210n.2, 221–22, 223
Thanksgiving 235
Thar Desert 73–74, 75, 83, 86, 138
theka 162–63
theology of embodiment 149
Theosophical Society 92, 217–19, 220–22
  influence 220–21
thick description 13–14
thirunangai 257–58, 261–62, 263, 305–9, 312–14
  non- 305–6
  trans- 307, 310–11, 314–15
Thomas, Rosie 354–55
Thoothukudi 160*f*
THR Raaga 458–59
thumri(s) 29, 33, 34, 35, 37, 38, 133n.7, 165
tihai 237*f*
TikTok 468–69
Tilak, B. G. 146
Tipitaka 391n.5
tippani 442
tirmanam 198, 199, 200*f*, 207
Tirukkural 454–55
Tirunelveli 106–7
Tiruppugal 462–63
toka 321

INDEX 519

Tönnies, Ferdinand 4, 18–20, 19n.2
Toppo, Biju 179–80
Toppur, Sonali 291, 291n.2, 299–300, 300f, 301
Tora 45
Toronto 467
"Tottiram Ceyvene" 99–101, 100f–7f, 102, 104–5, 107, 108, 109
tovil
   deva 391–92, 393–96
   yak 391–96, 403
tradition(s) 22–23, 37–39, 59, 86, 92, 93, 129–30, 155, 163, 212, 260, 277, 281, 287–88, 354–55, 356–58, 379, 391n.3, 409–10, 416, 421–22, 430, 441, 476
   bearers 333–34
   Black 430
   Brahminical high-scriptural 4–5
   classical and folk 438
   courtly 38
   courtly love 22
   devotional 144–45
   drumming 392
   grace note 107
   great 4–5, 252
   imagined 308
   Indian classical 252
   living and inclusive 439
   low-country 392–93
   music and dance 288–89
   musical 12n.1, 83
   oral 42, 92, 398
   oral textual 75–76
   regional 392–93, 398
   religious 144–45
   staged 393–95
   up-country 392–93
traditional 80–81, 94, 306–7, 339–40, 359, 360, 366–67, 393–95, 413n.1, 451–52
   audience 280
   caste profession 391n.3
   codes of modesty 119
   context(s) 84, 269–70
   custodians 215
   development initiatives 77
   Eastern 430–31
   education 80–81
   entertainers 281–82
   folk 353
   form 413–14
   form and practice 115
   grip 201
   ideal(s) 263, 353
   lifeways 246
   means of livelihood 77
   music 84–85
   musical patronage 75–76
   neo- 356–58
   non- 82–83, 84, 355–56
   norms and relationships 12
   patronage 80–81, 82, 83
   patrons 76–77, 80–81
   pedagogical system 218–19
   performance 75
   repertoire 281–82
   rhythms 270n.7
   salutation 413
   social relationships 18–19
   songs 282, 283
   spaces 305, 307
   teacher-student relationships 416, 425
   values and customs 11–12
   village patronage 86
   village patrons 74–75
trance 42–43, 50, 52, 54–55, 56–57, 61–65, 69
   -induced singing 14
   -like behavior 67–69
   -like ecstasy 56–57
   -like state 59
   state(s) 48, 60–65, 69–70, 197
   -ers 65, 67–69
trans 306–7
   -feminine 257–58, 261–62 (*see also* feminine)
   -gender 257–58, 261–62, 305–7, 308, 314–15
   -ing 307
   local 410n.1
   -masculine 315
   national 270–71, 273–74, 306–7, 427–30, 432, 437–38, 455–56, 467n.2, 468, 469, 470, 476
   -regional 12–13
   -*thirunangai* 307, 310–11, 314–15 (*see also thirunangai*)

tran-tali 444–45, 451
trauma 14, 407–8, 441
Trautmann, Thomas 3, 3n.2
Tribal Music of India: The Muria and Maria Gonds of Madhya Pradesh 245–46
tribe(s) 5–6, 129, 169, 171, 176–77, 181–246, 280
  Scheduled 176, 181, 245–46
  -al 7–8, 13, 171, 176–77, 180–81, 181n.3, 183–85, 183n.8, 187, 190, 191–92, 245–46, 261, 319
  -al dance 182–84, 191*f*, 259
Trinidad and Tobago 408
Trisuli 371
Trump, Donald 408–9, 445–47
trumpet(s) 157, 161–62
Tukaram 148–49, 150, 152–54
tumbi 428–29, 432
Turino, Thomas 90–91, 145n.4, 339
Turkey 41
Turkistan 160–61
Turner, Victor 13–14
Turtle Island 439
2Point9 Records 432–33
Tyagaraja 106–7

'Umar 127–28, 130–31, 130n.5, 135–36, 136*t*, 137, 138
'Umar-Marui 130–31, 131n.6, 138–40
'Umarkot 130–31, 130n.5
UNESCO 439
  -Intangible Cultural Heritage List 439
"U'n'I (Mere Dil Vich Hum Tum)" 432–33
United 6 359–60
United Kingdom (UK) 1–3, 26, 58, 415, 433, 437–38, 443, 465
United States (US) 1–3, 12, 26, 58, 179–80, 209, 235, 243, 408–9, 427–29, 432, 433, 437–38, 440–41, 442, 445–47, 470–71
  continental 432–33
  politics 441
  presidential election 408–9
  southwestern 23
unity in diversity 267, 371

untouchability 172–75, 260
urban
  akhara 190–91
  areas 105, 106, 182–83, 365
  association 368, 370–71
  audience 323
  centers 279, 280
  Christian idiom 109–11
  Christian settings 108
  Christians 103–4, 106–7, 109–11, 182
  church services 98
  congregations 106–7
  cosmopolitan(ism) 20, 26–27, 339
  culture 108
  environment 18–19
  experience 12, 18
  folklorized performances 327–30
  India 22n.10, 26–27
  Indian(s) 175–76
  Indian sensibility 109
  landscape 366
  life 13, 191–92, 367
  merchants 340
  modern expressions 108–9
  musical styles 368–69
  plains 344–45, 348
  rural and urban 12–13, 94, 259, 270–71, 306–7, 348, 364–65, 369–70
  rural-urban migration 368–69, 372–73
  spaces 11, 13, 18–19
  staging 93, 93n.2, 180, 199
  troupes 190–91
  woman 364, 367
  -ity 375
  -ization 12, 13, 109, 319
Urdu 22, 43
  dialects 279–80
  essays 32
  -inflected Hindi 436–37
  -language 334
  text 47
  translations 127–28
'urs 52
urulakkai 378, 380, 385–86
US Capitol Hill 235
ustad 281–82
Uttar Pradesh 343

Uttarakhand 334–35, 337–38, 338f, 339–40, 340n.1, 343–44, 345
-i 338–39, 343, 344–45
uttararanga 144t, 145–46, 148, 151

vadyam 6
vai 43
Vaishya 171, 172t
Valia, Hardarshan 248
van Oostrum, Duco 115
vanaprastha 379
vannama(s) 418n.8, 420, 420n.11, 422
Vanniyar 308
varkari 144, 144t
    bhajan 148, 152f, 153
    contexts 150
    kirtan 144–45, 144t, 148, 149, 150
    kirtankars 144–45, 150
    performance 150, 154
    philosophy 144–45
    pilgrimage site 147, 150
    practice 145n.3
    religious tradition 144–45
    saint(s) 148
    songs 145n.3
varna 170, 171, 172t
Vasudevan, Aniruddhan 305, 307, 314–15
vattama 400
    daeveni 399f
    palamu 399f
    tunveni 399f
Vedas 156–57
Vedic 156–57
    literature 157
    term 169n.1
Veerasingam, Yogeerswaran 459
Vellalar 456
    Christian(s) 97–98, 99, 106–7
    Isai 170–71
Venugopal, Tulika 471, 472–73, 475
vernacular music industry 338–39, 349
ves 418–19, 419f
veshti 104
Victorian
    buildings 18
    cultural values 106
    sensibilities 105–6
    values 212

Vijayadasami 223
Villapuram/Villupuram District 305, 307, 310–11
Vimeo 468–69
vina(s) 156–57, 158, 159–60, 160f, 162, 258
    dhrupad techniques 164–65
    ekatantri 158–59, 160
    rudra 158–60, 159n.3, 163, 164
    tritantri 160
violence 172–74, 267–68, 273, 278, 301–2, 408–9, 410, 415, 445–47
    Hindu Nationalist 142, 143
    police 371
violin 156
viraha 366, 370
Virgin Records 17
visal 44
*vistar*s 165–67
"Vithoba Rakhumai" 148, 150
Vitthala/Lord Vitthala 144–45, 144t, 145n.3, 148
vocal style 163, 164, 165–67, 354, 384
Vrindavan 157

Wade, Bonnie 161–62
wahdat al-wujud 45
waheguru 237f, 239–40
wajd 42, 50
Webb, Edward 97–98, 102
Weber 12
Weidman, Amanda 155, 351
Wellawatte 413
Wesley, John 106–7
West Asia 162
    -n innovations 160–61
    -n musical elements 160–61
    -n paired *tabl* drums 162
    -n sources 162
Western 106–7, 269–70
    academic setting 386–87
    anti- 267
    arts 92
    behaviors 356–58
    classroom 385
    clothing 356–58, 359
    colonial knowledge constructions 8
    colonialism and racism 3

Western (cont.)
  cultural model 109–11
  culture 108
  dance 3, 421–22
  harmonic organ
    accompaniment 109–11
  harmonic practices 3n.3
  harmony 103–4
  hymn-like performances 98
  hymnody 105
  hymns 99–101, 106–7
  instruments and tuning systems 337–38
  intellectuals 4–5
  major scale(s) 98, 105, 106–7
  mimicry 95
  modernity 38–39
  notation 3–4
  scholars 158
  sensibility 109
  spaghetti-inspired film 357
  staff notation 30f, 60–61, 65, 253
  style 99, 108–9, 111–12
  -er(s) 91, 382–84
  -ization 85, 106–7, 106–7n.5, 108, 135–36, 269n.5
  -izing 108
  -ness 92
Western Ghats 176
Western music 3, 397
  art 5–6, 167, 382–83
  canon 3
  classical 155
  scholarship 12–13
  theorist 252
  theory 95

Western musical values 108
White, Emmons 3–4, 102
White, Ruth 102
Wijegoonawardane, Pabalu 395–96
Wild West 433–34
Willard, Augustus 3–4
Wolf, Richard 245n.1
world music pedagogical texts 8
"Wrecking Ball" 359–60

xenophobic 408–9

"Ya Farid" 47, 48, 49
Yagnik, Alka 358
yak beraya 392–93
yak tovils 391–96
yakkha 392
yakku 390–92, 395–96, 397–98, 398n.9, 403–5
Yama 350
Yamuna 343
Yankee, Daddy 428, 433–34, 435
yappu 463
Yazid 136t
Yoga 221–22
Yogi B 458–59, 461–62
YouTube 185–86, 189, 190, 227, 251, 335–36, 340n.1, 359–60, 367, 432–33, 468–69, 470–71

Zimbabwe 430
zither 160, 162, 368
Zoorasamharam 463f
Zoroastrian(s) 407–8
Zumba 466